Internet Marketing

Strategy, Implementation and Practice

We work with leading authors to develop the strongest educational materials in business and management, bringing cutting-edge thinking and best learning practice to a global market.

Under a range of well-known imprints, including Financial Times Prentice Hall, we craft high quality print and electronic publications which help readers to understand and apply their content, whether studying or at work.

To find out more about the complete range of our publishing please visit us on the World Wide Web at: *www.pearsoneduc.com*

Internet Marketing

Strategy, Implementation and Practice

DAVE CHAFFEY
RICHARD MAYER
KEVIN JOHNSTON
FIONA ELLIS-CHADWICK

FINANCIAL TIMES
Prentice Hall

An imprint of Pearson Education

Harlow, England · London · New York · Reading, Massachusetts · San Francisco · Toronto · Don Mills, Ontario · Sydney
Tokyo · Singapore · Hong Kong · Seoul · Taipei · Cape Town · Madrid · Mexico City · Amsterdam · Munich · Paris · Milan

Pearson Education Limited
Edinburgh Gate
Harlow
Essex CM20 2JE
England

and Associated Companies throughout the world

Visit us on the World Wide Web at:
http://www.pearsoneduc.com

First published 2000

ISBN 0 273 64309 6

The programs in this book have been included for their instructional value. The publisher
does not offer any warranties or representation in respect of their fitness for a particular purpose,
nor does the publisher accept any liability for any loss or damage (other than for personal injury
or death) arising from their use.

Many of the designations used by manufacturers and sellers to distinguish their products are
claimed as trademarks. Pearson Education Limited has made every attempt to supply
trademark information about manufacturers and their products mentioned in this book. A list
of trademark designations and their owners appears on p. xviii.

British Library Cataloguing-in-Publication Data
A catalogue record for this book is available from the British Library

Library of Congress Cataloging-in-Publication Data
Internet marketing: strategy, implementation, and practice / David Chaffey...[et al.].
    p. cm.
  Includes bibliographical references and indexes.
  ISBN 0-582-38119-3
  1. Internet marketing. 2. Internet. I. Chaffey, Dave, 1963-

HF5415.1265.I57 2000
658.8'4—dc21
                                                              00-022942

10 9 8 7 6 5 4 3 2
04 03 02 01 00

Typeset by 30
Printed in Great Britain by Redwood Books Limited, Trowbridge, Wiltshire

CONTENTS

Part 3 INTERNET MARKETING: IMPLEMENTATION AND PRACTICE

PREFACE

Introduction

The Internet – opportunity and threat

The Internet represents a tremendous opportunity. For customers, it gives a much wider choice of products, services and prices from different suppliers and the means to select and purchase items more readily. For organisations marketing these products and services it gives the opportunity to expand into new markets, offer new services and compete on a more equal footing with larger businesses. For those working within these organisations it gives the opportunity to develop new skills and to use the Internet to improve the competitiveness of a company.

At the same time, the Internet gives rise to many threats to organisations. For example, start-up companies such as Amazon (books) (*www.amazon.com*), Expedia (travel) (*www.expedia.com*), AutoByTel (cars) (*www.autobytel.com*) and CDNow! (CDs) (*www.cdnow.com*) have captured a significant part of their market and struck fear into the existing players. Indeed the phrase 'amazoning a market sector' has become an often-used expression among marketers.

The Internet – how to react?

With the success stories of companies capturing market share together with the rapidly increasing adoption of the Internet by consumers and business buyers has come a fast-growing realisation that all organisations must have an effective Internet presence to prosper, or possibly even survive! But, how is an effective Internet presence achieved in a medium that is alien to most companies? Are existing marketing concepts, theories and models still valid? What is the effect on channel and market structures? How should the Internet be used to support existing business and marketing strategies? How should the web site be structured and designed? How should the site be promoted online and offline? How can the Internet be used to communicate with customers and build loyalty? How can we assess whether we are achieving these objectives? The aim of this book is to answer this type of question so that graduates entering employment and practitioners can help the companies for which they work to compete successfully using this new, digital medium in conjunction with existing media.

The Internet – skills required?

This book has been written to help marketers develop the knowledge and skills they need in order to be able to use the Internet effectively. Specifically, this book addresses the following needs:

- There is a need to know to what extent the Internet changes existing marketing models and whether new models and strategies can be applied to exploit the medium effectively.

■ Marketing practitioners will need practical Internet marketing skills to market their products effectively. Knowledge of the new jargon – terms such as 'portal', 'clickthrough', 'cookie', 'hits', 'page impressions', 'digital certificate'– and of effective methods of site design and promotion will be necessary, either for direct 'hands-on' development of a site or to enable communication with other staff or suppliers who are implementing and maintaining the site.

■ Given the rapidly changing market characteristics and best practices of Internet marketing, web-based information sources are needed to update knowledge regularly. This text and the supporting companion web site contain extensive links to web sites to achieve this.

The content of this book assumes some existing knowledge of marketing in the reader, perhaps developed through experience or by students studying introductory modules in marketing fundamentals, marketing communications or buyer behaviour. However, the text outlines basic concepts of marketing such as the modern marketing concept, communications theory, buyer behaviour and the marketing mix, and there is, at the end of each chapter, a comprehensive list of further reading materials. This includes widely used marketing texts as well as electronic media sources.

The structure and contents of this book

The book is divided into three parts, each covering a different aspect of how organisations use the Internet for marketing to help them achieve competitive advantage. Table P.1 indicates how the book is related to existing marketing topics.

Part 1 Internet marketing fundamentals (Chapters 1–4)

Part 1 relates the use of the Internet to traditional marketing theories and concepts, and questions the validity of existing models given the differences between the Internet and other media.

■ *Chapter 1 An introduction to Internet marketing* reviews the relationship between the Internet and the modern marketing concept, the benefits the Internet can bring to adopters, differences from other media and its impact on different elements of the marketing communications mix.

■ *Chapter 2 Key Internet marketing concepts* looks at communications theory, buyer demographics and buyer behaviour in the Internet context and the impact of the Internet on the marketing mix. It also introduces the elements of effective web site design and promotion, in view of the characteristics of the medium.

■ *Chapter 3 How does the Internet work?* explains the main technical terms marketers need in order to understand the operation of the Internet, intranets, extranets and the World Wide Web. The chapter summarises the steps a user must take to access the Internet and the steps an organisation must take to host a web site.

■ *Chapter 4 Finding information on the Internet* briefly explains how to use portals, search engines and directories to find information, and considers marketing research strategies. It also gives many examples of web information sources.

Part 2 Internet strategy development (Chapters 5–7)

Part 2 describes the emerging models for developing strategy and provides examples of the approaches companies have used to integrate the Internet into their business strategy.

- *Chapter 5 Internet marketing strategy* considers how the Internet strategy can be aligned with business and marketing strategies and describes a generic strategic approach with phases of goal setting, situation review, strategy formulation and resource allocation and monitoring.
- *Chapter 6 The Internet marketing plan* defines the main elements of a plan to implement an Internet marketing strategy including defining customer orientation; integrating the Internet web site with extranets and intranets; defining the scope of marketing communications; brand migration; forming partnerships and outsourcing; legal issues; impact on organisational structure; budgeting and planning.
- *Chapter 7 Marketing channels, market structure and the Internet* assesses how the Internet changes market and channel structures through processes such as disintermediation and reintermediation; its impact on the value chain and supply chain; and reviews how resulting channel conflicts can be managed.

Part 3 Internet marketing: implementation and practice (Chapters 8–15)

Part 3 of the book explains practical approaches to implementing an Internet marketing strategy. Techniques for communicating with customers, building relationships and facilitating electronic commerce are all reviewed in some detail. Knowledge of these practical techniques will be essential for undergraduates on work placements involving a web site and for marketing managers who are dealing with suppliers such as design agencies.

- *Chapter 8 Creating and building the web site* explains the work involved in the different stages of building a web site, such as analysis of customer needs, design of the site structure and layout, and creating the site. These are explained from the perspective of delivering the best service quality possible for the customer. The chapter provides extensive references to further information and tools in this area.
- *Chapter 9 Web site promotion* describes the different online and offline promotion techniques necessary to build traffic to a web site and for other promotion objectives. Among the techniques covered are: banner advertising, affiliate networks, promotion in search engines and directories, co-branding and sponsorship, e-mail, loyalty techniques and PR.
- *Chapter 10 Relationship marketing using the Internet* details the benefits of using the Internet for building and sustaining 'one-to-one' relationships with customers, and looks at e-mail and web-based personalisation techniques for achieving this.
- *Chapter 11 Electronic commerce transactions* covers the concepts, systems and processes to enable payment for goods and services using the Internet. Practical issues of security, reliability, performance and privacy are considered from the viewpoint of how they can be implemented to make the customer experience of e-commerce favourable.
- *Chapter 12 Maintaining the web site and measuring Internet marketing effectiveness* defines a process for successful updating of a site and online and offline methods for assessing the effectiveness of the site in delivering business and marketing benefits.

- *Chapter 13 Business-to-consumer Internet marketing – the retail example* examines models of marketing to consumers, and provides many case studies of how retail businesses are tackling such marketing.
- *Chapter 14 Business-to-business Internet marketing* examines the different area of marketing to other businesses, and provides many examples of how companies are achieving this to support international marketing. It also discusses the different stages of the buying decision such as supplier search, product evaluation and selection, purchase, post-purchase customer service and evaluation and feedback.
- *Chapter 15 The future of Internet marketing* attempts to assess which currently emerging trends are likely to be significant in the future. It also considers the problems facing marketing managers as they try to select which trends to follow. Finally, it discusses ethical issues that arise from uneven adoption of the Internet among consumers.

Who should use this book?

Students

This book has been created primarily as the main student text for undergraduate and postgraduate students taking specialist marketing courses or modules which cover Internet and digital marketing, electronic commerce and e-business. The book is relevant to students who are:

- *Undergraduates on business programmes* which include modules on the use of the Internet and e-commerce. This includes specialist degrees such as Internet marketing, electronic commerce, marketing, tourism and accounting or general business degrees such as business studies, business administration and business management.
- *Undergraduate project students* who select this topic for final year projects/dissertations – this book is an excellent supporting text for these students.
- *Undergraduates completing a work placement* in a company using the Internet to promote its products.
- *Students at college aiming for vocational qualifications* such as the HNC/HND in Business Management or Computer Studies.
- *Postgraduate students* taking specialist masters degrees in electronic commerce or Internet marketing, generic MBAs and courses leading to qualifications such as Certificate in Management or Diploma in Management Studies which involve modules on electronic commerce and digital marketing.

Practitioners

There is also much of relevance in this book for marketing practitioners, including:

- *Marketing managers* responsible for defining an Internet marketing strategy and implementing and maintaining the company web site.
- *Senior managers and directors* wishing to understand the potential of Internet marketing for a company and who need practical guidelines for how to exploit this potential.
- *Technical project managers or webmasters* who may understand the technical details of building a site, but have a limited knowledge of marketing fundamentals and how to develop an Internet marketing strategy.

What does the book offer to lecturers teaching these courses?

The book is intended to be a comprehensive guide to all aspects of using the Internet and other digital media to support marketing. The book builds on existing marketing theories and concepts, and questions the validity of models in the light of the differences between the Internet and other media. The book references the emerging body of literature specific to Internet marketing. It can therefore be used across several modules. Lecturers will find the book has a good range of case studies, activities and exercises to support their teaching. Web site references are given in the text and at the end of each chapter to important information sources for particular topics.

Student learning features

A range of features have been incorporated into this book to help the reader get the most out of it. They have been designed to assist understanding, reinforce learning and help readers find information easily. The features are described in the order in which you will encounter them.

At the start of each chapter

- *Learning objectives:* a list describing what readers can learn through reading the chapter and completing the exercises.
- *Links to other chapters:* a summary of related information in other chapters.
- *Chapter introductions:* succinct summaries of the relevance of the topic to marketing students and practitioners, plus the content and structure of the chapter.

In each chapter

- *Definitions:* when significant terms are first introduced the main text contains succinct definitions in boxes for easy reference.
- *Web references:* where appropriate, web addresses are given to enable readers to obtain further information. They are provided in the main text where they are directly relevant as well as at the end of the chapter.
- *Case studies:* real-world examples of how companies are using the Internet for marketing. Questions at the end of the case study are intended to highlight the main learning points from the example.
- *Minicase studies:* short features which give a more detailed example, or explanation, than is practical in the main text. They do not contain supplementary questions.
- *Activities:* exercises in the main text which give readers the opportunity to practise and apply the techniques described in the text.
- *Chapter summaries:* intended as revision aids to summarise the main learning points from the chapter.

At the end of each chapter

- *Self-assessment exercises:* short questions which will test understanding of terms and concepts described in the chapter.
- *Discussion questions:* these require longer essay-style answers discussing themes from the chapter. They can be used either as topics for individual essays or as the basis for seminar discussion.

- *Essay questions:* conventional essay questions.
- *Examination questions:* typical short answer questions of the type that are encountered in exams. These can also be used for revision.
- *References:* these are references to books, articles or papers referred to within the chapter.
- *Further reading:* supplementary texts or papers on the main themes of the chapter. Where appropriate a brief commentary is provided on recommended supplementary reading on the main themes of the chapters. Further reading refers to the relevant chapters in widely used marketing texts, including: Brassington and Petitt: *Principles of Marketing*; Dibb, Simkin, Pride and Ferrel: *Marketing; Concepts and Strategies*; Kotler, Armstrong, Saunders and Wong: *Principles of Marketing*; Fill: *Marketing Communications – Contexts, Contents and Strategies*; Burnett and Moriarty: *Introduction to Marketing Communications. An Integrated Approach*; and Baker (ed.), *The Marketing Book.* (*See* References and Further reading, Chapter 1, for full details.)
- *Web site references:* these are significant sites that provide further information on the concepts and topics of the chapter. This list does not repeat all the web site references given within the chapter, for example company sites. For clarity, the web site address prefix 'http://' is omitted.

At the end of the book

- *Glossary:* definitions of all key terms and phrases used within the main text, cross-referenced for ease of use.
- *Index:* all key words and abbreviations referred to in the main text.

Support material

Free supplementary materials are available via the Pearson Education companion books web site at *www.booksites.net* to support all users of the book. This regularly updated web site contains advice, comment, support materials and hyperlinks to reference sites relevant to the text. There is a password-protected area for lecturers only to discuss issues arising from using the text; additional examination-type questions and answers; a multiple choice question bank with answers; additional cases with suggestions for discussion; a downloadable version of the Lecturer's Guide and OHP Masters.

Table P.1 Coverage of marketing topics in different chapters

Topic	Chapter														
	1	2	3	4	5	6	7	8	9	10	11	12	13	14	15
Advertising	✓			✓				✓	✓						
Branding						✓		✓					✓		
Buyer behaviour	✓	✓		✓				✓		✓	✓		✓	✓	✓
Channel and market structure	✓				✓	✓	✓						✓	✓	✓
Communications mix	✓	✓				✓				✓			✓	✓	
Communications theory		✓													
Customer service quality	✓	✓	✓					✓		✓			✓	✓	
Direct marketing	✓							✓	✓	✓					
Ethical marketing											✓				✓
International marketing					✓									✓	
Marketing concept	✓														✓
Marketing mix	✓	✓			✓	✓	✓			✓					✓
Marketing planning					✓	✓	✓	✓				✓			
Marketing research	✓		✓	✓		✓						✓			
Monitoring/measurement						✓				✓	✓	✓			
Public relations	✓									✓					
Promotion	✓			✓		✓	✓		✓	✓			✓	✓	
Pricing strategy					✓							✓			
Relationship marketing	✓									✓					
Sales												✓			
Sales promotions	✓									✓	✓	✓			
Segmentation		✓								✓	✓		✓	✓	
Services marketing	✓												✓	✓	
Strategy	✓	✓				✓	✓	✓	✓	✓	✓	✓	✓	✓	✓

Note: A large tick indicates fairly detailed coverage; a smaller tick indicates a brief direct reference or indirect coverage.

ACKNOWLEDGEMENTS

We are grateful to the following for permission to reproduce copyright material:

Figure 1.2 from Microsoft; Figure 1.6 from Toyota; Figure 1.7 from KPMG; Figure 2.2 uBid; Figure 2.7, Figure 11.7 and Figure 14.3 from Amazon UK; Figure 3.4 and Figure 4.1 AltaVista, reproduced with the permission of AltaVista, Alta Vista and AltaVista logo are trademarks of AltaVista Company; Figure 3.5 from DHL UK; Figure 4.3 from Netscape, Netscape screen shot © 1999 Netscape Communications Corporation, used with permission; Figure 4.5 from Deja; Figure 4.6 from RealNames; Figure 5.2 reprinted from The Internet and International Marketing, by Quelch, J. and Klein, L., *Sloan Management Review*, Spring 1996, 61–75, by permission of publisher, copyright 1996 by Sloan Management Review Association, all rights reserved; Figure 5.4 McDonald (1999), Figure 6.4 Bickerton *et al* (1998), and Figure 6.5 Friedman and Furey (1999), reprinted by permission of Butterworth Heinemann Publishers, a division of Reed Educational Professional Publishing; Figure 5.6 and Figure 14.8 from Cisco Systems; Figure 6.1 from Bell Atlantic; Figure 6.2 from Durex; Figure 7.4 from Screentrade; Figure 7.7 from Berryman *et al* (1998), reprinted by special permission from the McKinsey Quarterly, 1998 Issue 1, 152–4, copyright McKinsey & Company; Figure 7.8 from Brightware Contact Centre; Figure 8.4 from Orange; Figure 8.6 from Synetix; Figure 8.8 from The Halifax; Figure 9.5 from DoubleClick; Figure 9.6 from New Woman; Figure 9.7 from Scottish Amicable; Figure 9.8 from Beenz; Figure 10.8 from Brightware; Figure 11.10 from iShop; Figure 12.3 and Figure 12.4 from Webtrends; Figure 14.5 from e-Steel; Figure 14.10 from UK DCS; Figure 15.1 from CNET, reprinted with permission from CNET, Inc © copyright 1995–2000.www.cnet.com; Figure 15.4 from Letsbuyit; Figure 15.5 from Digital TV.

Whilst every effort has been made to trace the owners of copyrights material, in a few cases this has proved impossible and we take this opportunity to offer our apologies to any copyright holders whose rights may have unwittingly infringed

Trademark Notice

ABOUT THE AUTHORS

Dave Chaffey BSc PhD

Dave has extensive experience of working in industry, as a business analyst/project manager on marketing information systems for companies such as Ford Europe, WH Smith and the Halifax. He is currently a Senior Lecturer in business information systems and marketing in the Derbyshire Business School at the University of Derby where he co-developed the *BA (Hons) Internet Marketing* degree and *MSc Electronic Commerce management*. His research interests include strategic approaches to Internet marketing and methods of measuring the effectiveness of Internet marketing. Dave is course director for Chartered Institute of Marketing practitioner seminars including *Strategic Internet Marketing, Practical Internet Marketing, Internet-based Marketing Research, Building Online Customer Relationships, Digital Technologies for Marketing* and *Measuring Online Marketing Effectiveness*. Dave has developed a regularly updated web site of Internet marketing resources at *www.marketing-online.co.uk* to support the seminars and this book. Dave would like to acknowledge the work of Stephen Spelman in contributing two case studies to Chapter 7.

Richard Mayer MA DipM MCIM

Richard is a Senior Lecturer in marketing, at the University of Derby, specialising in strategic marketing and marketing communications. Previously product manager for Delta Crompton Cables, Richard was director of his own packaging business for four years. In addition, he is an examiner for the Chartered Institute of Marketing and has contributed to two published study revision kits on marketing communications strategy, and marketing fundamentals. Richard has considerable experience in conducting, marketing seminar/training programmes, in particular he is course director for the Chartered Institute of Marketing seminars in the *Fundamentals of Marketing and Marketing a Service* and he has conducted many in-company training courses throughout Europe.

Kevin Johnston BSc MBA

Kevin is a Senior Lecturer in the Derbyshire Business School at the University of Derby. He is Programme Leader for the *BA (Hons) Internet Marketing* degree. His teaching and research interests are strategic marketing (meaning the way in which marketing informs corporate strategy) and the role of marketing in executing corporate strategy. Within this field, his specific interests are the converging areas of relationship marketing, database marketing and Internet marketing and the strategic implications of the new paradigm they create. He is currently engaged in doctoral studies with the working title: '*a dialogue framework for open-market e-commerce*'.

Fiona Ellis-Chadwick BSc PhD (submitted)

Fiona has 20 years experience in retail management, development and promotions. Fiona's career took a dramatic change of direction when she became interested in the commercial potential of the Internet early in the 1990's. She gave up her retail consultancy business to pursue her interest in the Internet. Currently Fiona is a Marketing Lecturer at the University of Derby and is Programme Leader of the MSc in e-commerce management. She has recently completed a PhD titled *An Empirical Study of Internet Adoption among Leading United Kingdom Retailers and its Impact on the Future of the Internet Retail Market*. Her current research interests include the future role of the Internet within retailing in Europe and corporate adoption of the Internet for strategic marketing communications. Fiona is a member of Women In Computing (WIC) and following the completion of her PhD has plans to encourage women of all ages to develop their skills in this area.

**A Companion Web Site accompanies *Internet Marketing*
by Dave Chaffey, Richard Mayer, Kevin Johnston and Fiona Ellis-Chadwick.**

Visit the *Internet Marketing* Companion Web Site at
www.booksites.net/chaffey to find valuable teaching and learning
material including:

For students:
- Study material designed to help you improve your understanding
- Extensive links to useful web sites, including;
  - academic and practitioner-oriented articles
  - case study materials
  - examples of best practice
  - guidance on tools and techniques for effective web sites

For lecturers:
- A secure, password protected site with teaching material
- Downloadable Instructor's manual and Overhead Masters to assist in lecturing
- Links to articles, company sites, and internet marketing resources on the web
- Ask questions about the author

This regularly maintained and updated site will also have a syllabus manager, search
functions, and e-mail results functions.

PART 1

Internet marketing fundamentals

CHAPTER 1

An introduction to Internet marketing

Learning objectives

After reading this chapter, the reader should be able to:

- assess the contribution of the Internet to the modern marketing concept;
- appreciate the key differences between Internet marketing and traditional marketing;
- understand the reasons for the increase in the business significance of the Internet in the new millennium;
- comprehend how the Internet can be used in different marketing functions.

Links to other chapters

This chapter provides an introduction to Internet marketing, and the concepts introduced are covered in more detail later in the book, as follows:

- ▶ Chapter 2 explains key concepts of Internet marketing and how they are underpinned by marketing and communication theory. It also examines differences between marketing in the new media compared with traditional media.
- ▶ Chapter 3 describes the technical foundations of the Internet which enable it to function.
- ▶ Chapter 4 describes how the Internet can be used to find information and be used for marketing research.
- ▶ Chapters 5, 6 and 7 in Part 2 review how an Internet marketing strategy can be developed.
- ▶ Chapters 8, 9 and 12 in Part 3 describe how the strategy can be implemented through creating, promoting and maintaining a web site.
- ▶ Chapters 10 and 11 in Part 3 describe specific applications of the Internet for relationship marketing and electronic commerce.
- ▶ Chapters 13 and 14 in Part 3 describe best practice in Internet marketing in the business-to-consumer and business-to-business markets.
- ▶ Chapter 15 considers the future development of Internet marketing.

INTRODUCTION

How significant is Internet marketing to businesses? Today, the answer to this question varies dramatically according to who is answering. For companies such as electronics company Cisco, the answer is 'very significant' – Cisco sell over $10 million worth of hardware using the Internet each day. For fast-moving consumer goods (FMCG) companies such as Unilever the answer is 'insignificant' – the majority of their consumer sales will occur through traditional retail channels in response to promotional campaigns in traditional media. In 1998 UK advertising expenditure for Internet-placed advertisements was estimated at £8m., compared with £3 billion for television and radio advertisements.

Does the relative unimportance of the Internet to companies such as Unilever indicate that Internet marketing is of specialised interest only? We believe not, because the interesting question to ask is 'how significant will Internet marketing be to businesses in the future; in two, five or ten years' time?' This is the question many companies are asking themselves today, and is why it is important to understand this relatively new marketing phenomenon.

For example, Unilever is starting to use the Internet as part of brand building for its new products. In 1998 it launched its Mentadent toothpaste in the United States using traditional media campaigns and also offered samples in response to users clicking on an advertisement placed on health-related web sites. It received more than 40 000 requests for samples, far exceeding its expectations for this new medium. If businesses do not understand and start to apply the new marketing techniques and technology in this way, then they may not only miss an opportunity, but may even cease to exist.

The media portrayal of the Internet often suggests that it is merely an alternative for traditional advertising. In fact, the Internet can be readily applied to all aspects of marketing communications and can and will need to support the entire marketing process. As we move into the new millennium, organisations will use Internet technology in the form of intranets and extranets to support the operation of the internal and external value chains.

This book will cover all the different ways in which the Internet can be used to support the marketing process. Many organisations have begun this process with the development of web sites in the form of electronic brochures introducing their organisations' products and services, but are now enhancing them to add value to the full range of marketing functions. This chapter introduces the diverse uses of the Internet and provides links to where these topics are covered in more detail later in the book.

We would encourage a healthy cynicism in the reader of this book; the reader should adopt a questioning approach. When referring to the case studies and estimates of growth, ask what tangible benefits have been delivered and what the growth estimates are based on. Remember also, that for every success story, there may be unrecorded instances of companies failing to deliver the foreseen benefits. Case study 1.1 highlights the reasons for growth in Internet sales to both other businesses and consumers and describes some of the barriers which make estimation of the level of sales difficult.

The Internet and the marketing concept

The word marketing has two distinct meanings in terms of modern management practice. It describes:

1 *The range of specialist marketing functions* carried out within many organisations. Such functions include market research, brand/product management, public relations and customer service.
2 *An approach or concept that can be used as the guiding philosophy* for all functions and activities of an organisation. Such a philosophy encompasses all aspects of a business. Business strategy is guided by an organisation's market and competitor focus and everyone in an organisation should be required to have a customer focus in their job.

The modern marketing concept (Houston, 1986) unites these two meanings and stresses that marketing encompasses the range of organisational functions and processes that seek to determine the needs of target markets and deliver products and services to customers and other key stakeholders such as employees and financial institutions. Increasingly the importance of marketing is being recognised both as a vital function and as a guiding management philosophy within organisations. Marketing has to be seen as the essential focus of all activities within an organisation (Valentin, 1996). The marketing concept should lie at the heart of the organisation, and the actions of directors, managers and employees should be guided by its philosophy.

Modern marketing requires organisations to be committed to a market/customer orientation (Jaworski and Kohli, 1993). All parts of the organisation should co-ordinate activities to ensure that customer needs are met efficiently, effectively and profitably. Marketing encompasses activities traditionally seen as the sole domain of accountants, production, human resources management (HRM) and information technology (IT). Many of these functions had little regard for customer considerations. Increasingly such functions are being reorientated, evidenced by the importance of initiatives such as Total Quality Management (TQM), Business Process Reengineering, Just in Time (JIT) and supply chain management. Individuals' functional roles are undergoing change, from being solely functional to having a greater emphasis on process. Individuals are therefore being encouraged to become part-time marketers. Processes have a significant impact on an organisation's ability to service its customers' needs.

The Internet can be applied by companies as an integral part of the modern marketing concept since:

- It can be used to support the full range of organisational functions and processes that deliver products and services to customers and other key stakeholders.
- It is a powerful communications medium that can act as a 'corporate glue' that integrates the different functional parts of the organisation.
- It facilitates information management, which is now increasingly recognised as a critical marketing support tool to strategy formulation and implementation.
- The future role of the Internet should form part of the vision of a company since its future impact will be significant to most businesses.

Without adequate information, organisations are at a disadvantage with respect to competitors and the external environment. Up-to-date, timely and accessible information about the industry, markets, new technology, competitors and customers is a critical factor in an organisation's ability to plan and compete in an increasingly competitive marketplace.

Internet marketing defined

What then, is Internet marketing? Internet marketing or Internet-based marketing can be defined as the use of the Internet and related digital technologies to achieve marketing objectives and support the modern marketing concept. These technologies include the Internet media and other digital media such as cable and satellite together with the hardware and software which enable its operation and use.

> **Internet marketing**
> The application of the Internet and related digital technologies to achieve marketing objectives.

The term 'electronic commerce or e-commerce' is often used in a similar context to Internet marketing and has become a standard term recognised for business transactions conducted on the Internet. It is a term that encompasses a range of business activities such as selling online, online bill payments, home shopping/banking and improving market efficiency in dealings with suppliers and clients (Hoffman and Novak, 1997). Some authors such as Zwass (1998) extend the meaning of electronic commerce to incorporate 'sharing business information and maintaining business relationships'. For clarity, in this book, a narrower definition is used; electronic commerce is used to refer to trading of goods and services that is mainly achieved by paid-for transactions between a business and other businesses and consumers. Methods for achieving this are specifically considered in Chapter 11.

> **Electronic commerce transactions**
> E-commerce transactions are the trading of goods and services conducted using the Internet and other digital media.

Electronic commerce has numerous synonyms, such as online commerce, Internet commerce or trading and digital commerce. IBM use the term 'e-business' to encompass all the implications of electronic, Internet-related technologies on business functions, from HRM to marketing to corporate strategy. There are significant overlaps between e-business and Internet marketing activities.

CASE STUDY 1.1   **INTERNET: EUROPE SALES 'COULD TOP $1990BN'**

European sales over the Internet could rise by more than tenfold to $1990bn by 2001, according to a report published yesterday. The first annual survey of electronic commerce in Europe undertaken for KPMG, the management consultancy, showed that over half the 500 companies interviewed believed the Internet was vital to their global competitiveness.

The level of the sales forecast drew surprise from some analysts, who questioned its accuracy. One, who did not wish to be named, said KPMG's current Internet sales estimate of $187bn, extrapolated from the survey, was 'well wide of the mark'. He put the level of sales at about half this. KPMG said the companies surveyed were at present conducting an average of 1 per cent of their sales on the internet, and expected this to rise to 10 per cent by 2001, and to 17 per cent, or £3555bn, in 2003.

The 'explosion' in European e-commerce will occur for a number of reasons, the report said. Firstly, the passage of the year 2000 computer bug problem and introduction of the euro will free up company resources to concentrate on the Internet. Personal computer penetration, as well as the advent of interactive services via television, will stimulate consumer demand. A growing familiarity with the technology will also help. Thirdly, improvements to the telecommunications infrastructure will encourage usage and, finally, concerns about security will recede as technology improves.

Some 10 per cent of the KPMG survey sample, drawn from all the larger European and Scandinavian countries, were gaining at least 1 per cent of their revenues from the Internet. Of these, 80 per cent had board-level support for e-commerce, against 56 per cent for the other companies, and more than two-thirds (against 40 per cent) had integrated e-commerce into their supply chains.

Further, the Internet marketing budget for the leading 10 per cent was an average $222 000, compared with $129 000 for the other companies.

A quarter of those surveyed cited security issues as a 'significant barrier' to their use of the Internet. Among French companies, this figure jumped to two-thirds. The UK financial service industry was the least concerned about this issue. Almost a quarter of all respondents were concerned that too few potential customers were connected to the Internet.

Source: Christopher Price, *Financial Times*, 16 October 1998.

Questions

1 What factors will be responsible for the growth in Internet sales, according to the article?

2 What additional factors may assist growth?

3 Why do you think some commentators question these figures?

4 What are the potential barriers to these growth figures being attained? Include both reasons given in the article and other reasons.

5 Use the Internet to research the current estimate of European electronic commerce transactions. Attempt to explain the difference between the original and new estimates.

What business benefits can the Internet provide?

Case study 1.1 highlights the key reason why many companies are seeking to harness the Internet. The reason is an additional source of revenue made possible by an alternative marketing and distribution channel. The marketing opportunities of using the Internet can be appreciated by studying the strategic marketing grid (Ansoff, 1957) for targeting new markets and products (Fig. 1.1). The Internet can be used to achieve each of the four strategic directions as follows:

1 *Market penetration*. The Internet can be used to sell more existing products into existing markets. This can be achieved by using the power of the Internet for advertising products to increase awareness of products and the profile of a company amongst potential customers in an existing market. This is a relatively conservative use of the Internet.

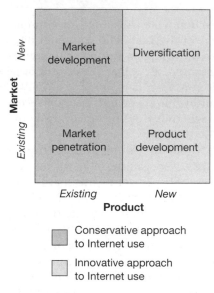

Fig. 1.1 **Market and product strategic grid**

2 *Market development.* Here the Internet is used to sell into new markets, taking advantage of the low cost of advertising internationally without the necessity for a supporting sales infrastructure in the customers' country. This is a relatively conservative use of the Internet, but it does require the overcoming of the barriers to becoming an exporter or operating in a greater number of countries (*see* Chapter 14).

3 *Product development.* New products or services are developed which can be delivered by the Internet. These are typically information products such as market reports which can be purchased using electronic commerce. This is innovative use of the Internet.

4 *Diversification.* In this sector, new products are developed which are sold into new markets.

Companies can use the Internet to adopt new approaches to selling products which involve positioning in one part of the grid presented in Fig. 1.1, or in multiple quadrants. Examples of these applications are in Activity 1.1, Using the Internet for new markets and products.

Activity 1.1 | ***Using the Internet for new markets and products.***

For each of the following companies identify which positioning the company has adopted relative to Fig. 1.1, Market and product strategic grid. Explain how the new markets or products are exploited.

1 The purchase by the book retailer WH Smith of the Internet bookshop (*www.bookshop.co.uk*) in 1998 for £9 million.
2 The PC seller Dell Computer (*www.dell.co.uk*), which estimates that over $6 million worth of sales are supported every day by the Internet (to support buying decisions or to order items online).

3 The Software company Microsoft, which has launched a range of new sites to help consumers purchase cars, holidays, shares and other items (*see* Chapter 7).

4 A UK company such as HR Johnson, which is selling tiles to international distributors (*www.johnson-tiles.com*) and has created an extranet to obtain orders over the Internet.

The lure of new sales has attracted many companies on to the Internet, but there are many other benefits of establishing an Internet presence. Consider the example of the parcel courier companies. These companies now provide a range of customer services over the Internet which were traditionally delivered by telephone operators, thus reducing operating costs. This is illustrated in Mini case study 1.1. In such situations, the online services may give better customer service if measured by convenience, but some customers will want the option of the personal touch, and phone services must be provided for this type of customer. Many companies will also reduce the costs of the printing and distribution of promotional material, price lists and other marketing communications.

Mini case study 1.1

Parcel couriers use the Internet to improve customer service and reduce costs

Federal Express

www.fedex.com

Key services
- Courier ordering
- Package tracking
- Delivery options
- Software downloads

Results
- 280 000–420 000 hits/week
- 13 000 packages/day tracked

United Parcel Services

www.ups.com

Key services
- Courier ordering
- Package tracking
- Rate calculations

Result
- 200 000–300 000 hits/week
- 1 million packages tracked and 500 000 phone calls avoided each month

---

In addition to increased sales and reduced costs, the Internet can be used to advantage in all of the marketing functions, for example:

- *Sales*. Achieved through increasing awareness of brands and products, supporting buying decisions and enabling online purchase, which is described in Chapter 11.
- *Marketing communications*. The use of the web site for the range of marketing communication is described in Chapter 2, and promotion of a company web site using banner advertising and other techniques is described in Chapter 9.
- *Customer service*. Supplementing phone operators with information available online and other techniques described in Chapters 2, 14 and 15.
- *Public relations*. The Internet can be used as a new channel for public relations (PR) and provides the opportunity to publish the latest news on products, markets and people (Chapter 2).

■ *Marketing research*. Techniques for finding a range of marketing information are described in Chapter 4. Assessing the strategic and operational value of the web site is covered in Chapter 12.

The Internet also changes the way in which companies do business with their trading partners. Extranets can be set up to reduce the costs of dealing with suppliers and provide marketing communications with suppliers. Such new ways of doing business are explained well by Ghosh (1998). The Internet offers a mechanism for companies to sell products direct to the customer. This process is known by American commentators as 'disintermediation', by Ghosh (1998) as 'pirating the value chain' or, in plainer language, as 'cutting out the middleman'. In Chapters 7, 13, 14 and 15 we also consider the important concept of Internet 're-intermediation' in which the intermediaries are created to link buyers and sellers.

Disintermediation

A company reduces the number of third parties it has to trade with. In particular it enables a company to sell direct to the customer.

To conclude this section, the benefits that are possible through use of the Internet are illustrated by Case study 1.2 about RS Components, which operates mainly in the business-to-business sector. A key phrase in this article articulated by the head of Internet trading is that the project *'isn't just about a site, it's about the whole integrated way of doing business on a very substantial scale'*. The use of extranets to form private links with customers, suppliers and distributors is an important issue of Internet marketing strategy, and is described in Chapter 7. The case study also shows some of the measures that can be used to assess the success of a web site (*see* Chapter 12). The benefits of an Internet presence can be summarised using the '6Cs' of, for example, Bocij *et al.* (1999):

1 *Cost reduction*. Achieved through reducing the need for sales and marketing enquiries to be handled by telephone operators and the reduced need for printing and distributing marketing communications material, which is instead published on the web site.
2 *Capability*. The Internet provides new opportunities for new products and services and for exploiting new markets.
3 *Competitive advantage*. If a company introduces new capabilities before its competitors, then it will achieve an advantage until its competitors have the same capability. For example, customers who transferred to Federal Express because of its new Internet services are likely to be less disposed to revert to an existing courier since they are 'locked in' to using the particular tools provided by Federal Express.
4 *Communications improvement*. These include improved communications with customers, staff, suppliers and distributors. This is a major topic within this book and is covered in more depth in Chapter 2.
5 *Control*. The Internet and intranets may provide better marketing research through tracking of customer behaviour and the way in which staff deliver services.
6 *Customer service improvement*. Provided by interactive queries of databases containing, for example, stock availability or customer service questions.

RS COMPONENTS

RS Components (*www.rswww.com*) is a distributor of electronic components for example in the motor trade. It launched a transactional site for the 107 000 products in its catalogue in February 1998. In its first six months 44 000 customers registered as users of the site and there have been 84 000 repeat visits. The average order value is £81 and the average site visit across all 280 000 site visits is 23 minutes.

Traditionally RS Components operated in the business-to-business sector by selling direct to garages or through distributors. A benefit of the new site has been that a tenth of all registrations were from private individuals who represent a new customer sector.

The web site uses personalisation software from Broadvision to tailor over 50 different versions of the home page to different types of visitors. Further capabilities that are unavailable via other channels are:

- the facility for online users to check on stock availability
- return to unfinished orders which are interrupted part-way through
- different parcels can be sent to different fulfilment addresses from a single order

The company has made a substantial investment and commitment to new media spending £2.5 million on the new system to date. Bernard Hewitt, head of Internet trading at RS Components, justified this expenditure saying:

'We're this committed to new media because we believe in the future. No one like us is doing anything close to what we're doing. It isn't just about a site, it's about the whole integrated way of doing business on a very substantial scale.'

Source: *Revolution* magazine, November 1998.

Questions

1 Explain how the company has used the Internet to achieve each of the '6Cs' of cost reduction, new capability, competitive advantage, communications improvement, improved control and customer service.

2 Compare the facility the Internet provides to measure the way the site is used with a traditional phone or fax-based ordering system.

3 What does the extent of the investment made by the company suggest about the directors' commitment to the Internet?

The Internet – a new marketing medium

A short history of the Internet

The Internet has existed since the late 1960s when a limited number of computers were connected in the United States to form the ARPAnet. This was mainly used to enable academics and military personnel to exchange defence information.

> **The Internet**
> The *Internet* refers to the physical network that links computers across the globe. It consists of the infrastructure of network servers and wide-area communication links between them that are used to hold and transport the vast amount of information on the Internet.

Why then has the Internet only recently been widely adopted for business purposes? The recent dramatic growth in the use of the Internet has occurred because of the development of the World Wide Web. This became a commercial proposition in 1993 after development of the original concept by Tim Berners-Lee, a British scientist working at CERN in Switzerland in 1989. The World Wide Web changed the Internet from a difficult-to-use tool for academics and technicians to an easy-to-use tool for finding information for businesses and consumers. How the World Wide Web works is described in more detail in Chapter 3. At this stage it can be considered as an interlinked publishing medium for displaying graphic and text information. This information is stored on server computers and then accessed by users who run web browser programs such as Microsoft Internet Explorer and Netscape Navigator, which display the information and allow users to select links to access other web sites (the process known as 'surfing').

Figure 1.2 gives an example of a web site accessed through the Internet Explorer web browser. This site has the web address or location '*www.marketing-online.co.uk*' and provides information on different aspects of Internet marketing. The significance of the components of different web addresses is explained in Chapter 3.

> **World Wide Web**
> The *World Wide Web* is a medium for publishing information on the Internet. It is accessed through *web browsers*, which display web pages and can now be used to run business applications. Company information is stored on *web servers*, which are usually referred to as *web sites*.

From the Internet to intranets and extranets

Intranet and extranet are two terms that have arisen in the 1990s to describe applications of Internet technologies that do not only involve communicating with customers, but rather with company staff (intranet) and third parties such as suppliers and distributors (extranet). While everyone connected to the Internet can access a company Internet web site, only those who have been given authorisation can access an intranet or extranet. This relationship between the Internet, intranets and extranets is indicated by Fig. 3.6. It can be seen that an intranet is effectively a private-company Internet with access available to staff only. An extranet permits access to trusted third parties, and the Internet provides global access.

Extranets provide exciting opportunities to communicate with major customers since tailored information such as special promotions, electronic catalogues and order histories can be provided on a web page personalised for each customer.

> **Intranet**
> A network within a single company which enables access to company information using the familiar tools of the Internet such as web browsers. Only staff within the company can access the intranet, which will be password protected.

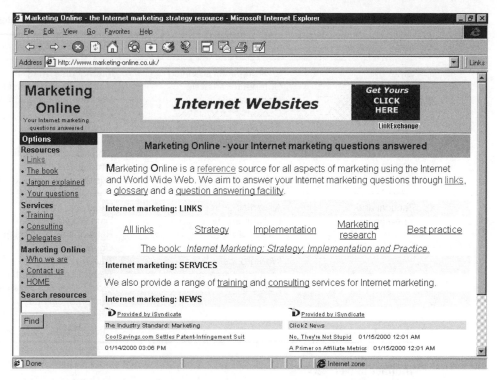

Fig. 1.2 A web site providing links to different Internet marketing information sources viewed using Microsoft Internet Explorer browser

---

Extranet
Formed by extending the intranet beyond a company to customers, suppliers, collaborators or even competitors. This is again password protected to prevent access by all Internet users.

Opportunities for using intranets and extranets to support the marketing process can be divided in two different ways. First, we must consider that the Internet can be used for marketing communications both within and beyond the company. As well as using the Internet to communicate with customers, companies find that internal use of an intranet or use of an extranet facilitate communication and control between staff, suppliers and distributors. Second, the Internet, intranet and extranet can be applied at different levels of management within a company. Table 1.1 illustrates potential marketing applications of both the Internet and intranet for supporting marketing at different levels of managerial decision making.

The scale of the Internet

How big is the Internet? This question can be answered from the perspectives of supply of information by organisations and individuals and demand for information by web users.

Table 1.1 Potential for using the Internet and the intranet to support marketing functions

Level of management	Internet	Intranet and extranet
Strategic	Environmental scanning Competitor analysis Market analysis Customer analysis Strategic decision making Supply chain management	Internal data analysis Management information Marketing information Database Operations efficiency Business planning Monitoring and control Simulations Business Intelligence (data warehouses)
Tactical and operational	Advertising/promotions Direct marketing Public relations Distribution/logistics Workgroups Marketing research Publishing	Electronic mail Data warehousing Relationship marketing Conferencing Training Technology information Product/service information Customer service Internet trading Sponsorship

Number of web servers

The information is supplied by the web sites stored on different web servers.

Figure 1.3 shows the dramatic growth in size of the Internet in terms of the number of hosts, or servers, connected to the Internet. The number of hosts exceeds the number of web sites since a web site may be made up of several hosts, or host computers may be used for other purposes. In 1999 it was estimated that there were approximately five million distinct web sites. This rapid growth is testimony to the popularity of the Internet as a means of communicating information.

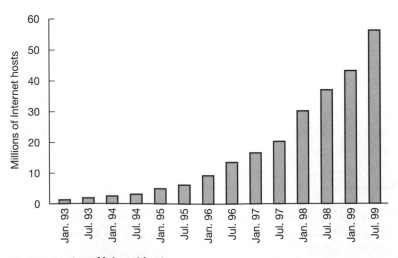

Fig. 1.3 Number of Internet hosts

Source: Internet Software Consortium (*www.isc.org*).

Market size – number of users

These web sites are accessed by a user population or audience. It can be seen from Fig. 1.4 that there has been a steady rise in the number of people online, although the rate of increase has not been as rapid as that for the number of servers. It is worth noting that for all the hype about the Internet, the current figure of about 200 million is less than 5 per cent of the global population. Within the developed world, it is shown in Chapters 2 and 13 that the proportion of adults with Internet access is between 5 and 50% for different countries in the developed world. In the business-to-business context, it is shown in Chapter 14 that for a developed country such as the UK, access levels have neared saturation in large companies, with SME access exceeding 50%.

Characteristics of users

In the early days of the use of the World Wide Web, the demographics of the overall Internet population was skewed towards predominantly male, relatively young, high income users (*see* Chapter 2). While this is still true to an extent, the explosive growth in number of users means that month by month the Internet population is becoming more similar to the average population. Despite this trend, the Internet still offers excellent opportunities for target marketing. Mini case study 1.2 shows how particular sites can be used to advertise to particular market segments.

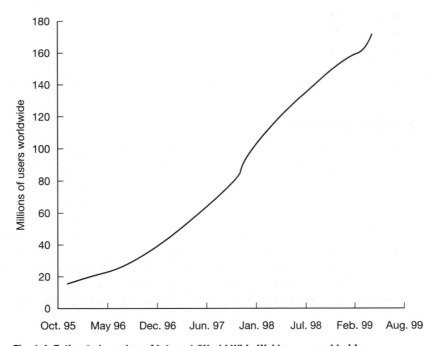

Fig. 1.4 Estimated number of Internet (World Wide Web) users worldwide

Source: Nua compilation (*www.nua.ie*).

Mini case study 1.2   **Target marketing using specialist sites**

The potential to use web sites to target special interest groups through advertising is illustrated by the demographic profiles of these three sites, which were developed by the Associated New Media design agency. The figures are based on profiling by NOP in August 1998. Page impressions refers to the number of separate pages viewed by different users. The examples show both general interest sites and specific interest sites.

This is London (*www.thisislondon.com*)

- 85 per cent ABC1
- 70 per cent 25–44
- 45 per cent female
- Four million page impressions

Ukplus (*www.ukplus.com*)

- 65 per cent ABC1
- 55 per cent 25–44
- 70 per cent male
- Six million page impressions

Soccernet (*www.soccernet.com*)

- 75 per cent ABC1
- 45 per cent 15–24
- 97 per cent male
- 15 million page impressions

The Internet and other new media

The generic term 'new media' is widely used to distinguish between the traditional delivery of information to consumers and digital or electronic methods of delivering this information. The Internet is only one of the new media. Other significant types of new media include digital television, mobile phones, CD-ROM and information kiosks. In this book we focus on the Internet and World Wide Web, but acknowledge that the importance of other digital forms of communication will increase through time. Note that there is a convergence of the way in which these new media are delivered, with the potential for all these information sources to be accessed via a World Wide Web browser. The concept of convergence and the future development of other digital media are explored in Chapter 15.

How do Internet marketing communications differ from traditional marketing communications?

Internet marketing differs from conventional marketing communications because of the digital medium used for communications. The Internet and other digital media such as digital television and satellite and mobile phones enable interactivity that has not been previously possible. The new medium and the way it is accessed also produce a different demographic profile to the overall population, and users of the Internet behave differently from how they would behave if they were using other media, as explained in Chapter 2.

Kiani (1998) has presented a number of differences between the old and new media, which are shown in Table 1.2. Annotations to the differences between the old and new media have been added to the table.

John Deighton of Harvard Business School identifies the following characteristics inherent in a digital medium (Deighton, 1996):

- the customer initiates contact;
- the customer is seeking information (pull);
- it is a high intensity medium – the marketer will have 100 per cent of the individual's attention when he or she is viewing a web site;
- a company can gather and store the response of the individual;
- individual needs of the customer can be addressed and taken into account in future dialogues.

Table 1.2 An interpretation of the differences between the old and new media

Old media	New media	Comment
One-to-many communication model	One-to-one or many-to-many communication model	Hoffman and Novak (1996) state that theoretically the Internet is a many-to-many medium, but for company-to-customer-organisations communications it is best considered as one to one
Mass marketing	Individualised marketing or mass customisation	Personalisation possible because of technology to monitor preferences and tailor content (Deighton, 1996)
Monologue	Dialogue	Indicates the interactive nature of the World Wide Web, with the facility for feedback
Branding	Communication	Increased involvement of customer in defining brand characteristics. Opportunities for adding value to brand
Supply-side thinking	Demand-side thinking	Customer pull becomes more important
Customer as a target	Customer as a partner	Customer has more input into products and services required
Segmentation	Communities	Aggregations of like-minded consumers rather than arbitrarily defined target segments

Source: After Kiani (1998).

17

We will now examine in more detail the two main conclusions arising from the views expressed on p. 17.

1 The Internet is a pull medium

It follows that the customer has to consciously decide to visit a particular site according to the particular information or experience he or she is seeking (Hofmann and Novak, 1996). That is, it is a pull medium, which contrasts with the push media used for mass marketing. The implication for marketers is that Internet marketing communications strategy should focus on the acquisition of site visitors.

The problem of encouraging site visitors is compounded since it is difficult for potential customers to find a company web site. It is estimated that there are over one billion web pages amongst which a company is competing for the attention of customers. It follows that promoting the location of the web site is critical for companies. There are two methods for this. First, *offline promotion* is used to provide users with the web addresses. This can be achieved by including the web address on traditional advertising newsletters, company stationery and other marketing communications. Second, *online promotion* is used to help users find the web site. Online promotion uses a number of methods, which are summarised in Fig. 1.5.

Staff monitoring web sites find that people visiting a web site most commonly use *search engines* or *directories*, so it is important that each company is listed with such directories. Search engines and directories are now commonly referred to as portals or Internet gateways, and are described in more detail in Chapter 4. Many larger companies now place banner advertisements (Chapter 9) with news services, search engines or other widely used sites to attract customers to their sites. A detailed coverage of how to promote web sites is supplied in Chapter 9.

2 It is an interactive, one-to-one medium

The interactive nature of the medium to which Deighton refers means that the Internet is ideally suited to developing relationships with customers. The Internet enables a one-to-one dialogue to be held with the customer (Peters, 1998; Allen *et al.*, 1998). Chapter 10 explains that when linked with well-known techniques from direct and database marketing such as customer profiling, the Internet can be used to build long-term relationships with customers in which a company learns their preferences and develops specific services and products to meet these needs.

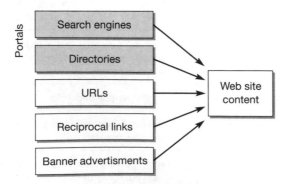

Fig. 1.5 Alternative methods of customer acquisition for a corporate web site

Given that attracting customers to the web site and then retaining their interest are important aims of Internet marketing communications, key elements for achieving this are often summarised as Content, Community and Commerce: content to capture and retain a customer's attention; community and interactivity to enable customers and a company to share information, values and beliefs; and commerce to support sales. How these elements can be applied is described in more detail in Chapter 2.

> **Content**
> Content is the design, text and graphical information that forms a web page. Good content is the key to attracting customers to a web site and retaining their interest or achieving repeat visits.

Internet marketing strategy

Part 2 of the book discusses integration between the Internet marketing strategy and broader marketing objectives and external influences on Internet marketing strategy (Chapter 5), describes the elements of an Internet marketing plan (Chapter 6), and explains how the Internet strategy must consider the implications for market and channel structures (Chapter 7).

As Quelch and Klein (1996) have noted, rather than following a defined strategy, many companies have followed a natural progression in developing their web site to support their marketing activities. Different levels of development of a web site can be identified, ranging from a simple static web site containing basic company and product information – sometimes referred to as brochureware – through a simple interactive site where users are able to search the site and make queries to retrieve information such as product availability and pricing, to an interactive site supporting transactions with users. An electronic commerce option for online sales may be available, together with other functions such as an interactive customer service helpdesk. Chapter 5 describes these different levels of web site development in more detail.

Typical current applications of web sites are shown in Table 1.3. This indicates that most companies who have a web site are at quite an early stage in its development, with the site being used for basic marketing information on the company

Table 1.3 Internet marketing applications in the UK

Use	Percent
PR/marketing information	70
Product catalogues	40
Customer contacts	27
Facilitating customer feedback	20
Detailed product information	18
Distribution of paid-for reports	10
Online orders	8
Paid-for advertisements	5

Source: *Business Computer World*/Spikes Cavell, February 1997.

and its products. A relatively small proportion of companies are using the Internet for sales of products or customer service.

Avoiding Internet marketing myopia

Theodore Levitt, writing in the *Harvard Business Review* (Levitt, 1960), outlined the factors that underlie the demise of many organisations and at best seriously weaken their longer-term competitiveness. These factors still provide a timely reminder of traps that should be avoided when embarking on Internet marketing.

1 Wrongly defining which business they are in.
2 Focusing on:
   ■ products (many web sites are still product-centric rather than customer-centric);
   ■ production;
   ■ technology (technology is only an enabler, not an aim);
   ■ selling (the culture on the Internet is based on customers seeking information to make informed buying decisions rather than strong exhortations to buy);
   rather than:
   ■ customer needs (the need for market orientation is a critical aspect of web site design and Internet marketing strategy); and
   ■ market opportunities (the Internet should not just be used as another channel, but new opportunities for adding value should be explored).
3 Unwillingness to innovate and 'creatively destruct' existing product/service lines.
4 Shortsightedness in terms of strategic thinking.
5 The lack of a strong and visionary CEO (Baker (1998) found that this was important to companies' using the Internet effectively).
6 Giving marketing only 'stepchild status', behind finance, production and technology.

Any organisation that sees and hence defines its business in anything other than customer-benefit terms has not taken the first step in achieving a *market orientation*. Any organisation that defines its business by what it produces is said to be suffering from 'marketing myopia'. Such myopia results from a company having a shortsighted and narrow view of the business that it is in.

If Internet marketing is to become integrated and fully established as a strategic marketing management tool, then the focus of attention needs to move towards understanding its broader applications within the total marketing process rather than just using it as a communication and selling tool. This is not to detract from the capability of the Internet to communicate and sell, but recognises that this is only one important aspect of the marketing process to which the Internet can contribute. The danger for those currently considering developing Internet technology is that the focus of such involvement will be too narrow and the true power of the Internet and its potential contribution to the marketing process will be missed. The broader implications of the use of the Internet for channel management and accommodating new market structures are considered in Chapter 7.

One of the elements of developing an Internet marketing strategy is deciding which marketing functions can be assisted by the Internet. There is a tendency amongst companies first using the Internet to restrict applications to promotion and selling. Further opportunities are available, and in the following sections, examples of the range of potential applications are given.

Market and marketing research (Chapters 4 and 9)

Alongside the constant monitoring of an organisation's marketing environment, there must also be research into customers' needs and wants (market research) and the monitoring of the effectiveness of marketing activity (marketing research).

The Internet provides a vehicle by which the marketer can gain rapid and often extensive access to secondary market and customer data. Such information is commonly held within an organisation's own intranet and databases. Further sources include trade associations, industry bodies, government departments and university libraries. Such sources are described in Chapter 4.

The Internet can be used to understand an organisation's macro and micro marketing environment. By monitoring information available on the Internet, organisations can attain more accuracy in their assessment of the competitive situation and the identification of potential market opportunities. The Internet also provides a channel through which closer relationships can be established between suppliers and customers, providing significant benefits in terms of efficiency and reliability to all parties.

Promotional activities (Chapters 2 and 9)

Promotion is the element of the marketing mix that is concerned with communicating the existence of products or services to a target market. Burnett (1993) defines it as:

> *'the marketing function concerned with persuasively communicating to target audiences the components of the marketing program in order to facilitate exchange'.*

A broader view of promotion is given by Wilmshurst (1993):

> *'Promotion unfortunately has a range of meanings. It can be used to describe the marketing communications aspect of the marketing mix or, more narrowly, as in sales promotion. In its very broad sense it includes the personal methods of communications, such as face to face or telephone selling, as well as the impersonal ones such as advertising. When we use a range of different types of promotion – direct mail, exhibitions, publicity etc we describe it as the promotional mix.'*

The main elements of the promotional or communications mix can be considered to be (as stated by, for example, Fill (1999)):

1 Advertising
2 Sales promotion
3 Personal selling
4 Public relations
5 Direct marketing

Most organisations use a combination of these methods to communicate with their target audiences in order to differentiate their products, remind, reassure, inform and persuade their customers and potential customers. The Internet provides organisations with a new media outlet that offers the opportunity to integrate all promotional mix elements. It has the benefit that a great depth and breadth of information can be readily provided on the web site. Internet promotions can work in the same way as any other form of promotion, and despite the medium still being in its infancy and the audience being smaller and more fragmented, Internet promotions are set to expand rapidly. In January 1998 Toyota used the Internet as part of an integrated promotional campaign for the launch of the Avensis, as described in Mini case study 1.3.

Toyota use the Internet as part of promotional mix for the Avensis launch

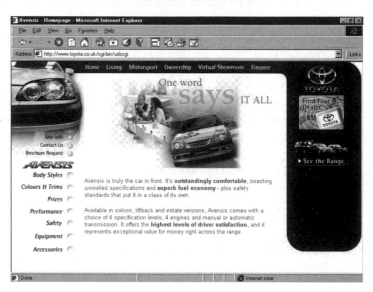

Fig. 1.6 Toyota Avensis promotion site

Toyota used the Internet for promotion of the Avensis at its UK launch in early 1998 by investing £100 000 in an online campaign. This used banner advertisements in search engines and other frequently visited general sites, such as newspapers, together with more targeted sites such as motor magazine sites. This promotion occurred in conjunction with traditional television and billboard campaigns. All elements of the campaign led to 12 000 page impressions a day, with the average visitor staying on the web site for 9.5-min. visits while enquiring about features, requesting a brochure, enquiring about the local dealer and finance. Note that the interaction achieved with customers is long in comparison with traditional media and that valuable direct marketing information such as names and addresses can be collected through requests for brochures.

Advertising (Chapter 9)

Since the Internet is a new medium, marketing staff are still undergoing a learning curve in terms of exploiting its full potential and integrating it with their offline promotional activities. Essentially, users have the choice of two options for advertising on the web. The first is to set up a web site and through this communicate key messages, images and buying information to the web site visitor. The second option is to use banner advertisements, which can increase brand recognition and communicate/reinforce brand values as well as providing a link to the web site.

Banner advertisements can be placed against reserved key words on search engines (entering the search keyword 'car', for example, might display a banner advertisement for the Avensis) or can be placed on media sites with more tightly defined niche audiences. The banners can provide opportunities for interaction and provision of further information. Additional messaging can be contained on the advertiser's own web site. While some Internet advertising is fairly primitive compared with that in other media, many advertisements have good creative execution and are integrated fully with offline campaigns.

> **Banner advertisements**
> A rectangular area of screen that promotes a brand and/or encourages the user to click on it and visit the relevant web site.

Sales promotion (Chapter 10)

The Internet provides marketers with an excellent channel through which to communicate sales promotions. Capital Radio in conjunction with Nestlé launched a telephone response promotion targeted at children revising for their GCSEs offering revision tips and a guaranteed answer within 24 hours to e-mailed queries. They received 10 000 phone calls per day over the two weeks that the promotion ran. However, on further investigation they discovered that they did not answer 90 000 calls per week, which proved to be an irritant to the caller and potentially detrimental to the brand. Capital put the information on the web and announced the new service on air. Altogether 3500 people downloaded the revision tips and a further 1000 entered a competition that required filling in a lengthy data capture form. Sales promotions that allow users to accumulate some kind of reward (possibly financial) for each time they interact with a company on the Internet is one promotional strategy that can be used to build longer-term loyalty. Similarly the inclusion of gifts such as mugs and pens or other collectibles can easily be incorporated on to a web site. Such examples demonstrate the power of the Internet to act as a channel for communicating sales promotion offers.

Public relations (Chapter 2)

Public relations (PR) activity on the web offers organisations scope for corporate communications, sponsorship, publicity and a direct vehicle for communicating press releases. The Internet provides scope for two-way interaction, clear targeting of key opinion formers and journalists and the potential for communicating strong corporate brand messages. Several PR agencies are investigating the potential for organisations to further exploit the potential for electronic PR.

The Internet can be used to facilitate traditional methods of PR. It can also be used to expand the depth and breadth of PR.

Most press agencies now use the Internet as a primary source of information. Press releases can be sent by e-mail to agencies with which a company is registered, and can also be made available on a company's web site.

With this new method of PR, a key difference is that a company can talk direct to the market via the corporate web site. Third party agencies and physical media still have a role, because of their credibility as independent sources of information and their wider circulation. Agency information can be supplemented by more detailed and timely information direct from the corporate web site. Another way in which the new PR is different is that traditional weekly and monthly publishing deadlines disappear as new stories appear by the minute. This has the obvious benefit that a company can make an immediate impact and be better aware of the changing marketing environment. The obvious problem of the new PR is that a company's competitors have these advantages too. So it is likely that there will be an increased need for defensive PR.

Direct marketing (Chapter 10)

Direct marketing is currently one of the fastest-growing fields of marketing. The techniques it utilises can be spread across all the elements of the promotional mix. The following extract clearly identifies the purpose and scope of direct marketing.

> **Direct marketing**
> Direct marketing is promotion using a range of media which include direct mail, e-mail and direct response campaigns using television, radio or print media. It is intended to reach individuals who are members of a defined target audience to assist in building profitable customer relationships. The media used may be complementary alternatives, indeed the actual mechanism by which a customer responds, be it e-mail, phone or by post is not important. What is most significant is that the information collected about the customers preferences and personal details is appropriate for maintaining an ongoing dialogue and delivering services.

Direct marketing on the Internet offers significant potential for customisation of products and services and personalising a message. The utilisation of databases and the interactivity of the Internet enable organisations to engage in one-to-one dialogue. As indicated above, the real benefit of direct marketing is its potential to use data to develop relevant dialogue and relationships with consumers. The Internet is currently not fulfilling its potential in this area with users of the Internet, but we will look at some examples of companies exploiting the potential for relationship marketing activity.

Electronic commerce transactions (Chapter 11)

The adoption of Internet-based commerce or e-commerce is currently variable, according to the suitability of a product for online sales. In some business-to-business sectors such as electronic components, the Internet is fast becoming the primary medium for product sales. The computer manufacturer Dell now sells personal computers worth $10 m. via its web site each day.

In other sectors, the Internet is also becoming a preferred method of purchase. The Microsoft Expedia site sells holidays and flights worth over $1 m. each day. Amazon, the largest Internet bookshop, saw revenue grow by over 800 per cent between 1996 and 1997 to a total of $239 m. Figure 1.7 indicates the variation in popularity of products purchased using the Internet.

Electronic commerce has implications for existing channels of distribution regarding the logistics involved in delivery of products and services, how products and services are ordered, taxed and paid for. For consumers, a significant benefit of online shopping is that it provides access to a global marketplace of online shopping sites.

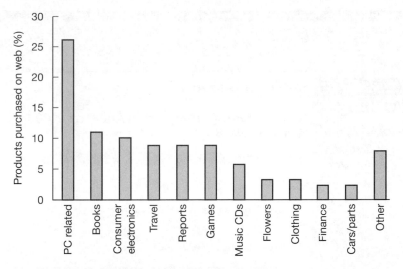

Fig. 1.7 Proportion of goods purchased online in Europe

Source: KPMG (1998), research carried out for 'Europe Gets Wired' report.

Concerns over security of transactions is one barrier that will need to be overcome before there can be any wider consumer use of electronic commerce. Organisations such as Mastercard and Visa are working with other partners to develop a Secure Electronic Transaction (SET) standard for securing payment-card transactions over the Internet. These issues, which will govern the adoption of electronic commerce, are investigated further in Chapter 11. In Chapters 13 and 14, examples are provided of how electronic commerce has been used in the business-to-consumer and business-to-business markets.

Services marketing (examples from Chapters 13 and 14)

The Internet provides both a communication and a distribution channel for the provision of faster and more effective service delivery. Access to organisational resources and information, the interactive nature of the Internet and the linkage of Internet technology to other IT hardware provide a wide range of opportunities for marketers to improve the service delivery process. An example of improved service delivery via the Internet is shown when the Royal Mail launched a web site that provides rapid access to information such as different types of postal services and a postal rates calculator where customers can enter the weight of their package and its destination to find out how much it will cost to send the package using each service. Users can request further information by entering their e-mail and postal address. Legal and General was one of the first UK insurers to set up a web page site. Now it has added a package of online financial products and services (Interplan) and plans an extranet for its representatives and agents. Account holders are able to access their accounts on the web site, make lump sum payments and increase/decrease monthly payments and withdraw any reserves. The company hopes to persuade more customers to link into Interplan to perform basic customer service such as notifying changes of address.

The potential to develop improved customer service online can provide customers with significant added value and also reduce costs. Software supplier Symantec

Fig. 1.8 Customer service for discussing software problems at the Symantec site
(www.symantec.com)

(*www.symantec.com*) has developed a customer service site that offers options for questions to be answered by support representatives and later reviewed by other customers with the same problem (Fig. 1.8), or even real-time chat. Most organisations can introduce customer care lines and customer information facilities that can easily be placed online. Cost savings, ease of access and immediacy of response are three potential benefits offered from improving online customer service.

SUMMARY

1 The growth in use of the Internet for marketing has been dramatic since the inception of World Wide Web browsers in the early 1990s.

2 The Internet is used to develop existing markets through enabling an additional communications and/or sales channel with potential customers. It can be used to develop new international markets with a reduced need for new sales offices and agents. Companies can provide new services and possibly products using the Internet.

3 The Internet can support the full range of marketing functions and in doing so can help reduce costs, facilitate communication within and between organisations and improve customer service.

4 Interaction with customers, suppliers and distributors occurs across the Internet. If access is restricted to favoured third parties this is known as an extranet. If Internet technologies are used to facilitate internal company communications this is known as an intranet – a private company internet.

5 Internet marketing involves a different demographic profile from the general population since it is largely restricted to computer users. The profile is skewed towards young, high-income males. Internet marketing also differs in that the customer is seeking information, and it is possible to set up interactive dialogues with customers that are tailored to the customers' preferences.

6 It is important for marketers to understand how visitors are likely to become aware of their web site. Online and offline promotion techniques can then be used to capture new visitors using these methods, which include:
- search engines;
- directories;
- banner advertisements placed in online media;
- links from other sites;
- typing in a web address (URL).

7 Many companies do not possess a clearly defined Internet marketing strategy. It is important that the strategy is integrated with the marketing strategy and includes clearly defined objectives, scope, branding, promotion methods and legal/technical constraints.

8 Electronic commerce is the term used to describe transactions between a business and third parties such as customers, suppliers and distributors. Transactions can include paid-for items or can be interpreted as the full range of transactions that occur as part of marketing communications.

9 The marketing benefits the Internet confers are advantageous both to the large corporation and to the small and medium-sized enterprise. These include:
- a new medium for advertising and PR;
- a new channel for distributing products;
- opportunities for expansion into new markets;
- new ways of enhancing customer service;
- new ways of reducing costs by reducing the number of staff in order fulfilment.

EXERCISES AND QUESTIONS

Self-assessment exercises

1 In what ways does Internet advertising differ from traditional advertising in terms of the cost, time and space that are available for communicating the marketing message?

2 Why have companies only started to widely use the Internet for marketing in the 1990s, given that it has been in existence for over thirty years?

3 What products appear suitable for sales in the 1990s given the current figures for sales by sector (e.g. Fig. 1.7)?

4 Explain what is meant by electronic commerce.

5 What are the main differences and similarities between the Internet, intranets and extranets?

6 How does the demographic profile of Internet users differ from the general population of a country?

7 What are the main methods by which a consumer will visit a web site using a web browser?

8 How is the Internet used to develop new markets and penetrate existing markets? What types of new products can be delivered by the Internet?

Discussion questions

1 'Estimates for the growth in the use of the Internet for electronic commerce tend to over-estimate this growth.' Discuss the validity of this statement and possible reasons for any overestimation.

2 The Internet is primarily thought of as a means of advertising and selling products. What are the opportunities for use of the Internet in other marketing functions?

3 'The World Wide Web represents a *pull* medium for marketing rather than a *push*-medium.' Discuss.

4 It is inevitable given the rapid adoption of the Internet that the Internet marketing strategy will not be well integrated with business and marketing strategies. Discuss the reasons for this poor integration and the problems this may cause.

Essay questions

1 You are a newly installed marketing manager in a company selling products in the business-to-business sector. Currently, the company only has a limited web site containing electronic versions of its brochures. You want to convince the directors of the benefits of investing in the web site to provide more benefits to the company. How would you present your case?

2 Explain the main benefits that a company selling fast-moving consumer goods could derive by creating a web site.

3 How can the Internet be used to support a company in implementing the modern marketing concept?

4 Examine the main similarities and differences in using the Internet and other media for advertising.

Examination questions

1 Briefly explain how the Internet can be used to support these different elements of promotion:
   (a) advertising
   (b) sales promotion
   (c) selling
   (d) public relations

2 Provide definitions of electronic commerce.

3 Internet technology is used by companies in three main contexts. Distinguish between the following types:
   (a) intranet
   (b) extranet
   (c) Internet

4 An Internet marketing manager must seek to control and accommodate all the main methods by which consumers may visit a company web site. Describe these methods.

5 In what ways does the balance between cost, time and space differ for a company advertising using a web site compared to a newspaper or television advertisement?

6 Imagine you are explaining the difference between the World Wide Web and the Internet to a marketing manager. How would you explain these two terms?

7 What are the main methods by which online and offline promotion of a web site can be achieved?

8 Explain how the Internet can be used to increase market penetration in existing markets and develop new markets.

REFERENCES

Allen, C., Kania, D. and Yaeckel, B. (1998) *Internet World Guide to One-to-One Web Marketing*. New York: Wiley and Sons.

Ansoff, H. (1957) 'Strategies for diversification', *Harvard Business Review*, September–October, 113–24.

Baker, P. (1998) *Electronic Commerce. Research Report 1998*. London: KPMG Management Consulting.

Bickerton, P., Bickerton, M. and Pandesi, U. (1996) *Cyber Marketing*. Oxford: Butterworth-Heinemann. Chartered Institute of Marketing series.

Bickerton, P., Bickerton, M. and Simpson-Holey, K. (1998) *Cyberstrategy*. Oxford: Butterworth-Heinemann. Chartered Institute of Marketing series.

Burnett, J. (1993) *Promotional Management*. Boston, MA: Houghton-Mifflin.

Bocij, P., Chaffey, D., Greasley, A. and Hickie, S. (1999) *Business Information Systems. Technology, development and management*. London: FT Management.

Deighton, J, (1996) 'The future of interactive marketing', *Harvard Business Review*, November–December, 151–62.

Fill, C. (1999) *Marketing Communications – Contexts, Contents and Strategies* (2nd edn). Hemel Hempstead: Prentice Hall.

Ghosh, S. (1998) 'Making business sense of the Internet', *Harvard Business Review*, March–April, 127–35.

Hoffman, D.L. and Novak, T.P. (1996) 'Marketing in hypermedia computer-mediated environments: conceptual foundations', *Journal of Marketing*, 60 (July), 50–68.

Hoffman, D.L. and Novak, T.P. (1997) 'A new marketing paradigm for electronic commerce', *The Information Society*, special issue on electronic commerce, 13 (January–March), 43–54.

Houston, F. (1986) 'The marketing concept: what it is and what it is not', *Journal of Marketing*, 50 (April), 81–7.

Jaworski, B. and Kohli, A. (1993) 'Market orientation: antecedents and consequences', *Journal of Marketing*, July, 53–70.

Kiani, G. (1998) 'Marketing opportunities in the digital world', *Internet Research: Electronic networking applications and policy*, 8(2), 185–94.

Levitt, T. (1960) 'Marketing myopia', *Harvard Business Review*, July–August, 43–56.

Peters, L. (1998) 'The new interactive media: one-to-one but to whom?', *Marketing Intelligence and Planning*, 16(1), 22–30.

Price, C. (1998) 'Internet: Europe sales "could top $1,990bn"', *Financial Times*, 16 October.

Quelch, J. and Klein, L. (1996) 'The Internet and international marketing', *Sloan Management Review*, Spring, 60–75.

Valentin, E. (1996) 'The marketing concept and the conceptualisation of marketing strategy', *Journal of Marketing Theory and Practice*, Fall, 16-27.

Wilmshurst, J. (1993) *Below the Line Promotion*. Oxford: Butterworth-Heinemann.

Zwass, V. (1998) 'Structure and macro-level impacts of electronic commerce: from technological infrastructure to electronic marketplaces', in Kendall, K. (ed.) *Emerging Information Technologies*. Thousand Oaks, CA: Sage.

FURTHER READING

Baker, M. (ed.) (1999) *The Marketing Book*. Oxford, UK: Butterworth-Heinemann.
Chapter 1, One More Time – What Is Marketing, by Michael Baker, reviews the meaning of marketing and marketing myopia. Chapter 30, The Internet: The Direct Route to Growth and Development, by Jim Hammill and Sean Ennis, reviews the impact of the Internet on different sizes and types of company.

Brassington, F. and Petitt, S. (2000) *Principles of Marketing* (2nd edn). Harlow, UK: Pearson Education. *See* companion Prentice Hall web site (*www.booksites.net/brassington2*).
Chapter 1, Marketing Dynamics, describes the marketing concept and the move from product orientation to marketing orientation.

Burnett, J. and Moriarty, S. (1999) *Introduction to Marketing Communications. An integrated approach*. Upper Saddle River, NJ: Prentice Hall.
See companion Prentice Hall web site (*cw.prenhall.com/bookbind/pubbooks/burnett/*). Particularly relevant are Chapter 1, Marketing Communication, and Chapter 2, The Marketing Mix and IMC.

Dibb, S., Simkin, S., Pride, W. and Ferrel, O. (1997) *Marketing. Concepts and strategies* (3rd European edn). New York: Houghton Mifflin.
See companion Houghton Mifflin web site (*www.busmgt.ulst.ac.uk/h_mifflin/*). *See* Chapter 1, An Overview of the Marketing Concept.

Hoffman, D.L., and Novak, T.P. (1997) 'A new marketing paradigm for electronic commerce', *The Information Society*, Special issue on electronic commerce, 13 (Jan.–Mar.), 43–54.
This was the seminal paper on Internet marketing when it was published, and is still essential reading for its discussion of concepts. Available online at Vanderbilt University (*ecommerce.vanderbilt.edu/papers.html*).

Kotler, P., Armstrong, G., Saunders, J. and Wong, V. (1999) *Principles of Marketing* (2nd edn). Hemel Hempstead: Prentice Hall, Europe.
See companion Prentice Hall web site for 8th US edn: *cw.prenhall.com/bookbind/pubbooks/kotler/*
Chapter 1, Marketing in a Changing World: Satisfying Human Needs, defines marketing and the marketing concept.

Strauss, J. and Frost, R. (1999) *Marketing on the Internet. Principles of online marketing*. New Saddle River, NJ: Prentice Hall.
Chapter 1, Introduction to the Internet, and Chapter 2, Internet User Characteristics and Behaviour, introduce Internet marketing and typical user characteristics.

WEB SITE REFERENCES

General sources on Internet marketing

Biz/ed Internet Catalogue (*www.bized.ac.uk/roads/htdocs/subject-listing/market.html*) has a range of online marketing resources.

Internet Marketing: A Strategic Framework (*web.ukonline.co.uk/Members/jim.hamill/topic4.htm*) gives a brief paper by Dr Jim Hamill, Reader in International Marketing, University of Strathclyde, Glasgow, Scotland, UK. Good summary of main work in this area, with references to Quelch and Klein, Sterne, Cronin etc.

MarketingNet (*www.marketingnet.co.uk*) includes extracts from the books *Cyberstrategy* Bickerton *et al.* (1998) and *Cybermarketing* (Bickerton *et al.* (1996)).

Marketing Online (*www.marketing-online.co.uk*) is a source for links to web sites concerned with Internet marketing strategy, implementation and practice. Produced by Dave Chaffey.

Project 2000 (*ecommerce.vanderbilt.edu*) was founded in 1994 by Tom Novak and Donna Hoffman at School of Management, Vanderbilt University, to study marketing implications of the Internet. Useful links/papers.

Reports on growth of electronic commerce (see also further references in Chapter 4)

Butler Group (*www.butlergroup.co.uk*) is a group of UK IT analysts who report on electronic commerce and business use of the Internet.

Durlacher Research (*www.durlacher.co.uk*) produces a quarterly newsletter covering the Internet services market in UK. Also contains information by industry and business size. Good for business-to-business marketing information. Also covers consumer access. Sponsored by BT.

KPMG Consulting Europe (*www.kpmg.co.uk*) is a source of regular reports on electronic commerce in Europe.

Sites giving general information on market characteristics of the Internet

CyberAtlas (*www.cyberatlas.com*) gives Internet statistics including demographics; updated monthly.

NOP Research Group (*www.nopres.co.uk*) is the main body conducting UK-based research on consumer behaviour and characteristics.

Iconocast (*www.iconocast.com*) gives monthly summaries of in-depth market research, online advertising and e-commerce reports from an American perspective.

Nua Internet Surveys (*www.nua.ie*) is the definitive source of news on Internet developments, and reports on company and consumer adoption of Internet and characteristics in Europe and worldwide.

Print media

e.Business Magazine (*www.ebusiness.uk.com*). A new magazine that contains many case studies of business and marketing use of the Internet in the UK.

Net Profit (*www.net-profit.co.uk*) is a monthly UK-based newsletter on Internet commerce with a European focus.

New Media Age (*www.nmg.co.uk*). A weekly magazine. Similar in context to *Revolution*.

Revolution magazine (*www.revolution.haynet.com*) has a web site for a monthly UK magazine on new media including Internet marketing.

CHAPTER 2

Key Internet marketing concepts

Learning objectives

After reading this chapter, the reader should be able to:

- evaluate the opportunities the Internet provides to vary the marketing mix;
- identify the potential of the Internet to enhance marketing communications;
- exploit the differences between the Internet and other marketing media.

Links to other chapters

This chapter provides a further introduction to Internet marketing, and the concepts introduced are developed further later in the book. The main related chapters are:

- ► Chapter 9, Web site promotion.
- ► Chapter 10, Relationship marketing using the Internet.
- ► Chapter 13, Business-to-consumer Internet marketing.
- ► Chapter 14, Business-to-business Internet marketing.

INTRODUCTION

In this chapter we introduce the key marketing concepts that are important in harnessing the Internet for marketing. As companies have started to exploit the Internet, many have naturally applied existing marketing concepts and approaches to this new medium. This approach will not maximise the possible benefits since the medium is fundamentally different from others. This chapter explores the ways in which this marketing medium differs and asks how traditional marketing concepts and approaches may need to be revised in recognition of the differences. In so doing we will highlight potential differences between the Internet and other marketing media and what the implications of this are for the marketing mix, marketing communications and the buying process.

The Internet as a new communications medium

Many companies, when starting to use the Internet for marketing, took the approach of simply re-publishing existing marketing materials in a new form. This approach, termed 'brochureware' or electronic brochures by, for example, Berthon *et al.* (1998), was a practical first step, but is now discredited since it fails to acknowledge the differences in this medium. These include the following:

- the medium itself is different in that it is digital, interactive, and a greater depth of information can be published on a web site;
- the demographics may be different;
- the culture of purchasers may be different;
- the markets may be different.

We will now consider each of these differences in greater detail.

The digital medium of the Internet

As a marketing medium the Internet is quite different from the mass media in several respects:

1 It is predominately a pull medium rather than a push medium

In traditional marketing communications it is usually an organisation that is aiming to provide or *push* information to a consumer. On the Internet, it is usually a customer who initiates contact and is *seeking* information. In other words it is a 'pull' mechanism.

2 It is a digital medium that enables interaction

Since the Internet is a digital medium that is mediated by software on the web server that hosts the web content, this provides the opportunity for interaction with the customer. This is a distinguishing feature of the medium (Peters, 1998). For example, if a registered customer requests information, or orders a particular product, it will be possible for the supplier to contact them in future using e-mail with details of new offers related to their specific interest. Deighton (1996) proclaimed the interactive benefits of the Internet as a means of developing long-term relationships with customers (*see* Chapter 10).

3 It offers potential for one-to-one or many-to-many rather than one-to-many communication

The interactive nature of the Internet lends itself to establishing dialogues with individual customers. Thus potentially it is a one-to-one communication (from company to customer) rather than the traditional one-to-many communication (from company to customers) that is traditional in marketing using the mass media, such as newspapers or television. Figure 2.1 illustrates the interaction between an organisation (O) communicating a message (M) to customers (C) for a single-step flow of communication. It is apparent that for traditional mass marketing in (a) a single message (M_1) is communicated to all customers (C_1 to C_5). With a web site with personalisation facilities (b) there is a two-way interaction, with

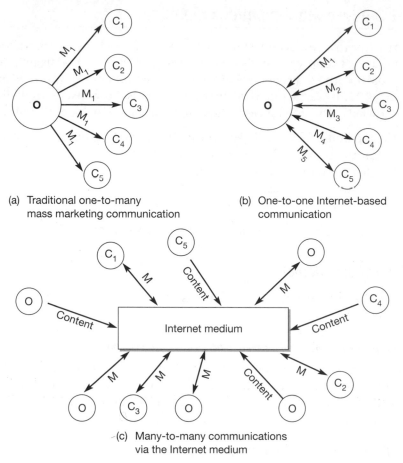

(a) Traditional one-to-many
    mass marketing communication

(b) One-to-one Internet-based
    communication

(c) Many-to-many communications
    via the Internet medium

Fig. 2.1 The differences between one-to-many and one-to-one communication using the Internet (organisation (O), communicating a message (M) and customers (C))

each communication potentially being unique. Note that many brochureware sites do not take full advantage of the Internet and merely use the Web to replicate other media channels by delivering a uniform message.

Personalisation
Web-based personalisation involves delivering customised content for the individual through web pages, e-mail or push technology. It is explored further in Chapter 10.

Hoffman and Novak (1997) believe that this change is significant enough to represent a new model for marketing or a new marketing paradigm. They suggest that the facilities of the Internet including the Web represent a computer-mediated environment in which the interactions are not between the sender and receiver of information, but with the medium itself. They say: *'consumers can interact with the medium, firms can provide content to the medium, and in the most radical departure from traditional marketing environments, consumers can provide commercially-oriented content to the media'*. This situation is shown in Fig. 2.1(c). This potential has not yet been fully developed since many companies are still using the Internet to provide standardised information to a general audience. However, some companies provide personalised Internet-based services to key accounts. An example is Dell (*www.dell.com*), with its PremierPages (Fig. 6.3). Furthermore some companies such as eBay (*www.ebay.com*) or uBid (*www.uBid.com*, *see* Fig. 2.2) are adopting the new paradigm by offering bespoke auction facilities. Here a user will state they have a product for sale (an example of a consumer providing content) and different offers will be made by many interested parties. At the end of the auction session, the highest bidder will take the goods on trust. Hoffman and Novak (1997) note that consumers can also take part in product design specification and in feedback on existing products.

Despite the reference to a new paradigm, it is still important to apply tried and tested marketing concepts such as the marketing mix and buying process to the Internet environment, as this chapter will illustrate. However, some opportunities will be missed if the Internet is merely treated as another medium similar to existing media.

4 The medium changes the nature of standard marketing communications such as advertising

In addition to offering the opportunity for one-to-one marketing, the Internet can be, and is still widely used for one-to-many advertising. On the Internet the overall message from the advertiser becomes less important, and typically it is detailed information the user is seeking. The web site itself can be considered as similar in function to an advertisement (since it can inform, persuade and remind customers about the offering, although it is not paid for in the same way as a traditional

Fig. 2.2 uBid (*www.ubidπ.com*), an Internet-based auction system

advertisement). Berthon *et al.* (1996) consider a web site as a mix between advertising and direct selling since it can also be used to engage the visitor in a dialogue. Constraints on advertising in traditional mass media such as paying for time or space become less important. A later section in this chapter explores the differences the Internet implies for different elements of the communications mix including advertising.

Peters (1998) suggests that communication via the new medium is differentiated from communication using traditional media in four different ways. First, *communication style* is changed, with *immediate*, or synchronous transfer of information through online customer service being possible. Asynchronous communication, where there is a time delay between sending and receiving information as through e-mail, also occurs. Second, *social presence* or the feeling that a communications exchange is sociable, warm, personal and active may be lower if a standard web page is delivered, but can be enhanced, perhaps by a personalised e-mail. Third, the consumer has more *control of contact,* and finally the user has control of *content*, for example through personalisation facilities such as My Excite (Fig. 10.5).

Although Hoffman and Novak (1996) point out that with the Internet the main relationships are not *directly* between sender and receiver of information, but with the web-based environment, the classic communications model of Schramm (1955) can still be used to help understand the effectiveness of marketing communication using the Internet. Figure 2.3 shows the model applied to the Internet. Three of the elements of the model that can constrain the effectiveness of Internet marketing are:

■ *encoding* – this is the design and development of the site content or e-mail that aims to convey the message of the company, and is dependent on understanding of the target audience;
■ *noise* – this is the external influence that affects the quality of the message; in an Internet context this can be slow download times, the use of plug-ins that the user cannot use or confusion caused by too much information on screen;
■ *decoding* – this is the process of interpreting the message, and is dependent on the cognitive ability of the receiver, which is partly influenced by the length of time they have used the Internet.

5 Changes to the distribution channel and marketplace enabled by the digital media

Chaterjee and Narasimhan (unpublished, quoted in Hoffman and Novak (1997)) note that the Web has extremely low entry and exit barriers for companies, reduces

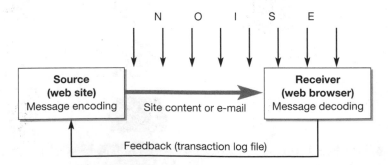

Fig. 2.3 The communications model of Schramm (1955) applied to the Internet

the need for intermediaries (although new intermediaries or cybermediaries may be promoted) and accelerates market change. Disintermediation and reintermediation and channel conflicts caused by these are considered further in Chapter 7.

Demographic differences

The characteristics of Internet users are currently quite different from those of the general population. This situation arises since the nature of the medium restricts its audience. For access from home, most users will have to be able to afford or identify a need for a personal computer or digital or cable TV with an appropriate set-top box. This restricts access to more affluent households. At work, the Internet may be available, but typically only to white-collar professionals who need it for their work. Public access to the Internet is available through some libraries and local council facilities, but the number of users is limited. Those studying at school or college usually now have access to the Internet. A summary of the number and characteristics of users is given in Case study 2.1.

CASE STUDY 2.1   **INTERNET USERS: NUMBERS AND DEMOGRAPHICS**

In the UK

The total number of UK users at the end of 1998 was estimated at 7–9 million in different surveys reported by CyberAtlas (*www.cyberatlas.com*). According to research conducted by National Opinion Poll (NOP) and *Marketing Magazine* (Denny, 1999) 20 per cent of adults are online. Six per cent have access only at home, 14 per cent only at work and 5 per cent at home and at work. The difficulty of estimating levels of usage was highlighted by a *Guardian*/ICM poll reported at the same time, which indicated that 34 per cent were online, with a further 14 per cent intending to be online in the course of the next year. These differences are partly explained by definitions of what is meant by 'online' and how regularly people use the Internet. These definitions can vary between anyone who has used the Internet at any time to those who have used it within the last six months or four weeks. It should be noted that such estimates may also include the many people who use e-mail, but do not access web sites.

At the time of the poll in late 1998 only 15 per cent of those online had bought products or services over the Internet, but 34 per cent said they would over the next year. Fifty-two per cent of users were put off buying goods online because of security risks, but the remainder were not concerned. Uses of the Internet include:

- sending e-mail (72 per cent);
- research (63 per cent);
- education (58 per cent);
- seeking information on products and services (53 per cent);
- hobbies and interests (53 per cent);
- games playing (32 per cent);
- planning holidays (24 per cent).

Web reference: NOP Research Group (*www.nopres.co.uk*)

▶

► **Case study** *continued*

The non-users

A survey from *Which Internet* reported that although 30 per cent of non-users intend to become connected to the Internet in the future, the majority (61 per cent of non-users or about 30 million individuals) believed they would never go online. Of those aged over 55, 85 per cent said they will never be connected to the Internet. Half of all non-users do not believe that the Internet is relevant to their needs, which is why they have not yet connected. A further 30 per cent have resisted because of the cost and the remainder because they are afraid of or do not understand the technology.

Web reference: *Which Internet* (*www.which.net*)

In Europe and the USA

A survey conducted by KPMG in 1998 (KPMG, 1998) showed that although Europe has similar levels of PC penetration to the USA (53 per cent of the population use a PC in the USA compared with 48 per cent in Britain, 45 per cent in Germany and 39 per cent in France), the levels of Internet access are much lower in Europe. It is estimated that the UK and Europe are approximately 14–18 months behind the USA in terms of usage of the World Wide Web. In the USA usage of the Web has exceeded 50 million or a quarter of the entire population.

An indication of the demographic profile of Internet users in the USA and Europe is available from the regular online surveys performed by the Graphic, Visualization, & Usability Center's (GVU) World Wide Web user surveys. These are the largest polls conducted on the Internet, often involving more then 10 000 respondents. They also give useful marketing-related information on how users use the Web, such as what prompts them to visit certain sites. However, they cannot be considered statistically representative since respondents opt to complete questionnaires themselves. In the latest survey the demographic characteristics are:.

- average age of user is 35.7 years old;
- 38.5 per cent female and 61.5 per cent male (22 per cent, 72 per cent Europe);
- 65 per cent access the Web from home (29 per cent Europe);
- average household income $53 000.

While early users tended to be students or technophiles, the growth in use has occurred as young professionals with high disposable incomes become connected at work or at home. This is reflected by these statistics. A general pattern in these surveys is that Internet users are 'becoming more normal': in other words, figures are approaching the mean in the general population, with the average age and proportion of females increasing, while average household income declines.

Web references: KPMG (*www.kpmg.co.uk*), GVU (*www.gvu.gatech.edu/user_surveys*)

Worldwide

Global figures of Internet user numbers and characteristics are summarised in regular reports by the USA-based analyst Cyberatlas and the Eire-based Nua Internet surveys. Latest figures suggest there are over 200 million users of the World Wide Web, which, to keep the figure in perspective, is little more than the population of Japan.

Web references: CyberAtlas (*www.cyberatlas.com*), Nua Internet Surveys (*www.nua.ie*)

Activity 2.1

Using the Internet for marketing research

1 You are to prepare a summary for a senior manager in your company explaining how the demographic characteristics of Internet users vary between the United States and Europe. You should visit the GVU web site (*www.gvu.gatech.edu*) and other surveys available from Marketing Online (*www.marketing-online.co.uk*).
   You should do the following:

   ■ Find and summarise the latest statistics giving breakdown by age, sex, income and occupation.
   ■ Read the report sections on how users access the Web, and on the implications of the behaviour of the users for how the web site should be defined.
   ■ Read the section on methodology of the GVU survey and explain how representative you believe it to be.

2 What is the total number of Internet users? Visit the Nua Internet Surveys web site (*www.nua.ie*) and the CyberAtlas site (*www.cyberatlas.com*). Locate the relevant sections on total number of users and summarise the total number of users in each continent. These are the figures that were used to compile Fig. 1.4. You should then comment on:

   ■ the distribution of Internet users in different parts of the world and the implications of this for the marketing effectiveness of the Internet;
   ■ the estimates for your own country and explanation of why the number of users is higher or lower than those for neighbouring countries;
   ■ the basis for estimating the number of users – what is the definition of a 'user'?
   ■ whether good quality information is available on the breakdown of users by demographic characteristics that could help marketers.

Cultural differences

There is a tendency to think of all customers on the Web behaving in a consistent way, by referring to them as surfers, users or customers. It is important to understand how different types of user interact with the message in this interactive medium. Two main types of psycho-segmentation are useful in understanding Internet users. A lifestyle-type segmentation was used by Bickerton *et al.* (1996), who suggest that the Internet marketer should cater for the following types of user:

■ *Techno-lusters*. Focused on the culture and technology.
■ *Academic buffs*. Originally one of the main types of user, now less significant.
■ *Techno-boffins*. Similar to the techno-lusters, but make more directed use of the technology for business purposes.
■ *Get aheads*. Use the Internet as a lifestyle accessory, use e-mail and use the Internet for product selection.
■ *Hobbyists*. People with specialist interests who use the Internet for purchase selection, such as golfers, fishermen, car enthusiasts.
■ *Knowledge traders*. Business-oriented users who turn to the Internet for news services and information on best business practice.
■ *Business bods*. General business users in management or procurement roles.
■ *Home users*. Members of families looking for education, entertainment or purchases.

Alternative classifications have been developed since the time of the Bickerton analysis, but as the Internet becomes more representative of the general population, more standard consumer classifications such as ACORN should prove more appropriate. For example, the Bickerton classification does not directly acknowledge the increasing number of retired users of the Web.

Market differences

For companies that do not currently operate worldwide, the Internet gives an opportunity to sell to overseas markets. As noted in Chapter 14, this will reduce the barriers to exporting for many small and medium-sized companies (Hamill and Gregory, 1997). Of course when companies are operating in new markets, the content of the company web site will have to acknowledge differences in areas such as:

- language;
- cultural characteristics and how these affect buying behaviour;
- legal and taxation differences.

How does the Internet relate to the marketing mix?

Many practitioners suggest that the marketing mix, the 4Ps, as stated by McCarthy (1960), is an essential part of marketing strategy. It is used as a device to define the marketing tools that should be used to achieve marketing objectives. It has also been extended to include two further elements: people and processes (Booms and Bitner, 1981) although others argue that these are subsumed within the 4Ps.

Current models of the marketing mix (Fig. 2.4) are applied frequently since they provide a simple framework for varying different elements of the product offering to influence the demand for a product. For example, to increase sales of a product the price can be decreased or the amount or type of promotion changed, or some combination of these elements can be varied. The Internet provides new

---

Using the Internet to vary the marketing mix

Product	Price	Promotion	Place	People	Processes
• Quality	• Positioning	• Marketing communications	• Trade channels	• Individuals on marketing activities	• Customer focus
• Image	• List	• Personal promotion	• Sales support	• Individuals on customer contact	• Business-led
• Branding	• Discounts	• Sales promotion	• Channel number	• Recruitment	• IT-supported
• Features	• Credit	• PR	• Segmented channels	• Culture/ image	• Design features
• Variants	• Payment methods	• Branding		• Training and skills	• Research and development
• Mix	• Free or value-added elements	• Direct marketing		• Remuneration	
• Support					
• Customer service					
• Use occasion					
• Availability					
• Warranties					

Fig. 2.4 The elements of the marketing mix

opportunities for the marketer to vary the marketing mix, so it is worthwhile to consider what these are.

The advent of the Internet provides opportunities to vary the elements of the marketing mix as follows:

- *Product* – the features of the product can be varied: in particular, customer service and brand values can be enhanced. New information-based products can be provided by the Internet such as specialised market information on subscription. Brand variants can be produced for some markets.
- *Price* – using the Internet as a new retail sales channel enables the price of products to be reduced since the number of items and the cost of distribution through a traditional network of shops can be decreased. Alternatively, if a price point can be maintained, the lower-cost route to the market can be used to increase profitability.
- *Promotion* – the Internet offers a new, additional marketing communications channel by which to inform customers of the benefits of a product and assist them in the buying decision. The Internet can be used to supplement the range of promotional activities such as advertising, sales promotions, PR and direct marketing. The Internet offers many advantages and some disadvantages as an alternative promotional medium and these are considered in more detail in the section on how the Internet will affect marketing communications.
- *Place* – the Internet also offers a new sales channel for distributing products through electronic commerce. This enables small UK companies such as Jack Scaife Ltd (a butcher) (*www.JackScaife.co.uk*) and E. Botham (a baker) (*www.Botham.co.uk*), which did not traditionally export, to enter overseas markets. The factors important in developing this new market are explored in Hamill and Gregory (1997).
- *People* – the Internet can be thought of as marginalising the role of direct customer contact from an organisation, but it is widely used to help recruit quality staff.
- *Processes* – the Internet must be integrated with other marketing processes such as telemarketing and direct marketing and the different processes of the value chain in order for it to be successful.

It is worth noting that the application of the 4Ps can lead to product rather than customer orientation – the latter being an important element of Internet marketing strategy and web site design. Lautenborn (1990) suggested that the 4Cs, of customer needs and wants (from the product), cost to the customer (price), convenience (relative to place) and communication (promotion) were important considerations when developing the mix. The Internet clearly helps in meeting customer needs using these techniques.

| Activity 2.2 | **How can the Internet be used to vary the marketing mix?** |

Review Fig. 2.4 and explain the *two* most important ways in which the Internet gives new potential for varying the marketing mix *for each* of product, price, promotion, place, people and processes. State:

- new opportunities for varying the mix;
- examples of companies that have achieved this;
- possible negative implications (threats) for each opportunity.

The Internet also represents threats to companies. These imply constraints on the elements of the mix. For example, the Internet will increase the transparency of prices of products. This is likely to lead to there being less opportunity for companies to charge a premium for quality products or customer service. Customers or potential customers will access such information through brokers or cybermediaries that offer a price comparison service (see Chapters 14 and 15). They already do so in some sectors that lend themselves to this type of service such as car insurance, where Screentrade (*www.screentrade.co.uk*) (*see* Fig. 7.4) has offered a comparison between ten different insurers since 1996. As the number of such services and the sectors they cover increases, the effect is likely to be an increase in price sensitivity on the part of customers. As the Internet continues to grow and electronic commerce increases, the sales volumes in traditional retail stores will decline and some may become untenable. In his book *eShock*, Michael de Kare-Silver (de Kare-Silver, 1998) suggests the effects could become apparent by as early as 2005 in the UK.

How can the Internet support marketing communications?

Of all the elements of the marketing mix, the role of promotion can be considerably enhanced through the use of the Internet. Marketing communications are traditionally divided into personal and impersonal communications with the customer. In this section, we make some general observations on the role of the Internet in different types of personal and impersonal marketing communications:

1 The Internet most readily lends itself to *impersonal* communications such as advertising, PR and sales promotions since this sort of communication can be achieved simply by publishing existing documents such as brochures. However, if the Internet is used in this way, it is simply being used in a similar way to other mass media such as television, radio or the print media. To maximise the use of the characteristics of the digital medium it should also be used to support *personal* communications and to develop long-term relationships with customers through its interactive facilities and communities (Deighton, 1996).

2 The Internet is of great value in *advertising*, since web sites provide the opportunity to give greater information on product features and benefits than do other media such as television and newspapers, where the advertiser has to pay for time or space. The web site itself can be considered an advertisement since it can fulfil the main objectives of advertising, namely to be able to inform, persuade and remind customers about the offering. Additionally, banner advertisements can be used to direct Web users to a web site or for brand building. The role of the Internet in advertising is discussed in Chapter 9.

3 In relation to impersonal methods of communication, the Internet also offers great scope for *PR and sales promotions*. The Internet significantly changes the nature of PR, since a company web site itself can act as a vehicle for PR. Through hosting a web site a company becomes a media owner and has the opportunity to publish what it deems to be newsworthy material without review by a media owner such as a publisher or a television company. Although the reduction in editorial control represents an opportunity for a company to make unfettered claims about itself and its products, it also enables a company's competitors to

monitor it, and possibly to denigrate its products on their web sites. Thus there is a need to monitor other companies' web sites for adverse publicity and take action accordingly. For example, the major software companies such as Microsoft, Lotus, Novell and Oracle feature product reviews by analysts, and strenuous rebuttals are published the next day. The Internet also provides a more dynamic medium in which news can be published immediately, without the delay necessary for review and incorporation in a weekly or monthly publication. The Internet offers many alternatives for sales promotions such as competitions and price reductions. Whereas conventional sales promotions are often used as a device to stimulate short-term sales, this is not necessarily the case with the Internet. While sales promotions can be used for this purpose, they are more often used as a technique to encourage repeat visits to the site.

4 Personal communications such as sales calls from the company to the purchaser are not really facilitated by the Internet, although this may be possible in the future if the use of *videoconferencing* becomes a routine business activity. Information available on the Internet can be used to support promotional material that is provided by the sales person, but printed material remains effective. Internet sites can also be used to facilitate or initiate the dialogue between potential buyers and salespeople. For example, Freeway (*www.freeway.ltd.uk*), a UK-based broker for new car sales, uses the web site to promote contact of the prospect by phone. Freeway asks users to specify when it will be convenient for one of the company's sales representatives to contact them (*see* Fig. 2.6). How such callback systems are used to integrate the Internet and telemarketing is discussed in Chapter 10.

5 Of all the personal communications techniques, *direct marketing* offers the most potential for use by the Internet. The Internet marketer should aim to capture the personal details of a customer including his or her e-mail address and then the marketer can establish a continuous dialogue with the customer. The content of the web site can also be dynamically updated to reflect the interest of the user. To date, this approach has been used mainly by information providers such as Yahoo! (*www.myyahoo.com*) and Excite (*www.excite.com*), but it is also used for some corporate accounts by companies such as Dell (*www.dell.com*). Direct marketing using the Internet and the wider topic of relationship marketing is of such significance to Internet marketing that it is described in more detail in Chapter 10.

6 *Brand activities* are media communications that use a combination of personal and impersonal techniques to enhance brand awareness and develop brand use. For Internet marketing, effective techniques in this area include:

- *Sponsorship* – sponsorship of another site can be used to promote a brand and drive traffic towards a company's own site. The 2000 BT Challenge (*www.btchallenge.com*) round-the-world yacht race will have each boat sponsored by companies such as Logica, Compaq and CGU. The exposure they receive on the BT Challenge site will result in more visits to these companies' sites and increase the profile of the companies. In the UK, The Sponsorship Company (*www.thesponsorship.co.uk*) developed a service for matching sponsors to a variety of events, many supported by web sites.

- *Exhibitions* – these usually provide personal contact between customer and company, and virtual exhibitions on the Internet are developing this through chat-rooms, videoconferencing and e-mail links between customers and suppliers.

■ Customer *feedback* on brands through discussion groups or samples. Such discussions are often used for pop bands. For example, Jeepster Records (*www.jeepster.co.uk*) has hosted chat sessions between fans and its artists such as Belle and Sebastian and Snow Patrol.

■ *Co-branded content* is created when a company enters an agreement with another web site to host content on that site. Examples of this include Virgin Net (*www.virgin.net*) hosting information on non-Virgin products or a search engine such as Excite (*www.excite.co.uk*) providing detailed information on Thomas Cook holidays on its sites. Both of these examples offer promotion to both brand owners.

Buyer behaviour

Standard models of consumer buyer behaviour have been developed by Bettman (1979) and Booms and Bitner (1981). In these models, consumers process marketing stimuli such as the 4Ps and environmental stimuli according to the consumers' personal characteristics such as their culture, social group and personal and psychological make-up. Together these characteristics will affect the consumers' response to marketing messages. For the Internet marketer, a review of the factors influencing behaviour is specially important since a single web site may need to accommodate consumers from different cultures and social backgrounds. Users will also have different levels of experience of using the Web.

Specific behavioural traits are evident on the Internet. Studies show that the World Wide Web is used quite differently by different groups of people. Lewis and Lewis (1997) identified five different types of web users:

■ *Directed information seekers*. These users will be looking for product, market or leisure information such as details of their football club's fixtures. This type of user tends to be experienced in using the Web and to be proficient in using search engines and directories. The GVU World Wide Web surveys (*www.gvu. gatech.edu*) indicate that more experienced users have a more focused way of using the Internet.

■ *Undirected information seekers*. These are the users usually referred to as surfers, who like to browse and change sites by following hyperlinks. Members of this group tend to be novice users (but not exclusively so) and they may be more likely to click on banner advertisements.

■ *Directed buyers*. These buyers are online to purchase specific products. For such users, brokers or cybermediaries who compare product features and prices will be important locations to visit.

■ *Bargain hunters*. These users want to find the offers available from sales promotions such as free samples or prizes. For example, the Cybergold site (*www.cybergold.com*) pays users a small amount to read targeted advertising.

■ *Entertainment seekers*. These are users looking to interact with the Web for enjoyment through entering contests such as quizzes (e.g. 'You Don't know Jack' at Won.net (*www.won.net* and *www.bezerk.com*)), puzzles or interactive multi-player games.

When designing a web site, marketers find it useful to provide information and navigation guides for each type of user who fits within the target audience. For a retail site this might include all the types of user listed above, whereas for a business-to-business site visitors will mainly be directed information seekers and buyers. Although it is suggested that there are generic types of users, the characteristics of users can, of course, vary with each session that they are logged on, varying for example according to whether they are using the Web for work or recreation.

An alternative view of how consumer behaviour in using a web site may vary relates to the stage they have reached in the adoption of a web site. The process of adoption (Rogers, 1983), summarised for example by Kotler *et al.* (1999), is made up of the following stages:

- awareness;
- interest;
- evaluation;
- trial;
- adoption.

Breitenbach and van Doren (1998) assess how a web user passes through each stage. While such a model may be suitable for some sites which will be visited repeatedly (such as a portal) it is less appropriate for a customer visiting a site a single time to make a one-off purchase.

The role of the Internet in supporting customers at different stages of the buying process should also be considered. Figure 2.5 indicates how the Internet can be used to support the different stages in the buying process. The boxes on the left show the typical stages that a new prospect passes through, according to, for example, Robinson *et al.* (1967). A similar analysis was performed by Berthon *et al.* (1998), who speculated that the relative communications effectiveness of using a web site in this process gradually increased from 1 to 6.

It is worth while reviewing each of the stages in the buying process referred to in Fig. 2.5 in order to highlight how effective the Internet can be when used at different stages to support the marketing communications objectives.

1 Generate awareness (of need, product or service)

Generating awareness of need is conventionally achieved principally through mass media advertising. The Internet is not very effective at this since it has a more limited reach than television, radio or print media. Although banner advertising is widely used, it is more limited in the message that it can convey. It can assist in generating brand awareness. Some companies have effectively developed brand awareness by means of PR and media mentions concerning their success on the Internet, with the result that even if a customer does not have a current need for a product, that customer may be aware of the source when the need develops. Examples of companies that have developed brand awareness include Amazon for books, Dell for computers, CDNow for records, Microsoft Expedia for Holidays and Autobytel for cars. In more specialised business-to-business sectors it may also be possible for a company to establish a reputation as a preferred web site in its sector.

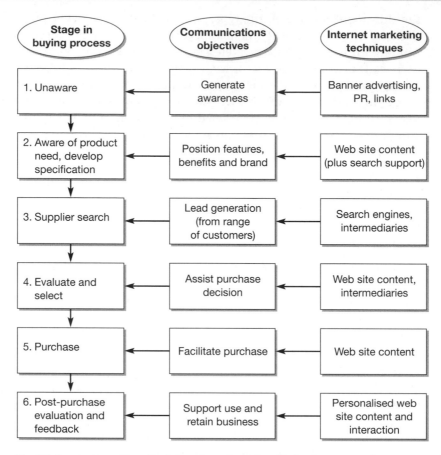

Fig. 2.5 A summary of how the Internet can impact on the buying process for a new purchaser

2 Position features, benefits and brand

Once a consumer is aware of a need and is considering what features and benefits he or she requires from a product, then he or she may turn to the Web to find out which suppliers are available or to find the range of features available from a particular type of product. Intermediaries are very important in supplier search and can also help in evaluation. For example, CNET (*www.computers.com*) (Fig. 15.1) provides detailed information and reviews on computers to help consumers make the choice. The prospect may visit sites to find out about, for example, features available in a digital television or characteristics of a place to go on holiday. If a company is fortunate enough to have such a customer, then it has an early opportunity to enter a dialogue with a customer and build the product's brand and generate a lead.

3 Lead generation

Once customers are actively searching for products (the directed information seeker of Lewis and Lewis, 1997), the Web provides an excellent medium to help them do this. It also provides a good opportunity for companies to describe the benefits of their web sites and obtain qualified leads. The Internet marketer must consider the methods that a customer will choose for searching and then ensure the company or its product is featured prominently.

4 Assist purchase decision

One of the most powerful features of web sites is their facility to carry a large amount of content at relatively low cost. This can be turned to advantage when customers are looking to identify the best product. By providing relevant information in a form that is easy to find and digest a company can use its web site to help in persuading the customer. Brand issues are important here also, as a new buyer will prefer to buy from a supplier with a good reputation – it will be difficult for a company to portray itself in this way if it has a slow, poorly designed or shoddy web site.

5 Facilitate purchase

Once a customer has decided to purchase, then a company will not want to lose the custom at this stage! The web site should enable standard credit-card payment mechanisms with the option to place the order by phone or mail.

6 Support product use and retain business

The Internet also provides good potential for retaining customers since:

■ value-added services such as free customer support can be provided by the web site and these encourage repeat visits and provide value-added features;
■ feedback on products can be provided to customers; the provision of such information will indicate to customers that the company is looking to improve its service;
■ e-mail can be used to give regular updates on products and promotions and encourage customers to revisit the site;
■ repeat visits to sites provide opportunities for cross-selling and repeat selling through sales promotions owing to the amount of information that can be displayed on the web site.

Internet marketing techniques to support different aspects of marketing communications have been categorised by Breitenbach and van Doren (1998). Their categories include the supply of in-depth product or company information, open communications (a two-way dialogue with the customer), real-time transactions and catalogue browsing, demonstrations ('try before buy'), club membership (or discussion forum), give-aways, entertainment (games or quizzes), virtual tours, instructional support and complementary services such as links and free customer support. The authors conducted a cross-industry survey of 50 company web sites, and found that of these techniques, those most commonly used include in-depth product or company information, open communications and complementary services. An example of customer support is shown in Fig. 2.6.

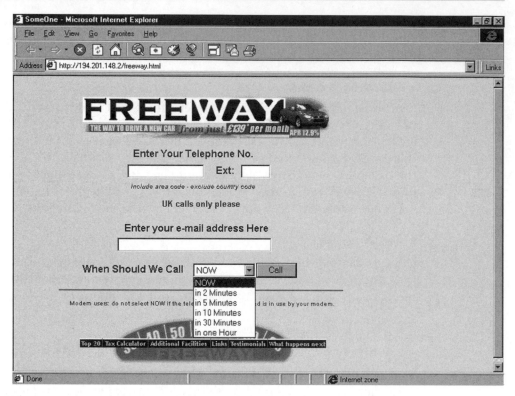

Fig. 2.6 Freeway (*www. freeway.ltd.uk*) **web site showing 'call-me' facilities for contacting customer by phone**

Key elements of effective web site design

To draw together the different ways in which the Internet can support marketing activities, the final section in this chapter will consider appropriate approaches to designing the web site to achieve marketing objectives. Creating and designing web sites is described in more detail in Chapter 8. The key success factors for a web site design strategy can be summarised as the 6Cs of capture, content, community, commerce, customer orientation and credibility. We will now consider these further:

- *Capture* – since there are estimated to be over one billion web pages (the search engine Altavista (*www.altavista.com*) references about 200 million web pages), it is highly unlikely that a casual user will visit an Internet site by chance. Web site designers must consider how to promote the web site to acquire these users. This can be achieved by online methods such as ensuring the web site can be easily located via search engines when the appropriate keywords are typed in or by means of banner advertisements to attract visitors to the site. There are also offline promotion methods such as including the company web address in advertisements and stationery. Such techniques are considered further in Chapter 9.
- *Content* – the content is the key to a web site, since this will be what attracts visitors to a web site and, if they recognise value, it will be what keeps them returning. Interactive content and personalisation to a user's preferences can

assist in generating return visits. How to develop a one-to-one relationship using the Internet with a customer is considered in Chapter 10.

- *Community* – the ability to develop specialised communities on a web site is one of the special characteristics of the Internet. If the web site designer can harness this, then it will be of great value in generating return visits to a site. For example, a users group based around an online discussion forum could be developed for a specialised business-to-business segment such as CAD software. This has been done by Delcam (*www.delcam.co.uk*). This will keep customers returning to a site where they can be informed of new products and offers. The value of online or digital communities has been reviewed by Hagel and Armstrong (1997) and is considered further in Chapter 10.

- *Commerce* – all content on a site and the way in which it is designed should be targeted at directly or indirectly generating additional sales transactions. However, many early sites did not offer the facility for online purchases, or the call to action was perhaps too subtle.

- *Customer orientation* – in accordance with the mantra of many marketing researchers and authors, who exhort companies to adopt a market orientation in marketing activities, customer orientation is key in web site design. To help customers find the information they need, the content should be targeted at particular customer segments. For example, the PC manufacturer Dell has an option on its home page for home users, small and medium-sized businesses and large corporate customers. The customer focus is also developed in the personalised content mentioned above. Customers may be any type of person who uses the site, not just people interested in buying a product. They may include new buyers, existing users of products or other users such as shareholders, the media and new staff.

- *Credibility* – since the Internet is a medium where there are likely to be many competitors in any sector (with over five million commercial web sites in 1999), it is important for companies to use the medium to establish that they are reliable and trustworthy. This can be achieved through a high quality brand identity and information about the company that summarises its pedigree. Case study 2.2 provides an example of an effective web site design strategy.

CASE STUDY 2.2   **AN EFFECTIVE WEB SITE DESIGN STRATEGY – AMAZON**

The USA-based site Amazon (*www.amazon.com*) is well known as one of the success stories of the Internet, at least in terms of its sales ($1 bn in 1999) and number of registered customers (2.5 million). It is also held up as an example of a site that is not yet profitable despite its being valued at about $10 bn in 1999. The company has certainly achieved success in terms of driving customers to its sites and this is a consequence of effective web site design. We shall now review the techniques it uses in relation to the 6Cs of Internet marketing using the less well-known example of the Amazon UK web site (*www.amazon.co.uk*). This site was formed in 1998 following the takeover by Amazon of *www.bookpages.co.uk*.

▶ **Case study** *continued*

Fig. 2.7 Amazon UK web site (*www.amazon.co.uk*)

1 Capture

When Amazon was launched in the UK it used offline media extensively to establish the Amazon.co.uk brand in the public awareness. This advertising targeted customers who were likely to own a PC with an Internet connection: for example, readers of broadsheet newspapers such as the *Guardian* and *Telegraph* and commuters on stations *en route* to London. Amazon also used banner advertising campaigns on search engines and news sites. Finally, traffic was built by using an affiliate model that has been successful in the United States. This involves links from other sites to the Amazon site in return for a proportion of any resulting sales. For example the Altavista search engine (*www.altavista.com*) offers links to Amazon about books related to keywords typed into the search engine.

2 Content

Study of Fig. 2.7 or a visit to the Amazon site will show that the content and navigation of the Amazon site are designed to provide customers with what they need. Users are able quickly to find a book that interests them by typing a keyword on the front page. Registered users can use the 'One-click' service which makes it very rapid to order a new book. Reviews of books by other customers, synopses and samples of text are all used to help the customer decide on a book. The site also has content such as gift wrapping and an e-mail-based book recommendation service to add value to a visit and help build the Amazon brand.

3 Community

Amazon provides several facilities that take advantage of the unique characteristics of the Internet medium to enable sharing of ideas between customers. These include:

- book reviews contributed by readers;
- a recommendation centre where readers join a particular interest group such as health and beauty or sport;
- recommendations based on what other similar readers have purchased.

4 Commerce

In addition to the benefits described above, the main proposition of the Amazon site is the discounting of books by up to 40 per cent. This is backed up by an easy-to-use system that stresses the security (out of three million orders received no instances of fraudulent use of customers' credit cards are known). Timely fulfilment supported by an e-mail summary of anticipated delivery assists commerce.

5 Customer orientation

Customer orientation is exhibited well in many of the facilities described above, with Amazon recognising the need to cater for new and existing users with many different interests.

6 Credibility

The promotion techniques referred to in the first point above are also useful in building the credibility of a company. The site shown in Fig. 2.7 does not have any clear design or brand features to enhance credibility. Often a tag line can achieve this. At one point the amazon.com site stated that it was 'the world's largest online bookstore'.

Questions

1 Summarise the main propositions of the Amazon brand that make it popular with customers.

2 How does the Amazon site make use of the interactive facilities of the Internet?

3 Give details on specific sites that Amazon could use to help promote the site using banner advertisements.

4 Given the cost of the facilities provided, why do you think the Amazon sites may not be profitable?

An alternative view of the factors that make a successful web site is provided by Kierzkowski *et al.* (1996), who identified what they describe as five critical success factors for successful digital marketers. They suggested it is necessary to:

- *Attract users*. This is equivalent to the capture element of design referred to above. Traffic-generating programs, described in Chapter 10, are necessary to achieve this.
- *Engage users' interest and participation*. This is primarily a function of the content of the site. Interest can be provided by giving value-added information.

Participation will be assisted through the use of interactive content such as competitions and games.

- *Retain users and ensure that they return to the site.* This is again a function of the content, but it is a vital aim that warrants stating separately. Breitenbach and van Doren (1998) claim that it is the unique features or services and free or value-added features of a site that will help a company to retain customers.
- *Learn about customer preferences.* This point stresses the need to make use of the unique facilities of the Internet to find out information about customer behaviour from monitoring log files of their pattern of use of the site and asking questions via onscreen forms. Online techniques about individual customers' preferences can be supplemented by focus groups that discuss the merits of a site and customers' needs. For example, Eddie Cheng of *Yellow Pages* has stated that the use of focus groups conducted via the Audited Bureau of Circulation (ABC), comprising over 800 site users, has significantly enhanced the performance of their site (*www.yell.co.uk*).
- *Relate back to customers with customised interactions.* Using the web site for direct-marketing purposes again takes advantage of the digital medium.

How does Internet marketing differ from conventional marketing?

Much of this chapter has taken the approach of reviewing how the Internet can be related to traditional marketing concepts and how it can be used to supplement or augment traditional techniques. Some concepts and models on the use of the Internet for marketing are, however, totally different. These are discussed in this section, which acts as a summary to this chapter and seeks to emphasise the concepts covered earlier in the chapter.

The Internet has been referred to as a new marketing paradigm (for example by Hoffman and Novak, 1997). This view suggests that it is a completely new model of the way in which marketing occurs. However, we have seen in this chapter that many established marketing models and concepts can be applied to the Internet. Why, then, is it suggested that the Internet is such a radically different medium? Hoffman and Novak (1996) suggest that the key difference is the way in which interactions occur between the different parties involved in the marketing process. Note that their comments refer specifically to the World Wide Web, which they refer to as a 'global hypermedia computer-mediated environment'. They see the World Wide Web providing a:

'many-to-many mediated communications model in which consumers can interact with the medium, firms can provide content to the medium and, in the most radical departure from traditional marketing environments, consumers can provide commercially oriented content to the medium'.

We will now consider these claims in turn:

1 It is a 'many-to-many' medium

This refers to the potential for the Internet to provide exchange of information between customers and suppliers. A many-to-many communication involves information being sent to many participants and implies interaction between participants in a discussion forum, chat forum or virtual community (discussed in Chapter 11). While these techniques are used quite frequently in a commercial context for customer support, they cannot be described as the predominant form of communication on the World Wide Web. This is currently one-to-many, and involves a company creating static information on a web site, which is accessed by many customers. This one-to-many arrangement is similar to that of traditional marketing by means of mass media advertising, for example. The current arrangement will change in the future, and already many sites are setting up specially configured web pages for customers to enable one-to-one communication. However, it can be argued that one-to-one marketing is not a 'paradigm shift', but merely a method of achieving direct marketing using a new, effective medium.

2 'Consumers can interact with the medium'

In marketing via traditional media consumers cannot directly control the message or easily request further information, but they can do so with the World Wide Web, and this represents a significant difference. For example, a user may view a banner advertisement from a financial services provider that encourages him or her to type in the amount of loan he or she is looking for to calculate repayment options. Furthermore, when interaction with a message occurs, the involvement of the consumer will be higher, leading to better recall of the message. It should be noted, though, that traditional media integrate different forms of media to achieve a similar effect. For example, if a consumer views an advertisement for a loan on television, he or she will be encouraged to phone for further information. This is arguably less effective than the web advertisement in which the call to action can be followed up immediately by the consumer.

3 'Consumers can provide commercially oriented content to the medium'

This is not possible with traditional marketing communications, and it is a significant difference which can be considered as an opportunity and a threat. One method by which consumers can provide content is to contribute to company or product-specific discussion forums and communities. When a user posts a message, that user is effectively adding content about the product being discussed. This has several possible benefits: testimonials from an independent customer are valuable assets; information about how to use a product can reduce the need for customer service phone help lines; and feedback or market research can be generated about customers' perceptions of products. A company may have to face negative comments, but this may be seen favourably by customers, since it indicates a willingness on the part of a company to listen to customers' needs.

A further important difference not referred to in the quotation (above) from Hoffman and Novak (1996) is that the Web is a 'pull' medium where the customer decides which content to view. This means that companies need to use a different approach to marketing, in which they have to provide signposts and a large volume of relevant information that reflects different customer needs rather than providing smaller volumes of less targeted information.

53

SUMMARY

1 The Internet possesses a number of characteristics that differentiate it from other media:
   ■ it is a *pull* medium in which customers seek information rather than a *pull* medium;
   ■ it enables interaction between a company and an individual on a one-to-one basis;
   ■ it has a limited reach (150 million regular Web users in 1999), with users being more affluent and younger than the wider population.

2 The Internet offers opportunities to vary the elements of the marketing mix in new ways.

3 The key elements of web site design are the 6Cs of:
   ■ *capture* – use online and offline promotion techniques to ensure customers visit a site;
   ■ *content* – provide relevant, interactive content to help retain customers and ensure they return;
   ■ *community* – facilitating dialogues between groups of customers can also help in retaining customers;
   ■ *commerce* – using the Internet to persuade customers to purchase by traditional channels such as in person or by phone, or by the new channel of buying online;
   ■ *customer* – the site should have segmented content for the different types of customers to which the web site appeals;
   ■ *credibility* – establishing a reputation as a trustworthy company to do business with.

4 The Internet mainly supports impersonal marketing communications and is particularly useful in assisting in supplier and product selection and product purchase through e-commerce.

5 Web site users are heterogeneous and the marketer should develop a site that attempts to provide suitable content and navigation for the full range of customers.

EXERCISES AND QUESTIONS

Self-assessment exercises

1 What is the difference for marketing communications between a 'pull' medium and a 'push' medium?

2 Describe two different models of online buyer behaviour.

3 How can the Internet be used to support the different stages of the buying process?

4 What are the '6Cs' of an effective web site design strategy?

5 Summarise the methods that can be used to attract customers to a web site.

6 What is meant by customer-oriented content?

7 Is the Internet best suited to personal or impersonal marketing communications?

8 What is the implication for the Internet of the 'price' and 'product' elements of the marketing mix?

Discussion questions

1 'Currently the Internet is mainly used as a "pull" medium, but in the future it will increasingly operate as a "push" medium.' Discuss.

2 'The Internet represents a completely new marketing paradigm.' Discuss.

3 Does a web site represent an advertisement, or should this term be restricted to banner advertisements on the Internet?

Essay questions

1 Explain how the Internet has developed cultural differences in its audience or 'netizens' in comparison with other media such as television and newspapers. How do companies that market using the Internet need to accommodate these cultural differences, and can they turn them to their advantage?

2 How can the different elements of the 'marketing mix' be applied to the Internet?

3 How can the Internet be used to support marketing communications?

4 What advantages does the Internet offer for retaining customers, in comparison with other media?

Examination questions

1 Explain why the World Wide Web is used primarily as a 'pull' medium rather than a 'push' medium for marketing communications.

2 Summarise the key differences between the Internet and other media in terms of audience characteristics and number.

3 Explain how 'one-to-many' communications differ from 'many-to-many' communications. How can the Internet facilitate 'many-to-many' communications?

4 For the following stages in the buying process, explain how the Internet can be used to help achieve the communications objective:
- supplier search;
- evaluation and selection;
- purchase;
- post-purchase.

5 Why are the following critical to the success of a web site:
- capture;
- content;
- community?

6 What is mass customisation and what advantages does it offer to Internet retailers and consumers?

7 Which types of customer may a web site need to appeal to if it is to have a broad audience?

REFERENCES

Berthon, B., Pitt, L. and Watson, R. (1996) 'Resurfing W³: Research perspectives on marketing communication and buyer behaviour on the World Wide Web', *International Journal of Advertising*, 15, 287–301.

Berthon, B., Pitt, L, and Watson, R. (1998) 'The World Wide Web as an industrial marketing communication tool: models for the identification and assessment of opportunities', *Journal of Marketing Management*, 14, 691–704.

Bettman, J. (1979) *An Information Processing Theory of Consumer Choice*. Reading, MA: Addison-Wesley.

Bickerton, P., Bickerton, M. and Pandesi, U. (1996) *Cybermarketing*. Oxford: Butterworth-Heinemann. Chartered Institute of Marketing Studies.

Booms, B. and Bitner, M. (1981) 'Marketing strategies and organisation structure for service firms', in Donelly, J. and George, W. (eds) *Marketing of Services*. New York: American Marketing Association.

Breitenbach, C. and van Doren, D. (1998) 'Value-added marketing in the digital domain: enhancing the utility of the Internet', *Journal of Consumer Marketing*, 15(6), 559–75.

Deighton, J. (1996) 'The future of interactive marketing', *Harvard Business Review*, November–December, 151–62.

de Kare-Silver, M. (1998) *eShock. The electronic shopping revolution: strategies for retailers and manufacturers*. Basingstoke, UK: Macmillan.

Denny, N. (1999) '34% to buy over net', *Marketing Magazine*, 14 January, p. 13.

Hagel, J. and Armstrong, A.G. (1997) *Net Gain: Expanding markets through virtual communities*. Boston, MA: Harvard Business School Press.

Hamill, J. and Gregory, K. (1997) 'Internet marketing in the internationalization of UK SMEs', *Journal of Marketing Management*, Special edition on internationalization, Hamill, J. (ed.), 13 (1–3).

Hoffman, D.L. and Novak, T.P. (1996) 'Marketing in hypermedia computer-mediated environments: conceptual foundations', *Journal of Marketing*, 60 (July), 50–68.

Hoffman, D.L. and Novak, T.P. (1997) 'A new marketing paradigm for electronic commerce', *The Information Society*, special issue on electronic commerce, 13 (January–March), 43–54.

Kierzkowski, A., McQuade, S., Waitman, R. and Zeisser, M. (1996) 'Marketing to the digital consumer', *The McKinsey Quarterly*, 3, 4–21.

Kotler, P., Armstrong, G., Saunders, J. and Wong, V. (1999) *Principles of Marketing* (2nd edn). Hemel Hempstead: Prentice Hall.

KPMG (1998) *Europe Gets Wired. A survey of Internet use in Great Britain, France and Germany*. London: KPMG.

Lautenborn, R. (1990) 'New marketing litany: 4Ps passes; C-words take over', *Advertising Age*, 1 October, p. 26.

Lewis, H. and Lewis, R. (1997) 'Give your customers what they want', *Selling on the Net. Executive book summaries*, 19 (3), March.

McCarthy, J. (1960) *Basic Marketing: A managerial approach*. Homewood, IL: Irwin.

Peters, L. (1998) 'The new interactive media: one-to-one but to whom?', *Marketing Intelligence and Planning*, 16(1), 22-30

Robinson, P., Faris, C. and Wind, Y. (1967) *Industrial Buying and Creative Marketing*. Boston, MA: Allyn and Bacon.

Rogers, E. (1983) *Diffusion of Innovations* (3rd edn). New York: Free Press.

Schramm, W. (1955) 'How communication works', in Schramm, W. (ed.) *The Process and Effects of Mass Communications*. Urbana, IL: University of Illinois Press.

FURTHER READING

Baker, M. (ed.) (1999) *The Marketing Book*. Oxford: Butterworth-Heinemann.
See Chapter 12, Managing the marketing mix, by Peter Doyle.

Berthon, B., Pitt, L. and Watson, R. (1998) 'The World Wide Web as an industrial marketing communication tool: models for the identification and assessment of opportunities', *Journal of Marketing Management*, 14, 691–704.

This is a key paper assessing how the Internet can be used to guide purchasers through the different stages of the buying decision.

Brassington, F. and Petitt, S. (2000) *Principles of Marketing* (2nd edn). Harlow, UK: Pearson Education, *See* companion Prentice Hall web site (*www.booksites.net/brassington2*).
Chapter 1, Marketing Dynamics, introduces the marketing mix and the '4Ps'. Chapter 3, Customer behaviour, describes the stages in the buying-decision process and reviews psychological and environmental impacts on this. Chapter 14, Communications and the Promotional mix, introduces communications theory.

Breitenbach, C. and van Doren, D. (1998) 'Value-added marketing in the digital domain: enhancing the utility of the Internet', *Journal of Consumer Marketing*, 15(6), 559–75. Highlights some of the differences the Internet brings to buying behaviour.

Dibb, S., Simkin, S., Pride, W. and Ferrel, O. (1997) *Marketing. Concepts and Strategies* (3rd European edn), New York: Houghton Mifflin.
See companion Houghton Mifflin web site (*www.busmgt.ulst.ac.uk/h_mifflin/*).
See Chapter 4, Consumer Buying Behaviour.

Fill, C. (1999) *Marketing Communications – Contexts, contents and strategies*. Hemel Hempstead: Prentice Hall, Europe.
This provides introductory chapters on communication theory.

Hanson, W. (2000) *Principles of Internet Marketing*. Cincinnati: South Western College Publishing.
Ward Hanson is a lecturer at Stanford Graduate School of Business and a Director of the Stanford Internet marketing project. This book covers a range of strategic and practical aspects of Internet Marketing and is supported by extensive references.

Hoffman, D.L. and Novak, T.P. (1997) 'A new marketing paradigm for electronic commerce', *The Information Society*, Special issue on electronic commerce, 13 (Jan.–Mar.), 43–54.
This was the seminal paper on Internet marketing when it was published, and is still essential reading for its discussion of concepts. Available online at Vandergilt University (*ecommerce.vanderbilt. edu/papers.html*).

Kierzkowski, A., McQuade, S., Waitman, R. and Zeisser, M. (1996) 'Marketing to the digital consumer', *The McKinsey Quarterly*, 3, 4–21.
Highlights differences between the Internet and other media. Available online at McKinsey Quarterly (*www.mckinseyquarterly.com*) (E-commerce section).

Kotler, P., Armstrong, G., Saunders, J. and Wong, V. (1999) *Principles of Marketing* (2nd edn). Hemel Hempstead: Prentice Hall, Europe.
See companion Prentice Hall web site for 8th US edn: *cw.prenhall.com/bookbind/pubbooks/kotler/*.
See Chapter 18, Integrated Marketing Communication Strategy.

McDonald, M. and Wilson, H. (1999) *e-Marketing: Improving Marketing Effectiveness in a Digital World*. Harlow, UK: Pearson Education.
This book summarises research and case studies conducted by Cranfield School of Management into how technology can be applied in marketing. Of particular relevance is Chapter 3 on the 'e-marketing mix' which includes a useful model (the 6Is) of how the Internet can impact service delivery.

Simeon, R. (1999) 'Evaluating Domestic and International Web Site Strategies', *Internet Research: Electronic Networking Applications and Policy*, 9 (4), 297–308.
Presents the AIPD (attracting, informing, positioning and delivering) model of strategies for web sites which compares to the models in this chapter. The model is applied to some US and Japanese banks.

Strauss, J. and Frost, R. (1999) *Marketing on the Internet. Principles of Online Marketing*. New Saddle River, NJ: Prentice Hall.
Chapter 1, Introduction to the Internet, and Chapter 2, Internet User Characteristics and Behaviour, introduce Internet marketing and typical user characteristics.

CHAPTER 3

How does the Internet work?

Learning objectives

After reading this chapter the reader should be able to:

- understand how the Internet has evolved;
- appreciate the different components needed for a company to host a web site and the different components needed for a consumer to access a web site;
- understand how the content on the World Wide Web is authored and structured;
- specify in broad terms how technology can be used to author, promote and measure the effectiveness of a web site;
- understand other Internet transport mechanisms such as Telnet and FTP.

Links to other chapters

Some of the terms and concepts discussed in this chapter are introduced in Chapter 1. Further details on some aspects of the technology introduced in this chapter are given in later chapters:

- ▶ Chapter 4, Finding information on the Internet.
- ▶ Chapter 8, Creating and building the web site.
- ▶ Chapter 9, Web site promotion.
- ▶ Chapter 11, Electronic commerce transactions.

INTRODUCTION

This chapter has the most technical content of the book. This is intentional in order not to obscure the marketing content in other chapters by description of technical terms. Why is this technical content necessary in a book focusing on marketing? First and foremost, a knowledge of the technologies behind the Internet is necessary to be able to apply it effectively for marketing purposes. An understanding of the technology makes it possible to appreciate the opportunities and limitations of using the medium for marketing. Second, many marketing staff or students who are on an industrial placement, and are given responsibility for developing or maintaining a web site, will, particularly in a small company, need to author web site copy and possibly update the web site. Here, a knowledge of the technology is necessary in order to complete these tasks. In a larger company, an outside company or technical staff may deal with the practicalities of developing the site. In this case, such in-depth knowledge of the web site is unnecessary, but a certain level of knowledge is required to talk to the technical people when specifying how the web site will be updated.

It is necessary to understand digital marketing technology from several perspectives:

- how to connect to the Internet as a user or consumer of information;
- once connected, how to use the tools to find relevant information (this is covered in the next chapter);
- how to host a company web site that can be accessed by customers;
- the opportunities the technology provides for developing effective content;
- how to promote the web site so that traffic is guided to the site;
- how to measure the effectiveness of the web site.

These different ways of using the technology form the main structure for this chapter, but we start with a historical overview of how the Internet has developed. For each method of using the technology we will introduce the benefits of the technology, the software and hardware that are needed and whether there are any additional costs. The last part of the chapter, which deals with the implementation of the strategy, provides further details on some of these topics such as authoring, promotion and measurement.

What is the Internet?

A brief history of the Internet

The history and origin of the Internet are well known. It started life at the end of the 1960s as the ARPAnet research and defence network in the USA, which linked servers used by key military and academic collaborators. It was established as a network that would be reliable even if some of the links were broken. This was achieved since data and messages sent between users were broken up into smaller packets and could follow different routes. Although the Internet has since been extended worldwide and is used extensively by the academic and defence communities it has only recently been catapulted into mainstream business and consumer use.

> **The Internet**
> The Internet refers to the physical network that links computers across the globe. It consists of the infrastructure of network servers and communication links between them that are used to hold and transport the vast amount of information on the Internet. The Internet enables transfer of messages and transactions between connected computers worldwide.

It was the advent of the World Wide Web, invented by Tim Berners Lee of CERN to help share research easily, that was responsible for the massive growth in business use of the Internet. The World Wide Web provides a publishing medium that makes it easy to publish and read information using a web browser and also to link to related information. Owing to its significance for Internet marketing, the features of the World Wide Web are described in a separate section later in this chapter.

Zwass (1998) describes a framework for the Internet consisting of three main levels. These are:

1 *Infrastructure*: the hardware, software, databases and telecommunications.
2 *Services*: Software-based services such as search engines, digital money and security systems.
3 *Products and services*: the web sites of individual companies and marketplaces.

Technical terms for transmission of information on the Internet

The technical terms for transmission of information on the Internet are described briefly since the reader will encounter them when using software to access the Internet and when talking to companies about connecting to the Internet.

The Internet functions through the use of a series of standard protocols that allow different types of machines to communicate with each other – it effectively ensures they are 'talking the same language'. When information is sent over the Internet by an e-mail or by downloading a web page, it is broken down into what are known as packets, which may follow different routes between the sender and the receiver. The passing of data packets around the Internet occurs via the TCP/IP protocol (Transfer Control Protocol/Internet Protocol). For a PC to be able receive web pages or for a server to host web pages it must be configured by a technician or configuration program to support this protocol. Another protocol that is important to the delivery of web pages is the http or hypertext transfer protocol; this is described later in this chapter in the section on the World Wide Web.

TCP/IP protocol

The passing of data packets around the Internet occurs via the TCP/IP protocol, or Transfer Control Protocol/Internet Protocol. For a PC to be able receive web pages or for a server to host web pages it must be configured to support this protocol.

Internet tools to access information

Over its lifetime, many tools have been developed to help find, send and receive information across the Internet. These tools are summarised in Table 3.1. In this section we will briefly discuss their relevance from a marketing purpose.

Of all the tools listed in the table, the World Wide Web (WWW) is most significant for marketers. It has become very popular with consumers and businesses because of its ease of use and the capability to display information clearly. E-mail is also significant since it is also used by many companies and consumers and can be used to contact them when required. The other tools either have been superseded by the use of the World Wide Web or are of less relevance from a marketing perspective.

In discussing the application of the Internet for marketing this book concentrates on the use of e-mail and the World Wide Web since these tools are now most commonly used by businesses for digital marketing. Many of the other tools such as e-mail, Internet relay chat (IRC) and newsgroups, which formerly needed special software to access them, are now available from the World Wide Web.

Table 3.1 Applications of different Internet tools

Internet tool	Summary
Electronic mail or e-mail	Sending messages or documents, such as news about a new product or sales promotion between individuals. A primitive form of 'push' channel.
Internet relay chat (IRC)	This is a synchronous communications tool that allows a text-based 'chat' between different users who are logged on at the same time. Of limited use for marketing purposes.
Usenet newsgroups	An electronic bulletin board used to discuss a particular topic such as a sport, hobby or business area. Traditionally accessed by special news reader software, these can now be accessed via a web browser from Deja News (*www.dejanews.com*).
FTP file transfer	The File Transfer Protocol is used as a standard for moving files across the Internet. FTP is available as a feature of web browsers, and is used for marketing applications such as downloading files – for example product price lists or specifications. Also used to update HTML (Hypertext Markup Language) files on web pages.
Gophers, Archie and WAIS	These tools were important before the advent of the World Wide Web for storing and searching documents on the Internet. They have largely been superseded by the Web, which provides better searching and more sophisticated document publishing.
Telnet	This allows remote access to computer systems. For example a retailer could check to see whether an item was in stock in a warehouse using a telnet application.
Push channel	Information is broadcast over the Internet or an intranet and received using a web browser or special program for which a subscription to this channel has been set up.
World Wide Web	The World Wide Web is widely used for publishing information and running business applications over the Internet. (It is described in detail in a later section of this chapter.)

Electronic mail or e-mail

E-mail is well known as a method of sending and receiving electronic messages. It has been available across the Internet for over twenty years. E-mails are typically written and read in a special mail reader program, which, in a large company, is often part of a groupware package such as Lotus Notes, Microsoft Exchange or Novell Groupwise. Smaller companies or individuals may use lower-cost or free mail programs such as Microsoft Outlook Express, Eudora or Pegasus mail. A relatively recent innovation is the use of web sites that provide free e-mail facilities and do not require any special software other than a web browser. Hotmail (*www.hotmail.com*) is one of the best known of the large number of portals (*see* Chapter 4) that now offer these facilities – for example Yahoo! (*www.yahoo.co.uk*)

and Excite (*www.excite.co.uk*). Some traditional businesses provide free e-mail and also Internet access as a value-added service for their customers – for example Dixons Freeserve (*www.freeserve.co.uk*), Virgin (*www.virgin.net*), BT Clickfree (*www.btclickfree.com*). E-mail tools do not warrant detailed discussion since they are well-known tools. A detailed description of e-mail is available in Chaffey (1998). Kennedy (1998) gives a practical description of Internet-based e-mail.

The main marketing application of e-mail is as a method of communicating with customers in a similar way to direct mail. As an outbound means of communication from a business, it is significant since it gives an electronic means of providing a customer with an update on new products and offers. Such updating is not possible using the web site since the latter is a pull mechanism that is reliant on a customer consciously deciding to visit. E-mails are also sent by a customer to a company requesting information such as product specifications or quotations. Autoresponders or mail-bots are mail tools that are used to automatically respond to these requests if appropriate. For example, an e-mail sent to *products@company_name.com* could automatically dispatch a summary of a company's products.

When measuring the effectiveness of an Internet marketing strategy, a company should record the role of e-mail in supporting the strategy. Measures could include:

- number of customer-support-related e-mails;
- number of requests for product information;
- number of new leads arriving through e-mail.

Since, in the digital medium, e-mail becomes one of the primary forms of communication, it is important that processes are in place, and staff are trained adequately to make best use of it. These aspects are discussed further in Chapter 10.

Internet relay chat (IRC)

Internet relay chat (IRC) is a low-cost Internet tool giving real-time communication between individuals. As a user in one location types in a comment, it is simultaneously available to those around the world who are 'tuned in' to a particular channel and they can then type in a reply. As with other tools mentioned in this section, IRC formerly required a special tool, but it has now migrated to the World Wide Web. Owing to the popularity of IRC sites, advertising is placed on these sites. The most popular Web-based chat channels are available at: 100.Hot.com (*www.100hot.com/chat*). An example of one of these is shown in Fig. 3.1.

Internet relay chat seems to be used more for recreational than for business use. In a marketing context, it is often inconvenient for a company and its customers to communicate simultaneously since the relevant people may not be available. Asynchronous delivery systems such as e-mail or discussion forums are more practical. For a company wishing to provide a customer support facility to view questions from other companies, discussion groups are more practical.

iChat (*www.ichat.com*) has attempted to carve a niche in the business-oriented chat market. Its iChat paging server offers the facilities of:

Fig. 3.1 Example of an online chat-room facility

- *rooms* – a standard chat facility for teams;
- *paging system* – for 'instant' transmission and display of important messages in a global enterprise where e-mail is not sufficiently rapid since users have to proactively access their in-boxes;
- *message boards* – similar to traditional bulletin boards.

Usenet newsgroups

There are over 35 000 Usenet newsgroups and they may be updated by up to three million messages each day. These can be thought of as electronic bulletin boards that are read by a closed community. Questions or statements are posted by one person who is looking for further information and the others will reply, and lists of related questions will be held together in what is known as a 'thread'. Usenet is mainly used by special interest groups such as people discussing their favourite pastime such as fishing or archery. They are not used very much by businesses, except as a means of studying consumer behaviour. There are some newsgroups for announcing the introduction of new products or staff vacancies. Newsgroups tend not to be used extensively by business people or consumers, since they have to be aware of them and to have the technical know-how to set them up. Setup can be difficult because a special piece of software known as a newsreader used to be required to read and contribute to newsgroups. When web browsers were developed, additional newsreaders were developed as extra modules. However, it was less clear how to access these than web browsers. Today, it is much easier to read and add to newsgroups since specialist web sites and search engines such as Altavista (*www.altavista.com*) enable users to access newsgroups without the need for special software. The best known web site for accessing newsgroups is Deja (*www.deja.com*).

The marketing applications of newsgroups usually involve obtaining marketing research in the form of feedback from customers. For example, a company manufacturing cat food may find comments in the rec.pets.cats newsgroups. These may be positive or negative comments about a brand, but each will be useful. Another example might be a pharmaceutical company which monitors the sci.med.pharmacy newsgroups to find news about new drugs that are being introduced by its competitors, or perhaps unofficial information from clinical trials.

Newsgroups are named in a particular format, broken down into several parts, the first part usually indicating the type of information or country to which it refers and the last part the specific topic:

- alt – for 'alternative', for example *alt.comedy.british* or *alt.music.kylie-minogue*;
- rec – recreation includes the largest number of groups; examples are *rec.climbing* or *uk.rec.climbing*;
- talk – discussions, for example *talk.politics.tibet*;
- biz – business; there are surprisingly few of these; for example *biz.marketplace.investors* is used to offer new investment products;
- comp – computer queries solved; an example is *comp.virus*;
- sci – these include a range of scientific discussions and opinions for example (*sci.med.cardiology*) or documents;
- soc – dealing with social issues for example (*soc.geneaology.misc*).

Activity 1.1

Usenet newsgroups

The following activity introduces you to newsgroups if you have not accessed them before. Follow the following stages:

1 Locate the Deja (*www.deja.com*) site. This is effectively a searchable database of all postings to the main newsgroups. It is also possible to post new contributions to this.

2 Type in the name of your favourite interest as a search word. Identify the newsgroups that relate to this.

3 Now go to one of these newsgroups and follow a particular theme or discussion.

4 If appropriate, either reply to an existing message or start your own thread by asking a question.

You should also explore some of the business-related newsgroups that exist. Most of these include the word business in their names. Repeat stage 2 by typing in 'business' and then reviewing the sites available.

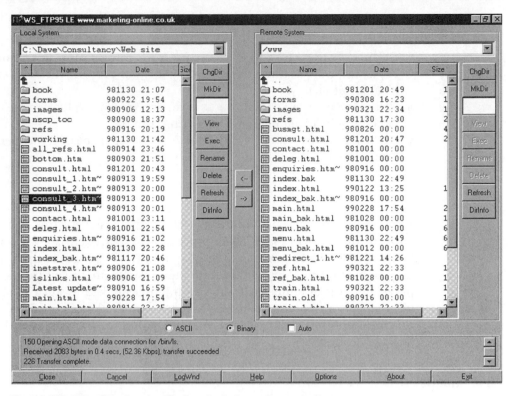

Fig. 3.2 WS_FTP utility showing file transfer between two web sites

FTP (File transfer protocol)

Marketing staff may use FTP in two different contexts:

1 FTP programs are used to upload, or transfer HTML web pages and graphics to a web site when a site is created or modified. Such facilities are now incorporated into many web authoring programs such as Microsoft Frontpage or Allaire Cold Fusion, but it is also worth knowing how to upload a file using a utility program such as WS_FTP. Figure 3.2 shows how files are transferred from a 'local' machine on which the web site (left window) has been created to a 'remote' computer (right window), which is the server on which the web site is located.

2 FTP can also be provided as a means of communicating with customers since large volumes of information such as price lists, catalogues or support information can be made available from a web site as a file, perhaps in Microsoft Word format, and then downloaded by customers or agents as required.

Gophers, Archie and WAIS

These tools have been almost completely superseded by the World Wide Web, and are only included here for completeness. All are concerned with structuring information so that it is easy to find. They have largely been replaced by the World Wide Web, since this provides a mechanism for publishing information that is easier to use and which is multimedia based rather than limited to plain text. The functions of these tools are as follows:

■ Gopher is a directory-based structure with information in certain categories. Type *'gopher://gopher.tc.umn.edu'* into your web browser location area to get an idea of this facility.
■ Archie is a database containing information on what is located on FTP servers. It would not be used much in a marketing context.
■ WAIS stands for Wide Area Information Service. It has been superseded by the World Wide Web.

Telnet

Telnet is used to navigate and transfer files between servers. It is frequently used as a means of deploying sales order processing systems across a wide-area network. For, example, if you purchase a holiday in a travel agency branch, your booking may be placed on a computer at head office using telnet to access the central computer. Telnet is of limited relevance to Internet marketing since in most cases it is impractical for individuals to use telnet to undertake electronic commerce. It is much easier if this facility is implemented within the browser using HTML, CGI or Java applications.

Push channel

Push technology was a prominent technology in 1997 since it was suggested that this would revolutionise the way people accessed the Internet. In fact, push tools have not superseded the 'pull' method of accessing information.

The idea behind 'Push' is that, rather than users having to search the Web to find what they want, users can subscribe to specialist services that broadcast content they have indicated as being relevant to them. Options are available to personalise information to the individual (for example Yahoo! *www.myyahoo.com*). In practice, this process is similar to a conventional television broadcast, with a subscriber choosing from a number of channels. The content is hosted on a server acting as a transmitter, which broadcasts information at intervals. Information is collected from the user's computer, when the user is not using it for other purposes: that is, when a screensaver would normally be used. One of the leaders in Push tools is Pointcast (*www.pointcast.com*).

Push was thought to be significant since Microsoft and Netscape introduced it, to much fanfare, in version 4 of their web browsers. Channels are available from content providers such as the *Financial Times*, the BBC and *Vogue* (see Fig. 3.3). However, users have to take the decision to subscribe to these channels, and this option has not proved popular, possibly due to the information overload that can occur with Push, although the information is targeted.

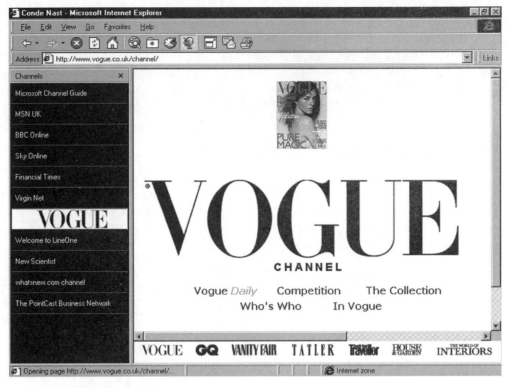

Fig. 3.3 Push channels available in Internet Explorer 4

What is the World Wide Web?

The World Wide Web, or 'Web' for short, is a medium for publishing information on the Internet in an easy-to-use form. If we take the analogy of television, then the Internet would be equivalent to the broadcasting equipment such as masts and transmitters, and the World Wide Web is equivalent to the content of different television programmes. The medium is based on a standard document format known as HTML (Hypertext Markup Language), which can be thought of as being similar to a word-processing format such as that of Microsoft Word documents. This standard has been widely adopted since:

- it offers hyperlinks that allow users to move readily from one document or web site to another – the process known as 'surfing';
- HTML supports a wide range of formatting, making documents easy to read;
- graphics and animations can be integrated into web pages;
- interaction is possible through HTML-based forms that enable customers to supply their personal details for more information on a product, ask questions or make comments.

> **Hyperlink**
> A method of moving between one web site page and another, indicated to the user by text high-lighted by underlining and/or a different colour. Hyperlinks can also be achieved through clicking on a graphic image such as a banner advertisement that is linked to another web site.

HTML is described in more detail in a separate section later in this chapter dealing with web content.

World Wide Web (WWW)
The most common technique for publishing information on the Internet. It is accessed through web browsers, which display web pages of embedded graphics and HTML/XML encoded text. Company information is stored on web servers, usually referred to as web sites.

Web browsers and servers

Web browsers are software to access the information on the World Wide Web that is stored on the web on web servers. The main browsers are Netscape Navigator or Communicator and Microsoft Internet Explorer (see Fig. 3.4). Browsers display the text and graphics accessed from web sites and provide tools for managing information from web sites.

Web browsers
Browsers such as Netscape Navigator and Microsoft Internet Explorer provide an easy method of accessing and viewing information stored as web documents on different servers.

Figure 3.4 shows the Microsoft Internet Explorer web browser. An indication of the options available through the menus is provided by the shortcut buttons:

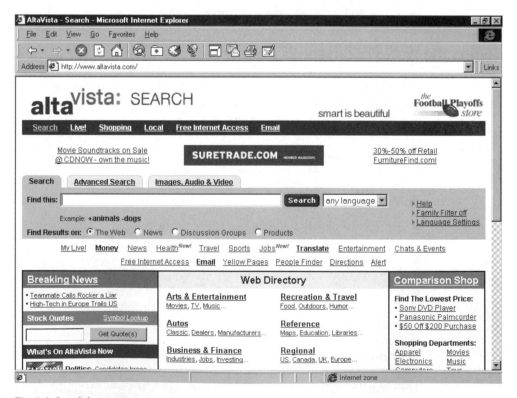

Fig. 3.4 A web browser

- *Back and Forward* – views the previous or the next page. Pressing the down-arrow gives an option of several pages.
- *Stop* – stops download.
- *Refresh* – repeats download of page elements if it has been updated.
- *Home* – loads the home page specified by the user. See the section on web pages later in the chapter.
- *Search* – displays a Microsoft-related search engine page by default.
- *Favorites* – displays a list of pages marked by the user for future reference. Often referred to as bookmarks. See the section in Chapter 4, Practical tips for managing information.
- *History* – provides a listing of all sites and pages visited on different days.
- *Fullscreen* and *Print* – self explanatory.
- *Mail* – starts a separate program to read and write mail.

In a more general sense the functions provided by web browsers are to:

- enable web addresses to be entered (by typing into the 'location' box), to set up communications links with sites and to download HTML pages;
- display web pages and interactive forms, and to run programs such as plug-ins and Java;
- enable navigation between sites by using 'forward' and 'backward' options and hyperlinks;
- record on the hard disk a copy of sites visited and the pages downloaded (caching), to enable quicker downloading and referencing in future;
- allow useful sites to be 'bookmarked' for later use; this process is referred to as 'Favorites' in Microsoft Internet Explorer;
- enable information to be saved to disk or printed for later use.

As mentioned earlier in the chapter, it is the combination of web browsers and HTML that has proved so successful in establishing widespread business use of the Internet. The use of these tools provides a range of benefits that can be turned to advantage by the marketer. The benefits include:

- They are easy to use since navigation between documents is enabled by clicking on hyperlinks or images. This soon becomes a very intuitive way of navigation, which is similar across all web sites and applications.
- They can provide a graphical environment supporting multimedia, which is popular with users and gives a visual medium for advertising.
- The standardisation of tools means there is a large and fast-growing target market.

Web servers are used to store, manage and supply the information on the World Wide Web. The stages that must be taken in order to host a web site using a server are described later in this chapter. A large site may be located across several computers with many processors. Such arrangements are sometimes referred to as 'web farms'.

New methods of hosting content, summarised by Spinrad (1999), have been introduced to improve the speed of serving web pages. These methods involve distributing content on servers around the globe. Two rival schemes that are emerging are Akamai Freeflow (*www.akamaitech.net*) and Sandpiper Networks Footprint (*www.sandpiper.com*). These are used by companies such as Yahoo!, Apple and other 'hot spot' sites likely to achieve many hits.

> **Web servers**
> Web servers are used to store the web pages accessed by web browsers. They may also contain databases of customer or product information, which can be queried and retrieved using a browser.

Web addresses (universal resource locators – URLs)

Web addresses refer to particular pages on a web server that is hosted by a company or organisation. The technical name for web addresses is uniform or universal resource locators (URLs). URLs can be thought of as a standard method of addressing, similar to postal or ZIP codes, which makes it straightforward to find the name of a site.

Web addresses are always prefixed by '*http://*' to denote the http protocol (explained below). Since web addresses always start with '*http://*', so references to web sites in this book and in most promotional material from companies omit this part of the URL. Indeed, when modern versions of web browsers are used, it is not necessary to type this in as part of the web page location since it is added automatically by the web browser. Although the vast majority of sites start with '*www*', this is not universal, so it is necessary to specify this.

Web addresses are structured in a standard way, as follows:

http://www.domain-name.extension/filename.html

The domain name (see page 81) refers to the name of the web server, and is usually selected to be the same as the name of the company; the extension will indicate its type. The extension is also commonly known as the global top level domain (gTLD). Note that gTLDs are currently under discussion, and there are proposals for adding new types such as .store and .firm.

Common gTLDs are:

- *.com* represents an international or American company such as Travelocity (*www.travelocity.com*);
- *.co.uk* represents a company based in the UK such as Thomas Cook's *www.thomas-cook.co.uk/*;
- *.ac.uk* is a UK-based university (e.g. *www.derby.ac.uk*);
- *.org.uk* or *.org* are not-for-profit organisations (e.g. Greenpeace – *www.greenpeace.org*);
- *.net* is a network provider such as virgin Net (*www.virgin.net*).

The '*filename.html*' part of the web address refers to an individual web page, for example '*products.html*' for a web page summarising companies' products. When a web address is typed in without a filename, for example *www.bt.com*, the browser automatically assumes the user is looking for the home page, which, by convention is referred to as *index.html*. When creating sites, it is therefore vital to name the home page *index.html*.

Web pages

The information, graphics and interactive elements that make up the web pages of a site are collectively referred to as *content*. The saying 'content is king' is often applied to the World Wide Web, since the content will determine the experience of the customer and whether that customer will return to a web site in future. Useful or enjoyable content will also attract favourable reviews and will generate word of mouth recommendations that are valuable in promoting a web site. Content also determines the marketing effectiveness of the site, since appropriate offers, contact points or calls to action must be available to achieve measurable outcomes. As was mentioned in Chapter 2, the content of a site must be oriented to all the potential users of a web site.

> **Content**
> Content is the design, text and graphical information that forms a web page. Good content is the key to attracting customers to a web site and retaining their interest or achieving repeat visits.

How are web pages displayed?

Web pages are displayed according to this sequence:

1 User requests web page by clicking on a hyperlink or typing in URL into web browser.
2 Request is sent across Internet from web browser to web server using http.
3 Information is returned using http from web server to web browser.
4 Information is displayed as the different elements of a web page described later in this section.

The information transfer stage is achieved by http (hypertext transfer protocol), which is a standard used to allow computers to transfer and receive web pages and their embedded graphics. When a user clicks on a link while viewing a web site, the web browser he or she is using will request information from the server computer hosting the web site using the http protocol. Since this protocol is important for delivering the web pages, the letters http:// are used to prefix all web addresses.

> **HTTP (hypertext transfer protocol)**
> HTTP or hypertext transfer protocol is a standard that defines the way information is transmitted across the Internet.

A description of how web pages and sites are built forms the content of Chapter 8, so this section gives a brief introduction to some of the concepts, terms and techniques involved with building web sites. For now, it is sufficient to list the components that can make up a web page. Each of these will be downloaded separately when a web page is requested. These are illustrated in Fig. 3.5. The main elements that make up a web page are:

- text information;
- static graphical images;
- animated graphical images;
- interactive form elements;
- plug-in components.

Each of these design elements will now be reviewed in turn.

Use of the different content elements by the DHL Red Planet site

Fig. 3.5 DHL Red Planet web site (*www.dhl.co.uk*) **showing different content elements of a web page**

The Red Planet site uses a variety of different screen elements to present a web-specific brand variant that is intended to be a memorable and efficient solution to ordering and monitoring parcel services. The different types of screen elements are as follows:

- *text information* – the central part of the screen is text based and uses underlined hyperlinks to repeat some of the menu options on the menu panels to the left and right as well as giving topical 'what's new' information;
- *static graphical images* – these are used to form the menu options on the left and right (.GIF images);
- *animated graphical images* – the 'SpeedBooking' branding at the bottom of the screen is animated using an animated .GIF image; the text in the static graphic elements such as 'Services' and 'Shipping Tools' uses Javascript 'rollover' images, which means that the menu options change colour when the user moves the mouse over them or selects them; this shows the current context;
- *interactive form elements* – the 'Warp Speed' menu option at the top of the screen uses a 'drop-down menu list' to select options. This uses a CGI-based form, as do the 'Search' options in search engines;
- *plug-in components* – these are small programs that are loaded: the sideways scrolling text at the bottom of the screen labelled 'Welcome to DHL Red Planet' is an example of this.

Text information (HTML and XML)

Web page text has many of the formatting options available in a word processor. These include applying fonts, emphasis (bold, italic, underline) and placing information in tables. Formatting is possible since the web browser applies these formats according to instructions that are contained in the file that makes up the web page. This is usually written in HTML or hypertext markup language. HTML is an international standard established by the World Wide Web Consortium (and published at *www.w3.org*) intended to ensure that any web page authored according to the definitions in the standard will appear the same in any web browser. HTML files can be authored in an ordinary text editor such as the Notepad program available with Microsoft Windows. Modern word processors also have an option to save formatted information in the HTML format. Alternatively, many software utilities are available to simplify the writing of HTML. Sources for these are described in Chapter 8.

HTML (Hypertext Markup Language)
HTML is a standard format used to define the text and layout of web pages. HTML files usually have the extension .HTML or .HTM.

A brief example of HTML is given in the box below. The HTML code used to construct pages has codes or instruction tags such as <TITLE> to indicate to the browser what is displayed. Each starting tag has a corresponding end tag usually marked by a '/', for example </TITLE>. The <TITLE> tag indicates what appears at the top of the web browser window.

Document as viewed in Web browser

The Power Company

The Power Company can solve many of your power needs. Select the options below for further information.

Information about The Power Company

- About our company
- Products
- Customer service
- Contact us

HTML source code

```
<HTML>
<HEAD>
<TITLE>The Power company – for all your power needs</TITLE>
</HEAD>
<BODY>
<CENTER><H1>The Power Company</H1></CENTER>
```

> *Document as viewed in Web browser* **continued**
>
> The Power Company can solve many of your needs. Select the options below for further information.
>
> ```
> <H2>Information about The Power Company</H2>
> <UL>
> <LI><A HREF="about.html">About our company </A>
> <LI><A HREF="products.html">Products </A>
> <LI><A HREF="service.html">Customer service</A>
> <LI><A HREF="contact.html">Contact us</A>
> </UL>
> </BODY>
> </HTML>
> ```

The simplicity of HTML compared with traditional programming languages makes it possible for simple web pages to be developed by non-specialists such as marketing assistants, particularly if templates for more complex parts of the page are provided. Interactive forms and brochures and online sales are more complex and usually require some programming expertise, although tools are available to simplify these.

XML is a more recent markup language, similar to HTML, which offers more flexibility for interactive pages.

Static graphical images (GIF and JPEG files)

Graphics produced by graphic designers or captured using digital cameras can be readily incorporated into web pages as images. GIF and JPEG refer to two file formats most commonly used to define graphics contained within web pages. GIF files are often used for small graphics and banner advertisements while JPEG files are used for larger images.

Animated graphical information (GIFs and plug-ins)

GIF files can also be used for interactive banner advertisments. Plug-ins are additional programs, sometimes referred to as helper applications, that work in association with the web browser to provide features not present in the basic web browser. The best known plug-ins are probably that for Adobe, which is used to display documents in .pdf format (*www.adobe.com*), and the Macromedia Flash and Shockwave products for producing interactive graphics (*www.macromedia.com*).

Interactive form elements (CGI and script elements)

Forms are used to collect information from customers, such as the keyword they wish to search on, or contact information for sending out product information. Information from forms is processed by simple programming languages known as scripts. This processing is particularly necessary in electronic commerce applications that require a great deal of interaction with the user, for example to specify and pay for the products. These scripts may be run by the web browser, when they are known as client-side scripts, or on the server (server-side scripts). Several different types of scripts are described in the following sections. Scripting languages include Javascript and VB Script from Microsoft. Java provides many of the features of a scripting language, but also provides further features present in a full programming language.

Common Gateway Interface (CGI) and Perl

In its early days, the Web was mainly used as a passive way of publishing information such as marketing information about company products. For a company with many products though, use in this way is limiting, since the user has to use hyperlinks to scroll through many screens of information for the product he or she wants. However, the CGI (Common Gateway Interface) was available to offer a way of providing interactivity to the web. CGI provides extensions to the web server, which allow scripts to be run that process information submitted through web-based forms. With a form built into the HTML document users can supply the name of the type of product they are interested in and a query can be performed, returning the details of the product. With this facility the Web is transformed from a passive document publisher into an interactive tool that can be used to write groupware applications that update, query and share databases and make commercial transactions possible. The scripting language Perl is commonly used for processing information generated by forms.

> **CGI (Common Gateway Interface)**
> CGI offers a way of providing interactivity through the web. With a form built into the HTML document users can supply the name of the type of product they are interested in and a query can be performed, returning the details of the product.

Other standards for dynamic content: Javascript, Java and Active-X

When browsers were introduced, they consisted of static web pages of text and graphics. These could not be used to implement the interactive functions of software applications. CGI was an early method of enabling user interaction through on-screen forms. There is now a range of competing methods that can be used to enable the user to interact with a web site by selecting menu options and entering data. The best known of these standards is the Java programming language.

> **Active-X**
> A programming language standard developed by Microsoft that permits complex and graphical customer applications to be written and then accessed from a web browser. An example might be a form for calculating interest on a loan. A competitor to **Java**.

> **Java**
> A programming language standard supported by Sun Microsystems that permits complex and graphical customer applications to be written and then accessed from a web browser. An example might be a form for calculating interest on a loan. A competitor to **Active-X**.

Intranets and extranets

The Internet is a well-established term, whereas the term '*intranet*' has only been used since the mid-1990s. Intranets arose because companies that experimented with using Internet tools to share company information between staff realised that intranets offered several benefits over traditional information systems. Early adopters found that intranets can be relatively:

■ quick to set up;
■ cheap to maintain;
■ easy to use and popular with users.

Intranets use the tried and tested standards and tools of the Internet, but within an organisation rather than between companies. Security measures are important to stop unauthorised access to company data. Intranets are widely used in large and medium-sized companies which operate from several locations, but are less useful for smaller companies. The quarterly internet newsletter produced by Durlacher Research (*www.durlacher.co.uk*) estimated in 1998 that 96 per cent of UK corporates had an intranet while only 54 per cent of medium and 34 per cent of small companies had an intranet.

> **Intranet**
> An intranet is a network within a single company which enables access to company information using the familiar tools of the Internet such as web browsers and e-mail. Only staff within a company can access the intranet, which will be password protected. Note that sometimes, when used loosely, 'intranet' is used to describe what is in fact an 'extranet' that allows access by people outside a company.

To derive full potential from an intranet, a company will want to share information with collaborators. The term *extranet* has been coined to describe an intranet that is extended beyond the boundaries of a company. The *extranet* can be accessed by authorised people outside the company such as collaborators, suppliers or major customers, but information is not available to everyone with an Internet connection – only those with password access. The relationship between intranets, extranets and the Internet is indicated diagrammatically in Fig. 3.6. Creating an extranet can be of great value in enabling marketing communications with other companies. Note that 'intranet' is sometimes loosely used to refer to extranets.

> **Extranet**
> An extranet is formed by extending the intranet beyond a company to customers, suppliers, collaborators or even competitors. This is again password protected to prevent access by general Internet users.

'Firewalls' are necessary when an intranet is created, to ensure that unauthorised access to confidential information does not occur. Firewalls are usually created as software mounted on a separate server at the point where the company is connected to the Internet. Firewall software can then be configured to accept links only from trusted domains representing other offices in the company. A firewall

> **Firewall**
> A specialised software application mounted on a server at the point where the company is connected to the Internet. Its purpose is to prevent unauthorised access into the company by outsiders. Firewalls are essential for all companies hosting their own web server.

has implications for marketers since staff accessing a web site from work may not be able to access some content such as graphics plug-ins.

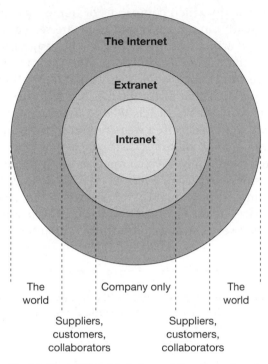

The Internet

Extranet

Intranet

The world | Company only | The world

Suppliers, customers, collaborators

Suppliers, customers, collaborators

Fig. 3.6 The relationship between intranets, extranets and the Internet

Connecting to the Internet as a user

To connect to the Internet and access the World Wide Web, a company or individual needs the following:

1 Hardware

- Computer to run the web browser and software required to connect to the Internet (mobile phones, personal digital assistants and set-top TV boxes are now also capable of this).
- Modem to connect to the Internet (from home or small companies), or a gateway server to the Internet (from a larger company).
- A digital or analogue connection to the Internet in the form of phone lines, cable or a wide-area network.

2 Software

- A web browser such as Netscape Navigator or Microsoft Internet Explorer that is compatible with the operating system of the computer to view the web pages.
- Connectivity software to use the TCP/IP standards of the Internet. For home users using Windows this is achieved by software known as Winsock. A standard PC or Apple computer will need to be configured with driver software to access the Internet using the TCP/IP protocol if these are not part of the operating system.

3 A service provider

■ An authorised connection to the Internet using an Internet service provider (ISP).

Figure 3.7 indicates the way in which companies or home users connect to the Internet. The diagram is greatly simplified in that there are several tiers of ISPs. A user may connect to one ISP, which will then transfer the request to another ISP, which is connected to the main Internet backbone. The Internet is denoted as a cloud on the diagram since this is not a single connection, but rather many different networks connected by routers that direct the message to its destination.

Service providers are usually referred to as ISPs or internet service providers. Providers who also provide some specialised web content to users such as America Online (AOL) or Compuserve are sometimes distinguished as OSPs or online service providers. ISPs are telecommunications companies that provide access to the Internet for home and business users. ISPs have two main functions. First, they can provide a link to a company or individual that enables them to access the World Wide Web and send Internet e-mail. Second, they can host web sites or provide a link from a company's web servers to enable other companies and consumers access to a corporate web site.

> **Internet service provider (ISP)**
> ISPs are companies that provide home or business users with a connection to access the Internet. They can also host web sites or provide a link from web servers to allow other companies and consumers access to a corporate web site.

For many years, service providers such as Compuserve charged according to the number of hours a user was connected to the Internet. This change was in addition to the charge the user incurred in making the connection to the ISP via a phone call. In recent years the cost of these services has been greatly reduced, now only amounting to the cost of a local telephone call – *see* Mini case study 3.2 for further details. With increased competition, lower flat-rate charges were introduced. In

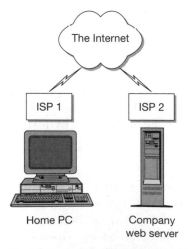

Fig. 3.7 Typical architecture linking home or business PC web users with company web servers via independent service providers and the Internet

1998 free services such as Freeserve from Dixons (*www.freeserve.net*), followed by, in 1999, Virgin (*www.virgin.net*), Tesco supermarkets (*www.tesco.net*) and BT (*www.btclick-free.co.uk*) changed the pricing model dramatically. With Freeserve signing up over one million customers in its first year many of the traditional paid-for services became untenable.

Mini case study 3.2

Free access to the Internet

In the USA Internet access via local telecommunications services is free of charge. In the UK, prior to 1998 the only way for the average consumer to access the Internet was through an Internet service provider (ISP) who charged approximately £10 per month for the service. Towards the end of 1998 British Telecom introduced a new pricing tariff offering discounts to customers based on total expenditure across a range of services. These changes shifted the charging structure for operators using low-call numbers like 0345. According to the telecommunications regulatory body OFTEL these changes enabled service providers to develop longer-term relationships with their customers through the offer of low-cost calls. A number of UK retailers began to utilise this opportunity by offering free Internet access to their customers. The main subscription and subscription-free ISPs are shown in Table 3.2. Dixons Freeserve was the first to be available and by 1999 it claimed to be the UK's largest Internet service provider with over 1.5 million users. A 1999 share issue valued the company at over £2 billion or over £2000 per active customer! Many other organisations have launched similar offers, Tesco, Barclays Bank, British Telecom and the Games Workshop providing users with free email addresses, web space and a range of other online services. The Disney Corporation bought 43 per cent of Infoseek (Web information services) in a bid to create a gateway known as a 'portal' to provide users with a starting point for their Internet access.

The advent of subscription-free ISPs such as Freeserve has helped slash the growth rate of subscription-based ISPs in Europe from more than 80 per cent to less than 1 per cent, according to a report by Durlacher.

Durlacher's Quarterly Internet Report for the second quarter 1999 found there are more than 95 subscription-free ISPs in the region, and that number will rise to as many as 200 by the end of 1999. The widespread adoption of the free ISP model has forced paid ISPs to re-price, differentiate their service, and add value to the offerings.

Table 3.2 Compilation of UK subscription-free and subscription ISPs

	Subscription-free ISPs			Subscription ISPs	
Company	Subscribers	Share (%)	Company	Subscribers	Share (%)
Freeserve	1 250 000	32	AOL	600 000	29
X-Stream	270 000	7	CompuServe	400 000	20
Currant Bun	250 000	6	Demon	175 000	9
breathenet	225 000	6	BT Internet	115 000	6
Line One	200 000	5	Global Internet	100 000	5
Other	1 735 000	44	Other	644 000	31

Source: Durlacher's Quarterly Internet Report, 2nd Quarter 1999.

▶ **Mini case study** *continued*

However, Durlacher's Nick Gibson believes that many subscription-free ISPs could also face a bleak future. *'Most subscription-free ISPs, including Freeserve, offer little to differentiate themselves and provide little or no barriers to exit for subscribers,' Gibson said. 'As long as users can switch accounts so easily, free ISPs leave themselves vulnerable to churn.'*

The process for setting up access to the World Wide Web from at home or within a company can be summarised as:

1 Select web browser software.
2 Buy appropriate hardware to run software.
3 Install modem or network card to connect to Internet.
4 Install browser software and configure computer to use TCP/IP and access ISP.
5 Set up firewall in a company environment.

Hosting a web site

The term used to describe the whole process of creating, managing and making available a web site is to 'host'. To host a web site, the following is required:

1 Hardware:
   ▪ A powerful server computer such as a high specification PC or workstation from a company such as Sun, IBM or Compaq.
   ▪ A gateway server to the Internet.
   ▪ A digital connection to the Internet in the form of a dedicated communications link.
2 Software:
   ▪ Web server software for sending web content to web browsers when they request it. The best-known software includes the Apache Server, Netscape server and Microsoft Internet Information Server (IIS).
   ▪ Tools to create content in HTML and graphics formats and using scripting languages such as Javascript. Tools include Webedit Pro, HotMetal Pro and Microsoft FrontPage. Server software such as IIS is also required to deliver the pages from the server.
   ▪ FTP tools to transfer the completed content to the web server.
   ▪ Tools to monitor the performance of the web site by producing reports from the server log file.
   ▪ Communications software supporting TCP/IP.
3 A service provider:
   An authorised connection to the Internet using an Internet service provider (ISP). The service provider may also provide the option to host the web site. This option is commonly taken up since this reduces the risk of outsiders accessing confidential information inside a company.
4 A registered domain name for the web site.

Domain name registration

If an individual or company wants to establish a web presence they will have to register a domain name that is unique to them. The URL becomes a marketing tool, which should be used on all company publications and advertisements. A unique name is in the form:

> *www.<company-name>.co.uk*

for a UK company such as Boots (*boots.co.uk*); or

> *www.<company-name>.com*

for an international or US company such as IBM (*www.ibm.com*).

A company should avoid siting its site on an ISP server that uses the name of the ISP such as:

> *http://unet/companies/<company-name>.co.uk.*

This name is less memorable and takes longer to type in. More importantly it reflects badly on the credibility of the company and its attention to quality.

Domain names can be registered via an ISP or at more favourable rates direct from the domain name services:

1 InterNIC – *www.internic.net*. Registration and information about sites in the .com, .org and .net domains.
2 Nomination – *www.nomination.uk.com*. This is an alternative registration service for the UK, allowing users to register in the (uk.com) pseudo-domain. (Also AlterNIC.)
3 Nominet – *www.nominet.org.uk*. Main co.uk site

Domain name
Indicates where the web server is located, and its use. Examples include .com and .co.uk. *See* the section earlier in the chapter on web addresses for details.

The process for hosting a web site

The process for hosting a web site can be summarised as follows:

1 Register domain name. This is best done as soon as possible to avoid conflicts with companies that have similar names or products (Chapter 8 provides some case studies of this).
2 Find an ISP to connect to the Internet or host the web server.
3 Find an appropriate server computer to enable the following standards:
   ■ http:// serving web pages;
   ■ ftp:// remote file access;
   ■ SMTP Internet e-mail.
   This server may be located inside a company, or more conventionally at the offices of an ISP.
4 Develop graphic and HTML content.
5 Upload to web server using FTP to transfer files.

The details of this process are described in Chapter 8.

SUMMARY

1 The Internet is a global communications network that is used to transmit the information published on the World Wide Web (WWW) in a standard format based on hypertext markup language (HTML).

2 Companies publish marketing information on the World Wide Web on web servers, which are often hosted by third party companies known as Internet service providers (ISP).

3 Consumers and business users access web servers using web browser software with a connection to the Internet that is also managed by an ISP.

4 Intranets are private networks used inside companies to share information. Internet-based tools such as e-mail, web browsers and servers are used as the method of sharing this information. Not all Internet users can access intranets since access is restricted by firewalls and password controls.

5 Extranets are similar to intranets, but they are extended beyond the company to third parties such as suppliers, distributors or selected customers.

6 There are many tools used to access the Internet to transfer information, but many of these have been superseded by facilities provided by the World Wide Web. The most important are:
   ■ e-mail;
   ■ FTP (file transfer protocol) software for uploading information to web servers;
   ■ Usenet newsgroups or bulletin boards for sharing information;
   ■ real-time chat facilities.

7 Web page content is made up of a range of elements:
   ■ text information (HTML);
   ■ static graphical images (GIF and JPEG);
   ■ animated graphical images (GIF);
   ■ interactive form elements (processed using CGI and Javascript).

8 To host a web site it is necessary to register a domain name, which is usually in the format: *http://www.<company_name>.<GTLD>*. GLTD is the top-level domain and may be co.uk or co.nz, for example or .com for a US or international company. Web server software is used to host the content, and FTP software is used to update the web server, which is often located at an ISP.

EXERCISES AND QUESTIONS

Self-assessment exercises

1 What is the difference between the Internet and the World Wide Web?

2 Describe the two main functions of an Internet service provider (ISP).

3 Distinguish between intranets, extranets and the Internet.

4 What are the elements of a web page?

5 What are stages involved in hosting a web site?

6 Explain the following terms:
- HTML
- CGI
- HTTP
- FTP

7 What is the difference between static web content written in HTML and dynamic content developed using a scripting language such as Javascript?

8 What software and hardware is required to access the Internet from home?

Discussion questions

1 'Without the development of the World Wide Web by Tim Berners Lee, it is unlikely that the Internet would have become a commercial medium.' Discuss.

2 'In the future the distinction between intranets, extranets and the Internet for marketing purposes is likely to disappear.' Discuss.

3 Discuss the merits and disadvantages of locating a company web site inside a company, in comparison with outsourcing it to an ISP.

4 'Extranets are potentially of more value to a company than a general access Internet web site.' Discuss.

Essay questions

1 Imagine you are a consultant with a new media agency. Create a summary guide for companies interested in setting up a site on the Internet, setting out the stages that are necessary in the creation of a web site and explaining the terminology of the tools used.

2 Research the development of 'push' technology. Explain the factors for its growth in popularity, and factors that have prevented it becoming a mainstream tool of Internet marketing.

3 Investigate the reasons for the migration of Internet tools such as e-mail, newsgroups and chat to the World Wide Web environment. What are the marketing implications for this trend?

4 What are the marketing benefits of using dynamic content development tools compared with writing static HTML sites? (This question should be considered in conjunction with Chapter 10.)

Examination questions

1 Imagine you are describing to a company the stages necessary for them to host a web site. Explain the main stages involved.

2 How would you explain to a friend what they need to purchase to access the World Wide Web using the Internet? Explain the hardware and software needed.

3 Why is the advent of the World Wide Web responsible for the increased use of the Internet in business?

4 Describe how the following tools would be used by a company hosting a web site:
- HTML
- FTP
- CGI

5 The existence of standards such as HTML and the HTTP protocol has been vital to the success and increased use of the World Wide Web. Explain why.

6 What marketing benefits does a web browser, as a means of accessing information, give to a customer?

7 Give two reasons why a marketing department would want to set up a contract for services with an Internet service provider (ISP).

8 Explain the differences between an intranet, an extranet and the Internet from a marketing person's perspective.

REFERENCES

Chaffey, D. (1998) *Groupware, Workflow and Intranets – Reengineering the enterprise with collaborative software*. Woburn, MA: Digital Press.

Durlacher (1999) *Quarterly Internet Report, Q2, 1999*. London.

Kennedy, A. (1998) *The Internet. The Rough Guide*. London: Rough Guides.

Spinrad, P. (1999) 'The new cool. Akamai overcomes the Internet's hotspot problem', *Wired*, 7 August, 152–4.

Zwass, V. (1998) 'Structure and macro-level impacts of electronic commerce: from technological infrastructure to electronic marketplaces', in Kendall, K. (ed.) *Emerging Information Technologies*. Thousand Oaks, CA: Sage.

FURTHER READING

Berners-Lee, J. (1999) *Weaveing the Web. The past, present and future of the World Wide Web by its inventor*. London, UK: Orion Publishing.
A fascinating, readable description of how the concept of the web was developed by the author with his thoughts on its future development.

Collins, S. (1998) *Doing Business on the Internet*. (2nd end). London: Kogan Page.
An introduction to Internet technology and some practical aspects of use.

Freedman, A., Glossbrenner, A. and Glossbrenner, E. (1998) *The Internet Glossary and Quick Reference*. New York: AMACOM.
Comprehensive.

Knight, J. (1999) *Computing for Business* (2nd edn). London: FT Management.
Chapter 3, Accessing the Internet, contains a succinct description of what the Internet is and how to use it for searching.

Russell, C. (1999) *Internet UK in Easy Steps*. Warwick, UK: Computer Step.
Basic book covering how to set up access and search. Useful sites are listed.

Turban, G., Lee, J. King, D. and Chung, H. (2000) *Electronic Commerce: A managerial perspective*. Upper Saddle River, NJ: Prentice Hall.
A comprehensive text on the infrastructure of the Internet and its use for electronic commerce transactions.

Zwass, V. (1998) 'Structure and macro-level impacts of electronic commerce: from technological infrastructure to electronic marketplaces', in Kendall, K. (ed.) *Emerging Information Technologies*. Thousand Oaks, CA: Sage.
Available online at: *www.mhhe.com/business/mis/zwass/ ecpaper.html*

WEB SITE REFERENCES

Bized (*www.bized.ac.uk/fme/internet.htm*) has an introduction, for MBA students, to the tools of the Internet and searching.

How Stuff Works (*www.howstuffworks.com/category-internet.htm*) has a straightforward description of how web pages are served and displayed.

Internet.com's Webopedia (*www.webopedia.com*) is similar to *whatis.com* but focuses on Internet related technology

The List (*thelist.internet.com*) is one of the largest worldwide lists of ISPs. May be useful for contacting with regard to work experience or surveys.

Whatis.com (*www.whatis.com*) is an online dictionary of computing terms including many Internet marketing terms, for example, for serving advertisements and assessing site effectiveness. A simple introduction to how the Internet works is available at *www.whatis.com/tour.htm*.

The World Wide Web consortium (*www.w3.org*) is an organisation that helps define the standards for the Internet. It contains many definitions, although in great technical detail.

CHAPTER 4

Finding information on the Internet

Learning objectives

After reading this chapter, the reader should:

- **possess knowledge of the different information sources available;**
- **know how to use the most effective information searching strategy;**
- **be able to use the appropriate search tools for finding information when conducting marketing research;**
- **be aware of the implications for marketers of the search techniques used by consumers.**

Links to other chapters

This chapter is related to:

▶ Chapter 2, which introduces the way in which consumers access web sites and buyer behaviour, distinguishing between different goals such as 'directed information seeker' and 'bargain hunter'.

▶ Chapter 3, which introduces the concepts of web sites and web addresses. Those unfamiliar with the Internet should read Chapter 3 before Chapter 4.

▶ Chapter 8 and Chapter 9 describe how a web site must be designed and promoted to ensure that consumers looking for information find it on the web site.

▶ Chapter 12 has brief coverage of how the Internet can be used to collect primary data through focus groups and through monitoring the use of the web site.

INTRODUCTION

Many new users of the Internet are discouraged when they first use it since, although there appears to be a great deal of potentially useful information, it often proves difficult to find relevant information. There are over one billion web pages containing information, so it is natural that useful information will be difficult to find. Fortunately there are techniques to make it easier to find this information. In this chapter, we review a number of methods using different searching tools and strategies to locate the particular information a user may be looking for. The techniques covered in this chapter are principally those used for finding information on the World Wide Web since, as explained in Chapter 3, this is the main source of business and consumer information.

After the main searching tools and techniques are introduced we describe the strategies for finding particular types of information needed by marketing researchers, such as:

■ company information (competitors and customers);
■ information about consumer characteristics from market research agencies;
■ economic and business environment information;
■ industry (vertical market) specific information.

An understanding of the techniques used to find information on the Internet is also required by those involved in promoting web sites, since online promotion techniques will target those using particular methods to find information on the Internet.

Alternative methods for finding information

Information can be found on the World Wide Web in four main ways:

■ typing in the web address of a known page (URL);
■ search engines;
■ directories (or web catalogues);
■ 'surfing'.

We will look at each of these in turn.

Web 'addresses' or URLs (universal resource locators)

The most efficient method of finding information on the Internet is through typing the web address or URL directly into the web browser. Knowing a web address is dependent on a word of mouth recommendation that a web site is worth visiting, seeing the web address in an advertisement or company promotional literature, or simply making a good guess. While the URL for a company such as IBM may be obvious (*www.ibm.com*), it is less obvious for a company with a longer name such as 'The Alliance and Leicester Building Society' (*www.allianceandleicester.co.uk*). The potential addresses for this could include *www.theallianceandleicester.co.uk* or *www.alliance-and-leicester.com*.

> **Uniform (or universal) resource locator (URL)**
> Text that indicates the address of a web site. It is typed into a web browser window, and the browser will then locate and load the web site. It is in the form of: *www.domain-name.extension/file-name.html*
>   These terms are described in Chapter 3.

When trying to guess URLs, users must remember that a large, multinational company is likely to have a web address domain name of .com, whereas a smaller company that mainly operates in one country such as the UK will end in .co.uk. If a company has several words to its name such as 'British Midland', try typing in the full address without any spaces, for example, *www.britishmidland.co.uk* or with dashes, *www.british-midland.co.uk.* You should also try the international site: *www.britishmidland.com*. In this example, both *www.britishmid-land.co.uk* and *www.britishmidland.com* will work. British Midland has also registered the name *www.iflybritishmidland.com* for marketing purposes.

Tips

Note that you do not need to type the *http://* prefix in modern browsers. It will be added automatically when you add the remainder of the web address.

If you do type the prefix '*http://*' it must be spelled exactly as given.

Activity 4.1

Web addresses

Try typing in the following:

- ■ *www.telegraph.co.uk*
- ■ *www.bbc.co.uk*
- ■ *www.altavista.com* (for this last one use the menu option in the browser of **File**, **Open** or Ctrl O.

Search engines

How search engines work

Search engines provide an index of the many words stored on the World Wide Web. Keywords typed in by the end-user on to a web-based form (*see* Fig. 4.1) are then matched against the index and the user is given a list of 'hits' – all corresponding to web pages containing the keywords. Clicking on a hyperlink for a listed site takes the user to the relevant web page. The list usually contains the title of the web page and a summary from the first line of a web page.

Search engines do not contain a completely comprehensive list of all web pages since it is necessary for a site to be registered with a search engine in order for it to be listed. To register, the site owner must contact the company operating the search engine by providing the URL on an electronic form. It is important, for promoting a web site, that it is included in as many search engine listings as possible. How to achieve this is described in Chapter 9 on web site promotion.

Search engines, spiders and robots

Search engines use special automatic tools known as spiders or robots to index web pages of registered sites. Users can search this index by typing in keywords to specify their interest. Pages containing these keywords will be listed, and clicking on a hyperlink will take the user to the site.

Search engine databases are regularly updated. Approximately once a fortnight or once a month, specialised software tools known as 'robots' or 'spiders' automatically search all sites that are registered with the search engine and check all the pages to update the index.

Mini case study 4.1 **A search engine – AltaVista**

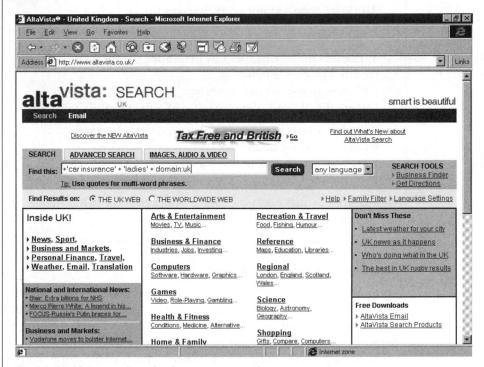

Fig. 4.1 AltaVista search engine (*www.altavista.co.uk***)**

This example uses AltaVista, one of the most popular search engines. Imagine you wanted to find out information on car insurance. You could start by typing in a general word such as 'insurance'. The problem with a non-specific search is that there is such a large volume of information on the web. The search above would return references to several million web pages. To narrow down a search it is best to use several key words. In this example you could type 'car insurance' for the UK or 'auto insurance' for the USA. To use the web efficiently it is necessary to know the *syntax* provided by search engines to narrow down the search. For example, if we were looking for special discounts on car insurance for women drivers from a UK-based insurer we could type '+"car insurance" +"ladies" +domain:uk'. This returns fewer pages (*see* example below), since we have indicated through use of the '+' symbol that both phrases must be present, and through enclosing the words in quotation marks that the words must appear in the order shown. 'domain:uk' indicates that we are only interested in sites based in the UK. Table 4.1 shows additional syntax that can be used to narrow down a search. For example, '-' can be used before a keyword to exclude this keyword from a search.

If you typed these keywords into AltaVista: '+"car insurance" +'ladies' +domain:uk', you would receive the following information:

> ► **Mini case study** *continued*
>
> **AltaVista found about 26 Web pages for you.**
>
> Result Pages: 1 2 3
>
> **1. Ladies Direct: Cheaper Car insurance for Women**
> Online Vehicle Insurance for...
> URL: *www.ladiesdirect.co.uk/ladies.html*
> Last modified 29-Oct-98 - page size 8K - in English [Translate]
>
> **2. Ladies Direct: Cheaper Car insurance for Women**
> Online Vehicle Insurance for...
> URL: *www.directravel.co.uk/ladies.html*
> Last modified 11-Feb-99 - page size 8K - in English [Translate]
>
> Notice that in this example, Ladies Direct is using two different sites to promote its products.

How are multiple keywords matched?

Typing in more than one keyword will usually assist in narrowing down the choice of web pages listed. The way in which search engines deal with multiple keywords often differs, and will even differ through time as the way in which search engines operate is improved. For example, AltaVista used to treat two words separately. If a user typed 'channel' followed by 'tunnel' the search engine would return all pages that contained 'channel' or 'tunnel'. This would typically return many irrelevant pages. To improve this, in 1998 the search engine was updated to include only those pages containing both 'channel' *and* 'tunnel'. Previously, this was only possible through typing 'channel tunnel' within quotation marks. To help avoid ambiguity with multiple keywords, many search engines offer the choice of using 'and' or 'or' to perform a search with multiple keywords. Others also allow the user to specify a phrase by placing it in quotes, for example 'great fire of London'. A good example of a search tool that provides flexibility in this area is Hotbot (*www.hotbot.com.*) This allows the user to select from:

- all the keywords typed;
- any of the words;
- an exact phrase;
- the page title.

Table 4.1 indicates the variation in options used to specify the search criteria for search engines. Some, such as Excite and Webcrawler, use boolean phrases such as 'and' and 'or' and 'not' to be typed into the search engine, while all of these allow a phrase to be defined in quotes. Some allow keywords prefixed by '+' and '-' to be included or excluded in a search. Finally the use of title:, or link: permits some engines to limit the search further.

Table 4.1 Summary of different options for search engines (*www.isleuth.com*)

Option	AltaVista	Excite	Infoseek	Webcrawler
Boolean		Yes		Yes
Phrase in quotes	"…"	"…"	"…"	"…"
Wildcard	*			
Word inclusion	+	+	+	
Word exclusion	-	-	-	
Words in title	title:		title:	
Links to URL	link:		link:	

What governs the order of web sites in a search engine listing?

The way in which the search engines order matches presented to the user differs in detail, but similar techniques are used to ensure that the most relevant documents occur at the top of the list. Documents are usually ranked according to:

- the occurrence of the keyword in the title;
- the number of occurrences of the keyword in the text of the web page;
- whether the keyword is in the 'meta-tags' or hidden keywords on a web page (these are explained in more detail in Chapter 9);
- how popular the page is with users.

Information on the main search engines and how they work is provided by Search Engine Watch (*searchenginewatch.com.*)

Others search engines (that are now also contact directory facilites) are:

- Excite (*www.excite.com*);
- Hotbot (*www.hotbot.com*);
- Infoseek (*www.infoseek.com*);
- Lycos (*www.lycos.com*);
- Excite (*www.excite.co.uk*);
- Northern Light (*www.northernlight.com*).

Meta search engines

Meta search engines submit keywords typed by users to a range of search engines in order to increase the number of relevant pages since different search engines may have indexed different sites. An example is the metacrawler search engine. (*www.metacrawler.com*). Another is Mamma (*www.mamma.com*), 'The Mother of all Search Engines'. The Netscape NetCenter (*www.netscape.com*) gives you a choice of search engine.

Tips

AltaVista syntax

- Use several words (or synonyms) to narrow down the search – London fire
- Use quotation marks to define a phrase – "Fire of London"
- Use + and – to include or exclude words – +"Fire of London" +1666 -Wren
- Use the European site *altavista.telia.com* for faster speed

Search engines

Type the following into the AltaVista search box (and hit return or enter), noting the number of web pages returned each time. Think about why the numbers increase and decrease.

1 channel tunnel
2 "channel tunnel"
3 "channel tunnel" fire
4 +"channel tunnel" +fire
5 +"channel tunnel" +fire -news

Web catalogues or directories

The best known directory is Yahoo! This is one of the most popular sites world-wide. Country-specific versions in the UK (*www.yahoo.co.uk*) and Germany (*www.yahoo.de*) are also popular in these countries.

Directories or catalogues
Directories provide a structured listing of registered web sites in different categories. They are similar to an electronic version of the *Yellow Pages*. Yahoo! and Yell are the best-known examples of directories.

Web catalogues such as *www.yahoo.co.uk* work differently from search engines in that they have a hierarchy of information stored under different categories. For example, to find a UK travel agent specialising in cheap flights you would move down the hierarchy to select:

Regional:Countries:United Kingdom:
Business:Companies:Travel:Agents:Direct

This would then lead you to the site of: *www.cheapflights.co.uk.* 'The best source for bargain air tickets from the United Kingdom.'

Yahoo! is often considered to be a search engine. This is understandable since it is based on an online form on to which keywords can be typed and then a button labelled 'Search' is pressed (*see* Fig. 4.2). Describing Yahoo! as a search engine is technically incorrect since Yahoo! operates quite differently from a search engine. Yahoo! is much more selective than a search engine since it is effectively only an index of the home pages of web sites (not all the pages on a web site). The search is based on matching the keywords a user types in against a category name in which the web site is placed, a site title and a short description.

The Yahoo! directory is created by humans since the entry for a particular category must be manually submitted via an onscreen form. The application to place a web page is then reviewed by a member of staff at Yahoo! who will visit a site and check its suitability for the category, and its quality. It is not guaranteed that the site submitted will be listed in the directory since Yahoo! wants to maintain the quality of its service. As a result Yahoo! is mainly used for listing home pages of established companies rather than start-up companies or home pages created by those at home. Contrast this approach with that of search engines. Here, the web address of the main page is submitted manually, but after this everything is automatic. The robots used by the search engine sites will then automatically visit this web address and add words to index from all linked pages on this site. As a result, a search engine will have many keywords from the pages of the site in its index whereas a directory such as Yahoo! will have in its index only words that are in the title of the site or company, or in the 25-word description of it. The implication of this is that since Yahoo! is less comprehensive than other sites, it is not necessarily the best source from which to find information that is not related to companies. It is arguably the best way to find information about companies whose name or products are well known. Note that company, product or service names you are searching for will only appear in a search of Yahoo! when the developers of a site remember to include them in the title or the 25-word description.

How do directories work?

Web directories provide a structured listing of web sites. They are grouped according to categories such as business, entertainment or sport. Each category is then subdivided further, for example sport is divided into football, rugby, swimming etc. Companies are listed in the directory if they register with the owner of the directory. This is usually achieved by filling in an electronic form giving the category in which they wish to be placed and the appropriate URL. A company will, of course, only be listed in Yahoo! if a company has registered it. Because the Yahoo! list is generated manually it may take several weeks before a web site is listed under Yahoo!.

Tips

Yahoo!

- Use a country-specific site such as *www.yahoo.co.uk* for speed.
- Restrict choices by selecting 'UK only'.
- Use either categories or search facilities to find relevant pages.

Activity 4.3

Web catalogues

1 Type in the name of a pop group or football team or other interest and search through the catalogue for it.
2 Now find this position in the hierarchy, starting at the top. For example:
   Regional:Countries:United Kingdom:Recreation and Sport:Sport:Football:FA Carling Premiership:Clubs:Arsenal FC
3 Or try this category to see which papers are online:
   /Regional/Countries/United_Kingdom/News_and_Media/Newspapers

Using Yahoo! to find information on car insurance

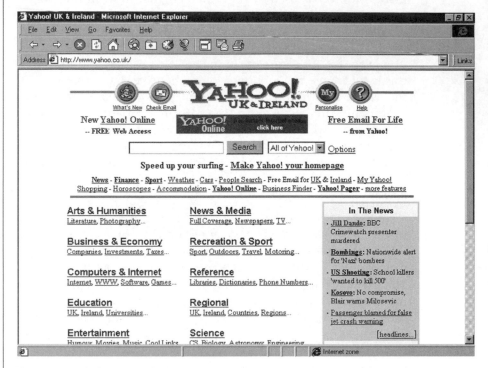

Fig. 4.2 Yahoo! directory web site (*www.yahoo.co.uk*)

When using Yahoo there would be two alternative ways of finding web sites concerned with car insurance.

First method

The first involves selecting from the category 'Business and Economy' and then choosing the options beneath this of:

- Companies, followed by
- Financial Services, followed by
- Insurance, followed by
- Automotive

This would then lead to the listings in this category (Regional > Countries > United Kingdom > Business and Economy > Companies > Financial Services > Insurance > Automotive) such as:

- New Car Net Insurance – fill in one form to receive four competitive insurance quotes from the UK companies. Quotes for mainland UK only.
- Car Insurance Centre – understand car insurance information and get quotes from multiple insurers.
- Avondale Fitzgerald Insurance – offering car and home insurance.

- Simply Direct – Lambeth Building Society offering low cost car insurance.
- Carquote UK – fill out one form and receive car insurance quotes from all the major UK insurance companies.

Note that each company has up to 25 words to describe the service on offer. They are not supposed to use any promotional text; it should be purely descriptive.

This method of finding sites may be useful when browsing, but is only efficient when you know the category you are looking for.

Second method

This involves typing keywords such as 'car insurance' into the box to the left of 'search'. It is probably the more widely used method. For country-specific sites such as those in the UK and Germany rather than searching 'All of Yahoo!' as is shown in Fig. 4.2, it is better to choose UK or Germany only. After you type 'Search' you will receive the following information:

This search was restricted to Regional > Countries > United Kingdom. For more matches, try an unrestricted search. Categories include Web Sites, Web Pages and News Stories

Yahoo! UK & Ireland Site Matches   (1 – 15 of 21)
Regional > Countries > United Kingdom > Business and Economy > Companies > Financial Services > Insurance > Automotive

- New Car Net Insurance – fill in one form to receive four competitive insurance quotes from the UK companies. Quotes for mainland UK only.
- Car Insurance Centre – understand car insurance information and get quotes from multiple insurers.
- Avondale Fitzgerald Insurance – offering car and home insurance.
- Simply Direct – Lambeth Building Society offering low cost car insurance.
- Carquote UK – fill out one form and receive car insurance quotes from all the major UK insurance companies.
- Regional > Countries > United Kingdom > Business and Economy > Companies > Automotive > Buyers' Services
- New Car Net – guide to new cars available in the UK; includes on-screen comparisons, motor insurance quotes, and links to manufacturers' sites.

Regional > Countries > United Kingdom > England > Counties and Regions > Norfolk > Cities and Towns > Norwich > Business and Shopping > Companies

- Avondale Fitzgerald Insurance – offering car and home insurance.

Regional > Countries > United Kingdom > Business and Economy > Companies > Financial Services > Insurance

- Eagle Star Insurance Company Limited – offers online quotes and immediate purchase of car, home and travel insurance.

Regional > Countries > United Kingdom > Business and Economy > Companies > Financial Services > Insurance > Homeowners

- Avondale Fitzgerald Insurance – offering car and home insurance.

> ▶ **Mini case study** *continued*

Regional > Countries > United Kingdom > Business and Economy > Companies > Financial Services > Insurance > Brokerages

- Admiral Insurance – UK motor insurance site for both new and existing customers. Car quotes available.
- InterSure Insurance Service – arrange immediate Insurance cover for Home or Car at very low rates. The system provides quotations from numerous UK insurance companies.

Regional > Countries > United Kingdom > Business and Economy > Companies > Financial Services > Insurance > Norwich Union Global

- Norwich Union Group UK - complete range of house, car, life, pension, savings, mortgage, investment, health and motorbike insurance for you and your family.

It should be evident from both examples that companies may occur in a number of categories. These can be:

- Business categories, for example **Business and Economy > Companies > Financial Services > Insurance > Automotive** or **Business and Economy > Companies > Financial Services > Insurance > Homeowners.**
- By towns, for example **England > Counties and Regions > Norfolk > Cities and Towns > Norwich > Business and Shopping > Companies.**
- By company, for example **Business and Economy > Companies > Financial Services > Insurance > Norwich Union Global.**

The implications of this for marketers are that great care should be taken in choosing the correct categories for a service and that a company with a diversity of products such as a financial services company should be represented in many categories. Since Yahoo! is one of the most popular sites, it is discussed in Chapter 9 in relation to how listing can be achieved.

The most widely used directories (that now also contain search engine capabilities) are:

- Yahoo! (*www.yahoo.com, www.yahoo.co.uk*);
- Lycos (*www.lycos.com*);
- Magellan (*www.magellan.com*);
- Infoseek Guide (*www.infoseek.com*).

Portals

Portal is a term that only came to prominence in 1998. It is now widely used to describe sites with the facilities of both search engines and directories. The latter also have other additional information. Portal is an appropriate term since it refers to a web site that is an individual's main access point to the information on the Internet. Portals are the sites users access most frequently to find the information they need.

Portal

A web site that acts as a gateway to the information on the Internet by providing search engines, directories and other services such as personalised news or free e-mail.

The term 'portal' originated in references to sites that were the default home pages of users. In other words, when users start their web browser such as Microsoft Internet Explorer, or Netscape Navigator, the first page they see is their personal home page. When users use a newly installed browser it will be set up so that the home page is that of the company that produces it. In the case of Microsoft this is usually *www.msn.com* (The Microsoft Network) or *www.microsoft.com*, and for Netscape it is *home.netscape.com.* Figure 4.3 shows the home page of the Netscape portal site. It can be seen that information is available in different categories, as for Yahoo!, and there is a search facility. It is also possible to search using other search engines.

The Netscape and Microsoft sites are very popular since millions of users use these browsers. It follows that the web sites that are loaded by default when the browsers are started will receive millions of hits and will act as users' gateway to the Internet. Figure 4.4 shows that the Netscape site and the two Microsoft sites therefore receive a lot of visitors. Of the other sites listed, the majority are search engines (Excite, Lycos, Infoseek and AltaVista) or directories (Yahoo!).

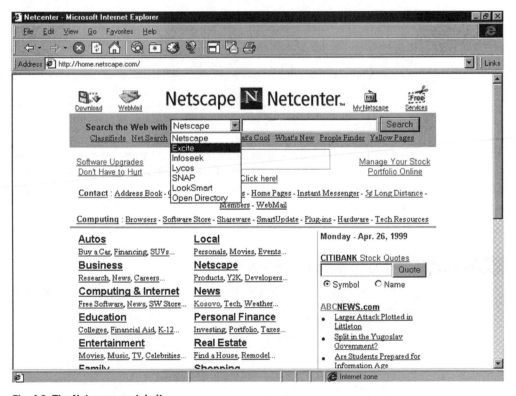

Fig. 4.3 The Netscape portal site

Activity 4.4

Why is Yahoo! the most visited web site?

From Fig. 4.4 it can be seen that Yahoo! is the most successful site, when measured by the number of visitors. From your experience of using Yahoo! and some of the other sites in the top 10, evaluate why it is successful. You should consider factors from a user's point of view in terms of how easy it is to find the site (including promotion methods), services offered, how easy it is to use the site and how good it is for its intended purpose.

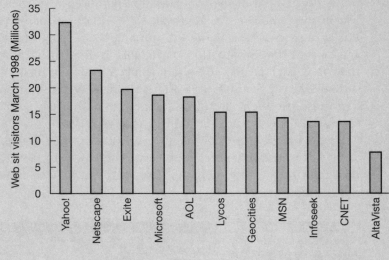

Fig. 4.4 Number of visitors to web sites in March 1998

Although the Microsoft sites and the Netscape home page are visited frequently since they are the default home pages of web browsers, it can be seen that several other sites are just as popular. These search engines and directories are also considered to be portals since they may be the first page after their home page that users choose when logging on to the Internet. Users who are familiar with using web browsers will know how to set their home page to be different from the default, and may set it to Yahoo!. Others may set their Favorite links (Explorer terminology) or Bookmarks (Netscape terminology) to their own home page.

Activity 4.5

Setting a different home page for a browser

This controls the web site that loads first when a browser is loaded. If you want to change the default page to the Yahoo! web page, do as follows:

Microsoft Internet Explorer

Choose View, Options, Navigation tab.
Set Page = Start Page and
Address = *www.yahoo.co.uk*

Netscape Navigator

Edit, Preferences (Netscape Navigator)

The section below on managing information shows how these options can be set to be 'Bookmarks' or 'Favorites'.

In addition to the two types of portals described above, there is one other significant category. This is portals provided by ISPs and IAPs such as Virgin Net, Freeserve, AOL and Compuserve. Some of the original services, such as the latter two, hosted a lot of information such as news and financial news that was originally available only to subscribers to the services. With the increased use being made of the Web, the providers have made public much of this information in order to increase the number of visits to their sites. However, the main users of this type of portal will be the subscribers to the service. Their browsers will be configured, when installed, to use the ISP's page such as Freeserve (*www.freeserve.net*) or Virgin Net (*www.virgin.net*) as the home page. Again, many of the users will not know how to change their default home page, nor will they want to do so. In this way a large ISP such as Freeserve may achieve millions of visits each month. The number of worldwide visitors to the AOL site (Fig. 4.4) bears testimony to the popularity of this type of portal.

A final type of site that could be considered to be a portal is that which has arisen from different free information services. For example, the BBC web site (*www.bbc.co.uk*) is one of the most popular sites for UK users. Elsewhere CNN or more specialist financial news sites are popular. These sites may contain facilities to search the Web, and the BBC also has a simple directory catalogue.

Portals are considered very important to companies looking to use banner advertising to promote their products, services and web sites using the Web. They have good potential for advertising since there are a large number of visitors. Advertisements for a broad audience can be served when users first visit the site. More specialised advertisements can be served after the user has typed in a keyword. For example, if the user types in 'insurance', an appropriate advertisement can be displayed. Owing to the importance of web sites, companies owning them have attracted significant investment which has increased, or some would say over-inflated, their stock prices. The value attached to these companies is particularly interesting since the value is greatly in excess of their turnover, and some are not returning a profit. For example in 1999 Amazon was valued at over $20 billion on a turnover of $1 billion, and it was not making a profit.

As the Internet continues to expand, the value of portals is likely to increase, and this has led to purchases and mergers between the main players. For example Lycos and Magellan have merged, and Infoseek has been acquired by Disney as part of the new Go portal.

To summarise this section, there are three main types of portal:

1 The search engines and directories.
2 The home pages of Internet service providers and access providers.
3 Information services.

Usenet newsgroups

Newsgroups were described in Chapter 3 as a long-established tool of the Internet. Newsgroups, as a source of information, are not used as frequently by the business community as are visits to web sites, but they can provide useful information in some market areas. They can be used for marketing researchers, particularly by retailers looking for feedback on their products. For example, a manufacturer of outdoor clothing could monitor customers' preferences for, or factors determining, their purchase of cagoules or footwear. This would be apparent if a user of the newsgroup *uk.rec.walking* started a thread on the topic by asking the question 'What is the best type of cagoule?'

An example is shown in Mini case study 4.3.

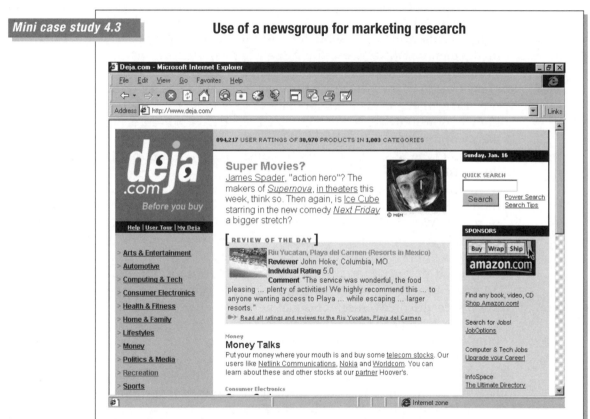

Mini case study 4.3

Use of a newsgroup for marketing research

Fig. 4.5 Deja web site (*www.deja.com*) for accessing Usenet newsgroups

This example reviews a 'thread' from the *uk.rec.walking* newsgroup. It is accessed using the Deja *www.deja.com* site. Users can search for topics or can follow the Yahoo!-like directory. The newsgroup is in the Recreation category.

In the newsgroup people will discuss anything to do with walking, from what climbs are recommended, through access rights to the weather (this being a UK-based newsgroup). Of interest to marketers might be the discussions that take place about gear used such as clothing or footwear. In this example the first person in the thread (Roy Smith) wants to know which insoles are useful for shock absorption. We look at comments from Giles Smith and Roy Smith. Note that the threads are indented according to which message is being replied to.

msg 1 Roy Smith 22 Apr 1999
    msg 2 Giles Smith 26 Apr 1999 (reply to msg 1)
        msg 3 Giles Smith 27 Apr 1999 (reply to msg 2)
            msg 4 Matt Smith 27 Apr 1999 (reply to msg 2)
                msg 5 Susan Smith 27 Apr 1999 (reply to msg 4)
    msg 6 Chris Smith 28 Apr 1999 (reply to msg 2)

Posting from Roy Smith 22 Apr 1999

I was wondering if anyone knows much about the pros and cons of various shock absorbing insoles? Probably the best known is sorbothane which, although it feels pretty hard, is supposed to be extremely efficient at absorbing shocks and therefore helps to prevent injury and reduce the general wear and tear on your joints. I have used sorbothane heel pads for several years now, not only in my hiking boots but also in my ordinary shoes. However I was wondering how long it lasts? The pads don't really look much different after a few years but it is safe to assume from that they are still just as capable of absorbing shocks as when they were new?

Reply from Giles Smith 26 Apr 1999

I used to use Sorbothane soles and heel pads from Spenco. They lastforever, I have a 10 year old pair of the heel pads. I have recently started using Smartfeet brand insoles, and love them. Theshock absorbtion properties of the material in them might not be as great asSorbothane or Noene, BUT, they are by far the most comfortable insoles Ihave ever used, and my feet are far less fatigued using them. Unless youhave bad problems with your leg or knee, I am guessing you will probablylike the Smartfeet brand insoles better than either of the others.Only bad part is that Smartfeet insoles are even pricier than the full-length sorbothane soles: $27/pr for the insoles, but that is significantlyless than orthotics for an orthotic like fit.

Reply from Matt Smith 27 Apr 1999

I use ordinary KSB insoles in my boots. I found the Sorbothane insoles too thick and they acted like a volume adjuster.

However I do use them in my trainers for playing Squash, and can recommend them for their performance. I used to get shin splints before but sinceusing them I don't have any problems (apart from losing!).

Someone said they deform in shape, well they are supposed to otherwise they couldn't absorb and disperse the shock.

The best method for researching a topic in a newsgroup is to use the Deja (*www.deja.com*) service (Fig. 4.5), which has an index of all messages posted to newsgroups. It is similar to a search engine or directory in that users can type in keywords that are matched against an index of all words in all the newsgroups or can choose from different categories to find information about a topic. Some of the search engines such as AltaVista also provide options for searching newsgroups.

'Push' information sources

'Push' was mentioned in Chapter 3 as an alternative method of publishing information on the Internet. In the 'push' model, rather than users having to search the Web to find what they want, users can subscribe to the services providing content they are interested in, and this information is broadcast to them at regular intervals such as daily or weekly. Information can be delivered in different ways. Typically push information is received when a user is not using his or her computer for other purposes. When the computer is not being used and the screensaver starts, information is downloaded and will then be displayed in the browser when the user next starts work. Such services do not appear to have been particularly popular. They were launched to great fanfare in 1997 when version 4 of Microsoft Internet Explorer and Netscape Navigator were launched. Internet Explorer has push channel options from information sources such as the BBC, *Financial Times*, *New Scientist* and *Vogue*. This service appears to have become unpopular since Microsoft removed the feature from its 1999 browser upgrade to Internet Explorer version 5. Reasons for this may include the difficulty of setting up channels, or the reduction in speed on the PC when channel features are used – or perhaps the fundamental model of regular delivery of information does not transfer well to the Internet. When using the World Wide Web, users may expect to find the information they need immediately.

Push information can also be delivered by e-mail newsletters. Here, users subscribe to an e-mail service and information is sent via e-mail on a regular basis such as monthly, weekly or daily. This type of approach appears to be more successful judging by the number of subscribers to these services. Examples of such push e-mail services concerned with Internet marketing include:

- Iconocast – weekly Internet marketing newsletter from the USA (subscribe at *www.iconocast.com*).
- Internet World weekly newsletter from publishers of *Internet World* magazine (subscribe at *www.internetworld.com*).
- Daily tips from the authors of the 'Dummies' series of books such as *Internet Search tips* (subscribe at *www.dummiesdaily.com*).
- Digests of the UK Netmarketing discussion group available from Chinwag Discussion Forums (*www.chinwag.com*).

Push e-mail services can also be used by publishers of conventional newspapers, or can be tailored for local information. For example, in the UK, UCI cinemas has a facility on its web site to send a weekly e-mail containing information on films and times for customers' local cinema (*www.uci-cinemas.co.uk*).

Such newsletters are also used to promote other products. This is done by integrating advertisements for products or sponsorships into the newsletter. Clicking on the newsletter links will take users to the accompanying web site. Mini case study 4.4 on Iconocast shows the types of advertisements in, and the content of, one of these newsletters.

Mini case study 4.4 **Iconocast – an example of a 'Push' e-mail newsletter**

ICONOCAST by Michael Tchong

'More concentrated than the leading brand'

Made possible in part by Business 2.0
The Magazine of Business in the Internet Age
Visit: http://service.imaginemedia.com/group/nett/8BSX.html
++++++++++++++++++++++++ 15-Apr-99 ++++++++++++++++++++++++

!!!!!!!!!!!!!!!!!!!!!!!!!!!! FLAG !!!!!!!!!!!!!!!!!!!!!!!!!!!!
NetGravity AdCenter for Agencies service offers the first
complete, end-to-end online ad solution for agencies to
manage and optimize online campaigns. AdCenter for Agencies
automates and manages the complete online advertising
process, including media planning and buying, trafficking,
ad targeting and delivery of detailed campaign performance
analysis. For more information, visit our Web site
http://www.netgravity.com or call 1-888-NETGRAVITY
!!

_____M a c r o v i e w
Rock and Row --> The Net music industry coalesces behind MP3

_____P a g e v i e w s
Usage Patterns --> Usage at work exceeds home viewing by 40%

_____R e a d e r I n t e r a c t i o n
Adam Smithline --> Rich media response will eventually drop!

_____T h e J a c o b y t e
Foundation Room, "Behind the Blue Door," DoubleClick, Lot 21

Practical tips for managing information

This section describes various techniques that marketing researchers can use to find and refer later to information collected from a web site.

1 Using bookmarks

The 'Bookmarks' feature in Netscape is known as 'Favorites' in Internet Explorer.

- Use **Favorites**, **Add To Favorites** (Internet Explorer), **Communicator, Bookmarks, Add Bookmarks** (Netscape Navigator) to retain a page for re-visiting later. These are personal bookmarks retained on the hard disk.
- Set Favorites to be home page. Choose **View, Internet Options, Navigation** tab. Set **Page = Start Page** and **Address = C:\Windows\Favorites** (Internet Explorer 4.0) or **Edit, Preferences** (Netscape Navigator).

2 Printing information

Choose File, Print.

3 Saving text for subsequent reading or printing

- All text on a web page can be saved to a text file by choosing File, Save As File, then Save File As Type Plain Text (.txt). This can then be later loaded into Word (remember to choose the extension .txt in Word).
- It is probably easier to save text by selecting it, using the copy option and then pasting it into a word processor. Select part of the text by selection with the mouse (left click and drag), then choose Edit, Copy. Select the target application such as a word processor and choose Edit, Paste. You can also select all the text in a document by this method using Edit, Select All. Using this technique has the benefit that some formatting of the document such as titles or tables may be retained and only relevant information needs to be highlighted.

4 Saving an image or diagram

Images are separate elements on the web page. Right mouse click on the image and choose Save Image As. This can then be loaded into an application such as Word using Insert, Picture. In more recent versions of Internet Explorer, diagrams are saved together with text for later viewing.

Activity 4.6

1 Save an entire page of your choice as a text file and load this file into Word.
2 Save an image as a file and load into Word.
3 Transfer the same page into Word using Copy and Paste.

Speeding up Web access

Using the World Wide Web can be frustrating: many refer to it as the 'World Wide Wait'. The following tips may help in speeding up access:

1 Use of browser

- Turn off image loading in your browser by choosing View, Internet Options, General tab (Internet Explorer). This may make some sites unusable but is useful if you are only interested in text information on a site!
- Use cached copies of pages stored on disk.
- Use bookmarks to return to sites you have accessed in previous sessions.

2 Tactical use of Internet

Use the Internet between 8 and 10 a.m. in Europe – access is much faster before midday when the USA wakes up.

3 Upgrade speed of connection to the Internet

This is a high-cost option. The user's modem can be upgraded to the fastest available (currently 56 600 bits per second) or alternative transmission methods can be used such as ISDN or fibre-optic cable.

4 Use specialised tools

Tools such as WebWhacker can be used to download all or part of a site, and it can then be viewed offline, at leisure when access to the web pages will be much faster.

Marketing research strategies

Marketing research is an important input to marketing and strategic decision making. It involves gathering information about the micro and macroenvironment.

Marketing research involves collecting two types of data: primary and secondary. Primary data consist of information obtained directly from interviews and discussions with or questionnaires completed by customers, and are generally new data. Secondary data consist of information obtained from internal or external sources that has been previously collected and collated. Market research should begin with the identification and assessment of secondary data sources. Such information is available from internal as well as external sources and will usually provide extensive data sourcing from which an initial understanding of the market and customers can be obtained. Primary research can then be conducted to verify findings and provide additional and potentially more relevant data. Brief coverage of how the Internet can be used to collect primary data through focus groups and through monitoring the use of the web site is provided in Chapter 12.

The Internet is well suited to secondary research since many of the traditional sources of information such as company reports, government reports, economic data and surveys from market research organisations such as AC Nielsen, MRB and NOP have now migrated online. Some data are provided free of charge, but other data must be paid for and accessed via an extranet.

Key questions to ask when searching for information sources via the Internet (which is well known for the great volume of poor quality data) are:

- Are they relevant?
- Are they accurate (what is the bias)?
- Are they up to date?

Accuracy will be dependent on the methods of collecting data and the sample size. The sample frame is also important: what are the characteristics of the sample and is it representative?

Useful information sources

When you are undertaking online marketing research for secondary data, the search strategy will vary according to the type of information you are looking for. These techniques can be used to find companies, markets and general business information. We would recommend the following:

1 Companies and different business markets

For information about companies and different business markets, directories such as Yahoo! or Yellow web may represent the best method since they provide the most comprehensive listing of companies and links to associated web sites. The companies will have registered their names, and keyword searches are peformed against company names. For smaller companies that have not been registered with Yahoo! search engines may be a better option.

- **Yahoo!**: (*www.yahoo.co.uk*)
- **Yellow Pages**: (*www.yell.co.uk*)
- **Real Names**: (*www.realnames.com*)

Tips | **Finding a company name**

You will probably not find a company web site the first time, every time, if you use a single method. A strategy for finding company information could be:

1 Type in the web address.
2 Use the RealNames translator, which suggests sites when you type in a company name.
3 Use a directory: Yahoo!, then Yellow Pages then Scoot or Thomson.
4 Use a search engine: AltaVista, then Excite, then Infoseek.
5 Telephone the company

Activity 4.7 | Find the following companies using each of the techniques above:

- Johnson Tiles
- Alliance and Leicester
- Boots the Chemist
- Others of your choice

RealNames

Fig. 4.6 RealNames service (*www.realnames.com***)**

RealNames was established in 1998 as a possible solution to the difficulty of match-ing company names to web addresses. It is essentially a specialised search engine facility that is intended to make finding companies and products easier. Centraal, the company that operates RealNames, will register company names and brands for $100, and it offers a searching service to consumers where the consumer types a company or product they are looking for and its search engine will then list matches (see Fig. 4.6). The search engine will also list companies that are not directly regis-tered with RealNames. In March 1999 there were 15 000 registered companies or brands registered with RealNames and three million other companies.

To increase the availability of RealNames, Centraal has completed distribution deals with search engine sites such as AltaVista (*www.altavista.com*) and Inktomi (*www.inktomi.com*). The RealName of a company is then displayed when the RealName matches the keyword typed into the search engine.

It remains to be seen whether this service creates a sufficient critical mass to be successful.

2 Products and services

For information about products and services use the search engines. As was explained earlier in the chapter, search engines have a much more comprehensive listing of web pages than the directories do. Searches may pick up the names of these products. But in Yahoo! product or service names will only be found if the company has included them in the 25-word text it provided summarising details about the company.

- AltaVista: (*www.altavista.com*)

3 Local companies

For companies that operate in a local area use local online databases. In the UK, the Yellow Pages or Thomson databases could be used to search locally. Electronic Yellow Pages offers a search by postcode or county. Thomson is better for nation-wide information.

- **Thomson**: (*www.thomson-directories.co.uk*)
- **Electronic Yellow Pages**: (*www.eyp.co.uk*)
- **Freepages**: (*www.scoot.co.uk*)

4 Industry information

Standard news media for each country are located in the Yahoo! hierarchy at:

/Regional/Countries/United_Kingdom/News_and_Media:Newspapers

Electronic media business information may be available in portals. For example Infoseek Industrywatch offers daily updates of industry news by industry areas such as finance, bio-technology, energy and chemicals (*www.infoseek.com*). Further information is available about companies and industries for the UK at UK Business Park (*www.ukbusinesspark.co.uk*).

You can also try searching newsgroups for industry information using DejaNews (*www.dejanews.com*). For example:

clari.biz.industry.textiles
clari.biz.industry.transportation
clari.biz.marketreport.europe
misc.industry.pulp-and-paper
uk.rec.fishing.sea

5 Market research data

Visit the main market research agencies:

- **Mintel** (*www.mintel.com*)
- **MORI** (*www.mori.co.uk*)
- **Euromonitor** (*www.euromonitor.com*)
- **Verdict** (*www.verdict.co.uk*)
- **AC Nielsen** (*www.nielsen.com*)
- **NOP** (*www.nopres.co.uk*)
- **Economist Intelligence Unit** (*www.eiu.com*)

For information on business-to-business and consumer levels of adoption try:

- **Durlacher** (*www.durlacher.co.uk*)

For summary information on consumer demographics, see:

- **Office for National Statistics** (*www.ons.gov.uk*)
- **Government Statistical Office** (*www.statistics.gov.uk*).

The range of UK government information can be accessed from the gateway *www.open.gov.uk*.

6 Educational information

UK educational information about business including student and staff resources is available at Bized Information Service (*www.bized.ac.uk*).

7 Full text electronic academic journals, abstracts and newspapers

The main UK-based electronic academic sources are listed below:

- **BIDS** (Bath Information Data Service) (*www.bids.ac.uk*) is the best known and most widely used bibliographic service for the academic community in the UK. Special login required.
- **NISS EBSCO** (*www.niss.ac.uk/ebsco*) – online journals covering a wide range of subjects
- **Emerald** (*www.emerald-library.com*) – full-text journal articles on the following subjects: marketing, general management, human resources, quality, property, operations, production and economics, library and information services, information management, training and education and engineering. From MCB Press.
- **International Digital Electronic Access Library** (*www.janet.idealibrary.com*) – full-text version of 178 Academic Press journals. Special login required.
- **Anbar** (*www.anbar.com*) – abstracts of 400 international management journals.
- **Clover** (*clover.niss.ac.uk*) – the Clover Newspaper Index is a comprehensive index that provides access to the quality daily and Sunday newspapers, including their supplements and colour magazines. Newspapers covered include: *Daily Telegraph, Financial Times, Guardian, Independent, The Times, Observer, Sunday Times, European, The Economist, Times Educational Supplement, Times Higher Educational Supplement, Times Literary Supplement.*
- **The Journal of Computer-Mediated Communication** (*www.ascusc.org/jmc*).

Other useful sites

1 Reference sites for Internet marketing and e-commerce

This section describes reference sites that may help you when researching digital marketing. To avoid the need to continuously use search engines or directories it is useful to identify *reference sites* that fit your interest. For example: CyberAtlas (*www.cyberatlas.com*) and Nua (*www.nua.ie*) are sites that are updated monthly on the latest business developments on the Internet. It is more efficient to visit these sites monthly than try to find the information yourself – the compilers of the site have done the searching for you.

A further useful reference site for business students and practitioners is Business Researchers Interests (BRINT). This site has research compiled on topics such as business process re-engineering, organisational learning and electronic commerce (*www.brint.com*). For example:

- **Electronic commerce** – *www.brint.com/Elecomm.htm*
- **Internet and WWW** – *www.brint.com/web.htm*

Other sites with articles and links are:

- **Marketing Online** (*www.marketing-online.co.uk*) is a source for links to web sites concerned with Internet marketing strategy, implementation and practice. Produced by Dave Chaffey.
- **Internet Marketing**: A Strategic Framework (*web.ukonline.co.uk/Members/jim.hamill/topic4.htm*) gives a brief paper by Dr Jim Hamill, Reader in International Marketing, University of Strathclyde, Glasgow, Scotland, UK.
- **Project 2000** (*ecommerce.vanderbilt.edu*) was founded in 1994 by Tom Novak and Donna Hoffman at School of Management, Vanderbilt University, to study marketing implications of the Internet. Useful links/papers.
- **MarketingNet** (*www.marketingnet.co.uk*) includes extracts from the books *Cyberstrategy* and *Cybermarketing* by Pauline Bickerton, a director of the company.

There are various online discussion groups and newsletters about Internet marketing that are useful for discussions about effective Internet marketing techniques:

- Iconocast – weekly Internet marketing newsletter from the USA (subscribe at *www.iconocast.com*).
- Internet World – weekly newsletter from publishers of *Internet World* magazine (subscribe at *www.internetworld.com*).
- Digests of the UK Netmarketing discussion group are available from Chinwag *www.chinwag.com*. This is recommended.

2 Management consultants

Management consultants are a useful source of information for detailed reports on electronic commerce. Many of these reports can be downloaded free of charge. Often the user requires Adobe Acrobat PDF reader to review these reports. You can try both global and country-specific sites.

- **KPMG** – *www.kpmg.co.uk, www.kpmg.com*
- **Andersen Consulting** – *www.andersen.com*
- **Ernst and Young** – *www.ey.com* (USA), *www.eyi.com* (global), *www.eyuk.com* (UK)
- **PricewaterhouseCoopers** – *www.pwcglobal.com, www.pwcglobal.com/uk*
- **IBM** – *www.ibm.com, www.uk.ibm.com/, www.ibm.com/e-business/*
- **Deloitte and Touche** – *www.dttus.com* (US site), *www.dc.com*. (Deloitte Consulting)

3 US/international business magazines

Most business magazines have a regular technology section and features on applying new techniques, for example e-commerce and online marketing.

- *The Economist* – *www.economist.com*
- *Business Week* – *www.businessweek.com*

- *Fortune* – www.fortune.com
- *Forbes* – www.forbes.com
- *Chief Information Officer Magazine* – www.cio.com/CIO/ciomaghome.html
- *Time* – www.pathfinder.com/time
- *Harvard Business Review* – abstracts only available at no charge: *www.hbsp.harvard.edu*
- *Mckinsey Quarterly* – full-text articles in categories on marketing, information technology, electronic commerce from Mckinseys consultants at *www.mckinseyquarterly.com*
- *Sloan Management Review* – abstracts only available at no charge at *mitsloan.mit.edu/smr*

The implications for marketers of the ways in which people find information

As a summary to this chapter, we set out some general conclusions about the methods by which end-users on the Internet find information. Methods of finding information have important implications for the way in which a web site is promoted. On the many different methods of finding information reviewed in this chapter we can make the following comments:

1 Since a great number of sources are used to find information, a company promoting its web site should aim to be represented on as many as possible. All the methods indicated in Fig. 1.5 should be used to drive traffic to the site. Methods for becoming listed on search engines and directories are described in Chapter 9. It is also important for a company to promote its web address in offline media.

2 Information contained on web sites should be available by a method accessible to users with different behaviour patterns as described in Chapter 2. The site should accommodate:
   - those with different behavioural traits such as directed information seekers and undirected information seekers (browsers) (Breitenbach and van Doren, 1998);
   - those at different stages of adopting a web site;
   - those at different stages of the buying decisions (e.g. Berthon *et al.*, 1998).

3 The role of push techniques such as e-mail newsletters should not be underestimated as a means of communicating with business customers.

SUMMARY

1 Uniform resource locators (URLs) or web addresses are the best method of finding information on the Internet – if you know a site contains the information you want!

2 Search engines such as AltaVista (*www.altavista.com*) provide the most comprehensive information listing for the Internet. They consist of an index to all pages in all web sites registered with the search engine. When a user types in keywords they are matched against the index and the sites with the most relevant information are listed in order.

3 Directories such as that of Yahoo! (*www.yahoo.com*) provide a more selective index of web sites than search engines. They consist of a *structured* listing of sites, grouped in categories. The categories and companies can be searched by typing in keywords.

4 A portal is a web site that acts as a gateway to the information on the Internet by providing search engines, directories and other services such as personalised news or free e-mail. Examples include Yahoo! (*www.yahoo.com*), Goto (*www.goto.com*) and Netscape (*www.netscape.com*).

5 Useful market research information can be found in Usenet newsgroups where consumers may discuss their experience in selecting and using products.

6 Push techniques can be used to receive information. A user will select the information he or she needs such as industry-specific news or share prices and this will then be sent regularly, either by e-mail or as a push broadcast which can be viewed in the web browser.

7 The Internet is a useful source of secondary marketing research data and can also be used for primary data collection.

8 Research strategies for secondary data will vary according to the type of information sought. Directories such as Yahoo! (*www.yahoo.com*) tend to be best for company information while search engines such as AltaVista (*www.altavista.com*) tend to be best for product or industry marketing research data.

EXERCISES AND QUESTIONS

Self-assessment exercises

1 Distinguish between search engines and directories. What do the differences between them contribute to their marketing effectiveness?

2 What is a uniform resource locator? How is it structured? Why is it one of the best methods of finding information on the Internet as compared with search engines and directories?

3 How can companies ensure their web sites are listed in search engines and directories?

4 How can searches performed using search engines be specified more precisely using multiple keywords and symbols?

5 Define 'portal'. How do portals differ from search engines and directories? What are the different origins of portal sites?

6 Describe three methods that are available to enable you to return to a web site you have visited in the past.

7 Describe newsgroups and their importance to marketers.

8 What methods are available to enable the content of web sites to be downloaded more rapidly?

Discussion questions

1 'Search engines are a more effective method of finding information than directories.' Discuss this assertion.

2 'The effectiveness of portals as measured by the number of site visitors is mainly dependent on the number of links to relevant web sites.' Discuss.

3 'The use of the Internet for finding out about companies and their products will make the use of paper-based phone and business directories obsolete in ten years.' Discuss.

4 'The increasing use of comparison shopping services will result in increased use of the web for retail purchases'. Discuss this statement using existing examples.

Essay questions

1 Examine the reasons for the growth in importance of portal sites. How do you expect their number and characteristics to change in the future?

2 Review the different methods for searching for information using the Internet. What should marketers do to ensure their company and products are publicised to customers who use the different methods?

3 Given the different types of searching behaviour exhibited by customers how can companies ensure that promotion of their web site is effective?

4 How are the different searching tools used to support different stages of the buying decision?

5 Assess the benefits and disadvantages of portals as a means of finding news, as compared with television teletext-type searches.

Examination questions

1 What facilities are provided by a portal web site? What is their importance to companies marketing products using the Internet?

2 Explain the differences between a web-based search engine and a directory in terms of the information searched when the keywords are typed in.

3 What are newsgroups? What might be their value to a marketing researcher in a pharmaceuticals company?

4 Briefly explain how a company can use the Internet to conduct market research about:
(a) its known competitors;
(b) unknown competitors.

5 Explain how a web-based product comparison service operates. Give three implications of such services for marketers.

6 Describe the order in which you would use different tools such as search engines, directories and entering a web address to find information about a *product*. Justify your answer.

7 Describe the order in which you would use different tools such as search engines, directories and entering a web address to find information about a *company*. Justify your answer.

8 Define push technology and explain how it differs from a search engine as a means of finding information.

REFERENCES

Berthon, B., Pitt, L. and Watson, R. (1998) 'The World Wide Web as an industrial marketing communication tool: models for the identification and assessment of opportunities', *Journal of Marketing Management*, 14, 691–704.

Breitenbach, C. and van Doren, D. (1998) 'Value-added marketing in the digital domain: enhancing the utility of the Internet', *Journal of Consumer Marketing*, 15 (6), 559–75.

FURTHER READING

Baker, M. (ed.) (1999) *The Marketing Book*. Oxford: Butterworth-Heinemann.
Chapter 7, Marketing research, by John Webb is recommended.

Brassington, F. and Petitt, S. (2000) *Principles of Marketing* (2nd edn). Harlow, UK: Pearson Education. *See* companion Prentice Hall web site (*www.booksites.net/brassington2*).
Chapter 6, Marketing Information and Research, describes the marketing research process and techniques for collection of primary and secondary data.

Campbell, D. and Campbell, M. (1995) *The Students Guide to Doing Research on the Internet*. Reading, MA: Addison Wesley. Mainly US sources.

Dibb, S., Simkin, S., Pride, W. and Ferrel, O. (1997) *Marketing. Concepts and strategies* (3rd European edn). New York: Houghton Mifflin.
See companion Houghton Mifflin web site (*www.busmgt.ulst.ac.uk/h_mifflin/*).
See Chapter 6, Marketing Research and Information Systems.

Kennedy, A. (1998) *The Internet. The Rough Guide*. London: Rough Guides.
A small book, but accessible style and packed with useful information about searching. Many sites are listed.

Knight, J. (1999) *Computing for Business* (2nd edn). London: FT Management.
Chapter 3, Accessing the Internet, contains detailed descriptions of how to use the Internet to find information efficiently.

Kotler, P., Armstrong, G., Saunders, J. and Wong, V. (1999) *Principles of Marketing* (2nd edn). Hemel Hempstead: Prentice Hall, Europe.
See companion Prentice Hall web site for 8th US edn: *cw.prenhall.com/bookbind/pubbooks/kotler/*.
See Chapter 8, Marketing Information and Marketing Research

Lehnert, W. (1999) *Light on the Internet.* Reading, MA: Addison Wesley Longman.
A readable book on searching and other introductory topics.

Strauss, J. and Frost, R. (1999) *Marketing on the Internet. Principles of online marketing*. New Saddle River, NJ: Prentice Hall.
Chapter 3, Online Research, discusses using the Internet for collection of both primary and secondary data.

Winship, I. and McNab, A. (1996) *The Student's Guide to the Internet*. London: Library Association Publishing.
Mainly English sources. Now updated.

Wright, C. (1999) *The Internet for Students*. London: Hodder & Stoughton.
Categorises UK academic sites by subject.

WEB SITE REFERENCES

Many web references are given in the section (*see* pp. 107–10). Useful information sources, in this chapter. Specific search engine references are given in that section.

AllSearchEngines.com (www.allsearchengines.com) aims to list all search engines and categorises them.

Ariadne magazine (*www.ariadne.ac.uk*) is an online quarterly journal reviewing information sources and search techniques available on the Internet. It has a regular column on search engines.

The Online Netskills Interactive Course (*www.netskills.ac.uk*) provides a free 'hands-on' tutorial to searching the Internet. Registration is required.

ResearchBuzz (*www.researchbuzz.com*) has news on new information sources and search engines.

SearchEngineGuide.Com (*www.searchengineguide.com*) is another categorised listing of over 1000 search engines.

Search Engine Watch (*searchenginewatch.com*).

The definitive source of information on how different search engines work. Some content has to be paid for, but the section on searching tips is fully available at *searchenginewatch.com/facts*. This contains advancing searching advice, tutorials and a comprehensive list of search engines. Another useful section explains how search engines work (*searchenginewatch.com/webmasters/ work.html*). In brief it contains everything you ever wanted to know about search engines, and possibly much you didn't.

Yahoo! search engine section (*dir.yahoo.com/Computers_and_Internet/Internet/World_Wide_Web/ Searching_the_Web/*) has many useful resources on how to search as well as referencing the engines themselves.

Internet strategy development

CHAPTER 5

Internet marketing strategy

Learning objectives

After reading this chapter, the reader should be able to:

- relate Internet marketing strategy to marketing and business strategy;
- identify opportunities and threats arising from the Internet;
- evaluate alternative strategic approaches to the Internet.

Links to other chapters

This chapter is related to other chapters as follows:

▶ Some of the terms and concepts discussed in this chapter are introduced in Chapters 1 and 2.

▶ Chapter 6 outlines how the Internet marketing strategy can be implemented through an Internet marketing plan.

▶ Chapter 7 describes, in more detail, the impact of the Internet on market structure and distribution channels.

INTRODUCTION

For many companies, developing a first version of their web site is not the result of a well-defined Internet marketing strategy; rather, it is a necessary response to a rapid market development. The decision to create the web site is reactive: a response to the development of sites by new companies in their sector, or by existing competitors, or a response to customer demands. After a site has been in existence for a year or so, marketing staff and senior managers in a company will naturally question its effectiveness. This is often the point at which the need for a coherent Internet marketing strategy becomes apparent. As a consequence of this approach, our starting-point in this chapter is not solely that of creating a strategy for a completely new site; rather, it involves assessing the current site and its effectiveness with a view to future improvements. To summarise, the possible starting-points for a company needing to develop an Internet marketing strategy will be:

1 Existing company, no web site.
2 Existing company with existing web site.
3 New web-based start-up.

119

The chapter will concentrate on the second situation since it is the most common. The strategic approaches can, however, be applied to all situations.

When discussing Internet marketing strategy it is useful to keep in mind that Internet strategy involves much more than the narrow focus of a strategy to develop a web site. Although this is our starting-point in this chapter, in Chapter 7 we examine broader issues of using the Internet strategically to redesign business processes and integrate with partners such as suppliers and distributors in new ways.

Integrating the Internet marketing strategy with business and marketing strategy

The integration of an Internet marketing strategy into business and marketing strategies represents a significant challenge for many organisations, in part because they have traditionally considered them separately and in part because the implications for change at an industry level and within the organisation are profound. The Internet is a recent and rapidly growing application and it is this recency and rapid growth that have created the need for its consideration as an important management agenda.

Figure 5.1 indicates the context of the Internet marketing strategy. The internal influences include corporate objectives and strategy, and these in turn will be among the influences on marketing strategy that should directly influence the Internet marketing strategy. There have been relatively few research surveys on how Internet strategies are developed, but anecdotal evidence suggests the approaches are *ad hoc*, with Internet marketing being influenced to some extent directly by corporate strategies.

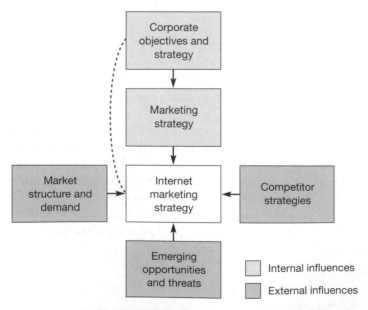

Fig. 5.1 Internal and external influences on Internet marketing strategy

Key external influences include the market structure and demand, competitor strategies and the current and evolving opportunities and threats. Methods for monitoring the external environment to anticipate external opportunities and threats and competitors' actions are covered in this chapter, as are methods of assessing the demand of the market for Internet-delivered services. In Chapter 7 we look in more detail at the influence of market and channel structure that should be assessed in order to define strategy.

Is a separate Internet marketing strategy needed?

It could be argued that companies do not require a separate Internet marketing strategy; rather, the Internet should be an adjunct to a strategic marketing plan. This argument would possibly be valid if the Internet was 'just another channel'. However, the potential significance of the Internet as a contributor to sales and reduced costs is such that it warrants separate attention. For example, for companies selling electronic components and hardware such as Cisco and Dell, the Internet warranted a separate plan in that it has radically changed the ways in which these companies operate, with a significant proportion of their sales now being generated via the Internet, and their costs have been greatly reduced as a consequence of using the Internet to re-engineer their businesses.

The Internet marketing strategy also warrants a separate strategic plan since it is a new medium, and companies will need to specify their response to this medium. They may be making a substantial investment in an Internet web site and will naturally want to ensure that the correct amount of money is invested and that it is used effectively. A plan to support investment in the Internet may occur either when the web site is first produced or when an upgrade is planned to the facilities the web site offers, and/or when new technologies or infrastructure are used. Such upgrades may need to occur more than once a year or, as a web site matures, they may be needed once every two or three years.

To summarise this section: a clearly defined Internet marketing strategy may be required for any of the following reasons:

1 As a detailed strategy that is part of the broader strategic marketing planning process.
2 As part of the investment proposal for a new web site.
3 As part of an investment proposal for upgrading a web site.
4 As a separate strategy for a company for which the Internet is a significant communications or sales channel.

Although it has been argued that the Internet should be considered as a separate *plan*, it should be remembered that it is important that the Internet strategy is an integral part of the marketing strategy in order that it supports the main thrusts of the marketing and business strategy.

Levels of web site development

Owing to the newness of the medium, few companies have a clearly defined strategy for their web site. This does not mean, however, that sites develop randomly. Rather, there is a logical way in which the facilities offered by a web site can be gradually developed.

Many companies have followed a natural progression in developing their web site to support their marketing activities. The following levels of development of a web site can be identified:

- **Level 0**. No web site
- **Level 1**. Company places an entry in a web site that lists company names such as Yellow Pages (*www.yell.co.uk*) to make people searching the web aware of the existence of a company or its products. There is no web site at this stage.
- **Level 2**. Simple static web site created containing basic company and product information (sometimes referred to as brochureware). With the average cost of a UK web site being £3000, many companies are currently in this category.
- **Level 3**. Simple interactive site where users are able to search the site and make queries to retrieve information such as product availability and pricing. Queries by e-mail may also be supported.
- **Level 4**. Interactive site supporting transactions with users. The functions offered will vary according to the company. If products can be sold direct then an electronic commerce option for online sales will be available. Other functions might include an interactive customer service helpdesk which is linked into direct marketing objectives.
- **Level 5**. Fully interactive site providing relationship marketing with individual customers and facilitating the full range of marketing functions.

> **Brochureware**
> Brochureware describes a web site in which a company has migrated its existing paper-based promotional literature on to the Internet without recognising the differences required by this medium.

The levels of sophistication of a web site are arbitrary and will vary according to different authors. Commentators in the United States, for instance in *Wired* magazine, talk of second and third generation web sites. Three generations of web site sophistication could be:

- *First generation*: simple static 'brochureware' site used for one-to-many communication.
- *Second generation*: simple interactive site, perhaps with product availability and pricing queries. The communication model is still one-to-many, with the company not collecting any information about the customer.
- *Third generation*: fully interactive, dynamic site with personalisation or mass customisation facilities for direct marketing, sales and customer service.

Quelch and Klein (1996) have noted how web sites develop for different types of company. They distinguish between existing major companies (*see* Fig. 5.2(a)) and start-up companies (*see* Fig. 5.2(b)) that start as Internet companies. The main

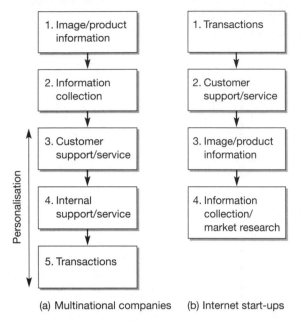

(a) Multinational companies   (b) Internet start-ups

Fig. 5.2 Levels of web site development in (a) the information to transaction model and (b) the transaction to information model of Quelch and Klein (1996)

difference appears to be that Internet start-ups are likely to introduce transaction facilities earlier than existing companies. However, they may take longer to develop suitable customer service facilities.

The approach of gradually developing a web site in response to competitive threats and according to the monetary and people resources available is likely to give the types of business benefits discussed in Chapter 1. However, such an approach tends to be reactive, and it is only through being proactive that opportunities can be identified and threats assessed in advance, with action being taken accordingly. The next section suggests how a more carefully planned strategic approach can be followed. This involves defining a company's goals, assessing the current market environment, reviewing alternatives and then selecting the best approach.

A generic strategic approach

If a site is developed without clearly defined strategic goals it will not be possible to identify how successful it is. Only through setting realistic goals and then assessing whether they are achieved can a company be sure of the contribution Internet-based marketing is making. Figure 5.3 shows the relationship between goal setting and measurement. First goals and objectives are defined in the Internet marketing strategy. These then form an input to the Internet marketing plan, which shows how these goals will be achieved. After the site has been designed and created, it is necessary to monitor it in order to assess whether strategic objectives have been achieved and feed this information back to influence future strategy and its implementation.

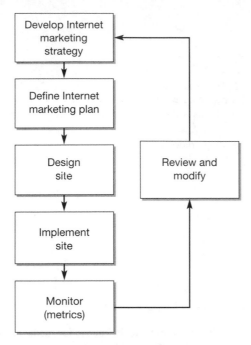

Fig. 5.3 A simple framework for Internet marketing strategy development

A more detailed approach has been suggested by McDonald (1999). In this there are four main phases, which relate to Fig. 5.3 as follows:

1 Goal setting (develop Internet marketing strategy).
2 Situation review (develop Internet marketing strategy).
3 Strategy formulation (develop Internet marketing strategy).
4 Resource allocation and monitoring (define Internet marketing plan and monitor).

The detailed model is shown in Fig. 5.4. In this chapter, we will review each of the four main stages in turn.

Strategic goal setting

Any marketing strategy should be based on clearly defined corporate objectives, but there is a tendency for Internet marketing to be conducted separately from other business and marketing objectives. This may be done because the Internet has not been integrated into company culture or management – it may be seen as a separate responsibility from marketing. It is best, of course, if the Internet marketing strategy is consistent with and supports business and marketing objectives. For example, business objectives such as increasing market share in an overseas market or introducing a new product to market can and should be supported by the Internet communications channel.

When an Internet marketing strategy is being defined, the objectives should be clearly stated in the Internet Marketing plan. These could include:

▪ cost reduction of 10 per cent in marketing communications within two years;
▪ increase retention of customers by 10 per cent;

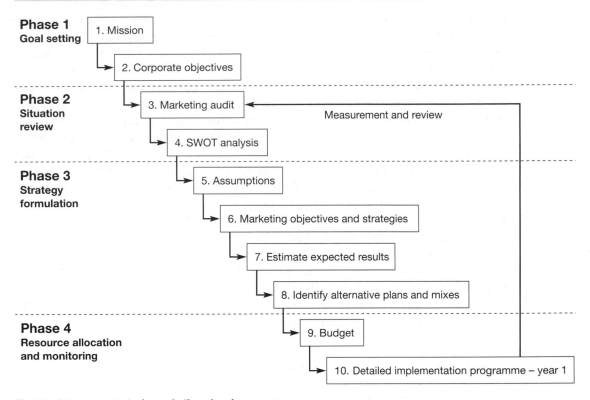

Fig. 5.4 A ten-step strategic marketing planning process
Source: MacDonald, 1999.

- increase by 20 per cent within one year the number of sales arising from a certain target market, e.g. 18–25 year olds;
- create value-added customer services not available currently;
- improve customer service by providing a response to a query within two hours, 24 hours per day, seven days a week.

Note that these objectives have numerical targets and times attached to them. In this way everyone is sure exactly what the target is, and can work towards it. With quantification of targets and milestones for when they will be achieved it is possible to review progress towards these targets, and when there is a danger that they will not be achieved, appropriate action can be taken to put the company back on target.

The Internet contribution

An assessment of the extent to which the Internet contributes to sales is a key measure of the importance of the Internet to a company. Companies that are likely to achieve a fair proportion of revenue from the Internet should set targets according to the anticipated growth in the medium. For example, Dell stated that, in 1999, $7 million of sales were 'via the Web'.

The Internet contribution is quite difficult to assess, so it is useful to consider the different ways in which a web site can contribute to sales. Some companies may only attribute sales actually placed on the web site to the Internet, but more forward-thinking companies will also consider how the Internet may have influenced the purchaser. Figure 5.5 indicates the different ways in which an online presence can contribute to sales. Traditionally, a purchaser would follow the real-world route, by evaluating the product, deciding to purchase, specifying his or her needs, and paying, and then the product would be dispatched to the customer. With an alternative online source of information, the buying process becomes more complex. As well as evaluating the product in the real world, customers with Internet access may well also evaluate the product online. As a result of visiting the web site, they then may decide to purchase. At this point, they have two choices: either they can purchase online (if the web site has these facilities), or they can place their order in the 'real world', perhaps by phone or fax. It is important to note that whatever alternative they take, their purchase is *determined by the web site*: in other words, the Internet has made a real contribution to sales. To measure contributions made in this way, Dell has an Internet-specific phone number, so they know when customers phone them to place their order that they are doing so in response to an evaluation made on the web site.

Mini case study 5.1 shows how Cisco has exploited the Internet through making it a central part of its marketing strategy.

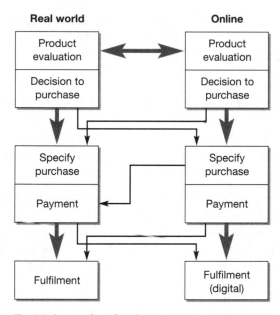

Fig. 5.5 Integration of real-world and online channels for product evaluation, purchase and fulfilment

Cisco Systems Internet contribution

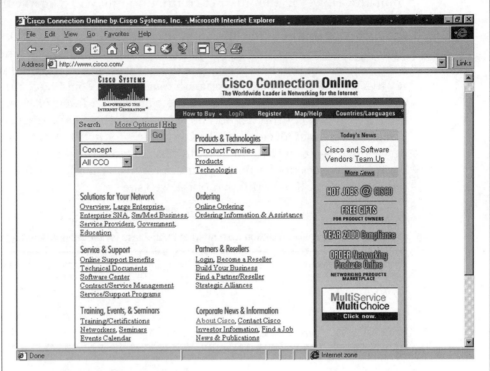

Fig. 5.6 Cisco Connection Online web site

Cisco Systems Inc., maker of computer networking gear, is now selling in excess of $22 million per day by electronic commerce (64 per cent of sales). This has been achieved by a strategy that identified the significance of the medium, set targets for the Internet contribution and then set up the web site and promotion to help achieve it. In 1999 Cisco sells more through online commerce than any other company ($22 million per day). Through using the Internet Cisco has achieved strategic benefits beyond increased revenue. It has also dramatically increased profitability. This has partly been achieved through the web site, which is thought to have been responsible for a 20 per cent reduction in overall operating costs.

Where sales are likely to be relatively homogeneous, as with a bookseller, the Internet contribution can be set in a general fashion for all products across the company. However, the Internet contribution may vary markedly for different product types or for different geographical or customer segments (*see* Activity 5.1, Internet contribution). In this case it may be useful to use a grid such as that in Table 5.1 to set objectives for the different product types. Take the example of a company selling watches. It may decide that it wants to use the Internet to sell a relatively low-value product to a youth market. This could have the growth profile shown for Product A. Markets where there are higher levels of Internet access such as Market B will contribute more to sales than other markets (such as Market A). The company may decide on a higher-value product that is targeted at an older age-segment – Product B might be in this category. In this example, the Internet contribution does not become significant for five years, so it is not worth investing heavily in promotion of this part of the web site.

Table 5.1 Percentage contribution from Internet to business for different product types and markets

Products or markets	Now	1 year	2 years	5 years	10 years
Product type A	5%	10%	20%	50%	100%
Product type B	1%	2%	5%	10%	25%
Market A	<1%	<1%	2%	10%	20%
Market B	2%	5%	10%	>25%	>50%

Activity 5.1

Internet contribution

Table 5.2 shows the Internet contribution for some companies taken from the world's top 100 Internet related companies. Note that there is a wide variety in Internet contribution according to the market sector in which the company operates.

Table 5.2 Selected Internet contribution to revenue

	Contribution to revenue (%)	Total Internet-based revenue ($m)
1 Cisco Systems	64	6400
2 Dell Computer	17	3000
15 Disney	1	240
17 Fedex	3	400
34 Thomas Publishing	14	40
36 LL Bean	4	45
59 Citigroup	11	700
68 New York Life	0.5	100
92 British Airways	1	200

Source: *Business 2.0*, May (1999) www.business2.com.

Potential business benefits

When defining the aims of Internet marketing, a company should conduct a comprehensive review of all the business benefits that could accrue. This can be of value in arguing the case for investment in a web site. Sterne (1999) identifies the following as the main benefits of setting up an Internet site:

- corporate image improved;
- improved customer service;
- increased visibility;
- market expansion;
- online transactions;
- lower communication costs.

Further benefits, and their relative importance, are highlighted in a 1998 report from Andersen Consulting (1999). Three hundred executives from European companies who were interviewed identified the following benefits as important:

- speed of transactions increased (73 per cent agreed);
- management of information improved (65 per cent agreed);
- increased service levels to customers (65 per cent agreed);
- removal of time constraints (65 per cent agreed);
- access to global markets (63 per cent agreed);
- removal of distance constraints (62 per cent agreed);
- ability to complete total transaction electronically (61 per cent agreed);
- access to full competitive arena (59 per cent agreed);
- opportunities for new revenues/services (57 per cent agreed);
- cost effectiveness (55 per cent agreed);
- more effective/closer relationships with business partnerships (54 per cent agreed);
- improved understanding of customer requirements (50 per cent agreed).

Such benefits can be converted into objectives that become part of the business or marketing plan described in the previous section. In such a review of potential benefits, it is useful to identify both tangible benefits, for which monetary savings or revenues can be identified, and intangible benefits, for which it is more difficult to calculate cost savings. These benefits can then be put into the marketing plan as critical success factors against which the success of the implementation can be

129

based. The types of benefits mentioned by senior managers from UK companies, who attended Strategic Internet Marketing seminars given by Dave Chaffey, are presented in Table 5.3.

Table 5.3 Tangible and intangible benefits from Internet marketing

Tangible benefits	Intangible benefits
Increased sales from new sales leads giving rise to increased revenue from: ■ new customers, new markets ■ existing customers (repeat-selling) ■ existing customers (cross-selling) Cost reductions from: ■ reduced time in customer service ■ online sales ■ reduced printing and distribution costs of marketing communications	■ Corporate image communication ■ Enhance brand ■ More rapid, more responsive marketing communications including PR ■ Improved customer service ■ Learning for the future ■ Meeting customer expectations to have a web site ■ Identify new partners, support existing partners better ■ Better management of marketing information and customer information ■ Feedback from customers on products

As an example of a company that has set targets and then recorded them in order to demonstrate the success of its web site, consider Mini case study 5.2.

Mini case study 5.2

$11 million in tangible benefits from Kodak's web site

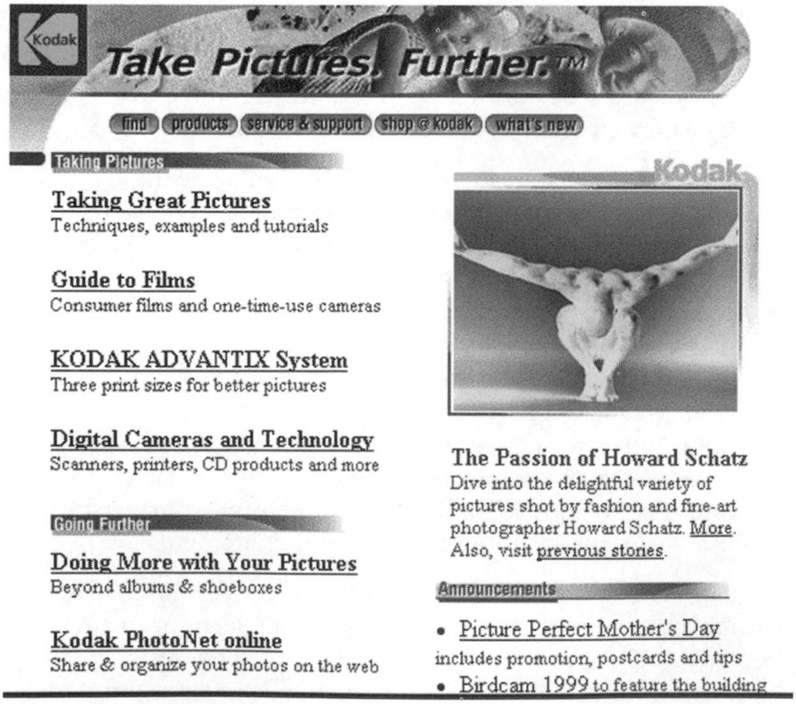

Fig. 5.7 Kodak web site

Kodak is an example of a company that recognised the threat posed by the new digital medium and has turned it to its advantage. Through promoting digital cameras and producing online services such as the 'Photo Net' referred to in Fig. 5.7, Kodak is now in a good position to gain revenues from new products and markets. In addition to gaining more revenue, Kodak has been able to improve customer service while also dramatically reducing costs.

Tim Nichols of Eastman Kodak estimates that $11 million in profits was created by Kodak's customer service site in 1996 through improved:

■ *Customer retention*. This is estimated at over $3.5 million since the site receives over 25 000 contacts per day and customer satisfaction surveys reveal that through having their problems successfully resolved, customers are likely to remain loyal.
■ *Cost avoidance*. Estimated at $1.6 million through savings on 55 000 software drivers downloaded rather than dispatched on disk; 201 000 information sheets on products that normally cost $5 to dispatch and 108 000 dealer location requests.
■ *Incremental sales*. Cross-selling of products while customers are searching the site is thought to account for nearly $3 million in extra sales.
■ *Product application assistance*. Higher conversion rates from potential buyers to actual buyers are thought to occur since customers have their queries answered by information on the web site. This is again thought to account for $3 million in sales.

Source: Web management strategies newsletter (*www.ioma.com*).

In Chapters 11, 13 and 14 we look at specific benefits for implementing e-commerce and the consumer and business-to-business markets.

Situation review

The situation review is best known as a marketing audit of the current effectiveness of marketing activities within a company and environmental factors outside a company that should govern the way the strategy is developed. We will consider internal and external audits separately, and will then present a structured analysis of the opportunities and threats presented by the new medium.

Internal audits

The internal audit will review the way in which the web site is currently used and will assess its effectiveness. The audit is likely to review the following elements of a web site, which are described in more detail in Chapter 12.

1 Business effectiveness

This will include the contribution of the site to revenue (*see* the section above on the Internet contribution), profitability and any indications of the corporate mission for the site. The costs of producing and updating the site will also be reviewed: that is, a cost-benefit analysis.

2 Marketing effectiveness

These measures may include:

- leads;
- sales;
- retention;
- market share;
- brand enhancement and loyalty;
- customer service.

These measures will be assessed for each of the different product lines produced on the web site. The way in which the elements of the marketing mix are utilised will also be reviewed.

3 Internet effectiveness

These are specific measures that are used to assess the way in which the web site is used, and the characteristics of the audience. They are described in more detail in Chapter 12. Such measures include hits and page impressions, which are collected from the log file, and also more conventional techniques such as focus groups and questionnaires sent to existing customers. From a marketing point of view, it should be noted whether the value proposition of the site to the customer is clear.

External audits

External audits consider the business and economic environment in which the company operates. These include the economic, political, fiscal, legal, social, cultural and technological factors usually referred to by the SLEPT acronym. Of these various factors, it is worth noting how three of these are particularly relevant to the Internet and should be monitored regularly since the way in which they vary will directly affect the viability of the Internet channel. The three most significant factors are:

1 *Legal constraints*. What are the legal limitations to online promotion and trade (*see* Chapter 11)?
2 *Social constraints*. What proportion of target customers are online? How do customers behave differently when they are online?
3 *Technological constraints*. What is the current availability of technology to access the Internet and how is it likely to vary in the future?

The external audit should also consider the state of the market in terms of customers and competitors. Pertinent factors for the Internet include:

- The size of the market, in terms of potential customers who have access to the Internet. This should be considered as the number and percentage of total potential customers.
- The type of marketplace. (Are customers purchasing through price comparison services? *See* the section on assessing threats, later in this chapter.)
- How the market share varies across different countries and for different products and services.

The way competitors of a company use the Internet medium should also be assessed. This should include:

- how competitors make use of intermediaries on the Internet and for fulfilment;
- how the channels of competitors make use of the Internet.

Conducting an audit of Internet-based competitors is more difficult than a traditional audit of competitors. Normally competitors will be well known. With the Internet, there may be companies that are quite significant operators in this medium, but which are newly established. This is particularly the case with retail sales. For example, successful new companies have developed on the Internet selling books, music, CDs and electronic components and hardware. As a consequence, companies need to review the Internet-based performance of both existing and new players. Companies should review:

- well-known local competitors (for example, UK/European competitors for British companies);
- well-known international competitors;
- new Internet companies local and worldwide (within sector and out of sector).

Competitors' sites can be reviewed using a more limited version of the Internet marketing audit discussed in the previous section. It will not be possible to assess the performance of the site in detail, by means of monitoring leads and log files. But it will be possible to assess the range of products and services available via the Internet, the volume of information available, the value proposition offered by competitors, the offers used and the graphic design and technical sophistication of their sites.

Web sites are available to assist benchmarking. In the UK Zenithmedia (*www.zenithmedia.co.uk*) presents the main operators in sectors such as finance, construction and industry. In the USA Netmarketing Online Magazine (*www.netb2b.com*) and Business 2.0 magazine (*www.business2.com*) review sites and classify them according to how successful they are. The relevant industry sections in a directory such as Yahoo! (*www.yahoo.com*) may reveal the names of competitors who are proactively promoting their web site (through an entry in the directory).

Chase (1998) advocates that when benchmarking, companies should review competitors' sites, identifying best practices, worst practices and next practices. Next practices are those that a company identifies by looking beyond its own industry sector to see what leading Internet companies such as Amazon (*www.amazon.com*) and Cisco (*www.cisco.com*) are doing. For instance a company in the financial services industry could look at what portal sites are providing and see if there are any lessons to be learnt on ways to make information provision easier.

In addition to assessing competitors when a company first sets up a web site, there should also be a regular review. This could occur annually, as part of the marketing planning process. However, it could be argued that, given the dynamic nature of the Internet and the speed at which companies change their marketing mix in order to gain tactical advantage, it is necessary to monitor more frequently. Some companies will employ a member of marketing staff to continuously scan their competitors' sites. This is particularly true for those in a business-to-business environment with a small number of clearly identified competitors. In this environment, it is also prudent to monitor customers' web sites frequently.

When undertaking scanning of available web sites, the key differences that should be watched out for are:

- new approaches from existing companies;
- new companies starting on the Internet;
- new technologies and design techniques on the site which may give a competitive advantage.

Assessing opportunities and threats

Companies should conduct a structured analysis of the external opportunities and threats that are presented by the Internet environment. They should also consider their own strengths and weaknesses in the Internet marketing environment. Summarising the results through SWOT analysis will clearly highlight the opportunities and threats. Appropriate planning to counter the threats and take advantage of the opportunities can then be built into the Internet marketing plan. An example of a typical SWOT analysis of Internet marketing related strengths and weaknesses is shown in Fig. 5.8. As is often the case with SWOT analysis, the opportunities available to a company are the opposite of the threats presented by other companies. The strengths and weaknesses will vary according to the company involved, but many of the strengths and weaknesses are dependent on the capacity of senior management to acknowledge and act on change.

In order to exploit opportunities to gain competitive advantage it is essential for companies to act quickly. Competitive advantage tends to be short-lived on the Internet since it is easy for competitors to monitor each other. When a company sees that its competitor has a better offer or service, it will counter with a similar

Fig. 5.8 A generic SWOT matrix showing typical opportunities and threats presented by the Internet

service. However, if a company is the first with a truly innovative service, then this will be valuable in capturing market share. Once customers have used a service, and are happy with the service, they may not return to their original supplier. There are probably still opportunities for companies to 'Amazon their sector' or build up a clear market leadership on the Internet.

Assessing threats

Figure 5.9 shows Michael Porter's classic 1980 model of the five main business forces that impact a company. Consideration of the effect of these forces is especially relevant to a company reviewing how the Internet may impact on its business. We will now review these factors in more detail, in the approximate order by which companies are most likely to be affected by them on the Internet.

1 Threat of new entrants

For a company to set up a rival service on the Internet is common. The examples of Amazon (books), Travelocity (travel), eBay (auctions), Security First National Bank (banking) are well known. The Internet represents a particular threat in this area because it is relatively easy to start up a business with limited capital since no retail distribution channel is required: goods are sold direct. In other words, the barriers to entry in any particular sector become lower since the Internet is a cheaper medium over which to do business. For business-to-business companies, the threat of new entrants is smaller if these require a manufacturing infrastructure.

2 Threat of substitute products and services

The Internet is particularly good as a means of providing information-based services at a lower cost. The greatest threats are likely to occur where product fulfilment can occur over the Internet, as is the case with delivering share prices, industry-specific news or software. This threat may not affect many business sectors, but is vital in some, such as newspaper, magazine and book publishing, music and software distribution.

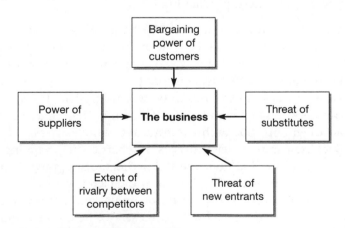

Fig. 5.9 Porter's five forces model
Source: Porter (1980).

135

3 Bargaining power of customers

The bargaining power of customers is greatly increased when they are using the Internet to evaluate products, and compare prices. For retail products or low-value business-to-business products, services are becoming available that make it easy to look at the cost of a particular product from several different distributors or to search for a similar product from several different manufacturers. Such services include Amazon 'Shop The Web' (*www.amazon.com*) and Yahoo! shopping (*www.yahoo.com*). The overall effect of such price comparison services will be to make the price of products more transparent and to make customers more price aware. Both of these outcomes are likely to drive down the price of retail products over time. *See* Chapters 7 and 15 for further examples.

Diamantopoulos and Matthews (1993) suggest there are two aspects of competition that affect an organisation's pricing. The first is the structure of the market – the greater the number of competitors and the visibility of their prices the nearer the market is to being a *perfect market*. The implication of a perfect market is that an organisation will be less able to control prices, but must respond to competitors' pricing strategies. The second is the perceived value of the product. If a brand is differentiated in some way, it may be less subject to downward pressure on price. As well as making pricing more transparent, the Internet does lead to opportunities to differentiate in information describing products or through added-value services. Whatever the combination of these factors, it seems clear that the Internet will lead to more competition-based pricing.

Kotler (1997) suggests that in the face of price cuts from competitors in a market, a company has the following choices:

(a) Maintain the price (assuming that Internet-derived sales are unlikely to decrease price).
(b) Reduce the price (to avoid losing market share).
(c) Raise perceived quality or differentiate product further by adding value services possibly using the Internet. Customer service is a key differentiator on the Internet.
(d) Introduce new lower-priced product lines.

In the business-to-business arena too, the bargaining power of customers is likely to be increased since they will become aware of alternative products and services that they may previously have been unaware of, and will then use this knowledge to negotiate. A further issue is that the ease of use of the Internet channel makes it easier for customers to swap between suppliers. If a specific EDI link has to be set up between one company and another, there may be reluctance to change this arrangement. But with the Internet, which offers a more standard method for purchase through web browsers, the barriers to swapping are lower. It should be noted, however, that there are still barriers to swapping since once a customer invests time in understanding how to use a web site to select and purchase products, he or she may not want to learn how to use another service. It is for this reason that a company that offers a web-based service before its competitors has a competitive advantage.

4 Power of suppliers

This is a relatively minor factor in terms of marketing, but the argument given above in relation to the bargaining power of customers can be reversed. The Internet tends to reduce the power of suppliers since barriers to migrating to a different supplier are reduced.

5 Extent of rivalry between competitors

The threats from existing competitors will continue, with the Internet perhaps increasing rivalry since price comparison is more readily possible, and new products, services and ways of selling or business models will occur using the Internet.

From the review above, it should be apparent that the extent of the threats will be dependent on the particular market in which a company operates. Generally, the threats seem to be greatest for companies that currently sell through retail distributors and which have products that can be readily delivered to customers across the Internet or via parcel courier. Containing threats that arise from changes to channel partnerships caused by disintermediation is discussed further in Chapter 7.

Strategy formulation

Since the Internet is a relatively new medium, and many companies are developing a strategy for the first time, a large number of strategic factors must be considered, in order to make best use of it. Many companies will not have had the resources or time to consider these. In this section we shall cover all the main strategic options that should be considered.

Amount of investment and commitment to the Internet

Arguably, the most important strategic decision taken by a company will be the extent of commitment given by the managing director, or senior management team, to the Internet. If the strength of this commitment (or a decision for more limited investment) is not clear, it will be very difficult for those implementing the system to have direction. Verbal and written commitment to the Internet medium is helpful in promoting the use of the Internet across the company, but of course it is financial commitment that is crucial. A 1998 report by KPMG consultants on the development of electronic commerce in Europe found that there was a correlation between the amount spent on the Internet and the revenues received. In a survey of 500 companies with a turnover of more than $300 million the leading 10 per cent of companies in terms of online revenues had an average expenditure on the Internet of $222 000 per year, compared with less than $130 000 in other companies (Baker, 1998). The leaders also tended to have the most management 'buy-in'.

The amount invested in the Internet should be based on the anticipated contribution the Internet will make to a business. It was explained earlier in this chapter that for some companies, such as Dell and Cisco, which committed to this channel early on, the Internet contribution is now over 50 per cent.

To decide on an appropriate investment in the Internet is, in part, an act of faith by senior managers since it will be based on forecast levels of use of the Internet. There are, however, models available to assist them in deciding on the amount of investment. Kumar (1999) suggests that a company should decide whether the Internet will primarily *complement* the company's other channels or primarily *replace* other channels. Clearly, if it is believed that the Internet will primarily replace other channels, then it is important to invest in the promotion and infrastructure to achieve this. This is a key decision as the company is essentially deciding whether the Internet is 'just another communications and/or sales channel' or whether it will fundamentally change the way it communicates and sells to its customers.

Figure 5.10 summarises the main decisions on which a company should base its commitment to the Internet. Kumar (1999) suggests that replacement is most likely to happen when:

- customer access to the Internet is high;
- the Internet can offer a better value proposition than other media (*see* the section on this topic later in this chapter);
- the product can be delivered over the Internet (it can be argued that this condition is not essential for replacement, so it is not shown in the figure);
- the product can be standardised (the user does not usually need to view to purchase).

Only if all three conditions are met will there be primarily a replacement effect. The fewer the conditions more met, the likely is it that there will be a complementary effect.

From an analysis such as that in Fig. 5.10 it should be possible to state whether the company strategy should be directed as a complementary or as a replacement

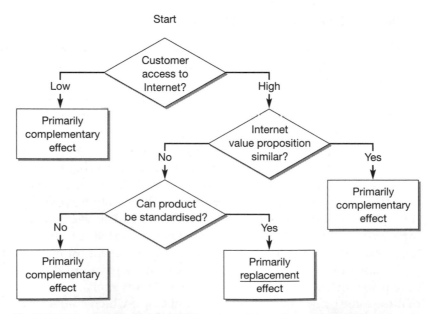

Fig. 5.10 Flow chart for deciding on the extent of dependence on the Internet
Source: After Kumar (1999).

scenario. As mentioned in relation to the question of the contribution of the Internet to its business, the company should repeat the analysis for different product segments and different markets. It will then be possible to state the company's overall commitment to the Internet. This can be achieved in the form of a matrix such as that in Fig. 5.11. If the future strategic importance of the Internet is high, with replacement likely, then a significant investment needs to be made in the Internet, and a company's mission needs to be directed towards replacement. If the future strategic importance of the Internet is low then this still needs to be recognised, and appropriate investment made.

An alternative model for considering the likely importance of the Internet to a company is provided by de Kare-Silver (1998). This model, developed for the retail sector, implies that commitment should be based on a single factor: the proportion of the target market who are likely to use the channel. Of course, the propensity of the target market to use the medium is dependent on a number of other factors, and de Kare-Silver gives guidelines suggesting how these should be assessed. These guidelines are known as the ES or 'Electronic shopping' test (*see* Mini case study 5.3).

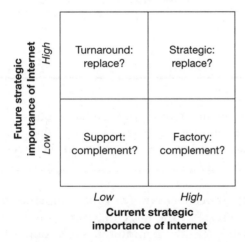

Fig. 5.11 Strategic Internet importance grid based on the McFarlan (1984) model for information systems investment

The Electronic Shopping or ES test

The ES test was developed by de Kare-Silver (1998) to assess the extent to which consumers are likely to purchase a retail product using the Internet. De Kare-Silver suggests factors that should be considered in the ES test:

1 *Product characteristics*. Does the product need to be physically tried, or touched, before it is bought?

2 *Familiarity and confidence*. Considers the degree to which the consumer recognises and trusts the product and brand.

▶ **Mini case study** *continued*

3 *Consumer attributes*. These shape the buyer's behaviour – is he or she amenable to online purchases (i.e. in terms of access to the technology and skills available) and does he or she no longer wish to shop for a product in a traditional retail environment? For example, a student familiar with technology may buy a CD online because he or she is comfortable with the technology. An elderly person looking for a classical CD would probably not have access to the technology and might prefer to purchase an item in person.

In his book, de Kare-Silver describes a method for ranking products. Product characteristics and familiarity and confidence are marked out of 10, and consumer attributes are marked out of 30. Using this method, he scores products as shown in Table 5.4:

Table 5.4 Product scores in de Kare-Silver's (1998) Electronic Shopping (ES) potential test

Product	Product characteristics (10)	Familiarity and confidence (10)	Consumer attributes (30)	Total
1. Groceries	4	8	15	27
2. Mortgages	10	1	4	15
3. Travel	10	6	15	31
4. Books	8	7	23	38

De Kare-Silver states that any product scoring over 20 has good potential, since the score for consumer attributes is likely to increase through time. Given this, he suggests companies will regularly need to review the score for their products.

De Kare-Silver also suggests strategic alternatives for companies that could be selected according to the percentage of the target market using the channel and the commitment of the company. The idea behind this suggestion is that the commitment should mirror the readiness of consumers to use the new medium. In other words, it is probably wasteful of resources if a company is a pioneer when only a small proportion of the channel are using the Internet. Alternatively, a company should not be resisting development when a medium to high proportion of the target market are using the Internet.

The strategic alternatives given in Fig. 5.12 range from those where there is a limited response to the medium such as 'information only' or 'subsume' in business through to spinning off the electronic commerce part of a company into a 'separate business' or even 'switching fully' to an Internet-based business. Although the 'switch fully' alternative may seem unlikely for many businesses, it is already happening. In the UK, the Automobile Association and British Airways have closed the majority of their retail outlets since orders are predominately placed via the Internet or by phone.

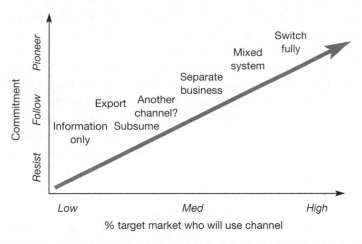

Fig. 5.12 Strategic options for a company in relation to the importance of the Internet as a channel
Source: de Kare-Silver (1998).

Activity 5.2

Assessing the strategic value of the Internet

Assess the likely future importance of the Internet for the following products over a 5– to 10-year time period:

- travel products;
- financial services;
- books;
- clothing;
- electronic components;
- industrial chemicals;
- management consultancy;
- engineering contracts.

You should use the terms described in the previous section to describe the strategic importance of the Internet, defining whether the role of the Internet for different products within each category will be complementary or replacement.

Market and product positioning

The Internet offers new opportunities for selling new products into new markets. These present strategic options that need to be evaluated. These options can be evaluated on the matrix shown in Fig. 1.1. As explained in Chapter 1, the Internet has great potential for selling an existing product into existing or new markets. As a starting-point, many companies will use the Internet to help sell existing products into existing markets. The Internet channel can help consolidate or increase market share for this sector by providing additional promotion and support facilities.

It is, however, the other quadrants in the matrix that offer the greatest opportunities for companies to make new sales that would probably not been achieved without a web site (or certainly at a lower cost per sale). The top-left quadrant, indicating opportunities for selling existing products into new geographical markets, represents a common approach taken by companies, particularly small or medium-sized enterprises (SMEs) that do not have existing sales channels into overseas countries. When assessing this alternative, companies will consider three main objectives that will need to be fulfilled in order successfully to exploit the new market. The objectives are to achieve adequate promotion, sales and fulfilment of the product. Whether the objectives can be achieved should be carefully analysed by asking questions such as:

■ Is an existing infrastructure in place for fulfilment?
■ What will be the impact on the existing channel such as agents/distributors?
■ Is the product standardised so that it is suitable for being purchased from a web site?

A less evident benefit of the Internet is that, as well as selling into new geographical markets, companies can also sell products to new market segments or different types of customer. This may happen simply as a by-product of having a web site. For example, RS Components, a company that is featured in Case study 5.1, found that 10 per cent of its web-site sales were to individual consumers rather than traditional business customers. The retailer Argos found the opposite was true, with 10 per cent of web site sales to businesses, its traditional market being consumer based. The Internet may offer further opportunities for selling to market sub-segments that have not previously been targeted. For example, a product sold to large businesses may also appeal to SMEs, or a product targeted at young people could also appeal to some members of an older audience.

In addition to assessing how existing products can be sold via the Internet, companies should also evaluate whether new products can be developed that can be promoted or sold via the Internet (the two right-hand quadrants in Fig. 1.1). These may differ from existing physical products and could include information products that can be delivered over the Web. Such products may not be charged for, but will add value to existing products. Ghosh (1998) talks about developing new products or adding 'digital value' to a web site. He states that companies should ask the following questions:

1 Can I offer additional information or transaction services to my existing customer base?
2 Can I address the needs of new customer segments by repackaging my current information assets or by creating new business propositions using the Internet?
3 Can I use my ability to attract customers to generate new sources of revenue such as advertising or sales of complementary products?
4 Will my current business be significantly harmed by other companies providing some of the value I currently offer?

In addition Ghosh (1998) suggests that companies should provide free sector-specific information on 'digital' value to help build an audience. He refers to this process as building a 'customer magnet'. There is good potential for customer magnets in specialised vertical markets served by business-to-business companies. For example, a customer magnet could be developed for the construction industry, agrochemicals, biotechnology or independent financial advisers.

Internet marketplace positioning

The advent of the Internet forces companies to reappraise the way in which they sell products, since new and existing competitors will take advantage of this new distribution channel, even if one company does not. For the company, this raises questions such as which new market structures will arise, which marketplaces it can operate in, and what the implications of the new marketplaces are for existing distribution strategy arrangements. Chapter 7 examines all these questions.

Setting the Internet marketing value proposition

Internet marketing consultants suggest that in the same way that any company or product will only be successful if it has a unique selling proposition, it is also necessary for companies to have a value proposition for their web site or Internet presence. This proposition should be clearly evident to customers using the site and should indicate reasons for purchasing from the company, or for visiting the site in the future. The proposition may be based on existing product differentiation in terms of quality or product features or cost. Ideally, the Internet web site should have an additional value proposition to further differentiate the company's products or services. Having a clear Internet value proposition has several benefits:

- It helps distinguish the site from its competitors (this should be a web site design objective).
- It helps provide a focus to marketing efforts, and company staff are clear about the purpose of the site.
- If the proposition is clear it can be used for PR, and word of mouth recommendations may be made about the company. For example, the clear proposition of Amazon on its site is that prices are reduced by up to 40 per cent and that a wide range of three million titles are available.
- It can be linked to the normal product propositions of a company or its product.

RS Components is a good example of a company with a clearly defined web site proposition which has built success as a result of this. This example is explored in Case study 5.1.

CASE STUDY 5.1   **RS COMPONENTS**

Fig. 5.13 RS Components web site (*rswww.com*)

RS Components UK, part of Electrocomponents plc, is Europe's leading distributor of electronic, electrical and mechanical components, instruments and associated tools. The company employs 2 000 people and dispatches over 21 000 parcels every day for UK distribution. RS Components UK sales for the 12 months ending 31 March, 1996 were £368 million.

Electrocomponents plc turnover for 1997 was £605 million. The company sells its products through its 3-in-1 catalogue, which is distributed three times a year and also available electronically on CD-ROM. Specialized catalogues for mechanical engineers and health and safety products have also been recently launched.

> 'We wanted to create a new channel for doing business online. Reliability, responsiveness and customer service are crucial to RS Components. The Internet channel had to be as robust and interactive as state-of-the-art technology allows, whilst also delivering fast and detailed access to 100 000 products. In only seven months we built a transactional, interactive Web site to carry out our core business online. Our supplier partners BroadVision and Cambridge Technology Partners were selected for their experience but also because they understood the particular challenges we faced in taking a multinational plc and putting its business on the web.' – Head of Internet Trading, Bernard Hewitt.

RS Components wanted to offer customers another convenient choice of how to do business with them, and to encourage customers' loyalty. They recognized that to keep customers coming back to the web site, they would have to offer something unique. Fast search and retrieval of 100 000 products, combined with personalized customer promotions, offers an immediate advantage over their printed catalogue and creates an instant reason to do business online. RS Components chose BroadVision because it is a robust and flexible application with personalization at its core. They believed that BroadVision created a new benchmark for e-commerce in the UK. In their first week of trading online, the site was able to support as many as 7 000 visitors in one day with up to 250 concurrent users.

> *'The Internet is a natural fit for RS Components' business model. We sell and deliver thousands of products to thousands of customers, quickly, reliably and at market prices. We have increased the ease and choice of how existing customers do business with us whilst reaching out to new customers cost effectively.'* – Head of Internet Trading, Bernard Hewitt.

A summary of the RS Components Internet Value Proposition according to David Sone is:

Product		Value
+		+
Information	=	Product selection
+		+
Services		Delivery, after sales

Solution

The business challenges:

- Build a superior catalogue-based web site which is also fully transactional and capable of supporting volume business online.
- Provide quick search and retrieval of detailed information on all 100 000 products, on all logical search criteria.
- Create an online business environment robust enough to support a customer base of 140 000 customers, 40% of whom already have easy Internet access.
- Integrate the web site all the way, through existing customer order processing for same day dispatch and next day delivery in line with telephone and fax ordering.
- Generate personalized promotions based on buying habits for effective customer interaction and cross-selling of product groups.
- Extend the reach of RS Components to potential customers not in receipt of the catalogue. BroadVision Solution, BroadVision One-To-One Application System Version 2.6 Applications Areas Business to consumer content, knowledge management, and commerce. Hardware platform, database and security integrated into IBM ES/9000 based customer order processing system (COP) Sun Ultra Server 4000, Oracle database, Verity Search '97 search engine.

▶ **Case study** *continued*

Benefits

- *Customised user interface*: Masks complex underlying technology.
- *Online order processing*: Automatic generation of correct pricing based on account or cash customer status.
- *Integration*: Seamless integration offers same day dispatch service as existing business channels.
- *Customer relationship marketing*: Personalized promotions to each individual customer according to purchase profile.
- *Merchandising*: Cross-promotion of product groups.

RS Components' Internet vision

The RS Components team headed by Bernard Hewitt, Head of Internet Trading and David Sones, Head of Technical Development, worked with BroadVision partner Cambridge Technology Partners to develop their vision for a new business channel via the Internet.

Significantly, the project had the blessing of CEO Bob Lawson, which ensured that the internal project team met with full and timely cooperation and input from every area of the business. RS created a new autonomous Internet Trading division to handle project development, headed by board-level directors who understand the Internet's potential as a channel for business.

Cambridge Technology Partners' consulting skills, together with BroadVision's One-To-One technology, ensured that the project objectives and time scales were precise and achievable. The site went live in seven months, a week earlier than anticipated.

The results

In the first eight months from when the site was introduced RS Components (*rswww.com*) recorded:

- 280 000 sessions (visits);
- 44 000 registered customers;
- 84 000 repeat visits;
- 23 minutes average time on site;
- £81 average order value.
- 10 per cent private rather than trade.

Source: Sun Microsystems UK web site (*www.sun.co.uk*)

Questions

1 What are the main business benefits that RS Components wanted to achieve through introducing a web site?

2 Explain what is meant by the 'Internet value proposition' in the case of RS Components.

3 The 'Broadvision' software used to implement part of the site is mentioned extensively. What do you think is the value of this software to the company?

4 What approach did the company take to implementing the system in terms of resources and organisational structure, given the strategic vision of the senior managers?

While it may be beneficial to have a unique value proposition for a web site, it may not be practical in some sectors. For example, a financial services provider that is competing in a very crowded sector, which has similar products, will find it difficult to make its proposition clear. Ideally, it should support the product, price or quality differentiation established as part of the core marketing strategy.

Activity 5.3

Internet value proposition

Visit the web sites of the following companies and, in one or two sentences each, summarise their Internet value proposition. You should also explain how they use the content of the web site to indicate their value proposition to customers.

1 CDNow (*www.cdnow.com*).
2 Boots the Chemist (*www.boots.co.uk*).
3 Renold's Chain (*www.renold.com*).
4 Harrods (*www.harrods.com*).

Planning, scheduling, resource allocation and monitoring

Once the Internet marketing strategy has been formulated, a more detailed strategy implementation plan will need to be drawn up. This is the Internet marketing plan described in Chapter 6.

SUMMARY

1 The development of web sites tends to follow a natural progression from basic static 'brochureware' sites through simple interactive sites with query facilities to dynamic sites offering personalisation of services for customers. It is the job of the Internet marketing strategist to develop a proactive rather than reactive strategy.

2 When a company web site is first conceived, how a company formulates strategies to deal with the opportunities and threats presented requires a separate, detailed Internet marketing strategy which is, however, integrated with the company's existing business and marketing objectives.

3 The Internet marketing strategy should follow a similar form to a traditional strategic marketing planning process and should include:
   - goal setting;
   - situation review;
   - strategy formulation;
   - resource allocation and monitoring.
   A feedback loop should be established to ensure the site is monitored and modifications are fed back into the strategy development.

4 Strategic goal setting should involve:
   - setting business objectives that the Internet can help achieve;
   - assessing and stating the contribution that the Internet will make to the business in the future, both as a proportion of revenue, and in terms of whether the Internet will complement or replace other media;

■ stating the full range of business benefits that are sought, such as improved corporate image, cost reduction, more leads and sales and improved customer service.

5 The situation review will include auditing of the existing web site for its current contribution and design and then benchmarking this against competitors' sites. Opportunities and threats will also be assessed at this time.

6 Strategy formulation will involve defining a company's commitment to the Internet; setting an appropriate value proposition for customers of the web site; and identifying the role of the Internet in exploiting new markets, marketplaces and distribution channels and in delivering new products and services.

EXERCISES AND QUESTIONS

Self-assessment exercises

1 Draw a diagram that summarises the stages through which a company's web site may evolve.

2 What is meant by the 'Internet contribution', and what is its relevance to strategy?

3 What is the role of monitoring in the strategic planning process?

4 Summarise the main tangible and intangible business benefits of the Internet to a company.

5 What is the purpose of an Internet marketing audit? What should it involve?

6 What does a company need in order to be able to state clearly in the mission statement its strategic position relative to the Internet?

7 What are the market and product positioning opportunities offered by the Internet?

8 What are the distribution channel options for a manufacturing company?

Discussion questions

1 Discuss the frequency with which an Internet marketing strategy should be updated for a company to remain competitive.

2 Discuss the value to marketers of models for web site development and evolution.

3 'A company that migrates its existing value proposition to the Internet will not take full advantage of the new medium.' Discuss.

4 'Setting long-term strategic objectives for a web site is unrealistic since the rate of change in the marketplace is so rapid.' Discuss.

Essay questions

1 Explain the essential elements of an Internet marketing strategy.

2 How should a company approach a review of the current impact on it of a web site?

3 What issues does the Internet raise in relation to dealing with distribution of products through channel partners?

4 Summarise the opportunities and threats presented by the Internet to a company that currently has either no site or a simple, static brochureware site.

5 What strategy tools and models are available to help in formulating a company's strategic approach to the Internet?

Examination questions

1 When evaluating the business benefits of a web site, which factors are likely to be common to most companies?

2 Use Porter's five forces model to discuss the competitive threats presented to a company by other web sites.

3 Which factors will affect whether the Internet has primarily a complementary effect or a replacement effect on a company?

4 Describe different stages in the sophistication of development of a web site, giving examples of the services provided at each stage.

5 Briefly explain the purpose and activities involved in an external audit conducted as part of the development of an Internet marketing strategy.

6 What is the importance of measurement within the Internet marketing process?

7 Which factors would a retail company consider when assessing the suitability of its product for Internet sales?

8 Explain what is meant by the Internet value proposition, and give two examples of the value proposition for web sites with which you are familiar.

REFERENCES

Andersen Consulting (1999) *Your Choice. How eCommerce could impact Europe's future*. Andersen Consulting. Report available from *www.andersen.com*.

Baker, P. (1998) *Electronic Commerce. Research Report 1998*. London: KPMG Management Consulting.

Chase, L. (1998) *Essential Business Tactics for the Net*. New York: Wiley and Sons.

de Kare-Silver, M. (1998) *eShock*. Basingstoke, UK: Macmillan.

Diamantopoulos, A. and Matthews, B. (1993) *Making Pricing Decisions. A study of managerial practice*. London: Chapman & Hall.

Ghosh, S. (1998) 'Making business sense of the Internet', *Harvard Business Review*, March–April, 126–35.

Kotler, P. (1997) *Marketing Management: Analysis, planning, implementation and control* (9th international edn). Upper Saddle River, NJ: Prentice Hall.

Kumar, N. (1999) 'Internet distribution strategies: dilemmas for the incumbent', *Financial Times*, Special Issue on Mastering Information Management, No 7. Electronic Commerce (*www.ftmastering.com*).

McFarlan, F.W. (1984) 'Information technology changes the way you compete', *Harvard Business Review*, May–June, 54–61.

McDonald, M. (1999) 'Strategic marketing planning: theory and practice', in Baker, M. (ed.) *The CIM Marketing Book* (4th edn). Oxford: Butterworth-Heinemann, pp. 50–77.

Porter, M. (1980) *Competitive Strategy*. New York: The Free Press.

Quelch, J. and Klein, L. (1996) 'The Internet and international marketing', *Sloan Management Review*, Spring, 61–75.

Sterne, J. (1999) *World Wide Web Marketing* (2nd edn). New York: John Wiley and Sons.

FURTHER READING

Baker, M. (ed.) (1999) *The Marketing Book*. Oxford: Butterworth-Heinemann.
Chapter 2, The Basics of Marketing Strategy, and Chapter 3, Strategic Marketing Planning: Theory and Practice, are highly recommended. Chapter 4 describes environmental scanning.

Brassington, F. and Petitt, S. (2000) *Principles of Marketing* (2nd edn). Harlow, UK: Pearson Education.
See companion Prentice Hall web site (*www.booksites.net/brassington2*).
Chapters 10 and 11 describe pricing issues in much more detail than that given in this chapter. Chapters 20, Strategic Management, and 21, Marketing Planning, Management and Control, describe the integration of marketing strategy with business strategy.

de Kare-Silver, M. (1998) *eShock*. Basingstoke, UK: Macmillan.
This business book reviews the implications of the Internet and the strategic options available to retailers and manufacturers. At the time of writing de Kare-Silver had just been appointed as director responsible for e-commerce at retailer Great Universal Stores (GUS).

Dibb, S., Simkin, S., Pride, W. and Ferrel, O. (1997) *Marketing. Concepts and strategies* (3rd European edn). New York: Houghton Mifflin.
See companion Houghton Mifflin web site (*www.busmgt.ulst.ac.uk/h_mifflin/*)
See Chapter 22, Marketing Strategy and Competitive Forces, and Chapter 19, Pricing Concepts.

Ghosh, S. (1998) 'Making business sense of the Internet', *Harvard Business Review*, March–April, 127–35.
This paper gives many US examples of how US companies have adapted to the Internet and asks key questions that should govern the strategy adopted. It is an excellent introduction to strategic approaches.

Kotler, P., Armstrong, G., Saunders, J. and Wong, V. (1999) *Principles of Marketing* (2nd edn). Hemel Hempstead: Prentice Hall, Europe.
See companion Prentice Hall web site for 8th US edn *cw.prenhall.com/bookbind/pubbooks/kotler/*.
See Chapter 3, Strategic Marketing Planning, and Chapter 12, Creating Competitive Advantage.

Kumar, N. (1999) 'Internet distribution strategies: dilemmas for the incumbent', *Financial Times*, Special Issue on Mastering Information Management, 7. Electronic Commerce (*www.ftmastering.com*).
This article assesses the impact of the Internet on manufacturers and their distribution channels. The other articles in this special issue are also interesting.

Stroud, D. (1988) *Internet Strategies, A Corporate Guide to Exploiting the Internet*. Basingstoke, UK: Macmillan Business.
Dick Stroud is a business strategy consultant who directs courses in Internet marketing for the Chartered Institute of Marketing. This book gives a personal view of how companies should define strategies, adapt and manage change.

WEB SITE REFERENCES

A Business Researcher's Interests (*www.brint.com/ecommerce*) has many articles on e-commerce strategy.

CHAPTER 6

The Internet marketing plan

Learning objectives

After reading this chapter, the reader should be able to:

- identify key components of an Internet marketing plan;
- understand key issues of budgeting for Internet marketing;
- assess different options for structuring and resourcing Internet marketing within an organisation;
- appreciate some of the legal constraints on web site production.

Links to other chapters

Chapter 5 should be read before this chapter since Chapter 5 describes how the Internet marketing strategy is developed, and the Internet marketing plan is based on this. More detail is provided on implementing aspects of the plan in later chapters, principally:

- ► Chapter 8, Creating and building the web site.
- ► Chapter 9, Web site promotion.
- ► Chapter 12, Maintaining the web site and measuring Internet marketing effectiveness.

INTRODUCTION

In Chapter 5 we introduced strategic objective setting and reviewed the different strategic approaches that can be adopted to exploit the Internet. This chapter covers the next stage after the strategy has been formulated, which is the development of an Internet marketing plan to achieve the strategic goals. We are now looking to define the tactics to achieve these objectives.

The Internet marketing plan is a short-term, operational planning device detailing both the implementation of the web site and associated marketing communications to achieve the aims of an Internet marketing strategy. The Internet marketing plan can be considered as being at the same level as an advertising plan, sales promotion or pricing plan.

> **Internet marketing plan**
> An operational plan to achieve an Internet marketing strategy through implementation of a new version of a web site and associated marketing communications.

The Internet marketing plan that is described in this chapter draws on elements of different books aiming to give guidance to practitioners implementing a site. These books include those by Bickerton *et al.* (1996, 1998), Sterne (1995, 1999), Bayne (1997) and Vassos (1996). Given the newness of the medium, there are few appraisals of methods of implementing an Internet marketing plan from an academic viewpoint.

This chapter introduces some aspects of implementing the strategy such as promotion and measurement that are covered in more detail in later chapters, but it also covers some issues that are not considered later such as setting the brand identity of the site and legal considerations. It covers practical issues of implementation such as how the Internet marketing function can be structured and how resources should be allocated for the implementation.

The structured framework provided uses the concept of a route planner with different decision points that reflect important choices that need to be made by those defining the strategy. Unlike those in a real-world route planner, the decision points here can arguably occur in any order, but we have tried to place them in a logical order.

Decision point 1: Who are the potential audience?

It was mentioned in Chapter 2 that customer orientation is one of the most important factors in achieving a successful web site. Analyst Patricia Seybold considers it sufficiently important that she has structured a whole book, *Customers.com* (Seybold, 1999), around the concept. Seybold (1999) offers eight guidelines for implementing an Internet strategy (available at Patricia Seybold consulting (*www.customers.com*) and considered in more detail in the business-to-business context in Chapter 14). She considers the first, and most important, to be to 'target the right customer'. What constitutes the 'right customer' will vary for different companies operating in different sectors, but some general principles can be established. First, some companies make the mistake of omitting some important types of site visitor. Table 6.1 summarises the different types of customers, staff or third parties that may visit a web site for information. For a web site to be effective, it should cater for all the different types of audience.

> **Customer orientation**
> Providing content and services on a web site consistent with the different characteristics of the audience of the site.

A survey conducted of the web sites of the top 100 US companies in 1998, and reported by *The Economist* on 4 March 1998, showed that only three – Sun Microsystems, Bell Atlantic and Sun Microsystems – managed to serve their customers, investors and potential employees alike. The survey, completed by Shelley Taylor & Associates, took into account the responses of three types of users – customers, prospective employees and shareholders – and asked over 200 questions. Complete Activity 6.1 to appreciate the difference between a site with good customer orientation, and one without.

Table 6.1 Different potential audiences for a web site

Customers vary by	Staff	Third parties
New or existing prospects	New or existing	New or existing
Size of prospect companies (e.g. small, medium or large)	Different departments	Suppliers
Market type (e.g. different vertical markets)	Sales staff for different markets	Distributors
Location (by country)	Location (by country)	Investors
Members of buying process (decision makers, influencers, buyers)		Media
		Students

Activity 6.1

Achieving customer orientation in a web site

Fig. 6.1 Bell Atlantic web site – best practice in customer orientation

Visit the web sites of the three leading companies in the survey reported in *The Economist* on 4 March 1998. The sites are:

■ Bell Atlantic (*www.bell-atl.com*), *see* Fig. 6.1
■ Sun Microsystems (*www.sun.com*)
■ AT&T (*www.att.com*)

Evaluate the home page and navigate the site, and assess how well the site meets the needs of all the different potential audience types described in Table 6.1. State which audience types the sites do not cater for so well.

Although Activity 6.1 has suggested that it is useful to provide content suited to the breadth of a site's audience, Seybold's assertion is that the effort of developing content should not be equally distributed. Rather, it should target those customers who can have the biggest impact on the company's profitability. These customers could be:

- *the most profitable customers* – provide better services to the top 20 per cent of customers and more cross-sales may result;
- *the largest customers* – an extranet could be produced to service these customers, and increase their loyalty;
- *customers who are difficult to target using other media* – an insurance company looking to target younger drivers could use the Web as a vehicle for this;
- *customers who are not brand loyal* – incentives, promotion and a good level of service quality could be provided by the web site to try and retain such customers;
- *decision makers* – the site should provide the type of information to establish the credibility of the company for decision makers.

A more rigorous segmentation will follow that of Wind and Cardazo (1974), who identify three macro-segmentation bases for organisations, namely their size, location and usage rate of products. These can then be subdivided into micro-segmentation bases considering issues such as products, decision-making unit and the buyer–seller relationship. As would be expected, the macro level and micro level typically correspond to the hierarchy of menu choices on a web site. Consumer markets will also follow geographic segments, but are then broken down according to demographics, psychographics, and behaviour segments. An example of such segmentation is provided by Scottish Amicable, the financial services provider, which put three typical customer profiles, of increasing age and responsibilities, on its home page, as a means of providing more detailed information.

Localisation

A specific aspect of customer orientation or segmentation is the decision whether to include specific content for particular countries. This is referred to as localisation. A site may need to support customers from a range of countries with:

- different product needs;
- language differences;
- cultural differences.

> **Localisation**
> Tailoring of web site information for individual countries or regions.

Localisation will address all these issues. It may be that products will be similar in different countries and localisation will simply involve converting the web site to suit another country. However, in order to be effective, this often needs more than translation, since different promotion concepts may be needed for different countries. Examples of a business-to-consumer site (Durex) and a business-to-business site (Gestetner) are featured in Activity 6.2. Note that each company prioritises different countries according to the size of the market, and this priority then governs the amount of work it puts into localisation.

Activity 6.2

Accommodating internationalx markets using localisation

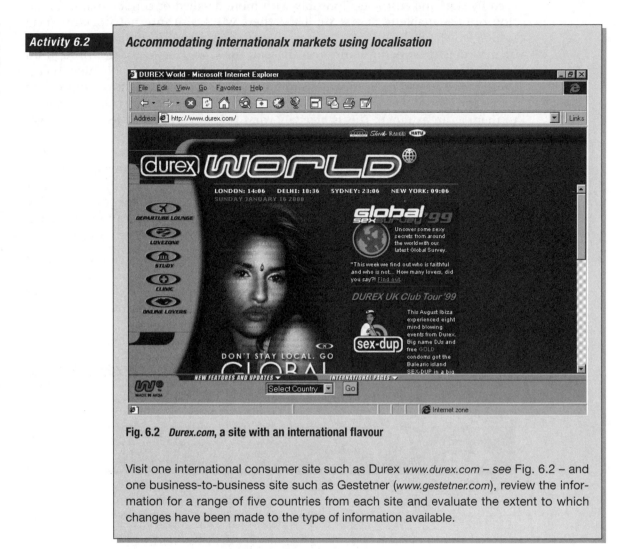

Fig. 6.2 *Durex.com*, a site with an international flavour

Visit one international consumer site such as Durex *www.durex.com* – *see* Fig. 6.2 – and one business-to-business site such as Gestetner (*www.gestetner.com*), review the information for a range of five countries from each site and evaluate the extent to which changes have been made to the type of information available.

Decision point 2: Integrating 'the nets'

When the Internet marketing plan is being defined, the role of intranet, extranet and Internet facilities should be reviewed. The facilities provided by each of the nets follow on from a review of customer orientation, since more detailed information may be provided for particular types of customer. The other reason for considering integrating the nets is the practical one of avoiding duplication and wasted effort. Take the example of a computer supplier. Staff will need to answer many questions by phone from customers enquiring about product specifications and prices, and will need to provide support to customers who have purchased products and are experiencing difficulties. Information on these topics is likely to be available to staff on an intranet in order that they can answer the queries. It is logical to review this

155

information for its relevance to customers and then make it available on the Internet web site. Why develop two customer support systems when one can be used by staff and customers (possibly with more detailed or confidential information only available to staff)? Similarly, there will be an internal stock ordering system which will be linked with a manufacturing system for controlling the status of new machines being built, and the data may well be available through an intranet. Again, much of the information on the intranet may be of value to customers, and in particular to large corporate accounts which need to monitor the status and cost of their orders. In this case, why not make the information available to them as an extranet? This is precisely what Dell has done with its PremierPages service, which is available for large corporate customers (*see* Fig. 6.3).

We will now review two models which can help companies discuss their options for integrating the Internet web sites with intranets and extranets. Figure 6.4 shows the model of Bickerton *et al.* (1998). In order to understand this model, it is necessary to recognise three different levels of use of a web site, as defined by Bickerton. These are similar to the increasing levels of sophistication of Quelch and Klein (1996) that were introduced in Chapter 5. The levels are as follows:

■ *Presentation*. This is the delivery of static information on the web site. It can be thought of as a 'brochureware' site, but may have additional depth of information.
■ *Interaction*. This stage involves methods of communicating with the customer such as the use of interactive forms and e-mail or discussion communities.
■ *Representation*. Representation occurs where the Internet replaces customer services that are normally delivered by human operators. In the case of a bank this stage

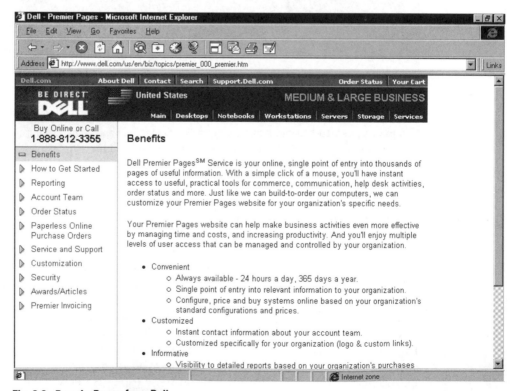

Fig. 6.3 PremierPages from Dell

would involve a customer performing online money transfers between bank accounts or bill payment. IBM has referred to this concept as 'web self-service'.

The grid in Fig. 6.4 shows three alternative strategies that a company could adopt. These strategies are more easily understandable and can be readily discussed through presentation in this form. Strategy A is that adopted by many small companies. They have a web site, which is initially an online brochure (Presentation stage). The marketing plan may then indicate that, six months from launch, interaction facilities may be introduced such as forms to give feedback on products. Finally, it may be planned that the site will be relaunched some 18 months to two years after inception and representation facilities will be included, such as online sales and customer service. Strategy B is one that is typically followed by larger companies. They may follow the initial stages of presentation and interaction, but will only provide their representation facilities to their largest customers. If an extranet is offered, with special login required, then this can be used to differentiate the service provided to favoured companies. This is the approach used by HR Johnson Tiles (*www.johnson-tiles.com*). They offer an extranet buying service that is only available to their larger customers. When the site was launched, they targeted 20 distributors with whom they wanted to do business over the Internet. So far, 12 have been persuaded to do that, resulting in £1 million in orders from the web site annually. A key feature of this extranet system is 'StockWatch'; by clicking on this button customers get a picture of the amount of stock available for the items they regularly order. Finally, strategy C may occur where a company has a great deal of information that is available on the internal company network, and which can be usefully made available to customers, either select customers via the extranet or a wider audience. Strategy C might be one adopted by a technology company such as Dell. Note that the strategy adopted by any single company could involve elements of A, B and C.

Figure 6.5 depicts an alternative model, derived from Friedman and Furey (1999), for comparing the role of open access, Internet-based information with restricted extranet information. This model is best applied in a business-to-

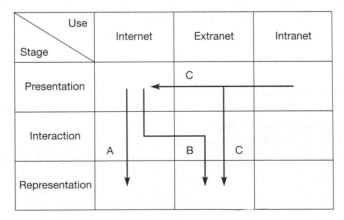

Fig. 6.4 Options for developing different types of IP-based service

Source: Bickerton *et al.* (1998).

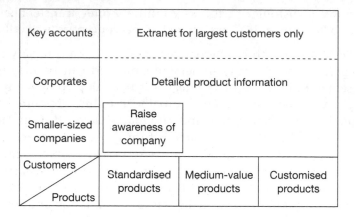

Fig. 6.5 A matrix for segmenting customer information on the Internet according to size of customer
Source: Friedman and Furey (1999).

business context. Their model considers the different types of products a company sells, from lower-cost standardised products through to higher-cost, customised products. These products are then considered in relation to the different sizes of company a company may serve. The core content of the site may appeal to smaller companies, which are perhaps unaware of the company or its products. This information will be provided by the Internet. At the other end of the spectrum, for key accounts which buy the full range of a company's products an extranet may be appropriate. This is again the case with Dell's PremierPages and is similar to path B, shown in Fig. 6.4.

Decision point 3: Defining the scope of Internet marketing communications

The Internet marketing plan should clearly state how the different aspects of marketing will be supported by the web site and the promotional activities necessary to attract customers to the site. It should explain how it will be used for different types of marketing communications and how online methods of communicating with customers will be integrated with current offline methods. For instance:

- Will we use the site URL on all offline campaigns?
- Will we update the site to be consistent with marketing messages in offline campaigns?
- How will PR be handled by the web site?
- How will the medium be used to build relationships with customers? Will it contain personalisation facilities?
- Will the site support sales staff meeting directly with customers?
- How will customer service be supported – what standards will be adopted to provide a good standard of 'electronic customer service'?
- Will online sales be supported – are there any plans for e-commerce?
- Will the site be used to support trade shows?
- How will the medium be used for sales promotions?

These issues are not discussed further at this stage since methods of promotion are described in detail in Chapter 9. E-commerce is described in Chapter 11 and one-to-one communications with the customer are described in Chapter 10.

Decision point 4: How do we 'migrate' our brands on to the Internet?

A successful brand is described by de Chernatony and McDonald (1992) as '*an identifiable product or service augmented in such a way that the buyer or user perceives relevant unique added values which match their needs most closely. Furthermore, its success results from being able to sustain these added values in the face of competition.*' It can be seen that the concept of brand is closely related to the value proposition of a web site, which may include unique value-added features that are often based on customer service. It is suggested by Schwartz (1999) that the Internet-based brand should emphasise service rather than product features. Dell, E*Trade and Amazon are examples of companies which have used this approach.

As well as the broader issues of branding, in terms of value added to a product, there is also a more specific issue of brand identity. Some of the characteristics of a successful brand name are suggested by de Chernatony and McDonald (1992): ideally it should be simple, distinctive, meaningful and compatible with the product. These principles can be readily applied to web-based brands. Examples of brands that fulfil most of these characteristics are CDNow, CarPoint, BUY.COM and e-STEEL. Others that suggest that distinctiveness is most important are Amazon, Yahoo!, Expedia, *Quokka.com* (extreme sports), E*Trade, and FireandWater (HarperCollins) books.

Brands that are newly created for the Internet such as Expedia and *Quokka.com* do not risk damaging existing brands, although it is suggested by de Chernatony and McDonald (1992) that new brand launches are risky activities, and less than 10 per cent of new brands prove successful. The new brand's dimensions such as its emotional and rational appeal to customers should also be reviewed. Online brands may need strong personalities to be prominent in the new medium. The Prudential's Egg brand is an example of such a site (Fig. 8.7).

A company has several options with regard to presenting its brands online. When a company launches or relaunches a web site, it has the following choices with regard to brand identity. These choices may apply either to individual brands or to the entire corporate identity.

1 Migrate traditional brand online

This is probably the most common approach. Companies with brands that are well established in the real world can build on the brand by duplicating it online. Sites from companies such as Ford, Orange and Disney all have identical brand identities and values that would be expected from customers' experience of their offline brands. The only risk of migrating existing brands online is that the brand equity may be reduced if the site is of poor quality in terms of performance, structure or information content. There may also be a missed opportunity, as explained below.

2 Extend traditional brand: variant

Some companies decide to create a slightly different version of their brand when they create their web site. The DHL site (*see* Fig. 3.5) is based on an online brand, 'Red Planet', which used the concept of a spaceship. Users order couriers and track progress of deliveries using controls as on a spaceship console. This approach illustrates well the advantages of a brand variant. The company is able to differentiate itself from similar competing services and can use its distinguishing features in online and offline promotion to differentiate the site from those of its rivals. Cisco uses a similar approach with its Cisco Online Connection brand. The use of an online brand variant helps raise the profile of the web site and assists the customer to think of the site in association with the company. The implications of extending existing brands have been considered by Aaker (1990). He suggests that there may be problems with recognition and also that brand trust and quality associations may be damaged. This can occur on the Internet if a company has, for example, poor quality service on a web site such as not responding to e-mails or slow download speeds.

3 Partner with existing digital brand

It may be that a company can best promote its products in association with a strong existing digital or Internet brand such as Yahoo!, Freeserve or LineOne. For example, the shopping options for record and book sales on Freeserve are branded as Freeserve although they are actually based on sites from other companies such as the record seller Audiostreet (*Audiostreet.com*) (Fig. 6.6). Freeserve is given brand prominence since this is to the advantage of both companies.

4 Create a new digital brand

It may be necessary to create an entirely new digital brand if the existing offline brand has negative connotations or is too traditional for the new medium. An example of a new digital brand is the Egg banking service, which is part of Prudential, a well-established company. Egg can take new approaches without damaging Prudential's brand, and at the same time it is not inhibited by the Prudential brand. Egg is not an entirely online brand since it is primarily accessed by phone. Egg are encouraging some of their 500 000 customers to perform all their transactions online. Another example of a new digital brand is the Go Network portal (www.go.com) created by Disney, which wished to be able to 'own' some of the many online customers who are loyal to one portal. It was felt that Disney could achieve this best through using a completely new brand. The Disney brand might be thought to appeal to a limited younger audience.

Decision point 5: Strategic partnerships and outsourcing

The marketing plan will describe how relationships will be built with other companies to help maximise the potential of the Internet. Such partnerships may take different forms. They may be straight contractual arrangements where a company is paid to design the web site, or they could be partnerships where there is no exchange of money, for example if the company agrees to provide reciprocal links

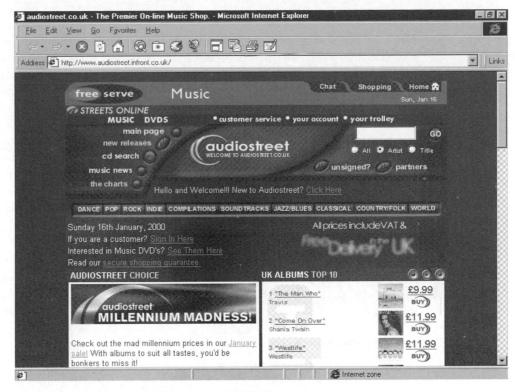

Fig. 6.6 Co-branding between Freeserve and Audiostreet

with the web site of another company. Partnership permits the sharing of skills and experience to help exploit the new medium. Some examples of partnerships that may have to be formed are:

- *Design/technology partnerships*. These are partnerships with companies that can provide site design, development and promotion skills. That may also include an ISP, chosen to host the web site.
- *Promotion partnerships*. These are relationships with media owners and advertising networks for the purpose of driving traffic to the site. Infomediary partners will provide information on customers or host product information on a price comparison site.
- *Reciprocal promotion*. Here promotion occurs through another site in exchange for promotion or co-branding.
- *Distribution partnerships*. Building on existing partnerships with distributors is important, in order to avoid the problems such as channel conflicts, referred to in Chapter 7.
- *Supplier partnerships*. Existing relationships with suppliers may have to be revised to deliver the product and service quality expected by customers ordering via a web site.
- *Legal advice*. Existing legal departments can be used, or it may be necessary to use a firm specialising in Internet marketing law.

We will now go on to identify what are probably the most important types of partnership – those with the consultants and agencies who provide advice and implementation input for the web site.

Acquiring web site skills and outsourcing

The marketing plan should identify the best partners for helping to implement the web site strategy. It will often be necessary to outsource some of the development and promotion of the web site since companies may not have staff with the necessary skills in-house in the marketing or IT departments, or staff may not have time for the additional work. Through outsourcing it may be possible to keep the costs of carrying out the work lower than they would be if new staff were recruited to do the work.

Companies to which work may be outsourced could be known companies which have been recommended, or they could have been evaluated from a choice of suppliers in a 'beauty contest'. If however a company is at the initial stage of considering outsourcing, the task would just involve consideration of the type of company that could perform the work. The main types of company or groups from within the company that can assist in implementing the site are:

1 In-company (marketing department)

It is possible for each function to be done in-house, but with the Internet being a new medium, it may be that staff do not have the experience or skills, or the time, do this.

2 Traditional marketing agency

Many marketing agencies, such as AKQA (*www.akqa.com*) now offer services to support web site development such as the functions listed in Table 6.2. They would argue that they are able to apply their experience of marketing in other media to the Internet.

3 New media agency

New media agencies tend to focus on web site design, development and promotion. Examples include Bluewave (*www.bluewave.com*), APL Digital (*www.apldigital. co. uk*) and Online Magic (*www.onlinemagic.com*). This is a new class of consultancy that has developed with the advent of the Web. They would argue that they have a good mixture of technical staff, graphical designers and even strategists who can make best use of the new medium, which needs quite different design and promotional techniques from other media.

4 IS or IT department

The IT department will have staff with the technical skills to develop a web site. They may, however, not have the necessary understanding of the business to develop a customer-focused web site. If these staff can work with the marketing department this may be a viable model for developing a web site; indeed some large companies have taken such an approach with success.

5 Management/IT consultants

With the realisation that the Internet will have a very large impact on some businesses, to get the most out of a web site may involve more than consideration of marketing in the narrow sense of the word. It may involve consideration of integration of a company's systems with suppliers and distributors and integration of existing sales order processing and stock control systems with a web site. It may also involve strategic input providing advice on how the web site can incorporate new opportunities and offset competitive threats. This type of input requires experience in how to apply IS to support business strategy and is beyond the scope of some new media agencies and traditional marketing agencies. Management consultants such as PricewaterhouseCoopers (*www.pwcglobal.com*), Ernst and Young (*eyi.com*), KPMG (*www.kpmg.com*) and Andersen Consulting (*www.andersen.com*), and IS suppliers such as IBM (*www.ibm.com*), Hewlett Packard (*www.hp.com*), Sun (*www.sun.com*) and Compaq (*www.compaq.com*) are all competing to provide this type of input to large corporations. Many of these sites are worth visiting, to read their surveys of industry adoption of e-commerce and 'thought-leadership' (opinions) on how the use of the Internet by business may evolve.

Kassye (1997) has classified the available suppliers as advertising agencies and new entrants (computer design studies and boutiques, PR firms, consultants and those involved in in-house development of campaigns).

As the market has evolved, two trends have been apparent within these different classes of company. First, many of the smaller 'one man and his dog' new media agencies have disappeared, as a result of the small profit margins and oversupply. Second, there have been many takeovers within the large companies. For example the UK new media agency Razorfish has been taken over by the US company CBHi. Mergers often involve the coming together of traditional marketing agencies and new media agencies, making best use of the skills available. Many international new media agencies such as USWeb/CKS (*www.uswebcks.com*) are developing, and the largest of these also offer strategic input to companies.

Most companies would formerly have kept some functions, such as strategy, in-house since they might have doubted the ability of consultants to understand their marketplace and company. Increasingly, however, strategy is outsourced, and many new media agencies offer this service as it is a lucrative one. Other functions, such as promotion, would be better handled by an outside agency experienced in this area. In Chapter 9 it is pointed out that technical online promotion methods such as registering with search engines are a specialised and time-consuming skill. Such a task, which can be contracted out for a modest amount, is ideal for outsourcing. Completing Activity 6.3 will assist you in understanding the best approach for outsourcing different functions.

Activity 6.3

Choosing the right functions to outsource

This activity involves assessing the most appropriate method of using partners to assist in developing different parts of the web site. For each of the functions 1 to 5 in Table 6.2 place a tick in the boxes corresponding to the partners it would be sensible to use to assist with this function. Now repeat the exercise putting a star in one box for each function to denote which you consider to be the best option. Explain your reasoning for selecting the best option.

▶ **Activity** *continued*

Table 6.2 Options for outsourcing different components of web site

Function	In-house	Marketing agency	New media agency	IT dept	Management /IT consultants
1. Strategy					
2. Design					
3. Content development					
4. Promotion					
5. Infrastructure					

Companies are learning the best approach for outsourcing as they gain experience in creating and managing web sites. In the short time during which web sites have been produced commercially, there seems to have been a trend away from using marketing agencies or new media agencies to design, develop and promote sites towards bringing content development and possibly control of promotion in-house. This means that new media agencies may only be involved in an initial prototyping phase, when their graphic designers will produce a design concept for the site based on a brief from the company. Although some companies have outsourced all the functions this approach is comparatively rare, because companies want to keep control of strategy. This trend has occurred as experience has increased within companies and there has been a desire to control the creative output more closely and reduce the costs of outsourcing. Another contributory factor has been the wide discrepancies in standard of service and cost amongst new media agencies. An apocryphal tale from the industry is of a company issuing a web site brief to five different agencies and receiving quotations ranging from a few thousand pounds to a hundred thousand pounds. Although it may be true that 'you get what you pay for', this cannot justify such a large discrepancy.

Legal issues

Legal issues need to receive recognition in an Internet marketing plan since it is vital to highlight the need for expert advice on these issues, and to budget for this. Such advice is particularly necessary if the Internet is used to promote and sell products overseas. Companies operating in countries of which they have no experience may be quite unaware of relevant legal issues. For example, Germany has specific laws that prohibit explicit comparisons between products, and Belgium has a law that discount sales may occur only in January and July. Legal issues on which companies will need to seek specific legal advice are:

1 *Domain name registrations and trade marks for new Internet brands*. There have been many disputes about ownership of company domains (URLs). Some examples of these and the legal principles used to settle such disputes are discussed in Chapter 9.
2 *Advertising standards*. Most countries have specific laws to prevent misrepresentation to the consumer and uncompetitive practices.

3 *Defamation and libel*. Information published on a site that criticises another company's people or products could represent libel.

4 *Copyright and intellectual property rights (IPR)*. Permissions must be sought for information or images sourced elsewhere in the same way as for any other medium.

5 *Data protection and privacy laws*. Sites must protect data held on consumers according to the local law. This topic is covered in more detail in Chapters 11 and 15.

6 *Taxation on electronic commerce*. Companies involved in e-commerce must collect sales tax from consumers. This issue is discussed in more detail in Chapter 11.

Decision point 6: Organisational structure

When a new web site is produced for a company, it will be common to produce it within the existing company structure, perhaps using outsourcing to make up a resource deficit. However, as the contribution of the web site to the company increases, the web site grows and more staff from different parts of the organisation are involved in developing the site, it may be necessary to plan new structures for Internet marketing. This issue has been considered by Parsons *et al.* (1996). They recognise four stages in the growth of what they refer to as the digital marketing organisation. These are:

1 *Ad hoc activity*

At this stage there is no formal organisation related to Internet marketing, and the skills are dispersed around the organisation. At this stage it is likely that there is poor integration between online and offline marketing communications. The web site may not reflect the offline brand, and the web site services may not be featured in the offline marketing communications. A further problem with *ad hoc* activity is that the maintenance of the web site will be informal and errors may occur as information becomes out of date.

2 *Focusing the effort*

At this stage, efforts are made to introduce a controlling mechanism for Internet marketing. Parsons *et al.* (1996) suggest that this is often achieved through a senior executive setting up a steering group, which may include interested parties from marketing, IT and legal experts. At this stage the efforts to control the site will be experimental, with different approaches being tried to build, promote and manage the site.

3 *Formalization*

At this stage the authors suggest that Internet marketing will have reached a critical mass and there will be a defined group or separate business unit within the company who manage all digital marketing.

4 *Institutionalising capability*

This stage also involves a formal grouping within the organisation, but is distinguished from the previous stage in that formal links are created between digital marketing and a company's core activities. Baker (1998) argues that a separate e-commerce department is needed, as the company may need to be restructured in order to provide the necessary levels of customer service over the Internet if existing processes and structures do not do this.

Although this is presented as a stage model with evolution from one stage to the next, many companies will find that true formalisation, with the creation of a separate e-commerce or Internet marketing department, is unnecessary. Small and medium companies with a marketing department of just a few people will not find it practical to have a separate group. Even large companies may find it is sufficient to have a single person or a small team responsible for Internet marketing, with the role of co-ordinating the different Internet marketing activities within the company using a matrix management approach. That many companies are not ready to move to a separate digital marketing department is indicated by the KPMG report (Baker, 1998). This found that over three-quarters of respondents were against establishing a separate e-commerce department.

Whatever the approach chosen, the Internet marketing plan should specify how the Internet marketing efforts will integrate with traditional marketing methods and how the process of controlling the web site will operate. The process, standards and responsibilities for managing the web site are described in more detail in Chapter 12.

Decision point 7: Setting the budget

We will spend some time describing the budgeting process since this is a practical skill that is required by all those responsible for web sites. To budget successfully requires two main ingredients. The first, which is relatively straightforward, is to be able to anticipate all the costs that are going to be involved. This is relatively easy since it is largely a matter of checking costs incurred for different tasks in previous projects. The second is assessing the magnitude of these costs. This is more difficult since site costs can vary dramatically.

Cost elements

Assuming a company does not have an existing web site, what are the main phases of development of the web site that should be budgeted for? The marketing plan should identify costs for:

- initial creation of site;
- initial promotion of site;
- ongoing maintenance of site;
- ongoing promotion of site;
- relaunch creation and promotion.

These phases are described in more detail in later chapters. The detailed cost estimates are best based on the different stages in building a web site that are described in Chapter 8 (*see* Fig. 8.1). These are:

1 Domain name registration.
2 Hosting web site.

3 Creating web site, including the stages of:
- analysis and design of content – finding out what is required for the target audience through a process of prototyping;
- creation of content by graphic designers and content developers;
- publishing content to test environment and then testing and revising content;
- publishing content on live web site.

4 Promoting the web site using online methods, such as banner advertising and registration with search engines (Chapter 9), and offline methods that promote the URL of the web site.

5 Maintaining the web site. This involves measuring the effectiveness of the web site, correcting errors and updating information as product prices, specifications and contact points and the like change. It can also be considered to include relaunches of the site.

Companies are able to manage their Internet marketing related costs better if they acknowledge that major revisions or relaunches of the site may be required at a frequency of every one to two years. This is highlighted by Case study 8.2 on Orange – *see* Chapter 8. Any users of major web sites such as those of Dell, British Airways or Amazon will be aware of the major changes that occur to the design and content of the site. These changes tend to be more frequent during the early life of the web site, and the sites subsequently stabilise, with less frequent relaunches or changes being added as revisions.

Site relaunch
The previous version of the web site is replaced with a new version with a new look and feel.

Further costs that must be considered are internal staff costs, capital costs such as new hardware and software and the costs paid to outside consultants. It will be possible to assess these when it has been decided which tasks to outsource (as described in a previous section of this chapter).

Actual costs

Bayne (1997) suggests several methods for estimating the actual costs for inclusion in the Internet marketing budget, based on the tasks outlined in the previous section. The Internet marketing budget can be based on:

- *Last year's Internet marketing budget.* This assumes the site has been up and running for some time.
- *Percentage of company sales.* It is difficult to establish this for the first iteration of a site.
- *Percentage of total marketing budget.* This is a common approach. Typically the percentage will start small (less than 5 per cent, or even 1 per cent), but will rise as the impact of the Internet increases.
- *Reallocation of marketing dollars.* The money for Internet marketing will come from that made available by cutting back other marketing activities. Bayne (1997) notes that this is a risky activity since if the Internet marketing fails then this has been a poor investment, but other promotional activity has been lost

too. In many cases, however, the marketing budget will be fixed and the creation and operation of a web site will require savings to made elsewhere. It may be possible for the marketing manager to argue that the initial creation of the web site is an exceptional cost and that more money should be made available, possibly from other budgets. For example, infrastructure costs could come from the IT budget.

■ *What other companies in your industry are spending.* It is definitely necessary to know this, in order to assess and meet competitive threats, but it may be possible that competitors are overinvesting. There is also a wide variation in expenditure according to the type of web site that is produced (*see* Table 6.3).

■ *Creating an effective online presence.* In the model of 'paying whatever it takes', a company spends sufficient money to create a web site that is intended to achieve their objectives. This may be a costly option, but for industries in which the Internet is having a significant impact, it may be the wise option. A larger than normal marketing budget will be necessary to achieve this.

■ *A graduated plan tied into measurable results.* This implies that there is an ongoing programme, into which investment each year is tied, in order to achieve the results established in a measurement programme (*see* Chapter 12).

■ *A combination of approaches.* Since the first budget will be based on many intangibles it is best to use several methods and present high, medium and low expenditure options for executives, with expected results related to costs.

It can be seen from these options that one of the key decisions is whether an addition to the marketing budget is necessary for the first web site. Other key decisions concern the amounts allowed for maintenance and promotion of the web site in comparison with the development budget, since these aspects of expenditure are often overlooked.

Maintenance

As a rule of thumb it can be said that maintenance of the site may cost between 25 and 50 per cent of the original cost of creating the site. This figure is of course dependent on the nature and type of updates, not to mention the technologies used to automate the process. It will be shown in Chapters 9 and 12 that the use of templates that help enforce the same look and feel across the site will assist in ensuring that most of the updates that need to be made will be detailed changes to text for promotions and product prices and specifications. It should be possible, with a well-managed process, to keep the cost of maintenance to a much smaller figure than 50 per cent.

Promotion

Promotion is discussed in more depth in Chapter 9. It can be established that there are many low-cost methods of promoting the site URL using existing company communications such as print or television advertisements or stationery. Such an approach will mean that only a small proportion of development costs are spent on promotion. However, to direct the desired number of customers to the site, it may be necessary to place advertisements that are specifically about the benefits of the site, and that do not merely add the URL to the foot of another advertisement. Similarly, it may be necessary to invest in online advertising methods such as banner advertisements or sponsorship of sites with related content since the use of search engines and directories is not an efficient way for customers to find a web site. Estimating the amount that must be spent to build an audience is very difficult, but for some applications it is clear that spending to advertise the site may cost from 50 to 100 per cent or more of the development costs. Since the Internet medium is so new, there is no research that gives an indication of the correlation between the amount of advertising and the number of visitors to a site. However, in Chapter 9, we do discuss the absolute costs of banner advertising and review the increasing use of sponsorship and co-branding of sites as a means of driving customers to sites.

The balance of expenditure on aspects of web sites is highlighted by an example reported in *Revolution* (1999): the design for a British Council web site to promote the UK in Hong Kong. The breakdown of the £29 000 web site was:

- £3900 on the design and development of identity and concepts;
- £5200 on sourcing and collating materials from different companies (an atypical expenditure);
- £18 850 for creating graphics, HTML template page authoring, CGI forms, site population and alpha testing;
- £1300 for amendments, beta testing and final delivery.

No mention was made of promotion costs.

Indicative figures for the costs of creating and promoting web sites are given in Table 6.3. Running costs are illustrated by the experience of HR Johnson Tiles (referred to earlier in this chapter in the section on Integrating 'the nets'). They claim running costs are low, the main component being the £8000 per year they pay to their service provider, UUNet.

Table 6.3 Sample expenditures on web site creation and advertising, UK

Company	Sector	Spend	Source
Ben and Jerry	Consumer, food outlet	£60 000 per year	*Revolution*, July 1999, p. 43
Hoover	Consumer, home appliances	£100 000 site creation	*Revolution*, July 1999, p. 45
Durex	Consumer, condoms	£60 000 banner advertising for launch of Avanti condom	Revolution, July 1999, p. 46
FT	Business, news	£6500 to advertise in AOL and MSN for budget coverage	*Revolution*, July 1999, p. 41
Heinz	Consumer, foodstuffs	£250 000 on phase 1 launch of sites for all products	*Revolution*, Oct. 1998, p. 20
Leeds United FC	Sport	£75 000–100 000	*Revolution*, Oct. 1998, p. 15

Achieving management commitment

One of the key factors in achieving success in Internet marketing, as for other strategy initiatives, seems to be having support from the senior managers in the company. If they have the vision to realise the impact of the Internet, they are more likely to commit to the investment to achieve success. If managers are cynical, treating the Internet as an irrelevance, then not only will they be unlikely to invest in the Internet, but they will not drive the initiative with enthusiasm and communicate this to staff. A KPMG survey reported by Baker (1998) showed that having board level support for the initiative was one of the key success factors for 'leaders' – companies in Europe achieving profitable web revenues. The survey also showed that there was a higher level of investment in such companies (Internet marketing budgets averaging $222 000 compared with $130 000), and the successful companies had integrated e-commerce into their supply chain.

Often the role of the marketing manager or Internet marketing manager within a company may be to lobby more senior managers within a company, explaining the benefits of investing in a web site and perhaps highlighting the consequence of not investing sufficiently.

Achieving staff commitment

Case study 5.1 on RS Components (*see* Chapter 5) highlights another important practical issue. This is the importance of integrating Internet marketing within the existing business. The strategic significance of the Internet needs to be communicated to staff. To do this RS Components set aside an area of their staff canteen and set up a stand staffed by members of the electronic commerce team. Other staff were then encouraged to learn about using the Internet and the services that the web site would provide. By this means all staff gained an understanding of the purpose of using the Internet and were more supportive of it. Additionally, integration of Internet marketing helps to support the adoption of an in-company intranet. More formal education and training, which explains the purpose of the Internet marketing strategy and provides practical training for those involved, is also necessary.

Decision point 8: The schedule

The schedule will be based on the detailed cost elements referred to in the previous section. It is important to register the domain name for the site as early as possible – there is then less risk of another company adopting the same name first.
The schedule can be structured as follows:

1 *Pre-development tasks*. These include domain name registration and deciding on the company to host the web site. They also include preparing a brief setting out the aims and objectives of the site, and then – if it is intended to outsource the site – presenting the brief to rival companies to bid and pitch their offering.
2 *Content planning*. This is the detailed analysis and design of the site, and includes prototyping.
3 *Content development and testing*. Writing the HTML pages, producing the graphics and testing.
4 *Publishing the site*. This is a relatively short stage.
5 *Prelaunch promotion*. This could include ensuring all new stationery and advertising material show the web address. This stage will also include specific advertising for the web site using either banner advertisements or traditional

advertisements. Briefing the PR company to publicise the launch is another source of promotion. Once the site has been completed it will need to be registered with different portals and search engines, as described in Chapter 9.

6 *Ongoing promotion*. The schedule should also allow for periodic promotion. This might involve discount promotions on the site or competitions. These are often reused each month.

Figure 6.7 gives an indication of the relationship between these tasks, and how long they may take, for a typical initial web site. The content planning and development stages overlap in that HTML and graphics development are necessary to produce the prototypes. As a consequence, some development has to occur while analysis and design are under way. These stages of development are discussed further in Chapter 8.

The box, 'A suggested Internet marketing investment plan', summarises the preceding discussion. Note that the points relating to strategic objectives and positioning are dealt with in other chapters, as indicated.

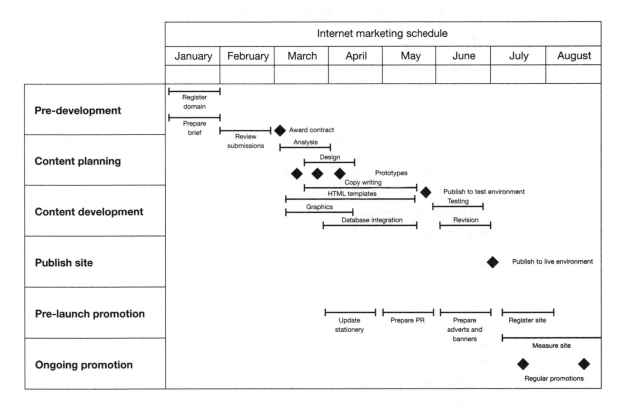

Fig. 6.7 Example web site development schedule

A suggested Internet marketing investment plan

1 Objectives statement (from Chapter 5)

- Corporate objectives of online marketing (mission statement).
- Detailed objectives: tangible and intangible benefits, specific critical success factors.
- Contribution of Internet to promotional and sales activities.
- Value proposition of web site to customer.

2 Strategic positioning (from Chapter 7)

- Impact of Internet on existing sales and promotion channels.
- Impact of Internet on market structure and representation needed.
- Strategic positioning in response to perceived impact.

3 Assessment of current position (from Chapter 5)

(a) Internal audits

- Internet marketing audit (business, marketing and Internet marketing effectiveness).
- Audience composition and characteristics.
- Web site contribution to sales and profitability.

(b) External audits

- Business and economic environment.
- The market and customer activity.
- Competition – threats from new services and new companies?

4 Assess opportunities and threats (from Chapter 5)

- Market and product positioning.
- Methods of creating digital value and detailed statement of customer value proposition.
- Marketplace positioning (buyer, seller and neutral marketplaces).
- Scope of marketing functions.

5 Partnering arrangements

- Promotion.
- Distribution.
- Development.

6 Integrating the 'nets'

Assessing the role and plans for integrating:

- Internet.
- Extranet.
- Intranet.

7 Channel choices (Chapter 7)

(a) Use of:

- Seller-controlled sites.
- Buyer-controlled sites.
- Neutral sites.

(b) Channel choices: split of sales between manufacturers and resellers.

8 Promotional and communications activities (Chapter 9)

Specifying online and offline promotion methods and costs such as advertising and PR. How will existing promotional activities be represented on the web site? Role of one-to-one marketing (Chapter 10).

9 New media branding

Options and risk assessments for brand:

- Migrate traditional brand online.
- Extend traditional brand: variant.
- Partner with existing digital brand.
- Create a new digital brand.

10 Measuring site effectiveness (Chapter 12)

Identify a measurement process and metrics covering:

- Business contribution.
- Marketing effectiveness (offline measures, e.g. leads, sales, brand enhancement).
- Internet marketing effectiveness (online measures, e.g. page impressions, visitors, repeat visits, registrations).

11 Resource requirements

- Budget including costs for development, promotion and maintenance.
- Time-scale.
- Staff.
- Outsourcing.

12 Implementation

- Project management.
- Team organisation and responsibilities.
- Risk assessment (identifying risks, measures to counter risks).
- Legal issues.
- Development and maintenance process.

SUMMARY

1 The Internet marketing plan is based on the Internet marketing strategy, and seeks to outline how the strategy should be implemented.

2 It should clearly state the intended audience of the web site and designate how much effort should be allocated to developing content for each. Different content may need to be developed for new customers, existing customers, customers in different countries, customers in companies of different sizes, potential investors and potential staff.

3 Localisation is the term used to describe the development of content for specific local markets and different countries.

4 The development of the Internet site, intranet and extranet should be integrated for efficiency since similar information may be made available in the different environments.

4 The marketing plan should outline how the web site will be used for different aspects of marketing such as advertising, PR, customer service, sales promotion and direct sales. The methods for promoting the web site (Chapter 9) should also be outlined.

5 When migrating a brand or corporate identity online, the options are:
- use existing brand;
- create a brand variant;
- partner with another brand;
- create a new brand.

6 Companies will need to form various partnerships to best exploit the Internet and will need to consider which aspects of site design, development and promotion to outsource.

7 There are many legal traps that a company promoting itself on the Internet can fall into if specialist legal advice is not obtained.

8 Companies need to consider whether the Internet is of great enough importance to their operation to restructure the organisation.

9 The balance between the cost of creating a web site and promoting it needs to be carefully considered in order to ensure adequate visitors to the site.

EXERCISES AND QUESTIONS

Self-assessment exercises

1 Summarise the main audience types a business-to-business site may need to accommodate.

2 What is localisation? Is it necessary?

3 What options are available to a company to reposition its corporate identity when it moves online?

4 Explain outsourcing. How can it be employed by a marketing manager responsible for a web site?

5 Describe the options for structuring digital marketing in a company according to Parsons *et al.* (1996).

6 Summarise the main costs incurred with the creation of a new web site.

7 Draw up a schedule summarising the main stages in developing a web site.

8 Suggest an appropriate balance of expenditure in a budget on: site creation, site promotion and site maintenance.

Discussion questions

1 'To create a new brand identity for a company on its web site is a dangerous practice.' Discuss.

2 'A company would be mad to opt for full-service Internet outsourcing (total outsourcing) where all aspects of the web site's development and maintenance are outsourced.' Discuss.

3 'The growing importance of the Internet makes it imperative that all large companies have a specific department responsible for digital marketing and e-commerce.' Discuss.

4 'Companies should spend a higher proportion of their web site budgets on promotion than on designing and developing the site.' Discuss.

Essay questions

1 Describe the different types of outsourcing that can be performed for creating and managing a web site. What are the advantages and disadvantages of outsourcing?

2 You have £50 000 available to spend on the design of a web site. Would you choose a new media agency, a traditional marketing agency or an IT services consultancy to implement the work? Justify your answer.

3 Describe the different types of legal problem that a manager responsible for a web site should guard against. Give an example of each.

4 What are the options available to a company for structuring the management of a web site?

Examination questions

1 What do you understand by the term 'customer orientation' of a web site? Give examples that would indicate good customer orientation.

2 Explain the term 'localisation'. Which types of business web sites would need to undertake localisation?

3 Why might a company restrict access to some part of its web site using an extranet? Give examples of services that could be provided.

4 Briefly summarise the different options available to a company when migrating an existing brand to the Internet.

5 Explain co-branding, and through an example explain the benefits it provides to both parties.

6 Which activities of web site creation can be outsourced? What benefits does this outsourcing give?

7 Summarise three of the main costs involved with building a web site.

8 Why should the relationship between the Internet web site, the extranet and the intranet be considered in a web site marketing plan?

REFERENCES

Aaker, D. (1990) 'Brand extensions: the good, bad and the ugly', *Sloan Management Review*, 31(4), 47–56.

Baker, P. (1998) *Electronic commerce. Research Report 1998*. London: KPMG Management Consulting.

Bayne, K. (1997) *The Internet Marketing Plan*. New York: John Wiley and Sons.

Bickerton, P., Bickerton, M. and Pardesi, U. (1996) *CyberMarketing*. Oxford: Butterworth-Heinemann. Chartered Institute of Marketing series.

Bickerton, P., Bickerton, M. and Simpson-Holey, K. (1998) *Cyberstrategy*. Oxford: Butterworth-Heinemann. Chartered Institute of Marketing series.

de Chernatony, L. and McDonald, M. (1992) *Creating Powerful Brands*. Oxford: Butterworth-Heinemann.

Friedman, L. and Furey, T. (1999) *The Channel Advantage*. Oxford: Butterworth-Heinemann.

Kassye, W. (1997) 'The effect of the world wide web on agency–advertiser relationships: towards a strategic framework', *International Journal of Advertising*. 16, 85–103.

Revolution (1999) 'How much is that web site in the window?' *Revolution*, April, 40–5.

Parsons, A., Zeisser, M. and Waitman, R. (1996) 'Organising for digital marketing', *McKinsey Quarterly*, 4, 183–92.

Quelch, J. and Klein, L. (1996) 'The Internet and international marketing', *Sloan Management Review*, Spring, 61–75.

Schwartz, E. (1999) *Digital Darwinism: Seven breakthrough strategies for surviving in the cutthroat web economy*. New York: Broadway Books.

Seybold, P. (1999) *Customers.com*. London: Century Business Books. Random House.

Sterne, J. (1995) *World Wide Web Marketing*. New York: John Wiley and Sons.

Sterne, J. (1999) *World Wide Web Marketing* (2nd edn). New York: John Wiley and Sons.

Vassos, T. (1996) *Strategic Internet Marketing*. Indianapolis, IN: Que. Business Computer Library.

Wind, Y. and Cardazo, R. (1974) 'Industrial marketing segmentation', *Industrial Marketing Management* (March), 153–66.

FURTHER READING

Baker, M. (ed.) (1999) *The Marketing Book*. Oxford: Butterworth-Heinemann. Chapter 3, Strategic Marketing Planning: Theory and Practice, is highly recommended.

Bayne, K. (1997) *The Internet Marketing Plan*. New York: John Wiley and Sons.
Presents many detailed templates to assist in developing a marketing plan. The most relevant chapters are:

- Chapter 5: Planning your Internet Marketing Budget (Cost Issues).
- Chapter 6: Forming the Internet Marketing Task Force.
- Chapter 9: Developing a Corporate Identity.
- Chapter 14: Launching your Internet Marketing Program.

Brassington, F. and Petitt, S. (2000) *Principles of Marketing* (2nd edn). Harlow: UK: Pearson Education.
See companion Prentice Hall web site (*www.booksites.net/brassington2*).
Chapters 20, Strategic Management, and 21, Marketing Planning, Management and Control, describe the integration of marketing strategy with business strategy and the development of marketing plans.

Dibb, S., Simkin, S., Pride, W. and Ferrel, O. (1997) *Marketing. Concepts and strategies* (3rd European edn). New York: Houghton Mifflin.
See companion Houghton Mifflin web site (*www.busmgt.ulst.ac.uk/h_mifflin/*).
See Chapter 23, Marketing Planning and Assessing Sales Potential.

Seybold, P. (1999) *Customers.com*. London: Century Business Books, Random House.
This business book suggest different tactics for using the Internet to provide better customer service. Patricia Seybold Group web site (*www.customers.com*) supports the book.

Vassos, T. (1996) *Strategic Internet Marketing*. Indianapolis, IN: Que. Business Computer Library.
- Chapter 5: Implementing the Initial Four Stages of Web Site Development.
- Chapter 6: Interactive and Database Web Site Strategies.
- Chapter 7: Advanced Web Site Development Strategies.

WEB SITE REFERENCES

Internet/e-commerce law. The following may be useful:

- UK Data Protection Act and related EU law
  www.open.gov.uk/dpr/dprhome.htm

- The Internet law newsletter
  www.legaltechnology.co.uk/internetlaw/

  Monthly newsletter and back issues giving UK/European cases and changes to legislation. From Jeffrey Green Russell (*jgrweb.com*), who provide legal services and advice to users and suppliers on all aspects of Internet law, computer software, hardware and related service contracts and disputes.

- Society for Computers & Law web site SCL Online
  www.scl.org/welcome.htm

  UK organisation, includes monthly magazine that has Internet and other computer-related cases.

- The Perkins Coie Internet Case Digest
  www.perkinscoie.com/resource/ecomm/netcase/index.htm

  Most comprehensive, covering international and US case law categorised by example, advertising, consumer, copyright etc.

- Internet Law and Policy Forum
  www.ilpf.org/

  International body steering Internet law development, good source of links.

CHAPTER 7

Marketing channels, market structure and the Internet

Learning objectives

After reading this chapter the reader should be able to:

- **assess the impact of the Internet on channel structures;**
- **suggest alternative strategies to deal with the conflicts that occur as the Internet is used as a channel;**
- **understand the Internet-based marketplace;**
- **explain the value of intranets and extranets for internal communications and for improving relationships with internal and external stakeholders.**

Links to other chapters

This chapter is related to other chapters as follows:

▶ This chapter is closely linked to the two previous chapters, which consider strategy.

▶ The discussion of the impact of electronic networks that link different business partners is also foundation material for Chapter 11 (electronic commerce).

▶ Further examples of the modified channel structures that are arising as a result of the Internet are given in Chapters 14 and 15.

▶ The impact of the Internet on pricing policy is discussed briefly in Chapter 5.

INTRODUCTION

This chapter completes consideration of the main influences on the Internet marketing strategy, which are shown in Fig. 7.1. The structure of the Internet marketing channel warrants separate attention since this medium causes dramatic changes such as disintermediation and reintermediation. This chapter discusses the potential channel conflicts and how to manage them. The chapter demonstrates that any consideration of Internet strategy must also take account of wider issues than the public web site strategy alone. The role of extranets to link to other organisations and the use of intranets for internal marketing communications have to be considered as part of an effective Internet marketing strategy.

The term 'virtual' is used extensively in this chapter, but what exactly does it mean? *Collins English Dictionary* explains it as '*having the essence or effect of, but not the appearance of*'. In the context of the Internet, 'virtual' usually refers to a separate, often parallel reality to an existing structure. Hence we have virtual worlds, virtual value chains, virtual marketplaces and virtual integration. Thus it is a structure that doesn't exist in the physical world.

This chapter is divided into two main parts. We start by considering the impact of the Internet on distribution channels and then review how a company should choose an appropriate representation in the evolving electronic marketplaces. Finally, we consider the impact of the Internet on value-chain integration and the role of the intranet in managing this.

The implications of the Internet for market structures

Figure 7.1 illustrates the relationships between businesses in the marketing microenvironment that need to be considered when one is assessing the impact of the Internet. These relationships include both those with channel partners such as wholesalers and retailers, who assist a company in delivering products and services to the customer, and also those with suppliers and other partners. The use of the Internet will affect each one of these linkages. It is the role of the marketer as part of strategy formulation to assess the action that is necessary to utilise the new method of communicating between businesses. It can be seen that there are many more business-to-business transactions than transactions between businesses and consumers. These business-to-business transactions usually occur over *extranets* with secure access using user names and passwords or digital certificates (*see* Chapter 11).

Channel structures

Channel structure is the term used to describe the way a manufacturer or selling organisation delivers products and services to its customers. The distribution channel will consist of one or more intermediaries such as distributors. For example, a music company is unlikely to distribute its CDs directly to retailers, but will use wholesalers who have a large warehouse of titles, which are then distributed to individual branches according to demand. A company selling business products may have a longer distribution channel involving more intermediaries.

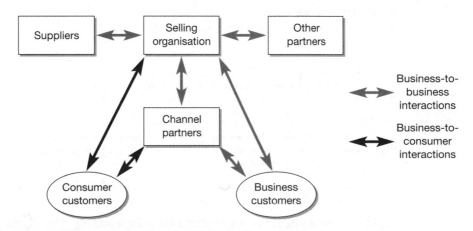

Fig. 7.1 Key players within a selling organisation's microenvironment

The relationship between a company and its channel partners (Fig. 7.1) can be drastically affected by the growth of the Internet. This occurs because the Internet offers a means of bypassing some of the channel partners. This process is known as disintermediation.

> **Disintermediation**
> The removal of intermediaries such as distributors or brokers that formerly linked a company to its customers.

Figure 7.2 illustrates disintermediation in graphical form for a simplified retail channel. Further intermediaries, such as additional distributors, may exist for this market or a business-to-business market. Diagram (a) shows the former position where a producer markets and sells its products by 'pushing' them through a sales channel. Diagrams (b) and (c) show two different type of disintermediation in which the wholesaler (b) or the wholesaler and retailer (c) are bypassed, allowing the producer to sell and promote direct to the consumer. The benefits of disintermediation to the producer are clear – it is able to remove the sales and infrastructure cost of selling selling through the channel. Benjamin and Wigand (1995) calculate that, using the sale of quality shirts as an example, it is possible to make cost savings of 28 per cent in the case of (b) and 62 per cent for case (c). Some of these cost savings can be passed on to the customer in the form of cost reductions.

The new intermediaries

Press (1993) speculated that as a marketplace the Internet has the potential to make markets more efficient, by making more information available, and Hoffman and Novak (1997) suggested that a highly developed form of price comparison shopping would develop. This is now a reality with the development of sophisticated product evaluators such as CNET (*www.computers.com*) (Fig. 15.1).

Sarkar *et al.* (1996) identify many different types of new intermediaries, who they refer to as cybermediaries. Some of the main intermediaries are:

■ Directories (such as Yahoo!, Excite).
■ Search engines (AltaVista, Infoseek).
■ Malls (BarclaySquare, Buckingham Gate).

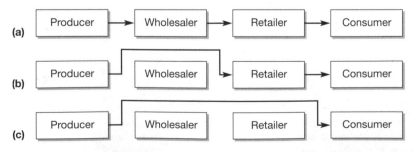

Fig. 7.2 Disintermediation of a consumer distribution channel showing (a) the original, (b) disintermediation omitting the wholesaler and (c) disintermediation omitting both wholesaler and retailer

- Virtual resellers (one that owns its inventory and sells direct, e.g. Amazon, CDNow).
- Financial intermediaries (offering digital cash and cheque payment services such as Digicash).
- Forums, fan clubs and user groups (referred to collectively as virtual communities).
- Evaluators (sites which act as reviewers or compare services). Examples of this type of cybermediary are found in Mini case study 7.1.

A further type of intermediary is the *virtual marketplace* or virtual trading community. Here the intermediary acts as the focus for bringing together buyers and sellers. An example of this type of intermediary is eSTEEL (Fig. 14.5)

Reintermediation
The creation of new intermediaries between customers and suppliers providing services such as supplier search and product evaluation.

Figure 7.3 shows the operation of reintermediation in graphical form. After disintermediation takes place, where the customer goes direct to different suppliers to select a product, this becomes inefficient. Take the example of someone buying insurance: to decide on the best price and offer, this person would have to visit, say, five different insurers and then return to the one from which he or she had decided to purchase. Reintermediation removes this inefficiency by placing an intermediary between the purchaser and seller. This intemediary performs the price evaluation stage of the buying process since its database has links that are updated from prices contained within the databases of different suppliers. In the

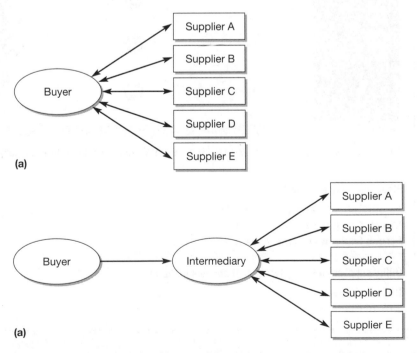

Fig. 7.3 Reintermediation process: (a) original situation, (b) reintermediation contacts

UK, Screentrade (*www.screentrade.co.uk*) offers this service, acting as a broker to several different UK insurers. For the marketer working for a supplier there are two important implications. First, it is necessary to make sure that your supplier is represented with the new intermediaries operating within your chosen market sector, as they are created. This implies the need to integrate, using the Internet, databases containing price information with those of different intermediaries. Second, it is important to monitor the prices of other suppliers within this sector (possibly by using the intermediary web site for this purpose).

Mini case study 7.1 **The growth of evaluator intermediaries on the Internet**

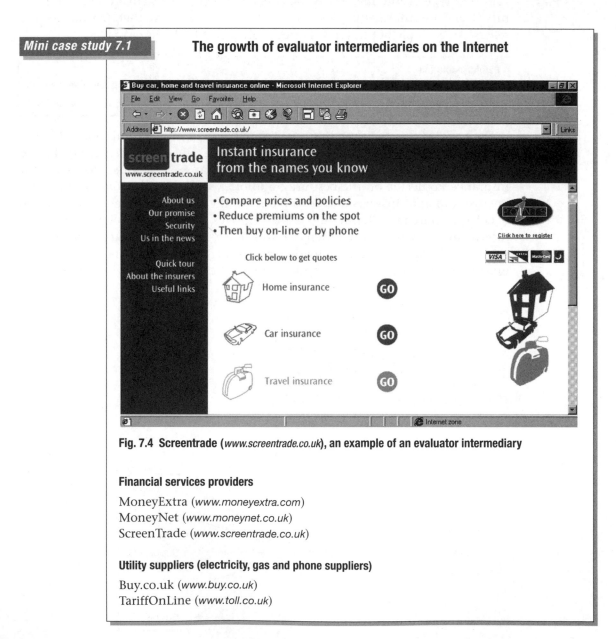

Fig. 7.4 Screentrade (*www.screentrade.co.uk*), an example of an evaluator intermediary

Financial services providers

MoneyExtra (*www.moneyextra.com*)
MoneyNet (*www.moneynet.co.uk*)
ScreenTrade (*www.screentrade.co.uk*)

Utility suppliers (electricity, gas and phone suppliers)

Buy.co.uk (*www.buy.co.uk*)
TariffOnLine (*www.toll.co.uk*)

Travel

Bargainholidays.com (*www.bargainholidays.co.uk*)
1 Travel.com (*www.onetravel.com*)
Co-op TravelOne (*www.holidaydeals.co.uk*)
Lastminute.com (*www.lastminute.com*)

Virtual marketplace
An intermediary site that brings together buyer and sellers to trade.

Implications of electronic distribution channels

There are two alternative, but contradictory, implications of channels becoming electronically mediated networks. Steinfield *et al.* (1996) suggest that networks may foster electronic marketplaces that are characterised by more *ephemeral* relationships. In other words, since it is easy to form an electronically mediated relationship, it is also easy for the customer to break it and choose another supplier. For example a buyer of steel using a virtual marketplace such as e-STEEL (Fig. 14.5), where price is a key determinant of purchase, may change supplier more readily since it is easy to select the new supplier. Counter to this is the suggestion that electronic networks may *lock in* customers to a particular supplier because of the overhead or risk in changing to another supplier. Here networks are used to strengthen partnerships. An example of this is the situation where the use of an EDI solution is stipulated by a dominant customer. For example, UK food retailer Tesco aims to use EDI and the Internet for all (including its smaller) suppliers (*see* Mini case study 7.2). Any suppliers that do not go along with this strategy may be sidelined. Such a system, where one channel member controls the channel, is conventionally known as a vertical marketing system (VMS).

Mini case study 7.2

Chivers Hartley Preserves uses EDI to link to its customers

Cambridge-based Chivers Hartley is a leading UK manufacturer of preserves, jellies and sauces. Brands such as Hartley's jam, Loyd Grossman pasta sauces and Haywards Pickles have contributed towards its £110m. turnover. It employs nearly 900 people in two sites in Histon and Bury St Edmunds. It processes branded and own-brand products for the major retail multiples and is also a supplier of ingredients. Every day, over 24 tonnes of jelly are dispatched to United Biscuits for the production of Jaffa Cakes.

Chivers Hartley has been using enterprise resource planning (ERP) software from software supplier JBA since 1994 to support 120 users. Chivers Hartley chose JBA because it wanted one system that could integrate its entire financial, manufacturing and distribution operations. It also needed a system that could handle traceability and also the batch and process manufacturing requirements of a food processing company (mixed mode manufacturing). Since 85 per cent of Chivers

> ▶ **Mini case study** *continued*

Hartley's business is conducted with retail multiples, which dictate that their customers must trade electronically with them for receiving orders and invoicing, electronic data interchange (EDI) was also a fundamental system requirement. The system also includes new applications such as Customer Returns and Distribution Requirements Planning (DRP). The project team members even created all the accompanying training manuals.

Over 90 per cent of Chivers Hartley's business transactions are via EDI. This is because so much of its business is with large customers, and they also have EDI in place. But with its increased use of industry standard integration software, management reporting systems and intranets, Chivers Hartley is now considering opening up its intranet to share business intelligence with other supply chain partners by allowing them direct access to its ERP legacy.

It is an especially valuable tool for the company's national account managers. They can now access key production information in order to provide accurate delivery dates when in discussion with buyers at the major multiples. The system is growing in its use at Chivers Hartley – currently it is used in sales and marketing, accounts and purchasing departments. However it is the finance function that has seen some exceptional performance improvements.

It is important for marketing managers to consider the impact of the introduction of electronic channels on the marketplace. Malone *et al.* (1987) noted two corollaries of the type of impact that the electronic networks described above may have:

1 *Ephemeral relationship impact.* Here the relationships are those of a marketplace, and revolve around issues such as price, quality and delivery of services. A buyer seeking to purchase will typically obtain a product after assessing the offerings of different suppliers. Malone *et al.* (1987) defined this activity as *electronic brokerage*. This activity is now performed by an *evaluator intermediary* such as e-STEEL.
2 *Lock-in relationship impact.* A hierarchical network develops with a well-defined structure in which the value chain does not change. A buyer seeking to purchase will typically obtain a product from a pre-determined supplier.

The popular conception is that the introduction of the Internet into a channel will tend to lead to more ephemeral relationships. This may yet prove to be the case as more intermediaries evolve and the use of intermediaries becomes an accepted way of buying. However, a review by Steinfield *et al.* (1996) seems to suggest that EDI and the Internet tend to cement existing relationships. Furthermore, more recent research by Kraut *et al.* (1998) indicates that the use of networks for buying may actually reduce outcomes such as quality, efficiency and satisfaction with suppliers. Personal relationships between the members of the buying unit and the supplier still seem to be important. It will be interesting to see which type of arrangement predominates in the future. It may well be that there is a role for both, according to the nature of the product purchased.

Virtual organisations and virtualisation

Benjamin and Wigand (1995) state that *'it is becoming increasingly difficult to delineate accurately the borders of today's organisations'*. A further implication of the introduction of electronic networks such as the Internet is that it becomes easier to outsource aspects of the production and distribution of goods to third parties (Kraut *et. al.*, 1998). This can lead to the boundaries within an organisation becoming blurred. Employees may work in any time zone, and customers are able to purchase tailored products from any location. The absence of any rigid boundary or hierarchy within the organisation should lead to a company becoming more responsive and flexible, and having a greater market orientation. This change also extends to 'virtual products' where mass production is replaced by the ability to tailor the product to the customer's need. An example of this is the customised jeans produced for some Levi customers (see Fig. 10.1).

Davidow and Malone (1992) describe the virtual corporation as follows:

'To the outside observer, it will appear almost edgeless, with permeable and continously changing interfaces between company, supplier and customer. From inside the firm, the view will be no less amorphous, with traditional offices, departments, and operating divisions constantly reforming according to need. Job responsibilities will regularly shift.'

> **Virtual organisation and virtualisation**
> An organisation that uses information and communications technology to allow it to operate without clearly defined physical boundaries between different functions. It provides customised services by outsourcing production and other functions to third parties. Virtualisation is the process whereby a company develops more of the characteristics of the virtual organisation.

Kraut *et al.* (1998) suggest the following features of a virtual organisation:

1 Processes transcend the boundaries of a single form and are not controlled by a single organisational hierarchy.
2 Production processes are flexible, with different parties involved at different times.
3 Parties involved in the production of a single product are often geographically dispersed.
4 Given this dispersion, co-ordination is heavily dependent on telecommunications and data networks.

All companies tend to have some elements of the virtual organisation. The process whereby these characteristics increase is known as virtualisation. Malone *et al.* (1987) argued that the presence of electronic networks tends to lead to virtualisation since they enable the governance and co-ordination of business transactions to be conducted effectively at lower cost.

What are the implications for a marketing strategist of this trend towards virtualisation? Initially it may appear that outsourcing does not have direct relevance to market orientation. However, an example shows the relevance. Michael Dell relates (in Magretta, 1998) that Dell does not see outsourcing as getting rid of a process that does not add value, rather it sees it as a way of *'coordinating their activity to create the most value for customers'*. Dell has improved customer service by changing the way it works with both its suppliers and its distributors to build a computer to the customer's specific order within just six days. This *vertical integration* has been achieved by creating a contractual vertical marketing system in which members of a channel retain their independence, but work together by sharing contracts.

So, one aspect of virtualisation is that companies should identify opportunities for providing new services and products to customers who are looking to outsource their external processes. The corollary of this is that it may offer companies opportunities to outsource some marketing activities that were previously conducted in-house. For example, marketing research to assess the impact of a web site can now be conducted in a virtual environment by an outside company rather than by having employees conduct a focus group (*see* Fig. 12.6).

The changing nature of customer–supplier relationships

We will now review how the advent of electronic linkages between customer and suppliers could affect the nature of these relationships.

A number of factors have been identified as causes of the breakdown in relevance of the traditional marketing model, which focused solely on the transaction process that was built around the classic four P's marketing mix described in Chapter 2. In the 1950s and 1960s the market for consumer and manufacturing goods operated in an economic environment where rising demand for goods and services meant that supply could not meet demand. In such an environment the needs of the customer were deemed secondary to the needs of the producer. Mass production and standardisation were the key drivers of business strategy. The limitations of this approach became evident in the 1980s and 1990s, when a combination of factors left many organisations exposed to the new market environment of increasing global competition. These included the global impact of economic change (in particular recession), more demanding and knowledgeable customers, increasing fragmentation of markets and significant improvements in and adoption of new technology.

Such changes led to the evolution and increasing adoption of a new type of customer–supplier relationship. This relationship recognised the need to see customers not as opportunities for single transactions but as opportunities for ongoing transactions based upon close understanding of customer requirements, an emphasis upon service and a building up of trust and commitment that would lead to win/win outcomes for both suppliers and customers. Early attention in relationship marketing focused on the development and cultivation of longer-term, profitable and mutually beneficial relationships between an organisation and a defined customer group. The concept was extended to encompass internal marketing, particularly the importance of employees, cross-functional organisation structures and a focus on process. It was further extended to recognise the importance and influence of other key stakeholder groups such as local communities, financial institutions and local/national governments etc. As a result new forms of organisation are emerging which are characterised by inter- and intra-organisational co-ordination. Businesses are restructuring around core processes and outsourcing those activities that add no value. New supply chain arrangements or structures are developing with preferred supplier status, partnerships and joint ventures or acquisitions. Such changes have occurred at the same time as evidence has emerged of increasing convergence of buyer power in many industry sectors. Such convergence has led to many organisations being 'squeezed' by buying organisations, and not necessarily in the best long-term interests of suppliers, customers or consumers. The new remit for many organisations as they enter the new millennium is to focus on maximising customer satisfaction and customer value and to focus activities and strategies on customer retention, not customer acquisition.

Managing channel conflicts

A significant threat arising from the introduction of an Internet channel is that while disintermediation gives a company the opportunity to sell direct and increase profitability on products, it can also threaten distribution arrangements with existing partners. Such channel conflicts are described by Frazier (1999), and need to be carefully managed. Frazier (1999) identifies some situations when the Internet should only be used as a communications channel. This is particularly the case where manufacturers offer an exclusive, or highly selective, distribution approach. To take an example, a company manufacturing expensive watches costing thousands of pounds will not in the past have sold direct, but will have used a wholesaler to distribute watches via retailers. If this wholesaler is a major player in watch distribution, then it is powerful, and will react against the watch manufacturer selling direct. The wholesaler may even refuse to act as distributor and may threaten to distribute only a competitor's watches, which are not available over the Internet. Furthermore, direct sales may damage the product's brand or change its price positioning.

To assess channel conflicts it is necessary to consider the different forms of channel the Internet can take. These are:

1 A communication channel only.
2 A distribution channel to intermediaries.
3 A direct sales channel to customers.
4 Any combination of the above.

To avoid channel conflicts, the appropriate combination of channels must be arrived at. For example, Frazier (1999) notes that using the Internet as a direct sales channel may not be wise when a product's price varies considerably across global markets. In the watch manufacturer example, it may be best to use the Internet as a communication channel only.

Internet channel strategy will, of course, depend on the existing arrangements for the market. If a geographical market is new and there are no existing agents or distributors, there is unlikely to be channel conflict, in that there is a choice of distribution through the Internet only or appointments of new agents to support Internet sales, or a combination of the two. Often SMEs will attempt to use the Internet to sell products without appointing agents, but this strategy will only be possible for retail products that need limited pre-sales and after-sales support. For higher-value products such as engineering equipment, which will require skilled sales staff to support the sale and after-sales servicing, agents will have to be appointed.

For existing geographical markets in which a company already has a mechanism for distribution in the form of agents and distributors, the situation is more complex, and there is the threat of channel conflict. The strategic options that are available when an existing reseller arrangement is in place have been described by Kumar (1999):

1 *No Internet sales*. Neither the company nor any of its resellers make sales over the Internet. This will be the option to follow when a company, or its resellers, feel that the number of buyers has not reached the critical mass thought to warrant the investment in an online sales capability.

2 *Internet sales by reseller only*. A reseller, who is selling products from many companies, may have sufficient aggregated demand (through selling products for other companies) to justify the expenditure of setting up online sales. The manufacturer may also not have the infrastructure to fulfil orders direct to customers without further investment, whereas the reseller will be set up for this already. In this case it is unlikely that a manufacturer would want to block sales via the Internet channel.

3 *Internet sales by manufacturer only*. It would be unusual if a manufacturer chose this option if it already had existing resellers in place. Were the manufacturer to do so, it would probably lead to lost sales as the reseller would perhaps stop selling through traditional channels.

4 *Internet sales by all*. This option is arguably the logical future for Internet sales. It is also likely to be the result if the manufacturer does not take a proactive approach to controlling Internet sales.

This strategy will need to be reviewed annually and the sales channels changed as thought appropriate. Given the fast rate of change of e-commerce, it will probably not be possible to create a five-year plan! Kumar (1999) notes that history suggests that most companies have a tendency to use existing distribution networks for too long. The reason for this is that resellers may be powerful within a channel and the company does not want to alienate them, for fear of losing sales.

Marketplace models

While previously 'marketplace' has tended to have a physical meaning, the Internet-based market has no physical representation – it is a *virtual marketplace*. Rayport and Sviokla (1996) use this distinction to coin a new term, *electronic marketspace*. This has implications for the way in which the relationships between the different actors in the marketplace occur.

> **Electronic marketspace**
> A virtual marketplace such as the Internet in which no direct contact occurs between buyers and sellers.

The new electronic marketspace has many alternative virtual locations where a company needs to position itself to communicate and sell to its customers. Thus one strategic decision is, 'What representation do we have on the Internet?' One aspect of representation that needs to be considered is the different types of marketplace location. Berryman *et. al.* (1998) have identified a useful framework for this (Table 7.1).

Table 7.1 Different types of marketplace

Marketplace	Examples of marketplace sites
Seller controlled	■ Vendor sites, i.e. home site of company with e-commerce facilities. ■ Intermediaries controlled by sellers.
Buyer controlled	■ Intermediaries controlled by buyers. ■ Web site procurement posting, e.g. Zygonet (*www.zygonet.com*), Respond.com (*www.respond.com*)* ■ Purchasing agents and aggregators, e.g. Powerbuy (*www.powerbuy.com*), Letsbuyit.com** (*www.letsbuyit.com*).
Neutral	■ Intermediaries not controlled by buyer's industry (e.g. industry net (*www.industry.net*). ■ Product specific search engines (e.g. CNET (*www.computer.com*)). ■ Information marts. ■ Business malls, i.e. Barclay Square (*www.barclaysquare.com*). ■ Auction space, e.g. uBid (*www.ubid.com*).

*See Fig. 13.3.
**See Fig. 15.4.

Source: After Berryman *et al.* (1998).

Seller-controlled sites are those that are the main home page of the company and are e-commmerce enabled. *Buyer-controlled sites* are either procurement posting on buyer-company sites or those of intermediaries that have been set up in such a way that it is the buyer who initiates the market making. This can occur through procurement posting, whereby a purchaser specifies what he or she wishes to purchase, this request is sent by e-mail to suppliers registered on the system and then offers are awaited. Aggregators are groups of purchasers who combine to purchase in bulk and thus benefit from a lower purchase cost. *Neutral sites* are independent evaluator intermediaries that enable price and product comparison.

To maximise the opportunity for sales, the creation of new neutral and buyer-controlled sites should be monitored to ensure the company is represented if appropriate and that product pricing is competitive. Companies may also want to consider creating new intermediaries for product selection. These intermediaries would be positioned as independent. They can either drive business to the main site (and possibly to competitors) or develop completely new services. An example of a company that is making good use of intermediaries created by itself to build new business is Microsoft (although it is not positioned as independent on all sites). This has the following sites, distinct from the main Microsoft site:

■ LinkExchange (*www.linkexchange.com*). Reciprocal banner advertisements.
■ CarPoint (*www.carpoint.com*). New and used car sales.
■ Expedia (*www.expedia.com*). Travel. Includes country-specific versions, e.g. *www.microsoft.co.uk*.

■ Investor (*moneycentral.msn.com*). Personal stock market investments.
■ Music Central (*musiccentral.msn.com*) CDs and downloadable music.
■ Microsoft Plaza (*shopping.msn.com*).

Mougayer (1998), though starting from a slightly different perspective to that of the marketplace, also makes the point that companies should not base their Internet strategies on a single web site. Successful companies will need several sites to locate promotional content, databases and services at several representation locations in the electronic marketspace. These could include:

■ a corporate web site for investor and partner information;
■ the main open consumer web site with transactional e-commerce facilities;
■ microsites or extranets within the main sites with restricted access to key customers;
■ versions of the corporate or main site in overseas markets;
■ an intranet web site for internal marketing communications;
■ microsites within partner sites such as those of intermediaries and distributors.

These various sites are summarised diagramatically in Fig. 7.5. This shows that the main transactional web site is only one representation location for the organisation. A large organisation may also have a corporate site. Both of these may have microsites providing specialised content, which may be provided at a premium or to favoured companies. An example of a microsite is shown in Fig. 7.6. In common with many others, this has extranet-based access to the premium content. Microsites may also set up on external sites such as those of distributors, who need to pass on product information direct to their customers. Representation is needed on evaluation intermediaries, as pointed out above, and also on portals. For example Virgin.Net has a collaborative arrangement whereby it hosts information for Thomas Cook as a microsite. The content of a microsite may either be located on the intermediary site and updated daily as a batch-transfer, or be linked direct from the main transactional site and transferred in real time.

Microsite
Specialised content which is part of a web site that is not necessarily owned by the organisation. If owned by the company it may be as part of an extranet.

Mougayer (1998) also points out that an organisation can set up its own intermediaries, which are used to direct traffic to the web site. This is acquisition by stealth since such sites are often not identified as belonging to their owners!

Markets can also be considered from a separate perspective – that of the type of commerce that occurs to arrange a sale. The different types of market are shown in Table 7.2.

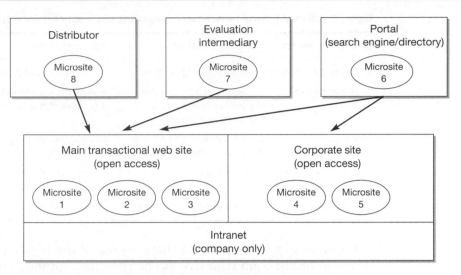

Fig. 7.5 Different representation locations in the electronic marketspace

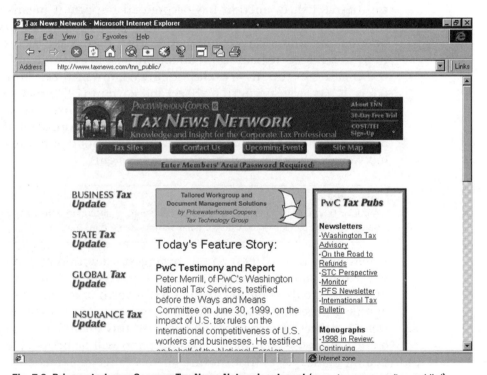

Fig. 7.6 PricewaterhouseCoopers Tax News Network extranet (*www.taxnews.com/tnn_public/*)

Table 7.2 Different types of commercial arrangement, and traditional and online examples

Commercial market	Examples – real world	Examples – online
1 Negotiated deal	Large engineering contract	Not common, but possible via e-mail
2 Brokered deal	Complex product, specialist knowledge important, e.g. insurance broking	Intermediaries on the Internet, screen trade e.g. Screentrade (*www.screentrade.co.uk*)
3 Auction	Traditionally expensive items such as houses	Lower-cost items e.g. eBay (*www.ebay.com*), Lastminute.co.uk (*www.lastminute.com*) (tickets)
4 Fixed-price sale	Traditional retail	Online retail, e.g. Tesco (*www.tesco.net*), Amazon (*www.amazon.co.uk*)
5 Pure markets	Commodity and stock markets	Online or e-trading

It can be seen from Table 7.2 that for each of the traditional types of arrangement, an online equivalent has also been created. Although the model cannot be considered to have changed, the importance of these different options has changed with the Internet. Owing to the rapidity with which new offers and prices can be published, auction has become an important means of selling on the Internet. eBay has achieved a turnover of several billion dollars from consumers offering items from cars to antiques. Many airlines have successfully trialled auctions to sell seats remaining on an aircraft just before a flight, and this has led to the creation of the site www.lastminute.com, which can broker or link to such offers. It has been suggested by Hagel and Rayport (1997) that a new type of broker known as an infomediary will develop as a consequence of the Internet. Infomediaries will act as brokers for consumer information. Such information might be collected by a banner advertising network that records the preferences of individuals who click on particular advertisements.

> **Infomediary**
> A business whose main source of revenue derives from capturing consumer information and developing detailed profiles of individual customers for use by third parties.

Berryman *et al.* (1998) go on to suggest a method by which companies can select the appropriate marketplace option. Figure 7.7 suggests that in the seller marketplace only companies with a well-known brand or a differentiated product or offer will be able to sell on their own web site. An example of such a company is Dell Computers. Companies will only visit this site to buy if they are aware of the brand. Other less well-known manufacturers will be better able to sell in malls or neutral marketplaces (not shown) where a range of companies is available. In the buyer marketplace procurement posting and purchasing agents will be most appropriate when the buyer is large, and therefore placing large orders.

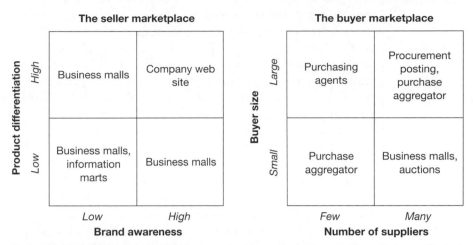

Fig. 7.7 Marketplace options for the buyer and seller marketplaces, and how they are affected by market and product factors

Source: Berryman *et. al.* (1998).

The Internet and value chain activities

Michael Porter's value chain is a framework for considering key activities between organisations and how well they can add value for the customer as products and services move from conception to delivery to the customer (Porter, 1980). The value chain is a model that describes different value-adding activities that connect a company's supply side with its demand side. By analysing the different parts of the value chain managers can redesign internal and external processes to improve their efficiency and effectiveness. The Internet provides a new way of improving the performance of companies by applying it to the value chain activities to add further value to the customer. In a marketing context it can be used to understand how to deliver better quality products to customers more efficiently through improving the logistics functions of an organisation.

Value chain analysis makes a distinction between *primary activities*, which contribute directly to getting goods and services to the customer (physical creation of a product, marketing and delivery to buyers, support and servicing after sale), and *support activities*, which provide the inputs and infrastructure that allow the primary activities to take place. Primary activities can be broken down into five areas:

1 *Inbound logistics* – receiving, storing and expediting materials to the point of manufacture of the good or service being produced.
2 *Operations* – transforming the inputs into finished products or services.
3 *Outbound logistics* – storing finished products and distributing goods and services to the customer.
4 *Marketing and sales* – promotion and sales activities that allow the potential customer to buy the product or service.
5 *Service* – post-sales service to maintain or enhance product value for the customer.

It should be apparent that the Internet provides a means of *integrating* these different value chain activities, a process sometimes known as vertical integration.

Through doing this the marketing process can be made more efficient, and services can be delivered to customers more readily. Rayport and Sviokla (1996) contend that the Internet enables value to be created by gathering, organising, selecting, synthesising and distributing information. They model the situation as a separate parallel *virtual value chain* mirroring the physical value chain. In a physical manner, the virtual value chain interprets different databases and applications that help deliver products to customers. A sales order processing system used to take customer and order details has a linkage to the accounting system for credit checking and processing accounts receivable. Thus there is an electronic linkage between the sales administration and infrastructure activities. Similarly the warehousing and distribution system keeps track of stock levels and actual and projected sales order levels. Information here can be used to generate automatically raw material orders and manufacturing orders. Here then is a clear linkage between inbound logistics and operations and also procurement and inbound logistics. Finally, the warehouse and distribution system will generate a 'picking list', which is used to select stock from the warehouse for delivery to specific customers. This illustrates a linkage between the sales and outbound logistics functions. Mini case study 7.3 gives an example of how this occurs in practice.

Secondary activities fall into four categories:

1 *Corporate administration and infrastructure* – this supports the entire value chain and includes general management, legal services, finance, quality management and public relations.
2 *Human resource management* – activities here include staff recruitment, training, development, appraisal, promotion and rewarding employees.
3 *Technology development* – this includes development of the technology of the product or service, the processes that produce it, and the processes that ensure the successful management of the organisation. It also includes traditional research and development activities.
4 *Procurement* – this activity supports the process of purchasing inputs for all the activities of the value chain. Such inputs might include raw materials, office equipment, production equipment and also information systems.

Intranets provide an infrastructure and a means of integrating these secondary activities with the value chain (*see* the discussion of intranets later in this chapter). The report by KPMG (Baker, 1998) shows that where marketing has input and control of the supply chain and value chain activities and uses e-commerce to automate them, the more effective will be the overall marketing process.

Developments in supply chain management

Supply chain and logistics management providers important ways of adding value to the customer, so it is useful to consider how this context is affected by the Internet.

1960s/1970s Physical distribution management (PDM)

Physical distribution management (PDM) focused upon the physical movement of goods by treating stock management, warehousing, order processing and delivery as related rather than separate activities. PDM was essentially about the management of finished goods but not about the management of materials and processes that impacted upon the distribution process. PDM was superseded by logistics management, which viewed manufacturing, storage and transport from raw material to final consumer as integral parts of the total distribution process.

1970s/1980s Logistics management (Just in Time – JIT)

The JIT philosophy is a relatively recent development of logistics management. Its aim is to make the process of distribution as efficient and flexible as possible in terms of material supply and customer service. Customers sought minimum order quantities and stock levels, and therefore manufacturers had to introduce flexible manufacturing processes and systems that interfaced directly with the customer – who could call an order directly against a pre-arranged schedule, with a guarantee that it would be delivered on time. However, neither of the above systems looked at the management of the total supply chain.

1980s/1990s Supply chain management

The supply chain is a shorthand term for the connected series of activities that deal with planning, co-ordinating and controlling materials, parts and finished goods from suppliers to customers, with payment and information as reverse flows. Effective management of the supply chain involved much closer integration between the supplier, customer and intermediaries and in some instances involved one organisation in the channel taking over functions that were traditionally the domain of the intermediary. Bottlenecks or undersupply/oversupply situations can have significant impacts on an organisation's profitability. The two primary goals of supply chain management are to maximise the efficiency and effectiveness of the total supply chain for the benefit of all the players, not just one section of the channel, and to maximise the opportunity for customer purchase by ensuring adequate stock levels at all stages of the process. These two goals impact upon the sourcing of raw materials and stockholding. A 1990s phenomenon was the rapid growth in global sourcing of supplies from preferred suppliers, particularly amongst multinationals and global organisations. The Internet will provide increased capability for smaller players to source raw materials globally and therefore to improve their competitivness. Quelch and Klein (1996) argue that the Internet will revolutionise the dynamics of international commerce and, in particular, will lead to the more rapid internationalisation of SMEs. The World Wide Web will reduce the competitive advantage of economies of scale in many industries, making it easier for smaller companies to compete on a worldwide basis. Global advertising costs as a barrier to entry will be significantly reduced as the Web makes it possible to reach global audiences more cheaply. Stockholding is an increasingly important part of organisations' competitiveness and profitability. Technology has enabled the introduction of faster, more responsive and flexible ordering, manufacturing and distribution systems that have reduced even further the need for warehouses to be located near to markets that they serve. Increasingly, centralised distribution depots are being developed that service whole regions. The Internet, by connecting the buyer directly with the supplier, will reduce the importance of the traditional intermediaries. The key criteria that should be included in an effective supply chain management system are a continuous focus on the distribution needs of each user in the supply chain and an effective planning, control and communications system that encompasses the entire logistics system. Information technology is an integral part of this process because it can be used for planning, monitoring, communicating, implementing and controlling the mechanisms for the total supply chain system.

1990s/2000s Technological interface management (TIM)

According to Hamill and Gregory (1997) the challenge facing suppliers, intermediaries and customers in the supply chain will shift from a focus on physically distributing goods to dealing with the process of collection, collation, interpretation and dissemination of vast amounts of information. The critical resource possessed by this new breed of 'cybermediary' will be information rather than inventory.

Hagel and Rayport (1997) take this one stage further by suggesting that customer information capture will serve customers rather than vendors in future. Currently customers leave a trail of information behind them as they visit sites and process transactions down the net. These data can be captured and then used by suppliers and agents to improve targeting of offers. As customers become more aware of the value of information and as technology on the Internet enables them to protect private information relating to site visits and transactions so the opportunity for intermediaries to act as customer agents and not supplier agents grows. The sole source of revenue of these new 'infomediaries' will derive from the value that they generate for their clients. Their revenues are likely to be either payments made directly by clients for services rendered or commission on revenues accruing to clients. Hagel and Rayport (1997) identify vendor-oriented infomediaries and customer-oriented infomediaries. Vendor-oriented infomediaries such as Doubleclick (*www.doubleclick.net*) supply information to businesses about customer behaviour and references from their advertising network, or provide new customer leads. Customer-oriented infomediaries provide information to customers and assist them in the buying process. Purchasing aggregators such as Letsbuy-it (*www.letsbuyit.com*) and Powerbuy (*www.powerbuy.com*) are examples of customer-oriented infomediaries.

Intranets

Intranets are also part of supply chain management and e-commerce fulfilment since they link all the systems in this process. At Marshall Industries, for example, a new customer order automatically triggers a scheduling order for the warehouse, an order acknowledgement for the customer and a shipping status when the order is dispatched (Mougayer, 1998). To enable different databases within a company such as a sales ordering system and an inventory control system to operate with each other and with databases in other companies requires an internal company intranet to be created that can then communicate across an extranet with applications on another company intranet (or internal network). Mini case study 7.3 reviews some of the issues involved. It is evident from the complexity of setting up these links that the Internet strategy involves much more than the web site, and that the strategy also needs to be linked into an IT or information infrastructure strategy for the company.

Mini case study 7.3 **Enterprise application integration links companies**

The middleware technology that is used to connect different software applications and their underlying databases is now known as 'enterprise application integration (EAI)'(*Internet World*, 1999). Such applications include a sales order processing system and a warehousing system. They also include software programs from different organisations.

Internet World (1999) reported on an example of EAI implementations in which the computer distributor Ingram Micro Inc. and the build-to-order PC manufacturer Solectron Corp. are integrating their respective applications so that Ingram can check the availability of parts with Solectron before placing an order to build a computer. This EAI project, the result of a strategic relationship between Ingram and Solectron set up in 1998, integrates several applications in each company.

Previously, Ingram placed orders without knowing if Solectron had the inventory to build systems in real time, making it difficult for Ingram to promise a delivery date to its customers. The new system helps Ingram realise its goal of guaranteed two-day delivery on orders. The driving force behind this EAI project has been improving customer relations. 'We and Solectron have an absolute passion for customer service', said Mr Carlson, CIO of Ingram. The link between Ingram and Solectron is Extricity Software Inc.'s Alliance (*www.extricity.com*) XML Server, which translates data from applications on each end of the connection.

Intranets are set up across a whole company, but are particularly beneficial in the marketing department. A marketing intranet has the following advantages:

- *Reduced product life cycles* – as information on product development and marketing campaigns is rationalised it is possible to get products to market faster.
- *Reduced costs* – through higher productivity, and savings on hard copy.
- *Better customer service* – responsive and personalised support, with staff accessing customers over the Web.
- *Distribution of information* – through remote offices nationally or globally.

Intranets are also used for internal marketing communications since they can include the following types of information:

- staff phone directories;
- staff procedures or quality manuals;
- information for agents such as product specifications; current list and discounted prices; competitor information; factory schedules; and stocking levels, information that normally has to be updated frequently and can be costly;
- staff bulletin or newsletter;
- training courses.

Intranets are popular since they can produce major cost savings, as is shown in the example of BT (Mini case study 7.4).

BT's intranet

As a large multinational company with over 125 000 staff, information management and internal communications are major challenges for British Telecom. Since 1994 it has developed an intranet with over two million pages, which is accessed by over 65 000 users and which is now described as BT's 'central nervous system'. Information available includes:

- product price-lists;
- operations manuals and policies;
- HR support and staff directories;
- training information;
- company news.

Much of this information was originally modified weekly and sent out as costly updates to staff around the world. The cost savings are substantial because there is now no need to run through the cycle of reprinting and distribution of hard copy. To take an example, the worldwide product pricing manual was regularly updated, and distributed around the globe. The annual direct cost of production and distribution was £800 000 before the introduction of the intranet. Indirect costs were estimated as much higher, at between £15 and £20 million. This figure was so high because individuals had to update their own manuals and there were costs involved in their spending time searching through their manuals. The overall savings made as a result of reducing these costs have been calculated at £305 million for 1995/96 and £747 million for 1996/97. In addition to these changes, there has been a change in the culture, with a move from information being pushed out from the centre of the organisation to people searching for or 'pulling' the information to their desktop as they need it.

Intranets are also necessary to enable Internet-based customer service to be delivered, when combined with *workflow* software. The software helps with managing the flow of information coming into the company and how it is processed as responses are made to customers. In Chapters 9 and 10 we will consider the importance of e-mail as a tool for communicating with customers over the Internet and will look at the need for service standards and the tools available to achieve them. For a good level of service quality it is necessary to have software applications that can handle both the inbound and the outbound e-mail. An example of a product that can assist a marketing manager through monitoring the replies to e-mails is shown in Fig. 7.8.

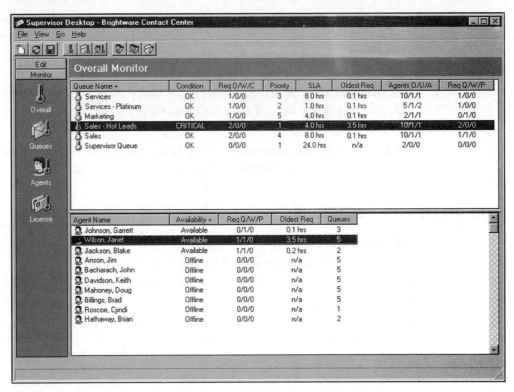

Fig. 7.8 Brightware Contact Centre (*www.brightware.com*) **for customer relationship management through e-mail**

SUMMARY

1 The use of the Internet has significant implications for the way in which relationships with channel partners such as wholesalers, distributors and retailers are managed. *Extranets* are often used to manage these linkages electronically.

2 The Internet can cause *disintermediation* within the channel as partners such as wholesalers or retailers are bypassed. The impact of these changes in the resulting channel conflicts needs to be carefully assessed. Alternatively the Internet can cause *reintermediation* as new intermediaries with a different purpose are formed to help bring buyers and sellers together in a *virtual marketplace* or marketspace.

3 The use of electronic distribution channels can lead to channel relationships becoming more short term, as the relationships are based on marketplace forces, or it can lead to a more rigid, hierarchical structure of stable trading relationships and possible 'lock-in' of customers. Both outcomes are found to occur, depending on product type.

4 Virtual organisations form as more non-core activities are outsourced, a trend known as virtualisation.

5 Customer–supplier relationships are affected by the fact that they are formed over an electronic medium. It is unclear whether relationships are strengthened or weakened by reduced personal contact.

6 New marketplace models develop in the electronic marketspace, and companies need to decide on their electronic representation. Are they represented on seller- or buyer-controlled sites or on neutral sites? What is the role of microsites and extranets in forming closer relationships with customers?

7 The impact of the Internet on value chain activities should be considered. Electronic or virtual integration of the supply chain can be used to improve the quality of service delivered to the end-customer.

8 Intranets have an important role in integrating the value chain and supporting internal marketing communications.

EXERCISES AND QUESTIONS

Self-assessment exercises

1 Explain disintermediation and reintermediation.

2 Describe three impacts of the Internet on supplier–customer relationships.

3 What is a virtual organisation?

4 What is meant by representation of a company within the electronic marketspace and how should a company position itself?

5 What is a microsite and what role can they play within the communications mix?

6 Explain the activities of the value chain. How can an Internet-enabled or virtual value chain be used to deliver better service to customers?

Discussion questions

1 'Disintermediation and reintermediation occur simultaneously within any given market.' Discuss.

2 'The use of the Internet to link suppliers and customers in a supply chain can only lead to strengthened relationships and "lock-in" of customers.' Discuss.

3 Discuss the implications of the increase of virtualisation for the marketer.

4 'All organisation are virtual organisations; it is a matter of degree.' Discuss.

Essay questions

1 Describe the types of channel conflicts that can arise through deployment of extranets, and suggest how they can be managed.

2 Examine the relationship between intranets, extranets and the Internet as a means of managing distribution channels electronically.

3 Write an essay on channel conflicts caused by the Internet and how they can be managed.

4 Using examples, show how can intranets can be used to manage internal marketing communications.

Examination questions

1 What options are available to a supplier, who currently fulfils customer orders through a reseller, to use the Internet to change this relationship?

2 What types of channel conflict are caused by the Internet?

3 What is a virtual organisation and how can the Internet support such organisations?

4 Name three options for a company's representation on the Internet in different types of marketplace.

5 Explain the term virtual value chain.

6 Briefly explain how an intranet can be used to assist the management of inbound and outbound e-mails and so improve customer service.

7 Explain the following types of commerce and give examples of how they are used by Internet-based companies:
   ■ brokered deal;
   ■ auction;
   ■ fixed price sale.

REFERENCES

Baker, P. (1998) *Electronic Commerce. Research Report 1998*. London: KPMG Management Consulting.

Benjamin, R. and Wigand, R. (1995) 'Electronic markets and virtual value-chains on the information superhighway', *Sloan Management Review*, Winter, 62–72.

Berryman, K., Harrington, L., Layton-Rodin, D. and Rerolle, V. (1998) 'Electronic commerce: three emerging strategies', *The Mckinsey Quarterly*, 1, 152–9.

Davidow, W.H. and Malone, M.S. (1992) *The Virtual Corporation. Structuring and revitalizing the corporation for the 21st century*. New York: HarperCollins.

Frazier, G. (1999) 'Organising and managing channels of distribution', *Journal of the Academy of Marketing Science*, 27 (2), 222–40.

Hagel, J. III and Rayport, J. (1997) 'The new infomediaries', *The McKinsey Quarterly*, 4, 54–70.

Hamill, J. and Gregory, K. (1997) 'Internet marketing in the internationalization of UK SMEs', *Journal of Marketing Management*, Special edition on internationalization, Hamill, J. (ed.), 13 (1–3).

Hoffman, D.L. and Novak, T.P. (1997) 'A new marketing paradigm for electronic commerce', *The Information Society*, Special issue on electronic commerce, 13 (January–March), 43–54.

Internet World (1999) 'Enterprise application integration – Middleware apps scale firewalls', *Internet World*, 17 May.

Kumar, N. (1999) 'Internet distribution strategies: dilemmas for the incumbent', *Financial Times*. Special Issue on Mastering Information Management, No 7. Electronic Commerce (*www.ftmastering.com*).

Kraut, R., Chan, A., Butler, B. and Hong, A. (1998) 'Coordination and virtualisation: the role of electronic networks and personal relationships', *Journal of Computer Mediated Communications*, 3(4).

Magretta, J. (1998) 'The power of virtual integration. An interview with Michael Dell', *Harvard Business Review*, March–April, 72–84.

Malone, T., Yates, J. and Benjamin, R. (1987) 'Electronic markets and electronic hierarchies: effects of information technology on market structure and corporate strategies', *Communications of the ACM*, 30(6), 484–97.

Mougayer, W. (1998) *Opening Digital Markets – Battle plans and strategies for Internet commerce* (2nd edn). New York: CommerceNet Press, McGraw-Hill.

Porter, M.E. (1980) *Competitive Strategy*. New York: The Free Press.

Press, L. (1993) 'The Internet and interactive television', *Communications of the ACM*, 54, 36–51.

Quelch, J. and Klein, L. (1996) 'The Internet and international marketing', *Sloan Management Review*, Spring, 60–75.

Rayport, J. and Sviokla, J. (1996) 'Exploiting the virtual value-chain', *The McKinsey Quarterly*, 1, 20–37.

Sarkar, M., Butler, B. and Steinfield, C. (1996) 'Intermediaries and cybermediaries. A continuing role for mediating players in the electronic marketplace', *Journal of Computer Mediated Communication*, 1(3).

Steinfield, C., Kraut, R. and Plummer, A. (1996) 'The impact of interorganisational networks on buyer–seller relationships', *Journal of Computer Mediated Communication*, 1(3).

FURTHER READING

Berryman, K., Harrington, L., Layton-Rodin, D. and Rerolle, V. (1998) 'Electronic commerce: three emerging strategies', *The McKinsey Quarterly*, 1, 152–9.
This definition of the different representation that companies can adopt on the Internet is a useful framework for companies wishing to make their products widely available on the Internet. Available online at *www.mckinseyquarterly.com*.

Brassington, F. and Petitt, S. (2000) *Principles of Marketing* (2nd edn). Harlow, UK: Pearson Education.
See companion Prentice Hall web site (*www.booksites.net/brassington2*).
Chapters 12 and 13 describe issues in channel strategy and structure.

Dibb, S., Simkin, S., Pride, W. and Ferrel, O. (1997) *Marketing. Concepts and strategies* (3rd European edn). New York: Houghton Mifflin.
See companion Houghton Mifflin web site (*www.busmgt.ulst.ac.uk/h_mifflin/*).
See Chapter 12, Marketing Channels.

Friedman, L. and Furey, T. (1999) *The Channel Advantage*. Oxford: Butterworth-Heinemann.
Business book containing extensive discussion of how to integrate the Internet into channel strategy.

Ghosh, S. (1998) 'Making business sense of the Internet', *Harvard Business Review* March–April, 127–35.
This paper gives many US examples of how US companies have adapted to the Internet and the resulting disintermediation and reintermediation.

Kotler, P., Armstrong, G., Saunders, J. and Wong, V. (1999) *Principles of Marketing* (2nd edn). Hemel Hempstead: Prentice Hall, Europe.
See companion web site for 8th US edn: *cw.prenhall.com/bookbind/pubbooks/kotler/*.
See Chapter 21, Managing Marketing Channels

Kumar, N. (1999) 'Internet distribution strategies: dilemmas for the incumbent', *Financial Times*, Special Issue on Mastering Information Management, 7. Electronic Commerce (*www.ftmastering.com*).
This article assesses the impact of the Internet on manufacturers and their distribution channels. The other articles in this special issue are also interesting.

Mohr, J. and Nevin, J. (1990) 'Communications strategies in marketing channels', *Journal of Marketing,* October, 36–51.

Sarkar, M., Butler, B. and Steinfield, C. (1996) 'Intermediaries and cybermediaries: a continuing role for mediating players in the electronic market place', *Journal of Computer Mediated Comunications*, 1(3).
A key paper reviewing the different types of intermediaries that can exist online. Available online at *www.ascusc.org/jcmc*.

Strauss, J. and Frost, R. (1999) *Marketing on the Internet. Principles of online marketing.* New Saddle River, NJ: Prentice Hall.
Chapter 5, The Net as Distribution Channel, gives a brief review of how the Internet impacts on distribution channels.

PART 3

Internet marketing: implementation and practice

CHAPTER 8

Creating and building the web site

Learning objectives

After reading this chapter, the reader should be able to:

- understand the work involved in the different stages involved in creating a site;
- describe the design elements that contribute to effective web site content;
- select appropriate tools to assist in web site development.

Links to other chapters

This chapter builds on Chapter 3, which introduces the stages involved in developing a web site. Other related chapters are:

▶ Chapter 6, which considers issues associated with the cost of web site development and maintenance. It considers which suppliers should be used for web site development.

▶ Chapter 9, which describes how to promote a web site. This topic is dealt with in a separate chapter because of its importance.

▶ Chapter 11, which includes details of processes and software tools for building electronic commerce solutions.

▶ Chapter 10, which includes details of software tools for personalisation.

▶ Chapter 12, which describes the maintenance of a site once it is created.

INTRODUCTION

This chapter describes the stages involved in creating a web site. It describes in more detail the practical work involved in the process of site creation that was introduced in Chapter 3. For example, in Chapter 3, it was noted that it is common to use an Internet service provider (ISP) to host the web site. However, the criteria that need to be considered when hosting a site were not detailed. These, and other similar practical details that are essential knowledge for anyone managing or maintaining a web site, are considered in this chapter. The main stages involved with setting up a web site are shown in Fig. 8.1.

Of the stages shown in Fig. 8.1, that of analysis and design is described in most detail in this chapter since the nature of the web site content is, of course, vital in providing a satisfactory experience for the customer and leading to repeat visits. Testing and promotion of the web site are described in subsequent chapters. An alternative model with more detailed stages can be found in a practical 'Internet marketing framework' presented by Ong (1995) and summarised by Morgan (1996).

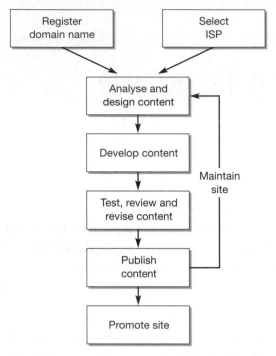

Fig. 8.1 Summary of process of web site development

Planning web site development

It is a natural mistake amongst those creating a new web site for the first time to 'dive in' and start creating web pages without forward planning. Planning is necessary since design of a site must occur before creation of web pages – to ensure a good quality site that does not need reworking at a later stage. Design involves analysing the needs of users of a site and then deciding upon the best way to build the site to fulfil their needs. Without a structured plan and careful design, costly reworking is inevitable, as the first version of a site will not achieve the needs of the end-users.

Conversely, it can be argued that not too much time should be spent on design and planning since web sites will constantly evolve. Experience of developing information systems for marketing and other applications has shown that an approach that involves too much up-front planning, analysis and design before development is started does not usually work well (Bocij *et al.*, 1999). The reason for this is that there may be a delay of several months, or even years, between the time the users are involved in discussing their needs from a system and the time they start to use the software. Over this time, the needs of the users, or the business itself, may have changed as market forces dictate. Additionally, when using the 'finished' system, the users may become aware of the need for features that were not originally envisaged, or there may be many errors or 'bugs' in the software. Problems such as these, which occur in the building of information systems, can be avoided by companies building web sites since a more natural approach is available, known as prototyping.

Web site prototyping

Prototypes are initial versions of a web site that contain the basic features and structure of the web site, but without all the content in place. The idea is that the development team and the marketing staff commissioning the work can review and comment on the prototype, and changes can then be made to the site that incorporate these comments. A further version or iteration of the web site can be made that can be commented on again. During prototyping, the prototype web pages are viewable only by staff inside the company – this is known as the test environment. This repeating or iterative approach is shown in Fig. 8.2.

The stages involved in developing the prototype are described in more detail later in this chapter. In brief, they involve the following:

1 *Analysis*. Understanding the requirements of the audience of the site and the requirements of the business, defined by business and marketing strategy.
2 *Design*. Specifying different features of the site that will fulfil the requirements of the users and the business identified during analysis.
3 *Development*. The creation of the web pages and the dynamic content of the web site.
4 *Testing and review*. Structured checks are conducted to ensure that different aspects of the site meet the original requirements and work correctly.

These are the four stages that are repeated during prototyping. There are also additional stages that occur at the start and end of the project and which are 'wrapped around' the prototyping effort (not shown in Fig. 8.2). There is an initial initiation stage, where the feasibility of producing the web site is reviewed. After the prototype has been developed to the point where it can be made available to its audience, it is published on the Web in a live environment. A separate promotion activity also occurs during prototyping and when the site is completed.

Prototypes and prototyping

A prototype is a preliminary version of part or a framework of all of a web site, which can be reviewed by its target audience, or the marketing team. Prototyping is an iterative process in which web site users suggest modifications before further prototypes and the final version of the site are developed.

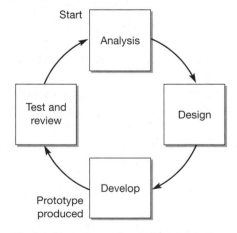

Fig. 8.2 Four stages of web site prototyping

The prototyping approach has the following benefits:

1 It prevents major design or functional errors being made during the construction of the web site. Such errors could be costly and time consuming to fix once the web site becomes live and could also damage the brand. Such errors will hopefully be identified early on and then corrected.
2 It involves the marketers responsible for the web site and ideally the potential audience of the web site in proactively shaping the web site. This should result in a site that more closely meets the needs of the users.
3 The iterative approach is intended to be rapid, and a site can be produced in a period of months or weeks.

When using the prototyping approach for a web site, a company has to decide whether to implement the complete version of the web site before making it available to its target audience or to make available a more limited version of the site. If it is necessary to establish a presence rapidly, the second approach could be used. This also has the benefit that feedback can be solicited from users and incorporated into later versions. Many companies will, however, prefer the security of the first approach in which the web site can be revised and market tested before a professional and complete version of the site is made available. This approach is less likely to cause damage to the brand or corporate image. It will still be possible for the company to make subsequent changes to the site based on feedback from users. An example of this is provided by Case study 8.2 on Orange, later in this chapter. Here new functions such as tariff calculators and customer service facilities were gradually introduced over a period of several years.

Initiation of the web site project

Before the analysis, design and creation of the web site, all major projects will have an initial phase in which the aims and objectives of the web site are reviewed, to assess whether it is worthwhile investing in the web site, and to decide on the amount to invest. This is part of the strategic planning process described in Chapters 5 and 6. This provides a framework for the project that ensures:

(a) there is management and staff commitment to the project;
(b) objectives are clearly defined;
(c) the costs and benefits are reviewed in order that the appropriate amount of investment in the site occurs;
(d) the project will follow a structured path, with clearly identified responsibilities for different aspects such as project management, analysis, promotion and maintenance;
(e) the implementation phase will ensure that important aspects of the project such as testing and promotion are not skimped.

> **Initiation of web site project**
> The phase of the project that involves a structured review of the costs and benefits of developing a web site (or making a major revision to an existing web site). A successful outcome to initiation will be a decision to proceed with the site development with an agreed budget and target completion date.

Domain name registration

It will be necessary to register a new domain name if the web site project will establish a new site or a promotional campaign that uses a new brand identity. The concept of domain names, more usually referred to as web addresses or URLs, was introduced in Chapter 3.

> **Domain name registration**
> The process of reserving a unique web address that can be used to refer to the company web site, in the form of *www.<company-name>.com* or *www.<company-name>.co.uk*.

Domain names are registered using an ISP or direct with one of the domain name services, such as:

1 *InterNIC* (*www.internic.net*). Registration for the .com, .org and .net domains. At the time of writing, registration has been deregulated so that it will be possible to register with any one of six companies.
2 *Nominet* (*www.nominet.org.uk*). Registration for the .co.uk domain. All country-specific domains such as .fr (France) or .de (Germany) have their own domain registration authority.
3 *Nomination* (*www.nomination.uk.com*). An alternative registration service for the UK, allowing registration in the (uk.com) pseudo-domain.

> **Activity 8.1**
>
> ### Domain name registration
>
> Think of a web site domain you might want to register. Go to the InternNIC site (*www.internic.net*) and use the tool provided to search to see whether the name is registered. Continue searching until you find a free name. Remember it is not necessary to include the http://www. prefix using this tool.
>
> How much would it cost you to register this name – both the initial cost and the ongoing costs each year? How often would you need to renew the registration?

The following guidelines should be borne in mind when registering domain names:

1 *Register the domain name as early as possible.* This is necessary since the precedent in the emerging law is that the first company to register the name is the one that takes ownership if it has a valid claim to ownership (*see* the Prince example in Mini case study 8.1). The mini case study also shows that if there is no claim to ownership, as in the 'One in a Million' case, then it will be possible for a company to retain ownership.

2 *Register multiple domain names* if this helps the potential audience to find the site. For example, British Midland may register its name as *www.britishmidland.com* and *www.britishmidland.co.uk*.

3 *Use the potential of non-company brand names* to help promote a product. For example a 1998 traditional media campaign for British Midland used *www.iflybritishmidland.com* as a memorable address to help users find its site.

4 *Avoid siting your site on an ISP server* that uses the name of the ISP such as: *www.<isp_name>.co.uk/<company_name<*. Such a name is not very memorable and takes quite a long time to type in. More importantly it reflects badly on the credibility of a company, as it indicates that it is too small to invest in a personalised domain name.

Mini case study 8.1   **Famous domain name clashes**

The 'One in a Million' case

In this case Richard Conway and Julian Nicholson from Manchester, UK, registered Internet domain names such as *ladbrokes.com*, *sainsburys.com*, *marksandspencer.com*, *spice-girls.net*, *buckinghampalace.org* under the name of their companies One in a Million and Global Media Communications. They then offered to sell the names to the various companies. In the court case it was claimed that Conway had written to Burger King, the hamburger chain, offering the domain name '*burgerking.co.uk*' for £25 000 plus VAT.

The case was brought by other companies that had also been affected by the purchase of related domain names. The companies included Marks & Spencer, Ladbrokes, J Sainsbury, Virgin Enterprises and British Telecommunications. They claimed that nine registered domain names constituted unlawful passing off and an infringement of trade marks.

The Deputy High Court judge granted the firms injunctions against the dealers using the names and ordered them to pay costs of £65 000. Since the companies were small, this judgment marked the end of the companies.

Source: *Electronic Telegraph*, Issue 919, Saturday 29 November 1997.

McDonald's Corporation pay out for domain name

In earlier cases, which were resolved without recourse to law, some companies have been prepared to pay for domain names. In the USA, Josh Quittner, a *Wired* magazine contributing writer and former *Newsday* reporter, managed to register the domain name *www.mcdonalds.com* since the company had only registered the domain *www.mcd.com*. Quittner used the registration to expose the loopholes in domain name registration and eventually persuaded McDonald's Corporation to donate $3500 to put a New York City school on the Internet.

Source: From Brunel (1996). Also available online at: *cla.org/RuhBook/chp3.htm#fn2*.

Prince v Prince

The UK training company Prince registered the domain name *www.prince.com* in 1995 after 12 years of trading under the name Prince. Prince first knew there was a problem when it received a letter from the US-based Prince Sportswear and tennis racket manufacturer in 1997 asserting that the UK firm had infringed its trade mark, and demanding that it give up the *prince.com* domain name. Prince UK brought a case on the advice of lawyer John Wood, suing Prince for making unjustifiable threats. The judge found that because of the precedent of the UK company using the brand name, the US company had no case. Since the finding Prince US has launched two sites, with the domain names: *www.princetennis.com* and *www.princegolf.com*.

Source: Computer Weekly News, 7 August 1997 (www.computerweekly.co.uk).

Selecting the right partner to host content

Selecting the right partner to host a web site is an important decision since the quality of service provided will directly impact on the quality of service delivered to a company's customers. The partner hosting content will usually be an Internet service provider (ISP – *see* Chapter 3) for the majority of small and medium companies, but for larger companies the web server used to host the content may be inside the company and managed by the company's IT department.

The quality of service of hosted content is essentially dependent on two factors: the performance of the web site and its availability.

The performance of the web site

The important measure in relation to performance is the speed with which a web page is delivered to users from the time when it is requested by clicking on a hyperlink. The length of time is dependent on a number of factors, some of which cannot be controlled (such as the number of users accessing the Internet), but primarily depends on the bandwidth of the ISP's connection to the Internet and the performance of the web server hardware and software.

Bandwidth gives an indication of the speed at which data can be transferred from a web server along a particular medium such as a network cable. In simple terms bandwidth can be thought of as the size of a pipe along which information flows. The higher the bandwidth, the greater the diameter of the pipe, and the faster information is delivered to the user. Bandwidth is measured in bits per second, where one character or digit, such as the number '1', would be equivalent to 8 bits. So a modem operating at 28 880 bits per second (28.8 Kbps) will transfer information at 3610 characters per second (28 800/8). When selecting an ISP it is important to consider the speed of the link between the ISP and the Internet. Choices may be:

- ISDN – from 56 Kbps to 128 Kbps;
- Frame Relay – from 56 Kbps to T1 (1.55 Mbps)
- Dedicated Point-to-Point – from 56 Kbps to T3 (45 Mbps): connected to the Internet backbone.

Some ISPs are not connected directly to the Internet backbone and are linked to it via other providers. Their service will be slower than that of servers directly connected to the main Internet backbone since information has to 'jump' several different network links.

Bandwidth

The speed at which data are transferred using a particular network media. Bandwith is measured in bits-per-second (bps).

■ Kbps (1 kilobit per second or 1000 bps – a modem operates at up to 56.6 Kbps).
■ Mbps (1 megabit per second or 1 000 000 bps – company networks operate at 10 or more Mbps).
■ Gbps (1 gigabit per second or 1 000 000 000 bps – fibre optic or satellite links operate at Gbps).

The speed of the site will also be affected by the speed of the response to a request by an end-user for information. This will be dependent on the speed of the server machine on which the web site is hosted and how quickly the server processes the information. If only a small number of users are accessing information on the server, there will not be a noticeable delay in meeting requests for pages. If, however, thousands of users are requesting information at the same time, there may be a delay, and it is important that the combination of web server software and hardware can cope. Web server software will not greatly affect the speed at which queries are answered, but these factors will: amount of memory (RAM) installed in the server; the speed of retrieving data from the hard disk; and the speed of the processors. Many of the search engines now store all their index data in RAM since this is faster than reading data from the hard disk.

A major factor for a company to consider when choosing an ISP is whether the server is *dedicated* to one company or whether content from several companies is located on the same server. A dedicated server is best, but it will attract a premium price.

The availability of the web site

The availability of a web site is an indication of how easy it is for a user to connect to it. In theory this figure should be 100 per cent, but sometimes, for technical reasons such as failures in the server hardware or upgrades to software, users cannot access the site.

To help companies decide on different providers rankings are made on different factors, as shown in Mini case study 8.2, Assessing ISP performance.

Mini case study 8.2   **Assessing ISP performance**

Several UK Internet magazines such as *Internet Works* (*www.iwks.com*) provide monthly performance assessments of different ISPs. Zeus Technology has a continuously updated survey for UK and US servers at *webperf.zeus.co.uk*, which indicates the vast variation in performance of web servers. It is clearly useful to compare figures between rival ISPs when choosing an ISP for the first time or switching between ISPs. There may be a trade-off between the quality of service, as indicated by these figures, and the cost of using the provider. The cost will have to be compared with the potential loss of business when a web server is unavailable, or when customers leave a site while waiting for information to download. Table 8.1 suggests speed of download is an important factor for customers.

Performance is assessed in several areas:

1. *Long-term availability trend for web server.* Availability varies quite considerably: from 99.82 per cent to 97.09 per cent for the top 50 ISPs. It is measured by another computer contacting or 'pinging' the ISP several thousand times each month to assess whether it is available.
2. *Variation of download rate from web server.* Download rate measures the length of time it takes to download HTML files, images and any other files such as plug-in content. It is usually measured as kilobits per second (Kbps), with the top 50 ISPs varying from 514 Kbps to 61 Kbps in the Zeus survey, so again there is a wide variation here.
3. *E-mail server availability and response.* E-mails will usually be handled by a separate computer or server, so the availability of the e-mail server needs to be assessed too.
4. *FTP server availability and response.* As explained in Chapter 3, the FTP method is used to upload completed web pages and graphics to the web server. The FTP server is, however, a separate server which a company such as Lotus or Microsoft might use when offering software downloads. Thus this figure can be disregarded by the majority of companies.

One of the leading ISPs in several surveys is UUNet (*www.uk.uu.net*). This company can be thought as a model for how other 'high-end' ISPs will operate in the future since it operates high quality services at a premium price. This is achieved through *service level agreements (SLAs)*. Further information on SLAs is available at *www.uk.uu.net/support/sla/*. The SLA will define confirmed standards of availability and performance measured in terms of the latency or network delay when information is passed from one point to the next (measured as London to New York). The SLA also includes notifying to the customer when the web service becomes unavailable and providing reasons for the unavailability and estimates of when the service will be restored.

Who is involved in a web site project?

The success of a web site will be heavily dependent on the range of people involved in its development, and how well they work as a team. As a result, the feasibility study will define how the project should be structured and what the different responsibilities will be. Typical profiles of team members follow:

- *Site sponsors.* These will be senior managers who will effectively be paying for the system. They will understand the strategic benefits of the system and will be keen that the site is implemented successfully to achieve the objectives they have set. Sponsors will also aim to encourage staff by means of their own enthusiasm and will stress why the introduction of the system is important to the business and its workers. This will help overcome any barriers to introduction of the web site.

- *Site owner.* 'Ownership' will typically be the responsibility of a marketing manager, who may be devoted full-time to overseeing the site in a large company; it may be part of a marketing manager's remit in a smaller company. The site owner is effectively the customer of the project manager for a web site in a larger company.

- *Project manager.* This person is responsible for the planning and co-ordination of the web site project. He or she will aim to ensure the site is developed within the budget and time constraints that have been agreed at the start of the project, and that the site delivers the planned-for benefits for the company and its customers. In smaller companies, the project manager may be the same person as the site owner.

- *Site designer.* The site designer will define the 'look and feel' of the site including its layout and how company brand values are transferred to the web. Further details are given later in the chapter in the section on designing site content.

- *Content developer.* The content developer will write the copy for the web site and convert it to a form suitable for the site. In medium or large companies this role may be split between marketing staff or staff from elsewhere in the organisation who write the copy and a technical member of staff who converts it to the graphics and HTML documents forming the web page and does the programming for interactive content.

- *Webmaster.* This is a technical role. The webmaster is responsible for ensuring the quality of the site. This means achieving suitable availability, speed, working links between pages and connections to company databases. In small companies the webmaster may take on graphic design and content developer roles also.

- *Stakeholders.* The impact of the web site on other members of the organisation should not be underestimated. Internal staff may need to refer to some of the information on the web site or use its services.

Case study 8.1, Internet marketing and new media jobs, indicates the type of skills needed for some of the different positions in Internet marketing. Note that there is a great deal of overlap between the skills required for different jobs, and that a number of different terms are used to refer to the different positions.

CASE STUDY 8.1   **INTERNET MARKETING AND NEW MEDIA JOBS**

The job advertisements below are taken from the New Media recruitment section of *Revolution* magazine in 1999. They are intended to show the range of careers available in Internet marketing and the skills required.

Web designer

Skilled and experienced web designers with a proven track record required to join dynamic sports media organisation. To be successful in this role you will have outstanding design skills, a strong feel for web structure and navigation and you will have closely worked with internet programmers on the design of high quality contemporary web sites. Excellent Photoshop, Flash, Director and knowledge of HTML with an awareness of the constraints of web graphics.

Web developer

A new and exciting long term contract requires us to appoint a highly skilled web developer on a permanent basis to initiate the project. You should be a confident self starter with at least 1–2 years' commercial experience. Your skills will include Visual Basic, SQL Programming, database to web site integration, excellent working knowledge of the Internet, HTML, Windows NT and VB Script.

Webmaster

Fantastic opportunity to join a newly formed team who will be responsible for the launch of an exciting and dynamic e-commerce web site. Based in luxury offices in the West End, you will be a 'key pin' in managing the site and updating it on a regular basis. Your skills set should include a broad understanding of web technology to include HTML and DHTML, Javascript, Perl and Director.

Online marketer

This job involves far more than just copywriting or co-ordinating promotions. Your day-to-day activities will be to manage online marketing campaigns, maintaining relationships with external partners including portal sites, ISPs and online promotional agencies. You will also be required to support the marcomms team on wider campaigns where required, write product descriptions and marketing materials. You must have between 1 and 3 years experience in sales, advertising, or other marketing related areas. Agency experience is a plus. Strong copywriting skills are a requirement and you must also have a strong interest and knowledge of the Web. Direct Web experience is preferred, but Web surfing experience is a must. Fluency in French or German is a plus.

Project manager

You will be responsible for a team of 3–4 designers/programmers, working with the production manager, account director and client. You should have excellent communication skills, as the position is client facing.

Discussion questions

1. Review all the advertisements for reference to communication skills. For each of the different positions, with whom is liaison necessary, both inside and outside the company?

2. Identify which of the jobs appear to be for a new media (advertising/design agency) company and which are for traditional companies promoting products and services.

3. Use a web search engine or visit the sites Adobe (*www.adobe.com*) and Macromedia (*www.macromedia.com*) to find out what is meant by 'excellent Photoshop, Flash, Director … skills'.

4. Why do you think the web site developer requires Visual Basic, SQL Programming and database to web site integration rather than simply straightforward HTML skills?

5. Each of the advertisements mentions the importance of experience. How can initial experience be gained, to avoid a 'Catch 22' situation?

The responsibilities of the different types of people involved in web site development are discussed further in Chapter 12 from a maintenance and updating perspective.

Analysis for web site development

Analysis involves using different marketing research techniques to find out the best method of designing and implementing the site. It is not a 'one-off' exercise, but is likely to be repeated for each iteration of the prototype. Although analysis and design are separate activities, there tends to be considerable overlap between the two phases, and for this reason they are shown together in Fig. 8.1. In analysis we are seeking to answer the following types of questions:

- What are the key audiences for the site?
- What should the content of site be?
- Which customer service capabilities will we provide for customers?
- How will the site be structured?
- How will navigation around the site occur?

These questions will not be answered in relation to site structure and navigation until after we have looked at site design and assessed different alternatives. We will consider these issues in the section on design. In this section we will consider briefly how to collect information about the needs of users of the site.

> **Analysis phase**
> Analysis refers to the identification of the requirements of a web site. Techniques to achieve this may include focus groups, questionnaires sent to existing customers or interviews to key accounts.

Methods of finding customer needs

Refer back to Chapter 2 for a review of how the different types of buyer behaviour exhibited on the Internet should be taken into account when conducting the analysis for a web site. For example Lewis and Lewis (1997) identify different behaviour types such as directed-information seekers and undirected information seekers (browsers). For the former group a search facility may be useful on the site, whereas a less formal approach will suit the browsers. It is also worth remembering that customers will be at different stages in adopting the web site (Breitenbach and van Doren, 1998): that is, they may be novices who need guidance or they may be experienced users who need short cuts to be productive. These issues are described in more detail in the section below on developing customer-oriented content.

It is also important to consider how the web site design and content will meet the needs of customers at different stages of the buying cycle. This issue was illustrated in Fig. 2.5 and is considered further by Berthon *et al.* (1998).

The methods for defining the needs of users of sites will vary according to whether the site is for a business-to-business or a consumer audience. For instance, focus groups are more likely to be successfully used for consumer sites (or low-value, high-volume business-to-business sites) with many customers purchasing low-value products. For a business-to-business site where a company is selling high-value products to a more select range of customers it is more appropriate to try to talk direct to key customers to find what their needs are. The method used will also depend on the type of distribution channel. If, for example, a product is pushed through many different distributors, then these will have valuable opinions as to what should be included within the web site. The following methods may be used to identify customer needs:

Interviews with marketing staff

When web sites are designed by an external marketing or design agency, their starting-point will often be informal interviews with marketing or account managers who are familiar with the customers' needs and who will also have their own ideas as to what they want to achieve through the web site. While this approach is common, it is also useful to involve customers in the process as soon as possible, since marketing staff may not be familiar with this new medium and may not be able to 'second-guess' the customers' needs or be aware of the full potential.

Questionnaire to companies

When the company setting up a web site has a limited number of business customers, sending out questionnaires to these customers may be a useful way of collecting information.

The type of questionnaire that could be sent out to customers is shown in the box 'Sample customer questionnaire'. In addition to finding out the type of services the customer is likely to use (questions 5 and 6), such a questionnaire is also useful for marketing research since questions 1 to 4 indicate how committed the customer is to the Internet and whether the Internet will be an effective medium for communicating to and making direct sales to the customer. If the customer is not connected to the Internet now, then questions on future use will give a crude assessment of the growth in significance of the Internet channel for a customer. Note that such questionnaires should also attempt to establish the use of the Internet by the different people involved in the buying decision (question 3 gives an indication of this).

Sample customer questionnaire

1 Is your company connected to the Internet?

☐ Yes   ☐ No

2 When do you anticipate using the following Internet services?

Access type	Now: how long?	Within 6 months	Within 1 year	Within 2 years	Never
Internet e-mail					
Access to web					
Host web site					
Host intranet					

► **Sample customer questionnaire** *continued*

3 **If your staff have access to the web, which ones?**

    ❏ All   ❏ Senior Managers   ❏ Technical staff   ❏ Buyers

    ❏ Other:_____

4 **Number connected in total?** _____

5 **Would you be interested in using the Internet to:**

    ❏ Receive updates about our company and its products via e-mail?

    ❏ Search for products in a web-based catalogue?

    ❏ Order products online?

    ❏ Read about customer support issues

6 **What aspects of a site are important to you when using a web site?**

    a._____

    b._____

    c._____

7 **What is your opinion of the Internet as a business tool?**

8 **Please add your e-mail and web site addresses if appropriate:**

    e-mail:_____   Web address:http://www._____

Informal interviews with key accounts

A similar means of collecting information will be through account managers or sales staff who have direct contact with customers. As well as asking the questions in the questionnaire, the interview should aim to assess the desire for personalised information provided by an extranet. Such information might give the client the opportunity to view the availability and prices of products for themselves and to view past orders. An example of such an extranet is that provided by the tile manufacturer HR Johnson Ceramics International (*www.johnson-tiles.com*).

Focus groups

The principle of using focus groups to help design web sites is similar to that for using them for testing television advertisements or feature films before they are released. Use of focus groups involves selecting a group that matches a typical audience profile and then asking them to comment on different aspects of the web site. Another similarity is that the focus group is usually used once there has already been considerable investment to develop the concept to a point where the group can meaningfully comment on it. This means that focus groups tend to be more useful in relation to minor modifications to an existing concept than for the more expensive option of completely revising the concept. As a result, focus groups are more often used to get ideas for improvements to existing sites that need a major revision. In 1998 *Yellow Pages* involved 800 customers in focus groups and as a result revised its site to make navigation easier.

Reviewing competitors' web sites

Benchmarking of competitors' web sites will be vital in positioning the web site to compete effectively with competitors who already have web sites. The importance of benchmarking, and some of the factors that need to be considered, are discussed in Chapter 5.

A review of other web sites suggests that, for most companies, the type of information that can be included on a web site will be fairly similar. The box, 'A web site marketing communications checklist' suggests the type of information that should appear on the web site. During analysis customers can be asked to view such a comprehensive list to evaluate which information they find most useful.

A web site marketing communications checklist

About the company
- [ ] History
- [ ] Contacts
- [ ] Office locations – addresses and maps
- [ ] Company annual reports (investor information)
- [ ] Financial performance (investor information)

Products and services
- [ ] Catalogue of products, prices?
- [ ] Online sales from product
- [ ] Current stock levels and delivery times
- [ ] Detailed technical specifications
- [ ] Customer testimonials and client list
- [ ] White papers
- [ ] Press releases
- [ ] Special offers
- [ ] Demonstrations
- [ ] Where to obtain them

(Consistent marketing message and branding applied throughout.)

Customer services
- [ ] Product returns
- [ ] Electronic help desk
- [ ] Frequently asked questions

Events
- [ ] Seminars
- [ ] Exhibitions
- [ ] Training

> ► **A web site marketing communications checklist** *continued*
>
> **General information**
>
> ☐ Contact us
>
> ☐ What's New or Media Centre (for PR)
>
> ☐ Job vacancies
>
> ☐ Index or site map
>
> ☐ Search
>
> ☐ Links to related sites

Many commentators such as Sterne (1999) make the point that some sites miss out the basic information that someone who is unfamiliar with a company may want to know, such as:

- Who are you?
- What do you do? What products or services are available?
- Where do you do it? Are the products and services available internationally?

In addition to specific needs for information that are identified during analysis, it can be suggested that there are some general requirements for web sites that companies should try and achieve through effective design. These general needs of customers, for which the web site should be designed to cater, are indicated in Table 8.1. It is apparent that it is not the promotions, design and branding that are perceived as important, but the basic qualities of good information: can it be accessed rapidly, is it easy to find, and is it relevant?

Table 8.1 Ten key reasons for returning to site

Reason to return	*Percentage of respondents*
1 High quality content	75
2 Ease of use	66
3 Quick to download	58
4 Updated frequently	54
5 Coupons and incentives	14
6 Favourite brands	13
7 Cutting-edge technology	12
8 Games	12
9 Purchasing capabilities	11
10 Customisable content	10

Source: Forrester Research poll of 8600 online households, 1998.

Designing web site content

Once analysis has determined the information needs of the site, the site can be designed. It will be shown that design is critical to a successful web site since it will determine the quality of experience users of a site have; if they have a good experience they will return, if not they will not! A 'good experience' is determined by a number of factors such as those that affect how easy it is to find information: for example, the structure of the site, menu choices and searching facilities. It is also affected by less tangible factors such as the graphical design and layout of the site.

> **Design phase**
> The design phase defines how the site will work in the key areas of web site structure, navigation and security.

Achieving a good design is important before too many web pages are developed since, if time is taken to design a site, less time will be wasted later when the site is reworked. Large sites are usually produced by creating templates comprising the graphical and menu elements to which content is added.

As mentioned previously, design is not solely a paper-based exercise, but needs to be integrated into the prototyping process. The design should be tested by review with the client and customer to ensure it is appropriate. The design of site layout, navigation and structure can be tested in two different ways. First, early designs can be paper based – drawn by the designer on large pieces of paper – or 'mock-ups' can be produced on screen using a drawing or paint program. This process is referred to as storyboarding. Second, a working, dynamic prototype can be produced in which users can select different menu options onscreen that will take them to skeleton pages (minus content) of different parts of the site.

> **Storyboarding**
> Using static drawings or screenshots of the different parts of a web site to review the design concept with customers or clients.

Since the main reason given in Table 8.1 for returning to a web site is high quality content, it is important to determine, through analysis, that the content is correct. However, the quality of content is determined by more than the text copy. It is important to achieve high quality content through design. To help in this it is useful to consider the factors that affect quality content. These are shown in Fig. 8.3. All are determined by the quality of the information.

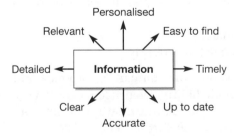

Fig. 8.3 Different aspects of high quality information content of a web site

| Activity 8.2 | **Content quality** |

Review Fig. 8.3 and Table 8.1 and summarise how the four most significant factors that control whether visitors return to the site (Table 8.1) relate to the different aspects of information quality (Fig. 8.3), and what action is necessary during the design phase to achieve these aspects. To take a simple example, the attribute 'updated frequently' is dependent on information being 'up to date'. The design action necessary to achieve this is to agree quality standards concerning who is responsible for updating information and setting targets for how often information is updated. You should present your answer in a table as follows:

Reason to return to site	Aspects of information quality	Design action required
1. High quality content 2. Ease of use 3. Quick to download 4. Updated frequently		

Developing customer-oriented content

In Chapter 2 it was suggested that a customer orientation to a web site is important, but how can this be achieved? For a web site to be effective, its content must be designed to accommodate the different characteristics of its customers. To achieve customer-oriented content, the web site design should enable different parts of the site to provide specific information and facilities for different customers who may be at different stages of the buying process. This is an integration of many of the concepts of Internet marketing communications described earlier in the chapter. Content of a site should be structured according to the following characteristics:

1 Familiarity of the customer with a product/company

For customers who are not familiar with a company, it is important to be able to answer their key questions readily:

- What does the company sell?
- How can its products be bought – where does it sell its products (channels and countries)?
- How can the company be contacted?
- Are there any special offers available currently?

As well as answering these questions, the company's corporate and brand identity should be apparent to establish credibility, even from a short visit. For customers who are repeat visitors to a site, updated information on products, prices or the market should be available, to encourage further repeat visits.

2 Familiarity of the customer with the Internet.

Some customers, perhaps a majority, will be novices to the Internet. It is important not to alienate them by asking them things they cannot do such as downloading a special add-in or plug-in which is necessary to view some content such as an animation of how a product works. Hoffman and Novak (1997) introduce the concept of flow (*see* the section on site management later in the chapter) as an important factor in effective web site marketing. They suggest that sites should be designed to enhance the flow experience, which they define as a 'process of optimal experience' that occurs when a consumer perceives a balance between his or her skills and the navigation facilities possible from the web site. If a customer has a positive flow experience then that customer will develop greater loyalty to a site and associated brands.

3 Familiarity of a customer with a company web site

Breitenbach and van Doren (1998) identify the following stages in adoption of a web site, which are similar in nature to stages in the product-buying process, namely awareness, interest, evaluation, trial and adoption. It is only at the adoption stage that the customer will become a regular user. This model is probably most suited to informational sites such as a news service or search sites such as portals for which a user is likely to become a regular user. Nevertheless, all types of sites will have experienced and inexperienced users, and navigation options should be available for both.

4 Stage of the customer in the buying process

The web site should support the different informational and functional needs of different people at different stages of the buying process, as explained in the section in Chapter 2 on varying the communications mix.

5 Type of customer

To help users find information, the site should be categorised in terms that are clear to the customer. Many sites contain lists of products and codes which are structured in a way that is not intuitive to a new customer. Menu options can be structured according to traditional market segments based on consumer demographics or, for the business-to-business sector, can be based on market size and type. Of course, this must be done in a subtle way – customers are unlikely to classify themselves as C2DEs. But, by adopting a customer focus, Orange, on its web site, provides not only a product menu option, but also options for customers with different needs such as those wanting tariff information, phone feature information or options for owners (*see* Case study 8.2).

A study of the advertising impact of web site content and its design has been conducted by Pak (1999). She reviewed the techniques on web sites used to communicate the message to the customer in terms of existing advertising theory. The study considered the creative strategy used, in terms of the rational and emotional appeals contained within the visuals and the text. As would be expected intuitively, the appeal of the graphics was more emotional than that for the text; the latter used a more rational appeal. The study also considered the information content of the advertisements using classification schemes such as that of Resnick and Stern (1977). The information cues are still relevant to modern web site design. Some of the main information cues, in order of frequency of use, were:

- performance (what does the product do?);
- components/content (what is the product made up of?);

ORANGE – CUSTOMER ORIENTATION ACHIEVES 12000 VISITORS TO SITE EACH WEEK

Orange first started using the Internet as a business tool in 1995. Since then, the site has been updated continually to reflect the needs of its customers. According to Nigel Shardlow, the new media manager at Orange (Shardlow, 1999), the site started off targeting a relatively limited audience. Doing so was thought to entail a lower risk than setting up a major site when the medium was relatively new. The initial audience was thought to be technical, consisting of students, academics and IT staff at organisations with Internet access. The initial content reflected this audience, the site providing a tool for finding out the Orange coverage area and another for asking technical queries.

In June 1996, the company decided to broaden the scope of the site, to provide more information on products and services such as a Talk Plan calculator that suggests to potential users which tariff is most suitable for them and a mechanism for looking up the nearest Orange dealership according to postcode. News and press releases and an interactive coverage map followed later in the year.

By the beginning of 1997 the amount of content on the site had made it difficult for customers to find the information they needed, so in June 1997 a complete restructuring of the site was necessary, to enable customers to find information more easily. Further information on products was added, but this time broken down into that appropriate for those looking for a phone for the first time,

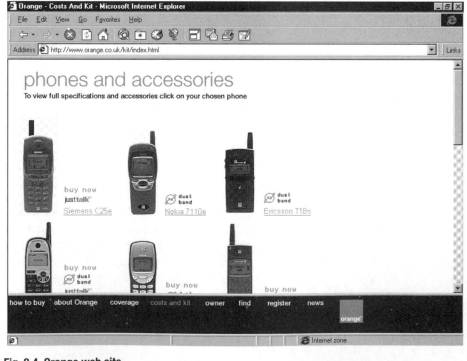

Fig. 8.4 Orange web site

existing phone owners and business users. The buying guide leads each type of person through a series of choices, available on onscreen forms, in order to put together a suitable package.

Today the site is seen as a useful tool not only for customers, but also for dealers, journalists, investors and potential employees. For dealers, it is a central place where up-to-date product and service information can be found; journalists use the site for researching and downloading press releases; and investors find corporate information such as interim and annual reports there. Many employees have now joined the company after making applications online. As a result of visits from all these different types of site customer, the Orange site now receives 12 000 visitors each week. So that it can keep customers informed without their having to remember to access the web site, Orange has registered 20 000 people and keeps them informed through regular e-mail bulletins.

The web site is today just one element of new media activity. To drive visitors two additional sites have been created, such as that for the Orange Prize for Fiction.

Web reference: Orange (*www.orange.co.uk*).

Questions

1 Why was the site not initially developed for a wide audience?

2 From reading the account above and through visiting the site, identify tools on the site that give users a service not readily available from other media.

3 Produce a table of the different types of customer the web site receives and the types of information and services that are oriented to these users.

4 What are the main benefits of registering at the site (for both Orange and its customers)?

- price/value;
- implicit comparison;
- availability;
- quality;
- special offers;
- explicit comparisons.

Aaker and Norris (1982) devised a framework in which the strategy for creative appeal is based on emotion/feeling and rational/cognitive appeal, is based on facts and logic.

Site structure

The design of the structure of a site is something that should be decided upon early in the development of the site, since it may be costly to redefine the structure at a later stage. The storyboarding method referred to earlier in the chapter can be used to develop the site structure. This can be done by having one diagram or 'map' that shows the structure of the site and other sheets that show the layout of individual pages. Figure 8.5 shows the structure of a web site that is arranged in a

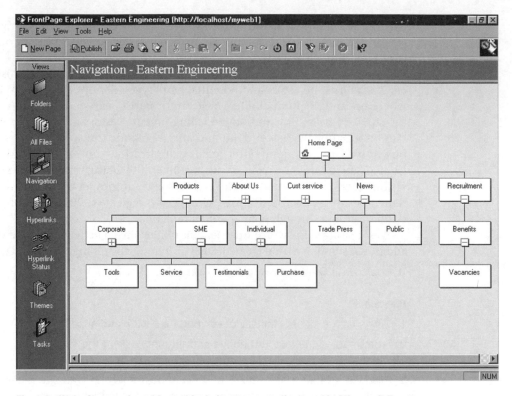

Fig. 8.5   Web site map for a hierarchical site structure displayed in Microsoft Frontpage

hierarchical or tree-like form. It is viewed in Microsoft Frontpage, which is used to help manage the different pages. This is a very common type of web structure since it is natural to have a top-level 'home page' with different options such as 'Products', 'What's New' and 'About the company'. On selecting one of these top-level menu options such as 'Products' the user will be presented with a web page with further options referring to that topic such as different types of product. Mini case study 8.3 illustrates this type of hierarchical web structure.

When deciding upon the structure of the site, it should be remembered that the user may not wish to work through the site in a systematic order by moving up and down the branches of each tree. Links should be available to move from one branch to another branch.

The ability to display a site structure is an important feature of web site design and construction tools since they facilitate this process.

The ease of moving from different points in the structure of the web site is critically dependent on the menu options available for moving from one part of the structure to another, and this is described in the following section. Alternative site structures are considered in Bickerton *et al.* (1998) and Sterne (1999)

Site navigation

Hoffman and Novak (1996) identify the concept of 'flow' as important in governing the reaction of a user to a site. Flow essentially describes how easy it is for the users to find the information they need as they move from one part of the site to the next. It broadly equates to ease of use in Table 8.1 and is mainly dependent on the navigation facilities of the site. Note that in some cases, if they are not 'directed-information seekers' (*see* Chapter 2), users may not know what information they are looking for!

Flow

Flow describes how easy it is for users of a site to move between the different pages of content of the site.

Flow is not simply a matter of navigating from one part of the site to another; it also concerns all interactions such as filling in forms. This is described in the section on service quality later in this chapter.

Navigation

Navigation describes how easy it is to find and move between different information on a web site. It is governed by menu arrangements, site structure and the layout of individual pages.

It can be suggested that there are three important aspects to a site that is easy to navigate. These are:

1 *Consistency*. The site will be easier to navigate if the user is presented with a consistent user interface when viewing the different parts of the site. For example, if the menu options in the support section of the site are on the left side of the screen, then they should also be on the left when the user moves to the 'news section' of the site.

2 *Simplicity*. Sites are easier to navigate if there are limited numbers of options. It is usually suggested that two or possibly three levels of menu are the most that are desirable. For example, there may be main menu options at the left of the screen that take the user to the different parts of the site, and at the bottom of the screen there will be specific menu options that refer to that part of the site. (Sub-menus in this form are often referred to as nesting.)

3 *Context*. Context is the use of 'signposts' to indicate to users where they located within the site – in other words to reassure users that they are not 'lost'. To help with this, the web site designer should use particular text or colour to indicate to users which part of the site they are currently using. Context can be provided by the use of Javascript 'rollovers', where the colour of the menu option changes when the user positions the mouse over the menu option and then changes again when the menu option is selected. Many sites also have a site-map option that shows the layout and content of the whole site so the user can understand its structure. When using a well-designed site it should not be necessary to refer to such a map regularly.

It should be noted that the three elements of web site navigation described above tend to support each other. To achieve simplicity, both consistency and context are required. To illustrate the importance of these factors *see* Mini case study 8.3.

Mini case study 8.3 **Elements of effective site design**

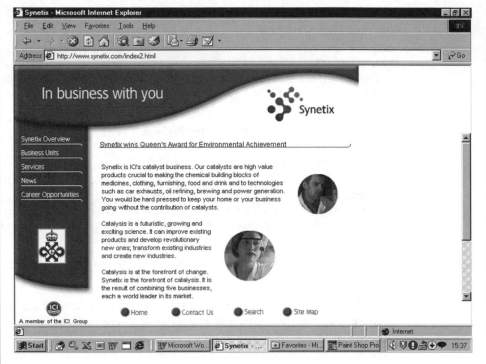

Fig. 8.6 Synetix web site (*www.synetix.com*), **illustrating different design elements**

This case study considers a business-to-business site – that of Synetix (*www. synetix.com*) – and looks at how well the ideas of consistency, context and simplicity are applied.

This site illustrates the following navigation characteristics:

1 *Consistency*. The menu options on the left side of the screen and at the bottom are always available to make it easy for the user to navigate around the site. The menu options at the left will vary according to which part of the site the user is in. Those at the bottom will always be available, whichever part of the site the user is in.

2 *Simplicity*. The menu options adopted are straightforward, with five available on the left and four at the bottom. The site also has a 'clean' design with relatively few graphics, which adds to the simple appearance and ease of use of the site.

3 *Context*. Context is provided by Javascript 'rollovers' – the colour of the menu option on the left changes when the user positions the mouse over the menu option and then changes again when the menu option is selected.

For further information on aspects of web design see the web site Web Pages That Suck (*www.webpagesthatsuck.com.*) This site describes its approach as 'learn good web site design through viewing bad web site design'.

Menu options

Designing and creating the menus to support navigation present several options, and these are briefly described here. The main options are:

1 Text menus, buttons or images

The site user can select menus by clicking on different objects. They can click on a basic text hyperlink, underlined in blue, by default. It should be noted that these will be of different sizes according to the size the user has selected to display the text. The use of text menus only may make a site look primitive and reduce its graphic appeal. Rectangular or oval buttons can be used to highlight menu options more distinctly. Images can also be used to show menu options. For instance, customer service could be denoted by a picture of a help desk. Whilst these are graphically appealing it may not be obvious that these are menu options until the user positions the mouse over them. A combination of text menu options and either buttons or images is usually the best compromise. This way users have the visual appeal of buttons or images, but also the faster option of text – they can select these menus if they are waiting for graphical elements to load, or if the images are turned off in the web browser.

2 Rollovers

'Rollover' is the term used to describe colour changes – where the colour of the menu option changes when the user positions the mouse over the menu option and then changes again when the menu option is selected. Rollovers are useful in that they help achieve the context referred to in the previous section, by highlighting the area of the site the user is in.

3 Positioning

Menus can be positioned at any of the edges of the screen, with left, bottom or top being conventional for western cultures. The main design aim is to keep the position consistent between different parts of the site.

4 Frames

Frames are a feature of HTML which enable menus to be positioned at one side of the screen in a small area (frame) while the content of the page is displayed in the main frame. Frames have their advocates and detractors, but they are commonly used on sites since they clearly and easily separate the menu from the content. Detractors point to poor display speed, difficulties in indexing content in search engines and inflexibility on positioning.

5 Number of levels

In a hierarchical structure there could be as many as ten different levels, but for simplicity it is normal to try and achieve a site structure with a nesting level of four or fewer. Even in an electronic commerce shopping site with 20 000 products it should be possible to select a product at four menu levels. For example:

- level 1 – drink;
- level 2 – spirits;
- level 3 – whisky;
- level 4 – brand x.

6 Number of options

Psychologists recommend having a limited number of choices within each menu. If a menu has more than seven, it is probably necessary to add another level to the hierarchy to accommodate the extra choices.

Graphic design

Graphic design of web sites represents a challenge since designers of web sites are severely constrained by a number of factors:

- *The speed of downloading graphics* – designers need to allow for home users who view sites using a slow modem across a phone line and who are unlikely to wait minutes to view a web site.
- *The screen resolutions of the computer* – designing for different screen resolutions is necessary, since some users with laptops may be operating at low resolution such as 640 by 480 pixels, the majority at a resolution of 800 by 600 pixels, and a few at higher resolutions of 1064 by 768 pixels or greater.
- *The number of colours on screen* – some users may have monitors capable of displaying 16 million colours giving photo-realism, while other may have only 256 colours.
- *The type of web browser used* – different browsers such as Microsoft Internet Explorer and Netscape Navigator and different versions of browsers such as version 4.0 or 5.0 may display graphics or text slightly differently or may support different plug-ins (*see* the section in Chapter 12 on testing).

As a result of these constraints, the design of web sites is a constant compromise between what looks visually appealing and modern and what works for the older browsers, with slower connections. This is often referred to as the 'lowest common denominator problem' since this is what the designer must do – design for the old browsers, using slow links and low screen resolutions. One method for avoiding the 'lowest common denominator problem' is to offer the user a 'high-tech' or 'low-tech' choice: one for users with fast connections and high screen resolutions, and another for users who do not have these facilities. This facility is mainly seen offered on sites produced by large companies since it requires more investment to effectively duplicate the site.

Despite these constraints, graphic design is important in determining the feel or character of a site. The graphic design can help shape the user's experience of a site and should be consistent with the brand involved. Look at the examples of financial services providers in Activity 8.3 (*see* Figs. 8.7 and 8.8) to see the effect of graphic design.

Activity 8.3

Giving a site character through graphic design

Both of the sites illustrated make extensive use of images of people to help differenti-ate and position their services. Visit these sites and other financial services sites and then discuss the following:

1 How successful do you think these sites are in using graphics for Internet-based marketing?
2 Discuss the use of the sites to highlight promotions on the two sites.
3 Evaluate the ease of use of the two sites.

Fig. 8.7 The Egg web site (*www.egg.com*)

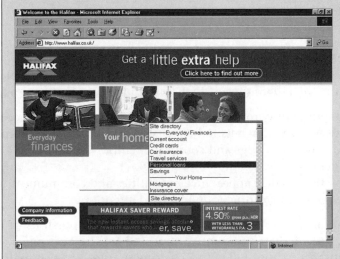

Fig. 8.8 The Halifax web site (*www.halifax.co.uk*)

Brand identity

As well as the technical constraints on the graphical design mentioned in the previous section, a further constraint is that the site should be consistent with the offline brand of the web site. The general wisdom, discussed in Chapter 6, is that the online brand identity should be similar to and should support the offline brand. However, Chapter 6 gave some examples, such as DHL (*www.dhl.co.uk*) and Cisco (*www.cisco.com*), where the companies had decided to differentiate their web offering by using a different brand from their offline brand. The brand can be damaged if the graphics are of poor quality or if the site is difficult to use in any way. This point emphasises again the importance of competent design.

Localisation

A further issue to be considered by the web designer is how to provide content for the different types of users in different countries. This is summarised by the slogan: 'act global, think local', sometimes contracted to 'glocalisation'. Localisation is primarily thought of in terms of translating the web content to different languages. However there are further issues such as ensuring the cultural tone of the web copy is appropriate and that the promotional techniques used are valid in specific countries. It may be decided that the amount of content developed will be in line with the likely volume of users of the web site. The Durex web site (*www.durex.com*) provides a good example of this (*see* p. 155), with more content being translated into French, for example, than into Croatian.

> **Localisation**
> Designing the content of the web site in such a way that it is appropriate to different audiences in different countries.

Service quality

The site designer should also consider how the design of a site affects the level of customer service the site delivers. The elements of service quality on which Parasuraman *et al.* (1985) suggest that consumers judge companies are:

- *reliability* – the ability to perform the service dependably and accurately;
- *responsiveness* – a willingness to help customers and provide prompt service;
- *assurance* – the knowledge and courtesy of employees and their ability to convey trust and confidence;
- *tangibles* – the physical appearance of facilities and communications;
- *empathy* – providing caring, individualised attention.

Service quality involves designing the interactive portions of the web site in order that they deliver the quality expected by the customers. Design should address two areas: those related to customers filling in online forms and those related to contacting customers through e-mail. We will relate both of these to the elements of service quality indicated in the guidelines for best practice set out below. These guidelines have been developed by Dave Chaffey in conjunction with delegates from European companies attending seminars on Practical Internet Marketing arranged by the Chartered Institute of Marketing.

Completion of online forms – best practice

1 *Information requested on forms should be kept to a minimum but must include contact information.* Early practice in relation to the information to collect through online forms seemed to be to collect as much as possible to help build up profiles of customers. There was a backlash against this, with users refusing to provide so much information. Many companies have now gone to the other extreme and capture the minimum information – usually just an e-mail address. Having this address will enable the company to keep in contact with the customer and work back to other information such as company name and position.

2 *Explain why information is being collected.* A customer will more readily provide personal information and spend time filling in a form if he or she knows why it is being collected. Alternatively, a suitable offering may be made, such as free information or a product trial, to provide an incentive to fill in the form.

3 *Indicate mandatory fields.* Extra information can be collected from customers if they have time by marking essential fields in a suitable way (perhaps by an asterisk).

4 *Validate.* Checks should be performed after the form is filled in to ensure that the user has filled in all mandatory fields. Fields should also be checked for validity – has the customer entered a valid e-mail address with the '@' symbol, is the postcode or zip code valid? The user should be clearly prompted with what information is wrong and why. Such validation can be performed using scripts such as Javascript.

5 *Provide 'opt-out'.* Check-boxes should be made available that the user can select if he or she does not want to receive further information through e-mail or communications through other media. This principle is important to 'permission marketing', which is advocated by those such as Seth Godin of Yahoo! (Godin, 1999) and Patricia Seybold (Seybold, 1999). It is suggested that users should be able to 'opt in' to giving information and being placed on mailing lists and then easily 'opt out'.

6 *Provide prompt confirmation.* After a user has filled in a form, a company should respond to acknowledge confirmation of receipt as soon as possible and describe what the follow-up actions will be. For example, if a customer has ordered a product, the confirmation note should thank the customer for shopping with the company and state clearly when he or she can expect to receive the product by courier.

Figure 8.9 shows an example of well-laid-out forms used to collect customer information by RS Components, the company featured in Case study 5.1 – see Chapter 5. Note that mandatory fields are marked with a square symbol and that the company informs customers of its obligations under the Data Protection Act 1984. In this form, the company is collecting information about the needs of the customer in order that site content and promotions can be matched with the customer's interests.

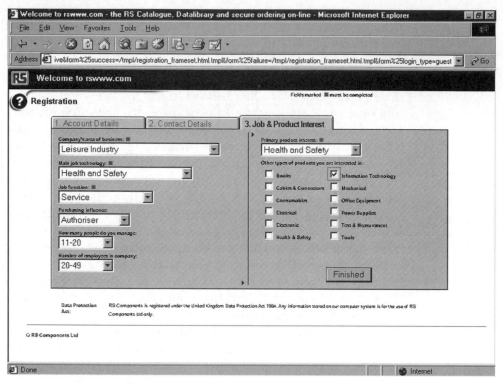

Fig. 8.9 Interactive forms best practice from RS Components (*rswww.com*)

Contacting customers via e-mail – best practice

1 *Keep e-mail communications relevant and targeted*. Junk mail is an apt term. Companies should ensure that the information sent is likely to be of interest to the recipient. One way to achieve this is to customise contact to groups of users. For example, Amazon will only send news about new books on aromatherapy to customers who have expressed an interest in or bought books on alternative health care.

2 *Keep contact timely*. In line with the previous guideline, e-mails should only be sent when there is something newsworthy to communicate to the customer, such as a major new product launch or a new series of seminars. Once a month is probably too frequent unless the communication is a newsletter. Once every few months is less likely to cause annoyance.

3 *Keep it personal*. Where appropriate the e-mail should be answered by a human to give a personal touch, and the name and contact e-mail and phone number of the person should be specified. This will enable rapid follow-up if necessary.

4 *Automate where possible*. The use of autoresponders or 'mail-bots' can be used to automate some standard queries. For example, a 'mail-bot' could be set up which, when an address such as '*support@company-name.com*' is contacted, automatically forwards the request to a customer services representative and also e-mails the customer saying that his or her query has been received, who is dealing with it and when the customer can expect to be contacted, for example

within 12 hours. Mail-bots should not be overused if this results in lack of personal contact.

5 *Provide opt-out.* For reasons suggested above, there should be details at the bottom of the message describing how it is possible for a user to opt out (unsubscribe) of receiving further messages.

Autoresponders or 'mail-bots'

Software tools or 'agents' running on web servers which automatically send a standard reply to the sender of an e-mail message.

To evaluate further the need for well-designed sensitive marketing communications, review the two examples in Activity 8.4.

Activity 8.4

Examples of e-mail communications

This case study contrasts two e-mail promotions which the companies concerned have sent out after the customer has purchased a product. Assess each of the e-mails in terms of best and poor practice by reviewing the items given in the list above 'Contacting customers via e-mail – best practice' and others you can think of. State which e-mail you think is the better promotional tool, and explain why.

Example 1

Dear Valued Customer

We'd like you to be the first to know that Amazon.co.uk is now offering 50% off list prices of selected UK bestsellers. This is in addition to the savings of up to 40% on thousands of other popular and harder-to-find books.

As from today, the daily top choice on the Amazon.co.uk homepage will also be offered at a 50% discount. Selected by our expert editors, these hand-picked recommendations include the best of the current fiction and non-fiction titles.

Visit us today to take advantage of our first 50% discount – Thomas Harris's new blockbuster "Hannibal", the sequel to "The Silence of the Lambs" – by following the link below:

http://www.amazon.co.uk/

This is not a sale or a short-term promotion. It is part of our ongoing commitment to provide our customers with terrific savings and consistently low prices. Whether you need summer holiday reading or a book for the train in winter, with such incredible discounts you'll be able to keep up with the latest and the best for up to 50% less.

Thank you for your custom in the past. We look forward to serving you in the future and hope that you will continue to enjoy Amazon.co.uk's unique shopping experience.

Warmest regards,

Dr Simon Murdoch
Managing Director
Amazon.co.uk
http://www.amazon.co.uk/

▶

> ► **Activity** *continued*
>
> **Example 2**
> ___
>
> Dear Dave Chaffey,
>
> As one of our most valued customers, we'd like to quickly thank you for shopping at Outpost.com, we really appreciate your business.
>
> Many of you have asked how you can secure a copy of the highly anticipated upcoming release of MICROSOFT OFFICE 2000. Great news: Outpost.com can get it to you on the release date, June 10th. You'll have a tough time finding a better price anywhere, and when you add in TruePrice FREE overnight shipping, our incredible price simply can't be beat!*
>
> Best of all, you can still preorder your copy of this incredible productivity tool that gets you completely organized and prepared for any professional situation. From Microsoft Word 2000 to Excel 2000, these are the programs you know you can depend on.
>
> Visit our Microsoft Office 2000 showcase for details on Office 2000 Standard, Premium, Professional, Small Business, and Developer editions, as well as details on UPGRADING your older edition.
>
> CLICK BELOW TO VISIT AND RESERVE YOUR COPY!
> http://www.outpost.com/shortcuts/m2k
>
> CLICK BELOW FOR MORE OUTPOST.COM SPECIALS:
> http://www.outpost.com/entry?site=mo:699
>
> Thanks for again for shopping at Outpost.com,
> THE OUTPOST.COM STAFF
>
> Outpost.com strives to only send email to those who want to receive it! If you would like to unsubscribe from all future special promotions from Outpost.com, simply send a message to remove@outpost.com with the word "remove" in the body of the message. We'll take care of you right away!
> *Dealers and resellers excluded from free shipping. Overnight delivery is not available in some locations. See site for details.

Further information on personalisation techniques such as the use of cookies and registration on sites is given in Chapter 12 on the section on measurement and in Chapter 10 on direct marketing techniques.

Development of graphic and text content

> **Development phase**
> Development is the term used to describe the creation of a web site by programmers. It involves writing the HTML content, creating graphics, and writing any necessary software code such as Javascript or ActiveX (programming).

It is often said, and has been suggested earlier in this chapter, that development of the site should not proceed until analysis and design are complete. Working in this way will ensure that development will be based on an agreed design, and there should be less need for changes to graphics and text as ideas of the design change. In reality, if a prototyping approach is used, some development is necessary as part of the prototyping proces, while analysis and design are taking place. This development will involve designing the layout of the web pages, the graphical elements and the navigation or menu structure.

Resources for web site development

It is not practical to provide full details of the methods of developing content – for two reasons. First, to describe all the facilities available in web browsers for laying out and formatting text, and for developing interactivity, would require several books! Second, the programming standards and tools used are constantly evolving so material is soon out of date. It is, however, recognised that students wanting to develop a career in Internet marketing or electronic commerce will often need to develop experience in 'hands-on' development of sites. To help such readers, this book presents a brief list of resources to help in 'hands-on' development in the box 'Some resources for web site development and testing'. An introduction to developing text content in HTML and XML and methods of displaying graphic images was provided in Chapter 3.

Some resources for web site development and testing

General resources

- *Netskills* – comprehensive HTML and CGI training guide at *www.netskills.ac.uk*.
- *Webmasters Reference.com* – guidance on and links to all aspects of development at *www.webreference.com*
- *Netscape developers page* – guidelines on development from the developers of Javascript: *developer.netscape.com*

Validation

Validation services test for errors in HTML code which may cause a web page to be displayed incorrectly or for links to other pages not to work.

- *Site viewer* – enables test viewing of web pages with different browser versions: *www.anybrowser.com/siteviewer.htm*
- *W3C HTML Validation Service* – check for errors in code online: *validator.w3.org*
- *CSE HTML validator* – check for errors in HTML code, offline: *www.htmlvalidator.com*

Sitemapping tools

These tools diagram the layout of the site, which is useful for site management, and can be used to assist users.

- *Elsop sitemapping tools* – siteMap and Linkscan tools for checking site links and mapping: *www.elsop.com*
- *Electrum Powermapper* – an offline tool for mapping a website: *www.electrum.co.uk*

▶

> ▶ **Some resources for web site development and testing** *continued*
>
> **Shareware**
>
> There are many listings of freeware or shareware, which has to be paid for once it has been evaluated. Some of the most comprehensive sites are:
>
> - Shareware.com (*www.shareware.com*).
> - Hensa UK Mirrors (*www.hensa.ac.uk*).
> - Tucows (*www.tucows.com*).

Testing content

Marketing managers responsible for web sites need to have a basic awareness of web site development and testing. There are a variety of reasons for this. First of all, they will have to communicate with their web development staff. This will require them to have an awareness of some technical jargon. Perhaps more importantly, for the web site to work well and be relatively error free, a number of essential steps are necessary following development. Managers need to check with their developers that these testing steps are conducted as the developers may not have the experience to understand their importance. These testing steps are described in Chapter 12 on maintenance of sites since they are an ongoing part of web site maintenance. In brief, the testing steps necessary are:

- test content displays correctly on different types and versions of web browsers;
- test plug-ins;
- test all interactive facilities and integration with company databases;
- test spelling and grammar;
- test adherence to corporate image standards;
- test to ensure all links to external sites are valid.

Testing often occurs on a separate test web server (or directory) or *test environment*, with access to the test or prototype version being restricted to the development team. When complete the web site is released or published to the main web server or *live environment*.

> **Testing phase**
> Testing involves different aspects of the content such as spelling, validity of links, formatting on different web browsers and dynamic features such as form filling or database queries.

Tools for web site development and testing

A variety of software programs are available to help developers of web sites. These can save much time when sites are being developed and will also help in site maintenance since they will make it easier for people not involved in the original development of the web site to be involved in web site maintenance. Tools are available with different levels of complexity, and managers must decide which are the most suitable to invest in. The types of tools to choose between are listed below. Although there are many rival tools, the ones listed here have been used for several years and are widely used, and skills in using these tools are often mentioned in advertisements for web design staff. Part of the purpose of listing these tools is to illustrate the range of skills a web site designer will need; an advanced web site may be built using tools from each of these categories since even the most advanced tools may not have the flexibility of the basic tools.

Basic text and graphic editors

Text editors are used to edit HTML tags. For example '<B>Products</B>' will make the enclosed text display bold within the web browser. Such tools are often available at low cost or free – including the Notepad editor included with Windows. They are very flexible, and all web site developers will need to use them at some stage in developing content since more automated tools may not provide this flexibility and may not support the latest standard commands. Entire sites can be built using these tools, but it is more efficient to use the more advanced tools described below, and use the editors for 'tweaking' content.

Examples

- Microsoft Windows Notepad (*www.microsoft.com*).
- Program File Editor (PFE).

Such tools can be downloaded and evaluated from shareware sites. Shareware must be paid for if a user decides to use it after evaluation. Freeware can be used free of charge.

Graphics editors, are used to create and modify GIF and JPEG pictures.

Examples

- Microsoft Windows Paintbrush (*www.microsoft.com*).
- Paintshop Pro (*www.jasc.com*).
- PhotoDraw 2000 (*www.microsoft.com*).
- PhotoImpact (*www.ulead.com*).

Specialised HTML and graphics editors

Specialised HTML and graphics editing tools provide facilities for adding HTML tags automatically. For example, adding the Bold text tag <B> </B> to the HTML document will happen when the user clicks the bold tag. Some of these editors are WYSIWYG.

Examples

There are many freeware and shareware editors in this category.

Basic tools

- Microsoft FrontPage Express (*www.microsoft.com*).
- Web Edit Pro (*www.luckman.com*).
- Modern versions of wordprocessors such as Microsoft Word and Lotus WordPro now have these facilities through using a Save As HTML option.

More advanced tools supporting Javascript and some site management facilities

- HotDog Professional (*wwww.sausage.com*).
- HotMetal Pro (*www.softquad.com*).
- HomeSite (*www.allaire.com*).

Advanced graphics tools

- Adobe Photoshop (extensively used by graphic designers, *www.adobe.com*).
- Macromedia Fireworks (a web-specific graphics package, with more limited functionality than Photoshop, *www.macromedia.com*).
- Macromedia Flash and Director-Shockwave (used for graphical animations, *www.macromedia.com*).

Site management tools

Site management tools provide the advanced HTML editing facilities of the previous category, but also provide tools to help manage and test the site, including graphic layouts of the structure of the site – making it easy to find, modify and republish the page by sending the file to the web site using FTP (*see* Chapter 3). Style templates can be applied to produce a consistent look and feel across the site. Tools are also available to create and manage menu options. Many of the tools that started as basic HTML editors have now been developed to incorporate the site management features.

Examples

- Microsoft FrontPage (*www.microsoft.com*).
- ColdFusion (*www.allaire.com*).
- Dreamweaver (*www.macromedia.com*).
- Fusion (*www.netobjects.com*).
- PageMill (*www.adobe.com*).

Database management tools for interactive site development

Database management tools provide an automated method of updating content in a site, often usable by non-specialists. Lotus Notes is an example of this. Documents such as PR releases or product information sheets are stored in a Lotus Notes database and automatically published to the web using the Domino facility (*see* Fig. 8.10). This is an efficient method of publishing content since the facility can be made available to people throughout the company.

Database management tools also include facilities for personalising content to certain users as part of one-to-one marketing (*see* Chapter 10). This category also includes some of the tools for creating electronic commerce catalogues that are mentioned in Chapter 11.

Examples

- ColdFusion (*www.allaire.com*).
- Fusion (*www.netobjects.com*).
- Lotus Notes/Domino (*www.lotus.com*).

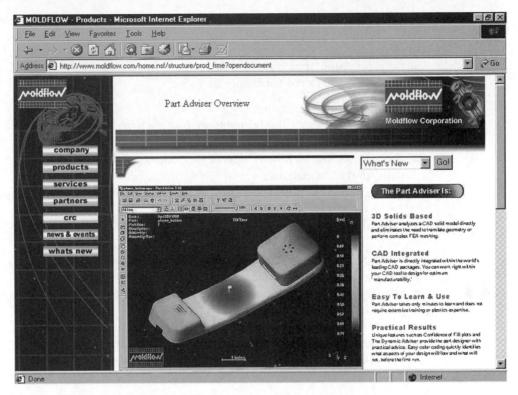

Fig. 8.10 Product information published through Lotus Notes/Domino by the Australian company Moldflow

Product information displayed using Notes is shown in Fig. 8.10.

Personalisation tools

Personalisation tools may overlap with those for database management. What distinguishes them is that they provide the ability to recognise each customer as he or she logs on to the web site and provide particular information and promotional offers specific to that customer, as explained, with examples in Chapter 9.

Promote site

Promotion of a site is a significant topic that will be part of the strategy of developing a web site. It will follow the initial development of a site and is described in detail in Chapter 9.

Success factors in developing web sites

To conclude this chapter, it is worth pausing to consider factors that contribute to a successful web site since they are not simply dependent on the skills of the developers. One method of identifying success factors for creating sites is to consider projects that have gone wrong and to learn from them. Bicknell (1998) reviewed the difficulties of building web sites – based on a survey of *The Times* European Top 500 companies. The very size of the companies meant that the projects they undertook were often major projects, and they included e-commerce facilities. The survey revealed that over a quarter of companies had cancelled e-commerce projects. Reasons cited for failure included:

- lack of real executive support;
- a failure to identify the business goals of systems;
- a lack of communication between marketing and IT departments;
- limited technical knowledge of developers of the system, either in-house or third-party companies;
- lack of integration between the e-commerce system and other systems.

From studying failures of projects to develop web sites, the following success factors can be suggested:

- management support necessary to promote project across company;
- clearly defined strategy and objectives;
- strong project management to ensure targets are achieved through effective planning and resourcing of the project;
- good skills and experience amongst developers of the project;
- co-operation amongst different parts of the business involved in the project and integration of information systems from the different areas.

SUMMARY

1 Careful planning and execution of web site implementation is important, in order to avoid the need for extensive reworking at a later stage if the design proves to be ineffective.
2 Implementation is not an isolated process; it should be integrated with the Internet marketing strategy. Analysis, design and implementation should occur repeatedly in an iterative, prototyping approach that involves the client and the user to produce an effective design.
3 A feasibility study should take place before the initiation of a major web site project. A feasibility study will assess:
    - the costs and benefits of the project;
    - the difficulty of achieving management and staff commitment to the project;
    - the availability of domain names to support the project;
    - the responsibilities and stages necessary for a successful project.

4 The choice of host for a web site should be considered carefully since this will govern the quality of service of the web site.

5 Options for analysis of users' requirements for a web site include:
    - interviews with marketing staff;
    - questionnaire sent to companies;
    - informal interviews with key accounts;
    - focus groups;
    - reviewing competitors' web sites.

6 According to surveys the main factors governing whether customers will return to a site are (in order of importance):
- high quality content;
- ease of use ;
- quick to download;
- updated frequently.

7 The design phase of developing a web site includes specification of:
- the structure of the web site;
- the flow, controlled by the navigation and menu options;
- the graphic design and brand identity;
- country-specific localisation;
- the service quality of online forms and e-mail messages.

EXERCISES AND QUESTIONS

Self-assessment exercises

1 Explain the term 'prototyping' in relation to web site creation.
2 What tasks should managers undertake during initiation of a web page?
3 What is domain name registration?
4 List the factors that determine web site 'flow'.
5 Explain the structure of an HTML document and the concept of 'tags'.
6 List the options for designing web site menu options.
7 What is a hierarchical web site structure?
8 What are the factors that control the performance of a web site?

Discussion questions

1 'Prototyping of web sites must involve the full range of their audience, but this is not practical in reality.' Discuss.
2 Discuss the relative effectiveness of the different methods of assessing the customers' needs for a web site.
3 Discuss the relative importance of the different reasons for returning to a web site given in Table 8.1. What are the implications of the list for the web site designer?
4 Discuss the merits of using automated tools to generate web site HTML coding rather than writing native HTML code.

Essay questions

1 Select three web sites of your choice and compare their design effectiveness. You should describe design features such as navigation, structure and graphic design.
2 Explain how strategy, analysis, design and implementation of a web site should be integrated through a prototyping approach. Describe the merits and problems of the prototyping approach.

3 Detail the importance of different aspects of navigation in controlling the experience of 'flow' on a web site.

4 When designing the interactive services of a web site such as online forms and e-mails to customers, what steps should the designer take to provide a quality service to customers?

Examination questions

1 What is web site prototyping? Give three benefits of this approach.

2 What controls on a web site project are introduced at the initiation phase of the project?

3 A company is looking to select an ISP. Explain:
   (a) what an ISP is;
   (b) which factors will affect the quality of service delivered by the ISP.

4 How are focus groups used to gain understanding of customer expectations of a web site?

5 Name, and briefly explain, four characteristics of the information content of a site that will govern whether a customer is likely to return to a web site.

6 When the graphic design and page layout of a web site are being described, what different factors associated with type and set-up of a PC and its software should the designer take into account?

7 What is meant by 'opt in'? Why should it be taken into account as part of web site design?

8 Explain the difference between a mark-up language and a scripting language.

REFERENCES

Aaker, D. and Norris, N. (1982) 'Characteristics of TV commercials perceived as informative', *Journal of Advertising*, 25(2), 22–34.

Berthon, B., Pitt, L. and Watson, R. (1998) 'The World Wide Web as an industrial marketing communication tool: models for the identification assessment of opportunities', *Journal of Marketing Management*, 14, 691–704.

Bickerton, P., Bickerton, M. and Simpson-Holey, K. (1998) *Cyberstrategy*. Oxford: Butterworth-Heinemann. Chartered Institute of Marketing series.

Bicknell, D. (1998) 'Top businesses find it hard to spin successful web projects', *Computer Weekly*, 10 September, 20–1.

Bocij, P., Chaffey, D., Greasley, A. and Hickie, S. (1999) *Business Information Systems. Technology, development and management*. London: FT Management.

Breitenbach, C. and van Doren, D. (1998) 'Value-added marketing in the digital domain: enhancing the utility of the Internet', *Journal of Consumer Marketing*, 15(6), 559–75

Brunel, A. (1996) 'Trademark protection for internet domain names', in Joseph F. Ruh Jr. (ed.) *The Internet and Business: A lawyer's guide to the emerging legal issues*. New York: The Computer Law Association of the United States.

Godin, S. (1999) *Permission Marketing*. New York: Simon and Schuster.

Hoffman, D.L. and Novak, T.P. (1996) 'Marketing in hypermedia computer-mediated environments: conceptual foundations', *Journal of Marketing*, 60 (July), 50–68.

Hoffman, D.L. and Novak, T.P. (1997) 'A new marketing paradigm for electronic commerce', *The Information Society*, Special issue on electronic commerce, 13, 43–54.

Lewis, H. and Lewis, R. (1997) 'Give your customers what they want', *Selling on the Net. Executive book summaries*, 19(3), March.

Morgan, R. (1996) 'An Internet marketing framework for the World Wide Web', *Journal of Marketing Management*, 12, 757–75.

Ong, C. (1995) 'Practical aspects of marketing on the WWW', MBA Dissertation, University of Sheffield, UK.

Pak, J. (1999) 'Content dimensions of web advertising: a cross national comparison', *International Journal of Advertising*, 18(2), 207–31.

Parasuraman, A., Zeithaml, V. and Berry, L. (1985) 'A conceptual model of service quality and its implications for future research', *Journal of Marketing*, 49, Fall, 48.

Resnik, A. and Stern, A. (1977) 'An analysis of information content in television advertising', *Journal of Marketing*, January, 50–3.

Seybold, P. (1999) *Customers.com*. London: Century Business Books. Random House.

Shardlow, N. (1999) 'Web blossoms for Orange', *Computing*, 14 January.

Siegel, D. (1997) *Creating Killer Web Sites* (2nd edn). Indianapolis, IN: Hayden Books.

Sterne, J. (1999) *World Wide Web Marketing* (2nd edn). New York: John Wiley and Sons.

FURTHER READING

Brassington, F. and Petitt, S. (2000) *Principles of Marketing* (2nd edn). Harlow, UK: Pearson Education. *See* companion Prentice Hall web site (*www.booksites.net/brassington2*).
Chapter 3, Customer Behaviour, describes the stages in the buying-decision process and reviews psychological and environmental inpacts on this.
Chapter 5, Customer Segmentation, describes methods of identifying different groupings of customers and communicating with them accordingly.

Knight, J. (1999) *Computing for Business* (2nd edn). London: FT Management.
Now includes a chapter on basic web site design.

Siegel, D. (1997) *Creating Killer Web Sites* (2nd edn). Indianapolis, IN: Hayden Books.
The state of the art guide to practical web site design and implementation issues when it was published. Useful information online at *www.killersites.com*.

Vassos, T. (1996) *Strategic Internet Marketing*. Indianapolis, IN: Que. Business Computer Library.
Chapter 5 describes implementing the initial four stages of web site development. Chapters 6 and 7 are on interactive and database web site strategies and advanced web site development strategies respectively.

WEB SITE REFERENCES

Web resources for developers are listed in two sections within this chapter:

- Resources for web site development lists some of the main sites directing site designers to other sites (*see* pp. 237–8)
- Tools for web site development and testing lists well-known tools for designing and implementing web sites. (*see* pp. 238–41)

Killer sites (*www.killersites.com*).
Site to support David Siegel's book (Siegel, 1997). Contains many useful tips.

Web Pages That Suck (*www.webpagesthatsuck.com*).
Gives a lighthearted review of design best practice by 'learning good web site design through viewing bad web site design'.

Yale University Press (*info.med.yale.edu/caim/manual/contents.html*).

Supporting site for Lynch, P. and Horton, S. (1999) *Web Style Guide. Basic design principles for creating web sites*. New Haven, CT: Yale University Press. (1999). Provides a large amount of detail on design.

ZD Net (*www.zdnet.com/enterprise/e-business/bphome/*).
Summaries of best practice in page design.

CHAPTER 9

Web site promotion

Learning objectives

After reading this chapter, the reader should be able to:

- identify effective methods for online and offline promotion;
- understand the importance of integrating online and offline promotion;
- relate promotion techniques to methods of measuring site effectiveness (in conjunction with Chapter 12).

Links to other chapters

▶ Chapter 4 describes how information can be found on the Internet. This is background for this chapter, which is about facilitating access for visitors to information on a company web site.

▶ Chapter 12 considers the measurement of site effectiveness in more detail. Part of the measurement process involves consideration of how well different online and offline promotion techniques are working.

INTRODUCTION

A company that has developed an easy to use web site with content appropriate to its audience is really only half-way to achieving a successful Internet marketing outcome. Promotion of the web site is necessary to generate traffic to the site. A separate chapter is devoted to this topic for two main reasons. First, the Web is a large place: there are estimated to be over five million web sites and approaching a billion web pages, so it is not easy for a company to distinguish its site or easy for its users to find it. The idea 'build a great site, and they will come' is not valid. Berthon *et al.* (1998) make the analogy with a trade conference. Here, there will be many companies at different stands promoting their products and services. Effective promotion of a stand is necessary to attract some of the many show visitors to that stand. The concept of 'visibility' can be applied to both the trade show and the Web. From those people noticing and visiting the stand it is then necessary to achieve a successful marketing outcome. In the context of the trade show this is done by obtaining a person's contact details so that marketing communications can continue. In the context of the web site the aim is similar: to capture the e-mail or company address of visitors so that the type of direct marketing described in Chapter 10 can occur. The second reason why this topic warrants a

247

separate chapter is that web site promotion is not straightforward. In fact it is quite different in detail from promotion in other media; all companies are still learning what works and what does not.

To be able to promote a site effectively, it is necessary to have some technical knowledge of how people find information on the Internet. Once this is understood, appropriate online promotion methods can be used to direct visitors to the site. For effective promotion, online techniques should be combined with offline methods. This chapter considers separately online techniques (of which banner advertising is the best known) and established offline techniques, and then briefly considers how they should be integrated.

> **Online promotion**
> Online promotion uses communication via the Internet itself to raise awareness about a site and drive traffic to it. This promotion may take the form of links from other sites, banner advertising or targeted e-mail messages.
>
> **Offline promotion**
> Offline promotion uses traditional media such as television or newspaper advertising and word of mouth to promote a company's web site.

The importance of promotion

It is useful for the person determining a company's web site strategy to assess the correct balance of annual investment on:

- site development;
- site maintenance;
- site promotion.

As mentioned in Chapter 6, the amount spent on maintenance for each major revision of a web site is generally thought to be between a quarter and a third of the original investment. The relatively large cost of maintenance is to be expected, given the need to keep updating information in order that customers return to a web site. What is surprising is that anecdotal evidence suggests that the proportion spent on site promotion is very low in comparison with promotion budgets for other media. Senior managers from UK companies attending seminars given by Dave Chaffey report that the figure for online site promotion in their companies is very low – usually between 0 and 5 percent. Delegates report that a small amount is spent on banner advertising, and most promotion of the web site simply occurs through placing the company's web address on advertisements placed in traditional media or on company stationery. In this chapter, we will use this division of online and offline media to look at the techniques available for promotion, at the same time remembering that it is necessary to use the two methods together for maximum effectiveness.

Online promotion techniques

Coverage of online promotion in UK trade magazines such as *Marketing Week*, *Marketing* and new media magazines such as *Revolution* and *New Media Age* tends to focus on the use of banner advertising as a mechanism to attract people to web sites. The reality is that banner advertising is currently limited in terms of value and the number of companies using it for promotion. In 1998, the value of banner advertisements placed in the UK was £15 million, while the cost of television advertisements placed was £2.2 billion. The number of companies placing banner advertising is measured in terms of hundreds rather than thousands. Most of the companies using banner advertisements were those for which the medium is most suitable for online sales. These include products such as books, computers and financial services. With the exception of computers, most of the advertisements were for consumers rather than for business buyers. This pattern does not mean, however, that advertising on the Internet is ineffective, since there are other lower-cost methods of drawing people to web sites. We will consider online promotion in two areas: banner advertisements and other methods of linking to sites. These techniques are often combined in what is known as a traffic-building campaign; this is a method of increasing the audience of a site using different online (and possibly offline) techniques.

> **Traffic-building campaign**
> The use of online and offline promotion techniques such as banner advertising, search engine promotion and reciprocal linking to increase the audience of a site (both new and existing customers).

Online advertising

It can be contended that each web site is in itself an advertisement since it can inform, persuade and remind customers about a company or its products and services. However, a company web site is not strictly an advertisement in the conventional sense since money is not exchanged to place the content of the web site on a medium owned by a third party. Advertising on the World Wide Web is generally acknowledged to take place when an advertiser pays to place advertising content on another web site. The simplest and most common model of advertising is shown in Fig. 9.1, where the advertiser places an advertisement on a range of sites in order to drive traffic to a corporate site.

Activity 9.1, Choosing appropriate locations for banner advertising (*see* p. 255), gives an   indication of the typical sites used for advertising a range of products. A section later in this chapter also explains how companies decide on the locations in which to advertise.

Janal (1998) considers how Internet advertising differs from traditional advertising in a number of key areas. These are summarised in Table 9.1.

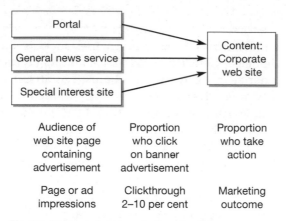

Fig. 9.1 Basic model for web site advertising

Table 9.1 Key concepts of advertising in the new and old media

	Old media	New media
Space	Expensive commodity	Cheap, unlimited
Time	Expensive commodity for marketers	Expensive commodity for users
Image creation	Image is everything Information secondary	Information is everything Image is secondary
Communication	Push, one-way	Pull, interactive
Call to action	Incentives	Information (incentives)

Source: After Janal (1998).

The main differences that should be noted are:

■ The cost of advertising in the new medium reduces as more space becomes available.
■ It is the customer who initiates the dialogue and who will expect his or her specific needs to be addressed. Web marketers need to promote their web sites effectively in order that customers find the information they are looking for.
■ The user's time is valuable and the time interacting with the user will be limited. So this time must be maximised.
■ Information is the main currency. Supplying information is arguably more important than appealing to emotions.

The advertisements placed on sites usually take the form of *banner advertisements*. These are so-called since they are usually placed across the top of the web page, as shown in Fig. 9.2. The power of banner advertisements is that they can be targeted at particular audience. In Fig. 9.2, for example, the banner is targeted at UK customers looking for travel insurance, on the basis of the two keywords they have typed into Yahoo! (holiday insurance). Companies will pay for banner advertising for two main reasons: (a) in the hope that the customer will click on the advertisement and then will be exposed to more detailed brand information on the company's web site; (b) all visitors to a page will see an advertisement, either noting it consciously or viewing it subconsciously. This can help to establish or

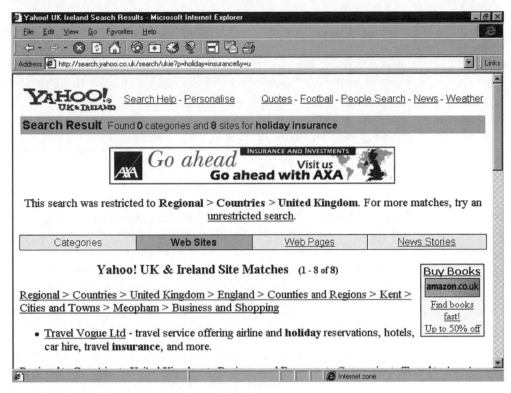

Fig. 9.2 Typical placement of a banner advertisement on Yahoo! directory

reinforce a brand image. Amazon (*www.amazon.com*) for example, advertised extensively on the Internet to help raise awareness of their brand.

> **Banner advertisment**
> A rectangular graphic displayed on a web page for the purposes of advertising. It is normally possible to perform a clickthrough to access further information. Banners may be static or animated.

Each time an advertisement is viewed, this is referred to as a page or advertisement (ad) impression (or 'ad exposure' according to I/PRO, *www.ipro.com*). Page impressions or page views are other terms used. 'Ad impressions' is used rather than 'hits' since, as explained in Chapter 12, referring to hits tend to inflate the number of people actually viewing a page. Since some people may view the advertisement more than one time, marketers are also interested in the *reach*, which is the number of unique individuals who view the advertertisement. This will naturally be a smaller figure than that for ad impressions.

> **Page and ad impressions and reach**
> One page impression occurs when a member of the audience views a web page. One ad impression occurs when a person views an advertisement placed on the web page. Reach defines the number of unique individuals who view an advertisement.

There is much discussion about how many impressions of an advertisement an individual has to see for it to be effective. Novak and Hofmann (1997) note that for traditional media it is thought that fewer than three exposures will not give adequate recall. For new media, because of the greater intensity of viewing a computer screen, recall seems to be better with a smaller number of advertisements. The technical term for adequate recall is *effective* frequency.

Effective frequency
The number of exposures or ad impressions (frequency) required for an advertisement to become effective.

When a user clicks on the advertisement, he or she will normally be directed to further information, viewing of which will result in a marketing outcome. Usually the user will be directed through to part of the corporate web site that will have been set up especially to deal with the response from the advertisement. When a user clicks on an advertisement, this is known as a *clickthrough*.

Clickthrough and clickthrough rate
A clickthrough (or an advertisement click) occurs each time a user clicks on a banner advertisement with the mouse to direct him or her to a web page that contains further information.

The clickthrough rate is expressed as a percentage of total ad impressions, and refers to the proportion of users viewing an advertisement who click on it. It is calculated as the number of clickthroughs divided by the number of ad impressions.

The purpose of banner advertising

Banner advertising is often thought of simply in terms of its function in driving traffic to a web site, as described in the previous section. There are, however, several outcomes that a marketing manager may be looking to achieve through a banner advertising campaign. Cartellieri *et al.* (1997) identify the following objectives:

- *Delivering content.* This is the typical case where a clickthrough on a banner advertisement leads through to a corporate site giving more detailed information on an offer. This is where a direct response is sought.
- *Enabling transaction.* If a clickthrough leads through to a merchant such as a travel site or an online bookstore the advertisement is placed to lead directly to a sale. A direct response is also sought here.
- *Shaping attitudes.* An advertisment that is consistent with a company brand can help build brand awareness.
- *Soliciting response.* An advertisement may be intended to identify new leads or as a start for two-way communication. In these cases an interactive advertisement may encourage a user to type in an e-mail address.
- *Encouraging retention.* The advertisement may be placed as a reminder about the company and its service.

These objectives are not mutually exclusive, and more than one can be achieved with a well-designed banner campaign. Zeff and Aronson (1999) stress the unique benefits of banner advertising as compared with those of other media. Using banners makes it possible to target Internet advertisements to groups of people, sometimes in a more sophisticated way than is possible with other media, as is shown by the example in Fig. 9.2 and Mini case study 9.1 on DoubleClick later in the chapter. The response to web-based advertisements can be tracked in more detail than that for advertisements in other media. This is explored further in Chapter 12. Zeff and Aronson (1999) also note that a web-based advertising campaign can be more responsive than a campaign in other media since it is possible to place an advertisement more quickly and make changes as required. Finally, since the advertisement can lead straight to a web site where more information and interactivity are available it should be possible to convey a more powerful message about a product.

How well does banner advertising work?

A key question about banner advertisement that marketers are struggling to answer is: 'How effective are banner advertisements in comparison with those other media?' In a landmark study conducted in 1997 for the Internet Advertising Bureau (*ww.iab.net*) in the USA, MBinteractive (*www.mbinteractive.com*) concluded that 'online advertising is more likely to be noticed than television advertising'. It was suggested that advertising banners performed so well because of the lower advertisement-to-editorial ratio on web pages (typically 90 per cent text to 10 per cent advertising for a single banner advertisement on a page) and because web users use the medium actively rather than passively receiving information. Boyce (1998) notes that for a television audience, the proportion who actually watch the advertisement may be as low as 25 per cent! Further evidence on the effectiveness of the Web for advertising, in comparison with television, is provided by an IPSOS-ASI survey published in February 1999, which suggested that banner advertisements and television advertisements are equally memorable. This conclusion was based on a survey of 7000 US consumers testing their recall of 45 banner advertisements on AOL sites, across a range of categories. The study tested consumers' advertisement recall after one viewing. It found that while 41 per cent recalled a 30-second television commercial after one viewing, 40 per cent recalled a static online banner advertisement. However, Marianne Foley, senior vice president of IPSOS-ASI Interactive, acknowledged that the study does not take into account the advanced features of advertisement impact such as communication and brand imagery and persuasion.

Whatever the arguments about effectiveness, it is clear that the use of the Internet is decreasing the amount of time that consumers spend on other home activities such as reading or watching the television. A study by Nielsen Media Research in 1998 found that households in the USA with access to the Internet are 15 per cent less likely to watch television than those without home Net access. This is confirmed in Europe by a report by Parry (1998), which showed that about a fifth of users said they were watching less television. This supported research from the Strategis Group of Washington, DC, which indicated that Internet use is displacing social and leisure activities such as watching television, reading and sleeping! Sixty-four per cent said they watch less television and video in order to surf the Net. Reading time is cut by 48 per cent of respondents, and a further 29 per cent spend less time sleeping. Perhaps disturbingly, social activities with family and friends were reduced by 26 per cent. The study was conducted using over 1000 US households, of which half were Internet users. Given these results, the implication is that expenditure on Internet advertising will increase in the future.

Locations for banner advertising

In Fig. 9.2 three main different locations for banner advertising were suggested. These alternatives will now be examined in more detail, in order to understand why the different alternatives are used. This section should be read in conjunction with Activity 9.1, Choosing appropriate locations for banner advertising. The main criteria on which the sites are chosen for advertising will of course be the size of the audience (or reach) and the composition of the audience. The three main types of locations are:

1 Portals

It was shown in Chapter 4 that there are different types of portal, but they are similar in that they all tend to have large audiences who visit the portals to gain access to the information on the Internet. This may be through search services such as Excite (*www.excite.com*) or AltaVista (*www.altavista.com*), or more structured directories such as Yahoo! (*www.yahoo.com*) or Yellow Pages (*www.yell.co.uk*). Alternatively the portals may be the home pages of ISPs such as AOL, Freeserve or VirginNet (*www.virgin.net*), to which the ISPs' users are directed when they first join the Web. By placing banner advertising on the home page of portals, advertisers get access to large but relatively undifferentiated audiences. This is similar to an advertiser placing a traditional advertisement in a prime-time television slot. A banner advertisement placed to reach a large, but non-specific, audience will be that displayed when the user first visits the portal. Yet portals offer greater advertising potential than other media since it is possible for companies to place specific advertisements that are related to the keywords that the user types in when performing a search. For example, if a user types in 'cheap flights', an airline such as British Airways or a flight broker can pay to display their banner advertisement (Fig. 9.2). This has the benefit that the advertisement is delivered to an audience that is pre-qualified as being interested in it. This is much less easy to achieve in other media, although it is possible to place advertisements in keeping with a special-interest programme, such as golf club advertisements in a live broadcast from a golf competition.

2 Generalised news services

It can be argued that news services overlap with the other two categories described here, but news services are presented separately since this type of site is commonly used (*see* Table 9.2). Such services are similar in audience to portals in that they have quite large audiences, but the audiences are arguably better differentiated, in that a certain type of person is likely to visit a certain type of news site. For example, the audience of the *Sunday Times* web site or the *Electronic Telegraph* web site is likely to be similar to that of their real-world equivalent. On this type of site, banners are not usually offered in response to keywords, but advertisements may be varied according to which section of the online newspaper is being read.

3 Specialised interest site

This category covers a range of sites, but examination of Table 9.2 shows that special interest online magazine sites are popular for banner advertising. Examples could include:

- men's lifestyle magazines – *FHM*, *GQ*.
- women's lifestyle magazines – *Vogue* and *Tatler*.
- science Fiction – *Fortean Times*.
- 'vertical portals', for example the online computing trade press – *Computer Weekly* and *Computing*.

Novak and Hoffman (1997) also identify three major types of advertiser supported sites. These are:

1 Sponsored content sites such as newspapers.
2 Sponsored search engines such as Infoseek and Excite.
3 Entry portals such as Netscape.

As noted above, it is increasingly difficult to distinguish between the second and third types identified by Novak and Hoffman, so it is felt that the classification mentioned given in this chapter is more appropriate for the type of sites on which advertisement placements occur.

Activity 9.1

Choosing appropriate locations for banner advertising

Table 9.2 Ranked value and placement of advertising, UK, February 1999

Advertiser	Value (£K)	Sites used for banner adverts
BT	81	www.beeb.com, www.capitalfm.co.uk, www.cricket98.co.uk, www.emap.com, www.esi.co.uk, www.excite.co.uk, www.fhm.co.uk, www.ft.com, www.loot.com, www.lycos.co.uk, www.moneyworld.co.uk, www.the-times.co.uk, www.thisislondon.co.uk, www.yahoo.co.uk
Amazon	65	www.bravo.co.uk, www.fhm.co.uk, www.forteantimes.com, www.freeserve.net, www.fcuk.co.uk, www.juiced.co.uk, www.lineone.net, www.thisislondon.co.uk, www.virgin.net, www.yahoo.co.uk, www.yell.co.uk
British Airways	59	www.aol.co.uk, www.economist.com, www.excite.co.uk, www.freeserve.net, www.lineone.net, www.lycos.co.uk, www.tatler.co.uk, www.ukplus.co.uk, www.vogue.co.uk, www.worldofinteriors.co.uk, www.yahoo.co.uk
HM Government	55	www.fhm.co.uk, www.jobworld.co.uk, www.juiced.co.uk, www.lineone.net, www.Sunday-times.co.uk, www.thisislondon.co.uk, www.topjobs.co.uk, www.whatcar.co.uk, www.yahoo.co.uk

Note: This list is compiled monthly by Fletcher Research (*www.fletch.co.uk*) and published in *Revolution* magazine.

Review the advertisers and the location they have used for banner advertisements given in Table 9.2, and then answer the following questions.

1 Comment on the total advertising spend by each company. How do you think it compares with that in other media?

▶ **Activity** *continued*

2 List the sites that are used by at least two of the advertisers. Why do you think each of these sites is popular?

3 For each advertiser review the sites where it has placed banner advertisements and try to deduce its advertising strategy. You should consider the following types of placement:
 ■ portal (categorise as search engine or directory or ISP);
 ■ media owner (general or specialist);
 ■ other specialist types.

4 Review of the Fletcher compilation shows that expenditure on business-to-business advertising using banner advertisements is low or non-existent. Why do you think this is?

Beyond the simple banner advertisement

The description of banner advertising to date has focused on simple static banner advertisements that are used to direct web users to particular sites. As the medium has evolved, other advertising techniques have been developed. These are summarised in Fig. 9.3.

We will now consider some of the variants of banner advertisements that have been developed to help attract attention and encourage clickthrough.

Animated banner advertisements

Early banner advertisements featured only a single image, but today they will typically involve several different images, which are displayed in sequence to help to attract attention to the banner and build up a theme, often ending with a call to

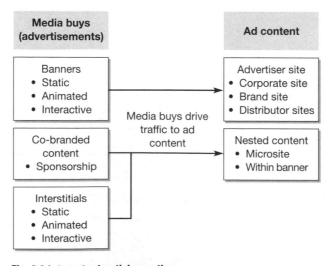

Fig. 9.3 Internet advertising options
Source: Jupiter Communications.

Fig. 9.4 Three different elements of an animated banner advertisement

action and the injunction to click on the banner. An example is shown in Fig. 9.4. This type of advertisement is achieved through supplying the creative elements of the advertisement as an animated GIF file with different layers or frames (Chapter 3), usually a rectangle of 468 by 60 pixels.

Interactive banner advertisments

The use of interactive banners is also increasing. These are intended to add value to the advertisement by providing a service that would normally only be available on the web site. Uses of interactive banners might include:

- Entering the amount of loan required to give an indication of its cost.
- Entering the destination of a flight to show the cheapest fare available.
- Buying a product.
- Filling in an e-mail address for further information on a product.

It can be seen that interactive advertisements may increase response since someone may fill in the form even though they might not bother to click on an advertisement.

Interstitials

Interstitials are quite different from banner advertisements in appearance. The term literally means 'in-between' other screens of information. Most often, they take the form of a 'pop-up' window that is displayed when a new web page is opened. Since they have to be removed by the user they are intrusive and have been reported as unpopular. However, some advertisers have found them to be quite effective. In early 1999, British Airways used a ten-second interstitial that received a clickthrough of 50 per cent, partly because of its novelty value.

Nested ad-content

Access to nested ad-content, sometimes referred to as a microsite, occurs when the person undertaking the clickthrough is not redirected to a corporate or brand site, but is instead taken to a related page on the same site as that on which the advertisement is placed. This route is relatively unusual, but may lead to less obtrusive advertising. For example, the nappy supplier Huggies placed an advertisement on a childcare site that led the parents clicking on this link to more detailed information on Huggies contained on the site.

Placing banner advertising

It is apparent from Table 9.2 that banner advertising is not usually directed at a single site; rather a banner campaign will be organised in which advertisements are placed in a range of locations. Banner advertisements can be placed through traditional advertising agencies since many are now seeking to integrate the Internet into their work. There is also a range of specialist services known as advertising networks that undertake this type of work.

Banner advertising requires a good knowledge of the media owners and their rates. Advertising networks such as Doubleclick (*www.doubleclick.net*) organise co-ordinated campaigns across several sites (*see* the section on advertising networks later in the chapter).

Paying for banner advertising

Banner advertising is typically paid for according to the number of web users who view the web page and the advertisement on it. These are the 'ad impressions' referred to earlier. Cost is then calculated as CPM or cost per thousand (*mille*) ad impressions.

> **CPM and run-of-site**
> Cost per 1000 ad impressions. CPM is usually higher for run-of-site advertisements where advertisements occur on all pages of the site.

Some representative banner advertising costs from 1999 are shown in Table 9.3. It can be seen that costs for the different sites are similar. The more expensive sites are likely to have a more specialist audience with a higher disposable income or to be related to specific keywords, as is the case with Yahoo!.

Table 9.3 Representative site audience characteristics and charges

Site name	Type of site	Media owner	Target audience	Monthly page impressions	Banner cost per 1000
Yahoo! home page (*www.yahoo.co.uk*)	Portal	Yahoo!	All web users	50 million	£21–70
New Musical Express (*www.nme.com*)	Special interest	IPC Magazines	18–30-year-old males	4.5 million	£30
Virgin Radio (*www.virginradio.com*)	Special interest	Ginger OnLine	20–44, 64% male, 36% female, ABC1	900 000	£25 (run of site)
Vogue magazine	Special interest	Conde-Nast	Women, 18–34, ABC1	600 000	£39
AOL (*www.aol.uk.com*)	Portal	AOL	All web users	125 million	£60
Megastar (*www.megastar.co.uk*)	'News'	Express Newspapers	18–35 males	2.2 million	£35

Source: Compiled from Media Owners Portfolio, *Revolution*, March 1999.

The cost of reaching customers on the Internet has been compared unfavourably with that for other media. For example, in 1998 Jupiter Communications (*www.jup.com*) quoted the average CPM as $35 for the Web, and $12 for television. However, Boyce (1998), in an article entitled 'Exploding the web CPM myth', has noted that the $35 is delivering a more targeted, qualified audience. This targeting occurs because of the placing of the advertisement on a special interest site, or because the advertisement is related to the specific keywords entered into a search engine. To reach a specialised audience on television could cost over $50 CPM!

When payment is made according to the number of viewers of a site it is important that the number of viewers is measured accurately. To do this independent auditors are required. The main auditing bodies are:

- the international auditing body BPA (*www.bpai.com*);
- Audit Bureau of Circulation, ABC (*www.abc.org.uk*);
- Internet Advertising Bureau, IAB (*www.iab.net*).

> **Web site auditors**
> Auditors accurately measure the usage of different sites in terms of the number of ad impressions and clickthrough rates.

Other payment models

Cartellieri *et al.* (1997) and Sterne (1999) note that other payment models are possible. They identify payment as occurring:

- *per exposure* – typically through ad impressions or possibly through the length of time the user views an advertisement;
- *per response* – payment only occurs according to the number of clickthroughs that occur;
- *per action* – payment according to a marketing outcome such as downloading a product factsheet, a new sales lead received when the user fills in an online form giving his or her name and address, or an actual purchase placed online.

The prevalent payment model is currently per exposure, as is clear from the compilation in Table 9.3. The IAB *Ad Revenue Report* (*www.iab.net*) for 1998 showed that CPM or impression-based deals accounted for 43 per cent of banner advertisements, and performance-based deals (based on outcome) for 5 per cent of revenues. The remaining 52 per cent were described as hybrid deals, perhaps involving some payment or sponsorship or being based on a product being sold as a result of a clickthrough.

Media owners and those selling advertising space prefer the CPM/exposure model since the cost is not related to the quality of the creative content. This model is similar to that used for payment in other media. Media owners are wary of the other two methods since these will be governed directly by the quality of the creative content; if this is poor there would be a low clickthrough, resulting in lower revenue for the media owner. Similarly if the offer is poor or the user is led through to a poor quality corporate site, then there are less likely to be follow-up actions. Media owners point out that the quality of the creative content or the destination web site is beyond their control – their function is merely to deliver viewers to the advertisement. To date, media owners have been able to control charging rates and have largely used a per exposure model. Large advertisers such as Procter & Gamble could require a return per response if the media owner was involved in the creative work. It is thought, however, that there is an overcapacity of Internet advertising, which is driving down prices, and this may give those placing advertisements more power to insist on new models (*see* the section later in the chapter on the future of online advertising).

Making banner advertising work

As with any form of advertising, certain techniques will result in a more effective advertisement. Discussions with those who have advertised online indicate the following are important to effective advertising:

1 *Appropriate incentives are needed to achieve clickthrough.* Banner advertisements with offers such as prizes or reductions can achieve higher clickthrough rates perhaps by as much as 10 per cent.

2 *Creative design needs to be tested extensively.* Alternative designs for the advertisement need to be tested on representatives of a target audience. Anecdotal evidence suggests that the clickthrough rate can vary greatly according to the design of the advertisement, in much the same way that recall of a television advertisement will vary in line with its concept and design. Different creative designs may be needed for different sites on which advertisements are placed. Zeff and Aronson (1999) note that simply the use of the words 'click here!' or 'click now' can dramatically increase clickthrough rates because new users do not know how banners work! Animated banners, or those that change during a campaign, may also provide a better response.

3 *Appropriate keywords are needed.* Testing is also needed to ensure that the keywords typed into a search engine fit the required profile of audience for the advertisement. An example of this is displaying an advertisement for IBM's Lotus Notes product if the user types in the name of the competing product, 'Microsoft Exchange'. This could appeal to members of an audience who were not loyal to Microsoft.

4 *Placement of advertisement and timing need to be considered carefully.* The different types of placement option available have been discussed earlier in the chapter, but it should be remembered that audience volume and composition will vary through the day and the week.

5 *Consider the clickthrough quality, not just the quantity.* A UK bank stated that having a clickthrough rate of 10 per cent is of limited value if the profile of the person clicking through does not fit a certain investment product. It is much better to have a 0.1 per cent clickthrough rate with a good match, resulting in qualified customers signing up for the new product.

6 *Build the infrastructure to deal with the response.* A successful advertising campaign will naturally lead to visits to the company web site. The content should be right to give the audience what they expect after clicking on the creative components, and the company should be able to follow up any subsequent communications with customers. Are there people in place to deal with e-mails or send out promotional materials?

Advertising networks

Advertising networks are collections of independent web sites from different companies and media networks, each of which has an arrangement with an advertising broker to place banner advertisements. The advantage for the companies that are part of the network is that they do not need to deal directly with different companies wishing to advertise on their site. They simply have the broker, who acts as a single contact point. In addition, they do not need to manage the technical process of serving banner advertisements and monitoring their usage. Companies wishing to place advertisements benefit by being able to deal with a single agency, or broker. Figure 9.5 shows DoubleClick, one of the best known advertising networks, which operates both in the USA and through worldwide franchises. The network offers advertisements in a range of different areas such as automotive, finance, health and entertainment.

Mini case study 9.1

The DoubleClick advertising network

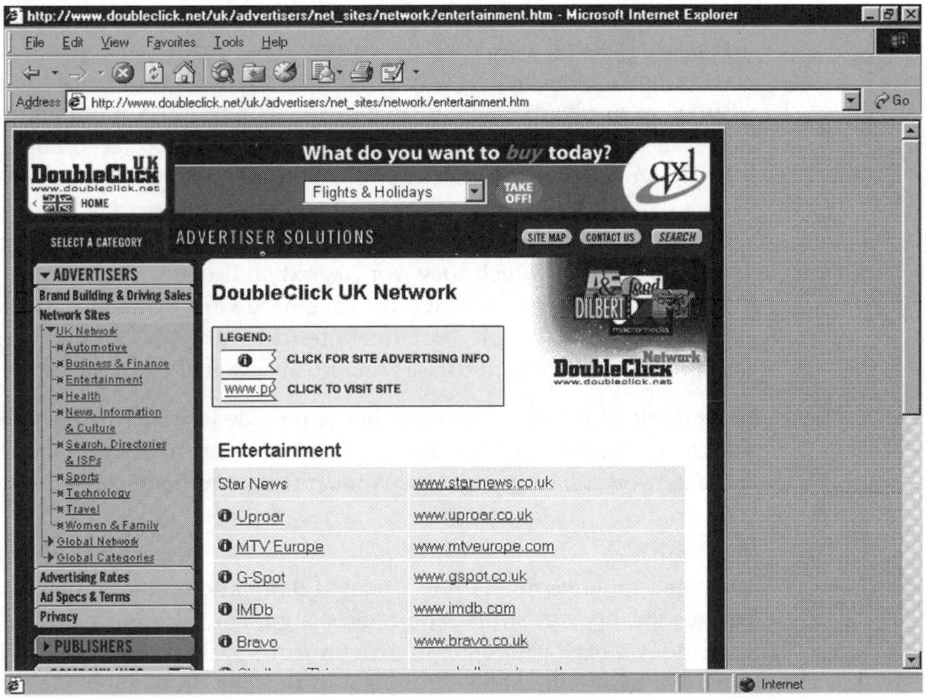

Fig. 9.5 The DoubleClick advertising network site, showing affiliated sites in the Entertainment category

DoubleClick offers advertisers the ability to dynamically target advertisements on the Web through its 'DART' targeting technology. This gives advertisers a core objective – that of reaching specific audiences. There are four basic categories of targeting criteria:

261

► **Mini case study** *continued*

1 *Content targeting.* Allows placement of advertising message on a particular interest site or within an entire interest category such as:
   ■ Automotive
   ■ Business and Finance
   ■ Entertainment
   ■ Health
   ■ News, Information and Culture
   ■ Search, Directories and ISPs
   ■ Sports
   ■ Technology
   ■ Travel
   ■ Women and Family

2 *Behavioural targeting.* An audience can be targeted according to how they use the Web. For example, advertisers can select business users by delivering advertisements on Monday to Friday between 9 and 5, or leisure users by targeting messages in the evening hours. Behavioural targeting includes psychographic aspects of advertising. For example, it has been shown that the impact of advertisements tends to decline after they have been viewed three or four times. It is possible through DoubleClick to save money on the total number of ad impressions by showing an advertisement to an individual up to a maximum number of times.

3 *User targeting.* This enables advertisements to be placed according to specific traits of the audience including their geographic location (based on country or Zip code), domain type (for example, educational users with addresses ending in .edu or .ac.uk can be targeted), business size or type according to SIC code or even by the company for which they work, based on the company domain name.

4 *Tech targeting.* This is based on user hardware, software and Internet access provider. For example, engineers tend to use UNIX operating systems and graphic designers tend to use Macintosh systems.

An example of the use of DoubleClick is provided by New Woman Online, which is part of the DoubleClick UK network. DoubleClick provides information on all the sites in the network. The entry for New Woman Online contains the following information:

Site overview

Launched in November 1996. Updated daily and contains news, fashion, health features, beauty tips, articles on blokes, a guide to shopping on the web and chat. It includes a back catalogue of articles from past issues and prizes and competitions. The site is one of few lifestyle web sites for UK women.

Monthly site statistics

Impressions: 40 000
Demographics: Gender: 86 per cent female
Median age: 28 years median age
Socio-economic group: ABC1
Traffic by country: 91 per cent UK

Targeting options

1 *Run of site*. Advertise throughout the whole of the New Woman site, taking advantage of the different areas available from the Feature Stories, Today, Bloke, Health, Beauty, The Shop, Caf and Directory, Bloke Jokes and the Chat Room.

2 *Category package*. One or more of the areas given above.

3 *Combination package*. A combination of the two above.

4 *Site sponsorships*. High-visibility, sponsorship positions available on both a temporary or permanent basis.

Note that many of the targeting facilities offered by DoubleClick are also available through other advertising brokers and media owners. This is because software for serving advertisements can be purchased by media owners that provides many of the features indicated above. The best known ad serving software is sold by a separate company, NetGravity (*www.netgravity.com*), which sells AdServer, a widely used online server, to serve advertisements to customers. This will also target users according to their interests and location, for example according to country domain, keywords typed into a search engine, or parts of a site visited (if a magazine).

Fig. 9.6 Composite image of NewWoman site (*www.newwomanonline.co.uk***), showing three main banner advertisements**

> **Ad serving**
> The term for displaying an advetisement on a web site. Often the advertisement will be served from a web server different from the site on which it is placed.

Affiliate networks

An affiliate network is different from an advertising network although the broad aim of the two is the same: to use advertisements placed on many sites to link to a web site. The use of affiliate networks is best illustrated by the example of the Amazon bookshop, which is perhaps the best exponent of this online marketing technique. According to Schiller (1999), Amazon has over 300 000 affiliates, who offer small banner advertisements on their sites that when clicked will take the user of their site through to the Amazon site (*www.amazon.com*). The network includes many major portals, for example, Yahoo! (Fig. 9.2). Each partner earns up to 15 per cent commission every time a customer clicks on the advertisement and then buys a book or other item at Amazon. Amazon claims that nearly a quarter of its revenue is derived in this way, which illustrates the effectiveness of this method. This is effectively a no-cost method of advertising or one in which payment is only made where there is a definite outcome – the purchase of an item.

> **Affiliate network**
> Collection of web sites that link to an online retailer in exchange for commission on purchases made from the retailer.

Note that the links between Amazon and the partners work well since when a user clicks on the advertisement he or she is taken directly through to a relevant book or listing of books. For example, a user visiting a gardening site and wanting to learn about lawn care would be taken through to the listing of all books related to this on the Amazon site. Links to Amazon also occur on search engines such as AltaVista (*www.altavista.com*), where links to Amazon are given according to the types of keywords typed in. An unusual example of an affiliate arrangement is that of Jesper Lindhart, a 19-year-old student in Copenhagen, who has not merely linked to the UK-based Internet Bookshop, but has translated the site into Danish!

Activity 9.2

Affiliate networks

Visit one of the Amazon sites (*www.amazon.com, www.amazon.co.uk* or *www.amazon.de*) and find out how you could join the affiliate network. Summarise:

1 The mechanism for linking to the Amazon site.

2 The contractual arrangement between Amazon and its partners, including payment.

3 Your understanding of the reasons for the success of the scheme.

The future of online advertising

It was mentioned in a previous section of this chapter that currently expenditure on online advertising in the UK is low compared with advertising expenditure in other media. However, it is generally expected that this figure will increase rapidly. It is worth pausing to consider the factors that determine the amount of advertising on the web. The main factors are the size and composition of the audience and the effectiveness of the medium for advertising. As explained in Chapter 2, the size of the audience is increasing rapidly as new, lower-cost methods of accessing the Internet become available. The characteristics of the audience are well known, in particular their relatively high income, although the characteristics of the audience are becoming more like those of the general population as time proceeds. However, the number of users, and hence the size of the audience, is likely to be constrained by the cost of buying devices to access the Internet. With PC owner-ship nearing saturation in the USA and elsewhere, there will continue to be a sizeable majority who do not have access to the Internet. This situation is only likely to change when the Internet becomes accessible via standard consumer products such as phones and televisions. The Internet will only become suitable for mass market advertising when this development occurs, and this is likely to be some years away. Perhaps a bigger barrier to the growth of Internet-based advertis-ing is the nature of the medium. Although there is the benefit that the user pays close attention to the message when using the computer, there is also the disad-vantage that the message is being delivered using a limited space on the screen, and with limited use of sound and motion.

A further issue to take into account when considering the future effectiveness of banner advertising is the fact that the efficacy of advertising may decline as users become familiar with advertisements. It has been suggested that there is a novelty element that causes new users to click on advertisement. If this is the case, it would be expected that over time, clickthrough rates will decline. This effect has already been recorded (although it will be offset by new users continually joining the Internet). Another effect concerns advertising inventory, which is always increasing as new sites go online and the size of existing sites increases. The likely effect of this will be to dilute the effectiveness of advertising and increase competi-tion on those selling advertising space. This is likely to result in lower advertising costs. Certainly there have been no large increases in the cost of advertising space in the short history of the medium. Accurate surveys of the average expenditure on advertising are only available from the USA, owing to the higher amount of advertising spend there. The 'Online Advertising Report' from AdKnowledge in January 1999 found that for the previous two years the cost of advertising had declined from nearly $40 CPM to approximately $35 CPM, a decline that is consis-tent with increasing advertising inventory and uncertainties over the value of Internet advertising.

Both of these effects may discourage advertisers, although any decline will be offset by a reduction in CPM and the fact that more companies will be looking to advertise. Possible evidence of this effect is suggested by a survey from the US Association of National Advertisers, who reported in June 1999 that there had been a 7 per cent drop in the number of US companies advertising online over the past year. Companies cited the inability to prove a return on investment, unreliable measurement information and high CPM rates as the major disincentives to advertising online.

Despite these reservations about the future of Internet advertising, Table 9.4 suggests that the Internet is now being used for advertising across a range of sectors: not just technology, but also consumer products such as financial services and cars. This suggests there will be further increases in the use of the medium for these areas. The compilation in Table 9.4 is consistent with the IAB *Ad Revenue Report* (*www.iab.net*) for the third quarter of 1998 in the USA. This reported that the leading categories for online advertising spend were consumer-related (27 per cent), computing (24 per cent), financial services (16 per cent), telecommunications (11 per cent) and new media (7 per cent).

Table 9.4 Relative expenditure of different advertisers by sector

Business sector	Number of companies in top 50 advertisers	Examples (position in brackets)
IT (hardware and software)	12	IBM (1), Microsoft (3), Hewlett-Packard (4)
Media	10	United News and Media (11), BBC (30)
Financial services	8	Citigroup (9), Legal and General (16), Nationwide (17)
Communications	5	BT (2), UUNET 19), Orange (48)
Automotive	4	Ford (8), BMW (21), General Motors (31)

Source: Based on a tabulation of the top 50 advertisers between March 1998 and February 1999, based in turn on research by Fletcher Associates (*www.fletch.co.uk*), *Revolution*, May 1999.

Some of the major companies that have prospered by advertising in traditional media are concerned as to how they can exploit the new medium. This is evidenced by the Future of Advertising Stakeholders (FAST) Summit, which was held in August 1998 and involved such major advertisers as Proctor & Gamble (the main sponsors), Kraft, Heinz, Glaxo-Wellcome, Coca-Cola and Unilever. The executives at the conference decided upon the need to investigate consumer acceptance of online advertising and set up 'FAST forward', a committee that will report on such issues. The results of such research and details of further conferences are available at the FAST Summit Site (*www.fastsummit.com*) and will also be reported at Internet World Magazine (*www.internetworld.com*) and Nua Surveys online (*www.nua.ie/surveys*).

Other online promotion methods

Promotion in search engines and directories

Another aspect of traffic building is maximising the number of users who find a web site when searching using keywords, in a search engine, directory or a portal. Note that this differs from paid-for advertising on a search engine site, as discussed in an earlier section of this chapter. Here we are referring to a company web site being listed in a list of web sites if a user types in a specific keyword such as 'agro-chemicals'. What a company is trying to achieve is inclusion in the list of the top ten sites displayed when a keyword is typed in. The reason for this is that research shows that most users will only bother looking at the first ten names – they will not look at subsequent pages.

This promotion technique is particularly important in view of the number of web users who use such facilities for finding information. Achieving good search rating listings is a skilled job, which is often dependent on a webmaster who is familiar with the techniques for achieving good listings in search engines. The webmaster will refer to sources such as Search Engines Watch (*www.searchenginewatch.com*), which describes how the search engines work and gives tips on how to get the site as high as possible in the search engine listing. There are a number of barriers that make this difficult:

1 The site has to be registered with each of the main search engines, and there are hundreds of potential search engines that customers may use. In practice it is only necessary to be listed in all the main search engines. According to MediaMetrix (*www.mediametrix.com*), the main search engines in April 1999 for combined usage at home and work (expressed as a percentage of all users) were:
   ■ Yahoo! 50.5 per cent
   ■ MSN 38 per cent
   ■ Infoseek 32 per cent
   ■ Netscape 31 per cent
   ■ Excite 25 per cent
   ■ Lycos 24 per cent
   ■ AltaVista 16 per cent
   ■ Snap 11 per cent
   ■ Hotbot 11 per cent
2 Each of the search engines uses different criteria to order the list of results or 'hits' associated with the keywords the user types in.
3 The techniques used to register and the procedures for producing the listings vary through time, so a repeat registration with a search engine may be necessary quite frequently.
4 There are a large number of web sites indexed by search engines. The webmaster may be competing for visibility with as many as 150 million web pages, as listed in AltaVista. Imagine the position of a company selling home insurance: if a user types in the keywords 'home insurance' there may be hundreds of companies offering this service, but users are not likely to view any more than the first ten in the search engine listing.

Given these difficulties, many companies find that the webmaster may not have the time to keep up with the changing techniques, so a better solution is to outsource the promotion of a site through search engines to other companies. For example, in the UK the following companies offer what they call 'traffic-generating' or 'visibility' programs:

■ Sitelynx (*www.sitelynx.co.uk*);
■ Web Promote (*www.webpromote.co.uk*);
■ Web Marketing (*www.web-marketing.co.uk*);
■ Hyperlink Services (*www.hyperlink.co.uk*).

A payment of, for example, £100 per month will ensure that a company and its products are visible via search engines and may include other services such as ensuring links refer to the site from other web sites (other than search engines). Companies or individuals who are unable to pay for such a service can use free submission engines such as *www.webpromote.com*, which provide submission to several search engines.

It is also useful for companies to understand the criteria used to determine whether a site is listed in a search engine, since these may affect page design. These criteria were introduced in Chapter 4, but are described in more detail here in the context of promotion. It is important to note the following:

1 Registration of a site with a range of search engines is essential, otherwise the site will not be listed. As explained in Chapter 4, a site will only be listed if it has been recently visited and indexed by a spider or robot from a web site. These visits will only occur if a site has been registered with a search engine. Registration can be achieved manually by visiting each of the search engines given in Chapter 4 and following links to 'submit your site or URL'. To make this easier there are services that automatically submit a URL to several search engines. It is generally thought that this procedure is inferior to handing submissions to individual search engines since some specific details required may be omitted.

    Some useful services to help promote sites have been collected together under the Microsoft Network Site Link Exchange site (*www.linkexchange.com/*). These microsites include:

    ■ *submitit.linkexchange.com* – SubmitIt! – software that automates the process of linking to search engines;
    ■ *positionagent.linkexchange.com* – a web-based tool for which a web address and keyword can be typed in to review one's position in the top ten search engines;
    ■ *www.linkexchange.com* – a free advertising network, which operates to enable sites to exchange banner advertisements. The largest of such networks is the LinkExchange banner network with over 450 000 sites in 32 languages. Advertisers using this service choose who sees their banner and what banners appear on their site according to site content and language. For every two advertisements that appear on a company site, that company's advertisement is displayed on another site, free of charge.

2 The keywords in the title of a web page that appears at the top of a browser window, as indicated in the HTML code by the <TITLE></TITLE> keyword, are significant on search engine listings. If a keyword appears in a title, that site is more likely to be placed high in a listing than if the keyword is only in the body text of a page. It follows that each page on a site should have a specific title giving the name of a company and the product, service or offer featured on that page.

3 The number of occurrences of the keyword in the text of the web page will also determine the listing. Copy can be written to increase the number of times a word is used. However, search engines make checks to ensure that a word is not repeated many times, as in: 'cheap flights... cheap flights... cheap flights... cheap flights... cheap flights... cheap flights... cheap flights... cheap flights...', and will not list the page if this type of 'spamming' occurs!

4 Some search sites such as Google (*www.google.com*) use the popularity of the site to enhance the position in the listing.

5 If a site uses a great deal of graphical material, perhaps on the home page, it is less likely to be listed high in a listing. The only text on which the page will be indexed will be the <TITLE> keyword. There are two methods to adopt to ensure graphical information does not affect a site's listing. First, additional text can be added to the page, and second, graphical images can have hidden text associated with them. This hidden text is not seen by the user (unless graphical images are turned off), but will be indexed by the search engine. For example text about a company name and products can be assigned to a company logo using the 'ALT' tag as follows:

<IMG NAME= 'Logo' SRC= 'logo.gif' ALT="Eastern Engineering – lathes and milling machines">

6 Information generated 'on the fly' when a user requests a page from a database will not be featured at all in the search engine index. Information from a database should be mirrored on a server where it will be indexed. The Lycos search engine has a facility for finding this information. It is in the 'Lycos Invisible Web Catalog' at *dir.lycos.com/Reference/Searchable_Databases/*.

7 The use of frames can make it difficult for search engines to index a site. The Thomas Cook example below shows that the information on the subsidiary frames is not available in the home page for indexing. No relevant words such as holidays or flights are available on which the search index can build its index.

```
<HEAD>
<TITLE>Thomas Cook On-Line</TITLE>
</HEAD>
<frameset rows="*,90" BORDER="0" FRAMEBORDER=0 FRAMESPACING=0>
        <FRAME SRC="/cgi-
bin/udscgi?BV_EngineID=0.930841559.195.92.21.128.0&BV_Operation=Dyn_Frame&BV_SessionID=
655869710&form%25destination_type=template&BV_ServiceName=ThomasCook&form%25destin
ation=%2fhomec.t" name ="TCmain">
        <FRAME SRC="/cgi-
bin/udscgi?BV_EngineID=0.930841559.195.92.21.128.0&BV_Operation=Dyn_Frame&BV_SessionI
D=655869710&form%25destination_type=template&BV_ServiceName=ThomasCook&form%25dest
ination=%2flinks.t" name ="TCnavigate" marginwidth ="0" marginheight ="0" scrolling ="no">
</frameset>
```

8 The use of 'meta-tags' is important for some search engines, such as AltaVista, in determining the position in which a site is listed by the search engine. They are also used to specify the first line of text displayed in conjunction with the web address in the search engine site listing. The text of this line can be important in encouraging users to visit a site. Some examples of the use of meta-tags are illustrated in Mini case study 9.2. Note, however, that meta-tags are only one of the factors that search engines take into account, and they are not used by directories such as Yahoo!.

Using meta-tags to promote web sites

Meta-tags are part of the HTML file, typed in by web page creators, which is read and displayed by the browser. They are effectively hidden from users, but are used by search engines when robots or spiders compile their index. In some search engines, if a keyword is typed in by the user that matches the meta-tag on a site, then this site will be listed higher up in the search engine listing. To see meta-tags such as those listed here you should view the source of the HTML file using a web browser. In Microsoft Internet Explorer, choose View, Source.

There are two important meta-tags that are specified at the top of an HTML page using the <meta name = " > HTML keyword:

1 The "keywords" meta-tag highlights the key topics covered on a web page:

Example: <meta name="keywords" content="book, books, shop, store, book shop, bookstore, publisher, bookshop, general, interest, departments,">

2 The "description" meta tag denotes the information that will be displayed in the listing of web sites in the web browser when a web page is found:

Example: <meta name="description" content="The largest online book store in the world.">

Other meta-tags are used to give other information such as the type of tool used to create the web page.

Some examples of meta-tags

1 *BBC home page* (*www.bbc.co.uk*)
<META NAME="Keywords" content="bbc online, BBC, online, British Broadcasting Corporation, home, homepage, internet, tv, television, radio, public-service, public service,">
<META NAME="Description" content="The BBC Homepage – Your gateway to BBC Online">

2 *Cisco* (*www.cisco.com*)
<META NAME="Keywords" CONTENT="Cisco, networking equipment, net-work hardware, network management, routers, LAN, WAN, ATM, software, servers, switches, internet, intranet, extranet, ISDN, network security, local area network, wide area network, hubs, token rings, business networks, ethernet, firewalls, Cisco Systems">
<META NAME="Description" CONTENT="Cisco is the leading supplier of network-ing equipment and network management for the Internet. Products include routers, hubs, ethernet, LAN/ATM switches, dial-up access servers and software.">

3 *Disney* (*www.disney.com*).
<META name = KEYWORDS content=Disney, Family, Kids, Shopping, Disney's Blast Online, Wonderful World Of Disney, The Disney Store Online, Pooh Gram, Disneyana, Walt Disney Pictures, Walt Disney World, Disney Interactive, Walt Disney Records, Disneyland, Walt Disney Home Video, Disney Channel, Disney Books, Walt Disney Television, Disney Cruise Line, Disney Vacation

Club, Disney Adventures Magazine, Walt Disney Classics Collection, Walt Disney Theatrical Productions, Star Watch, Mickey Mouse, Winnie the Pooh, Minnie Mouse, Donald Duck, Goofy>
<META name=DESCRIPTION content=Disney.com is the best place on the Web for what's new at Disney – movies, theme parks, vacations, games and activities, and other products and services.

4 *McDonald's* (*www.mcdonalds.com*)

Note the coverage of different spelling variants and the use of the additional 'Content' meta-tag.

<META NAME="KEYWORDS" CONTENT="*www.mcdonalds.com*, mcdonalds.com, mcdonald's, mc, mcdonalds, mc donalds, mc donald's, donalds, corporation, mcdonaldland, happy, meal, Big Mac, McMuffin, Ronald, Food, Franchise, Hamburger, Cheeseburger, Quarter Pounder, fry, fries, RMHC, RMCC, ronald, stock, MCD">

<META NAME="SUBJECT" CONTENT="www.mcdonalds.com, mcdonalds.com, mcdonald's, mc, mcdonalds, mc donalds, mc donald's, donalds, corporation, mcdonaldland, happy, meal, Big Mac, McMuffin, Ronald, Food, Franchise, Hamburger, Cheeseburger, Quarter Pounder, fry, fries, RMHC, RMCC, ronald, stock, MCD">

<META NAME="DESCRIPTION" CONTENT="McDonald's is a fast food restaurant chain serving such favorites as Egg McMuffin sandwiches for breakfast and Big Mac sandwiches and french fries for lunch and dinner. Kids look for the Golden Arches to enjoy a Happy Meal, may visit with Ronald McDonald. McDonald's offers franchising and career opportunities.">

5 *Nokia* (*www.nokia.com*)

<META NAME="keywords" CONTENT="nokia, Nokia, NOKIA, mobile phones, cellular, telecommunications, wireless networks, fixed networks, datacom, GSM, multimedia terminals, monitors, handsets, customer services, press releases, financial information, student exchange, open positions, employment opportunities, career opportunities with Nokia">

< META NAME = "description" CONTENT = "Nokia is the world's leading mobile phone supplier and a leading supplier of mobile and fixed telecom networks including related customer services." >

6 *British Airways* (*www.britishairways.com*)

No meta tags observed!

Useful sites, which describe how a company may ensure its site is promoted adequately in search engines, are listed at Yahoo! in the category:

www.yahoo.co.uk/Computers_and_Internet/Internet/World_Wide_Web/Information_and_Docume ntation/Site_Announcement_and_Promotion/

Notable sites explaining how to achieve listings are:

- Search Engine Watch (*www.searchenginewatch.com*);
- Northern Web (*northernwebs.com/set/*);
- Web Promote (*www.webpromote.com/tools/freesubmit.asp*).

Links from other sites: co-branding and sponsorship

Given the large number of web sites indexed in search engines and the difficulty this causes in providing visibility for a web site, it is important for companies to consider other low-cost methods of generating web site traffic. A relatively straightforward method is for them to make sure that their site has links from as many other related sites as possible, using hyperlinks. This is sometimes referred to as a 'link-building campaign'. A good starting-point for this process is to see how many sites are currently linking to their site. There are two methods for achieving this. First, a log-file analyser program such as WebTrends (*see* Chapter 12) can be used to indicate what are known as the *referring sites*. Second, some search engines such as AltaVista and Infoseek provide a facility that allows the user to type 'link:' followed by the URL, which then lists other web sites that are linked to the site specified.

Once sites that are currently linked to the site are identified, there are various options:

1 Review the different types of site and contact sites similar to those already linked to the site, and request the other sites to display a link to the company's site. Sometimes payment may be involved, but more usually other sites will provide a link in return for the company site providing a link back to them. These are known as reciprocal links.
2 Place more prominent advertisements on existing link sites. These may be paid for or may be by reciprocal arrangement (banner exchange).
3 Enter a co-branding agreement where the company places content on the linking (referring) site that provides value to that site's audience and increases the likelihood that the audience reading this content may visit the company's site.

Portals offering product and price comparison services

A closely related method of promotion for companies selling products using e-commerce is to ensure that the products are listed on infomediary or portal sites offering product comparison. The promoter of a site needs to check that a company's products or distributors selling its products are represented in as wide a range of these as is practical. There are several examples of these services in Chapter 15.

Sponsorship

> **Co-branding**
> An arrangement between two or more companies where they agree to jointly display content and to conduct joint promotions using brand logos or banner advertisements.

Co-branding or promotion partnering is seen as a cost-effective method of promotion, which can be used for longer periods than banner advertisments. The practice has become so widespread that *Revolution* magazine now has a monthly feature that lists co-branding arrangements. Examples from the June 1999 'dealwatch' include:

▪ *WhatCar* magazine and *AutoHunter* have joined together to encourage online car sales through reciprocal links between their sites (this is an example of two-way co-branding).

- The British Tourist Authority has signed a contract with Avis to offer visitors to the BTA web site special offers on UK car rental. The deal involves banner advertisements and sponsorship on 29 pages of the BTA sites linking to a special offer page on the Avis site (this is an example of one-way co-branding).
- The portal and ISP, AOL UK, has formed links with the online wine retailer Chateau online and the travel agency Thomas Cook, who are both 'anchor tenants', providing promotion of both companies in the relevant shopping channels.

A further example of how online and offline sponsorship can be combined is provided by Fig. 9.7. The financial services provider Scottish Amicable sponsors the Barbarians Rugby club and uses its web site to build a community of interested fans made up of existing and potential new customers. The competition is a good method of generating repeat visits, which should ensure that the fans will be made aware of new services, and their visits should increase their perception of the brand.

The growth of Internet-based sponsorship has been compared to the transition between radio and television advertising by, for example, Kassye (1997) and Cartellieri *et al.* (1997). Kassye (1997) points out that there was much initial scepticism about the likely success of both new media. In part this was due to initial technical difficulties, but the low level of initial users was the main reason for this scepticism. In fact the growth of the Internet has been much more rapid than that of television in terms of the rate of penetration, as is shown in Table 9.5.

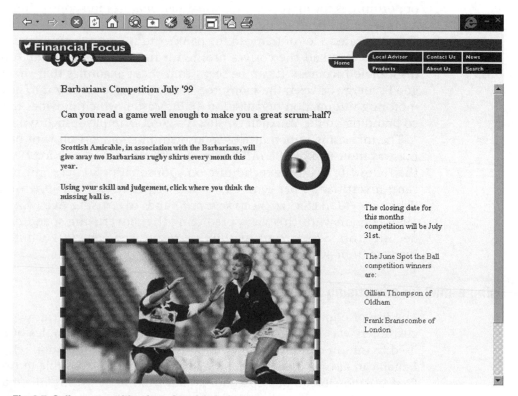

Fig. 9.7 Online competition from Scottish Amicable

Table 9.5 Years to reach audience of 50 million in the United States for different media

Medium	No. of years
Radio	13
Broadcast TV	13
Cable TV	9
Web	5

It is inevitable that with the growth of a new medium, there will be a long learning phase during which companies work out which promotion methods work best. There may also be long-term trends in the way companies are involved with developing the content for the medium. With broadcast television, for example, many of the early programmes were directly controlled by sponsors. Kassye (1997) gives the examples of the Colgate Comedy Hour, the Texaco Hall of Fame and the Kraft Music Hall. By the 1950s direct sponsorship had greatly declined, as it was felt that the revenue from advertising was maximised by having a range of advertisers during commercial breaks. This trend has partly reversed, with the direct sponsorship of drama serials and film presentations now being common. The current use of sponsorship in broadcast TV content has meant that this model has directly transferred to the Web.

Sponsorship, as well as taking the form of a promoter sponsoring a site, for example the sponsorship of the Guardian site (*www.footballunlimited.co.uk*) by the brewer Carling, which also sponsors the Football Premiership, can also make use of opportunities for involving individual personalities in sponsorship. For example, an investment bank in the Isle of Man sponsored a round-the-world yachtsman. This generated a lot of traffic to the bank's site amongst people interested in yachting, who also had the correct profile for investing (mainly mature, with high disposable incomes). It can be seen from these examples that there needs to be good synergy between the sponsored site and the sponsor for it to be effective. The motoring information organisation TrafficMaster, which provides traffic news and co-branding on the Vauxhall car site, is a good example of such synergy.

The increasing importance of sponsorship in comparison with banner advertising was indicated by the *IAB Ad Revenue Report* (*www.iab.net*) for 1998, which gave the following figures: expenditure on sponsorship, 30 per cent; banners, 53 per cent; investitials, 6 per cent; and others 11 per cent. The *eAdvertising Report* published by eMarketer (*www.emarketer.com*) and Advertising Age (*www.adage.com*) in 1999 concurs with this view, predicting that advertising spend on banners will decline from 52 per cent in 1998 to 26 per cent by 2001 while sponsorships increase from 40 per cent to 58 per cent.

Using e-mail for advertising

The use of e-mail for communicating and building long-term relationships with customers was introduced in Chapter 8 by means of examples of e-mails being used to inform customers of new product or market information relevant to them. E-mail can also be used for paid-for advertising. This is possible in two main ways. First it is possible to buy space for an advertisement within an e-mail newsletter. Such newsletters have the benefit that they are highly targeted, and the audience will view the advertisment as part of the e-mail (although they may skim over it). Such advertising is primarily text based, although more graphical advertisements are likely to develop with the more frequent use of HTML-based e-mail packages, which permit more sophisticated formatting of e-mail (which could include graphical advertisements). There are many opportunities for advertising, particularly for technology-based products. For example, the Search Engine Watch newsletter (from *www.searchenginewatch.com*), an e-mail newsletter that gives advice on how to boost a site's position in search engines, is read by over 60 000 webmasters. For those interested in Internet marketing there are several newsletters such as Michael Tchong's Iconocast (*www.iconocast.com*) or Internet.com's Internet World's Weekly digest (*www.internetworld.com*). Such newsletters can be sponsored – Iconocast is sponsored by *Business 2.0* magazine – and also advertisements can be placed within the news items contained in the e-mail and separated by exclamation marks from the main news item (*see* Mini case study 9.3).

Mini case study 9.3 **Examples of e-mail based advertisements**

The text-based advertisements below are taken from the Iconocast e-mail newsletter, which is a US-based weekly newsletter summarising the use of the Internet for different commercial applications. The advertisements are interspersed with the news information. They are clearly directed at those seeking specialised techniques of reaching new customers using the web.

!!!!!!!!!!!!!!!!!!!!!!!!!!!!! FLAG !!!!!!!!!!!!!!!!!!!!!!!!!!!!!!!!!
YOUR BRAND MAKES AN IMPACT on Mplayer.com with rich media advertising. Mplayer.com is an online games and entertainment site with 3 million affluent members who spend huge amounts of time online. Reach them with rich, innovative campaigns. See what all the fuss is about at: http://www.mplayer.com/advertising/
or mailto:advertising@mplayer.com
!!!

!!!!!!!!!!!!!!!!!!!!!!!!!!!!! FLAG !!!!!!!!!!!!!!!!!!!!!!!!!!!!!!!!!
SUPER STICKY. SUPER TARGETED. SUPER RESPONSE. Email powered by Mail.com makes site visitors everyday site users. For a valuable, super-targetable audience. The Mail.com ad Network, including CNN, Rolling Stone, CBS and many other top sites, lets you pinpoint users by profession, affinity and rich, declared profiles. To advertise, email us at adsales@staff.mail.com. To get free email for your site, emailpartner@webmail.com. Or call (212) 425-4200.
!!!

!!!!!!!!!!!!!!!!!!!!!!!!!!!!! FLAG !!!!!!!!!!!!!!!!!!!!!!!!!!!!!!!!!
FREE PERFORMANCE APPRAISAL OF YOUR E-COMMERCE WEB SITE
Are you losing customers or revenue because your web site is too slow or slower than your competitors? Are your Internet providers delivering the speed and service they promised? Measure, assure and improve your web-site quality of service from 35 cities worldwide – for one week, for free.
http://www.keynote.com/adv/ic.html From Keynote Systems, the Internet Performance Authority
!!!

Relevant e-mail lists

- Liszt (*www.liszt.com*) – a site giving a categorised list of the tens of thousands of specialist mailing lists;
- Kim Bayne's personal site (*www.wolfBayne.com/lists*) – Kim Bayne's Marketing Lists on the Internet;
- Online Advertising (*www.o-a.com*) – online advertising list;
- Clickz (*clickz.com/list*) – online advertising related list;
- Internet Advertising Organisation (*www.internetadvertising.org*) – representative e-mail lists.

Loyalty techniques and online incentive schemes

Air Miles and storecards are well known as methods of generating loyalty from customers by offering special promotional offers or the perception of 'getting something for nothing'. Given the success of these techniques, it is no surprise that many companies have tried to migrate these marketing concepts online. Online these incentives are sometimes referred to as 'e-centives', but this is probably one use too many of the 'e'-prefix.

One of the forerunners in the use of online incentives has been Cybergold. In the USA, sites such as Cybergold (*www.cybergold.com*) have operated the concept of 'pay per view' for some years. This is not, however, a conventional pay per view where the customer pays to view a boxing match for example, but it is the customer who is paid to view advertising material after completing an online questionnaire which will profile his or her interests. The concept of this site has now been extended to include loyalty: Cybergold credits are offered as bonus points.

Case study 9.1, Online loyalty schemes, illustrates some of the online loyalty schemes that have been developed in Europe.

It is useful to apply concepts of the adoption and diffusion processes to new promotional techniques such as these loyalty schemes. The process of adoption (Rogers, 1983) follows the stages of:

- knowledge;
- persuasion;
- decision as to whether to trial product;
- implementation of trial;
- confirmation of product as valuable.

Note that here the adoption model can be applied both to the companies using these techniques and to the members of public who are using them.

Across the whole population, through time, a diffusion process (represented by a bell curve) can be identified for those trialling new products, in the categeries innovators, early adopters, early majority, late majority and laggards (Rogers, 1983). Many of the new Internet promotion initiatives such as the loyalty scheme are at the high-risk 'innovators' stage in terms of both companies and customers whereas others such as banner advertising are at a later stage of early adopters. The application of diffusion theory to the new Internet technologies as a whole is described in Chapter 15.

Case study 9.1

ONLINE LOYALTY SCHEMES

Fig. 9.8 Beenz online loyalty scheme

Although there are plans to migrate the Air Miles incentive scheme online, at least three online incentive schemes have already been developed in the UK: Ipoints (*www.ipoint.co.uk*), Beenz (*www.beenz.com*) and Zoom (*www.zoom.co.uk*). These differ from the Air Miles model in several ways. According to Aaron O'Sullivan, director of Ipoints (Schofield, 1999), the scheme has benefits because it is more immediate than schemes such as Air Miles – you can join the scheme, check your points and redeem them online. The lower overheads of electronic trading enable larger rewards. Ipoints allocate 7–10 per cent of the sales value for rewards compared with 1–2 per cent for offline schemes. Ipoints are offered on sites such as Amazon (*Amazon.co.uk*) and Screentrade (*www.screentrade.co.uk*), and can be redeemed elsewhere.

Beenz (Fig. 9.8) was launched in early 1999. Although it is similar to Ipoints, its founder Phil Letts has a different vision for the service, seeing it more as a global currency than as a loyalty scheme limited to a single country. To accentuate this, he uses terms such *earning, saving* and *spending* Beenz to describe how they are used. He does not see Beenz as a pure loyalty scheme but as a rewards system, which may be tied into other loyalty schemes. Schofield (1999) stated that within six months of start-up Beenz had developed a network of over 150 sites offering Beenz, 22 sites redeeming them and 20 000 account holders. The company has a staff of 50 and intends to spend a $1 million per month during 1999 on promotion and development of the concept. A company wanting to use Beenz for promotion purchases a

► **Case study** *continued*

set number of Beenz, and when a user earns Beenz he or she is sent a secure e-mail from beenz.com with a unique code, which is pasted into an 'offer' window on the web site. In this way the units are credited to the customer and removed from the retailer. Arguments against the Beenz scheme posted on the UK NetMarketing discussion group by, for example, Scott Reid of Miller Brothers Electrical Ltd, who have considered using the Beenz scheme, include:

■ The concept of customer loyalty runs against a trend of shopping on the Internet, which is to find an item as cheaply as possible. Given this, customers will be price sensitive, but less concerned about other incentives.

■ It is difficult to establish the value of such points. Different sites showed very different values: one offered 4 beenz free when you bought a toaster costing £17.99 and offered a reduction of £5 per order for 50 Beenz, while another site offered 50 Beenz with every CD purchased.

■ There may be a cost to the retailer of offering beenz or from similar schemes.

Zoom points follow a different model in that they can only be awarded and redeemed on the Zoom shopping mall. This mall includes sites related to the parent company, Arcadia Group. These include Top Shop, Principles, Dorothy Perkins and Burton. The scheme also includes other 'e-tailers' on the mall, such as Amazon, Interflora, Jobsearch and the online auction company, QXL, all of which will also be able to offer these points. This scheme is more similar to signing up to a loyalty scheme with a single supermarket.

Questions

1 Summarise the difference between the three schemes described.

2 These schemes are all new ventures at the time of writing. Visit the sites and assess the relative success of the three companies in terms of the number and type of merchants and customers who have signed up or other measures you think are useful.

3 Compare these sites with more established US sites such as Cybergold (*www.cybergold.com*), my points (*www.mypoints.com*) and Net centives (*www.netcentives.com*).

4 Assess the long-term viability of such schemes, stating the success factors and risks for such ventures.

Site announcements

The term 'site announcements' is usually used to describe how to announce a new or revised site. There are a number of methods possible, some of which will need to be repeated, not merely used at the launch or relaunch of a web site. A good source that summarises these techniques is available at ep.com epage auctions and classifieds (*www.ep.com/faq/webannounce*). This is based on the frequently asked questions (FAQ) posted regularly to the newsgroup *comp.infosystems.www.announce*. The main methods recommended are:

1 *'What's New' web pages*. These are sites, or parts of sites, devoted to new sites. For example Netscape has a 'what's new' at *www.netscape.com/home/whats-new.html*,

and Open Market provides a daily listing of new commercial sites on the Web at *www.directory.net*. E-map has a *www.whatsnew.com* site.

2 *Directories and search engines*. These are described in an earlier section of this chapter.

3 *Newsgroups*. The only official place for site announcements is at *comp.infosystems. www.announce*, but subtle announcements that are felt to be of value to members of a newsgroup could carefully be placed in more specialised newsgroups.

4 *Newsletters*. Special interest print or e-mail newsletters, as described above.

5 *Books and magazines that list web sites*. An example is *The Internet: The Rough Guide*. (Kennedy, 1999). Typically, only specialist sites or sites of general interest are suitable for listing in print. Specialist magazines or associated web sites serving vertical markets would be useful for vertical markets. For example, a civil engineering company could aim to place a news item about the relaunch of its web site in *New Civil Engineer*.

On-site promotional techniques

In addition to ensuring promotion on other sites to attract an audience to a site, the promotional campaign must also recognise the need to keep the audience once it arrives. To achieve this a variety of devices can be used, both to increase the length of site visit, and to make users return. A measure of a site's ability to retain visitors has been referred to as site 'stickiness' since a 'sticky' site is difficult to drag oneself away from. Activity 9.3 is intended to highlight some of the methods that can be used to achieve the objective of repeat visits.

Activity 9.3

Methods for enhancing site stickiness and generating repeat visits

This activity is intended to highlight methods of on-site promotion which may cause people to visit a web site, stay for longer than one click and then return. For each of the following techniques, discuss:

1. How the incentives should be used.
2. Why these incentives will increase the length of site visits and the likelihood of return to the site.
3. The type of company for which these techniques might work best.

Techniques

- Sponsorship of an event, team or sports personality.
- A treasure hunt on different pages of the site, with a prize.
- A screensaver.
- A site-related quiz.
- Monthly product discount on an e-commerce site.
- Regularly updated information indicated by the current date or the date new content is added.

279

Note that as well as 'up-front' incentives there are some simple techniques that make a site 'fresh', which can be used to generate repeat visits. These include:

- daily or weekly update of pages with a date on the web site to highlight that it is updated regularly;
- regular publication of industry or product-specific news;
- the use of e-mails to existing customers to highlight new promotions.

Offline promotion techniques – put the URL everywhere

Offline promotion methods usually involve highlighting the existence of the web site and encouraging customers to visit it, using existing methods of advertising in the traditional media. The normal technique will involve printing the web address (URL) of the web site in a printed or television advertisement. Here, the Internet is acting as a method of facilitating a direct response. Rather than viewers of the advertisement being encouraged to ring a freephone number to give their name to obtain further information, they can be directed to the web site instead. The Internet provides a more informal type of direct response advertising, which may appeal to some people. However, it can be argued that the Internet is not as effective at establishing a dialogue as asking a person to ring a freephone number, in that the person's contact details are less likely to be captured than if he or she rings. This could explain why many financial services advertisements in newspapers often contain a freephone number, but no web address!

There are some tricks to offline promotion that can be used to help customers in finding the information they need on the web site. When advertising in traditional media such as a newspaper or magazine it is beneficial not to give as the address the home page, but a specific page that is related to the offline promotion and the interests of the audience. For example:

- in an American magazine: Jaguar (*www.jaguar.com/us*);
- in an advertisement for a phone from a company that sells other products: Ericcson (*www.ericcsson.com/us/phones*);
- for a specific digital camera: Agfa (*www.agfahome.com/ephoto*).

Providing the specific page enables the user to be sent direct to the relevant information without having to navigate through the corporate site – which can be difficult for companies with a diverse product range. A further advantage of using a specific web address is that, if there is no other way of navigating to that page on the site, it can then be established how many people arriving at a site on this page have viewed the orginal advertisement. For brand building and establishing the credibility of a site, it is, however, more normal not to give a specific web address.

A similar technique is to use a sub-domain different from the main domain, or to register a completely different domain name, which is in keeping with the campaign, as in the following example:

- Canon's *www.csci.canon.com/6000* (rather than *www.canon.com*);
- Honda's *www.drivehonda.com* rather than *www.honda.com*;

- HarperCollins' *www.fireandwater.com* rather than Harpers and Collins Publishers;
- NTL *www.askntl.com* to highlight that the site has the answers to questions such as: Who are NTL? What are their services?

Increasingly, promotion of the web site in the offline media does not simply consist of flagging the existence of the web site as an afterthought by including the URL at the bottom of an advertisement, but highlights the offers or services available at the web site, such as special sales promotions or online customer service. Amazon commonly advertises in newspapers to achieve this.

Other forms of offline promotion

The URL can also be publicised by other methods, for example by including it on stationery such as company letter heads and business cards, even if this requires reprinting of these items. In brief, the web site URL should be put on all printed marketing communications! The marketing message can be reinforced if the web address is associated with text to differentiate the offering of the web site. For example, mail-shots from RS Components contain the message, 'Order by eight, arrive next morning'.

When a web site is first developed, or when a major new version of it is developed, there are excellent opportunities for promoting the web site offline. The launch of the site represents news that can be used to generate PR in trade papers and other sources. If personal selling is involved with the product, then sales staff should be briefed to inform customers of the services the web site can offer, and the customers can be involved in defining the features of the site. It is worth remembering that, in a business-to-business context, different influencers of the buying team may visit the site to assess the credibility of the company to deliver on promises.

It is worth remembering that, in addition to the methods described below, word of mouth is playing an important role in promoting sites, particularly consumer sites, where the Internet is currently a novelty. A report by Opinion Research Corporation International, ORCI, reported on a study amongst US consumers that showed that the typical Internet consumer tells 12 other people about his or her online shopping experience. This compares with the average US consumer, who tells 8.6 additional people about a favourite film and another 6.1 people about a favourite restaurant! Parry (1998) reported that for European users, word of mouth through friends, relatives and colleagues was the most important method by which users found out about web sites, being slightly more important than search engines and directories or links from other sites.

Thus the role of opinion leaders, and multi-step communications with target audiences receiving information about the Internet experience from opinion leaders, the mass media and the Internet, appear to be perhaps even more important in relation to the Internet than for other media. Dichter (1966) summarised how word-of-mouth communications work. To exploit such communications, it is necessary for marketers to use appropiate techniques to target and adapt the message for the opinion leaders when a product or service is at an early stage of diffusion (Rogers, 1983).

Purchase follow-up activities

Offline communications or e-mail following a purchase offer good prospects for repeat business. However, it seems that not all online retailers are taking full advantage of this opportunity. Petersen (1999) reports on a survey by US consultants Rubric in which mystery shoppers shopped at 50 high-profile e-commerce sites. The mystery shoppers reported that 84 per cent of the sites did not follow up a sale with a related marketing offer, 96 per cent did not employ personalisation and 75 per cent did not recognise a 'repeat customer', that is one who visited the site again. One of the best sites was that of Cyberian Outpost, *www.outpost.com*. There is a sample e-mail message from this company in Chapter 8, in Activity 8.4.

Integrating online and offline techniques

As a conclusion to this chapter, it is worth reiterating the power of integrating online promotion techniques with established offline techniques. It was stressed in Chapter 2 that the aim of the web site is not usually to force the customer to purchase by the online route, rather it is to facilitate the buying process. If the customer is more comfortable making a phone call to order the product or obtain assistance then the web site should help them in this. A good example of combining online and offline communication techniques is the use of callback techniques.

Callback services

Television and newspaper advertisements commonly feature a direct response option via a freephone number. This concept has translated to the Web and is increasingly being used by companies with call-centre operations that can handle this type of enquiry in volume. It is usually referred to as a callback service. The example of Freeway, the car sales company, was given in Chapter 2. RealCall is a service offered by several rival suppliers to any company with a web site. It can be seen from Fig. 9.9 that it provides a form, to be filled in by the customer so that he or she can be called by a service representative at a later time. This has the advantage, for the customer, that the company pays the phone bill, but on a practical level, home users accessing the Internet from home using a modem and a single phone line will be unable to receive a phone call while online, and may forget about the request later. The callback mechanism is consistent with the general philosophy of using the Internet to facilitate communications with the customer and of using the method that suits the customer best.

> **Web callback service**
> A facility available on the web site for a company to contact a customer at a later time as specified by the customer.

Fig. 9.9 RealCall telephone callback scheme

Sales promotions

The Internet offers tremendous potential for sales promotions of different types since it is more immediate than any other medium – it is always available for communication, and tactical variations in the details of the promotion can be made at short notice. A good example of a sales promotion is that offered by RS Components on its home page and on the customer-specific pages of the site. It specifies discounts on different featured products each month on the home page, and then tailors promotions to groups of users according to their product interests. The Web has the advantage that if a promotion does not seem to be working well, it can be changed rapidly. Sales promotions will often be combined with some of the online techniques featured in the earlier discussion, such as methods for enhancing site 'stickiness' and generating repeat visits.

The relative importance of offline and online promotion techniques

It is worth remembering that the Web does not operate in a vacuum: an online promotion very often supports an offline promotion. Consider Table 9.6. This shows that in the business-to-business market the Web is currently the least important source for specifying equipment for new projects – magazines are far more important. However, this represents a promotion opportunity – mention of the web address in a magazine, together with an indication of the value proposition of the site, plus the more detailed depth of information the customer will find on the web site give more effective promotion than the use of the web in isolation or the use of the magazine on its own. The survey also reveals that the use of the Web as a secondary source of information is growing dramatically.

Table 9.6 Primary sources business professionals use for specifying projects

Source	1998 (%)	1999 (%)
Web	5	12
Magazines	39	39
Sales rep	20	12

Source: Cahners Business Information via *cyberatlas.com*, March 1999.

In conclusion it is useful to consider the relative strengths and weaknesses of the different means of communication described in this chapter. Activity 9.4 is intended to be contentious since it suggests that it is the offline promotion techniques that may be most effective, even though the bulk of this chapter has been devoted to the novel online techniques. The reason for this is open for discussion, but it is worth remembering that we spend most of our time currently in the real, offline world, not in the online world!

Activity 9.4

Which are the best promotion techniques?

The best promotion techniques will, of course, vary according to the market involved. Here, we take the example of a business-to-business site that has traditionally relied on a combination of personal selling and traditional media to reach its customers. Now it has a web site, which are the best methods for it to use to attract customers to the web site?

Table 9.7 Suggested importance of different promotion techniques for a business-to-business site relying on a combination of personal selling and traditional media to reach its customers

Technique	Promotion type	Strength	Weakness
1. Word of mouth promotion by sales force	Offline		
2. List URL in magazine PR or advertisements and on company stationery	Offline		
3. Place product and company information on a 'vertical portal' for this industry	Online		
4. Run a link-building campaign identifying industry-related sites that will link through to site (possibly with sponsorship)	Online		
5. Provide banner advertisement that pops up when industry-specific keywords are typed in	Online		
6. Register site with search engines and directories	Online		

Table 9.7 suggests an order for the relative importance of different methods of promotion. For the purpose of this exercise, the purpose of this web site is to entice a visitor to the site (not to make a sale). You are asked to:

1 State your own order for the relative importance of the techniques.
2 Add to the table the strengths and weaknesses of each promotion technique and explain the order you have chosen.
3 Consider whether the order of the list would differ for a new as opposed to an existing customer.

Measuring effectiveness

This important topic, which is closely linked with promotion – since we need to measure the success of the different promotion techniques used – is covered separately in Chapter 12.

SUMMARY

1 Online promotion techniques include:
   - banner advertising;
   - advertising in e-mail newsletters;
   - co-branding and sponsorship.

2 Offline promotion involves promoting the web site address and highlighting the value proposition of the web site in traditional media advertisements in print, or on television.

3 Banner advertising is used to drive traffic to sites by placing advertisements on specific-interest sites or displaying advertisements when particular keywords are entered. Advertising can also occur through sponsorship of a web site. When a user clicks on an advertisement (a clickthrough) he or she is taken to a web site that provides further information. Banner advertising can also be used for other purposes such as brand building or offering incentives.

   Banner advertisements are usually paid for according to the cost per 1000 people viewing the advertisement (CPM).

4 Companies should ensure their web sites are listed as near to the top as poss-ible in the most popular search engines. This task is best outsourced since search engine listings are dependent on several factors.

5 Referring links from related sites are also important in building traffic to a site.

6 For companies selling products online it is vital that their products are included in as many as possible of the price comparison shopping sites such as Yahoo Shopping.

7 Reciprocal links or co-branding, whereby companies agree to promote each other's site and services, are relatively low-cost forms of online advertising.

8 In addition to using the various methods for driving traffic to the web site, companies must ensure that the content and promotional offers on the site are sufficient when the user arrives. Methods such as loyalty schemes should be devised to keep the content and offers fresh and relevant.

9 Promotion works most effectively when online and offline techniques are combined to give a consistent marketing message.

EXERCISES AND QUESTIONS

Self-assessment exercises

1 Briefly explain and give examples of online promotion and offline promotion techniques.

2 Explain the different types of payment model for banner advertising.

3 Which factors are important in governing a successful online banner advertising campaign?

4 How can a company promote itself through a search engine web site?

5 Explain the value of co-branding.

6 Explain how an online loyalty scheme may work.

7 How should web sites be promoted offline?

8 What do you think the relative importance of these Internet-based advertising techniques would be for an international chemical manufacturer?
(a) Banner advertising.
(b) Reciprocal links.
(c) E-mail.

Discussion questions

1 Discuss the analogy of Berthon *et al*. (1998) that effective Internet promotion is similar to a company exhibiting at an industry trade show attracting visitors to its stand.

2 Evidence seems to suggest that banner advertising is not widely used for advertising business products and services. Discuss the evidence available and attempt to explain the limited amount of business-to-business banner advertising.

3 Discuss the merits of the different models of paying for banner advertisements on the Internet for both media owners and companies placing advertisements.

4 'Online promotion must be integrated with offline promotion.' Discuss.

Essay questions

1 Compare the effectiveness of different methods of online advertising including banner advertisements, e-mail inserts, site co-branding and sponsorship.

2 Is a web site an advertisement?

3 Compare the different models of payment for banner advertising and explain which are likely to be the most significant now and in the future given the pattern of more banner advertising inventory (space on web sites) and reduced clickthrough rates (fewer users clicking on banners).

4 You have £10 000 from the Internet marketing budget to spend on a single online promotion method. Do you choose banner advertising, promotion in search engines or sponsorship? Justify your answer.

5 Review the major findings of the 1997 *IAB Advertising Effectiveness Study Executive Summary* at *www.mbinteractive.com*. Use other surveys to assess the validity of the observations made in this report, which represents one of the most thorough surveys of the effectiveness of the Internet for advertising.

Examination questions

1 Give three examples of online promotion and briefly explain how they function.

2 Describe four different types of site on which online banner advertising for a car manufacturer's site could be placed.

3 Clickthrough is one measure of the effectiveness of banner advertising. Answer the following:
   (a) What is clickthrough?
   (b) Which factors are important in determining the clickthrough rate of a banner advertisement?
   (c) Is clickthrough a good measure of the effectiveness of banner advertising?

4 What is meant by co-branding? Explain the significance of co-branding.

5 What are 'meta-tags'? How important are they in ensuring a web site is listed in a search engine?

6 Name three ways in which e-mail can be used for promotion of a particular web site page containing a special offer.

7 Give an example of an online loyalty scheme and briefly evaluate its strengths and weaknesses.

8 Which techniques can be used to promote a web site in offline media?

REFERENCES

Berthon, B., Pitt, L. and Watson, R. (1996) 'Resurfing W³: research perspectives on marketing communication and buyer behaviour on the World Wide Web', *International Journal of Advertising*, 15, 287–301.

Boyce, R. (1998) 'Exploding the web CPM myth', IAB web site (*www.iab.net*).

Cartellieri, C., Parsons, A., Rao, V. and Zeisser, M. (1997) 'The real impact of Internet advertising', *The McKinsey Quarterly*, 3 44–63.

Dichter, E. (1966) 'How word-of-mouth advertising works', *Harvard Business Review*, 44 (November–December), 147–66.

IPSO-ASI (1999) Banner ads and TV ads equally memorable. Press release of survey reported at Nua Internet Surveys (*www.nua.ie/surveys*) 14 February 1999. *See also www. ipsosasi.com.*

Janal, D. (1998) *Online Marketing Handbook. How to promote, advertise and sell your products and services on the Internet.* Van Nostrand Reinhold. ITC.

Kassye, W. (1997) 'The effect of the world wide web on agency–advertiser relationships: towards a strategic framework', *International Journal of Advertising*, 16, 85–103.

Kennedy, A.J. (1999) *The Internet: The Rough Guide.* London: Rough Guides.

Nielsen (1999) Homes with net access watchless TV. Press release of survey reported at Nua Internet Surveys (www.nua.ie/surveys) 14 August 1998. *See also www.nielsen.com.*

Novak, T. and Hoffman, D. (1997) 'New metrics for new media: towards the development of web measurement standards', *World Wide Web Journal*, 2(1), 213–46.

Parry, K. (1998) *Europe gets wired. A survey of Internet use in Great Britain, France and Germany, Research Report 1998.* London: KPMG Management Consulting.

Rogers, E. (1983) *Diffusion of Innovations* (3rd edn). New York: Free Press.

Petersen, S. (1999) 'Handle e-customers gently', *PC Week*, 13 July, 19.

Schiller, B. (1999) 'Online alliances help firms spread their reach', *Net Profit*, June, 9.

Schofield, J. (1999) 'Beenz meanz money', *Guardian*, 11 July.

Sterne, J. (1999) *World Wide Web Marketing* (2nd edn). New York: John Wiley and Sons.

Zeff, R. and Aronson, B. (1999) *Advertising on the Internet* (2nd edn). New York: John Wiley and Sons.

FURTHER READING

Allen, C., Kania, D. and Yaeckel, B. (1998) *Internet World Guide to One-to-One Web marketing*. New York: Wiley and Sons.
This is a readable book describing different techniques for forming and building customer relationships using the Internet. The chapter on 'push' techniques is dated.

Brassington, F. and Petitt, S. (2000) *Principles of Marketing* (2nd edn). Harlow, UK: Pearson Education.
See companion Prentice Hall web site (*www.booksites.net/brassington?*).
Chapter 15, Advertising, provides the conceptual underpinning of and describes best practice in advertising in traditional media.
Chapter 16, Sales Promotion, introduces traditional methods of sales promotion, many of which can be applied to the Internet.

Burnett, J. and Moriarty, S. (1999) *Introduction to Marketing Communications. An integrated approach*. Upper Saddle River, NJ: Prentice Hall.
See companion Prentice Hall web site (*cw.prenhall.com/bookbind/pubbooks/burnett/*).
Particularly relevant are Chapter 1, Marketing Communication, Chapter 2, The Marketing Mix and IMC, and Chapter 9, Advertising.

Dibb, S., Simkin, S., Pride, W. and Ferrel, O. (1997) *Marketing. Concepts and strategies* (3rd European edn). New York: Houghton Mifflin.
See companion Houghton Mifflin web site (*www.busmgt.ulst.ac.uk/h_mifflin/*).
See Chapter 16, Promotion – An Overview, and Chapter 17, Advertising, Publicity and Sponsorship.

Fill, C. (1999) *Marketing Communications – Contexts, contents and strategies* (2nd edn). Hemel Hempstead: Prentice Hall, Europe.
This has useful chapters on promotion techniques.

Janal, D. (1998). *Online Marketing Handbook. How to promote, advertise and sell your products and services on the Internet*. Van Nostrand Reinhold. ITC.
Covers promotion and has several chapters on driving traffic to your site.

Kotler, P., Armstrong, G., Saunders, J. and Wong, V. (1999) *Principles of Marketing* (2nd edn). Hemel Hempstead: Prentice Hall, Europe.
See companion Prentice Hall web site for 8th US edn (*cw.prenhall.com/bookbind/pubbooks/kotler/*).
See Chapter 19, Mass Communications: Advertising, Sales Promotion and Public Relations.

Novak, T. and Hoffman, D. (1997) 'New metrics for new media: towards the development of web measurement standards', *World Wide Web Journal*, 2(1), 213–46.
This paper gives detailed, clear definitions of terms associated with measuring advertising effectiveness.

Strauss, J. and Frost, R. (1999) *Marketing on the Internet. Principles of online marketing*. New Saddle River, NJ: Prentice Hall.
Chapter 6, Marketing Communications on the Net, describes banner advertising and sponsorship in some detail.

Vassos, T. (1996) *Strategic Internet Marketing*. Indianapolis, IN: Que. Business Computer Library.
Chapter 10 is entitled Driving Traffic to Your Site.

Zeff, R. and Aronson, B. (1999) *Advertising on the Internet* (2nd edn). New York: John Wiley and Sons.
A comprehensive coverage of online banner advertising and measurement techniques and a more limited coverage of other techniques such as e-mail based advertising.

WEB SITE REFERENCES

Internet marketing related e-mail newsletters

- Iconocast (*www.iconocast.com*).

  US-based newsletter of Internet marketing news.

- Internet World (*www.internetworld.com*)

  US-based newsletter of Internet marketing news.

- Nua: e-mail (*www.nua.com*)

  Newsletter of European and worldwide Internet marketing news.

- Online Advertising discussion list (from *www.o-a.com*).

Internet advertising-related links

- AdKnowledge (*www.adknowledge.com*).
  Site of analysts AdKnowledge, who specialise in consultancy on advertising campaigns.

- Advertising Age (*www.adage.com*).

- Clickz (*www.clickz.com*)
  A US-focused online magazine: 'the ultimate resource for doing business online' which includes articles on advertising management, banner campaigns and banner design.

- DoubleClick (*www.doubleclick.net*).
  The main advertising network worldwide, with offices in many countries. Its site describes how it uses its 'DART' technolology to target customers.

- Fletcher Associates (*www.fletch.co.uk*)

- Internet Advertising Bureau (*www.iab.net*).

- Internet.com (*www.internet.com/mediakit*).

- I/PRO (*www.ipro.com*).
  Provides services to audit web site effectiveness through studies of the site traffic. Example reports held on its site indicate the types of approach used.

- MediaMetrix (*www.mediametrix.com*), now merged with RelevantKnowledge (*www.relevant-knowledge.com*).
  These claim to be the world leaders in 'media measurement'.

- Nielsen-Netratings (*www.nielsen-netratings.com*).
  Nielsen have acquired NetRatings, and this site is an interesting resource on the current levels of activity and success of banner advertising. The site shows the creative content of the ten most popular banners each week and gives information on the main advertisers.

289

CHAPTER 10

Relationship marketing using the Internet

Learning objectives

After reading this chapter, the reader should be able to:

- synthesise the underpinning concepts of relationship, direct and database marketing that are converging to create the new paradigm of one-to-one marketing on the Internet;
- evaluate the potential of the Internet to support one-to-one marketing and the range of techniques and systems available to support dialogue with the customer over the Internet;
- assess the characteristics required of tools to implement one-to-one marketing.

Links to other chapters

- ▶ Chapter 8 has guidelines on how to achieve suitable standards of e-mail interaction and data collection in the section on service quality.
- ▶ Chapter 9 describes methods of acquiring customers for one-to-one marketing.
- ▶ Chapters 13 and 14 give examples of one-to-one marketing in the business-to-consumer and business-to-business markets.

INTRODUCTION

Relationship marketing, direct marketing and database marketing are convergently evolving to create a powerful new marketing paradigm. This paradigm is often referred to as one-to-one marketing. This involves a company developing a long-term relationship with each customer in order to better understand that customer's needs and then deliver services that meet these individual needs. The interactive, multimedia interface of the Web provides an ideal environment in which to conduct this relationship, and databases provide a foundation for storing information about the relationship and providing information to strengthen it by leading to improved, often personalised services.

Relationship marketing theory provides the conceptual underpinning of one-to-one marketing since it emphasises enhanced customer service through knowledge of the customer, and deals with markets segmented to the level of the individual. Direct marketing provides the tactics that deliver the marketing communications and sometimes the product itself to the individual customer. Database marketing provides the technological enabler, allowing vast quantities of customer-related data to be stored and accessed in ways that create strategic and tactical marketing opportunities. To harness the power of the Internet for one-to-one marketing, companies need to be able to apply all these related areas of theory.

This chapter begins by exploring relationship and one-to-one marketing in the context of the evolution of marketing and then relates this to the new reality of the busy, confident and demanding customer, empowered by technology. We then review how one-to-one marketing on the Internet can be implemented using techniques such as personalisation, e-mail and push technology, married to more traditional direct marketing techniques such as data mining and neural networks. The need to avoid the potential clash between direct marketing techniques and a relaxed Internet culture is also explored.

Relationship marketing

Relationship marketing is best understood within the context of the historical development of marketing. In early medieval or feudal societies marketplaces were mainly developed where people traded for agricultural purposes and to meet their basic needs. Suppliers mainly traded within a limited area and knew a small number of customers well. Effectively, one-to-one marketing was in operation. With the Industrial Revolution, the large-scale production of more widely distributed, standardised products changed the nature of marketing. Whereas marketing was previously largely by word of mouth it became a mass-marketing monologue from suppliers to customers with the aim of convincing customers of the need for standardised goods. The ultimate expression of this was, of course, the mass production of the Model T Ford. During the twentieth century, differentiation of products and services became more important, and this highlighted the need for feedback from customers about the type of product features required. This philosophy led to the promulgation by Jerome McCarthy at the University of Michigan in 1960 of the 4Ps of Product, Price, Place and Promotion, which have long since been a mainstay of the teaching and practice of marketing. The 4Ps model applies to the aggregate market: that is, where the market is considered as a homogeneous whole.

> **Mass marketing**
> One-to-many communication between a company and potential customers, with limited tailoring of the message.

Since the late 1980s and the rise of the relationship approach to marketing, the limitations of the 4Ps model have increasingly been highlighted. With increasing competition, the focus of marketers on meeting the customers' needs has increased, and the ultimate goal is to be able to hold details about each customers' preferences and produce customised products and services to meet this need. Such a customised service is illustrated by Mini case study 10.1. Gummesson (1987) argues that the 4Ps approach to marketing is limited in theory, takes little notice of interrelationships and co-operation, and heavily exaggerates areas such as advertising and competition. Ultimately the 4Ps model reveals itself as being product-centric rather than customer-centric, and a creature of the heyday of mass marketing.

Mini case study 10.1

Levi-Strauss personalise jeans

Fig. 10.1 Levi Strauss Original Spin (*www.levi.com/originalspin*)

Levi's provide a truly personal service that dates back to 1994, when Levi Strauss initiated its 'Personal Pair' programme. Women who were prepared to pay up to $15 more than the standard price and wait for delivery could go to Levi's Stores and have themselves digitised – that is, have their measurements taken and a pair of custom jeans made and then have their measurements stored on a database for future purchases.

The programme achieved a repeat purchase rate significantly higher than the usual 10–12 per cent rate, and by 1997 accounted for a quarter of women's jean sales at Levi's Stores. In 1998 the programme was expanded to include men's jeans and the number of styles for each was doubled – to 1500 styles. This service has now migrated to the Web and is branded as Original Spin.

Tailoring of products has been described as *'complicated simplicity'* by Ira Matahia, chief executive officer of Brand Futures Group, as reported in *The Times* of 19 December 1998. She says:

> *'As consumers crave individually tailored products from DIY pottery shops to person-alised perfume formulas to PC-generated greeting cards, there will be a strong demand for unique items. For businesses this means the end of a mass audience oriented approach and the beginning of an audience-of-one approach.'*

The need for more consumer choice has to be balanced against the concept of the accelerating lifestyle of the 'busy customer', who can be characterised by phrases such as:

- 'cash rich, time poor';
- 'time is money';
- 'value for *time*';
- personal disposable *time*.

According to Cross (1994), over 50 per cent of consumers feel too time pressured to enjoy traditional shopping. Foley *et al.* (1997) comment on the lack of time available to sift through hundreds of television and print advertisements and 'a preference for communications which are personalised and directed specifically to their needs, typically based on past transactions'. Maling (1999) notes that '*A number of companies are beginning to withdraw from TV and return to other media and that shakedown will continue*'.

The fragmentation of media audiences also makes the mass-marketing model untenable. The cosy scenario of the nuclear family sitting around the single television set watching family fare accompanied by mass-marketing communications is now becoming unrealistic. The first reason for this change involves social factors. In the 1960s, according to Schultz *et al.* (1994), 60 per cent of families included three or more members and 20 per cent included five or more. By the 1990s, the nuclear family of mother, father and two children comprised only 7 per cent of households, 60 per cent had two or fewer members, and more than half of all households were singles. Then there are the technological factors. The gradual increase in the number of television channels in the UK over the last few decades from one to five is soon to be dwarfed by the hundreds of channels provided by digital television. A huge increase in the number of magazine titles available has also occurred in the last decade. The ability to reach large sections of the population through a small number of vehicles is now a thing of the past. This is not necessarily a problem for sophisticated marketing organisations as the audiences of the fragmented media are very tightly targeted to niche markets – thus aiding segmentation. A further, more intractable problem is the diversity of activities available that do not necessarily rely on advertising such as pay-per-view cable, videos, surfing the Internet and computer games. Additionally, 'channel hopping' with a remote control means that any advertising that is transmitted is easily avoided.

Relationship Marketing (McKenna, 1993) was a seminal text in bringing the approach of one-to-one marketing from the academic to the business domain. In this book McKenna describes the key elements of this approach as:

- Own the market by selecting a specific market segment and attempting to dominate it by developing highly appropriate products and services for the market.
- Commit to a deep relationship with customers in this market to help develop appropriate products by integrating customers into the product design process.
- Be adaptive by using monitoring, analysis and feedback to respond flexibly to the environment.
- Develop partnerships with suppliers, vendors and users to help maintain an edge in the segment.

Relationship marketing reflects the shift in attitude from 'making a sale' to 'gaining a client'. It is also referred to as customer relationship management (CRM).

> **Relationship marketing**
> 'Consistent application of up to date knowledge of individual customers to product and service design which is communicated interactively in order to develop a continuous and long term relationship which is mutually beneficial' (Cram, 1994).

In *The One-to-One Future* (Peppers and Rogers, 1993) the authors advise the following:

- Focus on share of the customer rather than market share – this means increasing the revenue from each customer as far as possible.
- Focus on customer retention, which is more cost effective than acquisition.
- Concentrate on repeat purchases by cross- and up-selling; these also help margins increase.
- To achieve the above use dialogue to listen to customer needs and then *respond to them* in order to build trusting and loyal relationships

They also recommend stages to achieve these goals which they popularise as the 5Is (as distinct from the 4Ps) (Peppers and Rogers, 1997):

- *Identification*. It is necessary to learn the characteristics of customers in as much detail as possible to be able to conduct the dialogue. In a business-to-business context, this means understanding those involved in the buying decision.
- *Individualisation*. Individualising means tailoring the company's approach to each customer, offering a benefit to the customer based on the identification of customer needs. The effort expended on each customer should be consistent with the value of that customer to the organisation.
- *Interaction*. Continued dialogue is necessary to understand both the customer's needs and the customer's strategic value. The interactions need to be recorded to facilitate the learning relationship.
- *Integration*. Integration of the relationship and knowledge of the customer must extend throughout all parts of the company.
- *Integrity*. Since all relationships are built on trust it is essential not to lose the trust of the customer. Efforts to learn from the customer should not be seen as intrusive, and privacy should be maintained. (Privacy issues are considered in the final section of this chapter.)

> **One-to-one marketing**
> A unique dialogue occurs directly between a company and individual customers (or groups of customers with similar needs).

Though the books mentioned above predate the large-scale commercialisation of the Web the characteristics identified are remarkably compatible with the kind of dialogue-facilitated, customer-centric relationship that the Internet can support so well. This was not lost on Peppers and Rogers, who revisited the themes of *The One-to-One Future* with an exploration of the technological possibilities of the Internet, the Web and databases and *Real-Time* by McKenna (1999). In *Enterprise One-to-One* Peppers and Rogers (1997) highlight the importance of:

- using the technology to achieve *mass customisation* of the marketing message (and possibly the product);

- the learning relationship – here a continuous dialogue is established where the company responds directly to the needs of the customer with services responding to his or her demands;
- incentive for and convenience in establishing the dialogue. There must be a clear reason or offer for the customer to engage in the dialogue, and it must be easy to do so;
- acknowledging the privacy of the customer and the demands on her or his time.

These goals translate particularly well to the Internet, and in the next section we will consider how these are actually achieved. The web site representing Peppers and Rogers (Fig. 10.2) is a good source of information about the concept of one-to-one and tools and techniques to achieve the goals.

Mass customisation

Mass customisation is the ability to create tailored marketing messages or products for individual customers or a group of similar customers (a bespoke service) yet retain the economies of scale and the capacity of mass marketing or production.

Mass customisation can range from minor cosmetic choices made by the customer (for example, the choice of colour, trim and specification available to the customer via the multimedia kiosks in Daewoo's car showrooms) to a collaborative process facilitated by ongoing dialogue. Peppers and Rogers (1993) give the example of Motorola, which can manufacture pagers to any of over 11 million different specifications.

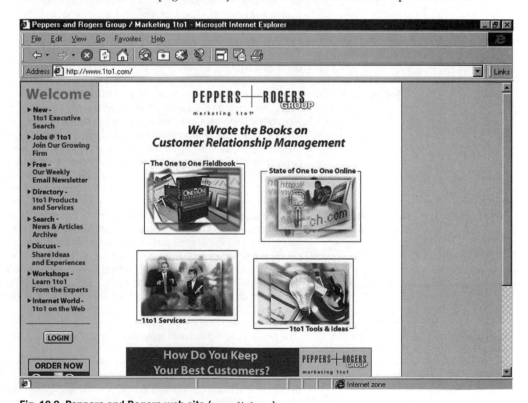

Fig. 10.2 Peppers and Rogers web site (*www.1to1.com*)

Benefits of the one-to-one approach

One-to-one marketing can increase customer loyalty, which has a number of benefits. Loyalty or retention within a current customer base is a highly desirable phenomenon for the following reasons:

- no acquisition costs (which are usually far higher than 'maintenance' costs);
- less need to offer incentives such as discounts, or to give vouchers to maintain their custom (although these may be desirable);
- less price sensitive (loyal customers are happy with the value they are getting);
- loyal customers will recommend the company to others ('referrals');
- individual revenue growth occurs as trust increases.

Table 10.1 summarises the differences between the two paradigms discussed in this section.

Table 10.1 A summary of different concepts for the transactional and relationship paradigms

Transactional paradigm concept	Relationship paradigm concept	Comments and examples
Market segment	Individual customer	Raphel (1997) describes the success story of AMC Kabuki 8 movie theatres in San Francisco. Despite the competition from the giant multiplexes, AMC is flourishing because of its understanding of the cinematic preferences of its customers so they can be informed in advance of ticket sales. 'The most failure-prone fault-line in transactional marketing is the statistical customer – the hypothetical human who is composed of statistically averaged attributes drawn form research' (Wolfe, 1998).
Duration of transaction	Lifetime relationship	The pursuit of customer loyalty 'is a perpetual one – more of a journey than a destination' (Duffy, 1998).
Margin	Life-time value	To support the Huggies product in the 1970s, Kimberley-Clark spent over $10m. to construct a database that could identify 75 per cent of the four million expectant mothers every year in the USA, using information obtained from doctors, hospitals and childbirth trainers. During the pregnancy, mothers received a magazine and letters with advice on baby care. When the baby arrived a coded coupon was sent, which was tracked to learn which mothers had tried the product. The justification was the life-time value of these prospective customers, not the unit sale (Shaw, 1996).
Market share	Most valued customers and customer share	Rather than waging expensive 'trench warfare' where profit objectives are linked automatically to overall market share, companies have now realised that, as 80 per cent of their business often comes from 20 per cent of their customers (the famous Pareto law), then retaining and delighting that 20 per cent will be much more cost effective than trying to retain the loyalty of the 80 per cent. Reichheld (1996) conducted research indicating that an increase in customer retention of 5 per cent could improve profitability by as much as 125 per cent.
Mass market monologue	Direct marketing dialogue	'The new marketing requires a feedback loop' (McKenna, 1993).
Passive consumers	Empowered clients	'Transactional marketing is all about seduction and propaganda and it depends on a passive, narcotised receptor, the legendary "couch potato"' (Rosenfield, 1998).

One-to-one on the Internet

Achieving one-to-one marketing on the Internet has the well-known advantages of relationship marketing – that is, it is targeted and personalised but these benefits are built on in the Internet medium since it can:

- *Target more effectively*. Traditional targeting, for direct mail for instance, is often based on mailing lists compiled according to criteria that mean that not everyone contacted is in the target market. For example, a company wishing to acquire new affluent consumers may use post-codes to target areas with appropriate demographics, but within the postal district the population may be heterogeneous. The result of poor targeting will be low response rates, perhaps less than 1 per cent. The Internet has the benefit that the list of contacts is *self-selecting* or pre-qualified. A company will only aim to build relationships with those who have visited a web site and expressed an interest in its products by registering their name and address. The mere act of visiting the web site and browsing indicates a target customer. Thus the approach to acquiring new customers with whom to build relationships is fundamentally different, as it involves attracting the customers to the web site, where the company provides an offer to make them register. All of those who register are interested in the product (or offer). This is very different from contacting many customers, only a small proportion of whom may be interested.
- *Increase depth, breadth and nature of relationship*. The nature of the Internet medium enables more information to be supplied to customers as required. For example, special pages such as Dell's Premier Pages can be set up to provide customers with specific information. The nature of the relationship can be changed in that contact can be made more frequently with a customer. The frequency of contact with the customer can be determined by customers – whenever they have the need to visit their personalised pages – or they can be contacted by e-mail by the company.
- *Lower cost*. Contacting customers by e-mail or through their viewing web pages costs less than using physical mail, but perhaps more importantly, information only needs to be sent to those customers who have expressed a preference for it, resulting in fewer mail-outs. Once personalisation technology has been purchased, much of the targeting and communications can be implemented automatically.

In the previous section it was noted that some of the goals suggested in *Enterprise One-to-One* by Peppers and Rogers (1997) translate particularly well to the Internet. Let us now consider how the Internet can be used to achieve each of these goals in more detail:

1 Using the technology to achieve mass customisation of the marketing message (and possibly the product)

An online bookseller, for example, such as Blackwell's (*www.blackwells.co.uk*), can automatically send communications to customers based on their behaviour and products they purchase when using the Web. If a customer has previously purchased books related to cookery, or has searched for books in the cookery section of the site for instance, then that customer could be automatically notified when a major new cookery book is published. This could be achieved by a specific e-mail that promotes this book. Note that it is not an individually tailored e-mail, but one that is sent to all customers with a similar profile who have a similar interest: thus it is mass customisation of the offer. Blackwell's also uses personalisation technology from Broadvision that makes it possible to tailor the information displayed on screen to groups of users according to particular rules (*see* the section later in this chapter on personalisation).

2 The learning relationship

The Internet provides a number of methods by which a company can learn about a customer's needs:

- Tools summarise products purchased on site and the searching behaviour that occurred before these products were bought.
- Online feedback forms about the site or products are completed when a customer requests free information.
- Questions asked through forms or e-mails to the online customer service facilities.
- Product evaluation – Marshall Industries (*www.marshall.com*) invite customers to comment on prototypes of new products.

3 Incentive and convenience in establishing the dialogue

The incentive to start a dialogue on the Internet is often the provision of free information – and the medium is suited to the cheap delivery of information to the customer. For example, on the Peppers and Rogers web site (Fig. 10.2) if a customer provides an e-mail address then that customer will be sent a monthly e-mail newsletter related to one-to-one. It is very easy for the initial contact to be established – the customer only needs to fill in his or her e-mail address. It is also straightforward for communications to continue as the messages are received in the in-box.

4 Acknowledging the privacy of the customer and the demands on her/his time

Ethics and legal codes place constraints on companies in the way they conduct direct marketing – these are covered later in the chapter. However, it is very necessary to acknowledge customer privacy in relation to one-to-one marketing, in order for it to be effective. This is a very difficult balance to achieve. One of the most important principles is respecting customers' preferences concerning 'opt-in' and 'opt-out'. This is most relevant to e-mail, which is covered in a later section, but should be emphasised at the outset. The principle of opt-in is that communications are only sent to customers if they have agreed to receive information, for example by filling in an online form. The principle of opt-out is that customers will not be contacted if they have asked not to be contacted. For example, if a customer is on an e-mail list and asks to be removed from the list, that customer will no longer be sent messages.

Opt-in and opt-out

With opt-in, the customer is only contacted when he or she has explicitly asked for information to be sent. With opt-out, the customer is not contacted if he or she has explicitly asked not to be contacted.

Achieving one-to-one marketing online

Online one-to-one marketing uses a number of techniques to achieve personalisation. Personalisation utilises the power of web technology to customise content and the one-to-one dialogue in line with the individual's preferences. Godin (1999) has coined the term 'permission marketing' to describe how one-to-one Internet marketing should be conducted, and he contrasts it with what he describes as traditional 'interruption marketing'. Relatively unobtrusive advertising is needed to start the relationship, and this is followed by a need for opt-in, to enter the dialogue, and then for opt-out when there is no need for it to continue.

> **Personalisation**
> Web-based personalisation involves delivering customised content for the individual, through web pages, e-mail or push-technology.

In the following sections we proceed through the different stages that are involved in achieving personalisation via the Web.

Stage 1: Attract customers to site (acquisition)

The strategy for achieving one-to-one marketing online should start with consideration of how to acquire customers who want to communicate in this way. These may be either new or existing customers. For new customers, the goal is to attract them to the site using all the methods of site promotion described in Chapter 9 such as search engines, portals and banner advertisements. These promotion methods should aim to highlight the value proposition of the site, for example by means of incentives such as free information or competitions. To encourage new users to use the one-to-one facilities of the web site, information about the web site or incentives to visit it can be built into existing direct marketing campaigns such as mailshots.

The strategy to entice existing customers to use the web site for one-to-one is more complex. Companies can just leave them to find the site in the same way as new customers, but it is better, of course, to proactively encourage them to visit the site. To do this, marketing communications using other media are required as part of an integrated marketing campaign. In the business-to-business environment, mailshots can be sent to customers highlighting what is available on the site, whereas for consumers media campaigns should feature the web site prominently.

Stage 2: Provide incentive

As explained in Chapter 9, the first time a customer visits a site is the most important since if he or she does not find the desired information or experience, that customer may not return. The quality and credibility of the site must be sufficient to retain the customer's interest so that he or she stays on the site. To initiate one-to-one, an offer or incentive must be prominent, ideally on the home page. There are any number of incentives that can be used to achieve this. Some common offers are shown in Table 10.2.

Stage 3: Capture customer information to maintain relationship

Once the user has decided the incentive is interesting he or she will click on the option and will then be presented with an online form such as those shown in Fig. 10.3 or Fig. 9.9. The user will be prompted to provide various items of

Table 10.2 Some examples of some offers intended to initiate one-to-one marketing

Offer	Example	Web sites
Free information	Subscribing to a free monthly newsletter on one-to-one marketing. Downloading a report. Logging in to an extranet or password-restricted area such as the Virgin Megastore VIP Lounge.*	www.1to1.com www.ft.com www.virginmega.com
Access to a discussion forum	A community with messages posted about industry or product topics.	www.camcable.co.uk
Product purchase	Purchasing a product will enable a retailer to collect a customer's e-mail and real-world addresses, and these can subsequently be used for one-to-one marketing.	www.rswww.com www.amazon.com www.outpost.com
Download of free software or screensaver	The user has to fill in a form and give his or her e-mail address, and contact details before being permitted to go the file download area.	www.cognos.com www.lotus.com www.oracle.com www.brasdirect.co.uk
Loyalty schemes Competitions and games	These integrate well with one-to-one. Treasure hunts, quizzes, etc.	www.beenz.com www.vnunet.com www.disney.com

*See Fig. 10.3.

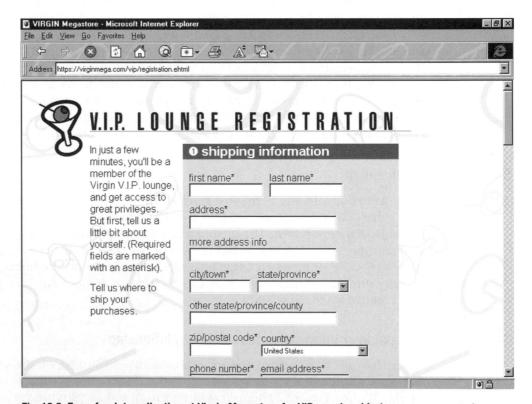

Fig. 10.3 Form for data collection at Virgin Megastore for VIP membership (*www.virginmega.com*)

information. The crucial information that must be collected is a method of contacting the customer. Ideally this will be both an e-mail address and a real-world address. The real-world address is important since from the post-code or zipcode it may be possible to deduce the likely demographics of that person. Some companies, such as Peppers and Rogers (*www.1to1.com*), take the attitude that the e-mail address is the only piece of information that needs to be collected since this can be used to maintain the one-to-one relationship online. Apart from the contact information, the other important information to collect is a method of profiling the customer so that appropriate information can be delivered to the customer. For example RS Components (Fig. 8.9) ask for:

- industry sector;
- purchasing influence;
- specific areas of product interest;
- how many people you manage;
- total number of employees in company.

Customer profiling
Using the web site to find out customers' specific interests and characteristics.

A company must decide carefully on the number of questions asked. It is, of course, a balance between the time taken to answer the questions and the value of the offer to the customer. If the offer is valuable, the customer may be prepared to fill in a lengthy questionnaire. There are a number of practical issues in designing such forms that are described in Chapter 8 in the section on service quality.

Other methods of profiling customers include collaborative filtering and monitoring the content they view. With collaborative filtering, customers are openly asked what their interests are, typically by checking boxes that correspond to their interests. A database then compares the customers' preferences with those of other customers in its database, and then makes recommendations or delivers information accordingly. The more information a database contains about an individual customer, the more useful its recommendations can be. An example of this technology in action can be found on the Amazon web site (*www.amazon.com*), where the database reveals that customers who bought book 'x' also bought books 'y' and 'z'. Moviecritic (*www.moviecritic.com*) is another example of this. This uses LikeMinds software from Andromedia (*www.andromedia.com*). An individual first spends time rating a minimum of 12 films. Then, comparing individual ratings with those of others with similar tastes, the site recommends films an individual is likely to enjoy. The more films an individual rates, the more appropriate the recommendations are.

Similar filtering is performed by 'intelligent agents'. For example Autonomy (*www.autonomy.com*) monitors users' clicks and stores the results in a database to match the content with areas in which they have shown interest.

Collaborative filtering
Profiling of customer interest coupled with delivery of specific information and offers, often based on the interests of similar customers.

Mini case study 10.2   XOOM.com uses personalisation technology to enter Web top 20

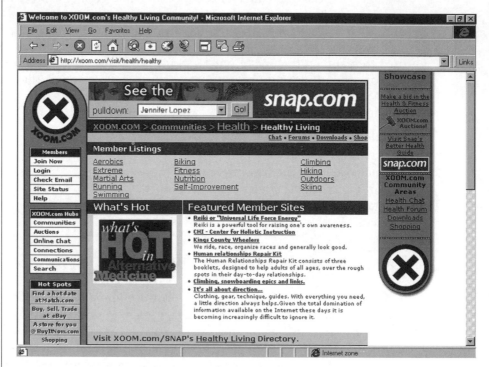

Fig. 10.4 XOOM.comsite, showing the health-related community

Autonomy's technology automatically connects XOOM.com visitors to relevant sites and helps home page builders find other members with similar interests

The company

XOOM.com offers one of the largest personal web page hosting services on the Internet. In January 1998 XOOM.com was not even one of the 100 most-visited sites on the Web. But by July it had become the second fastest-growing site and by December 1998 was the thirteenth most visited site on the Web, according to Media Metrix. During 1998 alone, XOOM.com's reach grew ten-fold – from 1.7 per cent in January to 29.5 per cent across all of its properties in December. By February 1999, XOOM.com had more than 7 million registered members, adding approximately 20 000 new members per day during the prior quarter. Of XOOM.com's more than seven million members, more than one million take advantage of the company's offer of free, unlimited web hosting space.

The problem

Owing to the extraordinary volume of its traffic, XOOM.com needed a highly scalable content management solution able to provide users with a highly personalized experience: a system able to automatically organize information across

XOOM.com's service and deliver it quickly, accurately and dynamically. More importantly, XOOM.com wanted to provide home page builders and visitors with an intuitive way to find other members with similar interests.

The solution

Autonomy provides advanced search and auto-suggest features across every web page posted by XOOM.com members. XOOM.com recently launched its XOOMBar, a menu-bar that appears at the top of every XOOM.com member page and contains a link to the Autonomy advanced search and suggest feature. XOOM.com chose Autonomy because of Autonomy's unique advanced pattern-matching technology, which is able to read and analyse the ideas in any piece of text. When a XOOM.com member explores other members' web pages to find people who share his or her interests, Autonomy's software understands the concepts underlying those interests. This unique understanding enables the software to automatically suggest other web pages created by like-minded owners, creating a dynamically linked community of relevant and personalised web sites.

To make this dynamic community possible, XOOM.com implemented Autonomy's Content Server™, a scalable and highly effective engine that allows large volumes of information to be organised and presented to users on an individual basis. Autonomy's Content Server™ effectively eliminates the need for XOOM.com to hire hundreds [of] employees to manually tag and categorise this information, saving XOOM.com time and money, and ensures that XOOM.com members' information would be more easily found than if one million members attempted to categorise their own web sites using widely varying and incomplete keyword indexing.

According to Bob Ellis, XOOM.com's publisher, 'Autonomy's technology helps our members zero in on other people with similar interests by creating automatic hyperlinks between related personal web pages. It allows XOOM.com to create and manage a much more intuitive web community structure. For example, a XOOM.com member who enjoys Himalayan summit climbing can find other members who share his interest and then go one step further and find sites about climbing gear.'

Source: Autonomy web site (*www.autonomy.com*).

Stage 4: Maintain dialogue consistent with customer's profile

To build the relationship between company and customer there are three main Internet-based methods of physically making the communication. These are:

1 Send e-mail to customer.
2 Display specific information on web site when the customer logs in. This is referred to as personalisation.
3 Use push technology to deliver information to the individual.

Information on these techniques of maintaining dialogue is given in subsequent sections. Dialogue will also be supplemented by other tools such as mailshots, phone calls or personal visits, depending on the context. For example, after a customer registers on the RS Components web site, the company sends out a letter to the customer with promotional offers and a credit-card sized reminder of the user-name and password to use to log in to the site.

As well as these physical methods of maintaining contact with customers, many other marketing devices can be used to encourage users to return to a site (*see also* Chapter 9 and Table 10.2). These include:

- Loyalty schemes – customers will return to the site to see how many loyalty points they have collected, or convert them into offers. An airline such as American Airlines, with its Advantage Club, is a good example of this.
- News about a particular industry (for a business-to-business site).
- New product information and price promotions.
- Industry-specific information to help the customer do his or her job. Snap-on Tools, a manufacturer of professional-grade tools for automobile repair businesses, adds new value for its customers by supplying them with regulatory information about subjects such as waste disposal at no fee. This strengthens Snap-on's relationship with its customers. Synetix provides technical information for chemical-plant designers to help with their day-to-day design work.
- Personal reminders – 1-800-Flowers has reminder programmes that automatically remind customers of important occasions and dates.
- Customer support – Cisco's customers log on to the site over one million times a month to receive technical assistance, check orders or download software. The online service is so well received that nearly 70 per cent of all customer enquiries are handled online.

While adding value for their customers by means of these various mechanisms, companies will be looking to use the opportunity to make sales to customers by, for example, cross- or up-selling.

Technologies for implementing one-to-one

When reviewing the tools to implement one-to-one it is important to keep in mind that the relationship is more important than the technology. This was expressed well by Jim McCann, founder and president of 1-800-Flowers, in *Upside* magazine, November 1997:

> *'Despite our name, 1-800-Flowers, we're in the "social expression" business, like the people who sell greeting cards and chocolates. Flowers are symbolic, timeless, not hi-tech. And yet we conduct 10 per cent of our business on-line. We're using this new channel to reach a growing market segment that is embracing new technology and is motivated by convenience. But we've never lost sight of customer satisfaction, which we handle the old-fashioned way: one-to-one.'*

Belfer (1998) comments, 'Technologies such as datamining, datawarehousing and electronic commerce are lauded as the IT sledgehammer to crack the marketing walnut' in the article appropriately entitled 'IT are from Mars, Marketing are from Venus'. This article highlights the need for the marketing department to work closely with the IT department in the selection and implementation of personalisation tools.

Technology can also be used to enhance the relationship if the web site is constructed so that 'flow' (*see* Chapter 8) can be achieved as the customer uses the web site, thus making the use of the web site an enjoyable experience. A web site should provide something 'to do', not merely to read. The active involvement of the user, who is participating in a dialogue, creates a strong bonding experience. This is the same idea as that of the 'soft lock in' (Vassos, 1996), in which a satisfying online experience generates a loyalty effect.

Web page personalisation

Personalisation involves delivering customised content for the individual through web pages, e-mail or push technology. To be able to display personalised web pages such as Dell's Premier Pages, a web site needs to be able to identify an individual when her or she arrives at the site. There are three potential ways of doing this. The first is to use the IP or network address number of the computer accessing the site (for further discussion *see* Chapter 12). This is not reliable since for many ISPs this number is generated dynamically each time a user logs on, so it will not be the same from one user session to the next. The second method is to use a cookie (*see* Mini case study 10.3). This is more reliable, but will not work if the user logs on from a different location (from home rather than at work, for example). The final and best method is to require the user to log in using a user name and password. This extranet approach is used by many e-commerce sites such as RS Components (*rswww.com*) but some use only a cookie-based system. An example of personlisation achieved with a portal is shown in Fig. 10.5.

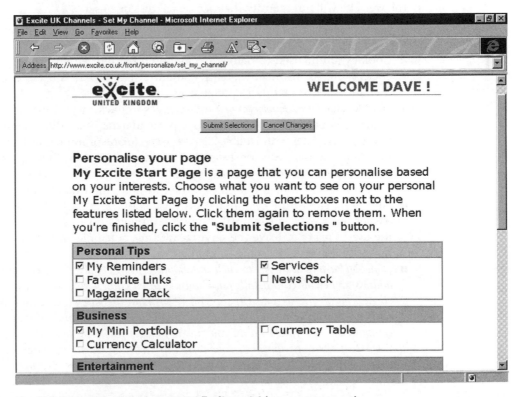

Fig. 10.5 **Personalisation of content at Excite portal** (*www.excite.co.uk*)

What are cookies?

A 'cookie' is a data file placed on a computer which identifies an individual computer. The cookie is placed on the computer via the web browser by the web site you visit. This is a powerful technique from a marketing point of view since it is used to identify a particular customer and tailor the web session accordingly – a key goal of personalisation.

Note that without the use of cookies it is not possible to uniquely identify an individual since log files (*see* Chapter 12) simply record an IP address, and this may differ between sessions if a user connects using an ISP. 'Cookie' derives from a Unix term, 'magic cookie', which meant something passed between routines or programs that enables the receiver to perform some operation. Eric Raymond in the *New Hacker's Bible* makes the analogy with a ticket for collecting dry cleaning.

Cookies are stored as individual text files in the directory \windows\cookies on a personal computer. There is usually one file per company. For example: *dave_chaffey@british-airways.txt*. This file contains encoded information as follows:

FLT_VIS |K:bapzRnGdxBYUU|D:Jul-25-1999| british-airways.com/ 0 425259904 29357426 1170747936 29284034 *

The information in the cookie file is essentially an identification number and a date of the user's last visit, although other information can be stored.

Cookies are specific to a particular browser and computer, so if a user connects from a different computer such as one at work or starts using a different browser the web site will not identify that person as the same user.

Some examples of cookie use

- Cookies can be used to deliver personalised content when linked with preferences expressed using collaborative filtering. The cookie is used to identify the user and retrieve that user's preferences from a database.
- DoubleClick (*www.doubleclick.net*) uses cookies to track the number of times a particular computer has been shown a particular banner advertisement. When advertisers register with DoubleClick they create one or more target audience profiles. When a user visits a registered site a banner dynamically matches that user to the target user profile. On any future visits by that user the DoubleClick server retrieves the ID number from the cookie and stores information about the visit.
- 'Shopping carts' in e-commerce sites use cookies to store the items the user wishes to order at a site until the user completes his or her purchases. When the user is ready to leave the server reads the cookie file and initiates a transaction based on what is in the shopping cart.
- *'Amazon customises itself to each individual visiting its pages. You enter your name, address and credit card details once and thereafter can buy any book just by clicking a single icon on the screen. (On subsequent visits to the site, credit card details can be retrieved from a secure database using the identification number in the cookie.) The computer system watches what you buy and judges your tastes and then starts offering titles it thinks may appeal to your taste... It creates a learning relationship that gets smarter and smarter the more you use it... The reason this is a compelling model is that it makes the customer more loyal to you. I buy books from Amazon and, in all*

probability, I could get them cheaper somewhere else. But why would I bother? I know Amazon, it's easy to use and to buy somewhere else I would have to go through the business of entering my address and credit card details again' (Don Peppers, *Sunday Times*, 13 June 1999).

Privacy concerns about cookies

Antagonism exists towards the cookie, because there is a lack of disclosure – the cookies are passed surreptiously and thus users have the feeling that their privacy has been invaded. Scare stories have been spread, to the effect that cookies contain personal and credit card details, but this is not the case unless the webmaster has made an error. Normally they only contain an identification code, which is used to retrieve these details from a database.

A study of almost 60 000 Internet users at the University of Michigan for the Hermes project (*www-personal.umich.edu/~sgupta/hermes*) indicated that over 81 per cent felt that cookies were undesirable.

Despite these concerns, the cookie is becoming ubiquitous at major commercial sites as a means of tracking users.

For additional information about cookies visit:

- Netscape communications (*www.netscape.com/newsref/std/cookie_spec.html*).
- Cookie central (*www.cookiecentral.com.*)

Personalisation systems must provide not only a method of identifying the customer, but also a method of delivering appropriate content to the user. This is often delivered in line with predetermined rules based on the customer's profile. For example, a customer of the RS Components site may have specified an interest in office equipment. The database will then execute a rule: 'If customer interested in office equipment, then display the office equipment sales promotions.' For a company that has a special account with a supplier, the database will display the account information for that customer. For instance, when a customer clicks the 'order history' button the database will perform a query that retrieves all orders for that specific customer.

Mini case study 10.4   **Tools for implementing personalisation**

Some of the main tools used to implement personalisation include:

- Broadvision (*www.broadvision.com*).
- Engage Profileserver (*www.engage.com*).
- LikeMinds (*www.andromedia.com*).
- GroupLens (*www.netperceptions.com*).

These sites provide good examples of the application of this technology as it develops.

► **Mini case study** *continued*

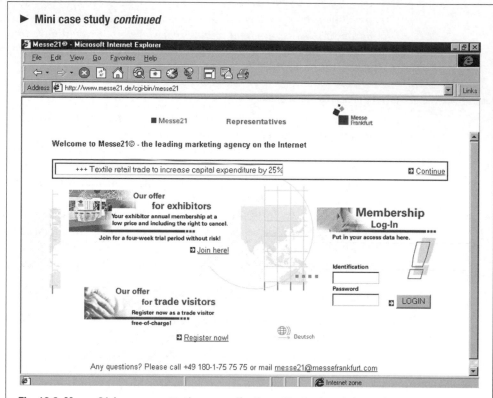

Fig. 10.6 Messe 21 (*www.messe21.de***): personalisation of trade show information according to interest in using broadvision technology**

Figure 10.6 gives an example of the use of personalisation by Messe Frankfurt as a means of enabling businesses around the world to access information about international trade fairs. The extranet, available in English and German, enables its members to access personalised information about trade shows and events, based on their industry and business objectives. Leveraging the targeted information available on this site, members determine the most effective ways to display their products at trade shows around the world. Personalisation can be used either by those wishing to visit trade fairs or by companies exhibiting.

E-mail

Outbound e-mails are sent out to customers, whose e-mail addresses are stored on a mail server. When a customer registers interest in receiving a standard newsletter, for example, that customer's address will be added to the list of addressees on a mail server and the newsletter will be sent out regularly. For tailored e-mails, integration with a database storing the customer profile is required. An e-mail announcing a special offer for one product such as that in Fig. 10.7 may only be of interest to a subset of customers – in this case, those likely to visit a particular cinema. The database will need to pass on a limited number of addresses to the mail server.

Guidelines for best practice when implementing e-mail can be found in Chapter 8 in the section on service quality.

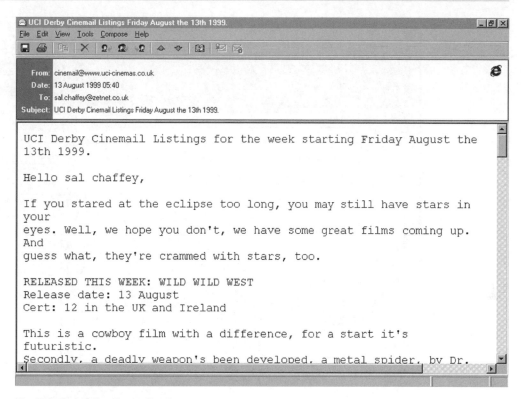

Fig. 10.7 Promotional e-mail

In the same way as mailing lists can be purchased for mailshots in the real world, lists of e-mail addresses can be purchased that target particular types of users. Some of these are compiled by unscrupulous operators, who obtain the e-mail addresses from web pages or newsgroups and then sell them in bulk – $500 dollars for 100 000 addresses. These may give a low CPM, but are likely to be completely untargeted. To avoid this approach the US company NetCreations has introduced a new approach through its PostMasterDirect Service (*www.netcreations.com*). Here consumers can opt to receive information about particular topics. This approach also works well in a business-to-business context when Internet users will be interested in industry or product news.

Managing inbound e-mail has become a major issue for companies operating over the Internet. In a study by Buchanan e-mail on 27 January 1999 reported by Nua Surveys (*www.nua.ie*), 361 UK companies were contacted by e-mail and only 62 per cent replied. On average the replies took two days. The survey also reviewed the quality of responses. In 28 per cent of cases, none of the customers' questions were addressed.

A number of tools have been developed to assist in managing both inbound and outbound e-mail to improve service quality. Examples from Peppers and Rogers (*www.1to1.com*) are as follows:

- Brightware (*www.brightware.com*) develops tools for managing inbound e-mail flow by directing e-mails to the correct people to action them (Fig. 10.8), and provides monitoring tools to check that replies are dispatched promptly.

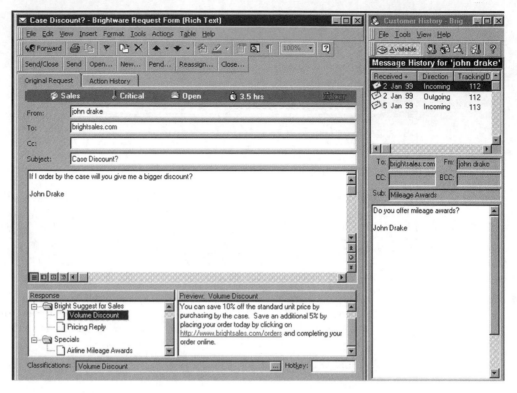

Fig. 10.8 Inbound e-mail management tool from Brightware (*www.brightware.com*)

- Media Synergy (*www.mediasynergy.com*) is an outbound e-mail personalisation tool.
- Digital Impact (*www.digital-impact.com*) (outbound) provides targeted e-mail based on customer profiles. According to the company, clients including The Gap, BMG Music, and The Sharper Image report dramatic increases in online sales, repeat purchases and customer loyalty.
- Post Communications (*www.postcommunications.com*) technology (outbound) provides e-mail marketing programs that use database marketing to target existing or new customers. Clients include Palm Computing, a 3COM company, CDNOW, Harlequin, Hewlett-Packard, Seagate, Selfcare and other market leaders.

Push technology

Push technologies allow a company to push information, advertising and other content out to a customer without requiring that customer to directly visit that company web site to get it. Similar terms are 'netcasting', 'webcasting' or 'channels'. Channels are available from content providers such as *Financial Times*, the BBC and *Vogue*, as shown in Fig. 3.3. Users sign on to a particular channel of interest and specify preferences for updates such as frequency and content. The information is sent to the user's desktop at a time when the computer is not being used intensively, such as when a screensaver is in operation. Users may alter their profile whenever they choose, and the marketer must react in real time.

> **Push technology**
> The delivery of web-based content to the user's desktop without the user being required to visit a site to download information. E-mail can also be considered to be a push technology.

'Lufthansa Airlines (www.lufthansa.com) uses push to alert consumers to fare discounts. Their launch of a pushed airfare-discount alert service is the first phase of what the airline hopes will be an extensive push strategy. "It turns traditional marketing upside down" says Roland Conrady, vice president of new media at Lufthansa in Cologne, Germany. "A customer subscribing to our channel will receive exactly the information he is looking for. There's no better way of marketing"' (Allen *et al.*, 1998).

Push technology can also perform a delivery function, for example when it is involved in the automatic transmission and installation of software updates.

Push was hailed as breakthrough technology in the mid-1990s when Microsoft and Netscape introduced it, to much fanfare, in version 4 of their web browsers. However, users have to decide to subscribe to these channels, and this option has not proved popular, possibly owing to the lengthy downloads, 'bandwidth hogging' and information overload that can occur with push, although the information is targeted. In version 5 of the Microsoft web browser, the active desktop, which was part of the push technology delivery, has been removed. Pointcast, one of the innovators, suffered a major fall in its stock prices and is now just part of a larger company. Push was also perceived as going against the Internet culture and as representing a retrograde step to the culture of mass marketing media such as television, as is illustrated by the following quotation:

'Remember way back when, to the days when we first saw the Web and dreamed of a revolution in communication, media, perhaps even human consciousness? Remember the many-to-many publishing model? Remember the democratic free-flow of information? Remember why you wanted to work on the Web in the first place? If we allow push media to become the status quo, we can kiss our Web dreams goodbye.' Julie Petersen's Awaken site *(www.awaken.org/push.html)*

Databases

Databases effectively provide the 'brains' behind the web site, enabling customer profiling and personalisation and predictive analysis through techniques such as Chi-squared automated interaction detectors (CHAID), neural networks and data mining. Without a database, a web server is 'dumb' and can only serve standard requested information. Personalisation is not possible. All of the reasons for which companies have applied database marketing, in order to assist them in learning about and targeting customers through other media, also apply to the Internet. This is clear from the definition of database marketing. Database marketing does not, however, constitute relationship marketing; it does provide 'the means by which a company identifies, maintains and builds up its network of customers' (DeTienne and Thompson, 1996).

> **Database marketing**
> The application of digital information collected about current and/or potential customers and their buying behaviour to improve marketing performance by formulating strategy and building personalised relationships with customers.

Analysing the customer base

The customer data collected from the web site using the techniques described in Chapter 12 need to be analysed in conjunction with data from other media. This process has been referred to as data fusion (Evans, 1998).

> **Data fusion**
> Data fusion is the combining of data from different complementary sources (usually geodemographic and lifestyle or market research and lifestyle) to 'build a picture of someone's life' (Evans, 1998).

Historic data from disparate sources are increasingly being stored in a single place for analysis – the data warehouse. The data can be 'mined' to identify patterns which help a company understand its customers better.

> **Data warehousing and datamining**
> *'Extracting data from legacy systems and other resources; cleaning, scrubbing and preparing data for decision support; maintaining data in appropriate data stores; accessing and analysing data using a variety of end user tools and mining data for significant relationships. The primary purpose of these efforts is to provide easy access to specially prepared data that can be used with decision support applications such as management report, queries, decision support systems, executive information systems and datamining.'* The Data Warehousing Institute (*www.dw-institute.com*)

Capital One Financial Corporation uses data mining to target low-rate loans at the appropriate targets so that it retains the customers, rather than having many customers leave after taking advantage of an initial offer (Souccar, 1999). Currently data mining is used in conjunction with direct mail, but as Internet access increases such communications will be made by e-mail and will appear on personalised web pages. The implication of this is that further integration is required between data-mining tools and web sites.

A neural network is a data-mining approach that operates in a way that is similar to the functioning of neurons in the human brain. A neural network can be used to identify patterns within data. Mini case study 10.5 gives an example of one application.

Mini case study 10.5   **Neural network builds profiles of web users**

'Aptex's SelectCast is a neural network-based tool that constructs behaviourally-based profiles of Web users. It then targets users with ads and personal promotions their behaviour dictates they will like. Using Aptex, marketers can finally achieve the one-to-one future.

'"Basically, your presence on any given site gives us a lot of information that allows us to begin profiling immediately", Theilmann [Michael, CEO of Aptex] explains. "If you're on a homepage. We might use the general behaviour-profile type for people at that site, but once you start clicking beyond that homepage we are building – in real time – a personal profile."

'That mathematical profile, or vector, is about a kilobyte per user. According to Theilmann, while SelectCast processes gigabytes – perhaps terabytes – of data every day for its customers in order to derive and improve the profiles contained in its vectors, it is necessary only to pass that data through its system. The system doesn't need to digest it. "We don't keep it in some master relational database – there's no massive database anywhere."

'"It's clustering based on interest to reach someone at a certain psychographic stage", explains Peter Rip of Knight-Ridder Ventures (Rip was VP and general manager of Infoseek's network division when the company first began to use Aptex's tools and the white paper he wrote about the success of the joint Infoseek–Aptex project has become part of Aptex'standard marketing pitch).

'That project ultimately become Ultramatch, an Infoseek service for ad buyers that targeted 22 user segments and promised significantly higher click-through rates on all of them. It worked in spectacular fashion, according to Rip and he believes that Aptex makes it possible for Web sites to identify even smaller segments – say, Webmasters looking for Java tools – for which advertisers would be willing to pay four or five times the going rate for search-engine ad inventory. In a market where the average ad can cost between $20 and $40 per 1,000 impressions, "you could get $200 CPMs on some microsegments", Rip says. SelectCast, the outgrowth of the Ultramatch project, is now available to any and all customers – or, at least, those that can afford its base $100,000 price tag.'

Source: Wired magazine (www.wired.com/wired/archive/6.05/one_to_onepr.html).

Despite the potential of using databases referred to above, it is worth remembering that many web sites have not yet progressed beyond brochureware status. Of those sites that are making strides in personalisation, many are not yet exploiting the data they are collecting. Bayers (1998) reports that much of the data Amazon collects about its customers, it is unable to mine.

Virtual communities

Virtual communities are a novel web concept in that they enable like-minded people from around the world to interact using e-mail or bulletin-board-type facilities. In a sense they are similar to user groups for some technical products such as software, or special interest groups created to fight a cause or share a problem. What the Internet provides is an easy mechanism for sharing views over a wide area.

Virtual community
An Internet-based forum for special interest groups to communicate.

Since the publication of the article by Armstrong and Hagel in 1996 entitled 'The real value of online communities' and John Hagel's subsequent book (Hagel, 1997) there has been much discussion about the suitability of the Web for virtual communities. For companies they provide an opportunity to get closer to their customers, although not through a strictly one-to-one model.

The power of the virtual communities, according to Hagel (1997), is that they exhibit a number of positive feedback loops (or 'virtuous circles'). Focused content attracts new members, who in turn contribute to the quantity and quality of the community's pooled knowledge. Member loyalty grows as the community grows and evolves. The purchasing power of the community grows and thus the community attracts more vendors. The growing revenue potential yet attracts more vendors, providing more choice and attracting more members. As the size and sophistication of the community grow (yet still remain tightly focused) its data gathering and profiling capabilities increase – thus enabling better targeted marketing and attracting more vendors... and so on. In such positive feedback loops there is an initial start-up period of slow and uneven growth until critical mass in members, content, vendors and transactions is reached. The potential for growth is then exponential – until the limits of the focus of the community as it defines itself are reached.

From this description of virtual communities it can be seen that they provide many of the attributes for effective relationship marketing – they can be used to learn about customers and provide information and offers to a group of customers.

When deciding on a strategic approach to virtual communities, companies have two basic choices if they decide to leverage them as part of their efforts in relationship building. First, they can provide community facilities on the site, or they can monitor and become involved in relevant communities set up by other organisations such as XOOM.com (Fig. 10.4).

If a company sets up a community facility on its site, it has the advantage that it can improve its brand by adding value to its products. Sterne (1999) suggests that minimal intrusion should occur, but it may be necessary for the company to seed discussion and moderate out some negative comments. It may also be instrumental in increasing word-of-mouth promotion of the site. The community will provide customer feedback on the company and its products as part of the learning relationship. However, the brand may be damaged if customers criticise products. The company may also be unable to get sufficient people to contribute to a company-hosted community. Communities are best suited to high-involvement brands such as those related to sports and hobbies and business-to-business (*see* Fig. 10.9).

Examples of communities in different areas include:

- hosting content such as personal web pages: Lycos Network Tripod (*www.tripod. com*); Yahoo! Geocities (*geocities.yahoo.com*) (grouped home pages),
- geographic: *Evening Standard Online* This is London (*www.thisislondon.co.uk*); Total New York (*www.totalny.com*);
- demographic: Senior Cyborgs (*www.online96.com/seniors*);
- personal interest: Motley Fool (*www.motleyfool.co.uk*) (personal investment); Travelocity (*www.travelocity.com*) (travel); Quokka.com (*www.quokka.com*) (extreme sports).

Privacy and data protection concerns

Direct marketing using the Internet is often associated with spam – a major infringement of privacy – and marketers have to fight misconceptions generated by this.

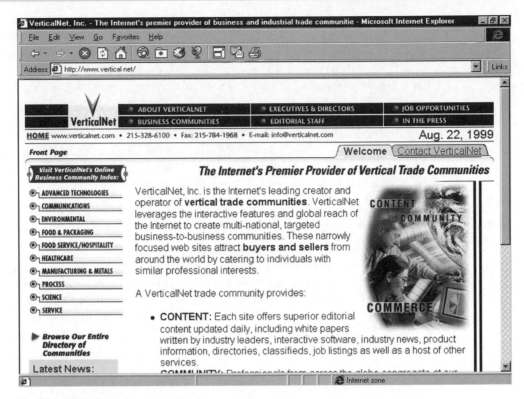

Fig. 10.9 Vertical.Net (*www.vertical.net*)

Spamming

The growth of Usenet newsgroups (*see* Chapter 4) on the Internet must have seemed like a golden opportunity for cynical direct marketers. These newsgroups are set up for people with a particular interest – sporting, political, recreational, etc. They are thus, in effect, lifestyle segments. The bulk mailing of newsgroups got e-mail direct marketing off to a bad start. A well-known incident is that involving Canter and Siegel, the infamous 'Green Card Lawyers', who spammed thousands of Usenet news groups with a message offering to help immigrants get US green cards. Bourne (1996) observed that, 'To say the least, traditional users of the net were dumbfounded and shocked. They fought back the only way they could. They flamed Carter and Siegel with thousands of messages, temporarily shutting down their service provider.'

Spamming
Bulk e-mailing of unsolicited mail.

Privacy issues marketers should consider when conducting one-to-one marketing are well covered by the Which? Web Trader code (*www.which.net/trader*). This is summarised in Chapter 11 with respect to e-commerce in Mini case study 11.5. The relevant items to note with respect to one-to-one marketing are in Clause 16, Data protection and privacy:

■ *Companies must meet the conditions of the Data Protection Act 1984.* This requires that the company must be registered and consumers can access their data. The eight principles of the Act are given in full in Chapter 15, but see also the office of the Data Protection Registrar online (*www.dataprotection.gov.uk*).

■ *Companies must say if they will send the consumer marketing material.* This refers to collecting details such as an address at the time of a sale. The person filling in the form should be notified at this point if marketing material will be sent, and ideally should be given the option to opt out.

■ *Companies must say if they will pass the consumer's details to others.* Again this should be stated on online forms on which customer details are collected.

■ *Consumers must be given the option to refuse marketing material.* This is opting out.

These issues are also covered by The British Code of Advertising Practice (BCAP), available at *www.asa.org.uk*. The main principles that apply to one-to-one marketing are:

■ Consumers must be notified of intended third-party use of their personal data.
■ Consumers must be given the opportunity to 'opt out' of such data rental.
■ Member companies must refrain from sending further mailings to a person who has indicated that he or she does not wish to receive any more mailings.
■ There is a 'global opt-out' registration scheme (mailing preference service – MPS and telephone preference service – TPS), which now includes e-mailing (eMPS).

Stone *et al.* (1996) report that opt-in offers, in which the customer must be proactive if he or she requires the product/promotion, tend to get a lower initial response but a higher retention rate as the customers registered have a genuine interest in the product rather than the incentive. This is important in the Internet context as a web site hit (visit) is implicitly a self-selecting opt-in. Rosalind Resnick, president of NetCreations Inc. (*www.netcreations.com*), is a leading advocate of opt-in or 'consensual' marketing. Her company provides the PostMaster Direct Response service, which allows marketers to send messages to targeted e-mail lists that comprise 100 per cent opt-in customers.

Integrating the Internet with other forms of direct marketing

Direct marketing is closely linked to one-to-one and relationship marketing since the aim of both is to communicate directly with customers with information tailored for them. The difference is really one of emphasis. Direct marketing has been viewed as a tactical vehicle in the form of a single campaign such as a mailshot that is aimed at achieving a direct response. Relationship marketing is a longer-term strategic communication with the customer that is aimed at understanding the customer's needs and then responding to them. Implementing relationship marketing will contain elements of direct marketing. However, the distinction between relationship and direct marketing over a period of time is becoming blurred. Integrated direct marketing involves using different media over a longer time period to achieve a response.

> **Direct marketing**
> Marketing to customers using one or more advertising media and aimed at achieving a measurable response and/or transaction.

The popular conception of direct marketing is of torrents of junk mail pouring through letterboxes urging consumers to buy items they don't need. Direct marketing originated with the first trade catalogues, which appeared soon after the invention of movable type by Gutenberg in the 1400s. They later became popular among wealthy settlers in the New World wishing to purchase wine, china and furniture from Europe. It may appear as if direct marketing has not moved on since this, but direct marketing is becoming increasingly diverse and covers everything from direct mail mailshots, catalogue marketing and telemarketing to direct-response television advertisements and the use of web sites. One of the challenges for today's direct marketer is to integrate the Internet into other forms of direct marketing. We will now consider how this integration is occurring.

Telemarketing and the Internet

In this section we briefly review the use of telephones in direct marketing and assess how the Internet can be used in conjunction with these.

Outbound telemarketing

Outbound telemarketing is known for its use for 'cold-calling' new prospects, but it is also used to increase the profitability of existing customers, either by encouraging them to spend more by up-selling or by cross-selling, often in conjuction with other media such as direct mail. If the target is accurate and a warm-up mailer has been sent this is a powerful technique. Misused, it has great potential to annoy and anger. Research by Datamonitor (*European Business Teleculture 98*) found that 70 per cent of customers have been annoyed by outbound calls, 20 per cent said it has destroyed their impression of a company, 14 per cent said that they would not use the company again, and 12 per cent told their families and friends about the experience, whilst 9 per cent were sufficiently annoyed to complain directly to the company. Outbound telemarketing can be thought of as the equivalent of 'spamming' on the Internet and there does not seem to be much potential to apply the Internet, other than by its decreasing the need for outbound telemarketing!

Inbound telemarketing

Inbound telemarketing is now widespread, and ranges from sales lines and carelines for goods and services to response handling for direct response campaigns. This technique can be used to up-sell and cross-sell to a customer who has called about something else. The Liederman and Roncorroni Group conducted a survey in 1995 showing that 22 per cent of all packaged goods in the UK now have a customer careline.

A web site can complement inbound telemarketing: product information may be available on the site that obviates the need for a customer to call. Alternatively, the information may not be readily understandable on the web site (a complex financial product, for example) and it may be necessary for the customer to phone the company. In this situation 'callback' facilities such as those illustrated in Fig. 9.9 provide good synergy between telephone and web. Callback facilities require integration between the web site and a call management system (using computer telephony integration – CTI) since the customer will specify a particular time he or she wants to be called. The callback is technically outbound since it originates from the company, but on a practical level it is inbound since it is initiated by the customer. Callback has the advantage that the customer does not pay for the phone call.

> **Callback systems**
> A facility on the web site enabling the customer to request an outbound phone call from a company.

In some circumstances it may not be appropriate to encourage the use of the Web in conjunction with telemarketing. Imagine for example that you have designed a direct-response television advertisement. Would you want customers to call a human operator to explain the benefits of a product or use a web site that does not have the sales skills? Furthermore, someone following up an advertisement on the Web may be distracted and investigate competitors' offers or go to an intermediary site to find the best price! Advertisements from financial services companies, for example, may give prominence to the direct-response phone number, but may provide no web address. This may be deliberate.

Call centres

According to Kislowski (1996) the renewed focus on the call centre is being driven primarily by three forces: customer demands for more convenient access to goods and services, business pressures to drive down costs, and the convergence of computers and telephones. The call centre is clearly important in supporting the outbound calls resulting from Internet callback systems.

> **Computer telephony integration (CTI)**
> The combined use of software and telephones to facilitate communication between a business and its customers, particularly through call centres.

An example of a company that has integrated its web site and call centre is the UK financial services company Clerical Medical, which set up a call centre in 1997 to manage requests arising from its promotional activity across all media, including its web site. This site is designed to enable independent financial advisers (IFAs) to find the information they need to service their clients. If they cannot find the information they need, they can request further information by clicking a screen button that triggers an e-mail message direct to the call centre. At the same time, customers can use a 'call-me' or callback button to get information from the call centre on their three nearest IFAs.

Finally it should be noted that some commentators have predicted the 'death of call centres' at the hand of the Internet since many of the routine enquiries currently handled by call centres such as bank account enquiries and transfers can readily be performed by customers with web-enabled PCs, digital television or a telephone.

SUMMARY

1 The three areas of relationship marketing, direct marketing and database marketing are convergently evolving to create a powerful new marketing paradigm known as one-to-one marketing.

2 Relationship marketing theory provides the conceptual underpinning of one-to-one marketing since it emphasises enhanced customer service through customer knowledge.

3 Direct marketing provides the tactics that deliver the marketing communications (and sometimes the product itself) to the individual customer. This approach is evolving rapidly with the advent of the Internet, the rise of call centres and advances in logistics.

4 Database marketing provides the technological enabler, allowing vast amounts of data to be stored and accessed in ways that create business opportunities.

5 One-to-one marketing on the Internet is effective since it provides an interactive, multimedia environment in which the customer opts in to the relationship.

6 Steps in implementing one-to-one on the Internet are:
- Step 1. Attract customers to site.
- Step 2. Provide incentive to start relationship.
- Step 3. Capture customer information to maintain the relationship and profile customer.
- Step 4. Maintain dialogue consistent with customer's profile.

7 Personalisation technologies enable customised e-mails to be sent to each individual (or related groups) and customised web content to be displayed or distributed using push technology.

8 Integration with databases is important for profiling the customer and recording the relationship.

9 Virtual communities have an important role to play in fostering relationships.

10 Marketers must be aware of the risk of infringing customer privacy since this is damaging to the relationship. Providing customers with the option to opt in and opt out of marketing communications is important to maintain trust.

11 Internet-based one-to-one marketing needs to be integrated with traditional communications by mail and phone.

EXERCISES AND QUESTIONS

Self-assessment exercises

1 Why is the Internet a suitable medium for one-to-one marketing?

2 Explain personalisation in an Internet marketing context.

3 What is meant by 'customer profiling'?

4 What is 'computer telephony integration'?

5 How can customer concerns about privacy be responded to when conducting one-to-one marketing using the Internet?

6 Explain the relationship between database marketing, direct marketing and relationship marketing.

7 What is a cookie?

8 How can a web site integrate with telemarketing?

Discussion questions

1 'Direct response television advertisements are more effective if customers are directed to a call centre rather than a web site.' Discuss.

2 'Cookies are a gross infringement of liberty and should not be used.' Discuss.

3 'Without a database behind it a web site is "dumb" and almost useless.' Discuss.

4 A recent development in online business that is attracting much attention and investment is the integration of call centres and web sites. Discuss the intended advantages of this facility.

Essay questions

1 Compare and contrast traditional transaction-oriented marketing with one-to-one marketing using the Internet.

2 Write a report summarising for a manager the necessary stages for transforming a brochureware site to a one-to-one interactive site and the benefits that can be expected.

3 Write a report evaluating which of these products/companies is most suitable for implementing personalisation on a web site:
 ■ Broadvision (*www.broadvision.com*);
 ■ Engage Profileserver (*www.engage.com*);
 ■ LikeMinds (*www.andromedia.com*);
 ■ GroupLens (*www.netperceptions.com*).

4 Explore the legal and ethical constraints upon implementing one-to-one marketing using the Internet.

Examination questions

1 Define and explain direct marketing within the Internet context.

2 What characteristics of the Internet make it so conducive to the direct marketing approach?

3 How does a company initiate one-to-one marketing with a company using the Internet?

4 Explain the concept of a 'virtual community' and how such communities can be used as part of relationship marketing.

5 Suggest three measures a company can take to ensure a customer's privacy is not infringed when conducting one-to-one marketing.

6 What is the role of a database when conducting one-to-one marketing on the Internet?

7 Describe how a web site can be integrated with inbound telemarketing.

8 Explore opportunities and methods for personalising the interactive web session and adding value for that individual customer.

REFERENCES

Allen, C., Kanian, D. and Yaeckel, B. (1998) *Internet World Guide and One-to-One Web Marketing.* New York: Wiley and Sons.

Armstrong, A. and Hagel, J. (1996) 'The real value of online communities', *Harvard Business Review*, May–June, 134–41.

Bayers, C. (1998) 'The promise of one-to-one (a love story)', *Wired,* 6 May.

Belfer, S. (1998) 'IT are from Mars, Marketing are from Venus', *Direct Marketing*, 61, 52–3.

Bourne, S. (1996) 'Business vs. the internet culture', InfoNation (*www.info-nation.com/culture.html*).

Cram, T. (1994) T*he Power of Relationship Marketing: Keeping customers for life*. London: Financial Times Management.

Cross, M. (1994) 'Internet: the missing marketing medium', *Direct Marketing*, 20(6) (October), 20–4.

DeTienne, K.B. and Thompson, J.A. (1996) 'Database marketing and organisational theory: towards a research agenda', *Journal of Consumer Marketing*, 13(5), 12–34.

Duffy, D. (1998) 'Customer loyalty strategies', *Journal of Consumer Marketing*, 15(5), 435–48.

Evans, M. (1998) 'From 1086 to 1984: Direct marketing into the millennium', *Marketing Intelligence and Planning*, 16(1), 56–67.

Foley, D., Gordon, G.L., Schoebachler, D.D. and Spellman L. (1997) 'Understanding consumer database marketing', *Journal of Consumer Marketing*, 14(1), 5–19.

Godin, S. (1999) *Permission Marketing*. New York: Simon and Schuster.

Gummesson, E. (1987) 'The new marketing: developing long term interactive relationships', *Long Range Planning*, 20(4), 10–20.

Hagel, J. (1997) *Net Gain: Expanding markets through virtual communities*. Boston, MA: Harvard Business School Press.

Kislowski, M. (1996) 'The increasingly important role of cell centres: strategies for the future', *Direct Marketing*, 59(5), 34–8.

McCarthy, J. (1960) *Basic Marketing: A managerial approach*. Homewood, IL: Irwin.

McKenna, R. (1993) *Relationship Marketing Successful strategies for the age of the customer*. Reading, MA: Addison-Wesley.

McKenna, R. (1999) *Real-Time. Preparing for the age of the never satisfied customer*. Boston, MA: Harvard Business School Press.

Maling, N. (1999) 'TV money spirited down the pan', *Marketing Week*, 11(5), 26–9.

Peppers, D. and Rogers, M. (1993) *Building Business Relationships one Customer at a Time. The One-to-One Future*. London: Piatkus.

Peppers, D. and Rogers, M. (1997) *Enterprise One-to-One: Tools for building unbreakable customer relationships in the interactive age*. London: Piatkus.

Raphel, M. (1997) 'How a San Francisco movie complex breaks attendance records with database marketing', *Direct Marketing*, 59(11), 52–5.

Reichheld, F.F. (1996) *The Loyalty Effect*. Boston, MA: Harvard Business School Press.

Rosenfield, J.R. (1998) 'The future of database marketing', *Direct Marketing*, 60(10), 28–31.

Schultz, D.E., Tannenbaum, S.L. and Lauterborn, R.F. (1994) *The New Marketing Paradigm: Integrated marketing communications*. NTC.

Shaw, R. (1996) 'How to transform marketing through IT', *Management Today*, Special Report.

Souccar, M.K. (1999) 'Epidemic of rate shopping spurs a search for remedies', *American Banker*, 164(4).

Sterne, J. (1999) *World Wide Web Marketing* (2nd edn). New York: John Wiley and Sons.

Stone, M., Woodcock, N. and Wilson, M. (1996) 'Managing the change from marketing planning to customer relationship management', *Long Range Planning*, 29(5) (October), 675–84.

Vassos, T. (1996) *Strategic Internet Marketing*. Indianapolis, IN: Que. Business Computer Library.

Wolfe, D.B. (1998) 'Developmental relationship marketing: connecting messages with mind, an empathetic marketing system', *Journal of Consumer Marketing*, 15(5), 449–67.

FURTHER READING

Brassington, F. and Petitt, S. (2000) *Principles of Marketing* (2nd edn). Harlow, UK: Pearson Education,
See companion Prentice Hall web site (*www.booksites.net/brassington2*).
Chapter 18 describes direct marketing techniques and their role within the marketing mix.

Burnett, J. and Moriarty, S. (1999) *Introduction to Marketing Communications. An integrated approach*. Upper Saddle River, NJ: Prentice Hall.
See companion Prentice Hall web site (*cw.prenhall.com/bookbind/pubbooks/burnett/*).
See Chapter 12, Communicating through Direct Marketing.

Kotler, P., Armstrong, G., Saunders, J. and Wong, V. (1999) *Principles of Marketing* (2nd edn). Hemel Hempstead: Prentice Hall, Europe.
See companion Prentice Hall web site for 8th US edn: *cw.prenhall.com/bookbind/pubbooks/kotler/*.
See Chapter 11, Building Customer Relationships, Customer Satisfaction, Quality, Value and Service, and Chapter 22, Direct and Online Marketing

Newells, F. (1996) *New Rules of Marketing: How to use one-to-one relationship marketing*. Homewood, IL: Irwin.

Payne, A., Christopher, M. and Peck, M. (1995) *Relationship Marketing for Competitive Advantage*. Oxford: Butterworth-Heinemann.

Payne, A., Christopher, M., Clark, M. and Peck (1998) *Relationship Marketing for Competitive Advantage* (2nd edn). Oxford: Butterworth-Heinemann.

Strauss, J. and Frost, R. (1999) *Marketing on the Internet. Principles of online marketing*. New Saddle River, NJ: Prentice Hall.
Chapter 7, Relationship Marketing through Online Strategies, briefly reviews the benefit of this approach, but with limited coverage of practicalities other than e-mail and privacy.

Database marketing

McCorkell, G. (1997) *Direct and Database Marketing*. London: Kogan Page.

Nash, E. (1993) *Database Marketing: The Ultimate Marketing Tool*. New York: McGraw-Hill.

Stone, M. and Shaw, R. (1988) *Database Marketing*. Aldershot, UK: Gower.

Tapp, A. (1998) *Principles of Direct and Database Marketing*. London: Financial Times Pitman.

Direct marketing

Katzenstein, H. (1992) *Direct Marketing*. New York: Macmillan.

Nash, E. (1995) *Direct Marketing: Strategy, Planning, Execution*. New York: McGraw-Hill.

Rapp, S. and Collins, T. (1987) *Maximarketing*. New York: McGraw-Hill.

Rapp, S. and Collins, T. (1990) *The Great Marketing Turnaround*. Englewood Cliffs, NJ: Prentice Hall.

Rapp, S. and Collins, T. (1994) *Beyond Maximarketing*. New York: McGraw-Hill.

Roberts, M.L. (1989) *Direct Marketing Management*. Englewood Cliffs, NJ: Prentice Hall.

WEB SITE REFERENCES

The sections on web and e-mail personalisation in this chapter list some of the main tools used for building and maintaining relationships online. These sites, particularly those for Broadvision (*www.broadvision.com*) and Net Perceptions (*www.netperceptions.com*), contain many examples of companies that have used these techniques.

Direct Marketing Resource Centre, US magazine (*www2.targetonline.com/dmcenter.html*).

Peppers and Rogers One-to-One marketing web site (*www.1to1.com*).
A site containing a lot of information on the techniques and tools of relationship marketing.

Data warehousing and data mining

Darling, Charles B., 'Data mining for the masses'.
(*www.datamation.com/plugin/issues/1997/feb/02mine.html*).

Inmon, W.H. 'Tech topic – what is a data warehouse?'.
(*www.cait.wustl.edu/cait/papers/prism/vol11_no1/*).

Thearling, Kurt, 'Data mining, database marketing'
(*www.santafe.edu/~kurt/index.shtml*).

pwp.starnetinc.com/larryg/articles.html

www.people.mephis.edu/~tsakagch/dw-web.htm

CHAPTER 11

Electronic commerce transactions

Learning objectives

After reading this chapter the reader should be able to:

- evaluate the drivers, enablers and inhibitors of e-commerce and the current and future impact of e-commence on business;
- understand the concepts, technologies and management implications of e-commerce;
- appreciate the economic, political and legal context within which e-commerce is developing and the likely changes that e-commerce will demand as it evolves.

Links to other chapters

▶ This chapter provides the background to Chapters 13 and 14, which explore the use of the Internet in consumer and business-to-business contexts.

▶ Chapter 6 has a short discussion on the implications of the Internet for product pricing.

▶ Chapter 7 is a closely related chapter that reviews the implication of the Internet for distribution channels and marketplaces in which e-commerce will occur.

INTRODUCTION

This chapter covers the concepts, systems and processes that enable electronic payment over the Internet. It examines the issues that companies need to consider when introducing e-commerce such as security, reliability and performance. It then explores the wider issues relating to e-commerce such as ethical and legal issues and government policy.

Commerce is, of course, as old as the time the first human being traded a bone for a shell. Electronic commerce or e-commerce is a new mode of commerce – commerce conducted over an electronic medium. It has, in fact, been around for over twenty years in the form of electronic data interchange (EDI), but the Internet now makes such a medium a mainstream commercial location to rival, or even exceed, traditional channels. This chapter defines e-commerce and examines its drivers, inhibitors and enablers. A key issue in the successful uptake of e-commerce is security. This chapter examines the risks and the requirements to address those risks. Standards and infrastructure are crucial requirements. The impact of e-commerce in consumer and business markets is examined, particularly the enablers of e-commerce for the general public such as home PCs, interactive digital television, smart cards and electronic wallets. Finally, the e-commerce commercial environment is analysed. How will governments address issues such as tariffs, taxation, legal, regulatory issues and international trade issues?

What is e-commerce?

Commerce is defined by the *New Oxford Dictionary of English* as: '*The activity of buying and selling, especially on a large scale*'. It can range from the smallest local supermarket purchase of groceries to huge international corporate purchases of supplies, the government issuance of bonds or the procurement of warships. In general usage it means more than payment. It encompasses the search for alternative solutions, the comparison of price, functionality, performance, image, perhaps the negotiation of a price, investigation of reputability and assurances and the shipping of the purchased item. Table 11.1 summarises the components of commercial transactions as part of the fulfilment cycle.

Electronic commerce, too, can have a broad or a narrow definition. Authors such as Kosuir (1997) and Zwass (1998) use broader definitions. Zwass (1998) defines e-commerce as: '*the sharing of business information, maintaining business relationships, and conducting business transactions by means of telecommunications networks*'. Kalakota and Whinston (1997) note that e-commerce has many definitions, according to the context. Their book and others on the topic, however, tend to focus on the business transactions and methods for implementing them using different security methods, for example. In this chapter the narrower definition of electronic commerce transactions is used since the broader aspects of electronic commerce such as those concerning strategy and marketing techniques are covered in other chapters in a marketing context. The narrow definition is consistent with the experience of the casual user of the Internet; e-commerce is what happens when you shift from browsing to buying.

> **Electronic commerce transactions**
> E-commerce transactions are the trading of goods and services conducted using the Internet and other digital media.

Electronic commerce has numerous synonyms, such as on-line commerce, Internet commerce and digital commerce. IBM uses the term 'e-business' to denote a broad, holistic concept encompassing all the implications of electronic, Internet-related technologies on business functions, from human resource management to marketing to corporate strategy.

As you read this chapter it will be apparent that the principal requirements, processes and risks of traditional commerce are essentially the same in e-commerce. It is the context and operation that are different. Table 11.1 shows that e-commerce has similar steps in a typical fulfilment cycle, but in a different medium. Note that Internet users will not necessarily conduct all stages of fulfilment via the Internet. For example, they may acquire product information online, but place their order using a fax. The different potential paths of purchase are indicated in Fig. 5.4, where it was argued that the Internet is crucially important for its role in facilitating the purchase, even if ultimately the purchase is not made online.

Table 11.1 Aspects of traditional and electronic commerce

Fulfilment cycle step (business-to-business)	Conventional shopping	Traditional mail order (multiple single-medium channel)	Electronic commerce (single multimedia channel)
Evaluate suppliers and product options	Shops, showrooms	Magazines, flyers	Portals, intermediaries, online catalogues
Select and specify product	Pick off shelf, take to counter	Order form, letter	Online form, e-mail
Send order to supplier	–	Fax, mail, telephone	E-mail, EDI
Supplier checks inventory	–	Printed form	Online database
Generate invoice	–	Printed form	EDI* or via credit card
Ship product	–	Shipper	Shipper or online distribution
Confirm receipt	Printed form	Printed form	E-mail
Schedule payment	Printed form	Printed form	EDI*, online database
Transfer payment	EFT-POS*	Mail (cheque), telephone (credit card)	EDI, EFT*

Note: *EDI: Electronic Data Interchange, EFT: Electronic Funds Transfer, EFT-POS: EFT at Point of Sale.

The electronic marketspace

Throughout history, the nature of a 'market' has diversified from a physical area in the centre of a medieval town to encompass global markets, consumer markets, niche markets and abstract markets such as the stock market and currency markets. Now the Internet provides an electronic marketspace in which transactions can occur. In a report by the Office of Technology Assessment (US Congress, 1994) it was stated that 'because electronic exchange transactions will increasingly be carried out electronically and online the network will in many instances serve as the market'. While it has been said in relation to traditional media that 'the medium is the message' (McLuhan, 1964), with the Web it is also true that the medium is the market (Hoffman and Novak, 1997).

The electronic marketplace (or marketspace as it is becoming known) is most evident in the trading of shares over the Internet and the development of electronic auction business such as eBay (*eBay.com*). Some say that the world's stock exchanges will eventually migrate completely to cyberspace, as a physical building simply represents an opportunity cost of available capital.

How important is e-commerce?

E-commerce still represents a small proportion of the time that people spend using the Internet. A study of online activities released by *Internet World* revealed the following breakdown of Internet usage: e-mail 32 per cent, research 25 per cent, news 22 per cent, entertainment 19 per cent, education 13 per cent and chatlines 8 per cent (*Observer*, 5 January 1997). However, in terms of monetary value, in the 1990s e-commerce has increased spectacularly, reaching economically significant levels from a zero base in a few years.

There is a plethora of statistics about the growth of e-commerce. Many sources disagree as to its size and growth at any one time but the overwhelming opinion is that e-commerce is already significant and will increase dramatically. A typical view reported by *Internet Business* in October 1998 is: *'Current figures support the view that the number and value of electronic transactions is growing at an exponential rate. The Organisation for Economic Cooperation and Development (OECD) predicts that electronic commerce will be worth over $200 billion by the year 2000. Research company Datamonitor predicts that by 2003 more than 245,000 companies and 640,000 companies worldwide will be trading on the Internet.'*

Uncertainty about the increase in volume of e-commerce is indicated by estimates from various research agencies reported by Nua Surveys (*ww.nua.ie*) of the volume of e-commerce in Europe by 2001. These vary from approximately $2 billion (Frost and Sullivan, November 1998) through $200 billion (Visa, March 1999) and $2000 billion (KPMG, October 1998) to $3000 billion (Activmedia, May 1999). Part of the variation is due to the difficulty in extrapolating when the growth is rapid and from a small base. Estimates also differ in that higher estimates tend to include both business and consumer e-commerce and traditional EDI, whereas lower estimates may exclude these. In Chapters 13 and 14 we look at more specific estimates for different sectors in the business-to-consumer and business-to-business markets.

How is this economic activity distributed across the globe? Countries are already jostling for positions, but clear leaders are emerging – pre-eminent amongst those being the United States. The USA's strengths of information technology and entrepreneurial culture and legislation are proving huge assets in this new arena. Table 11.2 lists the leading e-commerce countries according to their current economic importance on a global basis. Further estimates of consumer e-commerce are provided in Chapter 13.

Table 11.2 Relative significance of e-commerce in different countries

Category	Country
Superpower	United States
Contender	Germany, United Kingdom, Japan, Canada
Gateway	Singapore, Benelux, Hong Kong
Sprinter	Scandinavia/Nordic countries
Straggler	France, Australia, Italy, South Korea, Spain

Source: Forrester Research Inc, 30 April 1997 (*www.forrester.com*)

A history of e-commerce

> **Electronic Data Interchange**
> The exchange, using digital media, of standardised business documents such as purchase orders and invoices between buyers and sellers.

The concept of e-commerce transactions predates PCs and the World Wide Web. In the 1970s Electronic Data Interchange (EDI – the transfer of information, financial and otherwise, in a standard electronic format) and Electronic Funds Transfer (EFT) or Financial EDI over secure private networks became established modes of intra- and inter-company transaction. For decades many large companies such as banks, airlines, retail chains and manufacturers have benefited from increased back-office efficiency and improved supplier/vendor processes, helping them optimise inventories, operate more efficiently and improve customer service.

> **Financial EDI**
> An aspect of the electronic payment mechanism involving transfer of funds from the bank of a buyer to a seller.

However, these early solutions were expensive to implement. Despite massive efforts to create national and international standards for document formats, they were based on proprietary technologies, which tended to lock a company into one supplier since each EDI link tended to be set up specifically for a single supplier and buyer. This made it difficult to switch the connection to another supplier.

Business today demands adaptive and agile companies and value chains. The ability to connect with a variety of changing suppliers and distributors and to support rich, multimedia information transfer required an evolutionary step forward in corporate connectivity.

What e-commerce provides is a simpler, lower-cost method of conducting business electronically. This has given the potential for electronic trading to small and medium-sized companies (*see* Mini case study 11.1).

Mini case study 11.1   ### Internet enables electronic links for the smaller supplier

Tesco, the UK's largest grocery retailer, has a system known as Tesco Information Exchange (TIE) based on extranet technology. The system links multiple suppliers to Tesco enabling up-to-the-minute access to sales and tracking data for their products on special promotions within Tesco stores. The system is Internet based so providing affordable standard protocol solutions for small companies such as Kingcup mushrooms, which only employs 11 people at the height of the mushroom picking season, as well as the corporate giants such as Nestlé. Using the instant online data suppliers can precisely match supply to demand, thereby placing inventory management in the hands of the suppliers rather then the retailers, resulting in vast savings in administration costs.

Dixons, the UK electronics retail giant, is persuading some of its smallest suppliers to use a web-based trading system that links into Dixons' conventional EDI network, but does not have the up-front costs, and runs over the Internet. Dixons' effort is not just about running down costs through process automation, it is also about tracking inefficiencies in the supply chain by sharing sales information with manufacturers so that they will automatically predict product demand more accurately. The number of suppliers is significant: while Avon in the USA has 26 000, Dixons has fewer than 7500, of whom 374 are merchandise suppliers, and 320 of those already use EDI.

Within an organisation, to implement e-commerce is a significant step forward both conceptually and practically. A range of levels of sophistication of implementing e-commerce are available. These are similar to the evolutionary stages of implementing an Internet marketing strategy that were discussed in Chapter 5. Table 11.3 describes the levels of e-commerce sophistication an organisation may possess.

Table 11.3 Levels of e-commerce sophistication

Level	Characteristics
Primitive	Static web pages or 'brochureware'
	Searchable site with dynamic pages such as an online catalogue
	Integration with operational databases, e.g. inventory searching, package tracking, job postings
	Customer transaction through the Internet, e.g. selling products and services, buying and selling shares, applying for loans
Advanced	Full electronic commerce (i.e. integrated fulfilment cycle of ordering, shipping, billing)

It is evident that only the last two categories in Table 11.3 can be strictly described as e-commerce.

Reasons for the growth in e-commerce

In order to assess the prospects for e-commerce for a particular company's product offering, it is useful to understand the factors that contribute to users completing transactions online rather than by traditional means. The drivers, or reasons for implementing e-commerce from a consumer's standpoint, are as follows:

- increase in demand for choice (product depth, global reach, price choices);
- demand for information (detailed product information, inventory, order status);
- demand for interactive, online support;
- avoidance of travel and parking difficulties for consumer e-commerce;
- elimination of time constraints (that is, opening hours or delays between placing an order and delivery).

An example of the benefits that accrue to the customer is provided by Expedia UK (*expedia.msn.co.uk*), an online travel agent that puts the customer in charge, empowering him or her with comparative information and enabling the customer

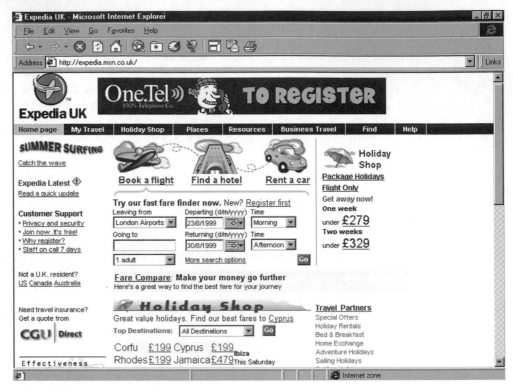

Fig. 11.1 Expedia UK (*expedia.msn.co.uk*) travel site

to deal directly with airlines, hotels and car rental companies (*see* Fig. 11.1). The benefits are summarised in an advertisement as: *'Imagine being able to plan your travel, buy your air tickets, make hotel reservations and book last-minute package deals yourself, in your own time, whenever you want to.'*

Now complete Activity 11.1 to examine another example of the factors contributing to online commerce. The suitability of particular products for e-commerce purchases from a consumer's point of view are reviewed in Chapter 13.

Activity 11.1

'Bras Direct: assessing the drivers for e-commerce'

Bras Direct was set up in 1996 as a mail order company offering a new way to buy branded lingerie. The *Daily Telegraph* of 8 September 1999 reported that '*Challenging Marks and Spencer's shares of the lingerie market is an ambitious task. But, if Bras Direct has its way women will soon buy underwear on the Internet as well as in the high street*'. It quoted the systems manager Mark Hooker as stating that: '*The Internet as an emerging sales vehicle was part of our strategy from the beginning*'. Around 10 per cent of the company's sales now come from the Web. Selling direct has a number of advantages for a company like Bras Direct. Since it is not limited by floor space it can afford to stock a wide inventory and size range.

1 Visit the Bras Direct site (*www.brasdirect.co.uk*) and then list the benefits evident for consumers of such a site and produce a separate list of problems for consumers or reasons why a customer might prefer to use the high street or mail-order facility.

2 From examining the site, what target market do you think the company is hoping to sell to?

3 The extract mentions two benefits of using the Internet for Bras Direct. Outline two further benefits.

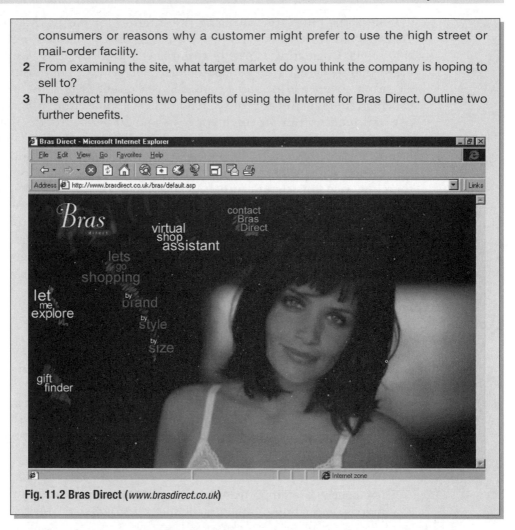

Fig. 11.2 Bras Direct (*www.brasdirect.co.uk*)

Activity 11.2

Conduct a focus group to investigate the feelings of fellow students regarding e-commerce purchases. Is it a 'brave new world' of greater choice and convenience or a world fraught with financial and privacy risks? Have you bought online? If not, why not? What would and wouldn't you buy? What are the implications of your results for the general market?

For the business customer, similar reasons for and against buying online may apply, but e-commerce also offers the business customer the following benefits:

■ lower purchasing overhead – especially for small value and repeat orders;
■ greater choice (greater product depth and global reach);
■ faster fulfilment cycle time (ordering, shipping, billing);
■ greater ability to supply information (inventory, order status, etc.);
■ lower cost than EDI;
■ ease of swapping between suppliers greater than with EDI.

One of the innovators in using the Internet for business buying is the GE Trading Process Network (TPN) at *www.tpn.geis.com*, which has been in operation since 1995. Originating as part of an intranet within GE, TPN Post is an Internet-based trading network that enables buyers and sellers to do business-to-business electronic commerce, including transactions. Current users of the TPN service have experienced up to 50 per cent reduction in cycle times from order to delivery, 30 per cent reduction in procurement costs and 20 per cent reduction in material costs. An example of its use is provided by Con Edison, a New York utility provider. A press release from GE TPN reported that Peter Deutsch, purchasing manager for Con Edison, anticipates that working with GE will allow Con Edison to reduce the sourcing cycle time significantly: '*Automating the transactional portions of the purchasing process and eliminating mailing and faxing time will allow us to serve our internal customers within Con Edison much more quickly.*' Deutsch expects to improve Con Edison's competitive position not only by getting better prices, but also by translating the sourcing cycle time gains into lower inventory levels, while increasing service level to his internal customers.

Drivers for suppliers

For the supplier, benefits from e-commerce are:

- a global reach, leading to more orders;
- reduced administration overhead (paperwork automation leading to a lower cost for each order made);
- reduced asset requirements (physical properties for companies with a retail network);
- integration between back office and online 'shopping' activities;
- integration of online 'shopping' activities with database marketing;
- less need for distribution via channel (disintermediation);
- reduced working capital (inventory).

These benefits are supported by a survey of US companies from the Information Technology Association of America conducted in 1998 (*see* Table 11.4).

Table 11.4 Benefits of e-commerce cited by US companies in 1998

Benefit cited	Percentage
Decreased overhead costs from interfacing external business systems for back-end functions	61
Increased sales from better targeting of specific products, incentives and advertising	43
Faster turnaround for transactions	39
Decreased costs from disintermediation	26

This survey shows that the streamlining of processes internally and externally is the principal benefit expected from a migration to e-commerce systems. Attracting particular interest is the opportunity to deal directly with the end-customer without the need for margin-reducing intermediaries – a process known as disintermediation.

Mini case study 11.2, Dell Computers, summarises the benefits of e-commerce for customer and supplier alike.

Dell Computers

Fig. 11.3 Dell Computers home page (*www.dell.com*), showing e-commerce offerings for different types of market

Dell is commonly quoted as one of the success stories of e-commerce, given that it achieves annual revenues of $3000 million via e-commerce or 17 per cent of its total turnover, but it is worth considering the history of the company and the drivers that apply in this case. Dell pioneered direct telephone sales of computers after noticing the increased sophistication of the consumer towards buying computers sight unseen. The CEO, Michael Dell, was quick to grasp the power of e-commerce since the company already had a direct sales model in place. This has enabled it to migrate to e-commerce more readily than companies such as Compaq and IBM, which used a well-developed channel to achieve the majority of sales.

The success of Dell is based not only on the 'front-office' links to customers, but also on 'back-office' links to warehousing and production, which have been vital in customer service. Dell has set up systems that are the envy of other computer manufacturers. Warehousing, supply chain integration and build-to-order manufacturing with quick customer fulfilment give Dell the edge in what has turned into a commodity business.

The benefits and disadvantages to Dell and its customers may be summarised as follows:

▶ **Mini case study** *continued*

Advantages to Dell

- cost savings;
- ability to develop relationships with customers;
- absence of need for intermediaries (although Dell has always sold direct);
- additional sales through use of another promotional and sales channel.

Disadvantages to Dell

- customer service may actually decline without personal contact by people;
- running a web site can be costly due to frequent updates (although this seems to be offset by sales occurring because of site).

Benefits for customer

- cost savings passed on to customers as lower prices;
- ease of purchase and monitoring delivery, particularly for corporate customers placing repeat orders;
- availability of up-to-date information on products and customer support;
- customisation according to the needs of major customers;
- staff can receive support direct from Dell without the need to go to an internal help-desk, who would then contact the supplier.

E-commerce enablers

The drivers for consumers, business people and suppliers act in conjunction with key enablers which have facilitated the use of the medium. These have been covered in other contexts, for example in Chapter 2, and so are covered only briefly here. They are:

1 Internet standards

A key enabler of the rapid and widespread uptake of the Internet for e-commerce, is the adoption of the Internet computer-to-computer 'language' as a global standard. The ubiquitous adoption of the Transmission Control Protocol/Internet Protocol (TCP/IP) standard as developed within the Open System Interconnect (OSI) layer framework confers interoperability. Organisations that adopt TCP/IP internally achieve a common platform-independent base for their information systems. Of course this benefit is greatly amplified by the adoption of TCP/IP by external partners and business customers.

2 Bandwidth development

Although performance is described above as an inhibitor, the enormous increase in bandwidth that has resulted from the replacement of existing telephone cable by fibre optic cable has been an essential part of creating a viable Internet backbone. Research and development is continuing at a ferocious rate, spurred on by government support such as the Internet2 programme – President Clinton's 'information superhighway'.

3 World Wide Web

The development of a user-friendly graphical interface to the arcane workings of the Internet itself was an absolutely necessary development in order for electronic commerce to diffuse from the IT departments of large corporations and financial institutions into small businesses, the high street and homes.

4 Diversification and proliferation of Internet access

For many people, their first taste of electronic commerce will not be through a home PC, but probably via digital television or WebTV when nothing on the television channels grabs their interest. Similarly, the general public will encounter e-commerce as currently familiar manifestations of technology such as cash machines (ATMs) and plastic cards take on new sophistication and functionality.

5 Development of 'off the shelf' e-commerce products

As electronic commerce grows in importance, support industries are developing to facilitate the creation of online trading business and expedite the evolution of smaller businesses on to the Internet. A key development is the availability of online shop front templates (for example, IBM HomePage Creator and BT Storefront – see Chapter 15). These provide a low-cost, simple development environment that enables non-experts to build virtual shops for themselves from standard components.

Inhibitors to e-commerce

It is also worth pausing to consider some of the inhibitors to e-commerce. For some markets, particularly where the target customers are likely to be technology shy, these may be considerable. Typical inhibitors are:

- technophobia;
- security fears;
- technology not user friendly;
- poor performance leading to slow download;
- inertia of habitual conventional shopping and purchasing;
- Internet access still limited;
- entrenched interests (for example, distributors who may be bypassed).

Since security is a major inhibitor this is considered in more detail in a later section of this chapter. Although the Internet has these significant inhibitors, it is worth remembering that it can help remove inhibitors to companies considering overseas export. How the Internet can help in this way is reviewed in Chapter 14.

Implementing transactions over the Internet

Over time and throughout history money has become increasingly abstract. Before the advent of money, trade was conducted by barter – three chickens for a pig, for example. The value being exchanged was intrinsic to the items, physical and very explicit. Interestingly, barter has a place in e-commerce:

'A typical transaction may involve a magazine publisher getting together with a television company and agreeing to provide each other with advertising space and airtime of equivalent value on their respective media. In another case, a computer retailer in need of a photocopier might arrange a straight swap with an appropriate supplier . . . ITEX, one of the USA's largest [barter] networks . . . has recently set up affiliated exchanges in Romania, New Zealand, Norway, Turkey and Canada' (Internet Business, May 1998).

The first money, in the form of silver and gold coins, also had intrinsic value as precious metals, but that value was abstract in that it was valuable because human beings desired it. Recognisably modern money in the form of notes and base metal coinage is clearly abstract in value and operates as a bearer certificate. That is, it has value because it can be redeemed by a bank or exchanged at a shop for goods and services at par value.

Electronic cash is a logical next step in that abstraction process. It has now even lost its physical existence – it is a stream of zeros and ones existing in cyberspace and pumped through the media just like any other data. *'Money is now an image'* (Kurztman, 1993).

Whatever the nature of the money involved, the requirements of a payments system remain the same: security, trust and convenience and efficiency of exchange. In the specific context of e-commerce the following more detailed list of attributes is desirable.

Payment system requirements

Payment systems have general requirements and specific security requirements (which are covered in a subsequent section in this chapter). Payment systems must:

- be secure (achieving privacy, authentication, integrity and non-repudiability);
- be easy for buyer and seller to use and understand;
- be straightforward for banks to administer;
- be scalable across different currencies and to different denominations;
- have low costs for implementing transactions.

Consumer requirements for payment systems are indicated by this extract from the American Bankers Association 1996 Payments System Task Force, 'The Role of Banks in the Payments System of the Future': *'Consumers' acceptance of new technologies will be driven largely by traditional concerns about liability, unauthorised access, exposure to fraud, fees, privacy and finality of payment.'*

We will now look at different types of payment system in the context of these requirements.

Types of payment systems

In considering the different types of payment systems it is useful to distinguish between those that are primarily targeted at consumers, and those that can be used for institutional or business buying.

Consumer payment systems

Perhaps the easiest way to understand electronic payment systems is to consider them in relation to existing payment systems. This provides a structure to the bewildering array of terms such as digital cash, microtransactions, Millicents and so on. Electronic payment systems can be divided into two basic types, those where no credit occurs and those where credit occurs. Before we look at these systems, it is worth reviewing the commonly used terminology for the different parties involved in the transaction:

- *Purchasers*. These are the consumers buying the goods.
- *Merchants*. These are the retailers.
- *Certification Authority (CA)*. This is a body that issues digital certificates that confirm the identity of purchasers and merchants.
- *Banks*. These are traditional banks.
- *Electronic token issuer*. Note that this term, which describes a virtual bank that issues digital currency, is less established than the other terms in this list, which are commonly used in electronic payment systems (e.g. Kalakota and Whinston, 1997). Many of the electronic tokens are dependent on digital certificates for security (described in a later section of this chapter).

Non-credit or pre-paid systems

Most of the non-credit systems operate using a pre-pay principle. In other words, before purchasing an item electronically, the purchaser must already have electronic funds available that can be immediately transferred to the merchant. These funds can exist in a variety of forms, known as electronic tokens. Electronic tokens are usually purchased from various electronic token issuers using a traditional payment device such as a credit card or by a transfer of cash into a personal account.

Electronic tokens
Units of digital currency that are in a standard electronic format.

Some examples of non-credit systems are:

1 Digital, virtual or electronic cash (e-cash)

Several companies have attempted to establish payment systems that replicate cash in that they are anonymous systems (from the retailer's perspective). The names to describe these systems are confusing, particularly since some of the concepts have a limited life. DigiCash (*www.digicash.com*) was one of the 'early runners' in this area, but this company filed for bankruptcy in 1998, and the technology and concept are now owned by eCash(*www.ecash.com*). Digital cash usually follows what is known as a bearer certificate system, where blank tokens are issued by the user and certified by the bank. It is a very secure system as the merchant must make an online real-time connection to the bank to ensure credit is available. This can make it difficult for small to medium retailers to implement. Cybercoin from CyberCash (*www.cybercash.com*) is a notational system using pre-paid funds that does not require inter-bank clearing. CyberCoin was terminated in 1998, and users migrated to instabuy (*www.instabuy.com*), a credit-card-based system. It is noteworthy that the CyberCash company (Fig. 11.4) increased the number of merchants using its credit-card based CashRegister service to over 15 000 in 1999. This indicates the relative popularity of credit card mechanisms over digital cash methods. Beenz and other loyalty-type tokens described in Chapter 9 can also be considered to be digital cash.

2 Microtransactions or micropayments such as Millicent

These are digital cash systems that allow very small sums of money (fractions of a penny) to be transferred, but with lower security. Such small sums do not warrant a credit card payment, because processing is too costly. The Digital Millicent scheme dating back to the mid-1990s is the best known of these, but has never been widely used in Europe. ECoin (*www.ecoin.net*) is a newer micropayment system that is becoming more popular. Such micropayment systems may become important for purchasing information or music to play on devices such as the Rio, a credit-card-sized personal stereo, which downloads CD-quality music direct from the Internet for a small charge.

3 Debit cards

Cards issued with standard bank accounts could theoretically be used for e-commerce purchase, but merchants prefer credit cards since the payment is secured by the bank. Debit cards have been used by Bank Austria to enable payments by teenagers who cannot have credit cards, but can use debit cards up to the limit of their accounts.

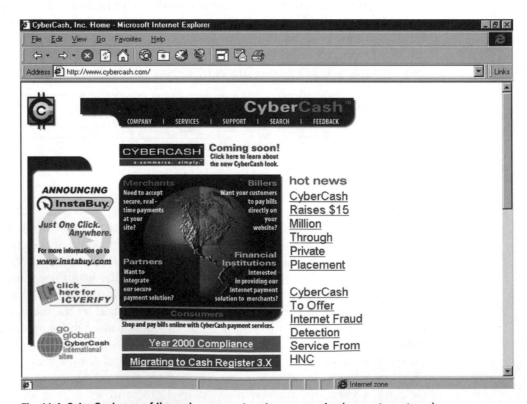

Fig. 11.4 **CyberCash, one of the major payment system companies** (*www.cybercash.com*)

4 Smartcards

These are different from the other items in the list since they are physical cards rather than virtual, so must be inserted into a smartcard reader before items can be purchased. Since such readers are not yet a standard feature of home PCs, the use of smartcards for purchase is limited to trials in areas such as Swindon (Mondex/ Mastercard) and Leeds (Visa Cash) where purchases across the Internet can be made from public kiosks in shopping centres that have smartcard readers. The Visa Cash system is a bearer certificate system (chip-card), cleared through the conventional banking system, where the issuing institution earns float. This was trialled in Leeds, with 60 000 cards in circulation and 1400 businesses accepting them. *Computing* (29 October 1998) reported that '*Ken Bignall, managing director of Visa UK, said that the Leeds programme has shown that an electronic purse adds real convenience for cardholders*'. For example, Visa Cash transactions have already replaced cash by up to 10 per cent in car parks, and have also proved popular in fast food restaurants, sandwich shops and newsagents. Visa plans to extend its coverage in these areas as well as to public transport. Note that these cards are not commonly used for the Internet currently, because of a lack of card-reading devices, but offer this potential.

Post-paid or credit-based systems

1 Digital/electronic cheques

These are modelled on conventional cheques except that they are authorised using digital rather than handwritten signatures. An example of a digital cheque payment system operating within the UK is the BankNet service *at mkn.co.uk/bank*, which is an online banking service between MarketNet and Secure Trust Bank plc. It offers the facility to write digitally signed cheques using public key/private key cryptographic techniques (defined in a later section of this chapter).

2 Credit cards such as Visa or Mastercard

These are the predominant means of making online payments. The reasons for this are that they fulfil well the requirements for a payment system and they are an existing standard.

Although a customer usually makes a credit card payment direct to the merchant, by filling in the card number and address on an online form, there may be some instances where it is more convenient for the customer to register his or her credit card details with a third party. This makes it easier for customers to make frequent purchases, and their credit card details do not have to be divulged to each retailer. Such a system is provided by Pay2See (*www.Pay2See.com*), which enables download-able products such as music and reports to be paid for. With Pay2See (*see* Fig. 11.5), it is only for the first purchase that a customer is asked for credit card details – to open an account. Credit card details are then stored at Pay2See.

In addition to the payment systems there are also digital wallets such as Microsoft Wallet (*www.microsoft.com/Wallet/default.asp*). This is not a form of digital cash, but rather a piece of software using a wallet analogy, and included with browsers such as Microsoft Explorer to make it easier for customers to adopt e-commerce. It has two

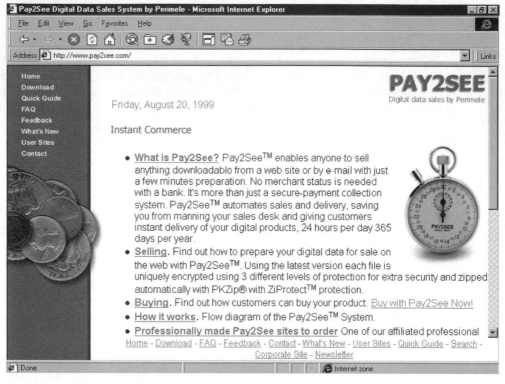

Fig. 11.5 Pay2See credit card based account payment system

elements, an address part for storing and retrieving ship-to and bill-to addresses and a payment part for securely storing and retrieving private payment information, such as credit cards, digital cash, electronic cheques or loyalty programme data. Note that it is designed to work with all the payment methods described above. Despite this, and despite backing by Microsoft, it is not widely used in Europe, because initially few merchants supported the standards on which it is based, such as SET and CyberCoin. It is also not clear to consumers why they need to use it when many sites offer credit card payment without the need to use this software.

Business payment systems

In addition to the methods described below, which are suitable for larger transactions, it is possible to use some of the consumer methods for business payments also. For example credit cards are becoming more widespread for business purchasing. Business payment systems are currently under development, and there is no simple clearly popular standard. They tend to be more complicated than business-to-consumer payment systems since they need to accommodate the following characteristics of the business-to-business situation:

- The system must provide facilities for different members of the buying organisation including the requisitioner, the authoriser and the purchasing department.
- The system must allow for repeat orders and complex orders comprising many items.
- The system must allow for specialised or bespoke orders.

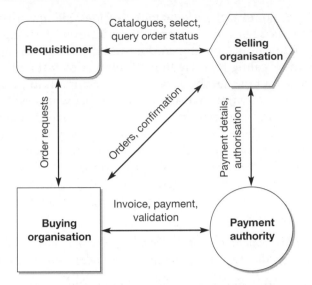

Fig. 11.6 The Open Buying on the Internet model for business-to-business e-commerce.

■ The system must have high levels of security for the potentially high value of the orders.
■ The bank or payment authority must be fully integrated into the system.

There are currently three main standards under development:

1 Open Buying on the Internet (OBI, *www.openbuy.org*), created by the Internet Purchasing Roundtable, is intended to ensure that different e-commerce systems can 'talk' to each other. It is managed by CommerceNet (*www.commerce.net*) and backed by, among others, 3M, Ford, Mastercard, Visa and Microsoft. Figure 11.6 shows the model proposed by OBI.
2 The Open Trading Protocol (OTP, *www.otp.org*) is intended to standardise a variety of payment-related activities including purchase agreements, receipts for purchases and payments. It is backed by, among others, AT&T, CyberCash, Hitachi, IBM, Sun and BT. Despite this impressive line-up the web site has not featured any updated press releases since 1998 and seems set to be eclipsed by OBI.
3 Internet-based EDI. Traditional EDI standards have also been extended for use on the Internet, but mainly through initiatives of individual suppliers rather than as a cross-industry move.

Managing security risks

Security is the principal issue in promoting e-commerce for both buyers and sellers, so this topic is covered in some detail. The current consumer opinion of Internet security is summarised well by Strom (1997), who says:

'The perception of insecure transactions will continue to prevent many shoppers from making their first [Inter]net-based purchases. While consumer attitudes about paying for goods and services online will slowly improve over the next few years, it will not be enough to fuel a rapid growth in e-commerce.'

However, there is a certain lack of logic and considerable inconsistency in the attitudes of consumers regarding Internet transactions. Although evidently extremely wary of credit card payment over the Internet, consumers apparently do not think twice about revealing their credit card number over the phone or allowing the card to be taken out of sight by a waiter in a restaurant. In these cases there is obviously no secrecy or attempt to disguise the number whatsoever. In contrast, the Internet has a large array of techniques available to make transactions secure. It cannot be assumed that these techniques are applied every time to every service – the basic e-mail, for example, is simply raw text and thus open to anyone who can access a user's account. However, when the appropriate hardware and software are applied a trading environment is created that can be used with confidence. The hype in the media of the perils of the Internet is being partially balanced by positive reporting of e-commerce:

> *'People are really terrified about putting their details out over the Internet but in reality the chances of crime are tiny'* (Beth Barling of Ovum, *Daily Telegraph*, 29 August 1998).

> *'It's as safe or unsafe as giving your credit card number over the phone or by fax'* (Wendy Grossman of Future Shopping, *Daily Telegraph*, 29 September 1998).

Such media coverage will gradually reduce the perception of risk, but for every positive story there may be several negative ones. The *Daily Telegraph* of 31 December 1998 reported that while businesses may be conscientious about data in transmission they may be less thorough about stored data:

> *'Ethical hackers' employed by IBM to test the security of Internet stores have found that 90 per cent are vulnerable to hacking attempts. In the unofficial survey the hackers managed to gain access to files containing customers' credit card details.'*

How, then, can companies break this perception of risk and aim to persuade Internet users to shop online? A clear and comprehensive, but also comprehensible description and explanation of the particular security arrangements and standards adhered to by a company on its web site would certainly begin to address this problem (*see* Mini case study 11.3) but a level of consumer understanding of the issues that does not yet widely exist is also needed. Eventually a critical mass of word-of-mouth reports of positive experiences of e-commerce may break through this obstacle.

Considering the origins of the Internet in a US Department of Defense national security project ('ARPANET') to create a computer network resilient to nuclear attack, it is ironic that security is now a major inhibitor to the growth of e-commerce. An Andersen Consulting survey of 3000 European executives carried out between December 1997 and July 1998 revealed that privacy and security issues, as well as the lack of a framework for commercial regulation, remained key barriers to developing e-commerce.

Consumer concern about Internet security is in marked contrast to their view of traditional EDI networks, which are perceived as very secure. Modern low-cost EDI transactions run over systems known as Value Added Networks (VANs) and Virtual Private Networks (VPNs). The vendors of these systems such as GE and AT&T are extremely careful about protecting the information that flows across these networks. As these major providers and others offer more and more Internet-based services it may become more difficult to protect this information.

Mini case study 11.3   **Quelling users' fears about security at Amazon.co.uk**

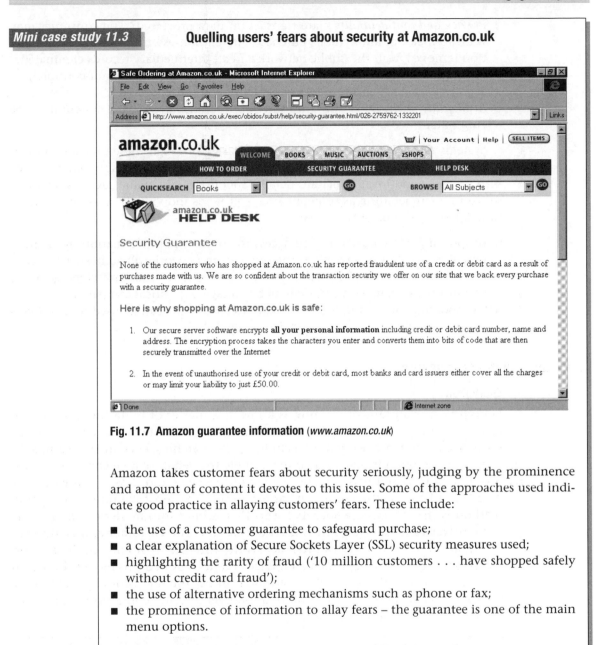

Fig. 11.7 Amazon guarantee information (*www.amazon.co.uk*)

Amazon takes customer fears about security seriously, judging by the prominence and amount of content it devotes to this issue. Some of the approaches used indicate good practice in allaying customers' fears. These include:

- the use of a customer guarantee to safeguard purchase;
- a clear explanation of Secure Sockets Layer (SSL) security measures used;
- highlighting the rarity of fraud ('10 million customers . . . have shopped safely without credit card fraud');
- the use of alternative ordering mechanisms such as phone or fax;
- the prominence of information to allay fears – the guarantee is one of the main menu options.

Requirements for security systems

When systems for e-commerce are devised, or when existing solutions are selected, the following attributes must be present:

1 *Authentication* – are the parties to the transaction who they claim to be? Ensuring that they are is achieved by the use of digital certificates, as explained on p. 346.

2 *Privacy and confidentiality* – are transaction data protected? The consumer may want to make an anonymous purchase. Are all non-essential traces of a transaction removed from the public network and all intermediary records eliminated?

3 *Integrity* – checks that the message sent is complete: that is, it is not corrupted.

4 *Non-repudiability* – ensures sender cannot deny sending message.

5 *Availability* – threats to the continuity and performance of the system must be eliminated.

Systems must also be protected against viruses, although these probably present less of a danger than hackers. Hackers can use techniques such as spoofing to hack into a system and find credit card details. Spoofing, as its name suggests, involves someone masquerading as someone else – either as individuals or as an organisation. Spoofing can be of two sorts:

■ IP spoofing can be used to gain access to confidential information by creating false identification data such as the originating network (IP) address. The objective of this access can be espionage, theft or simply to cause mischief, generate confusion and damage a corporate public image or political campaign.

■ Site spoofing, or fooling the organisation's customers, can be used to divert customers to a site that is not a *bona fide* retailer.

Methods of increasing security

Encryption

Encryption, as all fans of spy novels know, is a matter of mutating information using a technique (key) in such a way that it is only readable by someone who possesses the appropriate decryption technique (the matching key). In an e-commerce context, encryption is mainly used to scramble the details of an e-commerce transaction as it is passed between the sender and receiver and (less often) when the details are held on the computers at each end. The most common encryption method is the SSL (Secure Sockets Layer) that is built into modern web browsers such as Netscape Navigator. It is used to scramble the customer and credit card information when it is transmitted across the Internet. It would require a determined attempt to intercept such a message and decrypt it. SSL is more widely used than the rival S-SHTTP method. When SSL is in use the user is prompted with the message 'You are about to view information over a secure connection', and a key symbol is used to denote this security.

> **Secure Sockets Layer (SSL)**
> A commonly used encryption technique for scrambling data as they are passed across the Internet from a web browser to a web server.

Since, with enough computing power, time and motivation, it is possible to decrypt messages encrypted using SSL, much effort is being put into finding more secure methods of encryption. These are based around the concept of digital certificates or keys, which form the basis for the Barclaycard/Visa SET initiative, which is explained in Mini case study 11.4 (p. 347). First we review the concepts on which it is based.

> **Digital certificates (keys)**
> A method of ensuring privacy on the Internet. Certificates consist of keys made up of large numbers that are used to uniquely identify individuals.

Kalakota and Whinston (1997) describe two main methods of digital certificate encryption:

1 Secret-key (symmetric) encryption

This involves both parties having an identical (shared) key, which is known only to them. Only this key can be used to encrypt and decrypt messages. The secret key has to be passed from one party to another before use. This method is not practical for e-commerce since it would not be safe for a purchaser to give a secret key to a merchant since control of it would be lost and it could not then be used for other purposes. A merchant would also have to manage many customer keys.

2 Public-key (asymmetric) encryption

This is referred to as asymmetric encryption since the keys used by the sender and receiver of information are different. The two keys are related, so only the pair of keys can be used together to encrypt and decrypt information. Figure 11.8 shows how public-key encryption works in an e-commerce context. A customer would place an order with a merchant by automatically looking up the public key of the merchant and then using this key to encrypt the message containing the order. The scrambled message is then sent across the Internet and on receipt by the merchant is read using the merchant's private key. In this way only the merchant who has the only copy of the private key can read the order. In the reverse case the merchant could confirm the customer's identity by reading (using the customer's public key) identity information such as a digital signature encrypted with the private key of the customer.

Digital signatures

Digital signatures create a truly commercial system by using public key encryption to achieve authentication: the merchant and purchaser can prove they are genuine. The purchaser's digital signature is encrypted before the customer sends a message using his or her private key, and on receipt the public key of the customer is used to decrypt the digital signature. This proves the customer is genuine.

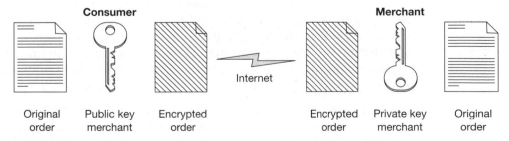

Fig. 11.8 Use of public-key encryption to send a secure message using the Internet

345

> **Digital signatures**
> A method of identifying individuals or companies using public key encryption.

The public-key infrastructure (PKI)

In order for digital signatures and public-key encryption to be effective it is necessary to be sure that the public key you intend to use to decrypt a document actually belongs to the person you believe is sending you the document. The developing solution to this problem is the issuance by a trusted third party (TTP) of a message containing owner identification information and a copy of the public key of that person. The TTPs are usually referred to as Certificate Authorities (CAs), and various bodies such as banks and the Post Office are likely to fulfil the role of CA. That message is called a certificate. In reality, as asymmetric encryption is rather slow, it is often only a sample of the message that is encrypted and used as the representative digital signature.

> **Certificate and certificate authorities (CAs)**
> A certificate is a valid copy of a public key of an individual or organisation together with identification information. It is issued by a trusted third party (TTP) or certificate authority (CA). CAs make public keys available and also issue private keys.

Sample certificate information could include:

- user identification data;
- issuing authority identification and digital signature;
- user's public key;
- expiry date of this certificate;
- class of certificate;
- digital identification code of this certificate.

It is proposed that different classes of certificates would exist according to the type of information contained. For example:

1 Name, e-mail address.
2 Driver's licence, national insurance number, date of birth.
3 Credit check.
4 Organisation-specific security clearance data.

It is apparent that for e-commerce to continue to grow and thrive, there is a critical requirement for the management of the vast number of public keys. This management involves procedures and protocols necesssary throughout the lifetime of a key – generation, dissemination, revocation and change – together with the administrative functions of time/date stamping and archiving. The successful establishment of a CA is an immense challenge of trust building and complex management. There are two opposing views on how that challenge should be met.

- *Decentralised*: market driven, creating brand-name based 'islands of trust' such as the Consumers Association. There is a practical need for a local physical office to present certificates of attestional value such as passports and drivers' licences. Banks and the Post Office have a huge advantage here.

■ *Centralised*: in the UK, the Department of Trade and Industry (DTI) has proposed a hierarchial tree ultimately leading to the government.

Secure Electronic Transaction

Secure Electronic Transaction (SET)
A standard for public-key encryption intended to enable secure e-commerce transactions, lead-developed by Mastercard and Visa.

This significant security protocol based on digital certificates has been developed by a consortium led by Mastercard and Visa, and allows parties to a transaction to confirm each other's identity. By employing digital certificates, SET allows a purchaser to confirm that the merchant is legitimate and conversely allows the merchant to verify that the credit card is being used by its owner. It also requires that each purchase request includes a digital signature, further identifying the cardholder to the retailer. The digital signature and the merchant's digital certificate provide a certain level of trust. Further technical details on SET are provided in Mini case study 11.4.

Mini case study 11.4   **What is SET and how does it work?**

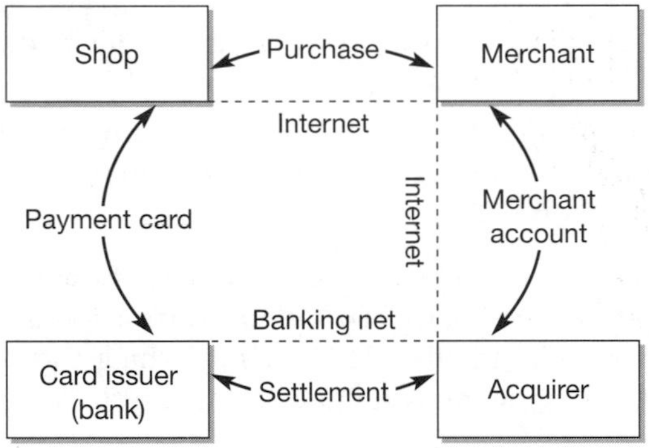

Fig. 11.9 SET payment mechanism via an intermediary between bank and merchant

SET is a standard for public-key encryption intended to enable e-commerce transactions that are more secure than those based on SSL. It was lead-developed by Mastercard and Visa, and has numerous other backers such as Microsoft.

SET is important because it offers protection from repudiation and unauthorised payments. A weakness is the rigidity of its rules – this is not a problem with standard forms completed by end-consumers but SET is possibly unable to cope with the *ad hoc* nature of many business-to-business transactions. The mechanism for SET is shown in Fig. 11.9. SET works as follows for a transaction between a customer and a merchant:

1 The customer selects items at a merchant's. Payment card details are entered to purchase items on an order form that is sent to the merchant.

> ▶ **Mini case study** *continued*

2 Payment information is forwarded from the merchant to the acquirer.

3 The acquirer decodes the customer's payment information and asks the card issuer for authorisation.

4 When the card issuer accepts the request for authorisation (this happens in real time in a process similar to that which occurs at a shop today), the acquirer sends the information back to the merchant, who then confirms the purchase to the customer.

5 The purchase price is then deducted as normal from the customer's account.

Even though the transaction process is complex it remains invisible to both the cardholder and the shop. A shopping transaction via the Internet can be completed in less than a minute.

Note that the acquirer is an intermediary who liaises between the bank and the merchant to remove the need for the merchant to have the infrastructure to link directly to the bank.

Source: DBS (Danish Payment Systems) (*www.setutility.com/facts/index.htm*).

From the consumer's viewpoint there are four stages necessary for the first transaction:

1 Obtain digital wallet or plug-in to communicate with merchant via SET.

2 Obtain digital certificates from CA.

3 Select item(s).

4 Authorisation and settlement process, involving transfer of digital certificates and authorisation, occurs automatically.

For future transactions, after the first, only stages 3 and 4 are necessary, but stages 1 and 2 are not straightforward for most Internet users.

For further information on SET see:

- Mastercard (*www.mastercard.com/set*) redirecting to *www.mastercard.com/shoponline /set/*
- Visa (*www.visa.com/set*) redirecting to *www.visa.com/nt/ecomm/security/set.html*
- (*www.setutility.com*), a tool for smaller merchants by which they can use the SET scheme without requiring the infrastructure to link directly to bank.

Although trials using SET have been running in the USA and Europe for several years, and there are a number of merchants offering the service in Scandinavia, there is still no firm evidence that the standard will be widely adopted. This is partly due to the practical difficulties of issuing certificates, but also because there is no great imperative for SET from consumers or retailers. Promotion by Microsoft, as part of the MS Wallet concept which is part of the Internet Explorer browser, may help acceptance. With the backing of the credit card issuers it can be expected to succeed in the long term once countries have well-established public-key infrastructures.

Firewalls

A firewall, like a firebreak in the forestry context, creates a break across which a threat cannot cross. Similarly, in computer networks a firewall creates a barrier between a local company network and the untrusted external network (the Internet). It is a system that allows access to the secure network only to users with specific characteristics. It thus not only performs a technical function but also forces the organisation to develop an access policy and provides a single 'check point' where access can be examined and audited. For very sensitive information (confidential, classified etc.) hardened firewalls isolate the secure network further by concentrating all security on to a stripped-down and well-tested computer. Maximum security, as is required at top secret military installations, is achieved by complete physical isolation from any external network. Firewalls are mainly used to prevent access by hackers who seek to obtain information about customers, such as credit card details.

Tools for implementing e-commerce

This section is intended as a brief practical guide that highlights the main issues involved in selecting tools to implement e-commerce. The constraints for implementing e-commerce are similar to those for creating an informational web site, but the constraints imposed according to the type, volume and cost of products to be sold by the site make the choice more complex. Assuming that there is no site initially, the main components that are needed for a functional e-commerce site are:

(a) Informational (background information on credibility of company details of its products).
(b) Catalogue of products and product selection mechanism.
(c) Payment and funds transfer/merchant mechanism.

Other functions of a web site such as customer service are not essential for an e-commerce web site and, although highly desirable, are not considered here.

For each of the components (a) to (c) two basic options have to be considered:

1. Where is the component located? Is it internal – within company – or external – with an ISP or other third party?
2. How is the component acquired/built? Namely, is it bespoke or tailor-made or is it a standard off-the-shelf product? With many packaged and consequently cheaper options available, there has to be a special business need to justify a bespoke solution. Financial services, or products that are difficult to offer in standardised form, might be examples of a specialist need. The off-the-shelf (OTS) packaged solution may be available online with creation/update through a web browser (e.g. IBM Home Page creator or iShop, which is seen in Fig. 11.10), or services may require the installation of separate software. An important consideration is the extent to which off-the-shelf options can be tailored. Specialist systems integrators will often be required for this.

There are many further constraints on e-commerce that will influence the purchase decision. These are considered in the next section.

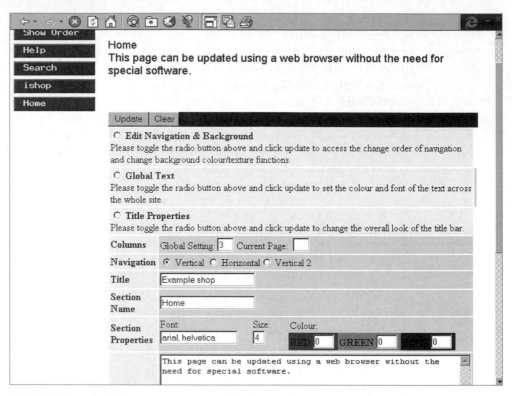

Fig. 11.10 Example of iShop e-commerce service for creating an e-commerce catalogue online

Constraints on selecting an e-commerce solution

1 Cost

For OTS software hosted in-house there will be a one-off purchase cost, plus the cost of maintenance or bug fixing updates. For outsourced solutions there will usually be several components to the cost. Questions to ask are:

(a) Is there a software purchase fee? What will upgrade costs be?

(b) What is the start-up/registration fee where no software purchase is involved?

(c) What is the cost per transaction? For example Secure Trading (*www.securetrading. com*) charges 5p per transaction regardless of size. Many others charge a variable percentage per transaction, for example 4–10 per cent dependent on volume of trade. This is usually negotiable.

(d) Is there a minimum monthly or yearly fee where there are few transactions?

2 Quality of service

Many of the following issues should be covered in the service level agreement offered by the ISP or merchant:

(a) *Performance of service.* What is the throughput in transactions per minute that can be supported? What is the average or maximum delay to authenticate a transaction?

(b) *Downtime* (measured against 100 per cent availability)

(c) *Security*. Are messages encrypted on a secure server? Are a range of security options available to suit customer preference? Is SSL used? Is SET possible? Can digital certificates be used (*see* earlier section on security)?

(d) *Cards supported*. Are all the major cards, and the less common cards such as Diner's Club, supported?

(e) *Currencies supported*. For example, is the euro supported? Are currency conversions up to date?

(f) How long does it take to set up an account? Registration and authorisation can take up to several months

3. Transaction method

This important choice of how the transaction is physically enacted can be broken down into the method by which the order is registered with the vendor and then how funds are transferred from the purchaser to the vendor. The choices are:

(a) *Traditional (phone/fax/mail)*. No e-commerce merchant software required – just a catalogue with product numbers and phone/fax numbers. This is not true e-commerce.

(b) *E-mail*. Internet Trading Systems available from Floyd SASSPay (*www.floyd.co.uk*) offers a simple e-mail solution. The orders placed on the web site are converted to an e-mail that is sent to the product vendor. This is then processed manually, as for any mail-order purchase.

(c) *Online transaction*. Here the order on the web site is seamlessly converted to an order on the sales order processing system within the company, and transfer of funds may also occur automatically. Does funds transfer occur via an integrated merchant server that transfers funds between a customer and supplier account?

Well-known merchant services or 'Payment Services Providers' include:

- Netbanx (*www.netbanx.com*);
- World Pay (*www.worldpay.com*);
- Secure Trading (*www.securetrading.com*).

4 Number of products required

Many of the OTS solutions are for smaller numbers of products in catalogues (*see* Volume of sales).

5 Volume of sales

This will affect the performance of the server required, the cost of per-transaction services and the suitability of the software. Examples are:

- Shopcreator Stall supports up to 10 products (*www.shopcreator.net*);
- IBM Home page creator (*see mypage-products.ihost.com/uk/en_US/*) supports 15–500 items;
- BT StoreFront – an online solution (*www.storecentre.bt.com*) – supports a small to medium number of products.

Higher-volume products for less than £1000 are:

- Shopcreator Store (*www.shopcreator.net*);
- Actinic Catalog (*www.actinic.com*);
- iShop (*www.ishop.co.uk*);
- Shop-assistant (*www.floyd.co.uk*).

Higher-cost products are:

- iCat commerce Publisher (*www.icat.co.uk*);
- Lotus Domino Merchant Server (*www.lotus.com*);
- Microsoft Site Server Commerce (*www.microsoft.com*);
- Actinic Supermall (*www.supermall.com*);
- Intershop Merchant (*www.intershop.co.uk*).

6 Cost of product

Low-cost products may require micropayments since the cost of processing a credit card may exceed the value of the product. A small-payment system for delivering relatively low-cost documents, images, software programs or music over the Internet is Pay2see (*www.pay2see.com*).

7 Configurability

Can the catalogue software be tailored to be consistent with the corporate style/look and feel of the remainder of a web site? Can HTML be tailored? Are Javascript or plug-ins possible?

8 Personalisation facilities

Must the e-commerce system recognise previous orders from customers and make recommendations according to their selections? If so, integration with a personalisation database will be required. This can add dramatically to the cost of a web site. Chapter 10 reviewed personalisation facilities such as Broadvision and Netperception GroupLens.

9 Integration with back-end systems

Requirements may include:

(a) Integration with stock control systems to determine availability is vital.
(b) Integration with stock control systems will allow price and product information changes to be updated rapidly. Is dual pricing (Internet and another channel), or pricing for different customers/countries supported?
(c) Integration with adequate fulfilment services, for example courier services that deliver product, is important for swift deliveries. Integration with the deliverer's tracking systems provides improved customer service.
(d) Integration with e-mail to confirm order to customer.

Fig. 11.11 Software Warehouse (*www.warehouse.co.uk*) shopping basket

Browser interfaces for catalogue and payment software

For ease of use, the software described in the previous section uses the familiar real-world store analogies of shopping baskets, carts and trolleys and checkouts. E-commerce catalogue software must be able to implement the electronic equivalent of these. Figure 11.11 illustrates the browser interface for an electronic shopping basket. This enables several products to be purchased with different numbers of each item. The purchaser can add items to the basket when browsing through the catalogue by clicking on an 'add to basket' option. After a shopper has put into the basket everything that he or she wants, he or she then proceeds to the *secure check-out* and arranges for payment, typically by entering a credit card number and address details.

Consumer and business markets for e-commerce

This section briefly contrasts and provides background information on the electronic commerce context for these two markets, which are covered in more detail in Chapters 13 and 14.

Business-to-business markets

Business-to-business e-commerce is more developed than consumer e-commerce. This phenomenon has been observed in all the major e-commerce markets such as the USA, Scandinavia and the UK. There are two good reasons for this:

1 *Familiarity with the technologies* and availability of in-house IT expertise dating from the days of EDI and EFT in the 1970s. The Internet reduces the costs of setting up, and removing, a network connection capable of supporting secure point-to-point connection. Thus this facility is made more applicable to a wider market.
2 *Account selling.* Supplier–customer relationships are often long term in nature and more relationship based that those in the consumer market. The nature of the relationship reduces risk in business-to-business e-commerce and makes participants less wary. Account transactions are usually repeat orders of high value and thus warrant the required capital investment.

In 1998 International Data Corporation (IDC) (*www.idcresearch.com*) predicted that the total value of goods and services purchased via the World Wide Web would surpass $10 billion, with business-to-business transactions accounting for two-thirds of that. BIS Strategic Decisions (*www.strategyanalytics.com*) has estimated that the amount of merchandise purchased electronically (including EDI and proprietary order entry) is 100 times greater than that purchased by the online consumer.

Consumer markets

The consumer market is less developed and more wary than the business market, owing to a relative lack of experience, skill and capital. However, it is growing rapidly. Forrester Research (*www.forester.com*) and Cowles/Simba found consumer spending online to be $1 billion in 1996, but Forrester forecast that it would grow to $6.9 billion by 2000. The *Which? Online* survey by MORI in 1998 found that 14 per cent of the UK population are using the Internet. Durlacher (1999) found that 30 per cent of residential Internet users had bought online: 13 per cent had bought software, 9 per cent books/magazines, 8 per cent computer hardware and 2 per cent clothes.

Drivers needed for further growth are:

▪ acceptable Internet access mechanisms;
▪ payment mechanisms perceived as convenient and secure;
▪ an attractive and usable media interface.

In order for Internet penetration to grow beyond its current bias towards higher-income professionals, the means of access must broaden from the usual mode of home and work PCs. Members of the public who would not be inclined to purchase a home PC other than as a machine for games such as Nintendo will be exposed to the Internet 'by stealth' through more consumer entertainment products such as interactive digital television and Web phones. The *Sunday Times* reported (1 December 1998) that:

'1998 saw the first commercial availability of web phones. All the major mobile phone companies are launching products that will enable people to browse the web using their mobile phone. Considering that, worldwide, only one in 10 000 people has access to a

PC and one in four has access to a telephone, the significance of this development is clear. In addition set-top boxes that provide access to the Internet from a standard TV and the rapid uptake of digital TV itself means that large numbers of non-PC owners will gain access to the Internet. The natural medium for a satellite-based web is the television, not the PC, and there are plenty of signs that television companies are beginning to understand this. If they can come up with devices that give you conventional television and a homogenised Web alongside it, they will start to pull in viewers, most of whom have never owned a home PC.'

In addition to the need for a non-threatening or simply socially appropriate mechanism of Internet access, such as digital television, another very important driver of consumer participation in e-commerce is the provision of an attractive and family-orientated interface. Services are now being offered that provide a range of information, entertainment, news and communication services tailored to the needs and preferences of the average family. One of the earlier services in the UK was LineOne, now joined by similar competitors such as Ukmax and those related to free ISPs such as Freeserve. Figure 11.12 gives an example of how such services attempt to make e-commerce more accessible.

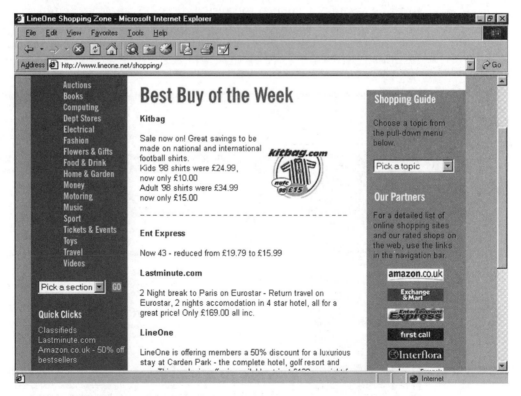

Fig. 11.12 LineOne (*www.lineone.net*) shopping options

The commercial environment for e-commerce

In this section we look at the influences on the marketing decisions of an organisation by considering the context in which those decisions are made. The environment in which an organisation operates includes economic and competitive conditions that are outside the marketing manager's control. As these factors have a critical bearing on the outcome of marketing decisions an ongoing assessment of the organisation's environment is vital. For an organisation developing an e-commerce capability the two most important areas of external influence are the economic infrastructure of a country, in terms of support by banks for the electronic payment systems mentioned in previous sections, and the legal framework within which the company operates. Some of the main issues raised by the legal framework are briefly reviewed in the final section of this chapter.

Legal status of banks

The Internet provides the opportunity for new virtual banks such as the US bank First Virtual and the European bank, first-e (*www.first-e.com*) (*see* Fig. 11.13), which must be carefully regulated to safeguard the income of potential customers. In the USA the Office of the Comptroller of Currency (OCC), the Office of Thrift Supervision (OTS) and the Federal Deposit Insurance Corporation (FDIC) have responsibility for the issues they will expect banks and savings institutions to

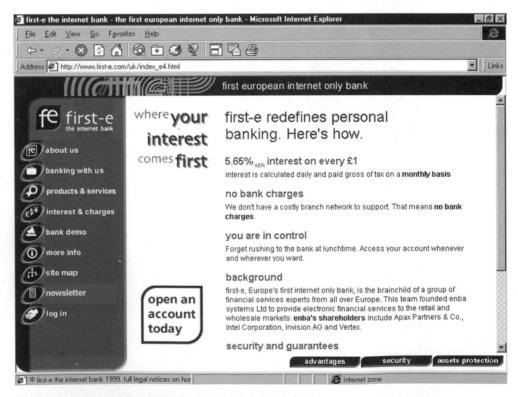

Fig. 11.13 The European virtual bank, first-e (*www.first-e.com*)

address before commencing operation of, or participation in, a company operating a stored-value system (*see www.fdic.gov/elecbank.pdf*).

The issues most frequently raised in relation to the issuance of electronic money by virtual banks that are not correctly registered are.

- Non-banks are subject to less scrutiny and regulation and thus more likely to create money that can be counterfeited (and that money is impossible to tell from the real thing, unlike real cash).
- Non-banks are at a competitive advantage as they do not carry the costs of the high level of regulation to which banks are subject.
- Because non-banks do not report to a central bank there is uncertainty, and consequently instability is created in the money supply.

Alan Greenspan, Chairman of the US Federal Reserve, has voiced his concern, saying:

'We could envisage proposals in the near future for issuers of electronic payment obligations, such as stored-value cards or digital cash, to set up specialised issuing corporations with strong balance sheets and public credit rating. Such structures have been common in other areas, for example in the derivative and commercial paper markets.'

This contrasts with the view of the Bundesbank Director, Edgar Meister, who said that in Germany the issuing of e-cash should be restricted to commercial banks and that it has major implications for monetary stability and control. The prospect of non-bank institutions 'printing' electronic money, compounded by the possibility of forgery of digital money, has obvious inflationary potential. This is a subject receiving ongoing attention from central banks, but it is not an urgent issue as the quantity of e-cash in their economies is a minute proportion of the total money supply. In the interim, voluntary reporting codes such as those that pertain to the issuance of travellers cheques are regarded as sufficient.

Tariffs and taxation

As the Internet is a truly global medium it could be argued that it makes little sense to introduce tariffs on goods and services delivered over the Internet. Such instruments would, in any case, be impossible to apply to products delivered electronically. This position is currently that of the USA. In the document 'A Framework for Global Electronic Commerce', President Clinton stated that: *'The United States will advocate in the World Trade Organisation (WTO) and other appropriate international fora that the Internet be declared a tariff-free zone.'*

Taxation

Tax jurisdiction determines which country is responsible for taxing income from a transaction. Under the current system of international tax treaties, the right to tax is divided between the country where the enterprise that receives the income is resident ('residence' country) and that from where the enterprise derives that income ('source' country).

Laws on taxation are evolving rapidly, and vary dramatically between countries. A proposed EU Directive intends to deal with these issues by defining the place of establishment of a merchant who actually pursues an economic activity from a fixed physical location. At the time of writing the general principle being applied is that tax rules are similar to those applying to a conventional mail-order sale. For the UK, the tax principles are as follows:

1 If the supplier (residence) and the customer (source) are both in the UK, VAT will be chargeable.
2 Exports to private customers in the EU will attract either UK VAT or local VAT.
3 Exports outside the EU will be zero-rated (but tax may be levied on import).
4 Imports into the UK from the EU or beyond will attract local VAT, or UK import tax when received through customs.
5 Services attract VAT according to where the supplier is located. This treatment is different from that which applies to products, and causes anomalies if online services are created. For example, a betting service located in Gibraltar allows UK customers to gamble at a lower tax rate than is applied to the same company in the UK.

The current tax laws, coupled with the ability to run a business in a country remote from its customers, are having a dramatic impact in some industries, particularly those where a service can be delivered across the Internet. Large UK bookmakers such as William Hill and Victor Chandler are offering Internet-based betting systems from 'offshore' locations such as Gibraltar. The lower duties in these countries offer the companies the opportunity to make betting significantly cheaper than if they were operating under a higher tax regime. Meanwhile the government will face a drop in its revenue from this source. This trend has been dubbed LOCI or Location Optimised Commerce on the Internet by Mougayer (1998).

Future taxation

'The United States believes that no new taxes should be imposed on Internet commerce' (President Clinton, 'A Framework for Global Electronic Commerce').

Given growth predictions, governments will at some point in the future be unable to ignore the revenue that would accrue from taxing e-commerce. This is already happening in the UK, with the government revising its betting duties to take account of revenues lost overseas. What form would such taxation take? One suggestion is a *bit tax*: that is, a tax rate (a minute fraction of a penny) on each bit of traffic transmitted. However, this approach is not a taxation on value – only on quantity. To be fair, the basic principle of taxing income or consumption should still apply. However, the issues of extraterritoriality and privacy greatly complicate the implementation of such measures. With a mail-order purchase, the product is physically shipped somewhere. If the product is downloaded over the Internet how does the merchant know where the buyer is located? Additionally, with e-cash, it is an anonymous transaction with third party intervention – an 'underground economy'. As the Information Society Project Office of the European Commission put it, *'how will governments be able to continue to raise funds in an increasingly information-based world in which value is generated through systems and global networks, rather than through clearly identifiable material production and exchange?'*

Contracts

The development of rules of contract law and evidence of the validity of commercial contracts are important elements in determining the validity of electronic commerce. *See www.abanet.org/buslaw/cyber* and *www.state.ma.us/itd/legal*.

The United Nations Commission on International Trade Law has completed work on a model law that supports the commercial use of international contracts in electronic commerce. An EU Directive on the protection of consumers in respect of distance contracts (that is, those without the simultaneous physical presence of both the supplier and the consumer) requires suppliers to provide customers, in a clear and comprehensible manner (perhaps on a sub-page of the web site), with the following information prior to the conclusion of any distance contract:

- the location and identity of the supplier and, in the case of contracts requiring payment in advance, his address;
- the main characteristics of the goods or services;
- the price of goods or services, including all taxes;
- delivery costs, where appropriate;
- the arrangements for payment, delivery or performance;
- the existence of a right of withdrawal;
- the cost of using the means of distance communication, where it is calculated other than at the basic rate;
- the period for which the offer or price remains valid;
- where appropriate, the minimum duration of the contract and whether the contracts for the supply of products or services are to be permanent or recurrent.

After the contract has been entered into, the supplier is required to provide written confirmation of the information provided. It remains to be seen whether e-mail confirmation will be sufficient.

Binding contracts

Until recently, digital signatures within an e-mail did not have a status in UK law. The draft UK law will accord digital signatures and associated contracts the same legal status as those signed conventionally. The EU Commission has also set out a draft Directive on electronic signatures relating to electronic contract formation and as to when such a contract is entered into.

Trade issues

Each month Cisco's web site receives about 150 000 order enquiries. How should it be classified for customs purpose? Is it eligible for NAFTA (the North American Free Trade Association)? What export control measures apply? Cisco gives customers the tools to find all this information on its web site. The company's primary domestic and international freight forwarders regularly update Cisco's database electronically with the status of each shipment, typically via EDI.

As a summary to this section, *see* Mini case study 11.5 on Which? Web Trader, a new initiative that aims to protect the rights of the consumer and improve the standard of customer service on the Internet. It highlights the many legal and ethical issues that e-commerce traders need to consider.

Mini case study 11.5

Which? Web Trader – Code of practice for web traders

The Web trader code of practice is intended to improve standards of service on the Internet and protect the rights of the consumer. This case study summarises the elements of the code to which companies must adhere if they have signed up to the code. Companies that have signed up include BarclaySquare, The CountryBookstore, EasyJet, Go and Comet.

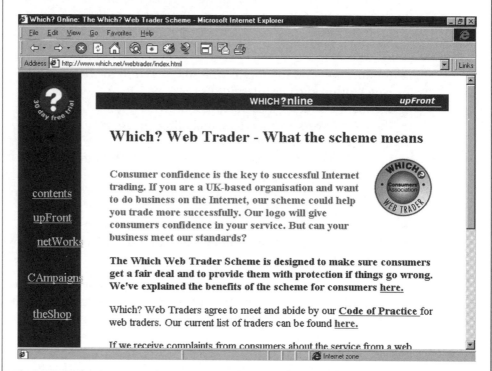

Fig. 11.14 Which? Web Trader code of practice (*www.which.net/webtrader*)

1 *Prices*. The price of all goods and services must be clear and easily found. There should be no hidden extras, such as taxes, packaging or delivery. Before agreeing the contract, the actual price the consumer must pay should be confirmed.
2 *Ways of paying*. The consumer should be informed of all the different ways of paying and clearly told how to pay.
3 *Delivery*. Delivery times should be agreed. If delivery within the agreed time is not possible, the consumer should be told immediately and another time for delivery arranged.
4 *Security*. The site must be secure for sending personal information.
5 *Advertising*. All advertising must meet the conditions of the Advertising Standards Authority code (*www.asa.org.uk*). Advertising material from organisations should be clearly identified.
6 *Promotions*. Any promotion you do must meet the conditions of the Sales Promotion Code (*www.asa.org.uk*).

7 *Consumer law*. Obligations under current consumer protection laws must be met including:
- the Sale of Goods Act 1979;
- the Supply of Goods and Services Act 1982;
- the Consumer Credit Act 1974;
- the Trade Descriptions Act 1968;
- the Unfair Contract Terms Act 1977 and the 1994 Regulations; and
- the Consumer Protection Act 1987.

8 *Company details*. Companies must provide on the website full contact details including your phone and fax numbers, an address for correspondence and your e-mail address, together with your company's registered name and address, company registration number and VAT number.

9 *Contracts*. You must set out the terms and conditions of your contracts clearly and in plain English. They must be easily found on the site. You must say that contracts do not affect the consumers' statutory rights.

10 *Refunds*. You must provide the option of a full refund, within a reasonable time, if the goods turn out to be faulty or different from those the consumer ordered. All refunds to be given as soon as possible, and at the latest within 30 days of agreeing to give the refund.

11 *Guarantees*. You must make it clear if you are providing a guarantee. If you are, you must make clear what is covered, for how long and that the guarantee does not affect the buyers' statutory rights. You must also say if an insurance company is backing the guarantee. If it is, you must give the name and address of the insurer and you must provide the policy.

12 *Receipts, bills and settlement mistakes*. You must provide a receipt with the goods. You must correct any mistakes in bills, receipts or payments as soon as possible.

13 *Legal advice and help*. Subscribers to Which? Online who have problems after buying online from a trader in the scheme will be entitled to free legal advice and help from Which? Legal Service. You must cooperate with Which? Legal Service to solve the problem.

14 *Handling complaints*. A system for handling complaints must be in place which is fair; confidential; effective; easy to use and well-publicised; speedy; informative; simple to understand and use; and checked to make sure that it is working well and getting better.

15 *Solving disputes*. Details of any procedure for solving disputes must be provided.

16 *Data protection and privacy*. Companies must meet the conditions of the Data Protection Act 1984. Companies must say if they will send the consumer marketing material, or pass the consumer's details to others. Consumers must be given the option to refuse marketing material.

17 *Customer support and service*. A customer service phone number must be available and cost of the calls and times stated.

18 *Customer feedback*. You must agree to invite Which? Online customers to post comments about their experience of using your service on Which? Online forum discussions. We will invite you to comment on relevant discussions.

Source: Which? Web Trader (*www.which.net/webtrader*).

SUMMARY

1 Electronic commerce covers a range of activities, from those associated with online buying and selling in the 'electronic marketspace' to online transactions, the narrower definition that is used in this chapter.

2 E-commerce transactions are an extension of electronic data interchange (EDI), which has been conducted for many years between larger companies and their suppliers. The Internet offers a lower-cost, more flexible approach that will extend the use of electronic purchasing to many more companies and individuals.

3 Key drivers for e-commerce amongst business and consumer purchasers are the availability of increased choice, lower costs and improved customer service.

4 For the business operating an e-commerce site, the benefits include lower costs, improved reach and the opportunity for disintermediation.

5 Enablers for e-commerce include the rapid adoption of the Internet and World Wide Web standards and the availability of off-the-shelf products for creating an e-commerce facility.

6 Electronic payment systems for consumers are divided into:
- pre-paid systems such as CyberCash, which require some form of digital token to be purchased before it is exchanged for a product;
- post-paid, credit systems such as electronic cheques and credit cards (the predominant mechanism for consumer purchases).

7 Standard payment systems for business-to-business transactions are under development since they are more complex, involving multiple orders, participation of different staff in the buying organisation and the need for integration with payment authorities (banks).

8 Security is a major barrier to e-commerce, and there are a number of initiatives under way to improve it:
- Credit card purchases are usually encrypted during transit using the SSL standards.
- More secure methods such as SET are based on digital certificates and digital signatures, which are used to identify purchasers and merchants.
- Firewalls are used to prevent unauthorised access to customer details residing on the merchant's secure server.

9 A 'public-key infrastructure' or method of issuing digital certificates is necessary for improvements in security, but this is embryonic. Banks, the Post Office and government agencies are possible as likely certificate authorities.

10 Tools for implementing e-commerce are reducing in cost as more off-the-shelf products become available. Some services such as IBM HomePage creator can be used online without the need for specialist software in-company.

EXERCISES AND QUESTIONS

Self-assessment excercises

1 Define 'e-commerce'.

2 What were the precursors of e-commerce? What distinguishes them from current e-commerce?

3 List the principal drivers and inhibitors for the growth of e-commerce.

4 Explain the importance of digital certificates to e-commerce. Explain what a Certification Authority is and why the Post Office is well placed to become one.

5 Which parties need to be able to exchange information in a business-to-business payment system such as Open Buying on the Internet?

6 What are the main payment systems for business-to-consumer e-commerce?

7 Create a time-line to show the evolution of payment systems from the days of bartering to the present, showing the increasing speed, globalisation and abstract nature of currency.

8 How does a firewall improve the security of e-commerce transactions?

Discussion questions

1 'The medium is the market.' Discuss in the context of the Web and e-commerce.

2 Discuss the prejudices and assumptions that exist about payment systems. Are credit card purchases more secure over the telephone than over the Internet?

3 The global and open nature of e-commerce creates a proactive approach to purchasing, where customers shop around for the best price. Do brands have any place in this environment?

4 A multinational company retails its products around the world. It has launched a transactional web site that now accounts for a significant proportion of its sales. On the web site, each product has a single global price (automatically recalculated to different currencies). However, the retail price in the high street varies from country to country. This is widely reported in the local press and is understandably creating resentment amongst those unable to purchase the cheaper way. Discuss these issues.

5 'E-commerce is providing a welcome boost to national economies, particularly the US economy. However, the Internet is inherently transnational and without a central management structure. It thus presents regulatory and taxation challenges for national governments.' Discuss.

Essay questions

1 You are responsible for building an e-commerce site for a company with an existing mail-order catalogue containing over 3000 products. You have been asked to prepare a briefing document for potential suppliers detailing the company's requirements from an e-commerce system. The document should refer to practical issues such as usability, security, cost and delivery time-scale.

2 Compare and contrast security for electronic and paper-based transactions. Particularly examine security aspects such as authentication, non-repudiation, auditability and integrity.

3 Many alternative electronic payment methods are touted, such as digital cash, electronic cheques, micropayments, smartcards and credit cards. Explain the different alternatives available in plain language in a report for your manager that reviews the main options available and recommends those that the company should support.

4 How should retailers attempt to overcome the fear of e-commerce amongst consumers?

Examination questions

1 The products most often purchased over the Internet are personal computers, books, travel, information, flowers, clothes and financial products. Suggest reasons for this.

2 What is a 'trusted third party', and how does the concept relate to the public-key infrastructure?

3 Draw a diagram explaining the information that needs to be exchanged between different parties when a business-to-business e-commerce purchase occurs.

4 Explain the concept and need for a 'public-key infrastructure'.

5 'Micropayments' are a totally new transaction mechanism. Explain the concept and how e-commerce technology enables this type of payment.

6 What is a digital signature? Why does it offer a more secure method of purchasing than encrypting credit card details in transit using SSL?

7 Some commentators predict e-commerce will revolutionise shopping and business purchasing. Others play down its impact and maintain that it will never seriously compete with the tactile, social world of conventional shopping. There are product areas where e-commerce has made serious inroads into traditional methods of customer information gathering, trial and transaction. Choose two examples and briefly describe the reasons for success.

8 Name three inhibitors to consumer e-commerce that will need to be reduced for further growth in this sector.

REFERENCES

Durlacher Quarterly Internet Survey Q2 (1999) (*www.durlacher.co.uk*)

Hoffman, D.L. and Novak, T.P. (1997) 'A new marketing paradigm for electronic commence', *The Information Society*, Special issue on electronic commerce, (13 January–March), 43–54.

Kalakota, R. and Whinston, A. (1997) *Electronic Commerce*: *A manager's guide*. New York: John Wiley and Sons.

Kosuir, D. (1997) *Understanding Electronic Commerce*. Seattle: Microsoft Press.

Kurztman, J. (1993) 'The death of money', *Harvard Business Review*, 15(16).

McLuhan, M. (1964) *Understanding Media*. New York: McGraw Hill.

Mougayer, W. (1998) *Opening Digital Markets – Battle plans and strategies for Internet commerce* (2nd edn). New York: Commerce Net Press (McGraw Hill).

Strom, D. (1997) 'The challenge of selling lemonade has never been this tough', excerpt from Decision Resources Information report (*www.strom.com/pubwork/e-commerce.html*).

US Congress, Office of Technology Assessment (1994) *Electronic Enterprises*: *Looking to the future*. Washington DC: US Government Printing Office.

Which report (1998) 'Controversy, conspiracy or control: are we ready for the e-nation? (*www.mori.co.uk/polls/1998/which/htm0*).

Zwass, V. (1998) 'Structure and macro-level impacts of electronic commerce: from technological infrastructure to electronic marketplaces', In Kendall, E. (ed.) *Emerging Information Technologies*. Thousand Oaks, CA: Sage Publications.

FURTHER READING

E-commerce

Kalakota, R. and Whinston, A. (1997) *Electronic Commerce: A manager's guide*. New York: John Wiley and Sons.
This book, despite the title, gives fairly technical coverage of techniques for securing e-commerce. It has good descriptions of encryption and public key cryptography.

Kosuir, D. (1997) *Understanding Electronic Commerce*. Seattle: Microsoft Press.
This book gives a more accessible description of e-commerce techniques.

Turban, E., Lee, J. King, D. and Chung, H. (2000) *Electronic Commerce: A managerial perspective*. Upper Saddle River, NJ: Prentice Hall.
A comprehensive test on the infrastructure of the Internet and its use for electronic commerce transactions.

Economics

Kelly, K. (1999) *New Rules for the New Economy*.

Schwartz, E.I. (1998) *Webonomics*. Harmondsworth, UK: Penguin.

Tapscott, D. (1995) *The Digital Economy: Promise and peril in the age of networked intelligence*. New York: McGraw-Hill.

Tapscott, D., Lowy, A. and Ticoll, D. (eds) (assoc. ed Natalie Klym) (1998) *Blueprint for the Digital Economy. Creating wealth in the era of e-business*. New York: McGraw-Hill.

WEB SITE REFERENCES

The section Types of payment systems has links to companies offering different e-commerce security solutions. The section Constraints on selecting an e-commerce solution gives links to companies providing e-commerce solutions.

Bloch, M., Pigneur, Y. and Segey, A., 'On the road of electronic commerce – a business value framework, gaining competitive advantage and some research issues' (*www.hec.unil.ch/mbloch/docs/roadtoec/ec.htm*).

A Business Researcher's Interests (*www.brint.com/ecommerce*) has many articles on e-commerce strategy.

Brint Institute, 'Electronic commerce & electronic markets' (*www.brint.com/elecomm.htm*).

Commercenet, 'Commercenet @ work' (*www.commmerce.net/about/*).

Davis, R., 'Electronic Money, or E-Money, and Digital Cash' (*www.exeter.ac.uk/~RDavies/arian/emoney.html*).
A comprehensive page of links to resources on e-money is maintained by Roy Davies at Exeter University.

Edward, G., 'The road to high volume electronic commerce: "take my transactions . . . please!"' (*policyworks.gov/org/main/m...ov/information/accessing/omb1.htm*).

'The emerging digital economy report' (*www.ecommmerce.gov/viewhtml.htm*).

Ferraro, A., 'Electronic commerce: the issues and challenges to creating trust and a positive image in consumer sales on the world wide web' (*www.firstmonday.dk/issues/issue3_6/ferraro/index.html*).

Financial Times, 'Middle men deleted as word spreads' (*www3.org/disintermediation.htm*).

Garcai-Sierra, A., 'Electronic commerce and the Internet' (*www.cf.ac.uk/uwcc/masts/ecic/netcom.html*).

Greenspun, P., *Philip and Alex's guide to web publishing*, Chapter 14: E-commerce (*photo.net/wtr/thebook/e-commerce.html*).

Greguras, F.M., 'An introduction to hot issues in electronic commerce' (*www.oikoumene.com/echotissues.html*).

'The gringo who stole e-commerce: a false sense of insecurity' (*www.connectingonline.com/articles/980105c.html*).

'Growth in e-commerce and EDI' (*www.uniforum.org/web/pubs/uninews/961104/inews2.html*).

Hage, C. (of C. Hage associates), 'Scenario 2: business on the Internet' (*www.cf.ac.uk/uwcc/matss/ecic/scenari2.html*)

Hoffman, D.L., Novak, T.P. and Chatterjee, P. 'Commercial scenarios for the web: opportunities and challenges' (*shum.huji.ac.il/jcmc/vol1/issue3/hoffman.html*).

How Stuff Works (*www.howstuffworks.com/ecommerce.htm*) has a basic introduction to e-commerce.

IBM, 'Electronic commerce – Internet business opportunities with ibm net.commerce' (*www.Internet.ibm.com/commercepoint/net.commerce*).

IBM, 'Point and click, buy and sell' (*www.ibm.com/e-business/commerce/*).

Jensen, M., 'Here there be tigers: profit, nonprofit, and loss in the age of disintermediation' (abstract) (*www.sfu.ca/scom/jensen.html*).

Konsynski, B., 'Centre for electronic commerce' (*www.emory.edu/business/welcome.html*).

Lundquist, E., 'Quit dissin' the web's middlemen' (*www8.zdnet.com.pcweek/opinion/0714/14last.html*).

McCann, J.M., Disintermediation sites (*www.duke.edu/~mccann/disinter.htm*).

Merkow, M., 'E-commerce watch' (*www.webreference.com/e-commerce/mm/*).

Merkow, M., 'Smartcards for smarter e-commerce' (*webreference.com/e-commerce/mm/ column10/index.html*).

Miers, D. and Hutton, G. (of Enix Consulting) 'Electronic commerce – the strategic challenges of electronic commerce' (*www.enix.co.uk.electron.htm*).

Net 101, 'Net 101 – 20 reasons to put your business on the world wide web' (*www.net101.com/reasons.html*).

Newsedge Corporation, 'Electronic transaction technology' (*www.newspage.com/browse/46537/46540/2945*).

Pery, C.T., 'Disintermediation' (*webopedia.Internet.com/term/d/disintermediation.html*);

(*150.108.63.4/ec/organization/disinter/disinter.htm*).

'Twenty questions about e-commerce' (*www.cnet.com/content/builder/business/e-commerce20/*).

US Federal Electronics Commerce Program Office (*www.ec.fed.gov/*)

Web Counsel, 'Beyond email, legal website based disintermediation by web counsel' (*www.webcounsel.com/disintrm.htm*).

Willmott, D., 'Disintermediation: the buzz word from hell' (*www.zdnet.com/pcmag/insites/willmott/dw970910.htm*).

CHAPTER 12

Maintaining the web site and measuring Internet marketing effectiveness

Learning objectives

After reading this chapter, the reader should be able to:

- identify the tasks necessary when managing a web site;
- understand terms used to measure site effectiveness;
- develop an appropriate process to collect measures of site effectiveness.

Links to other chapters

This chapter should be read in conjunction with these chapters:

▶ Chapter 4 outlines some of the Internet-based resources for marketing resource secondary data.

▶ Chapters 5 and 6 describe the development of an Internet marketing strategy and Internet marketing plan respectively. The aim of measurement is to quantify whether the objectives of these plans have been achieved.

▶ Chapter 8 describes how to set up a web site, and should be read before this chapter to introduce the reader to concepts of web site development.

▶ Chapter 9 describes methods of promoting a web site. It should be read before this chapter since the techniques of measuring a web site's effectiveness are aimed at assessing how well the different promotional methods are working.

INTRODUCTION

In the mid-1990s, a common sight when one viewed web sites was an 'under construction' logo showing a person digging a hole. Such logos are seen less frequently nowadays, since it has been realised that effective web sites are always under construction. The need for frequent updating does not necessarily indicate a poor site: it was shown in Chapter 8 that high-quality content was one of the key factors people gave for returning to web sites, with frequent update another important factor. This chapter outlines a suitable process for the updating of a web site, answering questions such as:

- How often does a web site need to be updated?
- What is a suitable process for managing maintenance of the site?
- Who is responsible for updating?

- What needs to be tested?
- How do we measure site effectiveness?

Measuring the effectiveness of the site is considered in some detail since a key part of managing the site is to see how popular the different areas of the site are, and then to adjust the content of the site if some areas are unpopular. Measuring effectiveness goes beyond this to ask whether the site is helping to achieve the strategic goals of the company. To answer these questions two main techniques are used. First, measures of the popularity of different parts of the site are collected online on the web server using specialist log file analyser software; second, measures that reflect the marketing impact of the site are collected. These measures include new enquiries, sales, savings that are made directly as a result of the site, and also the impact of the site on perceptions of the company and its products and services. To assess these marketing outcomes a process must be put in place to record these figures, such as when enquiries or orders are placed by different methods such as phone, fax or e-mail. Alternatively, surveys such as questionnaires or focus groups can be used, and these can be conducted offline or online.

The maintenance process

For effective control of a web site, it is important to have a clearly defined process for making changes to the content of the web site. This process should be understood by all staff working on the site, with their responsibilities clearly identified in their job descriptions. The main stages involved in producing a web page are to design it, write it, test it and publish it. A more detailed process is set out here, which distinguishes between review of the content and technical testing of the completed web page. A simple model of the work involved in maintenance is shown in Fig. 12.1. It is assumed that the needs of the users and design features of

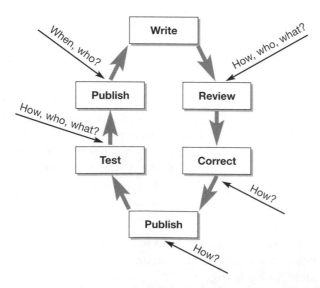

Fig. 12.1 A web document review and update process, with questions

the site have already been defined when the site was originally created, as described in Chapter 8. The model only applies to minor updates to copy, or perhaps updating product or company information. The different tasks involved in the maintenance process are as follows:

1 *Write*. This stage involves writing the marketing copy and, if necessary, designing the layout of copy and associated images.
2 *Review*. An independent review of the copy is necessary to check for errors before a document is published. Depending on the size of organisation, review may be necessary by one person or several people covering different aspects of site quality such as corporate image, marketing copy, branding and legality.
3 *Correct*. This stage is straightforward, and involves updates necessary as a result of stage 2.
4 *Publish (to test environment)*. The publication stage involves putting the corrected copy on a web page that can be checked further. This will be in a test environment that can only be viewed from inside a company.
5 *Test*. Before the completed web page is made available over the World Wide Web a final test will be required for technical issues such as whether the page loads successfully on different browsers.
6 *Publish (to live environment)*. Once the material has been reviewed and tested and is signed off as satisfactory it will be published to the main web site and will be accessible by customers.

How often should material be updated?

Web site content needs to be up to date, in line with customer expectations. The Web is perceived as a dynamic medium, and customers are likely to expect new information to be posted to a site straight away. If material is inaccurate or 'stale' then the customer may not return to the site.

After a time, the information on a web page naturally becomes outdated and will need to be updated or replaced. It is important to have a mechanism defining what triggers this update process and leads to the cycle of Fig. 12.1. The need for material to be updated has several facets. For the information on the site to be accurate it clearly needs to be up to date. Trigger procedures should be developed such that when price changes or product specifications are updated in promotional leaflets or catalogues, these changes are also reflected on the web site. Without procedures of this type, it is easy for there to be errors on the web site. This may sound obvious, but the reality is that the people contributing the updates to the site will have many other tasks to complete, and the web site could be a low priority.

A further reason for updating the site is to encourage repeat visits. For example, a customer could be encouraged to return to a business-to-business site if there is some industry news on the site. Such information needs to be updated at least weekly, and possibly daily, to encourage the customer to return. Again, a person has to be in place to collate such news and update the site frequently. The facility of being able to update prices regularly should be taken advantage of where possible. Some companies such as RS Components have monthly promotions, which may encourage repeat visits to the site. It is useful to emphasise to the customer that the information is updated frequently. This is possible through simple devices such as putting the date on the home page, or perhaps just the month and year for a site that is updated less frequently.

As part of defining a web site update process, and standards, a company may want to issue guidelines that suggest how often content is updated. This may specify that content is updated as follows:

- within two days of a factual error being identified;
- a new 'news' item is added at least once a month;
- when product information has been static for two months.

Responsibilities in web site maintenance

Maintenance is easy in a small company with a single person updating the web site. That person is able to ensure that the style of the whole site remains consistent. For a slightly larger site with perhaps two people involved, the problem more than doubles since communication is required to keep things consistent. For a large organisation with many different departments and offices in different countries, site maintenance becomes very difficult, and production of a quality site is only possible when there is strong control to establish a team who all follow the same standards. Sterne (1999) suggests that the essence of successful maintenance is to have clearly identified responsibilities for different aspects of updating the web site. The questions to ask are:

- Who owns the process?
- Who owns the content?
- Who owns the format?
- Who owns the technology?

We will now consider these in more detail, reviewing the standards required to produce a good quality web site and the different types of responsibilities involved.

Who owns the process?

One of the first areas to be defined should be the overall process for updating the site. But who agrees this process? For the large company it will be necessary to bring together all the interested parties such as those within the marketing department and the site developers – who may be an external agency or the IT department. Within these groupings there may be many people with an interest such as the marketing manager, the person with responsibility for Internet or new media marketing, a communications manager who places above-the-line advertising, and product managers who manage the promotion of individual products and services. All of these people should have an input in deciding on the process for updating the web site. This is not simply a matter of updating the web site; there are more fundamental issues to consider, such as how communications to the customer are made consistent between the different media. Some companies such as Orange (*www.orange.net*) and Ford (*www.ford.co.uk*) manage this process well, and the content of the web site is always consistent with other media campaigns in newspapers and on television. In Ford this has been achieved by breaking down the barriers between traditional media account managers and the Internet development team, and both groups work closely together. In other organisations, a structure is adopted in which there is a person or group responsible for customer communications, and they then ensure that the message conveyed by different functions such as the web site developers and the advertisement placers is consistent. Options for structuring an organisation to integrate new and old media are given in Parsons *et al.* (1996).

What, then, is this process? The process will basically specify responsibilities for different aspects of site management and detail the sequence in which tasks occur for updating the site. A typical update process is outlined in Fig. 12.1. If we take a specific example we can illustrate the need for a well-defined process. Imagine that a large organisation is launching a new product, promotional literature is to be distributed to customers, the media are already available, and the company wants to add information about this product to the web site. A recently recruited graduate is charged with putting the information on the site. How will this process actually occur? The following process stages need to occur:

1 Graduate reviews promotional literature and rewrites copy on a wordprocessor and modifies graphical elements as appropriate for the web site. This is the *write* stage in Fig. 12.1.
2 Product and/or marketing manager reviews the revised web-based copy. This is part of the *review* stage in Fig. 12.1.
3 Corporate communications manager reviews the copy for suitability. This is also part of the *review* stage in Fig. 12.1.
4 Legal adviser reviews copy. This is also part of the *review* stage in Fig. 12.1.
5 Copy revised and corrected and then re-reviewed as necessary. This is the *correct* stage in Fig. 12.1.
6 Copy converted to web and then published. This will be performed by a technical person such as a site developer, who will insert a new menu option to help users navigate to the new product. This person will add the HTML formatting and then upload the file using FTP to the test web site. This is the first *publish* stage in Fig. 12.1.
7 The new copy on the site will be reviewed by the graduate for accuracy, and needs to be tested on different web browsers and screen resolutions if it uses a graphical design different from the standard site template. This type of technical testing will need to be carried out by the webmaster. The new version could also be reviewed on the site by the communications manager or legal adviser at this point. This is part of the *test* stage in Fig. 12.1.
8 Once all interested parties agree the new copy is suitable, the pages on the test web site can be transferred to the live web site and are then available for customers to view. This the second *publish* stage in Fig. 12.1.

Note that, in this scenario, review of the copy at stages 2 to 4 happens before the copy is actually put on to the test site at stage 6. This is efficient in that it saves the technical person or webmaster having to update the page until the copy is agreed. An alternative would be for the graduate to write the copy at stage 1 and then the webmaster publishes the material before it is reviewed by the various parties. Each approach is equally valid.

It is apparent that this process is quite involved, so the process needs to be clearly understood within the company or otherwise web pages may be published that do not conform to the look and feel for the site, have not been checked for legal compliance, or may not work. The only way such a process can be detailed is if it is written down and its importance communicated to all the participants. It will also help if technology facilitates the process. In particular a workflow system should be set up that enables each of the reviewers to comment on the copy as soon as possible and authorise it. Tools such as Lotus Notes and the web management tools mentioned in Chapter 8 can help achieve this. The copy can be automatically e-mailed to all reviewers and then the comments received by e-mail can be collated.

The detailed standards for performing a site update will vary according to the extent of the update. For correcting a spelling mistake, for example, not so many people will need to review the change! A site re-design that involves changing the look and feel of the site will require the full range of people to be involved.

Once the process has been established, the marketing department, as the owners of the web site, will insist that the process is followed for every change that is made to the web site.

Who owns the content?

For a medium to large site where the content is updated regularly, as it should be, it will soon become impossible for one person to be able to update all the content. It is logical and practical to distribute the responsibility for owning and developing different sections of the site to the people in an organisation who have the best skills and knowledge to develop that content. For example, for a large financial services company, the part of the business responsible for a certain product area should update the copy referring to their products. One person will update copy for each of savings accounts, mortgages, travel insurance, health insurance and investments. For a PC supplier, different content developers will be required for the product information, financing, delivery information and customer service facilities. Once the ownership of content is distributed throughout an organisation, it becomes crucial to develop guidelines and standards that help ensure that the site has a coherent 'feel' and appearance. The nature of these guidelines is described in the sections that follow.

> **Content developer**
> A person responsible for updating web pages within part of an organisation.

Who owns the format?

The format refers to different aspects of the design and layout of the site commonly referred to as its 'look and feel'. The key aim is consistency of format across the whole web site. For a large corporate site, with different staff working on different parts of the site, there is a risk that the different areas of the site will not be consistent. Defining a clear format for the site means that the quality of the site and customer experience will be better since:

■ *the site will be easier to use* – a customer who has become familiar with using one area of the site will be able to confidently use another part of the site;

- *the design elements of the site will be similar* – a user will feel more at home with the site if different parts look similar;
- *the corporate image/branding will be consistent with real-world branding* (if this is an objective) and similar across the entire site.

To achieve a site of this quality it is necessary for written standards to be developed. These may include different standards such as those shown in Table 12.1. The standards adopted will vary according to the size of the web site and a company. Typically larger sites, with more individual content developers, will require more detailed standards.

Table 12.1 Web site standards

Standard	Details	Applies to
Site structure	Will specify the main areas of the site, for example products, customer service, press releases, how to place content and who is responsible for each area.	Content developers
Navigation	May specify, for instance, that the main menu must always be on the left of the screen with nested (sub-) menus at the foot of the screen. The home button should be accessible from every screen at the top left corner of the screen. See Lynch and Horton (1999) for guidelines on navigation and site design.	Web site designer/webmaster usually achieve these through site templates
Copy style	General guidelines, for example reminding those writing copy that web copy needs to be more brief than its paper equivalent. Where detail is required, perhaps with product specifications, it should be broken up into chunks that are digestible on-screen.	Individual content developers
Testing standards	Check site functions for: ■ different browser types and versions ■ plug-ins ■ invalid links ■ speed of download of graphics ■ spellcheck each page See Chapter 9 for details.	Web site designer/webmaster
Corporate branding and graphic design	Specifies the appearance of company logos and the colours and typefaces used to convey the brand message.	Web site designer/webmaster
Process	The sequence of events for publishing a new web page or updating an existing page. Who is responsible for reviewing and updating?	All
Performance	Availability and download speed figures.	

Note that it will be much easier to apply these quality standards across the site if the degree of scope for individual content developers to make changes to graphics or navigation is limited and they concentrate on changing text copy. To help achieve consistency, the software used to build the web site should allow templates to be designed that specify the menu structure and graphical design of the site. The content developers are then simply adding text and graphical based pages to specific documents and do not have to worry about the site design.

Who owns the technology?

The technology used to publish the web site is important if a company is to utilise fully the power of the Internet. This may not be evident when a simple brochure-ware site is produced, as this may require just an HTML editor. It becomes more significant when a company wants to make its product catalogue available for queries or to take orders online. As these facilities are added the web site changes from an isolated system to one that must be integrated with other technologies such as the customer database, stock control and sales order processing systems. Given this integration with corporate IS, the IT department (or the company to which IT has been outsourced) will need to be involved in the development of the site and its strategy.

A further technology issue to be addressed is providing an infrastructure which allows the content developers throughout the company to update copy from their own desktop computer. For example, companies that have standardised on Lotus Notes can use this so that individual content developers can readily contribute their copy and the process of checking can be part-automated, using workflow facilities, to send messages to testers and reviewers who can then authorise or reject the content. Some of the more sophisticated editing and publishing environments for maintaining a web site were described towards the end of Chapter 8.

As well as issues of integrating systems, there are detailed technical issues for which the technical staff in the company need to be made responsible. These include:

- availability and performance of web site server (*see* Chapter 8) ;
- checking HTML for validity and correcting broken links;
- managing different versions of web pages in the test and live environments.

Measuring Internet marketing effectiveness

Measurement is one of the most important activities that occur once a web site is published. As explained in Chapter 5, analysing the effectiveness of a site is crucial in assessing the strategy and then revising it to overcome problems. Given this, we will examine how we can measure the effectiveness of the Internet channel in some detail.

Measurement for assessing the effectiveness of Internet marketing can be thought of as answering three questions:

1 Are corporate objectives identified in the Internet marketing strategy being met (Chapter 5)?

2 Are marketing objectives defined in the Internet marketing strategy and plan achieved (Chapter 6)?

3 Are marketing communications objectives identified in the Internet marketing plan achieved? How effective are the different promotional techniques used to attract visitors to a site (described in Chapter 9)?

The measures can also be related to the different levels of marketing control specified by Kotler (1997). These include strategic control (question 1), profitability control (question 1), annual-plan control (question 2) and efficiency control (question 3).

We will describe measurement by reviewing measures collected online and offline separately. This is a natural division since offline measures tend to be traditional measures of marketing effectiveness such as the number of sales achieved, while online measures involve some novel technical methods such as analysing a web log file. Measures are often referred to as metrics to indicate a scientific approach to collecting and analysing data, but the two words are really synonymous. Often an individual *metric* records particular events that happen when customers use the web site such as which pages they visit or if they send an e-mail or place an order.

> **Internet marketing metrics**
> Measures that indicate the effectiveness of Internet marketing activities in meeting customer, business and marketing objectives.

The person creating a measurement programme will undertake three main activities: first, identifying how the overall measurement process will work; second, identifying the main measures; and third, designing techniques by which to capture the data to record the measures.

Although we have stated that measurement is an important part of maintaining a web site, it is worth noting that the reality is that measurement is often neglected when a web site is first created. This is natural since, when designing the first version of a site, the designers are concerned with issues such as what content to put on the site, how it will be laid out, and how users can navigate between the different pages. With many immediate issues such as these to be settled it is understandable that measurement is often not considered. Measurement will often become an issue once the first version of a site has been 'up and running' for a few months and people start to ask questions such as, 'How many customers are visiting our site, how many sales are we achieving as a result of our site and how can we improve the site?' The consequence of this is that measurement is something that is added after the first versions of a web site have been created. Fortunately, it is possible to do this, but it is probably easier and site performance information can be obtained earlier if measurement is built into site management from the start.

Creating a measurement process

A significant part of specifying the measurement process is highlighting the need for measurement of the web site's performance and then developing a measurement culture within the organisation. Measurement is part of a control process specified by Kotler (1997) that involves asking the questions: *What do we want to achieve? What is happening? Why is it happening? What should we do about it?* These questions correspond to the stages of goal setting, performance measurement, performance diagnosis and corrective action.

Measurement is not something that can occur on an *ad hoc* basis because if it is left to the individual some may forget to collect the data needed. A 'measurement culture' is one in which each employee is aware of the need to collect data on how well the company is performing and on how well it is meeting its customer's needs. Only by answering these questions and taking appropriate action can a company hope to be competitive. Fortunately, establishing such a culture may be straightforward in large companies, many of which will have undergone business process reengineering programmes that involve the development of metrics schemes such as the balanced scorecard (Kaplan and Norton, 1993).

Introducing measurement for a web site will typically involve the following stages:

1 Highlighting the need for metrics

This involves convincing the management team of the need for metrics since collecting metrics will add to the cost of maintaining a web site. Metrics can be justified in terms of the improved knowledge they provide about how well the site is performing and in terms of facilitating the process of making adjustments to the site to improve customer performance.

2 Identifying metrics

Relevant online and offline techniques such as those described in the following sections are identified. When identifying metrics it is useful to apply the widely used SMART mnemonic (*see*, for example, Obolensky, 1994). SMART metrics must be:

- **S**pecific;
- **M**easurable;
- **A**ctionable;
- **R**elevant;
- **T**imely.

Using SMART metrics avoids the following types of problem:

(a) Developing metrics for which accurate or complete data cannot be collected.
(b) Developing metrics that measure the right thing, but cause people to act in a way contrary to the best interests of the business to simply 'make their numbers'.
(c) Developing so many metrics that excessive overhead and red tape are created. Friedman and Furey (1999) contend that minimising the number of metrics to the key factors is important.
(d) Developing metrics that are complex and difficult to explain to others.

3 Introducing techniques to collect metrics and summarise results

Once the information needed has been determined, techniques must be devised to collect this information. These techniques will involve analysing information collected on the web server and measuring events that occur such as customers sending an e-mail or placing an order online. Since a great volume of data may be collected and it would be time consuming to review the detail, methods must also be devised to summarise the data and highlight the main trends.

4 Reviewing the metrics

A regular, structured method of reviewing metrics is required to evaluate performance.

5 Acting on the results

Many companies collect metrics, but unless the metrics are reviewed and the results acted on, collecting the data is a futile activity!

In the following sections we will concentrate mainly on deciding on the type of metrics required and how to collect them.

Which measures to use?

To measure the effectiveness of Internet marketing, a useful starting-point for deciding on the type of measures to use is to consider how they affect the business as a whole. The three measurement questions stated at the start of the section give us three levels of measures of increasing detail. We will now review these three levels of measures. Note that data for each of the measures described below may be collected directly online using the web site itself, or separate efforts must be taken offline to collect the data on which to base the measure. Online and offline methods of collection are described in subsequent sections.

Level 1: Business effectiveness measures

Business effectiveness measures assess how the Internet is affecting the performance of the whole business: in other words, what is the impact of the Internet on the business? Friedman and Furey (1999) say that: '*The use of performance metrics to bring channel activity in line with specific corporate goals is the cornerstone of effective channel management.*' Such measures are standard financial measures that are used to assess the health of a business, such as revenue and profitability. Here, however, we are looking at the contribution of the Internet to these measures. The concept of contribution was introduced in Chapter 5, and it was explained that there are different types of contribution, such as the amount of revenue achieved directly online, and the amount of revenue indirectly achieved online (due to the Internet influencing buying decisions). In summary these financial measures are:

- Direct online contribution to revenue (in percentage terms and absolute monetary amounts). It was shown in Chapter 5 that a company that is successful in exploiting the Internet such as Cisco has an online contribution of 64 per cent, equating to online revenues of over $6 billion each year.
- Indirect direct online contribution to revenue (in percentage terms and absolute monetary amounts).
- Profitability of web site (the direct revenue of the web site minus the operational cost of the web site – *see* Mini case study 12.1 for an assessment of the current status of web sites in general).
- Return on investment (ROI). This is a measurement over a longer period that calculates the return (amount of revenue) compared with initial investment and operational costs.
- Operational cost reductions. Cisco estimate that their web site has saved the business over 20 per cent of its operational costs, as compared with not having a site. These reductions are achieved through the need for fewer staff and lower materials costs.

Web site profitability

An Activmedia report of 30 June 1999 shows that ActivMedia estimates that 45.2 per cent of web sites now operate at a profit, with 19.3 per cent expecting to be profitable within 12 months. A further 9.1 per cent expect to be in the black within two years, and 5 per cent within five years. However, 20.6 per cent of sites do not expect ever to operate at a profit, according to the report.

In contrast, 52 per cent of speciality goods sites are currently profitable, as reported earlier this year by ActivMedia. Further, just 5.6 per cent of these sites do not expect to operate at a profit in the future.

Meanwhile, a focus group of 25 e-businesses by analyst Primary Knowledge, reported by Nua Surveys (*www.nua.ie*) on 26 July 1999, showed that while the majority recognised the need to implement effective ROI measurement strategies, most have not progressed beyond the planning stage. The survey found that, at present, e-businesses are relying on 'home-grown' measurement solutions and small-scale surveys, which do not accurately analyse or portray the overall consumer base. The report showed that these businesses are anxious to put ROI technology in place, to track all customer contact via the Internet, and to track the sources of the most profitable customers. Other measurement aims were not mentioned as important. These include the need to ascertain which customers present the greatest retention risk, to track where customers are lost in the transaction process, and the need to have adequately trained staff and sufficiently high-level technology.

As well as assessing financial measures, business effectiveness measures should assess whether the specific corporate objectives for the web site defined in the strategic plan have been achieved. These might include improving corporate awareness, or (for a services company) recruiting new staff of a better quality at a lower cost.

Level 2: Marketing effectiveness measures

Marketing effectiveness measures will reflect how well the web site is fulfilling the needs of the marketing manager. These will be more traditional marketing measures that describe a company's success in acquiring and retaining customers and making sales such as:

■ customer acquisition or new leads generated by the web site;
■ sales generated directly and indirectly by the web site;
■ impact on market penetration and demand (*see* Activity 12.1);
■ customer satisfaction and retention rates of clients who use the Internet, compared with those who do not;
■ incremental or cross-sales achieved through the Internet;
■ impact of Internet on customer satisfaction, loyalty and brand.

Internet sales will be expressed as:

■ Internet sales as a proportion of all sales made by company compared with sales by all companies operating in market (the Internet contribution);
■ Internet sales as a proportion of all Internet sales for company (the Internet market penetration).

Internet market penetration will be affected by previous representation in a country. This issue is evident from Activity 12.1.

Exploring market penetration in different geographical markets

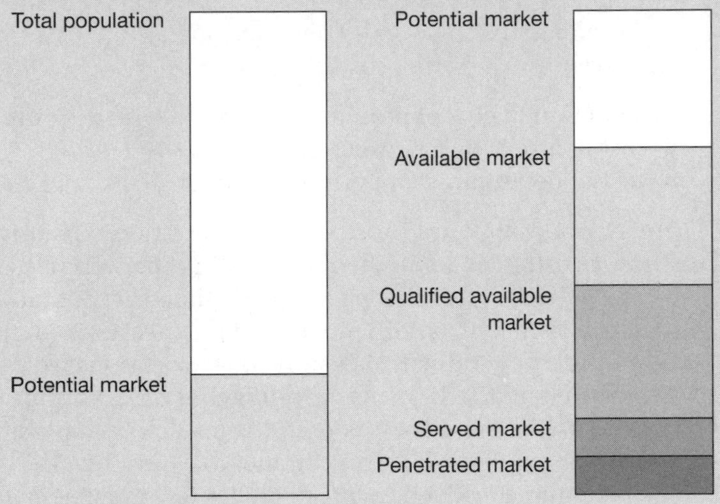

Total population

Potential market

Potential market

Available market

Qualified available market

Served market

Penetrated market

Fig. 12.2 The relationship between different types of demand

Explain the impact, on the following sectors of a geographic market, of customers gaining Internet access to a company web site:

1 The potential market.
2 The available market.
3 The qualified available market.
4 The served market.
5 The penetrated market.

You should consider two different geographic markets:

(a) One where there has been no previous geographic representation, e.g. sales offices, limited media campaigns; and
(b) One where there has been previous representation, e.g. sales office, distributors, promotional activities.

Use a standard marketing text such as Kotler (1997) to remind yourself of the terms. Thumbnail descriptions of the market terms are:

- *potential market* – the group of customers who express interest in a product;
- *available market* – potential customers who have income and access (i.e. Internet access) to information on products;
- *qualified available market* – available customers who are suitable for the product or service;
- *served market* – the part of the qualified available market that the company decides to operate in;
- *penetrated market* – customers who have purchased from the company.

As well as being interested in measures related to marketing outcomes, the marketing manager will also wish to know how the web site is helping to reduce costs. Cost reductions are unlikely to be monitored continuously, unlike the other measures described in this section. They are more likely to be measured by a one-off calculation, perhaps on a monthly or yearly basis. Methods of assessing cost reduction are covered in an earlier section of the chapter. These cost savings are distinct from reductions in overall company operating costs, which are part of business effectiveness. Marketing costs that could be measured include:

- reduction in cost of promotional material (lower printing costs);
- cost of acquiring a new customer;
- cost of developing/supporting an existing customer relationship through time.

The costs of supporting customers can be reduced mainly through salary reduction since if customers serve themselves using the web rather than phoning an operator, fewer employees will be required. Note that we have said these costs *could* be measured since it is difficult to obtain measures of some of these items if we cannot identify individual customers – for reasons we will see later in the chapter. Unfortunately the basic web site logging tools cannot easily identify individual customers. This is why it is useful to use more sophisticated techniques such as cookies or registration via an extranet to assess this.

Marketing effectiveness also includes less tangible benefits, beneficial elements, such as:

- corporate image and brand enhancement (see Chapter 6) through online PR;
- building long-term client relationships and reducing 'churn' of customers.

Level 3: Internet marketing effectiveness

Measures of Internet marketing effectiveness involve assessing how well the particular online techniques required for effective Internet marketing are working. These were introduced in Chapter 2.

- *Capture* – how effective are we in attracting customers to a site using online and offline promotion methods? Does the site use banner advertisements, offline advertisements with specific URLs? Does it use search engine meta-tags? How well do these work?
- *Content* – how well are customers supported with information and ease of use through the content and design of the site? Is the online proposition clear? (What are the unique offers/value of the site?) The speed and availability of the site, discussed in Chapter 8, will be covered in this area.
- *Customer orientation* – does the content suit its target audience: that is, in job-specific, industry-specific, or country-specific terms? Is it easy for a particular audience to find information? Is it relevant, accurate, up to date? How well are clients supported at different stages of the buying decision? What incentives are there for clients to return to the site at each stage?
- *Community and interactivity* – how well are the customer's needs as an individual met by providing community facilities and establishing an interactive dialogue?

Berthon *et al.* (1998) have described, in detail, a framework for defining the success of a web site whose aim is to sell products in terms of drawing the customer through different stages of the buying decision. This was discussed with reference to attracting customers to the web site in Chapter 2 (*see* Fig. 2.5). The main measures that can be defined are:

- *awareness efficiency* – target web-users/all web-users;
- *locatability/attractability efficiency* – number of individual visits/number of seekers;
- *contact efficiency* – number of active visitors/number of visits;
- *conversion efficiency* – number of purchases/number of active visits;
- *retention efficiency* – number of repurchases/number of purchases.

Online measurement methods

To paraphrase and update a well-known quote, 'I know that half my web site is making money . . . but I'm not sure which half'. Online metrics enable marketers to build a picture of which parts of their web sites are working well, and which are not.

Online web metrics are those that are collected automatically by software installed on the web server. When enabled, this web server software records a piece of information downloaded from a web site when someone visits a page, by writing a line of text in a server log file. For more details on the information contained in log files refer to Mini case study 12.2.

> **Online web metric and server log files**
> Online measures are those that are collected automatically on the web server, often in a server log file.

Lines in the web server log file measure what are colloquially referred to as 'hits'. These 'hits' describe the behaviour of different users visiting the site and show, for instance, their path through the site and which sites they previously visited. Some information is also provided on their characteristics, such as their country of residence and which browser they are using. The challenge for marketers is to take the vast amount of information stored in the server web file and convert it into useful marketing information. The intention of this section is to highlight which information is of value and which is less useful.

Note that the term 'hits' is quite widely used to indicate how successful a site is, but in fact it is misleading, and the term 'page impressions' should be used in preference. A hit is recorded for every piece of information downloaded from a web page, and this includes graphics containing company logos, graphics defining menu options and blocks of text. When one customer views the home page of a site, therefore, several hits could be recorded. The useful measure for the marketer is 'page impression' since this refers to one customer viewing one page.

> **Hits and page impressions (views)**
> A hit is recorded for each graphic or block of text requested from a web server. It is not a reliable measure of the number of people viewing a page. A page impression is a reliable measure, denoting one person viewing one page.

When a customer visits a site, he or she may simply visit the home page, or may browse through the site, visiting many pages. For the marketer not interested in this distinction, a more useful measure may simply be the number of people visiting the site each day or each month. These are known as site visits. Activity 12.2 'Measurement terms' will prompt you to think about the value of different terms used in a server log file.

Site visits (user sessions)
One site visit records one customer visiting the site.

Independent auditing of the popularity of a site is possible. This is particularly important for advertising, and as was mentioned in Chapter 9 on web site promotion auditing bodies are available. These include:

- the international auditing body, BPA (*www.bpai.com*).
- Audit Bureau of Circulation, ABC (*www.abc.org.uk*).
- Internet Advertising Bureau, IAB (*www.iab.org*).

Mini case study 12.2

Making sense of server log files

This case study considers in more detail the information contained in a web server log file. Each line in the log file corresponds to a single request made by a web browser to the web server. An example line in a common log format (CLF) is:

marketing-online.co.uk - - [05/Oct/1999:00:00:49 -000] "GET /index.html HTTP/1.0" 200 33362

The line above is broken into seven fields:

(1–3) The first three fields are the machine name of the computer making the request (marketing-online.co.uk) and the login details for accessing an extranet site (marked by two '-' symbols for most web sites which do not require a login).

(4) [Date]. The date and time the request was made.

(5) "Request". The path to the information resource requested by the client. This field also includes the protocol requested by the browser. In the example above, the browser requested the main index.html page, using HTTP/1.0.

(6) Status. The HTTP status code of the request (200 in our example). The HTTP/1.1 specification contains a more detailed explanation of the meaning of the status codes.

(7) Bytes. The number of bytes in the document that was requested (33 362 in our example).

See World Wide Web consortium (*www.w3.org/Daemon/User/Config/Logging.html#common-logfile-format*) for further details.

A log file will contain information for every piece of information downloaded. For example, the next line in the logfile might be for a graphic logo from the same page:

marketing-online.co.uk – - [05/Oct/1999:00:00:49 -000] "GET /logo.gif HTTP/1.0" 200 54342

In addition to the fields provided by the CLF, web servers should be configured to include additional fields. These include the referrer (the URL of the referring

---

location that brought the user to the web site) and the user agent (the browser name, version and machine type). The World Wide Web consortium (*www.w3.org*) defines an Extended Log File Format that specifies how to log additional data. Some web servers log different pieces of information in separate files. For example, in addition to the standard access log file, errors are in a separate error log file, referrer information in a referrer log and browser information in the agent log.

Caching and undercounting

It should be noted that the log file will only contain details of when information is actually transferred over the Internet. Such a transfer may not occur when a user has visited a page previously and then wants to view it again. In this case the page will often have been cached or stored on the hard disk of the user's machine by the web browser so it can be retrieved rapidly at a later time. Since it is retrieved directly from the user's hard disk it will not be registered in the log file of the web server. This type of caching can also occur when a web page is stored on a proxy server within a company or with an ISP. Proxy servers are used in order to save time when retrieving pages commonly requested by users. For example, if several users in an organisation access the front-page of the *Electronic Telegraph* each day, only the first user to access it will be recorded as a page impression at the *Electronic Telegraph*. The other users will access it from the proxy server within the company.

Web site auditors
Auditors accurately measure the usage of a site as the number of page impressions and visitors.

While the number of site visits may be useful in gaining an appreciation of the number of people visiting a site, and how this varies through time, much more information can be gleaned from the log file if a suitable tool is available to analyse it. The following information is available that gives details on how the site is used:

1 *Page impressions for different parts of the site.* The log file indicates which parts of the site are most popular and which are not successful. By carefully analysing these figures the following may be apparent:
   - Web pages that are difficult to find using the site navigation facilities may not be popular: action – consider modifying navigation.
   - Unpopular pages may not have a suitable incentive or offer to encourage users to visit that part of the site.
2 *Page impressions broken down by different time intervals.* How page impressions vary through time can be shown using different time intervals such as hours during the day, days of the week or through a month or year. *See* Fig. 12.3. Short-term trends may indicate something about the behaviour of the users that can be turned to advantage for promotion. A company offering life insurance found that the peak time in the week for visits was Monday lunchtime. This was thought to be because people at work were comparing offers after reviewing offers in Sunday's newspapers. As a result it was decided to place advertisements on a search engine at this time on Monday lunchtime.

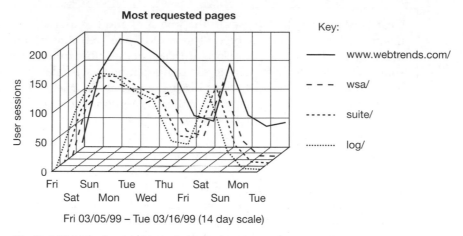

Most requested pages

Key:

——— www.webtrends.com/

– – – wsa/

······ suite/

·········· log/

Fri 03/05/99 – Tue 03/16/99 (14 day scale)

Fig. 12.3 WebTrends, showing variation in popular pages through a week

3 *Page impressions by domain.* The web analysis package may indicate a high level of interest in a company's products from a particular country in which the company does not currently have any distributor arrangements.

4 *Page impressions by browser type.* This information is of less value, but if it is found that many of a company's customers are still using older browsers, the designers of the company's site should test content on these browsers.

5 *Referring sites.* A knowledge of which sites are referring sites is useful when a company is considering a traffic-building campaign since it indicates how users are finding the company's site. Some may be using particular search engines, and sophisticated analysis tools can deduce which keywords were typed in to find the site. Knowledge of this can be used to target search engines for advertising or could suggest which keywords it is useful to include within copy or meta-tags (*see* Chapter 9).

6 *Exit pages.* It is difficult to interpret the meaning of this measure, but a knowledge of exit pages is potentially useful since a page with a high exit count may be successful because users have found the information they were looking for, or it may be a failure because users have become bored or frustrated and left the site. Figure 12.4 gives an example of the top exit pages for the WebTrends site.

7 *Document trails.* These summarise the most frequent routes through the sites. These results have implications for site design.

8 *Average length of visit.* This statistic is quoted quite widely, but it should be used with care since this value is difficult to evaluate. If a customer visits a particular site first thing in the morning and is then distracted, not visiting the site again until the afternoon, this would count as an 8-hour visit. So long as this limitation is understood, this metric is still of value in comparisons with other sites and in assessments of how this value varies through time.

Referring sites and exit pages

A log file may indicate which site a user visited immediately before before visiting a particular site. Exit pages give a summary of the main pages from which users left a site.

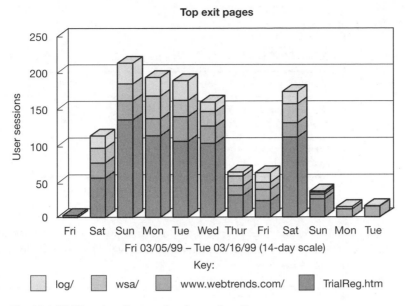

Fig. 12.4 WebTrends software, showing main exit pages

Activity 12.2

Measurement terms

1 Refer to the terms below, which define the level of usage of a site. For the measures marked with an asterisk, refer to Table 12.2, which shows some actual measures from a site. Explain the difference between the terms and how the numbers differ. For example, why is the number of hits greater than the number of site visits?

- Hits *
- Page impressions/views *
- Site visits/user sessions *
- Unique users *
- E-mails
- Registrations
- Online sales

Table 12.2 Summary web site metrics from WebTrends

Measure	Value
Number of hits for home page	8398
Number of successful hits for entire site	57 868
Number of page views (impressions)	24 437
Number of user sessions	2598
User sessions from United States	52.61%
International user sessions	20.51%
User sessions of unknown origin	26.86%
Average number of hits per day	4822
Average number of page views per day	2036

▶ **Activity** *continued*

Table 12.2 *Continued*

Measure	Value
Average number of user sessions per day	216
Average user session length	00:14:17
Number of unique users	2096
Number of users who visited once	1824
Number of users who visited more than once	272

Source: Based on WebTrends summary statistics (*www.webtrends.com*).

2 Visit the site of a supplier of a web site analysis tool and summarise the different facilities available. Which do you think would be valuable to a marketer and which could be disregarded?

The concept of site 'stickiness'

'Stickiness' is used to refer to the length of time a customer stays on a site. It is used as an additional measure to the more traditional measure of the number of visitors to the site.

The number of minutes on a site is difficult to determine by direct observation, since the time is measured between when a user first visits a site and when they leave to another site. If, however, they leave their desk or start word-processing they will still be counted as active on the site. As a result of this, this measure can only be thought of as an indication of how long users stay. Despite this, there maybe useful trends of increase or decrease in length of visit.

Tools for measuring web site performance

The majority of measurement tools are simply software that takes all the information contained in the server log file and summarises it using charts and tables. They differ in the sophistication of their analysis. A good tool will provide all the different breakdowns of page impressions mentioned in the previous section. Tools commonly used include:

■ WebTrends (*www.webtrends.com*).
■ Analog: a freeware tool (*www.statslab.cam.ac.uk/~sret1/analog/*).
■ WUsage (*www.boutell.com/wusage*).
■ Andromedia (*www.andromedia.com*). Makers of the Aria tool featured in Case study 12.1.
■ I/PRO site audit (*www.ipro.com*). Good examples are provided on this site.
■ Microsoft Site analyst for Microsoft Internet Information server (*www.microsoft.com*).
■ Superstats: a basic web analyser (*www.superstats.com*).
■ Hitbox (*www.hitbox.com*).
■ NetOutcome (*www.redeye.com*). This tool particularly focuses on finding out how a user behaves after clicking on a banner advertisement (discussed in Chapter 9).

All of these tools provide output that is accessible via a web browser, so reducing the need for large printed reports to be circulated.

CASE STUDY 1.1 **MEASURING PERFORMANCE AT THE CYBERIAN OUTPOST**

Fig. 12.5 The Cyberian Outpost (*www.outpost.com*)

With a half dozen antique shops in a three block radius, the sleepy little town of Kent, Connecticut, seems somewhat removed from the hustle and bustle of every-day American commerce. Scratch the surface a little deeper, however, and you'll find that at least one local business is different. Cyberian Outpost, Inc. (*www.outpost.com*) is a leading-edge Internet technology company serving up electronic commerce the way the Web promised.

Cyberian Outpost was founded in 1995 by its president, Darryl Peck, in a small warehouse with one other employee. The company is the world's first Internet-based computer retailer and is billed as "the cool place to shop for computer stuff," selling PC and Macintosh computer products, including hardware, software and peripherals, on line.

As with other Internet start-up companies, Cyberian Outpost has experienced explosive growth since it first introduced its Web site two and a half years ago. This fact is illustrated by Michael Starkenburg, Cyberian Outpost's chief technology officer, who says that traffic on the site has erupted in the time since he joined the company in August 1997.

► **Case study** *continued*

"Cyberian Outpost's philosophy is to be customer-centric, providing customers with competitively-priced products and unparalleled service," says Starkenburg. "These are the things that have helped us jump ahead in this market – something other Internet retailers are having trouble with."

When Starkenburg joined Cyberian Outpost, the Web site was receiving approximately 30,000 visitors per day – small potatoes in the Internet electronic commerce industry. Since then, however, traffic has grown so dramatically that Starkenburg will not even give the figures out for competitive reasons. "The exposure we've received from our partnerships with AOL, Excite, and CNet, among others, has helped us tremendously," he says.

However, this growth has created challenges to make the site as useful for shoppers as possible and for this, Starkenburg knew he'd need a top-notch Web site activity tracking solution.

"We'd been using Web Trends by e.g. Software, but as we experienced monumental growth, we needed a more sophisticated log analysis tool," says Starkenburg. "One issue is that traditional log file-based tools get really slow when there is a lot of data to crunch. Second, Cyberian Outpost had rapidly grown from one production server to more than ten, and Web Trends just wasn't able to combine all those logs without giving back incorrect calculations. Since we were growing the number of servers weekly, I knew we would quickly need to make a change."

Starkenburg opened up his search for the right product and looked at software from a number of companies. Ultimately, he chose Andromedia's ARIA, the industry's leading real-time Web site activity analysis software. Starkenburg went with ARIA for a number of reasons. "One of the products we looked at, Accrue, uses a flat data warehouse model, but it was similar to what we'd been using in that it pulls the hits in, puts them into a data warehouse, and then tries to count them, drastically slowing processing speeds," says Starkenburg. "This type of application also means that soon, you need massive amounts of disk space to store the data and keep it moving."

"Conversely, ARIA's object oriented architecture turns each hit into an incremental, real-time count, which is simply much faster," says Starkenburg. "Additionally, ARIA easily handles multiple servers. I am now getting one number that is consistent across my entire site – with just one hour's lag time. Before, I was only able to analyze my data once a week because it took so long."

Other features of ARIA that Starkenburg finds advantageous are scalability and customization. He states that ARIA will scale to meet Cyberian Outpost's growth in the years to come – sure to be phenomenal if the last two were any indication. As for customization, Starkenburg has big plans to further customize ARIA and use it to help track sales.

"It's all about selling more," says Starkenburg. "By using ARIA for product and content management, our company can immediately see what people are interested in and promote certain products accordingly. For instance, if ARIA tells us that lots of people are clicking on the digital camera we have on the home page, then we'll know that digital cameras are hot and we'll start merchandising more of them around the site. That's ARIA's trick – its simplicity."

In the future, Starkenburg plans to integrate ARIA into the bigger picture to help Cyberian Outpost calculate what shoppers actually purchased in relation to what they looked at. And that's the way the Internet promised electronic commerce would be.

Source: Andromedia (*www.andromedia.com*).

Questions

1 What is the proposition of the Cyberian Outpost?

2 What were the constraints imposed on the previous analysis tool?

3 How does the new tool help analyse marketing performance?

Measuring individual behaviour

None of the metrics described so far is able to identify the identity of the individual user, yet the ability to do so is often touted as one of the great benefits of the Internet! This inability is mainly a consequence of the design of the Internet – it was not designed with this marketing objective in mind. To be able to identify an individual, more effort is required by the owners of the web site.

Why should a company want to identify individuals? The business-to-business company with a high-value, low-sales-volume product would find it useful to identify the names of customers browsing sites looking at products. It would then be possible to phone them to arrange a sales visit. For a business-to-consumer company undertaking e-commerce such as a supermarket or a catalogue sales company it would be useful to identify a user who has purchased previously and then offer that user special promotional offers in line with his or her interest. It can be seen that this type of measurement is closely tied in with relationship marketing or one-to-one marketing and personalisation, which was introduced in Chapter 10.

Registration

The best way to identify an individual is to ask the individual to register at a site. This will normally require the user to type in his or her name and e-mail address and other relevant information such as product interests. To entice an individual to register is not easy. It requires:

■ a suitable incentive – most customers will only give information if they will receive something in return such as free information, a discount or entry to a competition;

■ a tacit agreement to enter into a medium to long-term arrangement with a customer so that he or she will enter the site again;

■ trust on the part of the customer, which will be based on his or her perception of a company's brand and credibility.

Registration works well for companies that can persuade customers to register. Electronics components reseller RS Components has persuaded over 100 000 customers to register, and it now requires them to enter a username and password to view product information on their site.

389

Once a customer has entered a site via a user name and password that customer's progress around the site can be monitored, and special content can be delivered as appropriate.

Cookies

Cookies are small text files stored on an end-user's computer to enable web sites to identify that user. They are useful tools in that a company can identify a previous visitor to a site, and build up a profile of his or her behaviour. They are covered in more detail in Chapter 10, and their implications for privacy are described in Chapter 15.

Cookies are most powerful when they can be combined with registration on a site. Used in this way, they can be related to an individual with a known name and interests.

Click-tracking

Java technology can be used to track individual users to a site. Table 12.3 shows the results of a visit to the Clickstream site (*www.clickstream.net*), part of the Green Cathedral agency. On this site this technology can be demonstrated for a user's visit to the site. It can be seen that for this demonstration each of the pages has been visited briefly only, suggesting nothing attracted the user's interest!

Table 12.3 Site for path visits

Date	Time	Web page	Time visited
07/24/1999	13:51:22	Clickstream Technologies Home Page	0h 0m 17s
07/24/1999	13:51:40	Product Information 1	0h 0m 7s
07/24/1999	13:51:47	Audience Tracking (Slide 01)	0h 0m 8s
07/24/1999	13:51:56	Audience Tracking (Slide 02)	0h 0m 3s
07/24/1999	13:52:00	Audience Tracking (Slide 01)	0h 0m 31s
07/24/1999	13:52:31	Technology Licensing	0h 0m 9s
07/24/1999	13:52:41	Product Information 3	0h 0m 3s
07/24/1999	13:52:45	Technology Licensing	0h 0m 9s
07/24/1999	13:52:54	Product Information 3	0h 0m 11s
07/24/1999	13:53:06	Technology Licensing	0h 0m 11s

Offline methods of metric collection

Offline measures usually relate to a conventional marketing outcome such as a new lead or a sale. It is not possible for these to be mutually exclusive with online measures recorded on the web server, so there is some overlap between the categories. Selected offline measures are shown in Table 12.4.

> **Offline web metric**
> Offline measures are those that are collated by marketing staff recording particular marketing outcomes such as an enquiry or a sale. They are usually collated manually, but could be collated automatically.

Table 12.4 Some offline measures of Internet marketing effectiveness

Measure	Measured through
Enquiries or leads (subdivided into new customers and existing customers)	Number of online e-mails Phone calls mentioning web site Faxed enquiries mentioning web site
Sales	Online sales or sales in which customers state they found out about the product on the web site. Sales received on a phone number only publicised on a web site
Conversion rate	Can be calculated separately for customers who are registered online and those who are not
Retention rates	Is the 'churn' of customers using the web site lower?
Customer satisfaction	Focus groups, questionnaires and interviews Mystery shoppers
Brand enhancement	Focus groups, surveys

An important aspect of measures collected offline is that the marketing outcomes may be recorded in different media according to how the customer has contacted the company. For example, a new customer enquiry could arrive by e-mail, fax or phone. Similarly, an order could be placed online using a credit card, by phone, fax or post. For both these cases what we are really interested in is, has the web site influenced the enquiry or sale? This is a difficult question to answer unless steps are put in place to answer this question. For all contact points with customers staff need to be instructed to ask customers how they found out about the company, or made their decision to buy. Although this is valuable information it is often intrusive, and a customer placing an order may be annoyed to be asked such a question. To avoid alienating the customer, these questions about the role of the web site can be asked later, perhaps when the customer is filling in a registration or warranty card. Another device that can be used to identify use of the web site is to use a specific phone number on the web site, so when a customer rings to place an order, it is known that the number was obtained from the web site. This approach is used by Dell on its site.

Evaluation of promotional methods

Assessing the effectiveness of the methods to lead customers to the web site, or the impact of the web site itself, can be carried out by traditional methods used to assess non-digital advertising. For example, *post-testing* methods of evaluating traditional advertisements can be used for banner advertisements, or for the web site itself. These methods include recall and recognition tests. The impact on brand awareness and activity amongst potential and current customers can be reviewed in terms of the following scale:

- Unaware
- Aware
- Attitude

- Preference
- Intention
- Trial
- Repeat

Kotler (1997) summarises the *communication effects* of copy by asking questions such as:

- How well does the page catch the reader's attention?
- How well does the page lead the reader to go further?
- How effective is the particular appeal?
- How well does the page suggest follow through or call to action?

Such questions can be applied to banner advertisements or the web site.

Pak (1999) has studied the advertising impact of web site content and its design (copy-testing). She reviewed the techniques on web sites used to communicate the message to the customer in terms of existing advertising theory. This work is described further in Chapter 8.

The impact of advertisements placed in traditional media can also be evaluated using the web site. In a crude form, a company might see an increase in number of site visits after a television campaign that promotes the web site URL, or even immediately after it was shown. If a company publicises a specific web address particular to one advertisement, it can then directly monitor how many enter the site in response to seeing that advertisement. The use of a web site can also be indicated by the number of phone calls arising directly from the site (with a callback system or a web-specific phone number).

A company such as DoubleClick (*www.doubleclick.net*) provides direct evaluation reports of banner advertisements in terms of number of clickthroughs. Further follow-up should take place, to see the behaviour of these customers when they visit the web site.

For specific sales promotions that take place over a period of time, such as a price reduction, it is possible to use the web site to directly evaluate the promotion. The number of page impressions before, during and after the sales promotion can be assessed. Some of the survey techniques described below could be used to assess the characteristics of the customers who responded and those who did not.

Customer satisfaction, customer loyalty and brand impact

Offline marketing research will also aim to determine the influence of the web site and related communications on customer perception of the company, its products and services. The options for conducting survey research include interviews, questionnaires and focus groups. Each of these techniques can be conducted offline or online. Offline methods are especially appropriate for companies with a smaller number of customers, who can be easily accessed, for example by sales staff. When surveys such as interviews are conducted they may not solely concern the impact of the web site, but questions about this could be part of a wider survey on customer perception of the company or its product.

This type of measurement will use the traditional techniques of survey-based marketing research, which seeks to collect primary data for gathering descriptive information about people's attitudes, preferences or buying behaviour.

> **Internet-based market research**
> The use of online questionnaires and focus groups to assess customer perceptions of a web site or broader marketing issues.

The techniques that are appropriate for conducting this type of research will need to target a sample of people who actively use the web site. The best place to find these customers is on the web site! As a result, online focus groups and questionnaires administered online are becoming more common. The use of Internet-based market research is relatively new, so there is little research on what works, and what does not. However, some general comments can be made for the different survey types.

1 Online questionnaires

These use onscreen forms to ask questions about the site. They may be in a feedback section of the site, or they may be available, on request, when a user arrives at the site. An example of an online questionnaire, relating to the use of the Levi Strauss European site, is shown in Fig. 12.6. This appeared in a separate window, which customers could open onscreen. Typical questions asked in such questionnaires are illustrated by Mini case Study 12.3. Such questionnaires tend to suffer from the fact that they use mainly closed questions, but they are quite quick for customers to fill in.

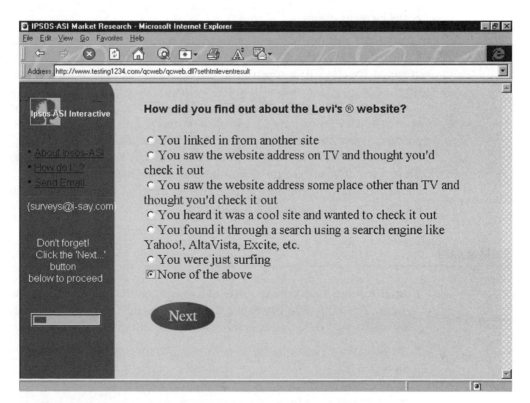

Fig. 12.6 Online questionnaire about the Levi Strauss European web site

| Mini case study 12.3 | British Airways questionnaire (*www.britishairways.com*) |

About the site

- How did you first hear about the British Airways Internet site?
- Did you find the information you needed?
- Overall, how would you rate the information contained in the British Airways site?

About you

- What was your age last birthday?
- Are you male or female?
- In which country do you live most of the time?
- What is your occupation?
- Where are you accessing from?
- What is the speed of your connection?
- When was the last time you flew with British Airways?
- Are you currently booked to fly with British Airways or one of our partners?
- Are you an Executive Club card holder?
- What is your e-mail address?

2. Online focus groups

Companies with more customers can use focus groups to assess the effectiveness of a web site. Traditional focus groups can be conducted, where customers are brought together in a room and assess the site. These tend to be expensive and time consuming, since rather than simply viewing an advertisement, the customers need to actually interact with the web site. This may be unrealistic if they are rushed. A more practical way of achieving this result is to use online focus groups. These are web-based focus groups, and they are used quite widely in the USA, but less widely elsewhere to date. One of the leading companies offering these 'virtual' focus groups is *www.w3focus.com*. These follow a bulletin board or discussion group form where different members of the focus group respond to prompts from the focus group leaders.

SUMMARY

1 Maintaining a web site requires clear responsibilities to be identified for different roles. These include the roles of content owners and site developers, and those ensuring that the content conforms with company and legal requirements.

2 To produce a good-quality web site, standards are required to enforce uniformity in terms of:
   - site look and feel;
   - corporate branding;
   - quality of copy.

3 A structured measurement programme is necessary to collect measures to assess a web site's effectiveness. Action can then be taken to adjust the web site strategy or promotional efforts.

4 Measures of Internet marketing effectiveness can be categorised as assessing:
- *Level 1. Business effectiveness* – these measure the impact of the web site on the whole business, and look at financial measures such as revenue and profit and promotion of corporate awareness.
- *Level 2. Marketing effectiveness* – these measure the number of leads and sales achieved via the Internet and effect of the Internet on retention rates and other aspects of the marketing mix such as branding.
- *Level 3. Internet marketing effectiveness* – these measures assess how well the site is being promoted, and do so by reviewing the popularity of the site and how good it is at delivering customer needs.

5 The measures of effectiveness referred to above are collected in two main ways – online or offline – or in combination.

6 Online measures are those obtained from a web server log file. They indicate the number of visitors to a site, which pages they visit, and where they originated from. These also provide a breakdown of visitors through time or by domain (country). A summary of the wide variation in online measures is given in Fig. 12.7. The cells labelled 'Dimensions' show the different ways in which each hit or page impression to the web site can be broken down. The categories give the detail of the breakdown.

7 Offline measures are marketing outcomes such as enquiries or sales that are directly attributable to the web site. Other measures of the effectiveness are available through surveying customers using questionnaires, interviews and focus groups. Table 12.5 summarises the online and offline measures and how they are collected.

Dimensions

	Time periods	Pages	Customer characteristics	Products	Browser type
Categories	Year	Individual pages	Domain (country)	Product types	Microsoft Internet Explorer
	Month	Entry pages	IP address	Service types	Netscape Navigator
	Week	Referring pages	* Real address		Other
	Day	Exit pages	* New or existing?		(Note different versions of each)
	Hour				

Measures are: hits, page impressions, site visits, site repeat visits, registrations, (length of visit), (spend).

Fig. 12.7 Breakdown of dimensions and categories of information related to online performance measures

Table 12.5 Checklist of online and offline performance measures of web site effectiveness

Measures collected online		Measures collected offline	
Measure	Collection method	Measure	Collection method
Traffic volume	Hits, page impressions, site visits, site repeat visits, registrations	Leads sourced from Internet (new and repeat)	Phone, e-mail, forms submitted, registrations
Variation	By time period, by browser type, by country, by unique visitor	Customer satisfaction with site	Questionnaires, focus groups, sales staff related to site information and usability, customer service
Document trails	Average, or example	Order value	Average and total order values
Feedback forms		Conversion rates	
Site performance	Download speeds and availability	Cost of transaction	Online or offline
		Cost savings (customer service and material cost avoidance) and profitability of site	
		Cross-sales	
		Brand impact and customer loyalty	
		Corporate image	

EXERCISES AND QUESTIONS

Self-assessment exercises

1 Why are standards necessary for controlling web site maintenance? What aspects of the site do standards seek to control?

2 Explain the difference between hits and page impressions. How are these measured?

3 Define and explain the purpose of test and live versions of a web site.

4 Why should content development be distributed through a large organisation?

5 What is the difference between online and offline metrics?

6 How can focus groups and interviews be used to assess web site effectiveness?

7 Explain how a web log file analyser works. What are its limitations?

8 Why is it useful to integrate the collection of online and offline metrics?

Discussion questions

1 'Corporate standards for a web site's format and update process are likely to stifle the creative development of a site and reduce its value to customers.' Discuss.

2 'There is little value in the collection of online metrics recorded in a web server log file. For measurement programmes to be of value, measures based on marketing outcomes are more valuable.' Discuss.

3 'The tools for analysing web server log files are not designed for marketing managers.' Discuss, using examples from these sites:

- WebTrends (*www.webtrends.com*).
- Analog (*www.statslab.cam.ac.uk/~sret1/analog/*).
- WUsage (*www.boutell.com/wusage*).
- I/PRO site audit (*www.ipro.com*).

4 'When developing metric programmes the objective should be to assess the contribution of the web site to the business rather than to evaluate the web site in isolation.' Discuss.

Essay questions

1 Explain why a web measurement programme needs to be carefully controlled by the marketing manager for it to be of value.

2 You have been appointed as manager of a web site for a car manufacturer and have been asked to refine the existing metrics programme. Explain, in detail, the steps you would take to develop this programme.

3 The first version of a web site for a financial services company has been live for a year. Originally it was developed by a team of two people, and was effectively 'brochureware'. The second version of the site is intended to contain more detailed information, and will involve contributions from 10 different product areas. You have been asked to define a procedure for controlling updates to the site. Write a document detailing the update procedure, which also explains the reasons for each control.

4 Visit the sites of the following web site analyser programmes. Write a report for the marketing manager in your company, evaluating the four alternatives and recommending the best alternatives. Note that the marketing manager has limited technical knowledge.

- WebTrends (*www.webtrends.com*).
- Analog (*www.statslab.cam.ac.uk/~sret1/analog/*).
- WUsage (*www.boutell.com/wusage*).
- I/PRO site audit (*www.ipro.com*).

5 Explain the value to a marketer of asking customers to register at a web site. What are the barriers to getting a customer to register, and how can the information be used once the customer has registered?

Examination questions

1 Why are standards necessary to control the process of updating a web site? Give three examples of different aspects of a web site that need to be controlled.

2 Explain the following terms concerning measurement of web site effectiveness:
(a) Hits.
(b) Page impressions.
(c) Referring pages.

3 Measurement of web sites concerns the recording of key events involving customers using a web site. Briefly explain five different types of event.

4 Describe and briefly explain the purpose of the different stages involved in updating an existing document on a commercial web site.

5 Distinguish between a test environment and a live environment for a web site. What is the reason for having two environments?

6 Give three reasons explaining why a web site may have to integrate with existing marketing information systems and databases within a company.

7 You have been appointed as manager of a web site and have been asked to develop a metrics programme. Briefly explain the steps you would take to develop this programme.

8 If a customer can be persuaded to register his or her name and e-mail address with a web site, how can this information be used for site measurement purposes?

REFERENCES

Berthon, P., Lane, N., Pitt, L. and Watson, R. (1998) 'The World Wide Web as an industrial marketing communications tool: models for the identification and assessment of opportunities', *Journal of Marketing Management*, 14, 691–704.

Friedman, L. and Furey, T. (1999) *The Channel Advantage*. Oxford: Butterworth-Heinemann.

Kaplan, R.S. and Norton, D.P. (1993) 'Putting the balanced scorecard to work', *Harvard Business Review* (September–October), 134–42.

Kotler, P. (1997) *Marketing Management – Analysis, planning, implementation and control*. Englewood Cliffs, NJ: Prentice Hall.

Lynch, P. and Horton, S. (1999) *Web Style Guide. Basic design principles for creating web sites*. New Haven, CT: Yale University Press.

Obolensky, N. (1994) *Practical Business Re-engineering. Tools and techniques for achieving effective change*. London: Kogan Page.

Pak, J. (1999) 'Content dimensions of web advertising: a cross national comparison', *International Journal of Advertising*, 18(2), 207–31.

Parsons, A., Zeisser, M. and Waitman, R. (1996) 'Organising for digital marketing', *Mckinsey Quarterly*, 4, 183–92.

Sterne, J. (1999) *World Wide Web Marketing* (2nd edn). New York: John Wiley and Sons.

FURTHER READING

Berthon, B., Pitt, L. and Watson, R. (1998) 'The World Wide Web as an industrial marketing communication tool: models for the identification and assessment of opportunities', *Journal of Marketing Management*, 14, 691–704.
This is a key paper assessing how to measure how the Internet supports purchasers through the different stages of the buying decision.

Brassington, F. and Petitt, S. (2000) *Principles of Marketing* (2nd edn). Harlow, UK: Pearson Education.
See companion Prentice Hall web site (*www.booksites.net/brassington2*).
Chapter 6, Marketing Information and Research, describes the marketing research process and techniques for collection of primary and secondary data.

Burnett, J. and Moriarty, S. (1999) *Introduction to Marketing Communications. An integrated approach*. Upper Saddle River, NJ: Prentice Hall.
See companion Prentice Hall web site (*cw.prenhall.com/bookbind/pubbooks/burnett/*).
See Chapter 18, Measuring IMC Performance.

Dibb, S., Simkin, S., Pride, W. and Ferrel, O. (1997) *Marketing. Concepts and strategies* (3rd European edn). New York: Houghton Mifflin.
See companion Houghton Mifflin web site (*www.busmgt.ulst.ac.uk/h_mifflin/*).
See chapter 24, Implementing Strategies and Measuring Performance.

Friedman, L. and Furey, T. (1999) *The Channel Advantage*. Oxford: Butterworth-Heinemann.

Chapter 12 is on managing channel performance.

Horgan, T. (1998) 'Developing your intranet strategy and plan', *CIO Magazine*. Website: *www.cio.com/WebMaster/strategy/printversion.html*.
This detailed paper covers many issues of site maintenance such as standards, responsibilities and tools that apply equally to an Internet web site.

Novak, T. and Hoffman, D. (1996) 'New metrics for new media: towards the development of web measurement standards', *World Wide Web Journal,* Winter, 2(1), 213–46.
Mainly covers metrics for advertising, such as ad-clicks and ad impressions, which are also referred to in Chapter 9.

Sterne, J. (1999) *World Wide Web Marketing* (2nd edn), New York: John Wiley and Sons.
Chapter 11 is entitled Measuring Your Success. It mainly reviews the strengths and weaknesses of online methods.

WEB SITE REFERENCES

The section Tools for measuring web site performance (*see* p. 386) lists commonly used log file analysis tools. Others are:

I/PRO (*www.ipro.com*) provides services to audit web site effectiveness through studies of the site traffic. Sample reports held on its site indicate the types of approach used.

MediaMetrix (*www.mediametrix.com*), now merged with RelevantKnowledge (www.relevant-knowledge.com), claim to be the world leaders in 'media measurement'.

CHAPTER 13

Business-to-consumer Internet marketing – The retail example

After reading this chapter, the reader should be able to;

- identify the key uses of the Internet from a retailer's perspective;
- understand the growth of Internet retailing and the impact of the Internet's design on the future of Internet retailing;
- consider the strategic implications of operating online, from a retail supplier's perspective;
- give examples of best practice in the world of online retailing;
- understand the future potential of the Internet Retail Market (IRM).

This chapter builds on concepts and frameworks introduced earlier in the book. The main related chapters are:

▶ Chapter 2, which provides an introduction to the characteristics of Internet consumer behaviour.

▶ Chapter 5, which introduces strategic approaches to exploiting the Internet.

▶ Chapter 8, which covers the issues that must be taken into account in designing a successful site.

▶ Chapter 12, which provides coverage of how metrics can be used to assess the success of a site.

INTRODUCTION

This chapter examines how consumers and businesses interact via the Internet. The focus of this chapter is on the use of the Internet for retailing. This specific area of marketing is chosen since it exemplifies the success factors for consumer Internet marketing. The principles developed can also be readily applied to other consumer marketing sectors such as travel and financial products, although these products have great opportunities for Internet sales since no physical product delivery is necessary. The chapter describes the origins of Internet retailing, current retail applications of the Internet, and how retail use of the Internet is likely to grow in the future. There is a whole range of businesses with active web sites, most of which are accessible without password control by the general consumer. However, some of these sites are clearly targeting a business audience. The chapter explores how businesses are interacting with domestic consumers around the globe – with people who are in the market to make a retail purchase via the Internet.

Using the Internet for business-to-consumer interactions is far removed from its original purpose as a military communication tool, which could operate without central authority in order to withstand nuclear attack. The Internet has rapidly evolved into a commercial trading environment/channel over the last decade. The expansion has spawned new styles of retail businesses, interactive communication and products in order to tempt customers to embrace the new virtual environment/channel. There have been some successes and some failures, and these are examined in this chapter in order to explore possible developments in the adoption of the Internet for business-to-consumer marketing. After looking briefly at the pioneer days of Internet retailing the chapter explores the Internet retail market (IRM) – a virtual environment, currently of unknown dimensions, a *virtual high street* consisting of: online retailers (both existing and new entrants), their customers and their virtual retail offer. We examine each of the components of the IRM in detail and then look at the activities involved in the IRM, such as the provision of information and interactive functions for the online consumer. The final section of the chapter explores the future of the IRM.

The pioneer days of Internet retail

Commercial use of the Internet has been acceptable since 1989 with the first commercial electronic mail communications (Kahin, 1995). In the early days the discovery of this new medium was likened to the gold rush era of the 1870s. Computer resellers, computer producers and Internet service providers were eager to extol the virtues and opportunities of using the Internet. Many of their proclamations heralded the introduction of exciting innovations. A number of companies began to provide goods and services for sale online. In 1994 Flowers Direct offered flowers for sale via the Internet: a service for end-users at the time who were mainly male with above average incomes living in the USA. In Europe Blackwell's Bookshop and Victoria Wine of the UK were amongst the first retailers to offer transactional services via the Internet.

Mini case study 13.1

BarclaySquare, evolution from an early attempt to develop a consumer site

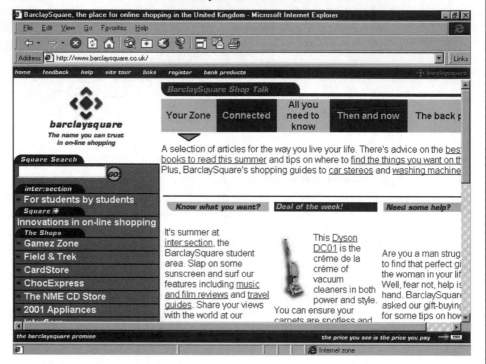

Fig. 13.1 BarclaySquare site in 1999

What is BarclaySquare?

In 1995 Barclays Merchant Services began to promote BarclaySquare as *'the UK's most exciting shopping centre development'* (Barclays Merchant Services promotional literature, 1995). The new retail development would have: a potential customer base of 35 million people with an expected growth rate of 10 per cent per month, unlimited *virtual* development space for expansion, opportunities for participating retailers to make substantial savings on fixed costs compared with a fixed-location operation in the real world, and a target audience of cash-rich, time-poor intelligent adults. The service provided the convenience of all-year-round shopping for consumers from their office or the comfort of home.

BarclaySquare eventually offered a good mix of core tenants, including Argos, Blackwells and Victoria Wine, and with the support of Barclays Merchant Services should have given customers confidence to use the innovative service. This was an excellent example of visionary management commitment to online retailing, but was it ahead of its time?

Many Internet innovations like electronic malls and push technologies (*see* Chapter 4) have been introduced and dismissed by media hype, which has focused on the next Internet gizmo.

> **Virtual or electronic mall**
> A web site that brings together different electronic retailers at a single virtual (online) location. This contrasts with a fixed-location infrastructure – the traditional arrangement where retail organisations operate from retail stores situated in fixed locations such as real-world shopping malls.

Electronic malls appeared, like Cyber Mall and BarclaySquare, where a variety of goods from various electronic retailers were available. These malls followed the format of fixed-location malls in the real world, grouping together an assortment of retailers in one *virtual* destination on the Internet. However, potential customers could view the product assortment of retailers located anywhere in the world from their workstations and laptops without the need to travel, and so the advantages for the consumer of retailers being in one destination were lost. Another facility to emerge was speciality malls, which were designed to facilitate comparison shopping, as all participating retailers had a similar product range. This approach was less than successful as the individual retailers were not able to derive any competitive advantage and as a result many electronic malls ceased to exist. Retailers, however, continued to develop their own Web presence through the 1990s in the form of *destination* web sites in a similar way to the development of a fixed-location destination store.

> **Destination store**
> A retail store in which the merchandise, selection, presentation, pricing or other unique feature acts as a magnet for customers (Levy and Weitz, 1995)

Nevertheless, European consumers struggled to locate their favourite online retailers. Towards the end of 1997 there was a notable increase in marketing communications activity. This often took the form of promotion by companies of their URLs on real-world point-of-sales materials and packaging. The Co-operative Wholesale Society and Debenhams printed their URLs on carrier bags during 1997. The following year saw an increase in the number of electronic retailers and consumers and a growth in revenue. Soon after the launch of digital television in the UK in 1999 there was a proliferation of television advertisements supporting company URLs. This is possibly explained by promoters' anticipation of increased numbers of end-users accessing the Internet via their own digital television sets or possibly advertisers aiming to increase awareness of companies' Internet activities. In many cases the URLs were not integrated into the communications messages, and the effectiveness of this strategy is unknown at the time of writing. Innovative methods of end-user Internet access are continuing to be developed, and are discussed in the final section of the chapter.

The Internet retail market (IRM)

There has been considerable speculation about the size, growth and future potential of the new virtual trading environment, especially in terms of predicted turnover as shown in Table 13.1.

Activity 13.1

Assessing the size of the IRM

Table 13.1 Conflicting views on the future value of the IRM

Year	Forecasts of retail turnover	References
1997	'According to a recent report by retail property consultants Healey & Baker, Where People Shop, by 1997 5 per cent of all retail spending in England Scotland and Wales will be done over the Net'.	Woolacott (1996)
Turn of the century	'By the turn of the century, in excess of 54 million people in the UK, France and Germany will have Internet access, and 7 per cent of UK's consumer shopping will be conducted via the Internet'.	Trafica (1998)
2000	'According to Forrester, online sales are expected to reach $6.6 billion by 2000'.	Field (1996)
2001	'Electronic sales accounted for 0.07 per cent of retail spending by UK customers. The figure is forecast to rise to £2 billion by 2001, though this will only represent 1 per cent of all retail spending.'	Verdict Research (1997)
2001	'Internet transactions will grow from $2.6 billion last year (1996) to $220 billion in 2001.'	The Economist (1997)
2003	'Online shopping will multiply its sales by 15 times to reach £6.1 billion in the year 2003.'	Retail Review (1999)
2005	'Electronic Commerce will total no more than $1 trillion – less than the annual flow of sales of the US direct-mail business today.'	Nevens (1999)

Although these forecasts indicate a general upward trend they have been shown to be over-optimistic in terms of electronic commerce's current trading performance. In addition, the criteria used for measuring e-commerce success vary, as we saw in Chapter 12. While few dispute the increase in the number of computers connected to the Internet, the actual number is somewhat unclear, having been measured in terms of registered domains (*see* Chapter 1). In 1986 there were 213 recorded domains and by 1998 there were 29 650 000 (Network Wizards – *www.nw.co./zone/ www/top.html*). The number of end-users or potential online customers is even less well defined, as the techniques for measuring the online market are currently considered to be 'an inexact' art form (Nua Ltd, 1997) and can only be indicative of a growing market of end-users. Until more reliable data are forthcoming, only vague predictions are available to speculate on the commercial potential of the Internet or electronic commerce (Whinston, 1997).

European businesses are regularly polled to examine their uptake of the Internet, with the objective of providing a better definition of the potential of IRM. However, the majority are recorded to be 'planning to offer Internet-based services some time in the near future', a finding that is of limited value for potential retail web site developers.

Questions

1 Explain the importance of being able to determine the value of the online market prior to development of a retail web site.

2 Discuss how the Internet strategy (Chapter 5) of the following types of retailers might be affected by this lack of accurate retail market information:

- A small to medium-sized mail-order retailer looking to expand its customer base overseas.
- A medium-sized multiple retailer with 100 outlets seeking to differentiate itself from the competition by offering a new product range online.
- A large multiple retailer with over a thousand outlets aiming to use the Internet to control costs by reducing the need for future investment in its fixed-location infrastructure.

Information about the value of the electronic commerce marketplace is obviously critical for retailers entering the IRM as it should help identify the sectors or variables that hold most potential for online retailing.

Of equal interest is an analysis of the types of retailers involved with this new market. These are:

1 Established retailers using the IRM strategically or tactically as a marketing tool.
2 Virtual merchants designing their operating format to accommodate the demands of online trading.
3 Intermediaries who link Internet technology and the retail supplier with the consumer.
4 Manufacturers using the Internet to take their goods direct to the consumer.

Any one of these types could become the archetypal *model Internet retailer* and could thus affect the IRM's future growth as a retail environment (*see* Fig. 13.2 for a model of the Internet retail market).

Virtual merchants
Retailers such as Amazon that only operate online – they have no fixed location infrastructure

Potentially, if virtual merchants proved to be highly successful, established retailers operating from fixed-location stores could find themselves replaced with a new electronic retail format (Van Tassel and Weitz, 1997). The implications are considerable, as ultimately the Internet could fundamentally alter the way that consumers shop and thus revolutionise the retail environment, transforming the local high street into a global *virtual high street*. However, if established retailers continue to dominate retail supply and develop their current integrated approach to retailing through the use of technologies such as EPOS, EFTPOS and loyalty cards, bringing them closer to the customer, then the Internet could be used to support these operations. In this scenario revolution is less likely to occur. Whichever type of retailer dominates may ultimately determine consumer demand for online shopping and thus the future development of the Internet.

Retail format
The general nature of the retail mix in terms of range of products and services, pricing policy, promotional programmes, operating style/store design and visual merchandising; examples of two differing formats are mail-order retailers (non-store) and department store retailers.

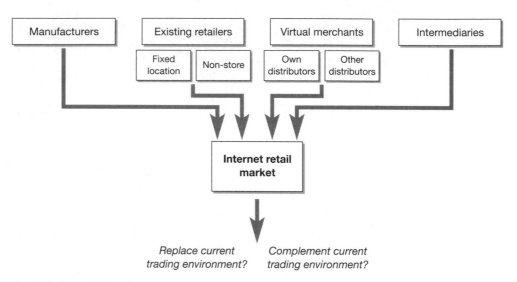

Fig. 13.2 A model of the Internet retail market

The online retailers

The first component of the IRM to consider is the retailers themselves. What type of retail organisations are using the Internet, and which sector is likely to have most influence on the future of the IRM? The question of whether the Internet will create a new retail format is interesting, and seeks to find out which companies will capitalise on the opportunity to exploit this new format. New entrants may benefit from financial freedom to develop an organisation suited to supporting the logistical demands of the new format, whereas established retailers can create competitive advantages from brand equity and high levels of customer service – effectively preventing new entrants from establishing a foothold in highly competitive retail markets. Tesco, for example, has been developing its online offering since mid-1990, and at the time of writing consumer demand outstrips supply in terms of accessibility. Many parts of the UK eagerly await the opportunity to shop online with the company. Clix of Loughborough, a new entrant to the grocery market, operates by using the model developed by Peapod and by *picking* customers' orders from Safeways. However, they can only offer the service in a limited area before the cost of delivery outweighs the convenience advantage for the consumer.

> **Picking**
> Selecting goods for customer orders.

According to Levy and Weitz (1995) retailers survive and prosper by satisfying customer needs more effectively than the competition, addressing customer needs through type of merchandise, variety and assortment of merchandise and levels of customer service. At present there are two main types of established retail company: (a) those operating from fixed-location stores, such as department and convenience stores; and (b) non-store-based operations, such as catalogue retailing and direct selling.

The fine details of these various operating styles have gradually evolved to accommodate current customer needs. Internet retailing has rapidly emerged, emulating non-store-based operations, and new entrants like Amazon (*Amazon.com*) demonstrate how the new medium can potentially completely redefine customer needs using the Internet and the World Wide Web to create a virtual retail environment with almost limitless dimensions and global coverage. However, the potential of Internet retailing is yet to be determined, and it would be naïve to imagine an overnight disappearance of the established *high street retailer*. Retailers will defend their existing territories through consideration of competitive forces and strategic options. It is the actions of retailers and their on- and offline behaviour in response to peer actions and new entrants' behaviour that are likely to shape the future of the Internet. Fundamentally, Shi and Salesky (1994) warn that value created by retailing on the Internet is unlikely to be additional but a redistribution of profitability from current retail channels to shopping via computers and interactive television. The rest of this section examines the wide range of retailers contributing to the IRM. These are as follows:

Established retailers operating from a fixed location

- *Small and medium-sized retailers* – it has been suggested that smaller retail organisations are the category most likely to adopt the Internet, owing to their greater flexibility (Auger and Gallaugher, 1997). Smaller companies have the opportunity to stand alongside large players. Jack Scaife Ltd (a butcher) (*www.jackscaife. co.uk*) and E. Botham (a baker) (*www.botham.co.uk*) are good examples of small organisations that have established an increase in turnover by retailing via the Internet to a new target audience. The advantages include access to a wider audience previously inaccessible and low-cost advertising, but the disadvantages include medium-term financial risk. Small-scale operators may be able to handle the picking and logistics owing to the small numbers involved but problems will arise when expansion is considered and the need to sustain a large operation becomes apparent.

- *Large retailers* across Europe have been quick to incorporate the Internet into their retail offer. Examples are Carrefour (*www.carrefour.fr*) (France), Benetton (*www.benetton.com*) (Italy) and Magnet online (*www.magnet.at*) (Austria). The Web offer varies considerably – some retailers offer their entire range of goods and services via the Internet while others present snapshots of their company history. The cause of this uneven rate of adoption is not entirely clear. According to Fletcher Research (*www.fletch.co.uk*), grocery retailers are not maximising the potential of their offer: they are missing opportunities to interact with customers by offering limited product ranges and by not keeping their web sites up to date. A number of large UK retailers have begun to develop *portal web sites* (*see* Chapter 4) as an attempt to attract customers to use their web sites as a gateway to the Internet and encourage customers to spend the majority of their online time in the retailer's own site in much the same way as they attempt to keep them in their retail stores.

Established retailers operating from a non-store base

Catalogue and *direct marketers* have the opportunity to extend their traditional methods of dealing with customers through using the Internet. The financial structuring of their operations is well suited to further investment in similar styles of operation. Another favourable condition is their growing international involvement and logistical infrastructure. But problems may arise from their target markets: these customers may not be comfortable with the new scenario of buying via the Internet.

New entrants operating from a non-store base

Virtual merchants – the Internet has distinct advantages over traditional marketing channels in that it reduces barriers to entry. The location issue, considered to be the key determinant of retail patronage (Finn and Louviere, 1990), is in the physical sense reduced, along with the need for sizeable capital investment in stores. It has been suggested that by removing the physical aspect to the retail offer the Internet may also provide the opportunity for increased competition (Alba *et al.*, 1997). New players, in the guise of 'virtual merchants', can easily combine commerce software with scheduling and distribution to bypass traditional retail distributors. Virtual merchants could therefore threaten existing distribution channels for consumer products. The Internet is thus likely to appeal to new entrants who have not already invested in a fixed-location network.

Probably the best-known virtual merchant is Amazon (*Amazon.com*), the self-proclaimed world's largest bookseller operating from a warehouse in Seattle and several web sites. Lack of profits has not deterred the company, which plans to move into a new product sector, groceries, where low margins and the high cost of picking customer goods mean that benefits are unlikely to come from the costs saved by retailing from a non-store location. The question raised by Amazon's plans is whether this virtual merchant has identified yet another way of deriving competitive advantage from the Internet. Whatever the outcome of this departure the company has a proactive approach towards retail adoption of the Internet, which could have widespread implications for the Internet's commercial future as a whole and for retailers in particular.

New online retail formats

n Intermediary or cybermediary – many existing businesses lack resources, in terms of both staff and technological infrastructure, to operate their web activities internally. This creates an opportunity for the intermediary to step in and provide the required technical skills. It seems likely that this will present opportunities for the intermediaries to monitor consumer activity and accumulate a certain level of control in the online retail channel. Eventually it is possible that the intermediaries could replace existing businesses. Intermediaries offering price comparison services are illustrated in Figs 15.1 and 15.2. The growth in importance of intermediaries has led to the use of the term reintermediation (Chapter 7) to describe the growth of these new formats. A good example of a new online retail format intermediary is Respond.com (www.respond.com) (Fig. 13.3). This is a site that is used to connect buyers and sellers by e-mail. The buyer fills out an online form giving

Fig.13.3 Respond.com (*www.respond.com*), **a new retail format**

details of the product he or she wants, together with its price. This form is then sent as an e-mail to suppliers who may be able to service the enquiry. E-mails are then sent by Respond.com to the consumer, providing him or her with an offer.

- *Manufacturers* of consumer goods could see the Internet as an opportunity to regain some of their power lost to retailers in the past by the shortening of distribution channels. The process of disintermediation suggests that manufacturers could exclude the retailer altogether and market directly to the consumer.

Disintermediation – shortening the value or supply chain by trading electronically and shifting the balance of power closer to the end-consumer (*see* Chapter 7 for a definition) – originated within the banking industry, when it was noticed that information technology and industry deregulation had reduced the need for banks as intermediaries. Consumers could obtain a loan from their local department store as easily as from their own bank. Some banks are now using the Internet to help them combat this trend by becoming a new type of intermediary, that is, a trusted third party broker in electronic commerce partnerships. Traditional travel agencies are another services sector that could be threatened by the shift in access to information, as connected consumers switch to making reservations online.

Cybermediaries
Organisations that perform the mediating tasks in the world of electronic commerce between producers and suppliers and consumers (Sarkar *et al.*, 1996).

The online consumers

The second component of the IRM to consider is the online consumers. Consumer demand for the Internet is a key factor that may ultimately drive widespread adoption of the Internet by retailers. Whether the consumer has access and how he or she uses or perceives Internet shopping will affect its ultimate success (Shirky, 1997). Internet retailing offers a retail experience that is totally different from that of fixed-location retailing (Westland and Au, 1998). Comparison and price shopping across a greater number of sites will be easier and could be achieved within minutes. Indeed, in the USA it is more common for consumers to use the Internet to find information about a product in the early part of the buying decision-making process, than for them to buy direct on the Web. They will then subsequently purchase the product through the fixed-location store or order by telephone or fax (Ernst and Young, 1999).

From a retailing perspective the use of the Internet is an elective activity whereby consumers require effort to access retail web sites and select products. As a consequence carefully planned shopping online may dominate, rather than impulse shopping. Also, online consumers incur costs that they can directly attribute to their shopping behaviour. Payment for call charges could mean that a *'virtual trip to the shops'* is a costly event. This suggests that web sites that are not well designed, and which require the potential customer to browse through many screens before locating his or her chosen products, could easily deter customers from ever returning to the site. The online customer also has to pay for the collection of mail, which could contain unsolicited advertising. Furthermore, the medium's inability to allow consumers to touch merchandise may be problematic, as the majority of consumers prefer the social and physical interaction of 'going to the shops' (KPMG and OXIRM, 1996). The Internet also places more demands on end-users, requiring them to understand the complexity of web site design. Additionally, the difficulties encountered in locating web sites and searching and sorting through the Internet may also deter some consumer segments from switching to cybershopping. Consumer behaviour is also likely to be affected by different gender approaches to the use of computers. The use of simpler digital television-based systems (as described in Chapter 15) may eventually reduce the impact of these issues.

Whatever format a retailer uses, on- or offline technology offers companies the opportunity to develop closer relationships with their target audiences. With the trend towards customer-oriented relationship marketing rather than transaction-oriented marketing, the building of long-term relationships is paramount. The type of target audience a company serves may affect its online success. In the 1980s physical location was the most important differentiator for the majority of retailers, hence the mantra *'location, location, location'*. On the Internet, from the retailer's perspective, location is of minor significance in the physical sense. However, physical location may be important from the consumer's perspective. If the customer's access is from home the cost of access is crucial. However, if the consumer is shopping from work, time is probably limited and access may be controlled or restricted, and all of these factors have design implications in relation to the speed and efficiency of the web site.

The sale of goods to individual customers via the Internet is increasing. The Internet marketplace has grown significantly since 1994. Online customers and

Table 13.2 Web user populations

Country	Internet population	Population	% Internet users
Sweden	3 300 000	8 900 000	37.08
Norway	1 340 000	4 400 000	30.45
Finland	1 400 000	5 150 000	27.18
United States	64 200 000	272 600 000	23.55
Australia	4 200 000	18 730 000	22.42
Canada	6 300 000	31 000 000	20.32
Switzerland	1 179 000	7 270 000	16.22
Denmark	682 000	5 300 000	12.87
United Kingdom	7 000 000	59 000 000	11.86
Ireland	370 000	3 600 000	10.28
Germany	8 400 000	82 000 000	10.24
Japan	11 500 000	126 100 000	9.12
Singapore	250 000	3 500 000	7.14
France	2 580 000	58 900 000	4.38
Italy	2 140 000	56 700 000	3.77
Belgium	369 000	10 180 000	3.62
South Africa	1 040 000	43 400 000	2.40
Brazil	2 700 000	171 800 000	1.57
Malaysia	250 000	21 300 000	1.17
Russia	1 000 000	146 000 000	0.68
Mexico	504 000	100 000 000	0.50
China	1 500 000	1 246 800 000	0.12

Source: US Government Population Statistics (*www.census.gov*).

retailer suppliers are quickly learning how to conduct themselves in the digital environment. Although online selling is still in its infancy and for many consumers and retail suppliers Internet technology is completely new, the size of the market for Internet trade is growing. The *Computer Industry Almanac* has reported that by the year 2000, just over 5 per cent of the world's population of six billion people will have Internet access. North America has the largest number of Internet users but, interestingly, it does not have the highest density of Internet users per head of population. This varies from country to country. According to a survey by the Oxford Institute of Retail Management (KPMG and OXIRM, 1996), '*the European experience of the Internet and retailers' exploitation of it is very much a patchwork quilt affair*', and penetration varies considerably. Sweden has the highest Internet penetration per head of population and China has one of the lowest. Table 13.2 shows a selection of countries and their levels of Internet adoption.

The online products

The third component of the IRM is the product offer. The nature of the products and the related shopping activity will govern the product groups most likely to succeed on the Internet. Intangible products and services such as flight reservations and banking services are well suited to online trading as they are less restricted by operational logistics than tangible goods like lawnmowers or cars. Moreover, the desired level of convenience, the depth of choice and the speed of delivery may all influence the attraction of the online product to the consumer. The Electronic Shopping test described in Chapter 5 (*see* Mini case study 5.3) can be applied to different products to assess their suitability for purchase over the Internet. Evidence from the US experience of Internet retailing indicates a preference for electronic products: among the goods sold by the top 100 US Internet retailers, electronic products have a greater representation than other product categories. In addition, banking services, books and magazines accounted for 47 per cent of Internet sales in the USA (Pavitt, 1997). At the other extreme, clothing retailers have a comparatively low representation. This seems to suggest that the most popular goods are either those associated with the computing industry, which is hardly surprising given the current Internet demographics, or products that consumers do not need to touch or see prior to purchase: books and music CDs. In Europe, UK grocery retailers have the greatest representation of online products. The next most popular categories are electrical products and books. It can be seen that UK non-store and mail-order companies are early adopters seeking to extend their catalogue method of retailing into the online world. Grocery retailers are well represented online even though their mode of operation is considered rather incompatible with the demands of Internet shopping because of complex logistics and the high cost of picking customer orders. A possible explanation is that in the UK the structure of the retail sector tends to be dominated by the food sector, which consists of a small group of very large food multiples. Case study 13.1 considers the issues further.

It is important to note that the home shopping market struggles to maintain about 5 per cent of all European retail sales. Unless online retailers can overcome consumer resistance to non-store-based formats, by offering higher levels of convenience, more choice and expediency of delivery, the retail potential of the Internet may be limited.

Internet retail marketing

This section of the chapter considers how the Internet can be actively used as a retail channel, for example for providing customer information, communicating via e-mail, collecting market research data, evaluation of online retail performance and online ordering and payment (Doherty et al., 1999).

The Internet retail channel

Traditionally, the term 'channel' described the flow of a product from source to end-user. This definition implies a passive unidirectional system whereby the manufacturer/producer marketed through a wholesaler or retailer to the consumer (Davies, 1993). Recent developments in information technology are changing this orientation by enabling retailers to focus their marketing efforts on managing customers more effectively (Mulhern, 1997). The potential role of the Internet in retailing could involve bringing the customer even closer to the retailer via a combined marketing/distribution channel, in effect an interactive 'retail channel'. This move may also suggest a shift towards a bi-directional retailer/consumer relationship, in which more power accrues to the customer (Hagel and Armstrong, 1997).

For some retailers the main function of a web site is to provide the end-user with information (see Fig. 13.5). For others, the main function is to transact with end-users via the Internet.

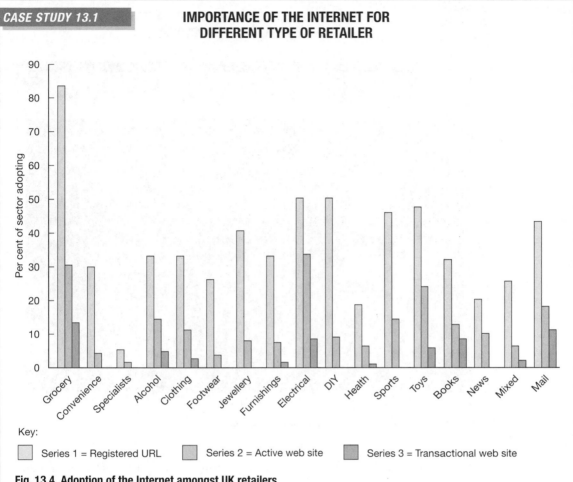

CASE STUDY 13.1

IMPORTANCE OF THE INTERNET FOR DIFFERENT TYPE OF RETAILER

Key:

Series 1 = Registered URL   Series 2 = Active web site   Series 3 = Transactional web site

Fig. 13.4 Adoption of the Internet amongst UK retailers

Source: Ellis-Chadwick (1999).

A research project looking at Internet adoption amongst a range of leading UK retailers (Doherty *et al.*, 1999) has identified different levels of uptake across product activity sectors. The three levels of involvement are: Registered URL – where a company has a registered URL but not an active web site; Active web site – one where various information is provided, but there is no form of interactive transaction; and Transactional site – one that has e-commerce facilities available for product purchase.

Questions

1 Apply the ES test (*see* Chapter 5) to the above product categories and see which, according to the test, are most likely to be successfully offered for sale online.

2 Compare your answers to question 1 with the figures for Internet activity presented in Fig. 13.4.

3 Explain why groceries have a comparatively high number of Series 3 Web sites.

CASE STUDY 13.2

WAITROSE USES THE INTERNET FOR A RANGE OF CUSTOMER INFORMATION

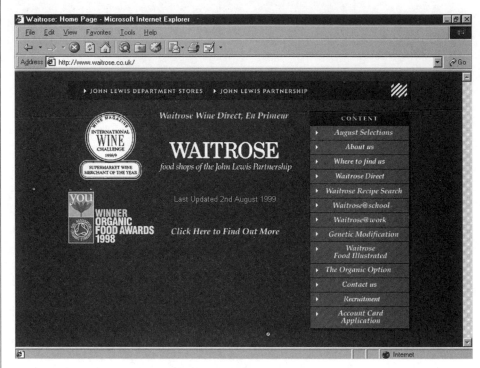

Fig. 13.5 Waitrose retail web site (*www.waitrose.co.uk*)

Grocery retailer Waitrose plc is part of the John Lewis partnership of retailers. The company web site offers a range of information, which is analysed in this case study.

Visit the Waitrose web site (*www.waitrose.co.uk*) and answer the following questions.

Questions

1 Suggest why this retailer may not wish to sell goods from the web site.

2 Describe the possible target audience of the Waitrose web site.

3 Identify three different types of information provided and discuss the suitability for the possible target audience.

4 Outline the benefits to the customer of this web site.

Conducting non-store-based transactions with consumers is not an innovation of the 1990s, nor is it an activity exclusive to the Internet. Probably the most notable example is the Minitel system in France. Since 1979 French *telephone subscribers* have enjoyed access to an interactive telephone directory and a range of retail services, for example buying wine and booking travel tickets via the Minitel system. In the UK Prestel similarly offered a small number of consumers the opportunity to shop digitally. This service did not achieve the level of success initially anticipated. Failure was due to the complex method and high costs involved in accessing the service.

Retail web sites are not limited to selling alone. A research project in 1999 (Doherty *et al.*, 1999) examined the use of the Internet by multiple retailers in the United Kingdom. This showed that only 3 per cent of retailers were offering customers the opportunity to buy goods and services online. Furthermore, the remaining retailers with active web sites offered a range of additional interactive services to end-users, including: information about products, financial services and novelty information features, recruitment features, marketing activities, communications via e-mail and capturing market research data via online questionnaires. It can therefore be argued that Internet retailing does not comprise merely buying and selling goods and services via computers and computer networks. It is in fact a new *retail channel*, which retailers can use for a range of activities.

Informational functions

Web sites also provide retailers with an important opportunity to give customers information. It has been suggested by Breitenbach and van Doren (1998) (*see* Chapter 2) that the behaviour of online consumers is similar to their behaviour offline. This is, however, unlikely to apply to all retail web sites. Many companies see the Web as a means of expanding customer services through offering their customers wider ranges of information than is possible in a store situation. One of the greatest advantages of the World Wide Web, according to UK retailers, is its ability to facilitate the dispersion of low-cost information. Retailers have been proactive about providing information on their web sites, and offer a wider range of different types of information than do other Internet marketers:

- *Product information* presented on retail Web sites includes product descriptions, specifications and prices, promotional information and promotional advertisements, colour swatches and graphical images.
- *Financial information* includes company reports, annual statements and investor information. The depth of coverage can vary considerably, as can the extent of accessibility. In some instances the consumer is required to provide address details so that reports can be mailed.
- *Company information* includes such items as history of the company, store locator, details of employees and company incentive schemes. For examples of these *see* the web sites of the following companies: store locators, Debenhams plc (*www.debenhams.co.uk*) (national), Levi Strauss UK Ltd (*www.levis.com*) (global); a company history, J Sainsbury plc (*www.j-sainsbury.co.uk*); an events diary, Waterstone's (*www.waterstones.co.uk*).
- *Educational information*. A number of companies have devoted parts of their web sites to providing educational information. Thorntons plc has a discovery zone aimed at a younger audience. Shell Oil also has an innovative, interactive, educational feature in its web site. The Co-operative Wholesale Society provides environmental information on *green* retailing issues.
- *Press releases* – often form part of the information provided in the corporate section of the web site – *see* Coats Viyella plc.

■ *Recruitment information* – recruitment features providing potential applicants with job details. Some companies provide the facility to request application forms or even to apply via e-mail.

Interactive functions

Interactive use of the Internet involves more than simply the provision of promotional information. It includes sophisticated functions such as the ordering of catalogues, promotional literature, samples and free gifts and encouraging customers to provide market research data:

■ *Marketing communication tool*. The Internet is a *'revolutionary new promotional tool'* (Fill, 1999). It is a channel for advertising. Traditional advertising channels such as television, radio, cinema and a variety of print media formats enable a one-to-many dialogue based on communication theory (Schramm, 1955) between senders and receivers. The communication process is normally constrained by time, namely, the speed of response amongst participants, but communication can become *'conversations at electronic speeds'* if conducted via interactive-based services such as the Internet. If the role of the Internet is marketing communication then Steuer's (1992) suggestion 'that the principal relationship be with the *"mediated environment"* itself rather than between senders and receivers' may be important to long-term adoption. If a web site is only a *static* electronic brochure of company product ranges the effect on this of changing relations might be limited.
■ *Direct communications*. As an interactive channel for direct communication and data exchange (Verity, 1995) the Internet enables focused targeting and segmentation opportunities for more closely monitoring consumer behaviour. E-mail provides a direct non-intrusive means of communication between firm and customer (Casserttari, 1995).
■ *Marketing research tool* – the Internet's interactivity facilitates the collection of consumer data, providing the opportunity to gather personal information from online consumers while they browse through online questionnaires and respond to e-mails. An interesting example is Fig. 10.1, where the online questionnaire explores individual preferences about styles of jeans.
■ *Sales channel*. The selling of goods and services online can take several different forms:
 – The order is placed online while the *delivery* and *payment* are made through the real world.
 – Online ordering where the *delivery* of goods is required in the real world and the payment facility has options – online or offline (e.g. electrical retailers Dixons).
 – The total process, namely the *order, payment and delivery* of the product, occurs via the Internet (e.g. purchasing of software).
 – Online bidding – the eBay web site (*www.eBay.com*) in the USA or the QXL site in the UK (*www.qxl.com*) offer end-users the opportunity to bid for goods online.

In summary, businesses may choose to utilise the Internet in a number of different ways to communicate and interact with their domestic consumers. The particular method that they adopt may vary, from just providing information to online transactions including ordering and payment for goods and services. The next section looks at the future of the IRM and briefly considers the factors that affect how a business might decide on the function and contents of its web site.

The future of the Internet retail market

A number of issues have been explored in this chapter, identifying the advantages and disadvantages of Internet retailing from both the consumer's and the supplier's perspective. Predictions about the potential of the IRM have yet to come to fruition. Business analysts International Data Corporation (IDC) predicted electronic commerce revenues would exceed $50 billion in 1997, whereas the actual figure was closer to $11 billion. Despite the optimistic tone of some of these predictions, there is little evidence to suggest that many companies have developed online trading. Indeed, KPMG and OXIRM (1996) observe that '*much of the debate still centres around the medium's potential rather than its actual performance, accessibility and content*'. Consumers are said to be fearful of lack of security, and logistical issues frustrate suppliers. So is this temporary flux likely to be overcome, and will the Internet mature and become a mainstream retail channel/environment?

Retailers appear to be testing the potential of the Internet, pushing away the boundaries by exploring the medium and its possibilities An example is Schuh Ltd. At the time of writing the success of a retail web site is often measured in terms of the site's ability to function effectively and without interruption. Producing graphical images that download rapidly, or three-dimensional views of car interiors, is more likely to attract the attention of the media and create valuable press coverage than to generate income through the web site. It seems retailers are less interested in the current profitability of their web operations than in being first in their sector to advance their image as being technologically aware and at the forefront of innovation. Dixons, Tesco, Waterstone's and Asda provide their consumers with free Internet access (*see* Mini case study 3.2 on free ISPs) but the fact that they are offering services that are not supported by the companies' core competencies suggests that the offer may not be sustainable as a long-term strategy. In addition the services offered may not comparable with the standards of service of the established ISPs. Post-adoption dissonance could have a negative effect on the consumer and subsequently on the long-term image of the retailer in the eyes of the consumer.

The future of the IRM is likely to be affected by the type of retail businesses that dominate the marketplace, the type of online services they offer, and the suitability of products for unseen sale (*see* the ES test in Mini case study 5.3 in Chapter 5). Therefore, it is important to consider which factors may affect how a business utilises the Internet. Operational factors that reportedly might influence adopter behaviour are:

■ *Accessibility* – current growth rates of domestic PC ownership and the basic desire to communicate suggest consumers have Internet access, and its use is forecast to expand exponentially (Haley *et al.*, 1996). Businesses may have internal capacity or may decide to employ a third party to manage their online access, outsourcing some or all of their Internet operations. However, this raises questions about the equality of access: do all target markets have the same level of PC ownership, and are all offline target segments realistic online target segments?

■ *Costs* – the Internet could ultimately replace the high street by satisfying all shopping needs online, from home. Such a change could reduce the enormous capital investment required of retailers in fixed-location stores. In addition this change could benefit the retailer by bringing about substantial savings in fixed operating costs. Web sites also provide a low-cost option for the display of customer information and a reduction in the cost of printed advertising. However, there are potential cost implications in relation to the initial cost of web site development, maintenance and support and the provision of a secure payment and trading environment. There are then ongoing development costs involved in ensuring that the web site provides current information and uses the latest technology. E-mail also offers the opportunity of low-cost communication, but responding effectively has cost implications.

■ *New markets* – it is predicted that companies can gain additional sales, either to existing customers or through attracting new ones via a whole new global marketplace. Van Tassel and Weitz (1997) suggest that '*the Internet turns local markets into global markets*'. Furthermore, the new communication opportunities of the Internet provide the potential and easy access for brand positioning and diversification into new product areas (McWilliam *et al.*, 1997).

■ *Technical considerations* – bandwidth, access connection speeds and network security are all reported to influence adoption, as is general global network reliability. In addition the complexity of the user interface, even although it has changed from arcane codes and network addresses to colourful graphical user interfaces (GUIs) driven by the click of a mouse button, still presents a barrier to the end-consumer. Web sites need to be of a logical design that caters for the comprehension abilities of specific target markets.

■ *Logistics* – establishing a new logistical infrastructure to service the needs of Internet customers may yet prove to be the biggest barrier to the business development of web sites designed to sell products to domestic consumers. Mail-order and direct marketing operators are probably, in logistical terms, the best positioned to exploit the commercial potential of the Internet, because they are non-store based and they have already established direct distribution systems (Shi and Salesky, 1994).

There are many examples of businesses that have managed to develop successful online operations. *See*, for example, Case study 13.3.

It can be seen from the brief discussion of operational factors likely to affect business adoption of the Internet that they may affect companies in either a positive or a negative manner. For example, mail-order companies could benefit from the existing structure of their organisation in terms of the logistical infrastructure it provides, but may not have the most suitable target audience, whereas wine merchants may find the reverse to be true.

The issue of how quickly, and to what extent, the IRM is likely to expand in the coming years still remains unclear. According to Doherty *et al.* (1999) three dominant and interacting themes are likely to affect retail adoption of the IRM:

■ internal inhibitors and facilitators;
■ environmental inhibitors and facilitators;
■ the Internet's comparative advantage over existing retail channels.

CASE STUDY 13.3   BLACKWELL'S ONLINE BOOKSHOP

Fig. 13.6 Blackwell's online bookshop

Blackwell's On-line Books have been operating successfully for a number of years, with an increasing annual growth in online sales. The company's academic target audience have generally had free access to Internet technology for longer than the average member of the public and are more likely to have the required searching abilities and computer skills. As well as having a suitable customer base, the company has experience in dealing with the complexity of the global logistics required for supplying customers around the globe.

Visit Blackwell's web site (*www.blackwells.co.uk*) and then answer the following questions.

Questions

1 Outline why the Blackwell's web site is a successful retail web site.

2 Discuss possible competitive advantages that its web site gives Blackwell's over other online booksellers.

3 Visit a virtual merchant's site, like that of Amazon (*www.amazon.com*), and compare its approach with that of Blackwell, as discussed in your answer to question 2. Discuss the different ways that these two companies have achieved success.

In considering these themes, a potentially important relationship can be identified. The authors suggest that retailers' current low levels of Internet activity will only increase significantly if they perceive that the environment and their organisation are ready to adopt the Internet as a retail channel. Their evaluation of the internal and environmental inhibitors and facilitators is then considered, in conjunction with their perception of the relative advantages to the company of using the Internet as a retail channel. The outcome of this process then gives the adopting business an overall perception of how valuable the Internet could be to the company as a means of interacting with domestic consumer. Therefore it is the outcome of this process that is likely to determine the progression of business adoption of the Internet and ultimately the long-term future of the IRM. Figure 13.7 gives a graphical model of the factors affecting the future development of the Internet.

It is possible to conclude, given current levels and extent of Internet utilisation, either that retail businesses do not perceive their organisations to be sufficiently well prepared internally to exploit the significant potential of the Internet or that the comparative advantages of using the medium are too limited. This lack of urgency and focus carries a risk from the threat of competition. For example, new

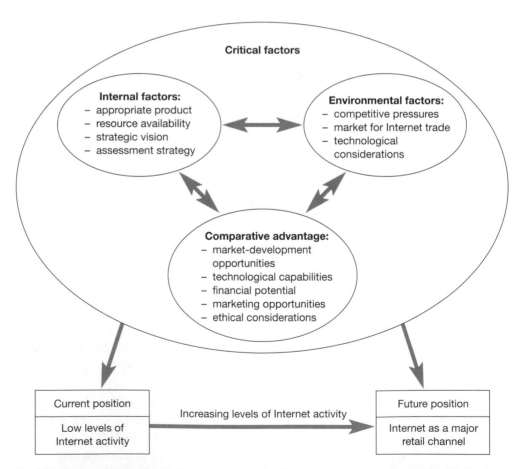

Fig. 13. 7 Factors affecting the likely uptake and application of the Internet as a channel for direct sales
Source: After Doherty *et al.* (1999)

entrants in the form of virtual merchants (such as the Internet bookshop Amazon.com) could not only drive the pace of development but also increase price competition through facilitating consumer search/price comparison. Furthermore, while the intensity of Internet rivalry is generally low, there are sectors, such as electrical goods and books, where the level of Internet activity is developing fast, and the threat could come from existing retailers. Finally, suppliers that manufacture retail merchandise for fixed-location outlets may exploit the potential shift in the balance of power in the online supply chain by trying to bypass intermediaries through offering their products direct to the customer.

The model presented in Fig. 13.7 provides details of factors likely to affect adoption. The factors presented in the model could be used for examining the facilitators and inhibitors of a company's web operations to provide a means of auditing the company's current position, the outcome of which could be translated into a coherent Internet retail marketing strategy.

SUMMARY

1 The Internet provides an innovative means of communication and interaction between businesses and consumers.

2 Retailers and virtual merchants use the Internet in a variety of ways and combinations: for market research, sales, payment and providing customer information.

3 Web sites focusing on the end-user vary in their function. Some offer a whole suite of interactive services whereas others just provide information. Internet shoppers face a number of options: how to access the Internet, whether to choose web content freely by using search engines such as Alta Vista (*www.altavista.com*) and hierarchical directories such as Yahoo! (*www.yahoo.co.uk*) or have it '*pushed*', for example by Tariff Online (*www.toll.co.uk*), whose web site offers to find the best option in terms of price for electricity and gas supplies in the UK.

4 Businesses offering online services need to consider their target audience and the logistics of getting goods and services to consumers as well as considering methods of payment if they are to operate successfully online.

5 The future potential of the Internet is unknown. However, at current rates of adoption it is likely that by the year 2010 the majority of the developed world will have some form of access to the Internet. In addition end-users' access to the Internet is increasing, using a variety of peripherals: via a computer at home or work, on the move via mobile telephone or in the family home. These increased uses will increase the opportunity to use the Internet from both the supplier's and the consumer's perspective. If end-users continue to be offered a range of services, which are effectively supported by retail suppliers, then it is likely that the Internet will mature into an important retail channel during the next decade.

EXERCISES AND QUESTIONS

Self-assessment exercises

1 Explain the term 'the Internet retail market'.

2 Describe the different types of retailers who might contribute to the Internet retail market.

3 Explain how the Internet retail channel differs from the traditional retail channel.

4 List the different types of business functions for which a retailer may use the Internet.

Discussion questions

1 Discuss the different approaches a consumer might take to shopping on- and offline.

2 Consider how the comparative advantages of using a web site devoted to online sales and ordering may vary between a fixed-location high street retailer and a virtual merchant.

3 Evaluate the potential of the Internet as a retail channel.

4 Discuss to what extent the Internet is likely to replace the traditional high street.

Essay questions

1 Select three web sites that demonstrate the different ways in which a retailer might use the Internet to interact with its online customers. Compare and contrast the contents of these web sites.

2 Imagine that an exclusive jewellery company in the Netherlands is wishing to sell its goods via the Internet. Write an executive summary covering the key discussion points for an executive planning board meeting. Consider the key factors that may facilitate and inhibit the progress of the web site.

Examination questions

1 Explain the different ways in which virtual merchants and established retailers might use the Internet.

2 The Internet is 'a revolutionary new promotional tool' (Fill, 1999). Discuss this statement from the perspective of a retail banker.

3 Discuss the critical factors that may affect business adoption of the Internet in a consumer market.

4 'Internet transactions will grow from $2.6 billion last year (1996) to $200 billion in the year 2001' (The Economist, 1997). Discuss the likelihood of this forecast being accurate. Give examples to support your argument.

REFERENCES

Alba, J., Lynch, J.C., Weitz, B., Janiszewski, C., Lutz, R., Sawyer, A. and Wood, S. (1997) 'Interactive home shopping. Consumer, retailer and manufacturer incentives to participate in electronic marketplaces', *Journal of Marketing*, 61 (July), 38–53.

Auger, P. and Gallaugher, J.M. (1997) 'Factors affecting the adoption of the Internet-based sales presence for small businesses', *Information Society*, 13(1), 55–74.

Breitenbach, C. and van Doren, D. (1998) 'Value-added marketing in the digital domain: enhancing the utility of the Internet', *Journal of Consumer Marketing*, 15(6), 559–75.

Casserttari, S. (1995) 'Discovering the missing pieces in your business strategy'. Paper presented to Conference, Internet for Business users, Madrid.

Davies, G. (1993) *Trade Marketing Strategy* London: Paul Chapman Publishing.

Doherty, N.F., Ellis-Chadwick, F. and Hart, C.A. (1999) 'Cyber retailing in the UK: the potential of the Internet as a retail channel', *International Journal of Retail and Distribution Management*, 27(1), 22–36.

Economist, The (1997) 'Hunt the Geek', 22 November.

Ernst and Young (1999) *The Second Annual Ernst and Young Internet Shopping Study*. New York: Ernst and Young.

Field, C. (1996) 'Window shopping: retailing over the Internet', *Computer Weekly*, 28 November, 52.

Fill, C. (1999) *Marketing Communications, Contexts, Contents and Strategies* (2nd edn). Hemel Hempstead: Prentice Hall Europe.

Finn, A. and Louviere, J. (1990) 'Shopping center patronage models: fashioning a consideration set segmentation solution', *Journal of Business Research*, 21, 277–88.

Hagel, J. III and Armstrong, A.G. (1997) *Net Gain: Expanding markets through virtual communities*. Cambridge, MA: Harvard Business School Press.

Haley, B.J., Carte, T.A. and Watson, R.T. (1996) 'Commerce on the Web: how is it growing?', *http://baylor.edu/ramsowers/ais.ac.96/program.htm*.

Kahin, B. (1995) 'The Internet and the national information infrastructure', in Kahin, B. and Keller, J. (eds) *Public Access to the Internet*. Harvard Information Infrastructure Project. Cambridge, MA: MIT Press.

KPMG and OXIRM (1996) 'The Internet: its potential and use by European retailers, a report by the Oxford Institute of Retail Management', No. 5114. London: KPMG.

Levy, M. and Weitz, B.A. (1995) *Retail Management* (2nd edn). Homewood, IL: Irwin.

McWilliam, G., Hammond, K. and Diaz A. (1997) 'Going places in Web town: a new way of thinking about advertising and the Web', *Journal of Brand Management*, 4(4).

Mulhern, F.J. (1997) 'Retail marketing: from distribution to integration', *International Journal of Research in Marketing*, 14, 103–24.

Nevens, T.M. (1999) 'The mouse that roared', *McKinsey Quarterly*, 1, 145–8.

Nua Ltd (1997) 'How many online?' *Nua Internet Surveys*, 1(11.4) (*www.nua.ie*).

Pavitt, D. (1997) 'Retailing and the super highway: the future of the electronic home shopping industry', *International Journal of Retail Distribution and Management*, 25(1), 38–43.

Retail Review (1999) 'General retailing', *Retail Review,* January.

Sarkar, M., Butler, B. and Steinfield, C. (1996) 'Intermediaries and cybermediaries: a continuing role for mediating player in the electronic market place', *Journal of Computer Mediated Communications*, 1(3), *www.ascusc.org/jcmc/vol1/issue3*.

Schramm, W. (1955) 'How communication works', in Schramm, W. (ed.) *The Process and Effects of Mass Communications*. Urbana, IL: University of Illinois Press.

Shi, C.S. and Salesky, A.M. (1994) 'Building a strategy for electronic home shopping', *The McKinsey Quarterly*, 4, 77–95.

Shirky, C. (1997) 'Attention strategy suggestion', *Communications of the ACM*, 40, 24.

Steuer, J. (1992) 'Defining virtual reality: dimensions determining telepresence', *Journal of Communications*, 42(4), 73–93.

Phillips Traffica Limited (1998) The net effect report, London.

Van Tassel, S. and Weitz, B.A. (1997) 'Interactive home shopping: all the comforts of home', *Direct Marketing*, 59(10), 40–1.

Verdict Research (1997) *Report on Homeshopping*. London: Verdict.

Verity, J. (1995) 'The Internet', *Business Week*, 14 November, 80–9.

Westland, C.J. and Au, G. (1998) 'A comparison of shopping experiences across three competing digital retailing interfaces', *International Journal of Electronic Commerce*, 2(2), Winter, 57–69.

Whinston, A.B. (1997) 'Electronic commerce: a shift in paradigm IEEE', *Internet Computing* (November–December), 17–19.

Woolacott E. (1996) 'Telly sales', *Computing*, 4 January.

FURTHER READING

Baker, M. (ed.) (1999) *The Marketing Book*. Oxford: Butterworth-Heinemann.
Chapter 28, Retailing, by Peter McGoldrick, describes retail formats, evolution and strategy.

de Kare-Silver, M. (1998) *eShock*. Basingstoke, UK: Macmillan.
This business book reviews the implications of the Internet and the strategic options available to retailers and manufacturers. At the time of writing de Kare-Silver had just been appointed as director responsible for e-commerce at retailer Great Universal Stores (GUS).

Dibb, S., Simkin, S., Pride, W. and Ferrel, O. (1997) *Marketing. Concepts and strategies* (3rd European edn). New York: Houghton Mifflin.
See companion Houghton Miffin web site (*www.busmgt.ulst.ac.uk/h_mifflin/*).
See Chapter 14, Retailing.

CHAPTER 14

Business-to-business Internet marketing

Learning objectives

After reading this chapter, the reader should be able to:

- identify the principal differences for marketers using the Internet in the business-to-business and business-to-consumer markets;
- identify the key uses of the Internet from a business perspective;
- consider the online buyer/supplier dialectic and the strategic implications of operating online or not operating online;

and should have:

- good understanding of the different applications of the Internet and the World Wide Web in the business-to-business context.

Links to other chapters

This chapter builds on concepts and frameworks introduced earlier in the book. The main related chapters are:

▶ Chapter 5, Internet marketing strategy.

▶ Chapters 6 and 7 – the use of extranets to build links with partners is important for the business-to-business market and is also covered in these chapters.

▶ Chapter 11, Electronic commerce transactions.

INTRODUCTION

Much of the media commentary on the commercial exploitation of the Internet has covered the way in which the Internet will affect consumers. While electronic commerce on consumer sites is predicted to increase dramatically, the forecasted volume of e-commerce on business-to-business sites dwarfs that of consumer sites. Several estimates suggest that the revenue of business-to-business e-commerce sites will be ten times that of consumer sites by 2001. Furthermore, of the top ten sites in the business2.com compilation of the most successful e-commerce sites (*see* Table 5.2), business-to-business companies such as Cisco, Dell and Marshall Industries dominate. Only two, Amazon and America Online, are exclusively consumer companies.

The use of the Internet for business-to-business marketing warrants separate study since many of the leading exponents of Internet marketing operate in this sphere. Furthermore, as for other media, the business-to-business market requires a different approach from that appropriate for other markets. To give one example of this, much media attention has focused on the use of banner advertising as a means of attracting customers to consumer sites, yet for many business-to-business sites it is an inappropriate technique.

This chapter starts by considering the differences between business-to-business and consumer markets. It then goes on to review the current state and size of the business-to-business Internet market, and finally reviews best practice through case studies of business-to-business sites.

Differences between business-to-business and business-to-consumer markets

As an introduction to this chapter we will start by considering the differences between business-to-business and business-to-consumer markets, and the implications of these differences for managers of business-to-business web sites.

Market structure

One of the main differences between business-to-business and business-to-consumer markets, which is important when considering the promotion of a web site, is the number of buyers. As Kotler *et al.* (1999) point out, there tend to be *far fewer but larger buyers*. What are the implications of this? First, with fewer buyers, the existence of suppliers tends to be well known. This means that efforts to promote a web site using methods such as banner advertising or listing in search engines are less important than for consumer brands. The buyers can be contacted directly, by post, or possibly by visits from sales representatives, to make them aware of the web site and how it can help them in their work. Of course, business-to-business suppliers with many potential customers will use promotion methods that correspond more closely to those of the retail market. Second, the existence of larger buyers is likely to mean that each is of great value to the supplier. The supplier therefore needs to understand the buyers' needs from the web site and will put effort into developing the web-based content and services necessary to deliver these services. The type of services needed to support the customer relationship are summarised well by Patricia Seybold in her book *Customers.com* (1999), in which she suggests principles for an effective business strategy for the Internet. Mini case study 14.1 assesses how these principles apply, particularly to the business-to-business market. To implement such principles for a business often requires the development of personalised web content such as that provided on Dell's Premier Pages, which are accessed using an extranet.

There may also be a correspondingly small number of competitors in a market. For example, there are five main train-makers in the world (such as ABB AdTranz, etc.). The fact that there are so few is significant from a market research point of view. To provide potential and existing clients with information, each manufacturer will publish information about new contracts, new products and testimonials from existing customers. This information will also be of great interest to competitors. The Web provides a means of finding such information more rapidly, and tends to give greater depth of information than other sources. This has led companies to employ staff specifically to find and summarise information from competitors.

With the need to put information on the Web in order to support customers and encourage loyalty, there is a danger of giving away too much information – 'giving away the crown jewels'. Thus, a careful balance needs to be struck between disclosing too much information and supplying less information than competitors. The use of extranets, where businesses have to log in to find information, is one solution to this, but passwords are notoriously insecure. An employee of a customer could be recruited on the basis of their access to a password or knowledge of competitors.

Figure 7.1 summarises the different interactions required between members of a business market and highlights the greater number of links in this market than in the business-to-consumer market.

Nature of the buying unit

Business purchases typically involve a more complex decision-making process than consumer purchases, since more people are involved. Webster and Wind (1996) identified the following participants:

- users;
- influencers;
- buyers;
- deciders;
- gatekeepers.

This complexity is needed in order to ensure financial control of and authorisation procedures for what may be expensive products. The content of the web site should therefore be designed to be suitable for the different members of the buying unit who are going to visit the web site. While the site should make the buying process straightforward, the content will mainly be tailored to the users, influencers and deciders. However, where the buyer is the same person as the decider, as may be the case for stationery, it is important to make the whole selection and buying process as easy as possible to encourage repeat purchases. Complete Activity 14.1 in order to understand how professional services companies design their web sites to appeal to different people. Note that it is not straightforward to tailor content for the different members of the buying unit since it is not practical to label the information under headings such as 'influencer' or 'decider', and their detailed information needs are difficult to identify.

Type of purchase

The type of purchase will vary dramatically according to scale. Companies such as train-makers will have low-volume, high-value orders; others selling items such as stationery will have high volume, low-value orders. With the low-volume, high-value purchase the Internet is not likely to be involved in the transaction itself since this will involve a special contract and financing arrangement. The high-volume, low-value orders, however, are suitable for e-commerce transactions and the Internet can offer several benefits over traditional methods of purchase such as mail and fax:

Tailoring the content for appropriate members of the buying decision

This activity involves assessing an e-commerce investment proposal from a chief information officer (CIO). It uses a web site to evaluate the suitability of various consultants as a potential partner.

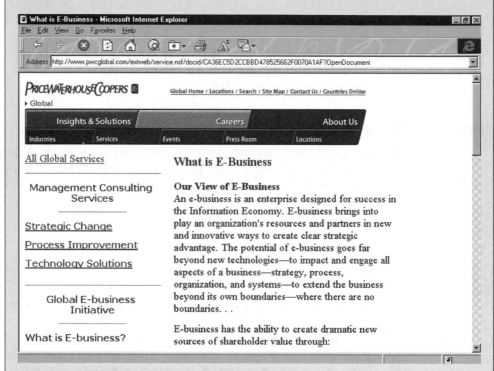

Fig. 14.1 PricewaterhouseCoopers web site (*www.pwcglobal.com*)

Scenario

An engineering company that sells gas turbines to the global market is intending to use the Internet to enable e-commerce integration with both its suppliers and its customers. It is looking to work with one of the leading professional services firms to specify and possibly implement such a system. The engineering company realises that since e-commerce is a relatively new concept, the experience in dealing with e-commerce projects may differ within the different firms. Different senior members of the company and some potential users of the system are planning to benchmark the different firms' web sites to assess their credibility and suitability for working on this project.

Task

Within a group of students identify different members of the buying decision team as follows:

■ Users (representatives of marketing and purchasing who will work with the chosen firm).
■ Influencers (Chief Information Officer and Chief Financial Officer).
■ Deciders (Chief Executive Officer).

Each team should visit one of the following firms' web sites:

1 Andersen Consulting (*www.andersen.com*)
2 PricewaterhouseCoopers (*www.pwcglobal.com*)
3 KPMG (*www.kpmg.com*)
4 IBM (*www.ibm.com*)
5 Ernst and Young (*www.ey.com*)

Each team should then prepare a one-page summary report or presentation summarising the suitability of the firm to work with the engineering company based on the information contained on the firm's web site.

A separate discussion group can be held to analyse which aspects of the web site design and content influenced the decision.

1 Easy for purchaser to assess whether item is in stock.
2 Order can be completed at any time of day or night.
3 Re-buys or repeat orders are easy to specify.
4 Delivery can be tracked online.
5 Purchasing history can be reviewed.

As was noted in Chapter 11, many of these advantages were previously available through EDI. The Internet offers these facilities at a lower cost, making them available to smaller companies, and gives them greater flexibility to switch to other suppliers.

Type of buying decision

The buying decision for technical business-to-business products and services will typically be more complicated and therefore more lengthy than that for consumer products (Turnbull, 1999), as is evidenced by Activity 14.1. There may be a lengthy period of supplier selection and product evaluation. To assist in this, many business-to-business specific portals similar to Yahoo! have been created that aim to unite buyers with sellers who have the products that match their requirements. Industry.Net (*www.industry.net*) is a good example of this (*see* Fig. 14.2). Such portals not only provide information about potential suppliers, but also enable searching of product specifications and standards and parts catalogues. Industry.Net has over 600 000 registered buying members and thousands of selling members. Virtual communities such as Vertical.Net (*see* Fig. 10.9) also help support members of a particular industry in their buying decisions. Many of the examples of such intermediaries are currently in the USA because the US market is large and it tends to be more developed, but examples of such intermediaries are starting to appear in other markets. For example, MarketSite is a new European service. This site (Fig. 14.3) is co-ordinated by British Telecom (BT), and has 40 selling merchants whose products range from office equipment and computing supplies to chemical and industrial components. The main buyer to have made a commitment to this service is Boots the Chemist.

Fig. 14.2 Industry.Net (*www.industry.net*) site for engineering products

Communication differences

Brougaletta (1985) and Gilliand and Johnston (1997) have reviewed the differences between organisation- and consumer-orientated marketing communications. Fill (1999) summarises these differences:

■ In an Internet context, the balance of the communications mix is different, with advertising and sales communication often merely being vehicles to support personal selling. The Internet will not greatly change this mix.

■ Below-the-line techniques tend to be more common than above-the-line techniques. The Internet can support these.

■ Message content. Business products tend to be higher involvement. The Internet can help here in providing the greater depth of information needed for a high-involvement product.

The nature of the business-to-business market

The Internet and the World Wide Web have created a dynamic online environment that, as will be seen in the final section of this chapter, is reaching all aspects of commercial trading. Companies managed by farsighted management teams have seized the opportunity to exploit the new business environment, and they have secured competitive advantage by being the first to offer a particular innovative online

Mini case study 14.1

Applying the principles of Customers.com to the business-to-business market

US industry analyst Patricia Seybold, in her book *Customers.com* (Seybold, 1999), offers guidelines for implementing an Internet business strategy (available at *www.customers.com*) that apply to both business and consumer markets, but are usefully applied to the business-to-business market. The eight critical success factors she suggests are:

1 *Target the right customers*. This first, and most important, principle suggests concentrating on either the most profitable customers – which is one of the tenets of one-to-one marketing (*see* Chapter 10) – or those that cannot be reached so well by other media. For example, the UK car insurer Swinton wished to target the young-driver market so it trialled a web site with a special 'Streetwise' brand. Alternatively, the right customers in the business-to-business context could be those who make the buying decisions. The web sites of management consultants such as those featured in Activity 14.1 are aimed principally at the senior managers in an organisation.

2 *Own the customer's total experience*. By managing the customer's entire experience it should be possible to increase the quality of service and hence promote loyalty. The total experience can be considered as all parts of the fulfilment cycle from product selection, purchase, delivery, set-up or installation to after-sales service. Examples of how the Internet can be used to improve the customer experience during this cycle are provided in the final section of this chapter. Note that since many services such as delivery are now outsourced, careful selection of partners is required, in order to ensure the delivery of quality service.

3 *Streamline business processes that affect the customer*. Seybold (1999) gives the example of Federal Express as a company that has used the Internet to re-engineer the service it delivers to customers – ordering, tracking and payment are now all available from the Fedex web site. For a financial services company such as Eaglestar selling insurance via the Web, streamlining the process has meant asking underwriters to reduce the complexity of the questions asked before a premium is calculated.

4 *Provide a 360-degree view of the customer relationship*. This means that different parts of the company must have similar information about the customer in order to ensure that it provides a consistent service. It implies integration of the personalisation facilities of a web site with other databases holding information about the customer. If these databases are not integrated then customer trust may be lost. If, for example, the web site offers a customer a product he or she has already purchased offline it will appear that the company does not understand that customer's needs. Integration of call centres with a web site is also evidence of the application of this guideline.

5 *Let customers help themselves*. This has the benefit of reducing costs, while at the same time providing faster, more efficient customer service. Mini case study 14.3 on Cisco (Fig. 14.8) illustrates these benefits well, for both the product-ordering and after-sales-support business processes.

▶ Mini case study *continued*

6 *Help customers do their jobs*. This guideline is similar to the previous one, but focuses more on providing them with the *information* needed to do their jobs. This is again a useful value-added facility of the web site, which helps encourage loyalty. Figures 14.9 and 14.10 give good examples of this principle in action.

7 *Deliver personalised service*. The importance of delivering personalised service to build a one-to-one relationship with the customer is discussed at length in Chapter 10.

8 *Foster community*. Business web sites afford good opportunities to create communities of interest since information can be generated that helps customers in their work and again encourages returns to the web site. Mini case study 14.3 refers to the community created between customers and engineers solving configuration problems as a 'self-inflating balloon of knowledge'. Independent business community sites are also important places for companies to have representation. Examples include Industry.Net (Fig. 14.2) and Vertical.Net (Fig. 10.9).

service. Some companies could fall behind as their management teams lack the required experience or vision of the future to embrace the Internet fully.

We now examine three different aspects of the current activity of the business-to-business market: (a) level of access to the Internet amongst businesses; (b) the proportion of companies that have a web presence; and (c) the volume of electronic commerce being conducted online.

Internet access levels

In Europe, the majority of large corporations are now online, giving employees web access and e-mail facilities. For the first quarter of 1998 Durlacher Survey (*www.durlacher.co.uk*) showed that access to the Internet in corporations was 94 per cent. Subsequent surveys have shown, however, that in many large companies access is only available to about 10 per cent of desk-based employees. Surveys by Durlacher have shown that a surprising number of small and medium-sized enterprises (SMEs) are now also online. The survey for the third quarter of 1997 showed that 39 per cent of SMEs had access, and medium companies 54 per cent. By the time of the survey for the second quarter of 1999, Internet use in SMEs had increased to 77 per cent, with free ISPs playing a role in this massive increase in access. Nearly half of the Internet-enabled SMEs in the UK still use a modem as their primary connection to the Internet. This is one reason why only 38 per cent of employees have access to the Internet (according to the survey for the second quarter of 1999).

Online presence

It is more difficult to assess the proportion of businesses that have a web site. While it is straightforward to monitor the number of Internet hosts or servers (as explained in Chapter 1), it is difficult to establish systematically how many of the 15 million servers have a business-to-business usage. In their survey of the second quarter of 1999 Durlacher found that, in the UK, retailers have a slightly lower Internet presence (61 per cent) than the rest of the supply chain. This is consistent with the research presented in Chapter 13. Nearly two-thirds (66 per cent) of distributors/wholesalers have an Internet presence, and 67 per cent of manufactures.

What is the financial performance of those sites that do have a web presence? An Activmedia report of 30 June 1999 shows that 35.2 per cent of US business-to-business web sites are currently operating at a profit, with an additional 19.1 per cent expecting to be profitable within 12 months. However, the study found that 31.5 per cent of companies with business-to-business web sites believe their web site may never operate at a profit, or never expected that it would do so!

It is often suggested that Europe is 18 months to two years behind the US market in terms of Internet adoption and innovation (*see*, for example, KPMG, 1998). Analysts and consultants produce reports with emotive titles such as 'Europe crawls while America runs' and 'Europe trails US in e-commerce market'. This picture does seem to be confirmed subjectively by the lack of intermediary sites such as Industry.Net (Fig. 14.2) and active e-commerce sites, but Europe is developing intermediary sites such as MarketSite (Fig. 14.3). Many examples of best practice do exist: for example, Marshall Industries and Cisco are often quoted as leading examples of e-commerce sites, but in Europe similar sites, such as RS Components, do exist.

Within Europe, the level of activities by business is variable, and not all companies have reacted. Adoption of the Internet amongst SMEs is much lower in France

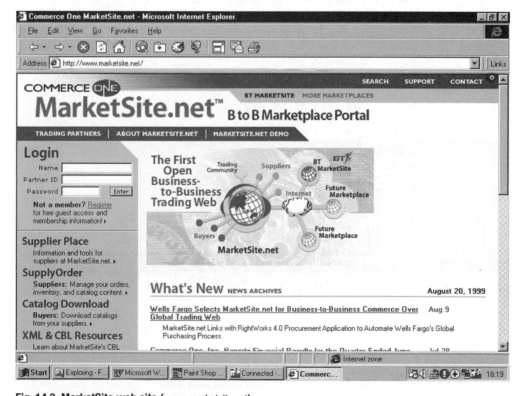

Fig. 14.3 MarketSite web site (*www.marketsite.net*)

than in Germany and the UK. In response to the deficiency the French Secretary of State for Industry, Christian Pierret, announced that the French government planned to spend as much as $8.2 million to assist these companies to get connected to the Internet. In contrast, Scandinavian companies, in particular those of Finland, have responded rapidly to the Internet.

Transactional e-commerce

The popularity of the Internet for business-to-business marketing is also indicated by the level of activity in business-to-business transactional e-commerce. Revenue transacted between businesses exceeds that in business-to-consumer transactions by a factor of 10. An indication of the importance of business-to-business commerce is provided by Fig. 14.4. Note that the figures include all e-commerce, not just that conducted using the Internet. It is evident that consumer goods (estimated at $2.9 billion in 2000, increasing to $26.0 billion in 2002) are dwarfed by the combined totals from business-to-business sectors such as petrochemicals, pharmaceuticals, construction and heavy industries. Some consumer products are, however, included within the figures for sectors such as computer/electronics and motor vehicles. Across all sectors a dramatic increase is forecast for a period of just two years.

There are many good reasons why the use of the Internet for e-commerce is greater for business-to-business than for business-to-consumer transactions:

1 Businesses are familiar with using the similar techniques of EDI (although this was beyond the reach of many SMEs).
2 There is more pressure on businesses to trade using e-commerce. Often, a major customer such as a supermarket may stipulate that its suppliers must use

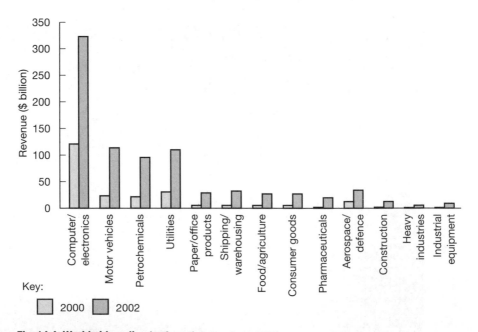

Fig. 14.4 Worldwide online trade estimates, June 1999

Source: Forrester Research (*www.forrester.nl*).

e-commerce for reasons of efficiency and cost. Alternatively, if a company's products are not available direct on the Internet then it may lose sales to other companies whose products are available.

3 Business-to-business relationships are often long term, making it more worth while for businesses to set up links between business partners.

4 The volume of transactions is often higher, thereby justifying the outlay.

5 Significant cost savings can arise through use of business-to-business e-commerce. Mougayer (1998) estimates that the average cost of producing and processing an invoice using a paper-based system is $100, which is 10 times greater than that for electronic processing.

Baker (1998), in a KPMG survey of over 500 large European companies, found that e-commerce was most widely used for business-to-business transactions with suppliers. In 1998 over 30 per cent used e-commerce for transactions with suppliers, and this figure was expected to rise to over 70 per cent by 2001.

International business-to-business marketing

The opportunity to achieve sales to new overseas markets is often used to champion the use of the Internet by businesses, but how practical is this in reality? While the Internet increases the potential market size, the smaller company may not have the infrastructure or resources to deal with international enquiries. Quelch and Klein (1996) point out that a company must have:

■ *'a 24 hour order taking and customer service response capability*;
■ *regulatory and customs-handling experience to ship internationally*;
■ *in-depth understanding of foreign marketing environments to assess the advantages of its own products and services.'*

Language and cultural understanding may also present a problem, and an SME is unlikely to possess the resources to develop a multi-language version of its site or employ staff with language skills. On the other hand, Quelch and Klein (1996) note that the growth of the use of the Internet for business will accelerate the trend for English to become the *lingua franca* of commerce. Additionally, the Internet will support the channel partnerships referred to in Chapter 7. Finally, the Internet will be used for market research about competitors and customers in overseas economies.

Hamill and Gregory (1997) highlight the strategic implications of the Internet that are relevant to business-to-business exchanges conducted internationally. The first is that there will be increasing standardisation of prices across borders as businesses become more aware of price differentials. Second, the importance of traditional intermediaries such as agents and distributors will be reduced by Internet-enabled direct marketing and sales.

There are many barriers to SMEs wishing to export overseas. What role can the Internet play in reducing these barriers? Hamill and Gregory (1997) identify barriers to SME internationalisation and propose how the Internet can assist. These findings are presented in Table 14.1.

Table 14.1 The role of the Internet in overcoming SME resistance to exporting

Barrier	How the Internet can assist
1 Psychological	Can help increase knowledge of overseas markets. Provides success stories of companies that have become exporters. International enquiries to prototype web sites can highlight demand.
2 Operational	E-commerce facilities can simplify the handling of international transactions. Can supply information on export issues.
3 Organisational	Overcomes lack of financial and staff resources for selling abroad. Provides knowledge of international markets and cultures. Creates networks of partners.
4 Product/market	Feedback from customers or market research facilitated by Internet may indicate the suitability of products for the overseas market.

Source: After Hamill and Gregory (1997) and Poon and Jevons (1997).

The KPMG survey reported by Baker (1998) showed that having board-level support for an e-commerce initiative was one of the key success factors for 'leaders' – companies in Europe that have achieved profitable Web revenues. The companies that have senior managers who have the vision to overcome the resistance factors listed in Table 14.1 are most likely to succeed in this new environment. The survey showed that there was a higher level of investment in the leading companies (Internet marketing budgets averaging $222 000 compared with $130 000), and the successful companies had integrated e-commerce into their supply chain.

Business-to-business case studies of best practice

This section illustrates best practice by reviewing how businesses are using the Internet to help different parts of the fulfilment cycle.

Supplier search

A Cahners Business Information survey of March 1999, reported in Table 9.6, illustrated the importance of integrated marketing communications as a means of providing information about a supplier and products. The survey showed that in the business-to-business market, the Web is currently the least important source for specifying equipment for new projects – magazines are far more important. However, this represents a promotion opportunity – mention of the web address in a magazine and an indication of the value proposition of the site, together with the more detailed depth of information the customer will find on the web site, gives more effective promotion than the use of the Web in isolation or the use of the magazine on its own. The survey also reveals that the use of the Web as a secondary source of information is growing dramatically.

The use of sites acting as intermediaries is also important in business-to-business transactions. As an example of this *see* Case study 14.1 – e-STEEL enables trading between buyers and sellers in a *virtual marketplace*. As explained in Chapter 7, the growth of such intermediaries means there is a need for marketers to be aware of when new intermediaries are established, and if relevant to make sure they are registered with the site as potential sellers. If a steel manufacturer is not registered with a site such as e-STEEL, then that manufacturer is missing out on potential business.

CASE STUDY 14.1

e-STEEL enables trading between buyers and sellers in a virtual marketplace

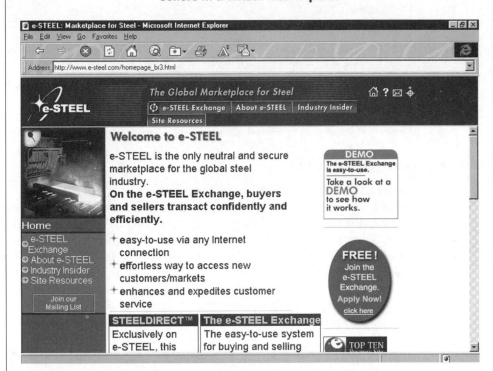

Fig. 14.5 e-STEEL marketplace for the global steel industry (*www.e-STEEL.com*)

e-STEEL Corporation was established in September 1998, as an e-commerce web site that allows buyers and sellers of steel to transact business with each other in a personalized, secure environment. As the intended global marketplace for the exchange of steel on the Internet, e-STEEL is completely independent – it does not own any of the products transacted on the system and is not affiliated with any industry participant. Companies are carefully screened to ensure that only legitimate, qualified steel buyers and sellers participate on the e-STEEL exchange.

e-STEEL is unique in that it offers a personalized negotiation site for buying and selling steel. Community and content features, such as market news, thought-leader forums, industry reports and stock information complement the transactional functionality of e-STEEL. This is the first implementation of its kind in the steel industry.

e-STEEL members can choose to conduct business with the entire universe of e-STEEL members, or familiar commercial partners, or they may deal exclusively with a single trusted mill or service center. Based on BroadVision One-To-One Enterprise, the site's STEELDIRECT™ technology supports member choices by enabling buyers and sellers to control their audience for pricing levels and product offerings at all times. When doing business on e-STEEL, each user completes a profile including trading credit references and preferences. Buyers and sellers may designate their partners for each potential transaction, or designate standard groups of partners through the e-STEEL site.

▶

> ► **Case study** *continued*

Questions

1 What benefits does such a site offer to buyers and sellers?

2 How does the site use the personalisation technology introduced in Chapter 10? Explore this using the demonstration facility on the site.

3 What other added value does the site offer to companies that register?

Source: Broadvision (*www.broadvision.com*).

Product evaluation and selection

One of the major challenges presented by the Internet to the marketer is that it empowers customers in product evaluation and selection. A greater amount of information is readily available on which purchasers can make their buying decision. This makes it imperative that each business makes efforts to provide better information than its competitors to assist the customer in the buying process. An example of a business that uses such a tool to help assist the buying decision is Marshall Industries. Figure 14.6 shows how the company provides an on-screen tool that helps show customers the range of products available that meet their needs, in this case for hard-disk drives.

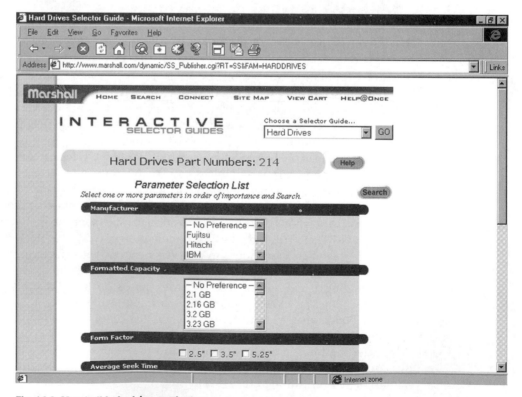

Fig. 14.6 Marshall Industries product

A further example of product evaluation is provided by the intermediary Wiznet, which connects buyers to over 50 000 manufacturer's industrial catalogues, 5 million data sheets and product specifications from 30 000 suppliers. Each week more than 130 000 product enquiries and 14 000 e-mail exchanges are facilitated.

Purchase

Mini case study 14.2 illustrates that even a large company may have previously failed to encourage all of its customers to order electronically. The Internet, with its lower cost and value-added features such as being able to search graphically and find information about availability and order status, has encouraged more customers to use this facility.

Mini case study 14.2   **Boeing uses PART web site to streamline ordering process**

The information you need, when you need it.

We are pleased to announce a new way for you to research and order parts from Boeing Spares.

To provide more value and better service to our customers, we have developed a way to use the sophisticated technology of the World Wide Web to give customers direct access to our extensive part information and ordering system. You can now order parts and view part information through a new World Wide Web site called the Boeing Part Analysis & Requirement Tracking (PART) Page.

Through the Boeing PART Page, current data such as part inventories, prices, part interchangeability and purchase order status are at your fingertips.

Fig. 14.7 Boeing PART web site

Owing to the volume and regularity of their orders the largest airlines, constituting 10 per cent of Boeing customers, and representing 60 per cent of its revenue, established EDI connections with Boeing over value-added networks. But not all customers did so, principally because of the capital investment required for such a facility. Boeing viewed the Internet as providing a great opportunity to encourage more of its customers to order electronically, and, to persuade its smaller customers to order in this way, in 1996 introduced its PART page on the Internet. This gave customers around the world the ability to check availability and pricing, order and track order status for nearly half a million parts. Less than a year later about 50 per cent of Boeing customers used it for 9 per cent of all parts orders and a much higher percentage of customer service enquiries, comprising about half a million transactions.

The Internet is also being used for new models of purchasing such as FastParts Inc., a subscribers-only Internet-based spot market for semiconductors and electronic components. It is patterned after the NASDAQ stock market model, which provides the trading facility and co-ordinates all trade fulfilment activities.

Post-purchase customer service

The Internet offers opportunities for businesses to improve the quality of customer service and at the same time to reduce costs. The quality of customer service can be increased since customers can find the right answer, more quickly, using information and diagnostic tools on the web site. For example, on the Dell site (*www.dell.com*) there is a software-based service that asks a series of questions that help diagnose the problem and then recommends possible solutions. Through providing web-based support or 'customer self-service' the company clearly has to employ fewer staff since straightfoward problems are solved by customers online. This is illustrated by Mini case study 14.3. Note that although costs can potentially be reduced, there is still likely to be a need for human service representatives in the foreseeable future. Cisco has had to double the number of service representatives, although the number of sales have increased by a greater extent.

Helping the customers do their job

The ability to help customers do their work is one of the key guidelines suggested by Seybold (1999). By providing value-added services this facility also encourages repeat visits and encourages customer loyalty. This section looks at two examples of this. The first, shown in Fig. 14.9, is Cyanamid, which offers guidance for crop growers on weed control.

A further example of the use of the Internet to provide improved information to a customer can be found in Mini case study 14.4.

Mini case study 14.3

Cisco excels in pre-sales and after-sales customer service

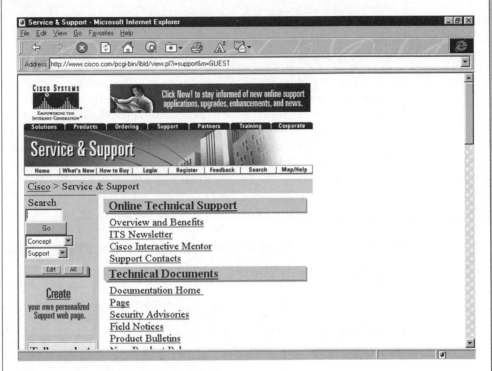

Fig. 14.8 Cisco customer service facilities (*www.cisco.com*)

Cisco is the leading site in the *Business 2.0* magazine compilation of the leading e-commerce businesses, with 64 per cent of its annual $6.4 billion revenue being derived through the use of the Internet (*see* Chapter 5 and Table 5.2 for further details). This success has not only been achieved through the proposition of the e-commerce part of the site. It has also been enabled by the quality of customer service provided on the site.

As is pointed out in *The Economist* (26 June 1999), during the early 1990s when Cisco was a relatively small company and growing rapidly, a bottleneck developed in after-sales support. This problem developed since Cisco electronic components such as routers and hubs need configuration after delivery. The queries that arise are highly technical and can cover a wide number of issues, as well as being numerous. The Web turned out to be the answer to this problem. Cisco took the decision to achieve as much of its support as possible online so that customers could resolve relatively straightforward queries themselves while the support engineers could deal with the most intractable problems. Susan Bostrom, head of Cisco's Internet Solutions Group, describes the idea as 'an almost instant success'; it became a 'self-inflating balloon of knowledge'. This occurred because Cisco customers not only accessed information on the site, but started to share their experiences with Cisco and other customers. The success of the scheme has been such that, today, more than 80 per cent of problems from customers and partners

▶

▶ Mini case study *continued*

are answered online. Although sales are six times greater than in 1994, the number of technical support staff has only doubled.

Sales support

Cisco also found it was receiving many enquiries arising from the complexity of specifying products. These sometimes arose from errors in catalogues, sometimes from customers ordering out-of-date equipment, but, whatever the source, one in three sales orders were filled in incorrectly. Today, over 60 per cent of Cisco's sales come from the Web, where customers order direct from an up-to-date catalogue accompanied by detailed information, which ensures they are selecting the right equipment. Over 55 per cent of sales now pass through the Cisco sales order processing system without the need for intervention.

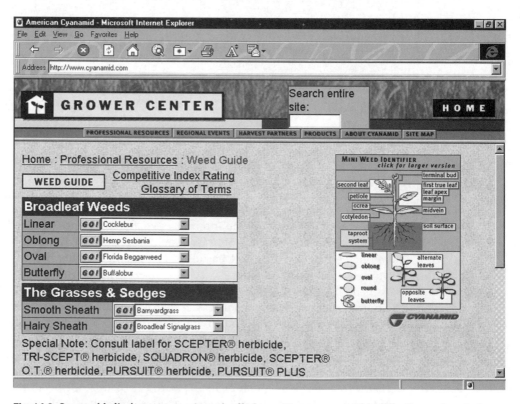

Fig. 14.9 Cyanamid site (*www.cyanamid.com*), offering guidance on weed identification and control

Mini case study 14.4

UK DCS uses online monitoring to reduce costs and improve customer services

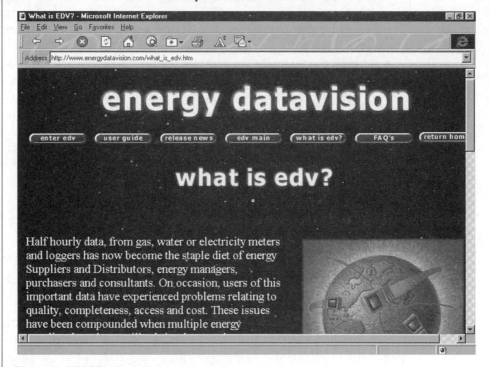

Fig. 14.10 UK DCS web site (*www.ukdcs.com*)

In June, 1999 Net Profit (*www.net-profit.co.uk*) reported on how UK DCS, an energy-monitoring company, has migrated its database online to provide a service to its business customers. Before it offered the web service, UK DCS monitored the energy consumption of companies through meters and sent detailed monthly reports by mail. It now offers information updated daily through the Web, and customers can also access an archive of data to compare usage.

The move to this new service has partly been driven by deregulation of metering, a move that has increased competition. The online service gives UK DCS an edge and also enables the company to reduce the cost of the service from £100 per month to £36–50 per month.

Product evaluation and feedback

The Internet has great potential for gaining feedback from customers about use of products as part of the relationship-building process examined in Chapter 10. However, this opportunity does not seem to have been seized upon since essential features such as transactional e-commerce and customer service are more important facilities to implement. An example of such feedback is a section on the Marshall Industries web site that is used to preview new products that are being finalised before release to market. Customers have the opportunity to sign up for trial use of products and then provide feedback.

SUMMARY

1 Business-to-business marketing via the Internet needs to be approached differently from business-to-consumer marketing since the well-known differences between business-to-business markets and business-to-consumer markets are magnified on the Internet. Some of the key difference are:

- The different market structure of sectors that have few customers representing significant value to a company requires significant investment in order that information is provided to sustain the business relationship online. This often requires the construction of *extranet-based* services for these customers.

- The buying decision is often complex and involves several people. Information on the web site must be available to facilitate this type of decision making. Selling businesses must make sure they are represented on intermediary sites such as Industry.net and MarketSite.

- The type of purchase is often suitable for *e-commerce* since complex and/or repeat orders and the ability to monitor purchase history are more necessary for business-to-business markets.

2 Seybold (1999) suggests that some of the most important tactics for businesses to consider when operating over the Internet are to:

- target the right customer, perhaps using extranets to deliver personalised service to larger accounts;

- use the Web to streamline the businesses processes that affect the customer such as product selection and ordering and so provide 'web self-service' facilities;

- help customers do their jobs by providing relevant information and nurturing communities within the industry sector.

3 There is now a high penetration of Internet access amongst businesses, but it may be restricted within businesses. The volume of business-to-business commerce greatly exceeds business-to-consumer business since there is a familiarity among businesses with previous use of EDI and a greater imperative for business-to-business e-commerce to reduce costs and maintain links between buying and selling businesses.

4 The Internet has promoted international business-to-business marketing, but there are many barriers to be overcome, particularly for SMEs.

5 Case studies illustrate how the Internet can be leveraged across the fulfilment cycle from supplier selection and product evaluation through to purchase and after-sales support.

EXERCISES AND QUESTIONS

Self-assessment exercises

1 Explain why the use of extranets is more important in business-to-business marketing than in business-to-consumer marketing.

2 Summarise how a business might employ the Internet and the World Wide Web to assist customers at different stages of the fulfilment cycle.

3 How does business-to-business marketing on the Internet differ from business-to-consumer marketing?

4 What are the implications of the different nature of business-to-business commercial transactions for business-to-business e-commerce?

Discussion questions

1 Discuss why a business might be cautious about trading via the Internet.

2 Consider how the comparative advantages of using a web site devoted to online sales and ordering may vary between a metal components manufacturer and an ice cream manufacturer.

3 'Business-to-business use of the Internet offers more opportunity for companies to benefit from its use by making savings on costs than by using the Internet to transact with their customers.' Discuss and support your answer with examples.

4 'Europe is two years behind the USA in terms of innovation and commerce using the Internet for the business-to-business market.' Discuss.

5 'For a company that has been too cautious to export internationally the Internet removes all barriers.' Discuss.

Essay questions

1 Select two web sites that demonstrate the different ways in which a business might use the Internet to interact with its online customers. Compare and contrast the contents of these web sites.

2 Assess the value of the Internet in interacting with customers at different stages of the fulfilment cycle.

3 Why should marketing communications be approached differently for business-to-business marketing on the Internet than for business-to-consumer marketing?

4 Compare and contrast e-commerce in the business-to-business and business-to-consumer markets.

5 Summarise and attempt to explain the differences in the extent of adoption of the Internet for use by businesses in Europe.

Examination questions

1 Describe two ways in which business-to-business marketing on the Internet differs from business-to-consumer marketing.

2 What is an extranet and what benefits can it bring to a supplier?

3 How does the buying decision for business-to-business marketing differ from that for business-to-consumer marketing, and what are the implications for a web site content developer?

4 What role can intermediaries play in the online business-to-business marketplace?

REFERENCES

Activmedia (1999) 'Two thirds of B-to-B sites to turn a profit', reported at Nua Online surveys June 30, (*http://www.nua.ie/surveys*) from *www/activmediaresearch.com*

Baker, P. (1998) *Electronic Commerce. Research Report 1998.* London: KPMG Management Consulting.

Brougaletta, Y. (1985) 'What business-to-business advertisers can learn from consumer advertisers', *Journal of Advertising Research*, 25(3), 8–9.

Fill, C. (1999) *Marketing Communications, Contexts, Contents and Strategies* (2nd edn). Hemel Hempstead: Prentice Hall Europe.

Gilliand, D. and Johnston, W. (1997) 'Toward a model of business-to-business communications effects', *Industrial Marketing Management*, 26, 15–29.

Hamill, J. and Gregory, K. (1997) 'Internet marketing in the internationalisation of UK SMEs', *Journal of Marketing Management*, 13, 9–28.

Kotler, P., Armstrong, G., Saunders, J. and Worg, V. (1999). *Principles of Marketing* (2nd edn). Hemel Hempstead: Prentice Hall Europe.

KPMG (1998) *Europe Gets Wired. A survey of Internet use in Great Britain, France and Germany.* London: KMPG Management Consulting.

Mougayer, W. (1998) *Opening Digital Markets. Battle plans and strategies for Internet commerce* (2nd edn). New York: CommerceNet Press, McGraw-Hill.

Poon, S. and Jevons, C. (1997) 'Internet-enabled international marketing: a small business network perspective', *Journal of Marketing Management*, 13, 29–41.

Quelch, J. and Klein, L. (1996) 'The Internet and international marketing', *Sloan Management Review*, Spring, 61–75.

Seybold, P. (1999) *Customers.com.* London: Century Business Books, Random House.

Turnbull, P. (1999) 'Business-to-business marketing: organisational buying, behaviour, relationships and networks', in Baker, M. (ed.) *The Marketing Book* (4th edn). Oxford: Butterworth-Heinemann.

Webster, F. and Wind, Y. (1996) 'A general model for understanding organizational buying behavior', *Marketing Management*, 4(4), 52–8.

FURTHER READING

Baker, M. (ed.) (1999) *The Marketing Book.* Oxford: Butterworth-Heinemann.
Chapter 6, Business-to-Business Marketing: Organisational Buying Behaviour, Relationships and Networks by Peter Turnbull, is recommended.
Chapter 23 by Stan Paliwoda, International Marketing – The Issues, discusses cultural and other issues.
Chapter 30, The Internet: The Direct Route to Growth and Development by Jim Hammill and Sean Ennis, reviews the impact of the Internet on small and medium-sized enterprises and on barriers to internationalisation.

Brassington, F. and Petitt, S. (2000) *Principles of Marketing* (2nd edn). Harlow, UK: Pearson Education.
See companion Prentice Hall web site (*www.booksites.net/brassington2*).
Chapter 4, Organisational Buying Behaviour, describes the stages in the business-to-business buying-decision process and the role of different members of the buying unit. Chapter 23 describes international marketing.

Dibb, S., Simkin, S., Pride, W. and Ferrel, O. (1997) *Marketing. Concepts and Strategies* (3rd European edn). New York: Houghton Mifflin.
See companion Houghton Mifflin web site (*www.busmgt.ulst.ac.uk/h_mifflin/*).

See Chapter 5, Organisational Markets and Buying Behaviour.

Kotler, P., Armstrong, G., Saunders, J. and Wong, V. (1999) *Principles of Marketing* (2nd edn).
Hemel Hempstead: Prentice Hall, Europe.
See companion Prentice Hall web site for 8th US edn (*cw.prenhall.com/bookbind/pubbooks/kotler/*).
See Chapter 7, Business Markets and Business Buyer Behaviour.

Leonidou, K. (1995) 'Export barriers: non-exporters' perceptions', *International Marketing Review*, 12(1), 4–25.

CHAPTER 15

The future of Internet marketing

Learning objectives

After reading this chapter, the reader should be able to:

- understand the factors that will govern the future development of the Internet;
- describe current trends in the use of the Internet;
- evaluate the significance of the Internet in comparison with other marketing channels;
- appreciate the cultural and social consequences of the availability and use of the Internet.

Links to other chapters

▶ This chapter does not link directly to any single chapter, but develops ideas from several previous chapters in the book.

INTRODUCTION

The purpose of this chapter is to review factors that will affect the future development of the Internet and to assess the implications for marketers. The trends encompass a range of issues, from technological developments that will introduce new methods of accessing the Internet and marketing using the Internet, through issues of concern over the infringement of privacy, to access to the Internet amongst different sections of society. One of the characteristics of the Internet to date has been the speed of change – the speed at which new technologies are introduced, new methods of marketing are employed and companies develop Internet-related revenue. This rapid rate of change makes it difficult to predict even a short time into the future, but awareness of the factors that will contribute to the future is important to marketers who need to anticipate the changing needs of consumers and responses by competitors. Techniques available for dealing with the rate of change with which new techniques are introduced are also described.

Factors governing future adoption of the Internet

It is necessary for marketers to understand the different factors that will affect how many people will use the Internet in future. By understanding these factors, marketers will be able to estimate how the nature of the audience on the Internet will change in the future. Suitable investment and appropriate tactics can then be developed to service this changing audience. We will consider separately the factors affecting the level of access to the Internet for the consumer audience and the business audience.

Factors affecting consumer adoption of the Internet

A useful insight into the factors affecting Internet adoption is provided by the *Which?* magazine 1998 Internet survey of UK users (*www.which.net*). This showed that about 14 per cent of the UK population was using the Internet in 1998 (approximately 8 million individuals). Significantly, of the non-users a large majority (61 per cent, 30 million individuals) said they would never use the Internet. The reluctance to go online increases with age: 85 per cent of those over 55 said they will never be connected to the Internet. When asked why they would remain non-users half of all non-users said they did not believe that the Internet is relevant to their needs. Of the non-users 30 per cent have resisted because of the cost and 16 per cent because they are afraid of, or do not understand, the technology. Part of the reluctance to access the technology appears to be based on ignorance, with 25 per cent of them not knowing that a computer is necessary to get online and only 37 per cent knowing that a telephone line is necessary.

Let us now look in a more structured way at the factors that are likely to affect an individual's decision to go online. The main factors can be considered to be:

1 Value proposition

The survey suggested that the most important inhibitor was that potential users did not perceive a need to be online. This is understandable since two key points for persuading people to use the Internet are that it is a source of information and that it is a way of buying. Sceptics are likely to take the attitude of, 'I have more than enough information from other media, and if I want to buy products, I have plenty of options for that too!' As the Internet matures and there is more publicity about the medium, then this perception is likely to change. The need will develop as consumers are exposed to offline promotion for web sites that explicitly champion the benefits of the Internet (*see* Mini case study 15.1) and word-of-mouth promotion as friends say how much money they saved by booking a flight or buying a computer online. Research mentioned in Chapter 10 showed that word of mouth is a very significant method of 'speading the news' about the Internet. As the online population grows, people may also be encouraged to move online to keep in contact via e-mail, or to take advantage of online price comparison services such as those mentioned in Case study 15.1. It can be argued, however, that none of these facilities is unique to the Internet – teletext services on television offer similar facilities already.

2 Cost of access

Cost is certainly a barrier for those who do not already own a home computer: a major expenditure for many households. The other main costs are the cost of using an ISP to connect to the Internet and the cost of using the media to connect (telephone or cable charges). At the time of the survey, consumers were having to pay £10 or £15 per month to access the Internet, a not inconsiderable sum. With the advent of free ISPs such as Freeserve this cost has been removed, and the cost of a local phone call to connect to the Internet is not a major barrier to use. The removal of ISP costs has made many go online, with Freeserve signing up more than a million customers in its first year of existence, many of them new to the Internet.

3 Ease of use

There are two aspects to ease of use. The first is ease of first connecting to the Internet using the ISP. The second is ease of using the Web once connected. Few would argue that both tasks are more difficult than recording a programme using a videocassette recorder, the oft-quoted example of technology that is difficult to use. Poor ease of use is likely to remain a barrier for the sizeable proportion (16 per cent) who mentioned this in the survey.

4 Security

While security is only, in reality, a problem for those who shop online, the perception generated by news stories may be that if people are connected to the Internet their personal details and credit card details may not be secure. It will probably take many years for this fear to diminish as using the Internet slowly becomes established as a standard way of purchasing goods.

5 Fear of the unknown

Many will simply have a general fear of the technology and the new medium. This is not surprising since many of the comments they have heard about the Internet are sensationalised reports of pornography and fraud.

How, then, will the perceptions that affect these factors change through time? With such a large proportion of people not planning to use the Internet, it will take a long time before the majority of people are convinced. Perhaps the biggest driver will be the unique benefits the Internet can offer. The personal experience of friends who have saved money on the Internet and do not find it too difficult to use or see it as a security risk will help adoption. This type of word-of-mouth information may not, however, transfer across social groups or age differences. With the personal computer likely to remain difficult to use, new easier-to-use Internet access appliances such as digital television may be necessary before the Internet is widely adopted. If and when the Internet becomes a standard feature of televison, the proportion of the population accessing it will increase to the 98 per cent who view television. This view is supported by a June 1999 report from the Henley Centre for Forecasting, which predicts that the Internet will only achieve its full potential if alternatives to the personal computer become available that will increase access from home. In the UK, the proportion of homes with personal computers increased from 10 per cent in 1995 to 30 per cent in 1998, but it is thought that it will reach a ceiling of about 40 per cent of households early in the new millennium.

Mini case study 15.1 **Freeserve highlights the proposition of the Internet**

A cross-media campaign in the summer of 1999 highlighting the benefits of the Internet available from the Freeserve portal was run by the UK free ISP Freeserve. This boldly proclaimed:

- £100 000 prizes.
- Last-minute holidays and breaks.
- Financial and company information.
- Best-selling books with up to 50 per cent off.
- Top 10 CDs from £9.99 with free delivery.
- Local information.

The offer was backed up by the tag line : 'I found it on Freeserve' (*www.freeserve.net*).

Factors affecting business adoption of the Internet for web access

We have described the business benefits of establishing an Internet presence extensively in this book. Here we look instead at the benefits of *access* and the levels of access to the Internet amongst businesses. Some of the factors mentioned in relation to consumers also affect the business community's access to the Internet. However, fears of security, difficulty in using the technology or fear of the unknown are unlikely to stop adoption except possibly in the case of some small businesses. To businesses, the value proposition of the ability to access the Internet is more likely to be well established. Medium and large businesses have used EDI to facilitate purchasing for many years, and the Internet is a natural extension of this. The benefits of cost reduction, ease of ordering and more rapid turnaround of purchasing using the Internet are clear. These clear benefits have resulted in extensive use of the Internet for digital purchasing, and this is why the amount of business-to-business commerce exceeds business-to-consumer commerce by a factor of 10. In the UK, the quarterly Durlacher Internet surveys (*www.durlacher.co.uk*) have been monitoring adoption of the Internet by businesses of different sizes. Surveys in 1999 showed that over 90 per cent of large corporations are connected, over 50 per cent of medium companies, and 35 per cent of smaller companies.

It is worth considering the penetration of Internet access within companies. Although the Internet may be used by senior managers and the purchasing department, its use may be deliberately limited for other staff. The Durlacher surveys suggest that in 60 per cent of companies accessing the Internet, the facility is available to less than 10 per cent of the workforce. This may be due to the cost of setting up access, but it is more likely to be done to prevent misuse of company time. Mini case study 15.5 highlights methods used to limit access to the Internet. This seems to suggest that Internet use throughout businesses will not become widespread, or it may be strictly controlled to, perhaps, 30-minute segments per day. At the time of writing, there are good opportunities for companies to sell direct to consumers at the workplace as well as for business-to-business marketers.

Future trends

In this section we examine some of the trends already evident today that seem set to be important to future digital marketers. It is, of course, much more difficult to speculate about the longer-term future where the trends are not evident today!

Digital brokers, transparent prices and the downward pressure on price

Arguably the most significant trend for both business-to-consumer and business-to-business markets will be the emergence of new intermediaries that simplify the buying process for both buyers and sellers. Mougayer (1998) stresses the importance of this type of intermediary, as does *The Economist* 1999 Business and the Internet survey (Symonds, 1999) and McKinsey consultants such as Berryman *et al.* (1998). As explained in Chapter 7, in the future, purchase will be facilitated by:

Neutral intermediaries

These are intermediaries who bring together buyers and sellers and who will create new digital marketplaces to help put buyers and sellers in touch. For business-to-business sites this trend is highlighted by sites such as Industry. Net in the USA (*www.industry.net*) (Fig. 14.2), which provides details of engineering companies for over 600 000 members. In Europe and elsewhere, the market tends to be smaller, so such services are just starting up. A good example of such a service is the MarketSite service (Fig. 14.3) co-ordinated by British Telecom (*www.marketsite.net*), which has 40 merchants selling goods ranging from office equipment and computing supplies to chemical and industrial components. The main buyer to have made a commitment to this service is Boots the Chemist. Intermediaries offering price comparison services are also likely to be very significant in the development of the Internet for retail marketing. The power of these services is already apparent from the popularity of late-booking holiday services facilitated by the television-based teletext services. On the Internet, the likely future of these services is indicated by US sites, the growth of which has been promoted by the size of the market that has driven such services. Two examples of these services are featured in Case study 15.1. The significance of the CNET (*www.computers.com*) site is indicated by the number of e-commerce retailers who are signed up to this service. For many products, between 50 and 100 suppliers are available. These services make it much easier for customers to compare prices – different prices are quite apparent. It is interesting to note that today retailers can sustain differences in price of over $100 for a $300 product. Such price differentials are not likely to persist in the future, as pricing becomes more transparent. The implications are that prices will be driven down – a worrying trend for manufacturers and retailers, but one that must be grasped as an opportunity before competitors do so.

Buyer-controlled sites

These present a slightly different model of buying, where procurement needs are posted. Examples of such sites in the UK include Zygonet (*www.zygonet.com*) and IT Network (*www.itnetwork.com*), where companies can post their buying requirements and then wait for offers to be made by different suppliers. It can be argued that these are not really new methods of buying; rather the World Wide Web has provided a means to make them more practical and therefore much more common. Mini case study 15.2 provides an example of a co-operative buying arrangement for consumers. While co-operative buying is not new for businesses, it is new for this type of consumer application.

Improved methods for facilitating purchasing using sites such as these will undoubtedly increase the adoption of the Internet for e-commerce since consumers will become aware of the lower prices made available by these buying methods. For business-to-business commerce it will be necessary to implement methods of making payment easier, such as the Open Buying Initiative (*see* Chapter 11).

CASE STUDY 15.1   **PRICE COMPARISON SERVICES: THE FUTURE WAY TO BUY**

This case study reviews two examples of existing Web-based services, which are thought to indicate the future development of purchasing on the Internet. You should visit both sites and select a product in which you are interested, in order to understand the convenience of this type of service. Then answer the questions below, which will prompt you to think about how these services will help shape the future of retail activity on the Internet.

CNET (*www.computers.com*) is marketed with the tag line, 'What to buy. Where to buy it'. It is effectively an online computing magazine with reviews of products, but it provides a value-added service of price comparisons that are linked to

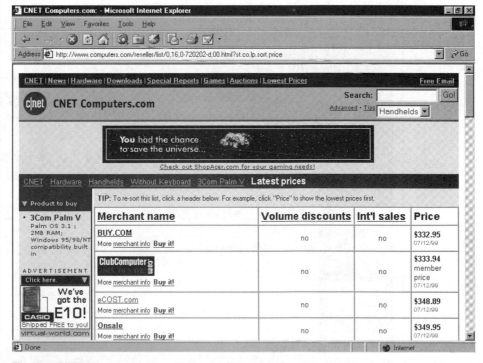

Fig. 15.1 CNET (*www.computers.com*) site, showing prices for a handheld computer from different suppliers

453

▶ **Case study** *continued*

reviews and details of suppliers. In Fig. 15.1, the user is interested in purchasing a Palm V handheld computer and has requested a list of lowest prices. The system is linked into a regularly updated database of suppliers and their prices, so the cheapest offer is readily apparent. Note that some suppliers such as ClubComputer.com pay a premium to CNET to have their logo displayed, and they are placed at the top of the list (which is not initially sorted in price order). The next stage in the purchase process is shown in Fig. 15.2.

Figure 15.2 shows the next stage in purchasing for a customer who has decided to buy this model of computer from BUY.com. The customer simply presses on the link marked 'Buy It!' in Fig. 15.1 and is then taken straight to the screen shown in Fig. 15.2. This makes the ordering process very straightforward.

Amazon is best known as a seller of books and music, but it has invested to diversify this position. In 1998 it acquired Junglee for the database technology associated with its price comparison software. The contribution of this service is indicated in Fig. 15.3. This shows how a consumer interested in purchasing a pair of jeans can type in different specifications such as the Levi's 501 brand and a maximum price and will be presented with a range of choices from different suppliers. As in the previous example, the user then has the option of going directly to the merchant's site to purchase the product. The model for payment will be that the intermediary, Amazon in this case, will receive a proportion of the product price (perhaps 10 per cent).

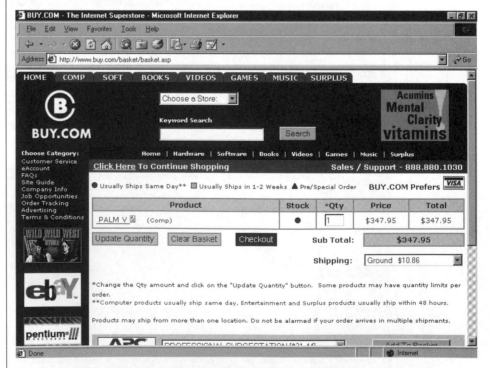

Fig. 15.2 Purchase screen for buying a handheld computer from BUY.com (*www.buy.com*)

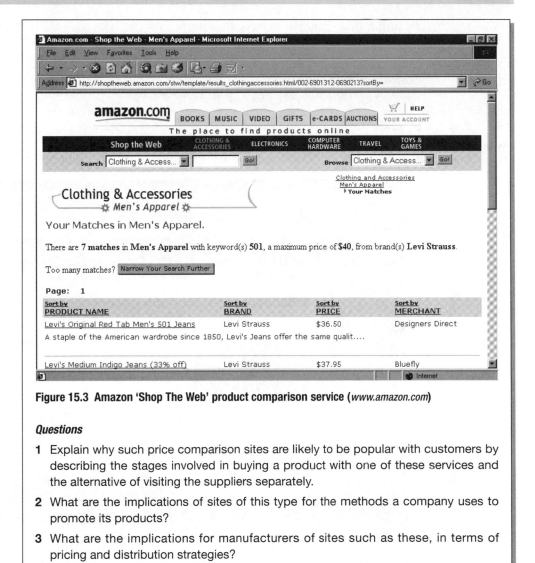

Figure 15.3 Amazon 'Shop The Web' product comparison service (*www.amazon.com*)

Questions

1 Explain why such price comparison sites are likely to be popular with customers by describing the stages involved in buying a product with one of these services and the alternative of visiting the suppliers separately.

2 What are the implications of sites of this type for the methods a company uses to promote its products?

3 What are the implications for manufacturers of sites such as these, in terms of pricing and distribution strategies?

In the future, some suggest that the task of searching for suppliers and products may be taken over by software agents that have defined rules or some degree of intelligence that replicate that in humans. An agent is a software program that can perform tasks to assist humans. On the Internet, agents can already be used for marketing research, by performing searches using many search engines, and in the future they may also be used to search for products or even to purchase products. Agents work using predetermined rules or may learn rules using neural network techniques. Such rules will govern whether purchases should be made ot not.

Some of the implications of agent technology for marketing are explored by Gatarski and Lundkvist (1998). They suggest that agent technology may create artificial consumers, who will undertake supplier search, product evaluation and product selection functions. The authors suggest that such actors in a supplier-to-consumer dialogue will behave in a more rational way than their human equivalent, and existing marketing theories may not apply.

> **Software agents**
> Software programs that can assist humans to perform tasks.

Mini case study 15.2

Letsbuyit.com, a co-operative buying service from Sweden

Fig. 15.4 Letsbuyit.com, online co-operative buying

Letsbuyit.com is a good example of the new types of buying model the Internet has inspired. Co-operative buying does occur offline for business-to-business buying, but it is rare for consumer buying. Letsbuyit.com covers a range of consumer products. It offers an initial discount of at least 20 per cent, with this set to increase once larger numbers of buyers are involved. The site was launched in Sweden, and its owners are anticipating roll-out to 12 countries in 2000.

How it works

Consumers join forces to buy many units of a product, rather than just one, thereby being entitled to volume discounts. If, for example, buyers are interested in purchasing a particular hi-fi, they will add their name to a list of buyers who are interested and then wait until a pre-set number have registered the intention to buy, at which stage the purchase will be fulfilled and the supplier will give all consumers a discounted price.

Integration of Internet, extranet and intranet

Traditionally, the control and management of these facilities may have occurred from different parts of an organisation. As explained in Chapter 7, this may give rise to conflicting strategies and duplication of effort and expenditure. As more companies develop experience of using these facilities there will be a realisation that there is considerable overlap in content between the three and the need for a coherent strategy.

Integration of digital media and the growth of digital television

A keyword used to describe this trend is convergence. Currently there are many separate solutions for digital media delivery. These include personal computers, digital television, WebTV, desktop and mobile (WAP) Internet phones and information kiosks.

> **Technology convergence**
> A trend in which different hardware devices such as televisions, computers and phones merge and have similar functions such as Internet access.

Mougayer (1998) identifies different types of convergence:

- *Infrastructure convergence* – this is the increase in the number of delivery media channels for the Internet such as phone lines, microwave (mobile phones), cable and satellite. These are now often being used in combination.
- *Information appliance (technology) convergence* – the use of different hardware devices to access and deliver the content of the Internet.
- *Supplier convergence* – the overlap between suppliers such as Internet service providers (ISPs), online access providers and more traditional media suppliers such as the telecommunications and cable companies.

Technology convergence may radically change the nature by which information is delivered to consumers. Steve Perlman, founder of WebTV, for example has said: '*the broadcast TV experience as we know it today will be an anachronism of the 20th century. Within a decade, almost all TV programming – essentially everything except for live events – will be available on demand and combined with interactive content*' (Maloney, 1999). It is still not clear what form mainstream digital television will take. Perlman outlines five main types of interactive television facility (Maloney, 1999):

1 Internet TV (basic Internet and e-mail access).
2 Response TV (interactive audience surveys).
3 Enhanced TV (web access, plus interactive television listing when the programming for the week can be viewed at any time using web-type facilities).
4 Digital VCRs (able to store and record digital video material and recognise user preferences).
5 Personal TV (personalised content on demand).

A study by Wade and McKechnie (1999) casts doubt on the likelihood of digital television having a major impact, at least as a sales channel. Their survey of consumers suggested that it is unlikely to lead to a significant increase in home shopping as a proportion of total retail sales within the foreseeable future. It will accelerate the trend from traditional mail order for some sectors such as books, CDs and holiday purchases.

Digital television
Information is delivered as binary information (0s and 1s), giving options for better picture and sound quallity and providing additional information services.

For the marketer, convergence has two main implications. First, it should result in more use of the Internet as a medium – for instance, there will be more users of the Internet as facilities are built into televisions, thus expanding the use of the Internet to those consumers who would be unlikely to purchase a computer. Second, it should be remembered that the mechanism for delivery of the content is likely to be quite different for the different delivery devices. For example, the display on a mobile phone will be black and white and a much lower resolution than that for a personal computer. Users of WebTV will not be controlling access to the content from a keyboard, and this will have significant implications for navigation, and in particular for how characters are input. Since different approaches are required for designing the display, navigation and content, efficient Internet marketing agencies will seek to use techniques and content creation technologies that work across all platforms with the minimum of duplication. Briefs given to agencies for Internet work should specify that the site content should be accessible via a variety of devices. It is also likely that the use of facilities to download channels more readily to a digital VCR will make it more difficult to reach consumers with advertisements since consumers may be able to fast-forward through them (as happens already with VCRs). New models of advertising will need to evolve, such as paying consumers to view them with 'online currency' such as beenz (*see* Chapter 9).

Mini case study 15.3   **WebTV**

WebTV (*www.webtv.net*) is now owned by Microsoft, and with their marketing and financial backing it is likely to increase in usage.

What is WebTV?

WebTV offers the following facilities:

■ Standard access to web sites as through a personal computer.
■ Facilities for sending e-mail and participating in online discussion groups.
■ Picture in Picture, which allows the television channel and web content to be viewed simultaneously.
■ Interaction with television listings and video material. Special Internet-based content and competitions related to some television programmes.

The simultaneous display of a television channel and the Web gives new opportunities for direct response advertising – if a consumer is interested in an advertisement, he or she can immediately call up the corresponding web site and even purchase a product. This provides a much more powerful interaction than is currently possible with direct response by phone.

Who is using it?

By the end of 1999 it was estimated that there would be over one million WebTV units in the countries in which it is currently available (the USA, Canada and Japan), giving approximately two million viewers. Research on usage behaviour indicates WebTV subscribers are online for more than 40 hours a month, 70 per cent more than typical users of personal computers. Typically, most subscribers have little or no Internet experience before they purchase a WebTV-based unit; about 30 per cent have PCs in their home, about half of which are online.

How does it work?

WebTV requires an existing television and access to a phone line, plus – to connect to the Internet – a 'set-top box' (a WebTV Internet unit), which is about the size of a VCR. The interactivity is controlled by a handset similar to a video remote control rather than a full-size keyboard. The Web is accessed by a WebTV browser, which is software different from PC-based browsers such as Microsoft Internet Explorer or Netscape Navigator. Consequently, content designed for WebTV needs to be tested separately from other content, and there are some minor differences in the implementation of Javascript and HTML, which may cause bugs (*see* the Web TV site (*developer.webtv.net*) for further details). Also graphic design needs to allow for the lower resolution of a television set than that of most PC monitors.

When future digital marketing efforts are being planned, it seems clear that it is best not to bet on any single technology platform, but to accept that consumers will require access to Internet-based information via a range of devices. The strategy adopted by the UK grocery retailer Safeway is consistent with this. In 1999, Safeway ran a pilot for customers at its Basingstoke, UK branch where customers are issued with handheld 3Com Palm computers for accessing the 'Easiorder' system. *Computing* magazine on 1 July (Ranger, 1999) reported that Roderick Angwin, Safeway's director of business IT development, considered that 'customers will want anytime, anywhere interaction. We have to provide this across a number of platforms. Customers might use a personal digital assistant on the way home, but a digital TV at home and a PC at work.' Such 'Easiorder' devices also provide the opportunity for one-to-one 'stealth-marketing' (so called since individual, tailored offers can be made to consumers without other customers or competitors being aware of the offers). Safeway keeps records of customers' purchases for the previous two years, amounting to 12 billion lines of information, and intends to use this to provide 'infotainment' services such as special offers and recipes.

Saturation

Access to the Internet will reach saturation as home PC ownership reaches a limit. This limit is approximately 50 per cent of households in the USA, but lower in Europe, for example 40 per cent in the UK. Access to the Internet in businesses will also reach a saturation point. The implication of saturation is that the dramatic rate of growth in new users of the Internet may begin to decline shortly, unless new methods of accessing the Internet are found. This is where digital television becomes important since this will provide a delivery mechanism to the 30 to 50 per cent of consumers in a country who have no perceived need for a personal computer. The use of the Internet will only continue to increase dramatically and it will only truly become a mass-market medium where it is accessed by most consumers in most countries, a situation that will arise once low-cost interactive digital television becomes widespread. When this will happen is difficult to assess. There have been trials in Europe for over five years, but the use of interactive digital television is negligible. There does seem to be a trend, however, for the digital content providers to move from pilots and trials to fully fledged services. With several suppliers investing in promotion, adoption should increase. In the UK, the main options available by the early part of the millennium will be:

■ Microsoft-backed WebTV (currently only in the USA, Canada and Japan).
■ Cable and Wireless Digital, launched in 1999. This will also require a set-top box for delivery. Like WebTV this solution will access existing web sites, which will need revision before they are suitable for television access
■ OpenTV. Companies supporting this medium will have to develop special content – effectively another web site. This will be delivered by phone lines to a modem in a set-top box. This option does not, however, represent access to information over the Internet. Nevertheless this option has major backing since it has been chosen by BSkyB as the interactive digital solution British Interactive Broadcasting, which was launched in 1999. Many retailers such as Dixons, Somerfield, Next, Ford, GUS, HSBC and *Yellow Pages* are already supporting the Open standard (*see* Fig. 15.5). With the need to develop content separate from that of the web site it seems unlikely that this method will be adopted by anything other than major retailers and manufacturers with the budget to achieve this. The launch of BIB is described in more detail by Clawson (1999).

With the emerging range of options for interactive digital marketing it is clearly going to become more difficult for companies to promote their products electronically. Although the technology is said to be converging, methods for delivering the content are diverging! It will be interesting to see how these two developments evolve over the next few years and which standard dominates. Will the web/HTML standard win because it is established as a standard, or will new standards such as XML or Open displace it? In future editions this book may be retitled 'digital marketing' rather than 'Internet marketing', but at the time of writing Internet is the term that is used since this is best understood and used most widely!

A two-tier Internet and broadband technology

A new high-speed network is being developed in the USA to act as a test-bed for a higher-speed Internetwork. Some speculate that this will evolve into a premium-price service for which consumers will pay for faster access to content. For home delivery, broadband techniques such as ADSL (Asymmetric Digital Subscriber Line) and cable delivery will increase the bandwidth of delivery channels to homes. The

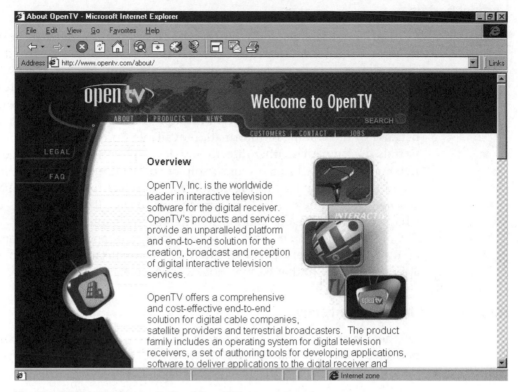

Fig. 15.5 Digital television web site of OpenTV (*www.opentv.com***)**

significance of ADSL is that it uses existing telephone lines, but allows continuous access to the Internet at the same time as voice or fax services. It will be up to 50 times faster than the ISDN existing 'high-speed' 128 kbps service. This will enable multimedia facilities such as videoconferencing across the Internet.

A number of rival techniques are currently being trialled to provide broadband facilities. The best known of these is the $9 billion Teledesic investment, which is partly financed by Bill Gates, Craig McCaw, Boeing and Motorola. Here, 100 low earth orbit satellites (between 300 and 1000 miles high, compared with a geostationary telecommunications satellite at 22 300 miles high) will provide 2 Mbps uplink and 64 Mbps downlink. Other alternatives are detailed in Platt (1999), including a less expensive proposal to deploy high altitude jet aircraft at 60 000 feet over major urban areas, which also provide broadband facilities, but to a more limited area.

eShock

Michael de Kare-Silver (1998) speculates that by 2005–7 the proportion of consumers using the Internet as their preferred form of purchase will account for 15–20 per cent of total purchases. This will lead to ever-decreasing margins for retailers, who will be forced to close substantial parts of their retail networks. This issue is discussed in more detail in Chapter 5. For banks, some staff reduction in call centres may be necessary as customers use 'web self-service facilities'.

Vertical portals

Vertical portals are generally business-to-business sites that will host content to help participants in an industry to get their work done by providing industry news, details of business techniques and product and service reviews. They are the modern equivalent of the trade press. They will act as magnets for a range of people involved in the buying process. They may gain importance if it becomes more difficult to access information through conventional, non-specialised portals, because of the volume of information available on the Internet. Control of these portals by companies either directly (by developing the content as customer magnets) or indirectly (through sponsorship or co-branding) will become important for recruiting and keeping existing customers. Examples include Vertical.Net (*www.vertical.net*) and Money World (*www.moneyworld.co.uk*). This topic was discussed in Chapter 4 and, from a promotion standpoint, in Chapter 9.

Consumer portals are likely to remain important and also to become differentiated to cater for users' personal interests. Personalisation of the portal, using an approach similar to that of myyahoo! will become a common feature.

Structuring of Internet marketing

As the contribution of the Internet to sales within companies increases and becomes more important to their bottom line, companies will reappraise the way they structure their marketing departments. Ideas include:

- Separate e-commerce or e-business department (*www.mckinseyquarterly.com*);
- the provision of a 'Chief Customer Officer' responsible for managing profitable customer relationships (*www.customers.com*);
- integration of marketing and IS departments.

Such ideas were discussed in Chapters 6 and 12. Mini case study 15.4 shows that such restructuring may need to encompass promotion, fulfilment and even procurement.

Mini case study 15.4
IBM reverses fortunes through e-business

IBM is well known as the manufacturer of mainframe and personal computers that suffered a major revenue loss, from $95 billion in 1985 to $30 billion in 1993. At the same time profits slumped from $10 billion to –$7 billion. According to IBM's senior e-business solutions specialist in Ireland, Barry O'Connor (reported in the *Irish Times* electronic commerce supplement of 9 June 1999), one of the reasons for reversing this trend is its change from a business to an 'e-business'. As an example, he gives the example of procurement. Here, purchasing is now possible with a one-day rather than a 30-day cycle time; contract length has reduced from 40 pages to 6 pages; maverick buying (where people fail to follow the proper channels) has reduced from 30 per cent to 2 per cent; and internal satisfaction from procurement has gone from 40 to 85 per cent. All this has been achieved with savings over a 12-month period of $4.2 billion.

On the fulfilment side, the average time taken to respond to enquiries has fallen from 20 minutes to immediate; the number of hardware orders processed manually has fallen from 70 per cent to zero, and the cycle time from order entry to delivery has decreased from between 27 and 44 days to 2 to 23 days. Savings through digitising such processes are reported to be $1.7 billion.

The speed of change is dramatic also. In 1998, IBM sold $15 million of goods and services on the Web each day, equivalent to $5 billion a year. By the end of 1999, it is thought that this value may increase to $10 billion.

These sales have only been achieved by extensive investment in traditional and new media promoting the e-business concept. In the UK, IBM regularly tops the monthly list of top spenders on banner advertising in *Revolution*. In the UK this amounts to £1 million per annum out of an industry total of £15 million.

The efforts by a company such as IBM to build its market using the Internet will also help fuel the growth of the Internet. For example, one of its services, launched in 1999, is HomePage Creator (*see mypage-products.ihost.com/uk/en_US/*), which provides 'the tools to create and publish a Web site right from your desktop' at a relatively low cost and without the necessity of hiring an Internet design agency. For £15 plus VAT per month a small company can set up a small web site of 5 pages and with facilities for e-commerce for 12 items. Storecentre, a similar concept from BT (*www.storecentre.bt.com*) based on the Intel iCat merchant software and available from BT for £112 per quarter, was also launched in 1999 to join similar products from smaller companies such as ShopCreator and iShop. Promotion by both established and new companies will help increase the use of such e-commerce facilities.

Selecting the right trends to follow

One of the great challenges of defining and managing the Internet marketing strategy for a company is to be able to assess which new techniques and marketing concepts may need to be applied for an effective web site. These new techniques may range from enhancements to marketing methods used on the Internet to the use of new technologies to enhance the customer's experience. Often the new marketing techniques will be allied to new technologies. Let us take an example. A new Internet marketing technique could be highlighted in the media, such as the use of one-to-one marketing or personalisation to help manage and develop customer relationship marketing (*see* Chapter 10 for further details). For this technique to be implemented effectively will require a large investment in software and hardware technology such as Broadvision or Engage. A manager who has read several articles in the trade and general press highlighting the issue faces a difficult decision. He or she must decide whether to:

- ignore the use of the technique, perhaps because it is felt to be too expensive or untried, or because he or she simply does not believe the benefits will outweigh the costs;
- enthusiastically adopt the technique without a detailed evaluation since the hype alone convinces the manager that the technique should be adopted;
- evaluate the technique and then decide whether to adopt it.

This behaviour on the part of the manager can be classified as demonstrating:

■ a cautious, 'wait and see' approach;
■ a risk-taking, early adopter approach;
■ an intermediate approach.

This diffusion process (represented by a bell curve) was identified by Rogers (1983), who classified those trialling new products as ranging from innovators through early adopters, early majority and late majority, to the laggards. Many of the new Internet promotion initiatives such as loyalty tokens are at the high-risk 'innovators' stage in terms of both companies and customers whereas others, such as banner advertising, are at a later stage of early adopters.

Early adopter

Companies or departments who invest in new marketing techniques and technologies when they first become available in an attempt to gain a competitive advantage despite the higher risk they entail than a more cautious approach.

The problem with being an early adopter is that being at the leading edge of using new technologies is often also referred to as being at the 'bleeding edge', owing to the risk of failure. New technologies will have bugs or may integrate poorly with the existing systems, or the marketing benefits may simply not live up to their promise. Of course, the reason for risk taking is that the rewards are high – if you are using a technique that your competitors are not, then you will gain an edge on your rivals. For example, RS Components (*www.rswww.com*) was one of the first UK suppliers of industrial components to adopt a one-to-one marketing and e-commerce system. This has enabled the firm to build up a customer base who are familiar with using the RS Components online services, and who are therefore less likely to swap to rival services in the future.

It may also be useful to identify how rapidly a new concept is being adopted. When a product or service is adopted rapidly this is known as rapid diffusion. The access to the Internet is an example of this. In developed countries the use of the Internet has become widespread more rapidly than the use of television for example. It seems that in comparison satellite and digital television are relatively slow-diffusion products!

The chief difficulty for the marketing manager evaluating new technologies is that the likelihood of a new technique becoming significant is not dependent on the amount of hype generated about that new technique. This is because it is in the interest of all the players to hype new techniques, from the newspaper and magazine publishers, the advertisers, the vendors of software and hardware to consultants advising on how to introduce the technology. It is only possible to increase revenues by hyping all techniques, regardless of their benefits. Some recent examples of Internet marketing trends that were hyped on the Internet were highlighted by Chip Bayers in *Wired* magazine (Bayers, 1999). He mentions the three trends of the late 1990s as:

■ *Community in 1996.* The use of special-interest information and dialogues on Web-based discussion groups or e-mail lists to help build customer loyalty (*see* Chapter 10 for further information).

- *Push in 1997*. The use of the Web to deliver channels of prescribed information that are automatically downloaded for the user's browser (*see* Chapter 3).
- *Portals in 1998*. Sites offering a gateway to information on the Internet such as search engines and ISP home pages. *See* Chapter 4.

Of these three technologies and techniques it can be argued that only portals seem to be a major technique which must be included in all companies' Internet marketing plans to ensure that their sites are promoted. Of the other two techniques, community is still seen as an element of Internet marketing, but one that works well in a limited number of product sectors such as that for youth-targeted products. Push is now largely confined to company intranets, although push channels are still offered by some web sites.

So, what action should marketing managers take when confronted by new techniques and technologies? There is no straightforward rule of thumb, other than that a balanced approach must be taken. It would be easy to dismiss many new techniques as fads, or classify them as 'not relevant to my market'. However, competitors are likely to be reviewing new techniques and incorporating some, so a careful review of new techniques is required. This indicates, as suggested in Chapter 6, that benchmarking of 'best of breed' sites within a sector and in different sectors is essential. However, by waiting for others to innovate and reviewing the results on their web site, a company is likely to lose 6 to 12 months. To be able to react more quickly companies need monitoring advice from industry pundits or consultants such as McKinsey (*www.mckinseyquarterly.com*), and must review magazine articles to identify new concepts earlier.

Ethical issues of Internet marketing

The nature of the marketing that will be effective on the Internet in the future will require a delicate balance to be struck between the benefits the individual (or companies) will gain from personalisation and the amount of information that they are prepared to permit companies to hold about them. For business-to-business marketing, which typically involves stronger relationships between buyers and sellers, the benefits to both parties of sharing information will be apparent. For example, when a supermarket chain such as Walmart makes its demand forecasts available to a supplier, it will clearly benefit both parties since more revenue will accrue to each. For business-to-consumer marketing the synergy is less clear, and the privacy issue is more of a barrier to the development of the Internet. It is on this aspect of privacy that we will concentrate.

Privacy

Privacy of consumers on the Internet covers three related issues: (a) collecting and holding personal information; (b) disclosing personal information to third parties; and (c) sending unsolicited e-mails to consumers.

Collecting and holding personal information

As mentioned in Chapter 10, one of the difficulties of using the Internet for personalised marketing is that it is not easy to identify the end-user in order to target them with specific promotional information. To do this, it is necessary to invade the user's privacy by planting cookies or electronic tags on the end-user's computer. By doing this it is possible to identify a user's preferences and behaviour, since each time that user visits a site, the cookie on the computer will be read to confirm the identity of the user.

It is possible to block cookies, but the user has to find out how to do this, and it is not a straightforward process. Many customers do not know that their privacy is being infringed. Cookies have a bad reputation since it is believed that they could be used to capture credit-card information or other personal information. In reality, this is unlikely to occur since cookies usually only contain an identification number that does not give away any personal secrets (*see* Chapter 10 for more details).

> **Cookies**
> Cookies are small text files stored on an end-user's computer to enable web sites to identify that user.

In the future, users will become more aware of cookies, and an increasing number of users may block cookies. This will reduce the effectiveness of one-to-one marketing. Industry groups are taking several initiatives to prevent this from happening. The first of these is TRUSTe (*www.truste.org*), an organisation sponsored by IBM and Netscape, with sites validated by PricewaterhouseCoopers and KPMG. The validators will audit the site to check each site's privacy statement to see whether it is valid. For example, a privacy statement will describe:

- how a site collects information;
- how the information is used;
- who the information is shared with;
- how users can access and correct information;
- how users can decide to deactivate themselves from the site or withhold information from third parties.

A recent UK initiative is the Consumers' Association/Which? Web trader code of practice (*www.which.net/webtrader/*), which aims to ensure 'consumers get a fair deal and to provide them with protection if things go wrong'. E-tailers who have signed up to this include BarclaySquare, Blackwell's, The Carphone Warehouse and EasyJet. Further details are given in Chapter 11.

Government initiatives will also define best practice in this area, and may introduce laws to ensure guidelines are followed. In the UK, the Data Protection Act 1984 covers some of these issues, and the 1999 European Data Protection Act also has draft laws to help maintain personal privacy on the Internet.

The Data Protection Act 1984 is defined by the Data Protection Registrar as:

'An Act to regulate the use of automatically processed information relating to individuals and the provision of services in respect of such information.'

The Act is mainly intended to cover the individual's rights to view the information stored on him or her and ensure that it is accurate.

The Data Protection Act is based upon eight general principles, which are set out in Case study 15.2.

THE DATA PROTECTION ACT 1984

The eight principles of this Act are:

1 The information to be contained in personal data shall be obtained, and personal data shall be processed, fairly and lawfully.
2 Personal data shall be held only for one or more specified and lawful purposes.
3 Personal data held for any purpose or purposes shall not be used or disclosed in any manner incompatible with that purpose or those purposes.
4 Personal data held for any purpose or purposes shall be adequate, relevant and not excessive in relation to that purpose or those purposes.
5 Personal data shall be accurate and, where necessary, kept up to date.
6 Personal data held for any purpose or purposes shall not be kept for longer than is necessary for that purpose or those purposes.
7 An individual shall be entitled:
  ■ at reasonable intervals and without undue delay or expense –
  ■ to be informed by any data user whether he holds personal data of which that individual is the subject; and
  ■ to access to any such data held by a data user; and
  ■ where appropriate, to have such data corrected or erased.
8 Appropriate security measures shall be taken against unauthorised access to, or alteration, disclosure or destruction of, personal data and against accidental loss or destruction of personal data.

Question

Assess each of the principles of the Act and state how a company with a Web presence should take action to ensure it complies with to the Act.

Source: Office of the Data Protection Registrar, UK (*www.dataprotection.gov.uk*)

A further method of regularising information held about consumers is to standardise the method of collecting information. At present it is inefficient for consumers to shop electronically, or give their details to different retailers. They have to type in the same information, such as name, address and credit card details, several times. What is being proposed is that a central body will hold such information in line with customers' wishes, and it will only be issued to retailers with the customers' consent. One of the first companies to suggest this was Firefly (*www.firefly.net*), which was acquired by Microsoft. It suggested the concept of an Internet passport known as the Open Profiling System, which would hold personal information.

It is obviously important for such information to be secure, so it will be necessary to link this technique with encryption and certification schemes. This role may be fulfilled by certification authorities such as banks, which also issue digital certificates (*see* Chapter 3). An alternative approach, being promoted by the credit company Visa (*www.visa.com*), is the use of smartcards or chips built into credit cards, which will store personal and medical information. In this approach, smartcard readers would need to be built into personal computers to validate the person and transfer all the information. The adoption of standards to allow certification of individuals will be a major breakthrough in establishing the more widespread use of e-commerce. It is difficult to forecast when this will happen, but probably not for several years since an infrastructure will be needed to make certificates readily available to customers and convince the majority of the need to use them. It may be that smartcards are a more practical solution.

> **Infomediary**
> Information brokers who hold information on individuals and then pass it on to trusted third parties.

Disclosing personal information to third parties

Customers may be quite happy to give personal information to a company with which they have formed a relationship. They are likely to be less than happy if this company then sells this information on to another company and they are subsequently bombarded with promotional material, either online or offline. For this reason the TRUSTe initiative mentioned in the previous section also lays down best practice for disclosing information to third parties. The other risk in this context is that of hackers accessing information held about a customer on servers within a company. For example, the infamous hacker Kevin Mitnick is known to have accessed over 20 000 credit card numbers on a company server.

Sending unsolicited e-mails to consumers

The sending of junk e-mail or 'spam' was referred to in Chapter 10. It is also covered by privacy rules such as the Data Protection Act.

Employee use of the Internet

Marketing managers may need to control the use of the Internet by staff. Staff will naturally need to monitor competitors' and customers' web sites as part of marketing research, but where does company research stop and personal research start? Mini case study 15.5 gives an example of a situation where it was felt that an employee was abusing access to the Internet. Given the potential for company time to be wasted (and estimates in the UK put this figure at up to £3 million for a large corporation), what actions can companies take to avoid this wastage? The main options employed to date are:

1 Only provide a single point of access to the Web in each department. It will be clear that staff on this machine are using the Web.
2 Restrict access to certain hours only, such as over lunchtime or after 6pm.
3 Use devices to filter content or only allow certain types of sites.
4 Use 'firewalls' to block certain types of interactive content such as plug-ins.

It is likely that, in the future, use of the Internet will be covered in employee contracts and more restrictions will be put in place. The access to the Internet by employees in different companies should be considered when marketing campaigns using this communications medium are planned. For instance, if it is unusual for procurers in the buying department to have Internet access, then other media will have to be used to reach them.

The first sacking for using the Internet?

The *Guardian* reported on 16 June 1999 the case of the first person to be sacked in the UK for using the Internet at work for personal gain. Lois Franxhi, 28, an IT manager, was sacked in July 1998 for making nearly 150 searches over four days in office hours for a holiday. As with many unfair dismissals, the case was not clear cut, with Mrs Franxhi claiming the company sacked her because of sex discrimination – she was pregnant at the time of the dismissal. The tribunal dismissed these claims, finding that the employee had lied about the use of the Internet, saying she had only used it for one lunchtime when, in fact records showed she had used it over four days.

Information haves and have nots

The social impact of the Internet has concerned many commentators since the Internet has the effect of accentuating the differences, both within a society, in a single country, and between different nations. The United Nations, in a 1999 report on human development, noted that parallel worlds are developing where *'those with income, education and – literally – connections have cheap and instantaneous access to information. The rest are left with uncertain, slow and costly access.'* It notes further that *'the advantage of being connected will overpower the marginal and impoverished, cutting off their voices and concerns from the global conversation'*. While the problem is easy to identify, it is clearly difficult to rectify: McIntosh (1999) rightly questions the likelihood of income redistribution and the impact of anti-poverty programmes. Developed countries with the economies to support it are promoting the use of IT and the Internet through social programmes such as the UK government's Computers for All initiative, which offers training to children and adults. While such government intervention can have benefits in the field of education, it can be hoped that the desire of companies to communicate with a larger market through new digital media will also help reduce the problem. Competition amongst ISPs in the UK has given rise to many 'free-access' services such as Freeserve, Barclays, Virgin and BT ClickFree, and this decrease in cost will increase the use of the Internet further. Coupled with this, the growth in interactive digital television services such as WebTV and OpenTV mentioned in previous sections of this chapter will help fuel access to information. If Internet access becomes a standard feature of television sets, the gap between information 'haves and have nots' will decline. In the longer term such facilities will become available worldwide in the same way that television is now widely used throughout the world.

How new digital media will affect the way we live is still unclear, but there is already evidence that significant changes will occur. A report published in June 1999 by the Henley Centre for Forecasting and commissioned by Cisco Systems found that the Internet is already having far-reaching effects on everyday life, and is, if anything, 'under-hyped', with six times more men than women taking to shopping on the Internet. The report states that: *'the Internet offers a male paradise for shopping, being quicker, less overt, more anonymous and currently offering products more suitable for them'*.

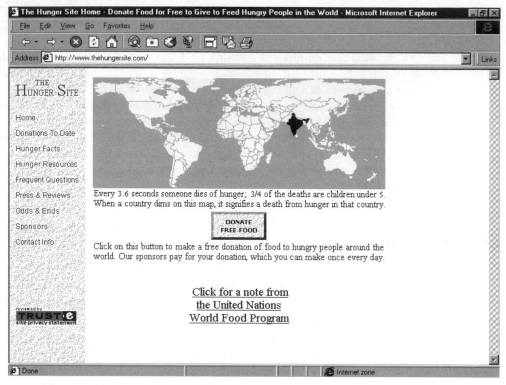

Fig. 15.6 The Hungersite (*www.hungersite.com*)

Although this book has concentrated on the new commercial opportunities offered by the Internet, the medium can also be used to assist causes in novel ways. In the Hunger Site (*www.thehungersite.com*, Fig. 15.6) each click from a site visitor confirmed that the sponsor's logo had been seen, and a half a cent was donated to the UN World Food Programme.

How significant will the Internet be?

Let us now finally return to the question posed at the beginning of the book, 'How significant will the Internet be for businesses?' Marketers are, of course, forced to answer this question since they have the difficult problem of deciding how much to invest in the Internet in order to maximise its benefit, while at the same time not wasting money from their budget, which has many other demands on it. Deciding on the impact of the Internet has been likened by Andy Grove, the CEO of Intel, to anticipating the force of an impending storm. He says (Grove, 1999), in the context of the technology industry:

'There's wind and then there's a typhoon. In this business you always have winds. But a ten times force is an element of one's business of typhoon force.

'Is the Internet a typhoon force, a ten times force, or is it a bit of wind? Or is it a force that fundamentally alters our business?'

So does the Internet fundamentally alter business? The temptation is to assume that any dramatic change will occur across all industries. Andy Grove still holds this view. Symonds (1999) reported that Andy Grove's view now is that in five years' time, *'all companies will be Internet companies or they won't be companies at all'*. The reality is likely to be that the extent of the impact of the Internet will differ according to the business in question. Let us now consider the factors that affect the impact of the Internet on business.

The Internet as sales channel

In Chapter 5, it was shown that models can be applied to evaluate the likely impact of the Internet on a business. The model of Kumar (1999) suggested that retailers and manufacturers should consider the following:

- The level of customer access – what proportion of customers are on the Internet?
- What is the value proposition of the Internet – can the Internet provide products, services or incentives differently or better than traditional media?
- Can the product be delivered over the Internet (though it can be argued that this is not essential)?
- Can the product be standardised (so that the purchaser does not usually need to view prior to purchase, and the product can be configured by choosing standard options, as with a car for example)?

De Kare-Silver (1998) simplifies this assessment by suggesting that although there are factors that determine the volume of purchases over the Internet, such as the characteristics of the product, the strength of the brand, and consumers' attributes and behaviour, the main consideration is the percentage of the target audience who purchase or decide to purchase using the Internet. Only when this audience becomes a large proportion of the population will the Internet become a typhoon. In the developed countries such as those of Western Europe, access to the Internet is still significantly less than 50 per cent. It was argued in an earlier section that with personal computer penetration in the home reaching saturation and the slow take-up of interactive digital television services it could be many years before access to the Internet reaches a scale similar to that for other media. This picture is accentuated if we look at the impact of the Internet on an international scale. The Internet user population in mid-1999 was estimated at 150 million. This represents just 2.5 per cent of the global population of six billion!

Using these models, it can be seen that only a limited range of products pass all the tests. Those that do are mainly consumer products that are already performing well on the Internet such as books, CDs, travel, insurance, financial stocks, home computers and cars. The impact of the Internet on businesses selling these products can be likened to a typhoon. For many other products, the Internet represents a wind that is currently of indeterminate strength. It is still not an important sales channel for fast moving consumer goods (the vast majority of which are still purchased at conventional retailers), clothing, high-value consultancy and engineering services and higher-value consumer goods such as refrigerators and washing machines.

When companies are deciding upon their future strategy for investing in the Internet, they need to consider all these factors, to decide not only what proportion of their target market use the Internet actively now, but how this is likely to increase in the future.

The Internet as communications channel

The discussion of the impact of the Internet to this point has concentrated on the Internet as a medium for achieving direct sales. Equally important is its role as a communications channel. What is clear already is that the Internet is having a significant role in influencing purchase. If someone wants to purchase a large-value item it is natural to go to the Internet to find out about competing products, and reduce the risk of not choosing the best product. To the manufacturer or retailer it does not matter if the item is then actually purchased by another channel such as phone, fax or by e-mail – the Internet has exerted a major influence in influencing the sale. This is why investment in Internet marketing communications is most important – not because many people will make their *purchase* online, but rather because many people will *decide* on their purchase online, often using the price/product comparison services highlighted earlier in this chapter. Online marketers should therefore concentrate on providing the depth and breadth of information to help customers decide between products. For service companies, the web site acts a vehicle for establishing the *credibility* of the company to deliver that service.

An interesting and disturbing effect for some retailers is that for products such as cars and clothing, where it is important to experience the product before purchase, consumers may still visit high street stores and malls to try the products and then purchase them online once they know the product options that are right for them. In the USA this development is already significant, with 50 per cent of the online population deciding on their car purchase online. Many local dealerships are just acting as test drive centres for consumers who subsequently purchase their cars over the Internet! The response to this phenomenon will be interesting.

When considering the future impact of the Internet it is worth remembering that through time, the technology awareness of the audience will increase. Younger users have better access to the technology, have skills developed from an early age, and may even no longer wish to shop for a product in a traditional retail environment. For example, a student familiar with technology may buy a CD online because he or she is comfortable with the technology. An elderly person looking for a classical CD would probably not have access to the technology and might prefer to purchase an item in person.

What is Internet marketing?

This may appear to be a strange question for the last chapter of this book, but it is posed here to highlight the change in the way the Internet is perceived, as a result of its impact on business. The way in which companies consider the impact of the Internet for marketing has changed in scope. Early books, such as those of Sterne (1995), Vassos (1996) and Bickerton *et al.* (1996), described how the Internet or specifically a web site could be used for marketing (while also acknowledging benefits to the whole business such as cost reduction). Today, as more management consultancy and technology companies offer services related to the Internet, their selling strategies have adopted a more holistic approach, explaining how the Internet can benefit the entire business. Certain vendors and consultants have coined their own terms to show the broad impact of the Internet. These terms include e-business, a term used by IBM and now in common use, and e-services from Hewlett-Packard. Books such as *Customers.com* by Seybold (1999) and *Opening Digital Markets* by Mougayer (1998) now emphasise the impact of the Internet on the entire business. Mini case study 15.4 on IBM gives an indication of the holistic nature of 'e-business'.

A further question that will occupy the marketer is the extent to which the Internet represents a major disruption to classical marketing theory and its application to marketing practice. As discussed at the end of Chapter 2, some authors such as Hoffman and Novak (1997) have suggested that Internet marketing represents a major 'paradigm shift' compared with other media, and that a revised model of marketing communications is necessary, from 'one-to-many' to 'many-to-many'. Others have suggested that existing marketing theories can be applied. The approach taken in this book is based on a belief that much existing marketing theory remains valid, even though practical implementation of the techniques may be very different. For example, the following marketing tactics are important on the Internet, but they are nothing new and are sought in other media:

- market segmentation;
- closely monitoring competitors through benchmarking;
- incentivised promotions;
- customer relationship management.

A significant strategic difference is the disruptive influence of the Internet – it can dramatically alter the balance of an industry in a short period. In some product areas, new entrants can rapidly establish a lead that it is difficult for traditional market leaders to recoup. New marketplaces such as the price comparison services can rapidly affect buying behaviour, and companies need to respond accordingly. To take the example of book retailing, it may be easier for a new company such as Amazon to use the new approaches that suit the new medium while for existing companies, such as Barnes and Noble, it will be more difficult and painful to make the transition. The speed of this change is implied in Bill Gates' book *Business @ the speed of thought* (Gates, 1999).

Companies' approaches to assessing the disruptive nature of the Internet will depend very much on the market. For some markets where all of Kumar's tests are successfully met, such as books, travel and financial services, the Internet does represent a new marketing paradigm where there will be much disruption of the existing order.

What the Internet certainly does represent is an opportunity for all those involved in its technical, commercial and social development to learn, influence and gain rewards. In the five years during which the Internet has been used extensively for commercial development there have been some major changes, such as the shopping comparison services replacing online malls, price reductions of 40 per cent on some products such as books, off-the-shelf e-commerce for a few pounds per month, and the dominance of portals as a means of finding information and online promotion efforts. Very few people were able to anticipate these developments at the outset. The next five years will certainly hold surprises, and it will be fascinating to see how the marketing use of the Internet and other digital media develops.

SUMMARY

1 The future impact of the Internet will be dependent on the proportion of consumers and business staff who have access to the Internet!

2 For consumers, the main factors affecting adoption will be:
   - *value proposition* – perceived need for an Internet connection;
   - *cost of access* – including both hardware and connection costs;
   - *ease of use* – including connection to the Internet and use of web sites;
   - *security* – security needs to be perceived as safe for e-commerce to be pervasive.
   The advent of affordable digital television may reduce some of these inhibitors.

3 For businesses the value proposition is clearer, and many businesses are already connected. Access may be restricted, for fear that employees may waste company time.

4 Future trends that will have a major impact on marketing use of the Internet include:
   - Digital brokers or intermediaries will help bring buyers and sellers together by offering product price and feature comparisons. These services will make price more transparent and drive down price.
   - Integration of the use of intranets, extranets and the Internet within a unified digital communications strategy.
   - Integration of digital media as part of technology convergence, including the growth of interactive digital television.
   - Saturation of personal computer usage at home will reduce the rate of Internet adoption until the use of interactive digital television becomes widespread.
   - The speed of Internet access will increase. Higher-speed, broadband technologies with performance guarantees may attract higher access charges, giving rise to a 'two-tier Internet'.
   - For some consumer products, the attraction of purchasing over the Internet may lead to pressure to reduce the number of high street retail shops.
   - As the importance of the Internet to businesses increases, restructuring of the marketing organisation may be necessary.

5 Selecting the right trends to follow will be difficult, owing to the narrow balance between opportunity and risk.

6 Constraints on the growth of the Internet may be imposed by legal and voluntary codes intended to protect consumer privacy. This may be difficult to reconcile with the benefits of personalisation.

7 The Internet may accentuate the divisions in society unless access to the Internet becomes more widely available.

8 The future impact of the Internet as a sales and communications channel is difficult to assess. Some commentators consider it a paradigm shift, while the approach adopted by most existing companies is to treat it as a new channel that, although different, shares many characteristics with other channels.

EXERCISES AND QUESTIONS

Self-assessment exercises

1 What are the implications of price comparison and intermediary sites for promotion strategy on the Internet?

2 What will be the main factors that govern the adoption of the Internet by consumers?

3 Explain the term 'technology convergence'.

4 What is a vertical portal? Why are they important to companies promoting a business-to-business service?

5 Explain the term 'early adopter'. What benefits and risks are faced by a company that is an early adopter?

6 What is TRUSTe? Explain its purpose.

7 What are the threats of unequal access to the Internet, both within and between countries?

8 On which companies will the Internet have the greatest impact?

Discussion questions

1 'It is inevitable that the transparency of information on products and price on the World Wide Web will drive down product prices.' Discuss.

2 'The Internet will only become a mass-market medium if the technology is made more consumer-friendly.' Discuss.

3 Discuss the statement by Steve Perlman, founder of WebTV, that 'the broadcast TV experience as we know it today will be an anachronism of the 20th century. Within a decade, almost all TV programming – essentially everything except for live events – will be available on demand and combined with interactive content'. What are the implications of this for marketers? Examine whether the initial use of digital television supports this statement.

4 'The Internet does not represent a paradigm shift in marketing communications. It is merely a supplementary channel with some unique characteristics.' Discuss.

Essay questions

1 Imagine you have been appointed as Internet marketing manager for a supplier of training shoes that currently has a web site, but no transactional e-commerce facilities. Develop a strategy for maximising your company's exposure on the Internet, taking into account some of the trends forecast in this chapter.

2 Research and review the range of techniques for broadband access to the Internet and devices for accessing the Internet from home, and forecast the impact of these on levels of Internet use over the next five years.

3 Research the current usage of WebTV using sites such as www.webtv.net, developer.webtv.net, www.nua.ie and www.cyberatlas.com. Evaluate its future potential for worldwide use and the implications of its widespread adoption for companies producing web sites.

4 What threats are posed by unequal access to the Internet, both within and between countries? What action can be taken to avoid unequal access, or is intervention unnecessary?

Examination questions

1 Explain the concept of a price comparison service and briefly review the possible impact on consumers and suppliers.

2 Name three factors that may inhibit consumer adoption of the Internet, and explain each.

3 What is technology convergence? What are its implications for digital marketers?

4 Explain the term 'vertical portal'. Why are vertical portals likely to be significant in the future?

5 In what ways does digital television differ from conventional television? What is it significance with respect to the Internet?

6 Why does interactive digital television such as WebTV give new opportunities for direct response advertising?

7 Name and briefly describe three risks a company operating a web site may face, in relation to infringing personal privacy.

8 Name two major differences between the Internet and other marketing communications channels.

REFERENCES

Bayers, C. (1999) 'Push comes to Shove', *Wired*, 110–13.

Berryman, K., Harrington, L., Layton-Rodin, D. and Rerolle, V. (1998) 'Electronic commerce: three emerging strategies', *The McKinsey Quarterly*, 1, 152–9.

Bickerton, P., Bickerton, M. and Pandesi, U. (1996) *Cyber Marketing*. Oxford: Butterworth-Heinemann. Chartered Institute of Marketing series.

Clawson, T. (1999), 'Forget the 140 channels, this is TV that does something', *Revolution*, January, 32–5.

de Kare-Silver, M. (1998) *eShock. The electronic shopping revolution: strategies for retailers and manufacturers*. Basingstoke, UK: Macmillan.

Gatarski, R. and Lundkvist, A. (1998) 'Interactive media face artificial customers and marketing theory must rethink', *Journal of Marketing Communications*, 4, 45–59.

Gates, B. (1999) *Business @ the Speed of Thought: Using a digital nervous system*. New York: Penguin Books.

Grove, A. (1996) *Only the Paranoid Survive*. New York: Doubleday.

Hoffman, D.L. and Novak, T.P. (1997) 'A new marketing paradigm for electronic commerce', *The Information Society*, Special issue on electronic commerce, 13 (January–March), 43–54.

Kumar, N. (1999) 'Internet distribution strategies: dilemmas for the incumbent', *Financial Times*, Special Issue on Mastering Information Management, No 7. Electronic Commerce (*www.ftmastering.com*).

McIntosh, N. (1999) 'The new poor', Guardian, 22 July, 19.

Maloney, J. (1999) 'Perlmania', *Wired*, 102–9.

Mougayer, W. (1998) *Opening Digital Markets – Battle plans and strategies for Internet commerce* (2nd edn). New York: CommerceNet Press, McGraw-Hill.

Platt, C. (1999) 'Ethernet at 60,000 Feet. Telecom's new jet age takes off', *Wired*, 7 June.

Ranger, S. (1999) 'Safeway says PCs are not the way', *Computing*, 1 July, 4.

Rogers, E. (1983) *Diffusion of Innovations* (3rd edn). New York: Free Press.

Seybold, P. (1999) *Customers.com*. London: Century Business Books, Random House.

Sterne, J. (1995) *World Wide Web Marketing*. New York: John Wiley and Sons.

Symonds, M. (1999) 'The net imperative'. *The Economist*, special Business and the Internet supplement, 26 June, 5–9.

Vassos, T. (1996) *Strategic Internet Marketing*. Indianapolis, IN: Que. Business Computer Library.

Wade, N. and McKechnie, S. (1999) 'The impact of digital television: will it change our shopping habits?' *Journal of Marketing Communications*, 5(2), 71–85.

FURTHER READING

Berners-Lee, T. (1999) *Weaving the Web. The past, present and future of the World Wide Web by its inventor*. London, UK: Orion Publishing.
A fascinating readable description of how the concept of the web was developed by the author with his thoughts on its future development.

Brown, D. (1997) *Cybertrends. Chaos, power and accountability in the information age*. London: Viking.
This gives an alternative view of the future and considers the impact of the Internet on government and society.

Clarke, D. (1999) 'Preparing for ecommerce with the TV, not the PC', *Computing*, 22 July, 16–17.
A good summary of the main digital television providers in the UK and Europe, this explores some of the design issues that will be presented by WebTV.

Dyson, E. (1998) *Release 2.1. A design for living in the digital age*. London: Penguin Books.
Discusses a range of ethical and privacy issues concerning the Internet.

Economist, The (1999) 'The Net imperative. A survey of business and the Internet', *The Economist* Special Survey, 26 June, 1–44.
This survey reviews several case studies in detail, presents e-commerce forecasts, and speculates on the future use of the Internet.

Gates, B. (1999) *Business @ the speed of thought: using a digital nervous system*. New York: Penguin Books.

WEB SITE REFERENCES

The US-based magazines *Wired* (*www.wired.com*) and *Business 2.0* (*www.business2.com*) have regular features on how new technology and marketing techniques are evolving. In the UK, the first Wednesday edition each month of the *Financial Times* (*www.ft.com*) has a technology supplement that often focuses on the Internet. Similarly the *Guardian Online* (*www.guardian.co.uk*) section (on Thursdays) has regular case studies of how 'web-entrepreneurs' are using the Internet by marketing in new ways. US analysts Jupiter (*www.jup.com* and *www.webtrack.com*) provide analysis of and predictions about the future adoption and direction of e-commerce. The Stanford Research Institute (*www.future.sri.com*) also has e-commerce predictions. The management consulting companies referred to in Chapter 4 also have regular reports on this topic.

A vision of the future provided by the advisers to the UK government is available from the Department of Trade and Industry Information Age initiative (*www.dti.gov.uk/infoage/index.htm*). The latest report on progress in the UK is provided by the 'e-commerce@its.best.uk' report, which is available at *www.cabinet-office.gov.uk/innovation/1999/ecommerce/index.htm*. Additional forecasting somewhat further into the future is available from the Government's Foresight E-Commerce Task Force, which is aiming to determine the impact that electronic commerce will have on business models by the year 2010! (*www.foresight.gov.uk*).

See also the following sites:

Sky Report (*www.skyreport.com*) and (*www.ee.surrey.ac.uk/Personal/L.Wood/constellations*).
These sites have information on high altitude broadband initiatives.

TRUSTe (*www.truste.org*).
This organisation promotes openness about the information held on web sites.

WebTV (*developer.webtv.net*).
This provides details of how to design content for the different needs of WebTV users.

GLOSSARY

Above the fold A term originally applied to printed media, which is used to indicate whether a **banner advertisement** or other content is displayed on a web page without the need to scroll. This is likely to give higher **clickthrough**, but note that the location of the 'fold' within the web browser is dependent on the screen resolution of a user's personal computer.

Access provider A company providing services to enable a company or individual to access the **Internet**. Access providers are divided into **Internet service providers (ISPs)** and **online service providers (OSPs)**.

Active Server Page (ASP) A type of **HTML** page (denoted by an .asp file name) that includes **scripts** (small programs) that are processed on a **web server** before the web page is served to the user's **web browser**. ASP is a Microsoft technology that usually runs on a **Microsoft Internet Information Server** (usually on Windows NT). The main use of such programs is to process information supplied by the user in an online **form**. A query may then be run to provide specific information to the customer such as delivery status on an order, or a personalised web page.

ActiveX A programming language standard developed by Microsoft, which permits complex and graphical customer applications to be written and then accessed from a **web browser**. ActiveX components are standard controls that can be incorporated into web sites and are then automatically **downloaded** for users. Examples are graphics and animation or a calculator form for calculating interest on a loan or a control for graphing stock prices. A competitor to **Java**.

Ad impression Similar in concept to a **page impression**; describes one viewing of an advertisement by a single member of its audience. The same as **ad view**, a term that is less commonly used.

Ad inventory The total number of **ad impressions** that a **web site** can sell over time (usually specified per month).

Ad rotation When advertisements are changed on a **web site** for different user sessions. This may be in response to ad **targeting** or simply displaying different advertisements from those on a list.

Ad serving The term for displaying an advertisement on a **web site**. Often the advertisement will be served from a different **web server** from the site on which it is placed. For example, the URL for displaying the advertisement is *http://ad.doubleclick.net*.

Ad space The area of a web page that is set aside for **banner advertising**.

Ad view Similar in concept to a **page impression**; describes one viewing of an advertisement by a single member of its audience. The same as **ad impression**, the term that is more commonly used.

Advertisement Advertisements on **web sites** are usually **banner advertisements** positioned as a mast head on the page.

Advertising broker *See* **Media broker**

Advertising networks A collection of independent **web sites** of different companies and media networks, each of which has an arrangement with a single advertising broker (*see* **Media broker**) to place **banner advertisements**.

Affiliate networks A reciprocal arrangement between a company and third-party sites where traffic is directed to the company from third-party sites through **banner advertisements** and links and incentives. In return for linking to the **destination site** the third-party site will typically receive a proportion of any resulting sale.

Agents Software programs that can assist people to perform tasks such as finding particular information such as the best price for a product.

Analysis phase The identification of the requirements of a **web site**. Techniques to achieve this may include **focus groups**, questionnaires sent with existing customers or interviews with key accounts.

Animated banner advertisements (animated GIFs) Early **banner advertisements** featured only a single advertisement, but today they will typically involve several different images, which are displayed in sequence to help to attract attention to the banner and build up a theme, often ending with a call to action and the injunction to click on the banner. These advertisements are achieved through supplying the ad creative as an animated **GIF** file with different layers or frames, usually a rectangle of 468 by 60 **pixels**. Animated banner advertisements are an example of **rich media advertisements**.

Announcements *See* **Site announcements**.

Archie A database containing information on what documents and programs are located on **FTP** servers. It would not be used in a marketing context unless one were looking for a specific piece of software or document name.

Audit (external) Consideration of the business and economic environment in which the company operates. This includes the economic, political, fiscal, legal, social, cultural and technological factors (usually referred to by the acronym SLEPT).

Audit (internal) A review of **web site** effectiveness.

Auditors *See* **site auditors**.

Authentication *See* **Security methods**.

Autoresponders Software tools or **agents** running on **web servers**, which automatically send a standard reply to the sender of an **e-mail** message. This may provide information to a standard request sent to, say, price_list@company_name.com, or it could simply state that the message or order has been forwarded to the relevant person and will be answered within two days. (Also known as mailbots.)

Availability *See* **Security methods**; **Site availability**.

Bandwidth Indicates the speed at which data are transferred using a particular network medium. It is measured in bits per second (bps).
Kbps (one kilobit per second or 1000 bps; a modem operates at up to 56.6 Kbps).
Mbps (one megabit per second or 1 000 000 bps; company networks operate at 10 or more Mbps).
Gbps (one gigabit per second or 1 000 000 000 bps; fibre-optic or satellite links operate at Gbps).

Banner advertisement A typically rectangular graphic displayed on a web page for purposes of brand building or driving traffic to a site. It is normally possible to perform a **clickthrough** to access further information from another **web site**. Banners may be static or animated (*see* **Animated banner advertisements**).

Behavioural traits of web users Web users can be broadly divided into **directed** and **undirected information seekers**.

Broadband technology A term referring to methods of delivering information across the **Internet** at a higher rate by increasing **bandwidth**.

Brochureware A **web site** in which a company has simply transferred ('migrated') its existing paper-based promotional literature on to the **Internet** without recognising the differences required by this medium.

Broker *See* **Media broker**.

Browser *See* **Web browser**.

Call centres A location for **inbound** and **outbound telemarketing**.

Callback service A direct response facility available on a **web site** to enable a company to contact a customer by phone at a later time as specified by the customer.

Catalogue Catalogues provide a structured listing of registered **web sites** in different categories. They are similar to an electronic version of *Yellow Pages*. Yahoo! and Excite are the best known examples of catalogues. (Also known as **directories**.)
The distinction between **search engines** and catalogues has become blurred since many sites now include both facilities as part of a **portal** service.

Certificate A valid copy of a **public key** of an individual or organisation together with identification information. It is issued by a **trusted third party (TTP)** or **certification authority (CA)**.

Certification authority (CA) An organisation issuing and managing **certificates** or **public keys** and private keys to individuals or organisations together with identification information.

Channel conflicts A significant threat arising from the introduction of an **Internet** channel is that while **disintermediation** gives the opportunity for a company to sell direct and increase the profitability of products it can also threaten existing distribution arrangements with existing partners.

Click-stream A record of the path a user takes through a **web site**. Click-streams enable **web site** designers to assess how their site is being used.

Clickthrough A clickthrough (ad click) occurs each time a user clicks on a **banner advertisement** with the mouse to direct them to a web page that contains further information.

Clickthrough rate Expressed as a percentage of total **ad impressions**, and refers to the proportion of users viewing an advertisement who click on it. It is calculated as the number of clickthroughs divided by the number of **ad impressions**.

Click-tracking Java technology can be used to track movements of individual users to a **web site**.

Co-branding An arrangement between two or more companies where they agree to jointly display content and perform joint promotion using brand logos or **banner advertisements**. The aim is that the brands are strengthened if they are seen as complementary. This is a reciprocal arrangement, which can occur without payment.

Common Gateway Interface (CGI) A method of processing information on a **web server** in response to a customer's request. Typically a user will fill in a web based **form** and the results will be processed by a CGI script (application). **Active Server Pages (ASP)** are an alternative to a CGI script.

Computer telephony integration The integration of telephony and computing to provide a platform for applications that streamline or enhance business processes.

Confidentiality *See* **Security methods**.

Content Content is the design, text and graphical information that forms a web page. Good content is the key to attracting customers to a **web site** and retaining their interest or achieving repeat visits.

Convergence A trend in which different hardware devices such as televisions, computers and telephones merge and have similar functions.

Cookies Cookies are small text files stored on an end-user's computer to enable **web sites** to identify the user. They enable a company to identify a previous visitor to a site, and build up a profile of that visitor's behaviour.

Cost models for Internet advertising These include per-exposure, per-response and per-action costs.

Cost per mille (CPM) Cost per 1000 **ad impressions**.

Cost per targeted mille (CPTM) Cost per targeted thousand for an advertisement (*see also* **targeting**).

Customer orientation Providing content and services on a **web site** consistent with the different characteristics of the audience of the site.

Cybermediaries Intermediaries who bring together buyers and sellers or those with particular information or service needs.

Cyberspace and cybermarketing These terms were preferred by science fiction writers and tabloid writers to indicate the futuristic nature of using the Internet, the prefix 'cyber' indicating a blurring between humans, machines and communications. The terms are not frequently used today since the terms **Internet**, **intranet** and **World Wide Web** are more specific and widely used.

Data fusion The combining of data from different complementary sources (usually geodemographic and lifestyle or market research and lifestyle) to 'build a picture of someone's life' (M. Evans (1998) 'From 1086 to 1984: Direct marketing into the millennium', *Marketing Intelligence and Planning*, 16(1), 56–67).

Data warehousing and data mining Extracting data from legacy systems and other resources; cleaning, scrubbing and preparing data for decision support; maintaining data in appropriate data stores; accessing and analysing data using a variety of end-user tools; and mining data for significant relationships. The primary purpose of these efforts is to provide easy access to specially prepared data that can be used with decision support applications such as management reports, queries, decision support systems, executive information systems and data mining.

Database marketing The process of systematically collecting, in electronic or optical form, data about past, current and/or potential customers, maintaining the integrity of the data by continually monitoring customer purchases, by enquiring about changing status, and by using the data to formulate marketing strategy and foster personalised relationships with customers.

Decryption The process of decoding (unscrambling) a message that has been encryted using defined mathematical rules.

Design phase (of site construction) The design phase defines how the site will work in the key areas of **web site** structure, **navigation** and **security**.

Destination site Frequently used to refer to the site that is visited following a **clickthrough** on a **banner advertisement**. Could also apply to any site visited following a click on a **hyperlink**.

Development phase (of site construction) Development is the term used to describe the creation of a **web site** by programmers. It involves writing the **HTML** content, creating graphics, writing any necessary software code such as **Java**script or **ActiveX** (programming).

Digital brand A digital brand is a brand identity used for a product or company online that differs from the traditional brand. (Also known as an online brand.)

Digital cash An electronic version of cash in which the buyer of an item is typically anonymous to the seller. (Also referred to as virtual, electronic cash or e-cash.)

Digital certificates (keys) A method of ensuring **privacy** on the **Internet**. **Certificates** consist of keys made up of large numbers that are used to uniquely identify individuals. *See also* **Public key**.

Digital signatures The electronic equivalent of written signatures that are used as an online method of identifying individuals or companies using **public key encryption**.

Digital television Information is received and displayed on a digital television using binary information (0s and 1s), giving options for better picture and sound quality and providing additional information services based on interactivity.

Direct marketing Marketing to customers using one or more advertising media aimed at achieving measurable response and/or transaction.

Direct response Usually achieved in an Internet marketing context by **callback services**.

Directed information seeker Someone who knows what information he or she is looking for.

Directories Directory **web sites** provide a structured listing of registered web sites in different categories. They are similar to an electronic version of *Yellow Pages*. Yahoo! and Excite are the best known examples of directories. (Also known as **catalogues**.)

Disintermediation The removal of **intermediaries** such as distributors or brokers that formerly linked a company to its customers. In particular disintermediation enables a company to sell direct to the customer by cutting-out the middleman.

Domain name The **web address** that identifies a **web server**. *See* **Domain name system**.

Domain name registration The process of reserving a unique **web address** that can be used to refer to the company web site.

Domain name system The domain name system (DNS) provides a method of representing Internet Protocol (IP) addresses as text-based names. These are used as **web addresses**. For example, www.microsoft.com is the representation of site 207.68.156.58. Domain names are divided into the following categories
- Top level domain names such as *.com* or *.co.uk*. (Also known as **Global (or generic) top level domain names (gLTD)**.)
- Second-level domain names. This refers to the company name and is sometimes referred to as the enterprise name, e.g. *novell.com*.
- Third-level or sub-enterprise domain names. This may be used to refer to an individual server within an organisation such as *support.novell.com*.

Download The process of retrieving electronic information such as a web page or **e-mail** from another remote location such as a **web server**.

Early adopters Companies or departments that invest in new marketing techniques and technologies when they first become available in an attempt to gain a competitive advantage despite the higher risk entailed than that involved in a more cautious approach.

E-business A term describing the use of digital and Internet technologies in the full range of business functions.

E-cash *See* **Digital cash**.

Electronic Data Interchange (EDI) The exchange, using digital media, of standardised business documents such as purchase orders and invoices between buyers and sellers.

Electronic cash *See* **Digital cash**.

Electronic commerce (e-commerce) The trading of goods and services using digital media.

Electronic commerce transactions Transactions in the trading of goods and services conducted using the Internet and other digital media.

Effective frequency The number of exposures or **ad impressions** (frequency) required for an advertisement to become effective.

Electronic mail (E-mail) Sending messages or documents, such as news about a new product or sales promotion between individuals. A primitive form of **push** channel. E-mail may be **inbound** or **outbound**.

Electronic mall *See* **Virtual mall**.

E-mail advertising Advertisements contained within e-mail such as newsetters.

Electronic marketspace A virtual marketplace such as the **Internet** in which no direct contact occurs between buyers and sellers.

Electronic Shopping or ES test This test was developed by de Kare-Silver to assess the extent to which consumers are likely to purchase a particular retail product using the **Internet**. (*See* **Eshock**.)

Electronic tokens Units of digital currency that are in a standard electronic format.

Encryption The scrambling of information into a form that cannot be interpreted. **Decryption** is used to make the information readable.

Enterprise application integration The middleware technology that is used to connect together different software applications and their underlying databases is now known as 'enterprise application integration (EAI)' (*Internet World*, 1999).

Entry page The page at which a visitor enters a **web site**. It is identified by a **log file analyser**. *See also* **Exit page** and **Referring site**.

EShock Michael de Kare-Silver speculates in his 1998 book of this name (Basingstoke, UK: Macmillan) that by 2005–2007 consumers using the **Internet** as their preferred method of making purchases will account for 15–20 per cent of total purchases. This will lead to ever-decreasing margins for retailers, who will be forced to close substantial parts of their retail networks.

Evaluating a web site *See* **Web site measurement**.

Exit page The page from which a visitor exits a **web site**. It is identified by a **log file analyser**.

Extranet An extranet is formed by extending the **intranet** beyond a company to customers, suppliers, collaborators or even competitors. This is password protected to prevent access by general Internet users.

File Transfer Protocol (FTP) A standard method for moving files across the **Internet**. FTP is available as a feature of **web browsers** that is sometimes used for marketing applications such as **downloading** files such as product price lists or specifications. Standalone FTP packages such as WSFTP are commonly used to update **HTML** files on **web servers** when **uploading** revisions to the **web server**.

Firewall A specialised software application mounted on a server at the point where the company is connected to the Internet. Its purpose is to prevent unauthorised access into the company by outsiders. Firewalls are essential for all companies hosting their own **web server**.

Flow Describes a state in which users have a positive experience from readily controlling their **navigation** and interaction on a **web site**.

Focus groups Online focus groups have been conducted by *w3focus.com*. These follow a bulletin board or discussion group form where different members of the focus group respond to prompts from the focus group leaders.

Form A method on a web page of entering information such as order details.

Frame A technique used to divide a web page into different parts such as a menu and separate content.

Global (or generic) top level domain names (gLTD) The part of the **domain name** that refers to the category of site. The gLTD is usually the rightmost part of the domain name such as *.co.uk* or *.com*.

Gopher Gopher is a directory-based structure containing information in certain categories.

Graphic design All factors that govern the physical appearance of a web page.

Graphic Interlaced File (GIF) GIF is a graphic format used to display images within web pages. An interlaced GIF is displayed gradually on the screen, building up an image in several passes.

Hit A hit is recorded for each graphic or block of text requested from a **web server**. It is not a reliable measure for the number of people viewing a page. A **page impression** is a more reliable measure denoting one person viewing one page.

Home page The index page of a **web site** with menu options or links to other resources on the site. Usually denoted by *<web address>/index.html*.

HTML (Hypertext Markup Language) A standard format used to define the text and layout of web pages. HTML files usually have the extension .HTML or .HTM.

HTTP (Hypertext transfer protocol) A standard that defines the way information is transmitted across the **Internet**.

Hyperlink A method of moving between one web site page and another, indicated to the user by text highlighted by underlining and/or a different colour. Hyperlinks can also be achieved by clicking on a graphic image such as a **banner advertisement** that is linked to another **web site**.

Inbound e-mail E-mail arriving at a company.

Infomediary An **intermediary** business whose main source of revenue derives from capturing consumer information and developing detailed profiles of individual customers for use by third parties. Defined from the article in *McKinsey Quarterly* (*www.mckinseyquarterly.com*).

Initiation of web site project This phase of the project should involve a structured review of the costs and benefits of developing a **web site** (or making a major revision to an existing web site). A successful outcome to initiation will be a decision to proceed with the site **development phase**, with an agreed budget and target completion date.

Insertion order A printed order to run an advertisement campaign. It defines the campaign name, the **web site** receiving the order and the planner or buyer giving the order, the individual advertisements to be run (or who will provide them), the sizes of the advertisements, the campaign beginning and end dates, the **CPM**, the total cost, discounts to be applied, and reporting requirements and possible penalties or stipulations relative to the failure to deliver the impressions.

Integrity *See* **Security methods**.

Interactive banner advertisements A **banner advertisement** that enables the user to enter information.

Intermediaries Online sites that help bring different parties such as buyers and sellers together.

Internet The physical network that links computers across the globe. It consists of the infrastructure of network servers and communication links between them, which are used to hold and transport the vast amount of information on the Internet. The Internet enables transfer of messages and transactions between connected computers world-wide.

Internet contribution An assessment of the extent to which the **Internet** contributes to sales is a key measure of the importance of the Internet to a company.

Internet marketing The application of the Internet and related digital technologies to achieve marketing objectives.

Internet marketing metrics *See* **Metrics for Internet marketing**.

Internet Relay Chat (IRC) A communications tool that allows a text-based 'chat' between different users who are logged on at the same time. Of limited use for marketing purposes except for special-interest or youth products.

Internet service providers (ISPs) Companies that provide home or business users with a connection to access the Internet. They can also host **web sites** or provide a link from **web servers** to enable other companies and consumers access to a corporate web site.

Interstitials Advertisements that are usually included within a 'pop-up window'.

Intranet A network within a single company that enables access to company information using the familiar tools of the **Internet** such as **web browsers** and **E-mail**. Only staff within a company can access the intranet, which will be password protected.

Java A programming language standard supported by Sun Microsystems, which permits complex and graphical customer applications to be written and then accessed from a **web browser**. An example might be a form for calculating interest on a loan. A competitor to **ActiveX**.

Joint Photographic Experts Group (JPEG) A compressed graphics standard specified by the JPEG. Used for graphic images typically requiring use of many colours such as product photographs where some loss of quality is acceptable. The format allows for some degradation in image quality to enable more rapid download.

Live web site Current site accessible to customers, as distinct from **test web site**.

Localisation Designing the content of the **web site** in such a way that it is appropriate to different audiences in different countries.

Log file A file stored on a **web server** that records every item **downloaded** by users.

Log file analysers Tools that are used to build a picture of the amount of usage of different parts of a **web site** based on the information contained in the **log file**.

Loyalty techniques Customers sign up to an incentive scheme where they receive points for repeat purchases, which can be converted into offers such as discounts, free products or cash. (Also known as **online incentive schemes**.)

Mailbots *See* **Autoresponders**.

Maintenance process The work involved with running a live **web site** such as updating pages and checking the performance of the site.

Marketspace A virtual marketplace such as the Internet in which no direct contact occurs between buyers and sellers. (Also known as **electronic marketspace**.)

Markup language *See* HTML, XML.

Mass customisation The ability to create tailored marketing messages or products for individual customers or a group of similar customers (a bespoke service) yet retain the economies of scale and the capacity of mass marketing or production.

Mass marketing One-to-many communication between a company and potential customers with limited tailoring of the message.

Measurement *See* **Web site measurement**.

Media broker A company that places advertisements for companies wishing to advertise by contacting the **media owners**.

Media buyer The person within a company wishing to advertise who places the advertisement, usually via a **media broker**.

Media owners The owners of **web sites** (or other media such as newspapers) that accept advertisements.

Meta search engines Meta search engines submit keywords typed by users to a range of **search engines** in order to increase the number of relevant pages since different search engines may have indexed different sites. An example is the metacrawler search engine or *www.mamma.com*.

Meta-tags Text within an **HTML** file summarising the content of the site (content meta-tag) and relevant keywords (keyword meta-tag), which are matched against the keywords typed into **search engines**.

Metrics for Internet marketing Measures that indicate the effectiveness of **Internet marketing** activities in meeting customer, business and marketing objectives.

Micropayments (microtransactions) **Digital cash** systems that allow very small sums of money (fractions of 1p) to be transferred, but with lower security. Such small sums do not warrant a credit card payment, because processing is too costly.

Microsite Specialised content that is part of a **web site** that is not necessarily owned by the organisation. If owned by the company it may be as part of an **extranet**. (*See also* **Nested ad content**.)

Microsoft Internet Information Server (IIS) Microsoft IIS is a **web server** developed by Microsoft that runs on Windows NT.

Navigation The method of finding and moving between different information and pages on a **web site**. It is governed by menu arrangements, site structure and the layout of individual pages.

Nested ad content This refers to the situation when the person undertaking the **clickthrough** is not redirected to a corporate or brand site, but is instead taken to a related page on the same site as that on which the advertisement is placed. (Sometimes referred to as **microsite**.)

Non-repudiability *See* **Security methods**.

Offline promotion *See* **Promotion (online and offline)**.

Offline web metric Offline measures are those that are collated by marketing staff recording particular marketing outcomes such as an enquiry or a sale. They are usually collated manually, but could be collated automatically.

One-to-one marketing A unique dialogue that occurs directly between a company and individual customers (or less strictly with groups of customers with similar needs). The dialogue involves a company listening to customer needs and responding with services to meet these needs.

Online brand *See* **Digital brand**.

Online incentive schemes *See* **Loyalty techniques**.

Online promotion *See* **Promotion (online and offline)**.

Online service providers (OSPs) An OSP is sometimes used to distinguish large **Internet service providers (ISPs)** from other access providers. In the UK, AOL, Freeserve, VirginNet and LineOne can be considered OSPs since they have a large amount of specially developed content available to their subscribers. Note that this term is not used as frequently as ISP, and the distinction between ISPs and OSPs is a blurred one since all OSPs are also **ISPs** and the distinction only occurs according to the amout of premium content (only available to customers) offered as part of the service.

Online web metrics Online measures are those that are collected automatically on the **web server**, often in a server **log file**.

Opt-in e-mail The customer is only contacted when he or she has explicitly asked for information to be sent (usually when filling in an on-screen form).

Opt-out e-mail The customer is not contacted subsequently if he or she has explicitly stated he or she does not want to be contacted in future. Opt-out or **unsubscribe** options are usually available within the e-mail itself.

Outbound e-mail E-mail sent from a company.

Outsourcing Contracting an outside company to undertake part of the **Internet marketing** activities.

Page impression One page impression occurs when a member of the audience views a web page. *See also* **Ad impression** and **Reach**.

Page request The process of a user selecting a **hyperlink** or typing in a **uniform resource locator (URL)** to rerieve information on a specific web page. Equivalent to **page impression**.

Page view *See* **Page impression**.

Performance of web site Performance or quality of service is dependent on its availability and speed of access.

Personalisation Web-based personalisation involves delivering customised content for the individual through web pages, e-mail or **push technology**.

Phone-me A **callback** facility available on the **web site** for a company to contact a customer by phone at a later time as specified by the customer.

Pixel The small dots on a computer screen that are used to represent images and text. Short for 'picture element'. Used to indicate the size of **banner advertisements**.

Plug-in A program that must be **downloaded** to view particular content such as an animation.

Portal A **web site** that acts as a gateway to the information on the Internet by providing **search engines**, **directories** and other services such as personalised news or free e-mail.

Privacy Concerns that affect the personal details of individuals or companies. *See also* **Security methods**.

Promotion (online and offline) Online promotion uses communication via the **Internet** itself to raise awareness about a site and drive traffic to it. This promotion may take the form of links from other sites, **banner advertisements** or targeted e-mail messages. Offline promotion uses traditional media such as television or newspaper advertising and word of mouth to promote a company's **web site**.

Prototypes and prototyping A prototype is a preliminary version of part or a framework of all of a **web site** that can be reviewed by its target audience, or the marketing team. Prototyping is an iterative process where web site users suggest modifications before further prototypes are made and the final version of the site is developed.

Public key A unique identifier of a buyer or a seller that is available to other parties to enable secure e-commerce using **encryption** based on digital certificates.

Public-key encryption An asymmetric form of **encryption** in which the keys or **digital certificates** used by the sender and receiver of information are different. The two keys are related, so only the pair of keys can be used together to encrypt and decrypt information.

Public-key infrastructure (PKI) The organisations responsible for issuing and maintaining certificates for public-key security together form the PKI.

Push technology The delivery of web-based content to the user's desktop without the need for the user to visit a site to **download** information. E-mail can also be considered to be a push technology. A particular type of information is a push channel.

Reach The number of unique individuals who view an advertisement.

RealNames A service for matching company names and brands with **web addresses**.

Referring sites A **log file** may indicate which site a user visited immediately before visiting yours. *See also* **Clickthrough**, **Destination site** and **Exit pages**.

Registration (individuals) The process whereby an individual subscribes to a site or requests further information by filling in contact details and his or her needs using an electronic form.

Registration (of domain name) The process of reserving a unique **web address** that can be used to refer to the company **web site**.

Reintermediation The creation of new **intermediaries** between customers and suppliers providing services such as supplier search and product evaluation.

Relationship marketing Consistent application of up-to-date knowledge of individual customers to product and service design, which is communicated interactively in order to develop a continuous, mutually beneficial and long-term relationship.

Rich media advertisements Advertisements that are not static, but provide animation, sound or interactivity. An example of this would be a **banner advertisement** for a loan in which a customer can type in the amount of loan required, and the cost of the loan is calculated immediately.

Robot A tool, also known as a **spider**, that is employed by **search engines** to index web pages of registered sites on a regular basis.

Run of site A situation where a company pays for **banner advertisements** to promote its services across a **web site**.

Sales promotions The Internet offers tremendous potential for sales promotions of different types since it is more immediate than any other medium – it is always available for communication, and tactical variations in the details of the promotion can be made at short notice.

Saturation of the Internet Access to the **Internet** will reach saturation as home PC ownership reaches a limit, unless other access devices become popular.

Scripts Scripts can run either on the user's browser (client-side scripts) (*see* **Web browser**) or on the **web server** (server-side scripts).

Search engines Specialised **web sites** that use automatic tools known as **spiders** or **robots** to index web pages of registered sites. Users can search the index by typing in keywords to specify their interest. Pages containing these keywords will be listed, and by clicking on a **hyperlink** the user will be taken to the site.

Secure Electronic Transaction (SET) A standard for **public-key encryption** intended to enable secure **electronic commerce transactions** lead-developed by Mastercard and Visa.

Secure HTTP Encrypted **HTTP**.

Secure Sockets Layer (SSL) A commonly used **encryption** technique for scrambling data such as credit card numbers as they are passed across the Internet from a **web browser** to a **web server**.

Security methods When systems for **electronic commerce** are devised, or when existing solutions are selected, the following attributes must be present:
1 *Authentication* – are parties to the transaction who they claim to be? This is achieved through the use of digital certificates.
2 *Privacy and confidentiality* – are transaction data protected? The consumer may want to make an anonymous purchase. Are all non-essential traces of a transaction removed from the public network and all intermediary records eliminated?
3 *Integrity* – checks that the message sent is complete, i.e. that it is not corrupted.
4 *Non-repudiability* – ensures sender cannot deny sending message.
5 *Availability* – how can threats to the continuity and performance of the system be eliminated?

Server log file *See* **Online web metrics**.

Service quality The level of service received on a **web site**. Dependent on reliability, responsiveness and availability of staff and the **web site** service.

Serving Used to describe the process of displaying an advertisement on a **web site** (**ad serving**) or delivering a web page to a user's **web browser**. *See* **Web server**.

Site *See* **Web site**

Site announcements Usually used to describe the dissemination of information about a new or revised **web site**.

Site auditors Auditors accurately measure the usage for different sites as the number of ad impressions and clickthrough rates. Auditors include ABC (Audit Bureau of circulation) and BPA (Business Publication Auditor) International.

Site availability An indication of how easy it is to connect to a **web site** as a user. In theory this figure should be 100 per cent, but for technical reasons such as failures in the server hardware or upgrades to software, sometimes users cannot access the site and the figure falls below 90 per cent.

Site measurement *See* **Web site measurement**.

Site re-launch Where a **web site** is replaced with a new version with a new look and feel.

Site statistics Collected by **log file analysers**, these are used to monitor the effectiveness of a **web site**.

Site 'stickiness' An indication of how long a visitor stays on a site. **Log file analysers** can be used to assess average visit times.

Site visits One site visit records one customer visiting the site. Not equivalent to **User session**.

Sitemapping tools These tools diagram the layout of the **web site**, which is useful for site management, and can be used to assist users.

SMART metrics SMART metrics must be:
- Specific;
- Measurable;
- Actionable;
- Relevant;
- Timely.

Smartcards Physical cards containing a memory chip that can be inserted into a smartcard reader before items can be purchased.

Software agents *See* **Agents**.

Spamming Bulk e-mailing of unsolicited mail.

Spider A tool also known as a **robot** that is employed by **search engines** to index web pages of registered sites on a regular basis.

Splash page A preliminary page that precedes the normal **home page** of a **web site**. Site users can either wait to be redirected to the home page or can follow a link to do this. Splash pages are not now commonly used since they slow down the process whereby customers find the information they need.

Sponsorship Sponsorship involves a company paying money to advertise on a **web site**. The arrangement may involve more than advertising. Sponsorship is a similar arrangement to **co-branding**.

Stages in web site development The standard stages of creation of a **web site** are **initiation**, feasibility, **analysis**, **design**, **development** (**content** creation), **testing** and **maintenance**.

Storyboarding Using static drawings or screenshots of the different parts of a **web site** to review the design concept with customers or clients.

Style guide A definition of site structure, page design, typography and copy defined within a company. *See* **Graphic design**.

Surfer An **undirected information seeker** who is often looking for an experience rather than information.

Targeting (through banner advertisers) Advertising networks such as DoubleClick offer advertisers the ability to target advertisements dynamically on the World Wide Web through their 'DART' targeting technology. This gives advertisers a means of reaching specific audiences.

Telemarketing using the Internet Mainly used for inbound telemarketing, including sales lines, carelines for goods and services and response handling for direct response campaigns.

Telnet A program that allows remote access to data and text-based programs on other computer systems at a different location. For example, a retailer could check to see whether an item was in stock in a warehouse using a telnet application.

Test web site A parallel version of the site to use before it is made available to customers as a **live web site**.

Testing content Testing should be conducted for **plug-ins**; for interactive facilities and integration with company databases; for spelling and grammar; for adherence to corporate image standards; for implementation of **HTML** in different **web browsers**; and to ensure that links to external sites are valid.

Testing phase Testing involves different aspects of the **content** such as spelling, validity of links, formatting on different **web browsers** and dynamic features such as form filling or database queries.

Traffic building campaign The use of **online** and **offline promotion** techniques such as **banner advertising**, **search engine** promotion and reciprocal linking to increase the audience of a site (both new and existing customers).

Transfer Control Protocol/Internet Protocol (TCP/IP) The passing of data packets around the Internet occurs via the TCP/IP protocol. For a PC to be able receive web pages or for a server to host web pages it must be configured to support this protocol.

Trusted third parties (TTP) Companies with which an agreement has been reached to share information.

Undirected information seeker A person who does not know what information they are looking for – a **surfer**.

Uniform (universal) resource locator (URL) Text that indicates the **web address** of a site. A specific **domain name** is typed into a **web browser** window and the browser will then locate and load the **web site**. It is in the form of:
http://www.domain-name.extension/filename.html.

Unsubscribe An option to **opt out** from an e-mail newsletter or discussion group.

Upload The transfer of files from a local computer to a server. Usually achieved using **FTP**. E-mail or web site pages can be uploaded to update a remote server.

Usenet newsgroup An electronic bulletin board used to discuss a particular topic such as a sport, hobby or business area. Traditionally accessed by special newsreader software, these can now be accessed via a **web browser** from *www.deja.com*.

User session Used to specify the frequency of visits to a site. Not equivalent to **Site visit**.

Validation Validation services test for errors in **HTML** code which may cause a web page to be displayed incorrectly or for links to other pages that do not work.

Value proposition of site The benefits or value of a **web site** that are evident to its users.

Vertical portals These are generally business-to-business sites that will host **content** to help participants in an industry to get their work done by providing industry news, details of business techniques and product and service reviews.

View *See* **Page impression**

Virtual cash *See* **Digital cash**.

Virtual community An Internet-based forum for special interest groups to communicate using a bulletin board to post messages.

Virtual mall A **web site** that brings together different electronic retailers at a single virtual (online) location. This contrasts with a fixed location infrastructure – the traditional arrangement where retail organisations operate from retail stores situated in fixed locations such as real-world shopping malls. (Also known as electronic mall.)

Virtual merchants Retailers such as Amazon that only operate online – they have no fixed location infrastructure.

Virtual organisation An organisation that uses information and communications technology to allow it to operate without clearly defined physical boundaries between different functions. It provides customised services by outsourcing production and other functions to third parties.

Virtualisation The process whereby a company develops more of the characteristics of the virtual organisation.

Visit *See* **Site visit**.

Web application protocol (WAP) A standard that enables mobile phones to access text from web sites.

Web addresses (universal resource locators – URLs) Web addresses refer to particular pages on a **web server**, which is hosted by a company or organisation. The technical name for web addresses is **uniform** or **universal resource locators (URLs)**.

Web browsers Browsers such as Netscape Navigator and Microsoft Internet Explorer provide an easy method of accessing and viewing information stored as **HTML** web documents on different **web servers**.

Web servers Web servers are used to store the web pages accessed by **web browsers**. They may also contain databases of customer or product information, which can be queried and retrieved using a browser.

Web site **Content** accessible on the **World Wide Web** that is created by a particular organisation on individual. The location and identity of a web site is indicated by its **web address (URL)** or **domain name**. It may be stored on a single server in a single location, or a cluster of servers.

Web site measurement The process whereby metrics such as **page impressions** are collected and evaluated to assess the effectiveness of **Internet marketing** activities in meeting customers, business and marketing objectives.

Webmaster The webmaster is responsible for ensuring the quality of a **web site**. This means achieving suitable availability, speed, working links between pages and connections to company databases. In small companies the webmaster may be responsible for graphic design and content developerment.

WebTV WebTV (*www.webtv.net*) is a web service delivered by television. It is now owned by Microsoft. Currently available in the USA, Canada and Japan only.

Wide Area Information Service (WAIS) An Internet service that has been superseded by the World Wide Web.

World Wide Web A medium for publishing information on the Internet. It is accessed through **web browsers**, which display web pages and can now be used to run business applications. Company information is stored on **web servers**, which are usually referred to as **web sites**.

XML An advanced markup language giving better control than **HTML** over format for structured information on web pages.

SUBJECT INDEX

Company and product names are in bold.

NAME INDEX